The Architecture of the M

This book is a comprehensive development and defense of one of the guiding assumptions of evolutionary psychology: that the human mind is composed of a large number of semi-independent modules. *The Architecture of the Mind* has three main goals. One is to argue for massive mental modularity. Another is to answer a 'How possibly?' challenge to any such approach. The first part of the book lays out the positive case supporting massive modularity. It also outlines how the thesis should best be developed, and articulates the notion of 'module' that is in question. Then the second part of the book takes up the challenge of explaining how the sorts of flexibility and creativity that are distinctive of the human mind could possibly be grounded in the operations of a massive number of modules.

Peter Carruthers's third aim is to show how the various components of the mind are likely to be linked and interact with one another—indeed, this is crucial to demonstrating how the human mind, together with its familiar capacities, can be underpinned by a massively modular set of mechanisms. He outlines and defends the basic framework of a perception / belief / desire / planning / motor-control architecture, as well as detailing the likely components and their modes of connectivity. Many specific claims about the place within this architecture of natural language, of a mind-reading system, and others are explained and motivated. A number of novel proposals are made in the course of these discussions, one of which is that creative human thought depends upon a prior kind of creativity of action.

Written with unusual clarity and directness, and surveying an extensive range of research in cognitive science, this book will be essential reading for anyone with an interest in the nature and organization of the mind.

Peter Carruthers is Professor of Philosophy at the University of Maryland, College Park.

The Architecture of the Mind

Massive Modularity and the Flexibility of Thought

Peter Carruthers

CLARENDON PRESS · OXFORD

OXFORD
UNIVERSITY PRESS

Great Clarendon Street, Oxford OX2 6DP

Oxford University Press is a department of the University of Oxford.
It furthers the University's objective of excellence in research, scholarship,
and education by publishing worldwide in

Oxford New York

Auckland Cape Town Dar es Salaam Hong Kong Karachi
Kuala Lumpur Madrid Melbourne Mexico City Nairobi
New Delhi Shanghai Taipei Toronto
With offices in
Argentina Austria Brazil Chile Czech Republic France Greece
Guatemala Hungary Italy Japan South Korea Poland Portugal
Singapore Switzerland Thailand Turkey Ukraine Vietnam

Oxford is a registered trade mark of Oxford University Press
in the UK and in certain other countries

Published in the United States
by Oxford University Press Inc., New York

© Peter Carruthers 2006

The moral rights of the author have been asserted

Database right Oxford University Press (maker)

Reprinted 2010

ISBN 978-0-19-920707-7

For Susan
the architecture of my life

Contents

List of Figures

Preface

This book has three main aims. One is to motivate and argue for a massively modular account of the architecture of the human mind. Another is to answer a 'How possibly?' challenge to any such approach. In the first part of the book (Chapters 1–3) the positive case for massive modularity is laid out. I also outline how the thesis of massive mental modularity should best be developed, and articulate the notion of 'module' that is appropriate to serve within such an account. And then in the second part of the book (Chapters 4–7) I take up the challenge of explaining how a massively modular mind could possibly display the sorts of flexibility and creativity that are distinctive of the human mind. Here the account that I provide finds a central place for representations of natural language sentences, among other things.

The third aim of this book is to give at least a sketch of the ways in which the various components of the mind are likely to be linked up to one another, and to interact with one another—indeed, this will be crucial to demonstrating how it is possible for the human mind, together with its familiar capacities, to be underpinned by a massively modular set of structures and components. Chapter 2 outlines and defends the basic framework of a perception / belief / desire / planning / motor-control architecture, as well as making proposals about many of the likely components and their modes of connectivity. And then in the chapters thereafter many specific claims about the place within this architecture of natural language, of a mind-reading system, and others are explained and motivated.

Although these three main strands in the book are mutually supporting, they are also to some degree independent of one another. Someone might find the arguments for massive modularity convincing, for example, while being unconvinced of my account of human flexibility, and while disagreeing with the overall architecture of components that I lay out. Or someone might think that the case for massive modularity is weak, while agreeing that my account of human flexibility and the component-architecture underpinning it are along the right lines—only requiring far fewer elements than a massive modularist would allege. And so on. But I believe that, taken together, the claims that I make under each of these three headings should add up to be (or rather multiply to be) an attractive overall package that is greater than the mere sum of its individual parts.

Our topic is massive modularity. But unfortunately there exists a wide variety of notions of modularity, put to work in a diverse range of literatures, extending from biology (Schlosser and Wagner, 2004), through computer science and artificial intelligence (Bryson, 2000, McDermott, 2001), to psychology (Karmiloff-Smith, 1992), to philosophy (Fodor, 1983, 2000; Samuels, 1998). Of these, Fodor's (1983) conception of a module has been especially influential, and many of the uses of the notion of modularity within cognitive science are to some degree variations upon it. In addition, a number of different researchers in cognitive science have argued for a form of *massive mental modularity*, and have done so in a variety of distinct ways (Tooby and Cosmides, 1992; Sperber, 1996; Pinker, 1997). But they, too, are by no means in complete agreement with one another about what modules, as such, *are*.

The way out of this morass is to line up the *arguments* for massive modularity with the *notion* of modularity that those arguments support. This is what I do in Chapter 1. I present and defend the cogency of three main arguments for massive modularity, while carefully teasing out the notion of 'module' that would be supported if those arguments are, indeed, cogent. The result is a notion of modularity that is some distance from Fodor's (in particular, modules needn't be informationally *encapsulated*). It is much closer to the use of the term 'module' in biology, and it is even closer to the notion used by researchers in artificial intelligence. On this account, a module is a functionally distinct processing system of the mind, whose operations are at least partly independent of those of others, and whose existence and properties are partly dissociable from the others. Moreover, modular systems must be *frugal* in their use of information and other cognitive resources, and they will have internal operations that are widely *inaccessible* to other systems. The thesis of massive mental modularity is then the claim that the mind is composed of *many* functionally isolable processing systems which possess such properties, and which have multiple input and output connections with others.

Chapter 2 then defends the major premise of one of the main arguments for massive modularity, claiming that the minds of non-human animals—from insects to chimpanzees—are massively modular in their organization. The chapter also locates those modules within a basic perception / belief / desire / practical reason / motor-control architecture, which will serve as the framework for the account of the structure of the human mind provided in later chapters. It also puts in place many specific ideas that will be needed in later chapters, including the claim that there is a limited capacity for mental rehearsal of action present in the minds of some of our primate cousins.

In Chapter 3 I discuss the modules that are likely to have been added, or enhanced, in the transition from the minds of the great-ape common-ancestors to our own. I defend the view that these are *multiple*, and argue at some length against the competing 'one major new adaptation' hypothesis. They include a mind-reading system, a natural language system, and systems for normative belief, reasoning, and motivation. In each case I discuss the probable internal organization of the module in question, and the ways in which it is likely to be embedded into the overall architecture of the mind.

Chapter 4 starts to take up the challenge of explaining the distinctive *flexibility* of the human mind in massively modular terms. It distinguishes a number of different kinds of flexibility, arguing that some are relatively easy to address while others are harder to explain. It then discusses how the language faculty may be responsible for flexibility of *content*, combining the outputs of other conceptual modules into a single representation that can then be mentally rehearsed, 'globally broadcast' (in the sense of Baars, 1988), and received as input by a whole suite of conceptual modules once again. Increasingly flexible *cycles* of modular processing thereby become possible, as do new kinds of reasoning.

Chapter 5 then tackles the problem of creativity. It advances the thesis that all forms of creative cognition reduce, ultimately, to creative *action*. In contrast with traditional views that see creative thought as prior to creative activity, I here argue the reverse. (Think of creative 'on-line' improvisation in jazz, to get a feel for the kind of thing that I have in mind.) The root of all creativity, I claim, lies in the creative activation and rehearsal of action schemata. The first manifestations of this ability are to be found in the problem-solving abilities of chimpanzees, and are then found—greatly enriched—in the pretend play of young children. Indeed, I claim that the *function* of childhood pretend play is to practice and further enhance that ability.

Chapter 6 turns to our capacity for science, and for abductive reasoning more generally (sometimes called 'inference to the best explanation'). Some people have claimed that our capacity for science is one of the remaining deep mysteries (comparable to the problem of consciousness, or the problem of the origin of the universe), and that it presents a formidable challenge for *any* cognitive theory to explain, let alone a massively modular one (Pinker, 1997; Fodor, 2000). Chapter 6 claims to solve this problem, in outline at least. Once again language and mental rehearsal play an important role in the account, as do principles employed in the interpretation of speech and the evaluation of testimony.

Chapter 7 discusses how the thesis of massive modularity can accommodate the distinctive features of human *practical* reasoning. This chapter is relatively brief, since most of the materials needed for the account have been put into place earlier in the book. What is new in the chapter is the suggestion that human practical reason can exploit the resources of our distinctively human *theoretical* reason. And I defend the belief / desire framework that I have adopted throughout against those who claim that, in the case of human beings, it is perceptions of *reasons*, rather than desires, that motivate our actions (Dancy, 1993, 2000; Scanlon, 1998). I also argue that conscious will is an illusion, developing one of the arguments of Wegner (2002). Chapter 8 then briefly summarizes the book's arguments and conclusions.

It hardly needs saying that this book is an ambitious one—indeed, it is almost absurdly so. For it takes as its goal nothing less than the elaboration and defense of a massively modular architecture for the human mind, to which many, many, different bodies of research are relevant. In consequence, there are numerous places where I have had to touch on topics on which I am by no means an expert. And there is, no doubt, a wealth of further evidence and theorizing out there in a variety of literatures that would be thoroughly germane to my project, if only I had the good fortune to know of it. Moreover, there are a wide range of kinds of expertise that are surely relevant to the evaluation of my various claims and proposals, some of which I simply don't possess. I can only console myself with the thought that *someone* has to step back from the details and paint the big picture, albeit taking big risks in doing so. And I hope that even if I have made many mistakes, and even if the architecture that I sketch in outline proves incorrect in many of its details, still what I have done might nevertheless be *roughly* along the right lines. At the very least, I hope that it will provide a useful foil and stimulus for the research of others.

It is worth remarking that many academic philosophers might fail to recognize what occurs within these pages as a form of philosophy. For the book contains very little that can be considered to be conceptual analysis, and most of the arguments are empirically grounded inferences to the best explanation, rather than deductive in form. If this is so, then so be it, and so much the worse for the philosophers in question. For by the same token much of the work of Aristotle, and of Hume, wouldn't count as philosophy, either. I believe that I have good role-models. And I believe that naturalistic philosophy, of the sort exemplified here, is the way (or at least, *a* way) that philosophy should be.

Many cognitive scientists, likewise, might fail to recognize what occurs within these pages as a form of science. For I report no new data or experiments. And although I do review a great deal of scientific data, I also make proposals and outline theories that go well beyond anything that the current evidence might strictly warrant, and many of the ideas that I defend are avowedly speculative. I can only plead that science always contains what might be called 'framework assumptions', as well as detailed theories closely grounded in the empirical data. And the examination and defense of those assumptions can be the work of naturalistically minded philosophers.

Again Hume (1739) provides us with a model. Although he, too, conducted no experiments, he saw himself as attempting to ground an empirical science of psychology, and the framework that he laid out has proven immensely influential amongst working psychologists ever since. (Even those of us who reject his associationism and empiricism can continue to find much that is of value in his work—see Fodor, 2003.) I should stress that the present book is a good deal less ambitious, of course. I am not attempting to *found* a massively modular framework for psychology, since much excellent work in that tradition already exists. Instead, I aim to lay out the best case for it, to defend it, and to show how it might be able to overcome its greatest difficulties. I thus see myself in the more modest role of 'under-laborer for science', championed by Locke (1690).

Acknowledgments

This book is the indirect product of twenty years of interdisciplinary theorizing and research, and the direct product of ten years of thinking about modularity issues. I have been heavily involved in interdisciplinary projects linking both philosophy and psychology since I began attending workshops and participating in reading groups while at the University of Essex through the latter half of the 1980s. (That was a time of transition for me. I was finishing up my work on Wittgenstein's *Tractatus*—which resulted in a pair of monographs at the close of the decade—while at the same time 'retraining' myself as a philosopher of psychology.) And in the year 1992 I was fortunate enough to secure funding from the Hang Seng Bank of Hong Kong to launch the Hang Seng Centre for Cognitive Studies at the University of Sheffield, where I then worked. In that same year I instituted a series of interdisciplinary colloquia, and began running (in collaboration with various others) a series of interdisciplinary workshops and for-publication conferences that lasted until the summer of 2004. The result has been a total of seven edited volumes of interdisciplinary essays (Carruthers and Smith, 1996; Carruthers and Boucher, 1998; Carruthers and Chamberlain, 2000; Carruthers, Stich, and Siegal, 2002; Carruthers, Laurence, and Stich, 2005, 2006, and one planned for 2007). It hardly needs saying that I have benefited immeasurably from conversations with the participants in these projects, from hearing their presentations, and from reading their work. They are, unfortunately, too numerous to list here. (I estimate that there are more than 250 of them.) But I should like to record my gratitude for all that I have learned from these colleagues over the years.

Some portions of the present book draw on previous publications of mine, to a greater or lesser extent. (I have been working out my ideas gradually as I have gone along, with frequent additions and changes of mind.) I am grateful to the editors and publishers of the pieces listed here for permission to reproduce material. And I am grateful, too, to all those who gave me advice and critical commentary on those items, at various stages of their production. (Again, they are too numerous to list; their names can be found in the acknowledgments sections of the original publications.) The publications are:

'The roots of scientific reasoning: infancy, modularity, and the art of tracking.' In P. Carruthers, S. Stich and M. Siegal (eds.), *The Cognitive Basis of Science*, Cambridge University Press, 2002, 73–95. 'Human creativity: its evolution, its cognitive basis, and its connections with childhood pretence.' *British Journal for the Philosophy of Science*, 53 (2002), 1–25; published by Oxford University Press. 'The cognitive functions of language.' *Behavioral and Brain Sciences*, 25 (2002), 657–719; published by Cambridge University Press. 'On Fodor's Problem.' *Mind and Language*, 18 (2003), 502–23; published by Blackwell Press. 'On being simple minded.' *American Philosophical Quarterly*, 41 (2004), 205–20; published by University of Illinois Press. 'Practical reasoning in a modular mind.' *Mind and Language*, 19 (2004), 259–78; published by Blackwell Press. 'Distinctively human thinking: modular precursors and components.' In P. Carruthers, S. Laurence, and S. Stich (eds.), *The Innate Mind: structure and contents*, Oxford University Press, 2005, 69–88. 'Why the question of animal consciousness might not matter very much.' *Philosophical Psychology*, 18 (2005), 83–102; published by Routledge. 'The case for massively modular models of mind.' In R. Stainton (ed.), *Contemporary Debates in Cognitive Science*, Blackwell, 2006, 3–21. 'Simple heuristics meet massive modularity.' In P. Carruthers, S. Laurence, and S. Stich (eds.), *The Innate Mind: culture and cognition*, Oxford University Press, 2006.

I should stress that the present book is far more than any sort of compilation of these previous publications, however. There is much in it that is new. And the last item listed, in particular, involved a very substantial change of mind concerning the nature of modularity. This required me to rethink much that I had previously written on the topic. I am especially grateful to Stephen Stich for forcing that rethinking on me over the course of a series of conversations. (Reading and commenting on drafts of Samuels, 2005, probably also had some significant effect in this regard.) And I am grateful to Randy Gallistel for a dinner-time tutorial that set me right on the architecture of practical reasoning in non-human animals, which again occasioned some important rethinking on my part.

Thanks to the following friends and colleagues for their comments on some or all of the first draft of this book: Greg Currie, Andrew Coward, Dustin Stokes, Jonathan Weisberg, and especially Mike Anderson, Keith Frankish, Paul Pietroski, and Richard Samuels. In addition, I am grateful for recent discussions with Isaac Carruthers, Erich Diese, Jerry Levinson, Louis Liebenberg, Joe Mikhael, Petter Sannum, and Mike Tetzlaff (the latter of whom also participated in writing one of the sections in Chapter 1, on languages of thought). Thanks also go to Shaun Nichols and Stephen Stich for permission to reproduce two figures from their 2003, printed here as Figures 3.1 and 5.1; to Daniel Felleman and David Van Essen for permission to reproduce their map of the visual areas in the macaque visual cortex from their 1991, printed here as Figure 1.3; and to Randy Gallistel for permission to reproduce his ant navigation figure from his 2000, printed here as Figure 2.6.

Some of the ideas in this book have been presented as talks at the following venues over the last half-dozen years. I am grateful to all those who participated in the discussions that followed these presentations:

Austin Texas (Human Behavior and Evolution Society), Georgetown (Philosophy), London (Royal Institute of Philosophy), Michigan (Ann Arbor, Cognitive Science), Paris (CNRS), Penn (Cognitive Science), Providence RI (American Society for Aesthetics, symposium on creativity), Rutgers (Cognitive Science), Sheffield (three conferences as part of a three-year project on the innate mind), Toronto (Cognitive Science), Tucson AZ (Towards a Science of Consciousness 2004, symposium), Washington DC (American Philosophical Association, Eastern Division symposium), Washington University in St Louis (Philosophy), and Western Ontario (Philosophy graduate conference).

In addition, an early version of some of the material in this book was presented to a graduate seminar at the University of Maryland in the Spring of 2003; and then a polished penultimate version of the book was presented to another group of students in the Fall of 2005. I am grateful to all the students involved for their discussion and critical comment, mentioning especially:

Mike Anderson, Bryan Baltzly, Matt Barker, Susan Bilek, Benedict Chan, Melissa Ebbers, Kent Erickson, Joel Gibson, William Kallfelz, Andrew Kania, Dimiter Kirilov, Ryan Millsap, Harjeet Parmar, Jeremy Pober, Chris Pyne, Natalia Romanova, Leyland Saunders, Elizabeth Schecter, Elizabeth Stoll, and Benedicte Veillet.

Finally, I am grateful to the General Research Board at the University of Maryland for an award that enabled me to take a year without teaching to complete the first full draft of this book, and to my Dean, Jim Harris, for his support.

1

The Case for Massively Modular Models of Mind

My goal in this chapter is to set out the positive case supporting massively modular models of the human mind. Unfortunately, there is no generally accepted understanding of what a massively modular model of the mind *is*. So at least some of our discussion will have to be terminological. I shall begin by laying out the range of things that can be meant by 'modularity'. I shall then adopt a pair of strategies. One will be to distinguish some things that 'modularity' definitely *can't* mean, if the thesis of massive modularity is to be even remotely plausible. The other will be to look at the main arguments that have been offered in support of massive modularity, discussing what notion of 'module' they might warrant. It will turn out that there is, indeed, a strong case in support of massively modular models of the mind on *one* reasonably natural understanding of 'module'. But what really matters in the end, of course, is the substantive question what sorts of structure are adequate to account for the organization and operations of the human mind, not whether or not the components appealed to in that account get described as 'modules'. So the more interesting question before us is what the arguments that have been offered in support of massive modularity can succeed in showing us about those structures, whatever they get called. This substantive issue will occupy the bulk of the chapter.

1 Introduction: On Modularity

We begin our discussion with a consideration of the range of things that can (and have) been meant by 'modularity'. I shall pay special attention to the work of Fodor (1983), which has been particularly influential in some areas of cognitive science.

1.1 A Spectrum of Options

In the weakest sense, a module can just be something like: a dissociable functional component. This is pretty much the everyday sense in which one can speak of buying a hi-fi system on a modular basis, for example. The hi-fi is modular if one can purchase the speakers independently of the tape-deck, say, or substitute one set of speakers for another for use with the same tape-deck. Moreover, it counts towards the modularity of the system if one doesn't have to buy a tape-deck at all—just purchasing a CD player along with the rest—or if the tape-deck can be broken while the remainder of the system continues to operate normally. It is important to stress, however, that independence amongst modules is by no means total. The different parts need to be connected up with one another in the right way, and coupled to a source of electrical power, in order for the whole hi-fi system to work; and the amplifier is an indispensable—but still distinct—component.

Understood in this weak way, the thesis of massive mental modularity would claim that the mind consists entirely of distinct components, each of which has some specific job to do in the functioning of the whole. It would predict that the properties of many of these components could vary independently of the properties of the others. (This would be consistent with the hypothesis of 'special intelligences'—see Gardner, 1983.) And it would predict that the components should be separately modifiable, being differentially affected by at least some other factors.[1] Moreover, the theory would predict that it is possible for some of these components to be damaged or absent altogether, while leaving the functioning of the remainder at least partially intact.

Would a thesis of *massive* mental modularity of this sort be either interesting or controversial? That would depend upon whether the thesis in question were just that the mind consists of some modular components, on the one hand; or whether it is that the mind consists of *a great many* modular components, on the other. Read in the first way, then nearly everyone is a massive modularist, given the weak sense of 'module' that is in play. For everyone will allow that the mind does consist of distinct components; and everyone will allow that at least some of these components can be damaged without destroying the functionality of the whole. The simple facts of cortical blindness and deafness are enough to establish these weak claims.

Read in the second way, however, the thesis of massive modularity would be by no means anodyne—although obviously it would admit of a range

---

[1] Sternberg (2001) develops this aspect of (weak) modularity into an elaborate and well worked-out methodology for the discovery of distinct modules in many different areas of cognitive science, relying on their separate modifiability by other factors.

of strengths, depending upon *how many* components the mind is thought to consist of. Certainly it isn't the case that everyone believes that the mind is composed of a great many distinct functional components. For example, those who (like Fodor, 1983) picture the mind as a big general-purpose computer with a limited number of distinct input and output links to the world (vision, audition, etc.) don't believe this, even though they may allow that the input systems themselves are composed of multiple parts.

In reply it might be said that almost everyone accepts that the mind contains lots and lots of *representations* (e.g. sentences in a 'language of thought'). And shouldn't each one of these count as a distinct component? If so, then the thesis of massive modularity (in the weak sense of 'module') will be accepted by almost all cognitive scientists—certainly by all who believe in local representations. The thesis of massive modularity is generally understood to apply only to *processing systems*, however, not to the representations that might be produced by such systems. And this is how I myself propose to understand it. So for these purposes, perceptual systems and inferential systems are candidate modules, but the individual percepts and beliefs produced by such systems are not.

It is clear, then, that a thesis of massive (in the sense of 'multiple') modularity is a controversial one, even when the term 'module' is taken in its weakest sense. So those evolutionary psychologists who have defended the claim that the mind consists of a great many different modular processing systems (Tooby and Cosmides, 1992; Sperber, 1996; Pinker, 1997) are defending a thesis of considerable interest, even if 'module' just *means* 'component'.

At the other end of the spectrum of notions of modularity, and in the strongest sense, a module would have all of the properties of what is sometimes called a 'Fodor-module' (Fodor, 1983). That is, it would be a domain-specific innately specified processing system, with its own proprietary transducers, and delivering 'shallow' (non-conceptual) outputs (e.g., in the case of the visual system, delivering a $2^{1}/_{2}$-D sketch; Marr, 1983). In addition, a module in this sense would be mandatory in its operations, swift in its processing, isolated from and inaccessible to the rest of cognition, associated with particular neural structures, liable to specific and characteristic patterns of breakdown, and would develop according to a paced and distinctively arranged sequence of growth. I shall need to comment briefly on the various elements of this account.

1.2 On Fodor-Modularity

According to Fodor (1983) modules are domain-specific processing systems of the mind. Like most others who have written about modularity since, he understands this to mean that a module will be restricted in the kinds of content that it takes as input.² It is restricted to those contents that constitute its *domain*, indeed. So the visual system is restricted to visual inputs; the auditory system is restricted to auditory inputs; and so on. Furthermore, Fodor claims that each module should have its own transducers: the rods and cones of the retina for the visual system; the eardrum for the auditory system; and so forth.

According to Fodor (1983), moreover, the outputs of a module are *shallow* in the sense of being non-conceptual. So modules generate *information* of various sorts, but they don't issue in *thoughts* or *beliefs*. On the contrary, belief-fixation is argued by Fodor to be the very archetype of a *non*-modular (or holistic) process. Hence the visual module might deliver a representation of surfaces and edges in the perceived scene, say, but it wouldn't as such issue in *recognition* of the object as a chair, nor in the *belief* that a chair is present. This would require the cooperation of some other (non-modular) system or systems.

Fodor-modules are supposed to be innate, in some sense of that term,³ and to be localized to specific structures in the brain (although these structures might not, themselves, be local ones, but could rather be distributed across a set of dispersed neural systems). Their growth and development would be under significant genetic control, therefore, and might be liable to distinctive patterns of breakdown, either genetic or developmental. And one would expect their growth to unfold according to a genetically guided developmental timetable, buffered against the vagaries of the environment and the individual's learning opportunities.

Fodor-modules are also supposed to be mandatory and swift in their processing. So their operations aren't under voluntary control (one can't turn them off), and they generate their outputs extremely quickly by comparison with other (non-modular) systems. When we have our eyes open we can't help but see what is in front of us. And nor can our better judgment (e.g. about the equal lengths of the two lines in a Müller-Lyer illusion) over-ride

---

² Many evolutionary psychologists understand domain-specificity somewhat differently. They tend to regard the domain of a module to be its *function*. The domain of a module is what it is *supposed to do*, on this account, rather than the class of contents that it can receive as input. I shall follow the more common *content* reading of 'domain' in the present chapter. But the two notions turn out to be intimately connected with one another when the notion of 'input' is elucidated properly, as we shall see shortly.

³ Samuels (2002) argues convincingly that 'innate', in the context of cognitive science, should mean something like 'cognitively primitive'. Innate properties of the mind are ones that emerge in the course of development that is normal for that genotype, but that admit of no cognitivist explanation. (For example, they aren't explicable as resulting from some sort of *learning* process.) So they are cognitively basic—they can be appealed to in the explanation of other mental properties, but don't themselves admit of a cognitive explanation (as opposed, e.g., to a biological one).

the operations of the visual system. Moreover, compare the speed with which vision is processed with the (much slower) speed of conscious decision-making.

Finally, modules are supposed by Fodor to be both isolated from the remainder of cognition (i.e. encapsulated) and to have internal operations that are inaccessible elsewhere. These properties are often run together with each other (and also with domain specificity), but they are really quite distinct. To say that a processing system is *encapsulated* is to say that its internal operations can't draw on any information held outside of that system in addition to its input. (This isn't to say that the system can't access any stored information at all, of course, for it might have its own dedicated database that it consults during its operations.) In contrast, to say that a system is *inaccessible* is to say that other systems can have no access to its internal processing, but only to its outputs, or to the results of that processing.

Note that neither of these notions should be confused with that of *domain specificity*. The latter is about restrictions on the input to a system. To say that a system is domain specific is to say that it only receives inputs of a particular sort, concerning a certain kind of subject matter. Whereas to say that the processing of a system is encapsulated, on the one hand, or inaccessible, on the other, is to say something about the access-relations that obtain between the internal operations of that system and others. Hence one can easily envisage systems that might *lack* domain specificity, for example (being capable of receiving any sort of content as input), but whose internal operations are nevertheless encapsulated and inaccessible (Carruthers, 2002a; Sperber, 2002; and see the discussion of the supposed logic module in Section 2 below).

The explanations just given depend crucially on the notion of the *input* to a system, however. And this, too, needs some elucidation. One option would see the notion of *input* as contrasting with that of *database*, or stored information of any kind (as proposed by Carruthers, 2003). In which case any sort of activated information generated by and received from other processing systems would count as input, provided that the receiving system could do something with that information. But understanding the notion of input in this way would deliver a highly counter-intuitive account of the notion of *encapsulation*. For suppose that a processing system were so set up that it could query a wide range of other systems for information in the course of its normal operations; but suppose that the system in question couldn't, itself, access any *stored* information. Then if 'encapsulation' meant 'processing that can't draw on any information besides the input', and 'input' just meant 'information received from another system (rather than accessed from a database)', then the system envisaged would count as an entirely encapsulated one! For while it can draw on information from many other systems in the mind, all of this would be categorized as 'input' to the system, and hence wouldn't count against the system's encapsulation. This is a conclusion that surely needs to be avoided.

Another way to see the point is to notice that the distinction between the database that a system can search, on the one hand, and the information that is made available to that system by other processing systems, on the other, can't bear the weight required of it. Imagine two systems A and B. System A conducts searches across all stored beliefs in the course of its own operations, and hence isn't encapsulated by the above account. System B doesn't do this, but queries a wide range of other systems, which collectively search all stored beliefs on its behalf. It is absurd to say that while System A is unencapsulated, System B is an encapsulated one (on the grounds that all of the information made available to it counts as *input*, and hence doesn't count against its encapsulation). For neither is in any meaningful sense isolated from information held or generated elsewhere in the mind.

It is better to understand the input to a system to be the set of items of information that can *turn the system on*. For example, the face-recognition system is turned on by representations of eye-like and mouth-like shapes related to one another in such a way as to form a rough triangle. And the mind-reading system is turned on by representations of behavior. As we shall see in Section 2, the mind-reading system might need to send queries elsewhere in order to do its work, seeking information from the folk-physics system, perhaps. But the answers to those queries don't count as input to the mind-reading system, because the latter can't be *activated by* mere representations of physical movement.

This account gives us plausible readings of both 'domain specificity' and 'encapsulation'. The domain of the mind-reading system includes intentional behavior, but not mere physical movements like the sight of a ball rolling down a hill, because only the former will cue the system into action. But if the mind-reading system operates by querying a wide range of other systems for information (including the folk-physics system, say), then it won't count as an encapsulated one. The terminology that has been introduced here is summarized in Figure 1.1, for ease of reference later on.[4]

---

[4] Note that this account also ties the *content* reading of 'domain' more closely to the *function* reading favored by some evolutionary psychologists. For the representations of behavior that turn the mind-reading system on—its inputs, and hence its content-domain—are (for the most part) the ones that it was *designed* to process, and hence also constitute its functional domain. (The qualification 'for the most part' is needed because of the distinction that Sperber, 1996, draws between the *proper* domain of a module—which is the set of inputs that it was designed to process—and the *actual* domain, which could be much wider. Geometric shapes moving around on a computer screen in the right sort of contingent way will cue me into interpreting their movements in intentional terms; but the mind-reading system wasn't designed to process the movements of geometric shapes.)

Input: The input to a system to be the set of items of information that can *turn the system on.* (The notion of *input* contrasts with that of *information accessed in the course of processing,* whether activated or stored.)

Domain specific: To say that a system is domain specific is to say that it only receives inputs of a particular sort, concerning a certain kind of subject matter.

Encapsulation: To say that a processing system is encapsulated is to say that its internal operations can't draw on any information held outside that system in addition to its input.

Inaccessible: To say that a system is inaccessible is to say that other systems can have no access to its internal processing, but only to its outputs, or to the results of that processing.

Figure 1.1. Some key terminology

2 What Massive Modularity could not be

There is nothing incoherent in the idea that the mind might consist of a great many Fodor-modules (or at least in systems that closely resemble Fodor-modules). Indeed, such an idea is consistent with Brooks's (1986) *subsumption architecture* for the mind. On such an account the mind consists of a whole suite of input-to-output modular processing systems, with the overall behavior of the mind, and of the organism that it governs, being determined by competition amongst such modules. Each module will receive its input from a set of sensory transducers (whether shared or proprietary), and will serve to control some specific type of behavior of the organism. The operations of each module will be mandatory, encapsulated, and inaccessible. And modules might be innate, each with its own specific neural realization, distinctive developmental trajectory, and characteristic patterns of breakdown.

I shall argue in Chapter 2, however, that a subsumption architecture isn't even plausible as an account of the minds of insects and arachnids, let alone of the human mind. Indeed, I shall argue that perception / belief / desire / planning architectures are well nigh ubiquitous in the animal kingdom. On such an account, perception gives rise to beliefs; a combination of perception and the organism's bodily states gives rise to desires; and then beliefs and desires are combined with one another within some sort of practical-reasoning system to select an appropriate behavior. I shall assume the correctness of this kind of view in the present chapter, returning to defend it in the chapter that follows.

If belief / desire architectures are presupposed, then it is obvious that by 'module' we can't possibly mean 'Fodor-module', if a thesis of massive mental modularity is to be even remotely plausible. In particular, some of the items in Fodor's list will need to get struck out as soon as we move to endorse any sort of central-systems modularity, let alone entertain the idea of *massive* modularity. (This is no accident, since Fodor's analysis was explicitly designed to apply to modular input and output systems like color perception or face recognition. Fodor has consistently maintained that there is nothing modular about central cognitive processes of believing and reasoning. See Fodor, 1983, 2000.) If there are to be conceptual modules—modules dealing with common-sense physics, say, or common-sense biology, or with cheater-detection, to name but a few examples that have been proposed by cognitive scientists in recent decades—then it is obvious that modules can't have their own proprietary transducers. Nor can they have shallow outputs. On the contrary, their outputs will be fully conceptual thoughts or beliefs.

Is this way of proceeding question-begging? Can one insist, on the contrary, that since modules *are* systems with shallow outputs we can see at a glance that the mind can't be massively modular in its organization? This would be fine if there were already a pre-existing agreed understanding of what modules are sup-posed to be. But there isn't. As stressed in Section 1, there are a *range* of meanings of 'module' available. And we surely shouldn't allow ourselves to become fix-ated on Fodor-modularity (as seems to have happened to most philosophers who write on these topics). On the contrary, principles of charity of interpretation dic-tate that we should select the meaning that makes the best sense of the claims of massive modularists. That is what I aim to do in this chapter.

What of domain specificity, in the context of a thesis of massive modularity? I once argued that this also needs to be dropped (or to be re-conceptualized in terms of functional rather than content domains), on the grounds that the practical-reasoning system should be considered as a distinct module, but one that would be capable of receiving any belief and any desire as input (Carruthers, 2004a). I now think, however, that practical reasoning is underpinned by a whole host of different systems, each of which is turned on by a specific sort of motivation, and each of which then searches for information in the service of that motivation within specific locations in the mind. (See Chapter 2.7 and 2.8.) So each such system can probably count as domain specific in character.

Although it may well be the case that *most* modules are domain specific, we could surely accept that some aren't, without thereby compromising the thesis of massive mental modularity. Sperber (1996), for example, hypothesizes the existence of a formal logic module, whose task is to deduce some of the simpler logical consequences of any set of beliefs that it receives as input. For example, when it receives as input any pair of propositions of the form, 'P' and 'P ⊃ Q', it immediately deduces the conclusion 'Q'. The operations of such a module might be entirely encapsulated (as well as sharing many other elements of Fodor-modularity). But it plainly couldn't be domain specific, since in order to do its job it would have to be capable of getting turned on by *any* set of beliefs of the right form.

While we should accept that most conceptual modules are likely to be domain specific, then, we shouldn't absolutely require it. Swiftness of processing, in contrast, surely needs to go, in the context of massive modularity (except perhaps in comparison with the speed of *conscious* thought processes, if the latter are realized in cycles of modular activity, as I shall argue in Chapter 4 that they are). For if the mind is *massively* modular, then we will lack any significant comparison-class. Fodor-modules were characterized as swift in relation to *central* processes; but a massive modularist will maintain that the latter are modular too.

It looks plausible that the claim of mandatory operation should be retained, however. Each component system of the mind can be such that it automatically processes any input that it receives. (Indeed, such a claim is almost analytic, if the input to a system is just the information that is capable of turning on its operations, as we suggested above.) And certainly it seems that *some* of the alleged central modules, at least, have such a property. As Segal (1998) points out, we can't help but see the actions of an actor on the stage as displaying anger, or jealousy, or whatever; despite our knowledge that he is thinking and feeling none of the things that he appears to be. So the operations of our mind-reading faculty seem to be mandatory. Another way to put the point is that the operations of a system are mandatory if they can't be *turned off at will*. And it seems very likely that most (if not all) of the component systems that make up the human mind are mandatory in this sense, and that conscious decisions shouldn't be capable of determining whether or not a given system continues operating. This is what explains Segal's point: just by reminding ourselves that this is only an actor, we can't stop the mind-reading system from processing the behavioral input that it receives.

Now what of claims of innateness, and of neural specificity? Certainly one *could* maintain that the mind consists almost exclusively of innately channeled processing systems, realized in specific neural structures. This would be a highly controversial claim, but it wouldn't be immediately absurd. Whether this is the *best* way to develop and defend a thesis of massive modularity is moot. Certainly, innateness has been emphasized by evolutionary psychologists, who have argued that natural selection has led to the development of multiple innately channeled cognitive systems (Tooby and Cosmides, 1992). But others have argued that modularity is the product of learning and development (Karmiloff-Smith, 1992; Paterson et al., 1999). Both sides in this debate agree, however, that modules will be realized in specific neural structures (not necessarily the same from individual to individual). And both sides are agreed, at least, that development begins with a set of innate attention biases and a variety of innately structured learning mechanisms.

My own sympathies in this debate are towards the nativist end of the spectrum. I suspect that much of the structure, and many of the contents, of the human mind are innate or innately channeled.[5] But in the context of developing a thesis of *massive* modularity, it seems wisest to drop the innateness-constraint from our definition of what modules are. For one might want to allow that some aspects of the mature language faculty are modular, for example, even though it is saturated with acquired information about the lexicon of a specific natural language like English. And one might want to allow that modules concerned with particular behavioral skills can be constructed by over-learning, say, in such a way that it might be appropriate to describe someone's reading competence as modular.[6]

Finally, we come to the properties of encapsulated and inaccessible processing. These are thought by many (including Fodor, 2000) to be the core properties of modular systems. And there seems to be no a priori reason why the mind shouldn't be composed exclusively out of such systems, and cycles of operation of such systems. At any rate, such claims have been defended by a number of those who describe themselves as massive modularists (Sperber, 1996, 2002, 2005; Carruthers, 2002a, 2003, 2004a). I shall leave the claim of inaccessibility untouched for the moment, pending closer examination of the arguments in support of massive modularity. But I do want briefly to argue that massive modularists shouldn't claim that the mind must consist exclusively of systems that are encapsulated. (I shall then return to this point at greater length in Section 6, in the context of an examination of Fodor's arguments.)

As we noted above, even where a system has been designed to focus on and process a particular domain of inputs, one might expect that in the course of its normal processing it might need to query a range of other systems for information of other sorts. Consider the mind-reading system, for example, which virtually every massive modularist would consider to be realized in

---

[5] What does it *mean* to say that some property of the mind is innate? Certainly not that it is built from a fully-specified genetic blueprint. For that isn't the way in which the development of any aspect of an organism occurs: it is always an interaction of genes and gene-environments (Carroll, 2005). Nor does it mean that the property is present at birth, nor universal in all members of the species. Rather, I endorse the analysis given by Samuels (2002). For the purposes of cognitive science, a trait is innate if (a) it emerges during the course of development that is normal for the genotype, and (b) it is cognitively *basic*, not admitting of a cognitive (e.g. learning-based) explanation.

[6] Indeed, recent theories suggest that there are *many* fine-grained motor-control modules constructed via learning, with different modules being constructed each time we acquire a new skill, or learn to manipulate a new tool (Ghahramani and Wolpert, 1997; Haruno et al., 2001).

a module (or collection of modules). This is designed to focus on behavior together with attributions of mental states, and to generate predictions of further behavior and/or attributions of yet other mental states. Yet in the course of its normal operations it may need to query a whole range of other systems for information relevant to solving the task in hand. In which case the system isn't an encapsulated one.

Consider an example used by Currie and Sterelny (2000) in their criticism of the view that the mind-reading faculty might be modular (which they take to require both domain specificity and encapsulation). They write:

If Max's confederate says he drew money from their London bank today there are all sorts of reasons Max might suspect him: because it is a public holiday there; because there was a total blackout of the city; because the confederate was spotted in New York at lunch time. Just where are the bits of information to which we are systematically blind in making our social judgments? The whole genre of the detective story depends on our interest and skill in bringing improbable bits of far-away information to bear on the question of someone's credibility. To suggest that we don't have that skill defies belief.

While the example perhaps shows that mind-reading isn't encapsulated, it shows nothing about lack of domain specificity; nor does it show that mind-reading isn't underpinned by a specialized function-specific processing system. (That is, it does nothing to show that mind-reading is just an aspect of some sort of holistic general-purpose cognition, as Currie and Sterelny believe.) This is because the skill in question arguably isn't (or isn't largely) a mind-reading one. Let me elaborate.

Roughly speaking, to lie is to assert that P while believing that not-P. So evidence of lying is evidence that the person is speaking contrary to their belief. In the case of Max's confederate it is evidence that, although he *says* that he drew money from the London account today, he actually believes that he didn't. Now the folk-psychological principle, 'If someone didn't do something, then they believe that they didn't do that thing', is surely pretty robust, at least for actions that are salient and recent (like traveling to, and drawing money from, a bank on the day in question). So almost all of the onus in demonstrating that the confederate is lying will fall onto showing that he didn't in fact do what he said he did. And this isn't anything to do with mind-reading per se. Evidence that he was somewhere else at the time, or evidence that physical constraints of one sort or another would have prevented the action (e.g. the bank was closed), will (in the circumstances) provide sufficient evidence of duplicity. Granted, many different kinds of information can be relevant to the question what actually happened, and what the confederate actually did or didn't do. But this doesn't in itself count against the domain-specificity and function-specificity of a separately effectible mind-reading system (although it *does* count decisively against its encapsulation).

All that the example really shows is that the mind-reading faculty may need to work in conjunction with other elements of cognition in providing us with a solution to a problem, querying other systems for information.[7] In fact most of the burden in detective-work is placed on physical enquiries of one sort or another—investigating foot-prints, finger-prints, closed banks, whether the suspect was somewhere else at the time, and so forth—rather than on mind-reading. The contribution of the latter to the example in question is limited to (a) assisting in the interpretation of the original utterance (Does the confederate mean what he says? Is he joking or teasing?); (b) providing us with the concept of a lie, and perhaps a disposition to be on the lookout for lies; and (c) providing us with the principle that people generally know whether they have or haven't performed a salient action in the recent past.

What we have so far, then, is that if a thesis of massive mental modularity is to be remotely plausible, then by 'module' we cannot mean 'Fodor-module'. In particular, the properties of having proprietary transducers, shallow outputs, fast processing, significant innateness or innate channeling, and encapsulation will very likely have to be struck out. That leaves us with the idea that modules might be isolable function-specific processing systems, all or almost all of which are domain specific (in the content sense), whose operations aren't subject to the will, which are associated with specific neural structures (albeit sometimes spatially dispersed ones), and whose internal operations may be inaccessible to the remainder of cognition. Whether all of these properties should be retained in the most defensible version of a thesis of massive mental modularity will be the subject of the remainder of this chapter.

In the sections that follow I shall be considering the main arguments that can be offered in support of a thesis of massively modular mental organization. I shall be simultaneously examining not only the strength of those arguments, but also the notion of 'module' that they might warrant.

3 The Argument from Design

The first argument derives ultimately from Simon (1962), and concerns the design of complex functional systems quite generally, and in biology in

---

[7] See Nichols and Stich (2003) who develop an admirably detailed account of our mind-reading capacities, which involves a complex array of both domain-specific and domain-general mechanisms and processes, including the operations of a domain-general planning system and a domain-general suppositional system, or 'possible worlds box'. I shall discuss their model in greater detail in Chapter 3.

particular. According to this line of thought, we should expect such systems to be constructed hierarchically out of dissociable sub-systems (each of which is made up of yet further sub-systems), in such a way that the whole assembly can be built up gradually, adding sub-system to sub-system; where the properties of sub-systems can be varied independently of one another; and in such a way that the functionality of the whole is buffered, to some extent, from changes or damage occurring to the parts.

Simon (1962) uses the famous analogy of the two watchmakers to illustrate the point. One watchmaker assembles one watch at a time, attempting to construct the whole finished product at once from a given set of micro-components. This makes it easy for him to forget the proper ordering of parts, and if he is interrupted he may have to start again from the beginning. The second watchmaker first builds sets of sub-components out of the given micro-component parts, and then combines those into larger sub-component assemblies, until eventually the watches are complete. This helps organize and sequence the whole process, and makes it much less vulnerable to interruption.

3.1 Modules in Biology

Consistent with such an account, there is a very great deal of evidence from across many levels in biology to the effect that complex functional systems are built up out of assemblies of sub-components (West-Eberhard, 2003; Schlosser and Wagner, 2004; Callebaut and Rasskin-Gutman, 2005). Each of these components is constructed out of further sub-components and has a distinctive role to play in the functioning of the whole, and many of them can be damaged or lost while leaving the functionality of the remainder at least partially intact. This is true for the operations of genes, of cells, of cellular assemblies, of whole organs, of whole organisms, and of multi-organism units like a bee colony (Seeley, 1995). And by extension, we should expect it to be true of cognition also, provided that it is appropriate to think of cognitive systems as biological ones, which have been subject to natural selection. (I shall return to examine this question in Section 3.2.)

West-Eberhard (2003) argues that a belief in massive biological modularity—in the sense of discreteness and dissociability amongst parts combined with integration within parts—is well nigh ubiquitous across the biological sciences. But not everyone uses the term 'module' to designate this same concept, however. Many other words are used to describe the same thing, including 'atomization' (Wagner, 1996), 'autonomy' (Nijhout, 1991), 'compartmentalization' (Maynard-Smith and Szathmáry, 1995; Kirschner and Gerhart, 1998), 'individualization' (Larson and Losos, 1996), and 'sub-unit organization' (West-Eberhard, 1996). But the phenomenon in question—and the belief in its omnipresence—is the same in each case.

West-Eberhard (2003) herself argues that in the context of evolutionary developmental biology, the most fruitful way of individuating modules is in terms of the developmental / genetic switches that lead to their development. For each such switch leads to a distinct or partly distinct compartment in the individual's phenotype, in which a distinctive set of genes is expressed, and which can hence become a target of natural selection. And developmental determination by switches must occur prior to the resulting modular system becoming an adaptation, as well as prior to any further shaping of the functional integration of the module through the evolutionary process.

The important point for our purposes, however, is that modular organization is a prerequisite of—or is at least an *extremely* common solution to—evolvability (Wagner and Altenberg, 1996; Raff and Raff, 2000; Wimsatt and Schank, 2004). Since the properties of modules are to some significant degree independent of one another, both they and the developmental pathways that lead to them can have distinctive effects on the overall fitness of the organism. But by the same token, since modules are separately modifiable, natural selection can act on one without having to make alterations in all (which would have potentially disastrous effects). So evolution can tinker with the separate components of the overall organism, at many levels of organization, responding to particular evolutionary pressures by factoring the overall fitness of the organism into the distinctive fitness-effects of the component modules. Since only a modular organization can enable this to happen, the question for us is whether or not it is appropriate to think of the mind as a *biological* system, subject to the same evolvability requirements as any other such system. We will turn to that question shortly.

Before we do so, I want to stress that biological modularity is always a matter of degree (Rasskin-Gutman, 2005). Hence the notion doesn't just apply to so-called 'mosaic' traits like eye-color that can vary quite independently of all others, as Woodward and Cowie (2004) allege. Biological systems like hearts and lungs are closely interconnected with many others, of course—each is tightly tied into the bilateral organization of the body, and presupposes the existence of the other, for example. Nevertheless, each follows a developmental trajectory that is significantly independent of the other; events like cancer can affect the one without affecting the other; and there can be genetic variations in each one that don't lead to alterations in the other. There is therefore an important sense in which hearts and lungs can be regarded as distinct bodily modules.

What we should expect, then, is that cognitive systems can be more or less deeply embedded in the developmental / genetic hierarchy, and more or less closely dependent upon other such systems. Some might be more like lungs—homologous across many species, and crucial to the functioning of the whole. (The cognitive modules that process basic spatial properties and relationships might be a good example, here.) And some might be more like eye-color—varying across individual members of the species, and comparatively peripheral in function. (Some genetic variations in personality type might be an example of this.) But all should be to some important degree discrete and dissociable, while displaying significant internal integration.

3.2 Did the Mind Evolve?

What sorts of properties of organisms are apt to have fitness-effects? These are many and various, ranging from gross anatomical features such as size, shape, and color of fur or skin, through the detailed functional organization of specific physical systems such as the eye or the liver, to behavioral tendencies such as the disposition that cuckoo chicks have to push other baby birds out of the nest. And for anyone who is neither an epiphenomenalist nor an eliminativist about the mind, it is manifest that the human mind is amongst the properties of the human organism that has fitness-effects. For it will be by virtue of the mind that almost all fitness-enhancing behaviors—such as running from a predator, taking resources from a competitor, or wooing a mate—are caused.

On any broadly realist construal of the mind and its states, then, the mind is at least a prime *candidate* to have been shaped by natural selection. How could such a possibility fail to have been realized? How could the mind be a major cause of fitness-enhancing behaviors without being a product of natural selection? One alternative would be a truly radical empiricist one. It might be said that not only most of the contents of the mind, but also its structure and organization, are acquired from the environment. Perhaps the only direct product of natural selection is some sort of extremely powerful learning algorithm, which could operate almost equally well in a wide range of environments, both actual and non-actual. The fitness-enhancing properties that we observe in adult minds, then, aren't (except very indirectly) a product of natural selection, but are rather a result of learning from the environment within which fitness-enhancing behaviors will need to be manifested.

Such a proposal is an obvious non-starter, however. It is one thing to claim that all the *contents* of the mind are acquired from the environment using general learning principles, as empiricists have traditionally claimed. (This is implausible enough by itself; see Section 4 below, briefly, and Chapter 2, at length.) And it is quite another thing to claim that the structure and organization of the mind is similarly learned. How could the differences between, and characteristic causal roles of, beliefs, desires, emotions, and intentions be learned from experience?[8] For there is nothing corresponding to them in the world from which they could be learned; and in any case, any process of learning must surely presuppose that a basic mental architecture is already in place. Moreover, how could the differences between personal (or 'episodic') memory, factual (or 'semantic') memory, and short-term (or 'working') memory be acquired from the environment? The idea seems barely coherent. And indeed, no empiricist has ever been foolish enough to suggest such things.

We have no other option, then, but to see the structure and organization of the mind as a product of the human genotype, in exactly the same sense as, and to the same extent that, the structure and organization of the human body is a product of our genotype. But someone could still try to maintain that the mind isn't the result of any process of natural selection. Rather, it might be said, the structure of the mind might be the product of a single macro-mutation, which became general in the population through sheer chance, and which has remained thereafter through mere inertia. Or it might be the case that the organization in question was arrived at through random genetic drift—that is to say, a random walk through a whole series of minor genetic mutations, each of which just happened to become general in the population, and the sequence of which just happened to produce the structure of our minds as its end-point.

These possibilities are so immensely unlikely that they can effectively be dismissed out of hand. Evolution by natural selection remains the only explanation of organized functional complexity that we have (Dawkins, 1986). Any complex phenotypic structure, such as the human eye or the human mind, will require the cooperation of many thousands of genes to build it. And the possibility that all of these thousands of tiny genetic mutations might have occurred all at once by chance, or might have become established in sequence (again by chance), is unlikely in the extreme. The odds in favor of either thing happening are vanishingly small. (Throwing a '6' with a fair die many thousands of times in a row would be much more likely.) We can be confident that each of the required small changes, initially occurring through chance mutation, conferred at least some minor fitness-benefit on its possessor, sufficient to stabilize it in the population, and thus providing a platform on which the next small change could occur.

The strength of this argument, in respect of any given biological system, is directly proportional to the degree of its organized functional complexity—the more complex the organization of the system, the more implausible it is that

---

[8] Note that we aren't asking how one could learn from experience *of* beliefs, desires, and the other mental states. Rather, we are asking how the differences between these states themselves could be learned. The point concerns our acquisition of the mind itself, not the acquisition of a *theory* of mind.

it might have arisen by chance macro-mutation or random genetic walk. Now, even from the perspective of common-sense psychology the mind is an immensely complex system, which seems to be organized in ways that are largely adaptive. (As evidence of the latter point, witness the success of our species as a whole, which has burgeoned in numbers and spread across the whole planet in the course of a mere 100,000 years or so.) And the more we learn about the mind from a scientific perspective, the more it seems that it is even more complex than we might initially have been inclined to think. Systems such as vision, for example—that are treated as 'simples' from the perspective of common-sense psychology—turn out to have a hugely complex internal structure.

Before leaving this topic I should stress that it remains possible that some properties of the mind might be 'spandrels' (in the sense of Gould and Lewontin, 1979). From the claim that the mind as a whole is an adaptation resulting from natural selection, it of course doesn't follow that every property of the mind is an adaptation likewise. For some might be by-products of those that *are* adaptations. And I should also stress that when they happen against the right background, small changes can sometimes have large adaptive effects without any need for a history of selection. Thus consider the hypothesis put forward by Hauser et al. (2002), concerning the evolution of the language faculty. They suggest that many of the systems that enable language in humans are shared with other animal species, such as the capacity to carve a speech stream into phonemes, and the capacity for vocal imitation (Hauser, 1996). Against a sufficiently rich background, it might then have needed but a small and relatively simple change—perhaps to enable a particular sort of recursion in the generation of mental representations—to make fully human language possible. And this change itself might either have resulted from a single random mutation, or be a spandrel of some other selected-for change. None of this is ruled out by the claim that the mind as a whole has been shaped by natural selection.

3.3 How many Modules?

The prediction of this line of reasoning, then, is that cognition will be structured out of systems that are to some significant degree dissociable, and each of which has a distinctive function, or set of functions, to perform.[9] This gives us a notion of a cognitive 'module' that is pretty close to the everyday

---

[9] We should expect many cognitive systems to have a *set* of functions, rather than a unique function, since multi-functionality is rife in the biological world. Once a component has been selected, it can be co-opted, and partly maintained and shaped, in the service of other tasks. By the same token, we should expect many sub-modules to be *shared* amongst more than one superordinate system. I return to this point in Section 3.4.

sense in which one can talk about a hi-fi system as 'modular' provided that the tape-deck can be purchased, can function, and can vary its properties independently of the CD player, and so forth. Roughly, a module is just a dissociable *component*.

Consistent with the above prediction, there is now a great deal of evidence of a neuro-psychological sort that something like massive modularity (in the everyday sense of 'module') is indeed true of the human mind. People can have their language system damaged while leaving much of the remainder of cognition intact (aphasia); people can lack the ability to reason about mental states while still being capable of much else (autism); people can lose their capacity to recognize just human faces; someone can lose the capacity to reason about cheating in a social exchange while retaining otherwise parallel capacities to reason about risks and dangers; someone can lose the capacity to name living things while retaining the capacity to name non-living things, or vice versa; someone can lose the capacity to name fruits and vegetables while retaining their ability to name animals; and so on and so forth (Sachs, 1985; Shallice, 1988; Hart and Gordon, 1992; Sacchett and Humphreys, 1992; Baron-Cohen, 1995; Farah et al., 1996; Tager-Flusberg, 1999; Stone et al., 2002; Varley, 2002).[10]

But just *how many* components does this argument suggest that the mind consists of, however? Simon's (1962) argument makes the case for hierarchical organization, but Samuels (2006) claims that the argument fails to establish modularity of mind in any interesting sense. At the top of the hierarchy will be the target system in question (a cell, a bodily organ, the human mind). And at the base will be the smallest micro-components of the system, bottoming out (in the case of the mind) in the detailed neural processes that realize cognitive ones. But it might seem that it is left entirely open how high or how low the pyramid is (i.e. how many 'levels' the hierarchy consists of), and whether the 'pyramid' has concave or convex edges. If the pyramid is quite low with concave sides, then the mind might decompose at the first level of analysis into just a few constituents such as *perception, belief, desire*, and *the will*, much as traditional 'faculty psychologies' have always assumed; and these might then

---

[10] In fact very few of these disorders are 'clean', with just the target capacity damaged and all else left intact. In most cases where one capacity is damaged, others will be damaged also. Where the damage results from an acquired brain-injury, this is hardly very surprising. For few such injuries are likely to affect just a single brain system. But even where the damage is genetic, we should not be surprised. For as Marcus (2004) points out, a very high proportion of the genes involved in building any one bodily system will also be involved in building others; so the vast majority of genetically based disorders should be expected to have broad effects. In addition, where modules share parts, damage to one of those parts will have an impact on the functioning of more than one superordinate system. And such sharing of parts is likely to be rife in cognitive systems, just as it is in biological ones.

get implemented quite rapidly in neural processes. In contrast, only if the pyramid is high with convex sides should we expect the mind to decompose into *many* components, each of which in turn consists of many components, and so on. (See Figure 1.2.)

There is more mileage to be derived from Simon's argument yet, however. For the range and complexity of the functions that the overall system needs to execute will surely give us a direct measure of the height of the pyramid and manner in which it will slope. (The greater the complexity, the greater the number of sub-systems into which the system will decompose at each level of organization, and the greater the number of levels.) This is because the hierarchical organization is there in the first place to ensure evolvability and robustness of function. Evolution needs to be able to tinker with one function in response to selection pressures without necessarily impacting any of the others.[11]

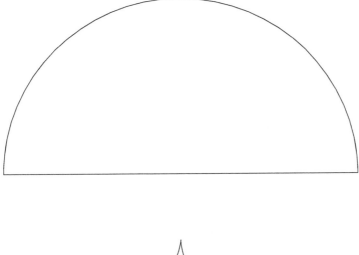

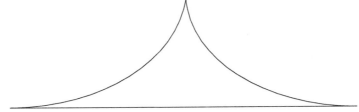

Figure 1.2. A convex deep 'pyramid' versus a concave shallow one

[11] So does learning, since once you have learned one fact, you need to be able to hold it unchanged while you learn others. Likewise, once you have learned one skill, you need to be able to isolate and preserve it while you acquire other skills; see Ghahramani and Wolpert, 1997; Manoel et al., 2002. I shall return to this point in Section 3.5.

Roughly speaking, then, we should expect there to be one distinct sub-system for each reliably recurring function that human minds are called upon to perform. (And whenever the function performed is complex, the sub-system in question should itself decompose into an array of sub-sub-systems, and so on.) But as evolutionary psychologists have often emphasized, the functions of the human mind are *myriad* (Tooby and Cosmides, 1992; Pinker, 1997). Focusing just on the social domain, for example, humans need to: identify degrees of relatedness of kin, care for and assist kin, avoid incest, select and woo a mate, identify and care for offspring, make friends and build coalitions, enter into contracts, identify and punish those who are cheating on a contract, identify and acquire the norms of their surrounding culture, identify the beliefs and goals of other agents, predict the behavior of other agents, and so on and so forth—plainly this is just the tip of a huge iceberg, even in this one domain. In which case the argument from biology enables us to conclude that the mind will consist in a *very great many* functionally distinct components, which is a (weak) form of massive modularity thesis.

If the argument for massive modularity depends upon counting (large numbers of) distinct cognitive functions, then it is important for us to know how *functions* are to be individuated for these purposes. How are we to tell, for example, whether identifying kin and identifying cheaters are two distinct functions (in which case we should expect two distinct processing mechanisms to underlie them), or whether they are really just one function (some generalized form of learning)? There are broadly two approaches that one can take to the individuation of cognitive functions. One is to do task analysis, showing that the abilities in question make structurally different demands on processing, requiring different sorts of algorithms in order to extract the knowledge or ability in question from the initial data or starting-point. This is the approach that will loom large in Chapter 2, where I shall argue on just these sorts of grounds that the learning challenges that animals face require *multiple* differently structured learning mechanisms, and not just one or a few.

There is, however, a second class of ways in which we can individuate cognitive functions, which enables us to keep the argument from general biological design separate from the argument from animal minds. This is by reflecting on the extremely powerful constraint that speed of processing places on the design of cognitive systems, as we shall see more fully in Sections 3.4 and 3.5 below. Wherever different materials need to be processed at the same time, it will be much more efficient to employ two distinct processing systems which can handle those materials in parallel, rather than relying upon a single general-purpose system which would have to tackle the tasks sequentially. For in the animal world generally, speed of learning, speed of decision-making, and speed of reaction time are crucial determinants of survival and reproduction. And just as we would therefore predict, and as everyone now acknowledges, the human brain is massively parallel in its organization and in its operations.

Before concluding this part of our discussion, let me note that it is important not to be misled by talk of 'mechanisms' and 'components' in the context of discussions of the massively modular mind. For these are supposed to be distinct functionally specialized cognitive systems, that is all. In particular, it is important not to think of modules as *objects*, by analogy with hammers and screwdrivers. (In this respect, comparing the massively modular mind to an 'adaptive toolbox' or to a 'Swiss army knife', in the way that evolutionary psychologists often do, is actually highly misleading.) For as Barrett (2006) argues, thinking in this way can lead critics of massive modularity—such as Woodward and Cowie (2004), and Buller (2005)—to attribute to modules properties that they don't (or at least needn't) have. In consequence, the critics end up attacking a straw man. Let me briefly elaborate.

If one conceives of modules by analogy with artifacts like a screwdriver, then one will naturally think that modules must be physically discrete from one another, that they aren't readily modifiable, and that they have been produced in accordance with some kind of design blueprint (in this case written in the genes). But modules are biological systems, and like most such systems they are likely to be built by co-opting and connecting in novel ways resources that were antecedently available in the service of other functions. In consequence, modules are likely to exhibit massive sharing of parts. This is still consistent with them being functionally specialized, as well as being independently effectible and independently disruptable. And modules (again like biological systems generally) are likely to show significant plasticity in the course of development and in response to environmental change. Moreover, they will develop through extensive and complicated gene–environment interactions, in which much of the 'information' that is used to build each system comes from the environment. Certainly it would be a mistake to think of modules as somehow 'pre-formed' in the genes (even in cases where they are significantly innate, given the sense of 'innate' sketched in Footnotes 3 and 5 above).

I have set out Simon's (1962) argument thus far as if it were an argument specifically about biological systems. But it is actually much broader, applying to complex functional systems quite generally, and to complex computer programs in particular.

3.4 Computer Science and AI

The basic reason why biological systems are organized hierarchically in modular fashion is a constraint of evolvability. Evolution needs to be able to add new functions without disrupting those that already exist; and it needs to be able to tinker with the operations of a given functional sub-system—either debugging it, or altering its processing in response to changes in external circumstances—without affecting the functionality of the remainder. Human software engineers have hit upon the same problem, and the same solution. (Although the language of modularity isn't so often used by computer scientists, the same concept arguably gets deployed under the heading of 'object-oriented programs'; see below.) In order that new functions can be added to a program, or in order that one part of it can be debugged, improved, or updated, but without any danger of introducing errors elsewhere, software engineers routinely modularize their programs. And for just these reasons, the automatic electronic control systems that manage complex telephone networks are always organized hierarchically out of modular sub-components, for example (Kamel, 1987; Coward, 2001).

Sometimes modularity is actually enforced by the computer language employed, although sometimes it isn't (Aaron Sloman, personal communication). Much low-level programming is still done using the language C, for example, which doesn't mandate modular organization. (Likewise for languages like Fortran.) But a good programmer will still try to write modular code, with well-defined interfaces between the different parts of the system. However, two of the most widely used languages nowadays are C++ and Java. Both support the use of well-defined interfaces *enforced* by the language, as do many other languages. Languages in this class are often described as 'object oriented'.

Thus many programming languages now require a total processing system to treat some of its parts as 'objects' which can be queried or informed, but where the processing that takes place within those objects isn't accessible elsewhere. This enables the code within the 'objects' to be altered without having to make alterations in code elsewhere, with all the attendant risks that this would bring; and it likewise allows new 'objects' to be added to the system without necessitating wholesale re-writings of code elsewhere. And the resulting architecture is regarded as well nigh inevitable (irrespective of the programming language used) once a certain threshold in the overall degree of complexity of the system gets passed.[12]

---

[12] Interestingly, since the need for modular organization increases with increasing complexity, we can predict that the human mind will be the *most* modular amongst animal minds, whereas the minds of insects (say) might hardly be modular at all. This is the reverse of the intuition shared by many philosophers and social scientists, who would be prepared to allow that animal minds might be organized along modular lines, while believing that with the appearance of the human mind most of that organization was somehow superseded and swept away.

AI researchers charged with trying to build intelligent systems, likewise, have increasingly converged on architectures in which the processing within the total system is divided up amongst a much wider set of task-specific processing mechanisms, which can query one another, make their outputs available to others, and many of which can access shared databases (personal communication: Mike Anderson, John Horty, Aaron Sloman). But many of these systems will deploy processing algorithms that aren't operated by any of the others. And most of them won't know or care about what is going on within the others. The fact that human designers of intelligent systems have converged on modular organization is evidence that the human mind, similarly, will be modular in its design.

In some respects the constraints on the design of computer-based systems are different from the constraints on the design of biological systems (especially brains), however. And this has implications for the sorts of modular organization that are likely to result. In particular, resource constraints are much more important in brains than within modern computers, and this differential has been increasing rapidly with developments in computing technology. Brains are very expensive to build and maintain, in comparison with other components of the body. Thus Aiello and Wheeler (1995) point out that the brain consumes energy at about eight times the rate that would be predicted from its mass alone (accounting for about 20% of the total). So adding extra processing power doesn't come cheap. Moreover, increases in brain size carry other sorts of cost as well, resulting from the consequent increases in head size. This is especially evident in the hominid line, where increased head sizes have resulted in much elevated dangers of maternal death during labor. They have also necessitated extended periods of maternal dependency, since hominid infants have to be born less mature than would be predicted from other biological measures (Barrett et al., 2002).

To some extent this resource constraint pulls in the opposite direction from the constraint of separate modifiability, and we should therefore predict that the actual design of the brain will involve some sort of trade-off between them (Coward, 2005). If minimizing energetic costs were the major design criterion, then one would expect that the fewer brain systems that there are, the better. But on the other hand the evolution of multiple functionality requires that those functions should be underlain by separately modifiable systems, as we have seen. As a result, what we should predict is that while there will be many modules, those modules should *share parts* wherever this can be achieved without losing too much processing efficiency (and subject to other constrains: see below). And indeed, there is now a great deal of evidence supporting what Anderson (forthcoming) calls 'the massive redeployment hypothesis'. This is the view that the components of brain systems are frequently deployed in the service of multiple functions.

A second sort of resource constraint, however, is speed. This often militates *against* sharing of parts, as we shall see. Brains are extremely slow in comparison with turn-of-the-century desktop computers. Information is propagated down the axons of the nerves in the human brain at speeds of only a few meters per second—below the 55 mph speed limit! So a signal passing down an axon of length ten centimeters, say (quite a common long-distance connection within the brain), will take around a tenth of a second on its own, even before time is allowed for electronic spread within the dendrites, and for synaptic transmission. The signal propagation rate within the microchip that forms the central processing unit of a standard desktop computer is about one *million* times greater than this (Christopher Cherniak, personal communication). Moreover, many real life processing tasks on which the organism's survival may depend will need to be *completed* within fractions of a second. (Think of reacting to an attack by a predator, for example.) The result is that we should predict massive *parallelism* in the functional organization of the brain. A great deal of evidence supports this prediction, too.

There are two sorts of circumstance in which speed constraints militate against modules sharing parts. One is where the processing sub-system in question would have to operate on different inputs, and generate distinct outputs, in the service of the two modules in question. For this means that the sub-system would then have to operate *sequentially*, significantly slowing the processing time for one of the two modules. Parts will therefore be shared, in general, only where the two containing systems need the *same* information to be generated from the *same* input at the same time. Otherwise we would expect two distinct sub-systems to evolve, which can operate in parallel. The other sort of circumstance in which speed counts against sharing is whenever the two down-stream consumer systems for a given sub-system are significantly spatially separated. In such cases it may be more efficient to build two distinct systems to do the job, even if they precisely replicate each other's processing. Hence parts are much more likely to be shared within two adjacent modules than within two distant ones.

How powerful is the pressure exerted on the design and organization of brains by energetic and temporal resource constraints? Notice that the length of any given neural connection is both positively correlated with mass (and hence with energy consumption) and negatively correlated with speed (since the distance traveled is greater). So if the pressure exerted by these resource constraints were powerful, then we would expect that the wiring diagram for the brain would minimize signaling distance. And indeed, it turns out that the wiring diagram for different areas of the cortex is almost as efficient in its layout as it is theoretically possible to be (Cherniak et al., 2004).

The resource constraints that distinctively constrain the design of brains (energetic and temporal), don't imply that the brain should be any *less* modular in its organization than other complex biological systems, then. But they do suggest that parts should be shared whenever this can be done without increasing signaling distances or processing time, and without too much loss of reliability. And they also suggest that there should be massive parallelism and duplication of structure whenever signaling distances get too great, or whenever different sorts of information need to be processed within the same brief time-frame. We should see these resource constraints as modulating and adding complexity to the 'one-function / one-module' principle that can be derived from the constraints of separate modifiability and separate evolvability, therefore, without altering that prediction in any fundamental way.

The biological argument for massive modularity, as discussed in Sections 3.1 through 3.3 above, might naturally be read as having the following form: (1) Biological systems are, when complex, massively modularly organized. (2) The human mind is a biological system, and is complex. (3) So the human mind will be massively modularly organized. But reflection on the *reasons why* biological systems are modular shows that the argument really has the following form: (1) Biological systems are designed systems, constructed incrementally. (2) Such systems, when complex, need to have massively modular organization. (3) The human mind is a biological system, and is complex. (4) So the human mind will be massively modular in its organization. And it now emerges that the argument from computer science and AI has exactly the same form, only with 'computational system' substituted for 'biological system' throughout.

So Simon's (1962) argument is really an argument from *design*, then, whether the designer is natural selection (in the case of biological systems) or human engineers (in the case of computer programs). It predicts that, in general, each element added incrementally to the design should be realized in a functionally distinct sub-system, whose properties can be varied independently of the others (to a significant degree, modulated by the extent to which component parts are shared between them). It should be possible for these elements to be added to the design without necessitating changes within the other systems, and their functionality might be lost altogether without destroying the functioning of the whole arrangement. And since there are *many* ancient and evolutionarily significant capacities of the human mind (as well as many capacities constructed by learning of various sorts—see Section 3.5), we should expect the human mind to be *massively* modular in its organization (using the weak sense of 'module').

3.5 A Design for Learning

The human mind (together with most animal minds and some AI systems, of course) is distinctive amongst designed systems in being designed for learning. Amongst the evolved modules that make up the human mind are many whose function is to generate and store new information of various sorts (both episodic memories and factual information), as well as building and retaining new skills. Indeed, many of the modules that make up human and animal minds are best characterized as learning systems of various sorts. (This will loom large in Section 4, when we come to consider a second line of argument in support of massive mental modularity, and again in Section 5, when we come to defend evolutionary psychology against its philosophical critics.)

So the argument from design suggests that the mind should contain multiple learning modules. But it might be objected again that a lot will turn, in evaluating that argument, on how the capacities of the mind are individuated. For example, if we treat 'learning who has cheated on a contract' as a distinct capacity from 'learning a social norm', then the design argument predicts that they will be realized in distinct modules. But if we just characterize both as 'learning', *simpliciter*, then why shouldn't there be just one system involved? Indeed, it might be urged that the argument from design is consistent with there being just *one* general learning mechanism in the human mind, which can be directed in the service of all the many different learning tasks.

In fact, however, the structure of the many different learning tasks that humans and other animals face is highly varied, and it is very doubtful indeed whether there could be just a single leaning mechanism capable of undertaking every one of them. (Stronger still, it is highly doubtful whether even the collective activity of a *few* leaning mechanisms would be adequate to the task.) These claims will be sketched in Section 4, and then developed at length in Chapter 2, in the course of presenting and defending what I call 'the argument from animals' in support of massive modularity. So at this point it should be acknowledged that the design argument gains strength from being integrated with the argument from animals. But even if we set this aside, it remains very implausible that there should be just one (or a few) mechanisms of learning.

Even if learning were everywhere and always the same—in such a way that the mechanism of learning that is used in one task could always in principle be used to undertake any other—we should *still* expect that the mind would contain many different versions, or instances, of that type of mechanism. One reason has to do with robustness of function: if there were just a single learning mechanism, then damage to it would cripple the organism; whereas if there are multiple learning mechanisms, each dedicated to a particular learning task, then damage to one can leave all the others intact. But the more important reason has to do with *speed* and *reliability* of learning, as I shall now argue.

If there were just a single learning mechanism, then it would presumably have to be deployed serially to undertake the various learning tasks. This would take time, and many opportunities for learning might consequently be lost. If there are multiple mechanisms, in contrast, then they can operate in parallel, greatly reducing the overall acquisition time. (And given the slow speeds characteristic of neuronal transmission—already mentioned in Section 3.4—this is a very significant constraint.) Nor would it be at all surprising that evolution should operate in this way. As Marcus (2004) points out, natural selection frequently operates through a process of copying sets of genes (and hence the structures that they build), before the new structure is turned to the service of a novel function.

For example, consider learning about the movements and interactions of physical objects (common-sense physics) and learning about the goals, thoughts, and intentions of human subjects (common-sense psychology). Even if we thought that the very same learning algorithms could serve both tasks equally well (which is actually *extremely* implausible), we should still predict the existence of two distinct learning mechanisms for these two domains. This is because events in those domains will vary independently of each other while often occurring simultaneously. If there were just a single learning mechanism, then it would need to operate on the physical and psychological aspects of a given event sequentially, or risk confounding them. This would retard learning, and might lead to many opportunities for learning being missed altogether when complex chains of events unfold in real time. The obvious design solution is to have two distinct copies of the learning system in question, each focused on a proprietary domain.

In addition to predicting that there will be multiple learning mechanisms, the argument from design predicts that, where the *products* of learning are multiple and complex, displaying significant internal organization, then those products themselves should have a modular character. Hence each learned element should have a realization that is distinct from the others, in such a way that new elements can be added through learning without interfering with those that already exist, and in such a way that the properties of any one element can be altered without altering the others. And the clearest examples of forms of learning that display such properties are learned skills of one sort or another, from reading and writing, through piano playing, cooking, to the various stages of kayak making.[13]

Consistent with these predictions, Ghahramani and Wolpert (1997) provide evidence of the modular decomposition of distinct visuomotor skills. They had subjects learn to reach to a perceived location that was displaced from actual (as if seen through a prism) from two distinct starting locations of their right hands, where the displacement was different for the two starting locations. The model they were testing assumed that a distinct module would be built for each of the two learned behaviors, and that subsequently a gating mechanism would take input from each of these modules (in the form of a weighted average) for starting positions of the hand that were intermediate between those that had been used in the initial training. The data that they obtained matched the predictions of this model very nicely, whereas those data proved inconsistent with a number of other models that assumed just a single learned system of some sort.

Likewise, Kharraz-Tavakol et al. (2000) set out to test the modular decomposition of acquired skills, on the assumption that if the different movements that make up a skill are stored as separate modules, then there should be transfers of learning to novel skills that recombine those movements in different ways. And this is just what they found, using a letter-writing task in which subjects first had to learn to write a letter from the Nashki alphabet (a precursor of the modern Arabic alphabet), and then had to learn to write that same letter rotated through 180 degrees. Manoel et al. (2002) produced further evidence in the same vein. They, too, had subjects learn to write a novel letter (this time a Chinese character), but then they embedded that task within a more complex character-writing assignment. They found, as predicted, that the sequencing and relative timing of movements from the original task remained invariant within the context of the new one, suggesting that it had been stored as a module that was left unaffected when embedded into a new skill.

The picture that emerges from these and other similar data, then, is that the components of acquired skills—like the modules of the mind more generally—are organized hierarchically out of motor-control systems that are constructed via learning. (See Wolpert et al., 2003, for a review.) So not only are the various learning systems of the mind realized in distinct modules, as the argument from design implies, but the products of those systems add yet further modules to the architecture of the mind, at least in the case of skill-learning.

[13] But memory, too, appears to display a modular organization, even when attention is confined just to long-term memory. Sites associated with memory are found in many different locations in the brain, with different regions associated with different forms of memory (Marcus, 2004). I shall return to develop this point in Chapter 2.6.

4 The Argument from Animals

Another line of reasoning supporting massive modularity starts initially from reflection on the differing task demands of the very different learning challenges that people and other animals must face, as well as the demands of generating appropriate fitness-enhancing intrinsic desires (Gallistel, 1990, 2000; Tooby and Cosmides, 1992, 2005). I shall provide just a sketch of this line of argument here. It will then be one of the tasks of Chapter 2 to establish its main premise: the massively modular organization of animal minds.

4.1 Extracting New Information

It is one sort of task to learn the sun's azimuth (its height in the sky at any given time of day and year) so as to provide a source of direction. It is quite another sort of task to perform the calculations required for dead reckoning, integrating distance traveled with the angle of each turn, so as to provide the direction and distance to home from one's current position. It is yet another sort of task to navigate via landmarks, recognizing each landmark and locating it on a mental map. And it is quite another task again to learn the center of rotation of the night sky from observation of the stars, extracting from it the polar north. These are all learning problems that animals can solve. But they require quite different learning mechanisms to succeed (Gallistel, 2000).

When we widen our focus from navigation to other sorts of learning problem, the argument is further reinforced. Many such problems pose computational challenges—to extract the information required from the data provided—that are distinct from any others. From vision, to speech recognition, to mind-reading, to cheater detection, to complex skill acquisition, the challenges posed are plainly quite distinct. So for each such problem, we should postulate the existence of a distinct learning mechanism, whose internal processes are computationally specialized in the way required to solve the task. It is very hard to believe that there could be any sort of *general* learning mechanism that could perform all of these different roles.

One might think that conditioning experiments fly in the face of these claims. But as we shall see more fully in Chapter 2, general-purpose conditioning is rare at best. Indeed, Gallistel (2000; Gallistel and Gibbon, 2001; Gallistel et al., 2001) has argued forcefully that *there is no such thing as* a general learning mechanism. Specifically, he argues that the results from conditioning experiments are best explained in terms of the computational operations of a specialized rate-estimation module, rather than some sort of generalized associative process.

4.2 *Acquiring New Desires*

Desires aren't learned in any normal sense of the term 'learning', of course. Yet much of evolutionary psychology is concerned with the genesis of human motivational states. This is an area where we need to construct a new concept, in fact—the desiderative equivalent of learning. Learning is a process that issues in true beliefs, or beliefs that are close enough to the truth to support (or at least not to hinder) inclusive fitness.[14] But desires, too, need to be formed in ways that will support (or not hinder) the inclusive fitness of the individual. Some desires are instrumental ones, of course, being derived from ultimate goals together with beliefs about the means that would be sufficient for realizing those goals. But it is hardly very plausible that all acquired desires are formed in this way.

Anti-modular theorists such as Dupré (2001) are apt to talk vaguely about the influence of surrounding culture, at this point. Somehow goals such as a woman's desire to purchase a wrinkle-removing skin-cream, or an older man's desire to be seen in the company of a beautiful young girl, are supposed to be caused by cultural influences of one sort or another—prevailing attitudes to women, perceived power structures, media images, and so forth. But it is left entirely unclear what the mechanism of such influences is supposed to be. How do facts about culture generate new desires? We are not told, beyond vague (and obviously inadequate) appeals to imitation (Campbell, 2002).

In contrast, evolutionary psychology postulates a rich network of systems for generating new desires in the light of input from the environment and background beliefs. Many of these desires will be 'ultimate', in the sense that they haven't been produced by reasoning backwards from the means sufficient to fulfill some other desire. But they will still have been produced by inferences taking place in systems dedicated to creating desires of that sort. A desire to have sex with a specific person in a particular context, for example, won't (of course) have been produced by reasoning that such an act is likely to fulfill some sort of evolutionary goal of producing many healthy descendants. Rather, it will have been generated by some system (a module) that has evolved for the purpose, which takes as input a variety of kinds of perceptual and non-perceptual information, and then generates, when appropriate, a desire of some

---

[14] This isn't meant to be a definition, of course. If there are innate beliefs, then evolution might also be a process that issues in true beliefs, but evolving isn't learning. What is distinctive of learning is that it should involve some method (not necessarily a *general* one, let alone one that we already have a name for, such as 'enumerative induction') for extracting novel information from the environment within at least the lifetime of the individual organism. And what distinguishes learning from mere triggering, is that it is a process that admits of a correct cognitive description—learning is a cognitive as opposed to a brute-biological process.

given strength. (Whether that desire is then acted upon, of course, will depend upon the other desires the subject possesses at the time, and on his or her relevant beliefs.)

One of the systems for generating new intrinsic desires is likely to be some sort of normative-reasoning module, as we shall see in Chapter 3. (And this will then prove to be of some importance in Chapter 7.) According to Sripada and Stich (2006) this will be a mechanism for figuring out the norms that are current in the agent's community, for building up a norms database, and for recognizing cases of norm compliance or non-compliance. But the mechanism will also attach intrinsic motivation to these norms, in such a way that agents become outraged and/or disgusted when one of the norms is breached, and feel guilty or ashamed when failing to comply with one themselves. And note that the existence of such a module fills the lacuna in Dupré's (2001) position. The result will be a set of intrinsic motivations that are just as varied as cultural norms are.[15]

4.3 Samuels's Challenge

What emerges from these considerations is a picture of the mind as containing a whole host of specialized learning systems, as well as systems charged with generating fitness-enhancing intrinsic desires. And this looks very much like *some* sort of thesis of massive modularity. Admittedly, it doesn't yet follow from the argument that the mind is composed *exclusively* of such systems. But as we shall see shortly (in Section 4.4), and again in more detail in Chapter 2, the argument can be further elaborated in such a way that the stronger conclusion is warranted.

There really isn't any reason to believe, however, that each processing system will employ a unique processing algorithm. On the contrary, consideration of how evolution generally operates suggests that the same or similar algorithms may be replicated many times over in the human mind / brain. (We could describe this by saying that the same module-*type* is tokened more than once in the human brain, with distinct input and output connections, and hence with a distinct functional role, in each case.) Marcus (2004) explains how evolution often operates by splicing and *copying*, followed by adaptation. First, the genes that result in a given structure or micro-structure (a particular bank of neurons, say, with a given set of processing properties) is copied, yielding two or more

---

[15] This isn't to say, of course, that *all* of the appeals to the alleged influence of culture on motivation and behavior, of the sort often made by anti-modularists like Dupré, are thereby accommodated within a modularist framework. There is no *rule* to the effect that a woman should be wrinkle-free, or that she should use wrinkle-removing creams, for example. The intrinsic desires involved in examples of this sort are better explained directly in terms of sexual selection.

instances of such structures. Then secondly, some of the copies can be adapted to novel tasks. *Sometimes* this will involve tweaking the processing algorithm that is implemented in one or more of the copies. But often it will just involve provision of novel input and/or output connections for the new system.

Samuels (1998a) challenges the above line of argument for massive processing modularity, however, claiming that instead of a whole suite of specialized learning systems, there might be just a single general-learning / general-inferencing mechanism, but one that operates on lots of organized bodies of innate information. (He calls this 'informational modularity', contrasting it with the more familiar form of *computational* modularity.) This sort of architecture would surely create a serious processing bottleneck, however. If there were really just one (or even a few) inferential systems—generating beliefs about the likely movements of the surrounding mechanical objects; about the likely beliefs, goals, and actions of the surrounding agents; about who owes what to whom in a social exchange; and so on and so forth—then it looks as though there would be a kind of tractability problem here. It would be the problem of forming novel beliefs about all these different subject matters in real time (in seconds or fractions of a second), using a limited set of inferential resources. Indeed (and in contrast to Samuels's suggestion) surely *everyone* now thinks that the mind / brain is massively parallel in its organization. In which case we should expect there to be distinct systems that can process each of the different kinds of information at the same time.

To the first of these objections Samuels (2006) replies: how do you know that the human mind *doesn't* contain serious processing bottlenecks? Well actually, I believe that it does contain such a bottleneck, specifically in *conscious* thinking and decision-making, which I argue are realized serially in *cycles* of operation of central / conceptual modules (see Chapters 4 through 7). But what is at issue here are those unconscious processes that might plausibly be realized in the operations of individual modules (whether computational or informational). And on this the evidence that we have suggests that most of these processes, at least, operate extremely swiftly. (See Gladwell, 2005, for a popular presentation.)

Samuels also claims that the parallel processing that takes place in the brain might be serving merely to *implement* a general-purpose inferencing system. But the only model that we have of how processing can be conducted in parallel in symbolic machines (i.e. machines that aren't of a distributed connectionist sort—see Section 6) is that the processing should be divided up into subroutines which can be executed in parallel before being pooled. And this appears to be just another variant on massive modularity. Moreover, it doesn't really solve the bottleneck problem. For even if the general processor were extremely swift (because organized in parallel), it would still have to deal sequentially with the many different learning and decision-making tasks that humans and animals routinely face, and on which their lives and reproductive opportunities frequently depend.

Samuels might try claiming that there could be a whole suite of distinct domain-general processing systems operating in parallel, all running the same general-learning / general-inferencing algorithms, but each of which is attached to, and draws upon the resources of, a distinct domain-specific body of innate information. This would get him the computational advantages of *parallel* processing, but without commitment (allegedly) to any *modular* processing. But actually this is just a variant on the massive-computational-module hypothesis. For there is nothing in the nature of modularity per se that requires modules to be running algorithms that are distinct from those being run by other modules, as we have just seen. What matters is just that they should be isolable systems, performing some specific function, and (as we shall see in Sections 5 and 6 below) that their internal operations should be computationally feasible. So one way in which massive modularity could be realized is by having a whole suite of processors, each of which performs some specific function within the overall architecture of the mind, and each of which draws on its own distinctive body of innate information relevant to that function, but where the algorithms being computed by those processors are shared ones, replicated many times over in the various processing systems.

Although possible in principle, however, this is a highly unlikely form of massive modularity hypothesis. For it does come with severe computational costs. This is because the difference between this 'informational module' hypothesis and the classic 'computational module' hypothesis just concerns whether or not the innate information is explicitly represented. The classical idea is that there will be, within the mind-reading faculty for example, an algorithm that takes the system straight from, 'x is seeing that P', to, 'probably x believes that P' (say). The information that people believe what they see is implicitly represented in the algorithm itself. Samuels's view, in contrast, will be that there is an intermediate step. Domain-general inference mechanisms will draw on the explicitly represented belief that people believe what they see, in order to mediate the inference from premise to conclusion. Imagine this multiplied again and again for all the different sorts of inferential transition that people regularly make in the domain of theory of mind, and it is plain that his proposal would come with serious computational costs. And it is equally clear that even if informational modules were the initial state of the ancestral mind / brain, we should expect that over evolutionary time these informational modules would be replaced by computational ones.

4.4 *Extending the Argument*

We should expect there to be lots of distinct systems (modules in the weak sense) charged with generating our beliefs and our intrinsic desires, then. But is there any reason to suppose that the mind should consist *wholly* of functionally isolable specialist systems, in the way that a thesis of *massive* (weak) modularity proposes? I believe that there is, although any attempt to establish the main premise necessary for such an argument will be deferred to Chapter 2, where we shall consider the architecture of animal minds. There I shall argue that not only do animal minds consist of large sets of belief-generating modules and desire-generating and emotion-generating modules, but that the systems charged with the selection, organization, and control of action are also fractionated along modular lines. There will therefore be nothing left that might be considered to be *non*-modular. For all of the main elements of a mind (perception, belief, desire, practical reason, and motor-control) will have emerged as modular in character.

If we suppose for present purposes that this main premise can be established, and that animal minds are massively modular (in the weak sense of 'module', at least), then from an evolutionary perspective it would be quite *extraordinary* if all of that structure had somehow been lost in the evolutionary transition from apes to hominids. (It would be rather as if we were to find that the ape respiratory and circulatory systems had no homologues, or near homologues, in ourselves.) For in general almost all biological structures are preserved in the evolutionary transitions from one species into another. And then provided that it is appropriate to extend normal biological and evolutionary principles to minds, we should expect the human mind to contain all or almost all of the modular systems that are present in animals. So the human mind should at least be *highly* modular in character.

But human minds do differ from animal minds, of course, and these differences might be thought to result from additions being made to the architecture of ancestral animals minds, rather than deletions. Indeed, I shall argue in Chapter 3 that this is so. But all of these additions come in the form of additional modules — for language, for mind-reading, for normative reasoning, and so on and so forth — rather than in the form of some sort of holistic, a-modular, belief-forming and general reasoning system. Or so it will be the burden of Chapter 3, and of the remainder of this book, to argue. For although humans do indeed have a sort of general reasoning capacity (which is put to use in science, for example), this is one that is actually realized in cycles of operation of, and interactions between, existing modular systems. Or so I shall argue in Chapter 6.

4.5 Taking Stock

Each of the arguments of Sections 3 and 4, then, predicts that the mind should be composed entirely or almost entirely out of a large battery of modular components (in the everyday sense of 'module'), many of which will be innate or innately channeled. Many of the innate systems will be learning systems.[16] They will have been designed by evolution, either to acquire and store information about some aspect of the environment (as the mind-reading system does, building up bodies of knowledge about different people's beliefs and goals), or to construct a much more detailed and fully specified cognitive module from environmental information (this seems like an accurate characterization of what the language-learning module does, for example), or to build a whole suite of acquired modules on an on-going basis (this seems like an accurate description of what the behavioral skill-acquisition modules do). And many of these systems should themselves fractionate into arrangements of further modules, which in turn (if the function that they execute is complex) are composed of yet further modules, and so on.

All of these component systems should run task-specific processing algorithms, with distinct input and/or output connections to other systems, although some of them may replicate some of the same algorithm types in the service of distinct tasks. And all of them should have properties that can be modified independently of the properties of the others, while many (though not all, perhaps) can be damaged or destroyed without undermining the functionality of the whole.[17] This looks like a thesis of massive modularity worth the name, even if there is nothing here yet to warrant the claims that the internal processing of the modules in question should be either encapsulated, on the one hand, or inaccessible, on the other. And it looks as if we have powerful reasons to believe such a thesis to be true, or at least to adopt it as a working hypothesis worthy of both further theoretical development and experimental investigation.

---

[16] Geary (2005) coins the term 'soft modularity' to describe innately-structured task-specific learning mechanisms.

[17] Compare bodily organs. An eye can be damaged or destroyed while leaving the rest of the organism almost fully functional; but the heart cannot. Still, however, the properties of the heart can vary independently of properties of the lungs; and factors that affect the functioning of the heart need not affect the functioning of the lungs.

5 In Defense of Evolutionary Psychology

Note that all of the arguments considered so far in this chapter presuppose the legitimacy and value of a science of evolutionary psychology. This is obviously the case in connection with the argument of Section 3 from hierarchical organization in biology. For this assumes that it is appropriate to think of the mind as an evolved system to which normal biological principles apply, which is precisely the guiding claim of evolutionary psychology. But it is also the case in connection with the argument from practices in AI and computer science. For the assumption here (if the argument by analogy is to work) must be that the mind is a *designed* system—presumably designed by processes of evolution with natural selection rather than by God, if we are to adopt a naturalistic framework. And likewise the argument of Section 4, from the task-specificity of learning mechanisms and desire-acquiring mechanisms, assumes that it is appropriate to apply the comparative method to the human case, applying lessons learned from study of the minds of animals (especially those fairly closely related to ourselves in evolutionary terms) to draw inferences concerning the likely organization of the human mind. And again, this is one of the leading assumptions made by evolutionary psychologists. The legitimacy of evolutionary psychology as a science will therefore form the subject of the present section.

I should stress at the outset, however, that I understand evolutionary psychology to be a broad church, defined only by its insistence that the mind is a biological / evolved system, and by its willingness to use adaptationist reasoning and the comparative method as heuristics in attempting to uncover the structure of the mind. Some people associate the term 'evolutionary psychology' with a more narrowly defined program—the so-called 'Santa Barbara school' of Cosmides, Tooby, and closely connected colleagues (Barkow et al., 1992). I use it much more broadly, to encompass the work of Boyd and Richerson (1985; Richerson and Boyd, 2004), for example, as well as the work of people like Miller (2000), Wilson (2002), and many others. It seems to me that the term 'evolutionary psychology' ought properly to be used in such a way as to coincide with the mandate of the methodologically diverse and inclusive Human Behavior and Evolution Society (HBES). As stated on their website, this reads in part: '[We] use modern evolutionary theory to *help* discover human nature—including evolved emotional, cognitive, and sexual adaptations' (emphasis added).[18]

[18] Leda Cosmides herself, too, shares this broad understanding of evolutionary psychology, and sees Boyd and Richerson, for example, as fellow-travelers rather than competitors (personal communication).

I should also stress that evolutionary psychology needn't be committed to the view that *every* useful, seemingly functional, aspect of the mind is an evolved adaptation. For as I noted in Section 3.2, some properties of the mind might be mere *spandrels* of evolved adaptations (Gould and Lewontin, 1979), and some might have appeared by mere happenstance against a richly prepared adaptive background (Hauser et al., 2002). All that evolutionary psychologists claim is that these will not, by any means, form the general case. And it is thus a reasonable initial presumption, when considering any evolutionarily ancient useful mental function, to assume that the mechanisms underlying it have been a product of natural selection. While not all such functions are necessarily adaptations, our default hypothesis in respect of any given case should be that it is.

One final qualification: I want to emphasize that my goal in the present section is only to correct misunderstandings and sketch replies to some of the more common objections to evolutionary psychology (especially by philosophers), not to embark on a full-scale defense. The latter would need to be the work of a separate (and equally long) book. There is now an *immense* body of scientific work in the evolutionary psychology tradition, of most of which the philosophical critics are simply ignorant. I cannot hope to survey that work here, or to defend its adequacy in any detail.

5.1 Some Misunderstandings of Evolutionary Psychology

The relatively recent movement of evolutionary psychology is the successor to a more long-standing program of work in sociobiology, which came to prominence in the 1970s and 1980s. Many philosophers have been critical of sociobiology for its seeming commitment to genetic determinism—flying in the face of the known flexibility and malleability of human behavior, and of the immense cultural diversity shown in human behavior and social practices (Kitcher, 1985; O'Hear, 1997; Dupré, 2001). Sociobiologists had a reply to some of these criticisms, in fact, since it isn't specific types of behavior but only behavioral *tendencies* that have been selected for, on their account. And which behavioral tendencies are actually expressed on any given occasion can be a highly context-sensitive—and hence flexible—matter.

The charge of genetic determinism is even less applicable to evolutionary psychology. For what such a psychology postulates, in effect, is a set of innate belief and desire generating mechanisms, as we shall see more fully in Chapters 2 and 3. How those beliefs and desires then issue in behavior (if at all) is a matter of the agent's practical reasoning, or practical judgment, in the circumstances. And this can be just as flexible, context-sensitive, and unpredictable-in-detail as you like (see Chapters 4 through 7). Supposing that there is a 'mind-reading' module charged with generating beliefs about other people's mental states, for example, those beliefs would then be available to subserve an indefinitely wide variety of plans and projects, depending on the agent's goals. Or suppose that there is a 'social status' module charged with generating desires for things that are likely to enhance the status of oneself and one's kin in the particular cultural and social circumstances in which agents find themselves. *How* those desires issue in action would depend on those agents' beliefs; *whether* those desires issue in action at all would depend upon those agents' other desires, together with their beliefs. There is no question of genetic determinism here.

There might seem to be a paradox inherent in the evolutionary psychologist's position at this point, however. For if it is behavior that ultimately influences the survival and reproductive success of individuals—as everyone acknowledges—then how could it *not* be behaviors and behavioral tendencies that are selected for in evolution, just as the sociobiologists supposed? Yet the apparent paradox is easily resolved within the framework of belief / desire psychology.[19] For mechanisms that generate reliable information / true beliefs will make fitness-enhancing behaviors more likely, provided that the organism's goals are for things that would enhance fitness; and vice versa for the mechanisms that generate such desires, on the assumption of reliable information. The point is just that the same item of information (e.g. the compass bearing of a food source) can be deployed in the service of a number of different goals; in which case mutations that enhance the reliability of that information, or the speed with which it is acquired, are likely to have a positive impact on a whole variety of fitness-enhancing behaviors. Similarly, a given goal can often be approached in a number of distinct ways, subserved by a variety of beliefs about the means to realize that goal; so mutations that make beneficial adjustments in goals are likely to manifest themselves in a range of fitness-promoting behaviors, also.

In addition to mistakenly alleging genetic determinism, philosophers are apt to have an overly narrow conception of the operations of natural selection as being wholly or primarily *survival based*. Many of us have a picture of natural selection as 'red in tooth and claw', 'survival of the fittest', and so on. And of course that is part—an important part—of the story. But survival is no good to you, in evolutionary terms, if you don't generate any offspring, or if your offspring don't live long enough to mate, or for other reasons aren't

---

[19] Note that a similar 'paradox' could be constructed for many of the mechanisms and processes within the human body that have no *immediate* impact on behavior or on the preservation of the life of the organism. Systems can have functions—contributing to the proper functioning of some wider arrangement—without those functions being specifiable at the behavioral / organismic level.

successful in generating offspring in their turn. In the human species, just as in other species, we should expect that sexual selection will have been an important force in our evolution, shaping our natures to some significant degree (Miller, 2000). In the animal world generally, sexual selection has always been recognized by evolutionary biologists as an important factor in evolution, and perhaps as the main engine driving speciation events. There is no reason to think that the human animal should have been any different.

In fact Miller (2000) makes out a powerful case that many of the behaviors and behavioral tendencies that we think of as distinctively human—story-telling, jokes, music, dancing, sporting competition, and so on—are products of sexual selection, functioning as sexual displays of one sort or another (like the peacock's tail). And as Miller (1997, 2000) also argues, when you have a species, such as our own, who are accomplished mind-readers, then sexual selection has the power to reach deep into the human mind, helping to shape its structure and functioning. Emotional dispositions such as kindness, generosity, and sympathy, for example, may be direct products of sexual selection. Consistently with this, it appears to be the case that members of both sexes, in all cultures, rate kindness very highly amongst the desired characteristics of a potential mate (Buss, 1989, 1994).

In addition to what one might call 'survival selection' and sexual selection, there is also *group* selection, for whose significance in human evolution a compelling case can be made out (Sober and Wilson, 1999). And as selection began to operate on the group, rather than just on individuals and their kin, one might expect to see the appearance of a number of adaptations designed to enhance group cohesion and collective action. In particular, one might expect to see the emergence of an evolved mechanism for identifying, memorizing, and reasoning about social norms, together with a powerful motivation to comply with such norms (Sripada and Stich, 2006). And with norms and norm-based motivation added to the human phenotype, the stage would be set for much that is distinctive of human cultures.

To see how some of this might pan out, consider an example that might seem especially problematic from the perspective of a survival-based evolved psychology. Consider Socrates committing suicide when convicted of treason (O'Hear, 1997), or a kamikaze pilot plunging his aircraft into the deck of a battle-cruiser. How can such behaviors be adaptive? Well no one necessarily claims that they are, of course.[20] Rather, they are the product of psychological

---

[20] Some such cases might indeed increase the inclusive fitness of the individual, by securing enhanced social status or special benefits for the kin of the person committing suicide; both were the case in wartime Japan, and are often the case amongst suicide bombers in the Middle East today.

mechanisms that are normally adaptive, operating in quite specific local conditions. An evolved mechanism charged with identifying and internalizing
important social norms may be generally adaptive; as might be one whose
purpose is to generate desires for things that will enhance social status. If we
put these mechanisms into a social context in which there is a norm requiring
sacrifices for the community good, for example, and in which the greatest
status is accorded to those who make the greatest sacrifices, then it is easy to
see how a suicide can sometimes be the result.

5.2 Is Evolutionary Psychology a Fruitful Research Program?

Many critics have claimed that evolutionary psychology is limited to constructing 'just-so stories' for the explanation of already known facts (such as: men
prefer pretty women), and that it fails to generate novel predictions (Gould
and Lewontin, 1979; Fodor, 2000; Dupré, 2001). This would be a serious
challenge to its scientific credentials, if true. For one of the vital good-making
features of a scientific research program is that it should be *fruitful*, generating
novel predictions and novel discoveries (Newton-Smith, 1981).

Fortunately, the charge is *not* true. To see this, one need look no further
than the topic of the present chapter. For evolutionary psychology predicts
that the mind should be massively modular in its organization, as we have
seen. This is certainly a novel and surprising prediction, which flies in the
face of both common-sense belief and the claims of more-orthodox forms of
cognitive and developmental psychology. Indeed, the prediction of a massively
modular mind is in direct conflict with the assumptions that dominated the
social sciences throughout much of the twentieth century, which Tooby and
Cosmides (1992) refer to as the 'Standard Social Science Model' of the mind as
a big general-purpose computer. So this was certainly no 'just-so story'. And
to the extent that the idea of massive modularity is even partially confirmed (as
we have seen already that it is), evolutionary psychology has proven fruitful.

But evolutionary psychology doesn't end with the prediction of massive
modularity in general, of course. It also proposes a research program for
uncovering the existence of such modules. The idea is that by reflecting on
comparative evidence from other mammalian (and especially primate) species,
and by considering the distinctive selection pressures to which our hominid
ancestors would likely have been subject, we can frame reasonable hypotheses
concerning the cognitive specializations that our minds will contain. These
can then be subjected to testing by the usual experimental methods.[21]

---

[21] Note that there is nothing in this methodology that requires all of the selection pressures on
human psychology to have been *stable* throughout the period of hominid evolution, as Buller (2005)

Here, too, evolutionary psychology faces the allegation that it is limited to constructing 'just-so stories' for the explanation of already known facts, and that it fails to generate novel predictions. Even supposing that no novel predictions are generated, however, it can still be true that evolutionary psychology can provide explanations of known facts that are better than those given by general-learning-theory competitors. Let me briefly elaborate on this point in relation to a pair of examples.

Consider mate selection first. Why do men tend to be more influenced by physical attractiveness, whereas women are more influenced by social standing and resources? This is a fact long-familiar to common sense, and since confirmed in numerous empirical studies. Evolutionary psychology says that after the point in hominid evolution when hominid females ceased to display visible signs of ovulation, the components of female physical attractiveness (clear smooth skin, luxuriant hair, firm body, lithe movements) would have been the best available indicators of female fertility (which peaks at about age 20) and lifetime reproductive potential (which peaks at about age 15). In contrast, male fertility and reproductive potential aren't well correlated with age. And for hunter-gatherer women in the ancestral past the status and resources of her mate would have been the best predictors of the survival and health of her children.

In contrast, proponents of general-learning-theory say something like this: differential power relations amongst the sexes mean that for women, their best chance of advancement is via a powerful male; while men can afford to objectify women as playthings. But why would this lead men to focus on physical attributes that happen to correlate with youth, rather than on others? And powerful women and leaders of feminist organizations actually set standards for a potential mate even *higher* than normal, not lower (Ellis, 1992).

---

assumes in his critique of evolutionary psychology. On the contrary, many human cognitive adaptations might result from evolutionary 'arms races' of one sort or another (e.g. between cooperators who need to detect cheaters, and cheaters who need to devise better means of outwitting cooperators), or from 'niche construction' (obvious examples would include adaptations to tools and other cultural products). In such cases the pressures are dynamic and shifting. But we still might be able to form reasonable hypotheses about the likely outcomes. Nor (*contra* Buller) does it need to be assumed that an evolved psychology will be monomorphic (or at most dimorphic, perhaps differing between the sexes). On the contrary, we might predict the existence of a number of balanced polymorphisms, just as Murphy and Stich (2000) suggest. And most importantly (and again *contra* Buller), there is nothing in the methodology that requires us to be able to identify the selection pressures on human psychology in advance of enquiry with anything approaching certainty. On the contrary, we should expect the process of enquiry to be messy and holistic, with a wide range of types of evidence, concerning not only ancestral environments but also comparative data from other species and present cognitive functioning, being brought to bear on one another. Here, as so often in science, our best hope is that we might bootstrap our way to knowledge on a recursive incremental basis. We shouldn't try to resolve one side of an interrelated set of issues before investigating the other.

Just as the female mate-choice rule seems to be: select a man four inches taller than yourself; so it seems to be: select a man of higher status and/or resources than yourself (Buss, 1994).

Now consider a second example: male sexual jealousy. Such jealousy is manifested in patterns of wife-beating, homicide, and divorce; and in practices worldwide designed to 'protect' and control women. Female jealousy, in contrast, tends to focus on alienation of attention and resources. Why? Evolutionary psychologists point out that maternity is always certain, paternity never so. There would therefore have been powerful selective pressure on men against investing in women and their children where those children might not be their own. (And note that mate-guarding strategies are common in any species where the male invests in offspring.) For women, in contrast, the main danger would have been loss of a partner and/or his resources. Proponents of general-learning-theory, however, say: what? Presumably something about the different power relations that obtain between the sexes again. Granted, there are such differences. But why should this lead men to focus on controlling especially the *sexual* activities of their women?

Not only can evolutionary psychology lead to better explanations of known facts than are provided by rival theories, as we have just seen, but it can also lead to the discovery that locally known facts are actually human universals. And that something is a universal, and not just true locally in the present time, can be both surprising and controversial. This is true in connection with both of the examples given above, as well as all three of the examples to be discussed below in another connection.

Evolutionary psychology can surely lead, in addition, to the prediction and confirmation of hitherto unsuspected phenomena. This is the crucial test of a worthwhile theory. For example, evolutionary psychology predicts that there should be a psychological mechanism that makes people unwilling to invest heavily in children who aren't their own; and that in consequence rates of child homicide and child abuse in families containing one step-parent will be much higher than in families containing two biological parents. (Although consistent with folk-belief—cf. the Cinderella story—these predictions have been strongly resisted by proponents of general-learning. And remember that the claim isn't that people will *always* reject children that aren't their own—only that there is a mechanism that produces some such motivation, which is then one motivation amongst others competing to control the person's behavior.) These predictions are in fact upheld. A child under two is 70–150 times more likely to be killed by a co-residing step-parent than by a genetic parent, across cultures (Daly and Wilson, 1988, 1995, 1998).[22] (Note that similar phenomena occur in many other animal species.)

Consider another example: evolutionary psychology predicts that maternal investment in offspring should be in accordance with Parental Investment Theory, being sensitive to the infant's health, the mother's marital status, and the mother's age, health, and access to resources. This was confirmed in a small-scale study of pre-term twins (Mann, 1992). And it is confirmed worldwide in patterns of abandonment and infanticide, which prove to be surprisingly common (Hrdy, 1999; Campbell, 2002). (Between 20% and 40% of all live births were abandoned throughout Medieval and Renaissance Europe, for example.)

Consider a third example: the Trivers-Willard hypothesis (confirmed for a wide range of animal species) is that in animals with greater male reproductive variance than female, high-fitness females should prefer male offspring and low-fitness females should prefer female offspring. Human males, too, have greater reproductive variance than do females. (Some males have many children with multiple partners, while some have none. Prior to the invention of contraception, in contrast, each fertile woman would have had some children, but with an upper limit on the number of children she can have, determined by her lifetime reproductive cycle.) The prediction is therefore that high-fitness women should prefer sons whereas low-fitness women should prefer daughters.

This was confirmed by Gaulin and Robbins (1989) in the US. High-income women with an investing male are more likely to breastfeed a male child, to do so for longer, and to have a longer birth interval before the next child. Low-income women without an investing male are more likely to breastfeed a *female* child, and for longer, and with a longer interval to the next birth. This surprising prediction was also confirmed by Bereczkei and Dunbar (1997) in Hungary, where Gypsies (who generally have low status and low incomes) not only give birth to more daughters and invest more in their daughters, but succeed in producing a higher number of their grandchildren through the female line.

Of course there is a great deal more that could be said on all of the above topics. And there are a great many more topics, too, on which evolutionary psychology has made novel predictions and generated novel experimental results. (For one example amongst many, consider Cosmides

---

[22] These data are criticized at length in Buller (2005); but see Daly and Wilson (2005) for a reply that is, to my mind, utterly devastating.

and Tooby's well-known 'cheater detection hypothesis'—see Cosmides and Tooby, 1992; Fiddick et al., 2000; Sugiyama et al., 2002; Stone et al., 2002. For another example, consider the prediction made by Fessler and Navarrete (2003) on evolutionary grounds, that women's sensitivity to *sexual* disgust should vary with their menstrual cycle—peaking with the period of greatest fertility—whereas their sensitivity to other forms of disgust should not. This surprising prediction was confirmed, suggesting that the disgust system is composed of a number of distinct modules.) All that I have been attempting to do here, is to establish that evolutionary psychology is at least a promising and progressive research program. To the extent that its detailed predictions are proving to be warranted, we have yet further reason to accept the hypothesis of massive modularity.

It should be stressed that there are also, of course, many objections to the thesis of massive modularity. Most of these have to do with the apparent *holism* of human central cognitive processes of inference and belief-formation (Fodor, 1983, 2000), and with the distinctive flexibility and creativity of the human mind. Replying to these objections will be the task of later chapters, beginning in Chapter 4.

6 The Argument from Computational Tractability

Perhaps the best-known of the arguments for massive modularity, however—at least amongst philosophers—is the argument from computational tractability. This derives from Fodor (1983, 2000) and will be presented in a moment. But it should be stressed that Fodor himself doesn't argue for or endorse massive modularity, of course. Rather, since he claims that we *know* that central processes of belief fixation and decision-making *can't* be modular, he transforms what would otherwise be an argument for massive modularity into an argument for pessimism about the prospects for computational psychology. (See Fodor, 2000.) The overall contention of the present book is that the knowledge-claim underlying such pessimism isn't warranted.

It is generally thought that the Fodorian argument, if it were successful, would license the claim that the mind is composed of *encapsulated* processing systems, thus supporting a far stronger form of massive modularity hypothesis than has been defended in this chapter so far (Carruthers, 2002a; Sperber, 2002). The argument can be summarized like this:

(1) The mind is computationally realized.
(2) All computational mental processes must be suitably *tractable*.

(3) Only processes that are informationally encapsulated are suitably tractable.

(4) So the mind must consist entirely of encapsulated computational systems.

The first premise of the argument is the claim that the mind is realized in
processes that are computational in character. This claim is by no means uncontroversial, of course, although it is the guiding methodological assumption of
much of cognitive science. Indeed, it is a claim that is denied by certain species
of distributed connectionism. But in recent years arguments have emerged
against these competitors that are decisive, in my view (Gallistel, 2000; Marcus,
2001). And what remains is that computational psychology represents easily
our best—and perhaps our only—hope for fully understanding how mental
processes can be realized in physical ones (Rey, 1997). I propose briefly to
defend the truth of this first premise here; and I shall then just *assume* its truth
for the purposes of the ensuing discussion.[23]

6.1 *The Language of Thought*

The Zeitgeist of the middle part of the twentieth century was behaviorism (Watson, 1924; Skinner, 1957). And in the year 1975 most philosophers
still assumed that the processes that underlie the apparently intelligent behaviors
of non-human animals, as well as much of the behavior of human beings, are
associationist ones, underpinned by some or other form of conditioning. And
it was widely assumed, too—especially amongst philosophers—that if there
is a language of thought at all, then that language is *English* (or more strictly,
the thinker's natural language; see Wittgenstein, 1953; Sellars, 1963; Davidson,
1973, 1975; Dummett, 1973). People assumed that it is only by manipulating
natural language sentences that humans come to have structured, content-
bearing, causally efficacious representations. Fodor (1975) effectively turned
the prevailing Zeitgeist on its head, doing for philosophy what Chomsky
(1959) and a number of others had done for psychology. He argued that
underlying the use of any natural language like English must be a universal language of thought—sometimes called 'Mentalese'—in which the real thinking
takes place; and that this language is very likely shared by non-human animals.

   It is important to understand the sense in which Mentalese representations
are supposed to be language-like. The idea is *not* that they consist of linear

---

[23] Note that nothing in the arguments of Sections 3 and 4 above requires that mental processes
should be computational in character. So the sort of weak massive modularity thesis to come out of
those arguments ought to be acceptable even to connectionists. The result would be a picture of the
mind as implemented in a nested hierarchy of a great many function-specific distributed connectionist
networks.

(spatially or temporally extended) strings of symbols. The crucial requirement is one of compositional structure (so that complex Mentalese representations are composed out of simpler ones, which can in turn figure as components of yet other complex representations) combined with processing systems that are sensitive to those structures. This idea can also be expressed as a *co-tokening thesis* (Fodor, 1998). Since a complex Mentalese representation is a composite of constituent representations, it can't be tokened unless all of its constituents are too. So the 'sentences' of Mentalese could perfectly well be mental models or mental maps of one sort or another, as long as they satisfy appropriate compositional-structure constraints (cf. Casati and Varzi, 1999).[24]

The thesis that there is a language of thought (LOT) has undoubtedly been a fruitful one across cognitive science, and I believe that it should continue to be so. The main challenge to the LOT thesis in the 1980s and 1990s came from certain forms of distributed connectionism, reviving and extending the earlier associationist tradition (Rumelhart and McClelland, 1986). On this sort of view, cognitive processes don't consist of algorithmic transformations of structured representations, as the LOT account would have it, but rather in the spread of activation through the nodes in a network. And although representations *can* be identified within distributed connectionist systems, consisting in *patterns* of activation across the system (Smolensky, 1991, 1995), these patterns don't satisfy the co-tokening requirement for LOT representations, and the outputs of the system aren't causally dependent upon the representational structures of those patterns (Fodor and Pylyshyn, 1988; Fodor and McLaughlin, 1990; Fodor, 1998).[25]

While wanting to defend the LOT hypothesis, I am happy to be concessive. It may well be that connectionist networks have some sort of role to play in certain aspects of cognition, particularly in pattern-recognition and in simple forms of statistical inference. But recent developments have presented

---

[24] It is important to distinguish between maps that are purely topographic in character, and those that contain labels for particular cities and mountains and so on. The former aren't compositional. You can't take a map that represents a river flowing from North to South and transform it into one that shows the same river flowing from East to West—all that you will have done is represent a different overall topology. But maps that contain labels *are* compositional. You can take a map in which the city labeled 'New York' is North East of the city labeled 'Philadelphia' and turn it into one that represents New York as due North of Philadelphia, by moving the marks that represent New York westwards.

[25] It is important to distinguish between *distributed* connectionist systems, in which there are no local representations, and neural networks more generally, which are also often described as 'connectionist'. For the latter often *do* contain local representations, with particular nodes assigned to represent a certain property, a certain class of entities, or a given individual. So neural networks often do contain structured representational states with causal efficacy, even if those networks are designed to build statistical associations amongst notes. In fact the *distributed* aspect of distributed connectionism can be pulled apart from the associationism.

decisive arguments against the ubiquity of connectionism and the associationist psychology that goes with it. I shall briefly review the work of Marcus (2001) and Gallistel (1990, 2000). (See also Davies, 1991, 1998.)

6.2 Recent Arguments for LOT

Marcus (2001) argues that connectionist architectures can successfully model human cognitive performance only if they implement representation-processing algorithms. He also argues that connectionist attempts to do away with complex representational structure face severe difficulties, whereas the attempts of some connectionists to accommodate complex representational structure aren't promising. He further argues that connectionist systems are unable to represent individuals as opposed to attributes. Taken together, his arguments provide a strong case in favor of the LOT alternative. I begin with a sketch of his argument concerning algorithmic processing.

Marcus points out that there is plenty of evidence that people can freely generalize universal one-to-one functions. That is, people can determine the value of such a function for any item in its domain, regardless of whether or not they have previously encountered that item. For example, English speakers can form the progressive of any English verb stem by affixing '-ing' to it, even if the verb stem is new to them.

Free generalization of a universal one-to-one function seems to require the execution of an algorithm that operates on instances of variables—what Marcus calls an 'algebraic rule'. Operations that rely on encoded one-to-one mappings between particulars (e.g., look-up tables) wouldn't suffice. Such operations don't permit generalization to novel particulars, since novel particulars are simply those for which there is no prior encoded mapping. On the other hand, free generalization comes naturally to a system that executes algebraic rules. For such rules are applicable to any input-variable instance, regardless of whether or not it is novel to the system.

Over the course of his book Marcus makes out a strong case that connectionist networks, trained by standard connectionist learning algorithms, can't freely generalize universal one-to-one functions. Or rather, he argues, in effect, that insofar as connectionist networks *can* generalize such functions, they turn out merely to *implement* a LOT-based algorithm. So the connectionist is presented with a dilemma: *either* connectionism is inadequate to account for core aspects of human and animal cognition, *or* the connectionist system in question has been set up in such a way as to implement a structure-dependent algorithm.

It is worth noting that connectionist networks also face the converse problem. Besides having difficulties in generalizing one-to-one functions, they also have trouble in learning novel items of arbitrary information (like a new word, or a new telephone number) without catastrophic forgetting of previous knowledge. This is because training a network on a novel set of inputs is apt to reconfigure all the previous weights in the system, which means that it no longer responds as it used to do when confronted once again with items from the original training set (McCloskey and Cohen, 1989). The only currently workable solution to this problem requires us to assume that each connectionist learning system is linked to a 'clone' of itself, which serves to present as input to the learning system, alongside the novel item to be learned, the output that it generates in response to self-generated noise (Ans et al., 2002). The input provided by the clone acts as something like an average over the previous training set. But there is no indication that any neural systems exist that possess such properties (Blackmon et al., 2005).

Marcus's other main argument against connectionism concerns our capacity to represent individuals as distinct from their properties. Humans are capable of having many different thoughts about one and the same individual thing, despite changes in its spatiotemporal and non-spatiotemporal properties. And many non-human animals, too, can do this—tracking the individual members of their social group, for example, through social, biological, and spatiotemporal changes (Cheney and Seyfarth, 1999; Daly et al., 2006).

If you want to represent a variety of facts, and changes in such facts, about various individuals, then it is quite natural to employ a LOT representational scheme. One class of representational constituents can be reserved for individuals and a distinct class of constituents can be reserved for properties of individuals. You can then devise representation-manipulating algorithms that are sensitive to the relevant distinction. The formal language and rules of predicate logic provide a familiar example.

As Marcus (2001) points out, however, it is by no means easy to achieve the same effect within connectionism. Of course specific activation patterns (or nodes) can be assigned to particular individuals; but then specific activation patterns (or nodes) will have to be assigned to represent properties. There will thus be no formal difference between representations assigned to individuals and representations assigned to properties—or none, that is, that can be read immediately off the representation itself. The problem will then be to get the system to 'know' that a particular activation-pattern is about an individual rather than a property. Regardless of the sorts of representation-level processes that you give the system, all that they will be capable of 'seeing' are sets of activation levels.[26]

---

[26] I am aware that connectionists might attempt to introduce the distinction in question, perhaps by assigning nodes to individuals and patterns to properties, or by having separate networks for individuals

If this is correct, then we should expect connectionist models to have difficulty with tasks that require picking out and tracking particulars. And Marcus shows that standard connectionist networks do indeed have difficulty with such tasks. He focuses on object permanence—the ability of an agent to believe that an object that he has recently seen, but no longer perceives, continues to exist—examining a variety of approaches to the problem. It turns out that the moral, here, is the same as the previous one: either connectionist networks can't account for object permanence at all, or they do so only by implementing a structure-dependent, LOT-involving, algorithm.

In sum, I take Marcus's arguments to provide the following case in favor of the LOT theoretical framework. First, an adequate model of human cognition must implement representation-manipulating algorithms. It must also assign formally special representations, or 'designators', to individuals. Moreover, if the model is to be able to represent a variety of facts, and changes in such facts, about various individuals, then it needs to construct the relevant representations, as needed, on an ongoing basis. Such representations will have designators and property representations as constituents. At this point, we need only add to Marcus's arguments the theoretical claim that the constituents of a representation can have content-appropriate causal roles only if they are tokened whenever that representation as a whole is tokened.

The cognitive capacities on which Marcus (2001) mostly focuses are, if not distinctively human, then relatively sophisticated ones (learning an algebraic rule; keeping track of individual things whose properties are changing). So even if his arguments are found convincing, it remains possible to doubt whether a LOT is ubiquitous throughout the animal kingdom. This lacuna is effectively addressed by Gallistel (1990, 2000), who argues that structure-dependent computational processes are *rife* amongst animals, including invertebrates. I shall mention here just the case of navigation by dead reckoning, in particular (which has already been discussed briefly in Section 5).[27]

The computations involved in dead reckoning are trivially easy, and easily implemented, using compositionally structured representations of distance, velocity, and direction, formalizable perhaps as ordered sets. Yet it is *immensely*

---

and for properties, to mention just two possibilities. To do so, however, would be to implement a LOT representation scheme. For instance, on the first option just mentioned, representations of individuals (activated nodes) would have to be tokened whenever representations having them as constituents are tokened.

[27] Gallistel (2000; Gallistel and Gibbon, 2001) also carries the argument into the very heartland of associationist psychology, as we have already noted in Section 4, and as we shall see in more detail in Chapter 2—arguing that learning by conditioning is best understood in terms of the computational operations of a special-purpose rate-estimation system, designed for foraging, rather than as resulting from the strengthening or weakening of associative connections.

hard to devise a connectionist network that operates without such representations while achieving the same effect. Indeed, it is not even clear that anyone has actually tried. Some 'connectionist' models are explicitly implementations of mathematical models (e.g. Hartmann and Wehner, 1995). And another that describes itself as a 'neural network model' (Samsonovich and McNaughton, 1997) is actually a theory of hippocampal place-cell dynamics, and assumes the existence of a cognitive map, with attendant compositional structure.

Moreover, it is very unlikely that any such network can do what an ant can do, which is compute the direction and distance in which it should travel towards a previously discovered food source when it ventures out from its nest once again (Collett and Collett, 2000). This seems to require structure-sensitive processes that can take a representation derived from the dead reckoning calculation—which might have the content, *Food is 64 meters NE of nest*—and combine it either with a desire for the nest or a desire for food, and either with the representation, HERE IS AT FOOD, or, HERE IS AT NEST, as appropriate, to calculate the correct direction and distance of travel necessary to achieve its goal.[28]

6.3 Is LOT Consistent with Massive Modularity?

I have argued that a language of thought (LOT) is at least extremely common amongst the processes that realize human and animal cognition, even if it isn't entirely ubiquitous. (Recall that I have allowed that *some* cognitive processes might be realized in distributed connectionist networks.) So the first premise in the Fodorian argument sketched in Section 6.1 is vindicated. But before returning to examine the remainder of that argument, I want to consider a challenge. This is that postulating a LOT should more properly be seen as inconsistent with massive modularity, rather than serving as a premise that supports it. This will help us to be clearer about what a commitment to LOT involves.

The seeming inconsistency is this. If there is a language of thought (LOT) underlying all or almost all mental processes, then wouldn't this be a sort of *Lingua Franca* of the mind, enabling any two different systems to 'talk to' one another in principle? But the massive modularist conception is that most if not all modules will only be capable to 'talking to' a limited range of other modules—namely, those with which they happen to be connected in respect of either input or output. And aren't these two ideas inconsistent?

---

[28] Throughout this book I adopt the familiar convention of using words in small capitals to designate mental representations, or tokens of Mentalese. I shall use quotation marks when referring to natural language words or sentences, and will generally use italics when referring to the *content* of either a Mentalese or a natural language expression.

In fact there is no inconsistency here. The simplest and most direct way to see this is to think of actual speakers of French. Even though all French speakers enjoy a common language, it doesn't follow that they are actually capable of talking to one another. For there might be impassible barriers of various sorts that prevent them from doing so. Put another way: two people who speak the same language might nevertheless be incapable to talking to one another for want of any workable channel of communication between them. But this reply—acceptable as far as it goes—still implies that if any two arbitrary modules *could* become connected, then they would be capable of understanding one another, just as would happen when any two arbitrary speakers of French are provided with a telephone line to link them. And this consequence is almost certainly false. Let me explain.

As we have seen, many mental modules are likely to employ computations that are domain-specific. They will have been designed to get turned on by a certain class of inputs, and might have been set up to query certain other systems for information at various points during their computations. This information, plainly, will be in a language that the module in question can understand. But if there are modules that a given module hasn't been set up to query or receive information from, then it is highly unlikely that the module in question could do anything with that information, even if a channel of communication were somehow to be created.

This is what massive modularity probably implies. But there is nothing here to conflict with the LOT thesis, properly understood. For the latter is really just a claim about compositional structure in representations, and in the computations defined over those representations. To say that all or most cognitive processes take place in a LOT is just to say that those cognitive processes are computational, involving the construction and transformation of compositionally structured representations. It doesn't by any means imply that the computations in question are defined over *all* structured representations, drawn from any arbitrary region of the mind. And if the mind is massively modular in its organization, quite the contrary is true. In consequence, it is probably misleading to talk about *the* language of thought, or to talk about 'Mentalese', as if it were a single representational system. We should more properly, in the context of a thesis of massive mental modularity, talk about *languages* of thought, or Mentales*es*.

6.4 Completing the Argument from Computational Tractability

I propose to assume, then, that the first premise of the Fodorian argument set out in Section 6.1 is correct: the mind is realized in computational processes. The second premise of the argument is the claim that if cognitive processes are to be realized computationally, then those computations must be suitably *tractable* ones. What does this amount to? First of all, it means that the computations must be such that they can *in principle* be carried out within finite time. But it isn't enough that the computations postulated to take place in the human brain should be tractable in principle, of course. It must also be feasible that those computations could be executed (perhaps in parallel) in a system with the properties of the human brain, whose basic neural processes operate at rates that are slower than those within modern computers by many orders of magnitude. Moreover, these computations must be effected within timescales that are characteristic of actual human performance (often seconds or fractions of a second). By this criterion, many computations that aren't strictly speaking intractable from the perspective of *computer* science, should nevertheless count as such for the purposes of *cognitive* science.

There is a whole branch of computer science devoted to the study of more-or-less intractable problems, known as 'Complexity Theory'. And one doesn't have to dig very deep into the issues to discover results that have important implications for cognitive science. For example, it has traditionally been assumed by philosophers that any candidate new belief should be checked for consistency with existing beliefs before being accepted. But in fact consistency-checking is demonstrably intractable, if attempted on an exhaustive basis. Consider how one might check the consistency of a set of beliefs via a truth-table. Even if each line could be checked in the time that it takes a photon of light to travel the diameter of a proton, then even after 20 billion years the truth-table for a set of just 138 beliefs (2^{138} lines) still wouldn't have been completed (Cherniak, 1986).

From the first two premises together, then, we can conclude that the human mind must be realized in a set of computational processes that are suitably tractable. This means that those processes will have to be quite *frugal*, both in the amount of information that they require for their normal operations, and in the complexity of the algorithms that they deploy when processing that information.

The third premise of the argument then claims that in order to be tractable, computations need to be encapsulated; for only encapsulated processes can be appropriately frugal in the informational and computational resources that they require. As Fodor (2000) explains it, the constraint here can be expressed as one of *locality*. Computationally tractable processes have to be *local*, in the sense of only consulting a limited database of information relevant to those computations, and ignoring all other information held in the mind. For if they attempted to consult all (or even a significant subset) of the total information available, then they would be subject to combinatorial explosion, and hence would fail to be tractable after all.

This third premise, in conjunction with the other two, would then (if it were acceptable) license the conclusion that the mind must be realized in a set of encapsulated computational processes. And when combined with the conclusions of the arguments of Sections 3 and 4, this would give us the claim that the mind consists in a very large set of encapsulated computational systems, each of which has its own function to perform, and many of which execute processing algorithms that aren't to be found elsewhere in the mind (although some do re-use algorithms that are also found in other systems for novel functions). It is therefore crucial for our purposes to know whether the third premise is really warranted; and if not, what one might put in its stead. This will form the topic of the next section.

7 What does Computational Frugality Really Require?

I have claimed that the first two premises in the Fodorian argument that we sketched in Section 6 are acceptable. So we should believe that cognition must be organized into networks of distinct computational systems, whose internal processes are appropriately *frugal*. The question is whether frugality requires encapsulation, in the way that is stated by the third premise of the argument. The idea has an obvious appeal. It is certainly true that *one* way to ensure the frugality of a set of computational systems would be to organize them into networks of encapsulated processors, each of which can look only at a limited database of information in executing its tasks. And it may well be the case that evolution has settled on this strategy in connection with many of the systems that constitute the human mind. It is doubtful, however, whether this is the *only* way of ensuring frugality, as we shall see. (See also Samuels, 2005.)

7.1 Heuristic Processes

The assumption of encapsulation (at least, as it is normally understood—see Section 7.3 below) may derive from an older tradition of thinking about the mind, in which information search had to be *exhaustive*, and in which algorithms should be designed to be optimally reliable. But this tradition is now widely rejected, since it gives rise to an insuperable 'Frame Problem' (Gigerenzer et al., 1999; Shanahan and Baars, 2005).[29] Most cognitive scientists now think

[29] The Frame Problem can be construed as a problem of *relevance*. It is the problem of determining which items of information from amongst the vast array available in memory or in the environment

that the processing rules deployed in the human mind have been designed to be *good enough*, not to be optimal. Given that speed of processing is always one constraint for organisms that may need to think and act swiftly in order to survive, evolution will have led to compromises on the question of reliability. Indeed, it will favor a *satisficing* strategy, rather than an optimal one. And likewise for information search: evolution will favor a variety of search heuristics that are good enough without being exhaustive.

These points are well illustrated by the research program pursued in recent years by Gigerenzer and colleagues (e.g. Gigerenzer et al., 1999). They have investigated the comparative reliability and frugality of a variety of rules for use in information search and decision-making, with startling results. It turns out that even very simple heuristics can be remarkably successful—such as choosing the only one of two options that you recognize, when asked which of two cities is larger, or when asked to predict which of two companies will do best in the stock market. In some cases these simple heuristics will even out-perform much fancier and information-hungry algorithms, such as multiple regression. And a variety of simple heuristics for searching for information within a wider database, combined with stopping-rules if the search is unsuccessful within a specified time-frame, can also work remarkably well—such as accessing the information that has worked best in the past with problems of this type (Take the Best), accessing the information in the order in which it was last used (Take the Last), or accessing the information that is partially activated (and hence made salient) by the context. Of course the question for us, at this point, is whether or not systems that deploy such simple heuristics must count as encapsulated in their operations. For if so, then the simple heuristics program will be perfectly consistent with the third premise of the Fodorian argument that we outlined at the outset of Section 6.

Consider the Recognition heuristic first. It works somewhat as follows. When you are required to decide which of two items scores higher along some dimension (e.g., which of two German cities is the larger), if you only recognize one of the two items, then select that one. (If both items are recognized, then some other heuristic must be employed.) This heuristic does appear to be fully encapsulated in its operation. For no other information in the mind either does or can influence the outcome, except perhaps information that is somehow implicated in the recognition process itself. Once the system

---

are relevant to the current task; and it is the problem of determining which inferences, from amongst the indefinitely many available, should be drawn from the information selected. Everyone now agrees that the Frame Problem can't be solved in a 'brute force' way. Rather, it needs to be evaded through the use of 'quick and dirty' heuristics of various sorts.

has received a judgment-task to process, it just has to look to determine which of the objects presented to it evokes recognition.[30] No other information needs to be consulted (nor can it be, indeed, or at least not internally within the operation of recognition heuristic itself), and the inferential procedure involved is a very simple one. So it would appear that instantiations of the recognition heuristic deserve to be counted as modules in something like the traditional Fodorian sense.

Now consider the Take the Best heuristic, however (Gigerenzer et al., 1999). Unlike Recognition, this heuristic does require the system to search for and consult some further information concerning the items in question. But it doesn't look at *all* the information concerning those items (let alone attempt to consider all the information contained in the mind). Specifically, it searches for the piece of information concerning the two target items that has most often been found in the past to discriminate between items of that type along the required dimension. Gigerenzer et al. (1999) have shown that this heuristic can perform almost as well as a bunch of fancier processing algorithms, but it can do so while being much more frugal in the information that it uses and the demands that it places on the computational resources of the system.

Notice that the relevant subset of total information available, that a system instantiating Take the Best can consult during processing, consists of its beliefs about relative cue validity together with its further beliefs concerning the cues in question. When it gets a query about the relative size of two German cities, for example, it must look first at its beliefs about which properties of cities have correlated best with size in the past. If having a top-division soccer team was the best predictor, then it will query the wider database: does either of these teams have a top-division soccer team? If it receives back the information that just one of them does, then it selects that one as the larger. If neither or both do, then it moves on to the next best predictor of size listed in its processing database. And so on. (And in order to operate tractably across all cases, there will have to be a stopping rule of the form: if the *n*th best predictor of size doesn't yield a result, then abandon the task altogether and move on to another one, or choose at random.) We might therefore be tempted to argue that a system instantiating Take the Best is encapsulated after all, with its dedicated database consisting of the items of information that it is permitted to consult.

Note, however, that which beliefs such a system *can* consult in the course of its processing is a function of what its beliefs actually *are*. If the system

---

[30] Hence the processing database for the system would consist in the set of concepts possessed, together with any information required for object recognition. This is likely to be a small sub-set of the total information contained within a mind.

had believed that having a high crime rate was the best predictor of city size, then *that* is the information that it would have sought out. And in principle any belief *could* have had an impact on processing. So it seems that our best hope of finding a place for the notion of 'encapsulation', here, would be to regard the specific beliefs that the system instantiating Take the Best happens to acquire as carving out a functionally individuated processing database from the wider set of stored information in relation to each dimension of comparison, such that the system *can* only consider that narrower set in answer to a given question. But it has to be admitted that this looks pretty forced and unnatural. And decisive reasons for rejecting this sort of approach will emerge when we consider the accessibility heuristic in the sub-section following.

7.2 'On the Fly' Modules?

Consider heuristic processes that rely upon such phenomena as the *salience* of a piece of information in a context, or the *accessibility* of that information given the recent history of its activation. Consider language comprehension, for example, on the sort of model provided by Sperber and Wilson (1996), in which accessibility of beliefs plays a major role. On their account, one of the factors in interpretation is saliency in the present environment, and another is relative recency (e.g. whether or not an item of information has been activated earlier in the conversation).

For example: Mary and Joan have been discussing a number of their mutual acquaintances. Mary says, 'I went to the zoo last Saturday with Paul.' Joan asks, 'Were the cheetah cubs outside?', to which Mary replies, 'Yes. He thought they were really cute.' Joan will of course interpret the pronoun 'he' here as referring to Paul. For even if John and Peter had also been mentioned previously, Paul is more salient because he has been mentioned *more* recently.

Might the comprehension process nevertheless count as an encapsulated one, although in principle *any* belief *might* be made salient by the present environment, or *might* have been activated previously? If so, then we shall have to think of the comprehension process, as it unfolds in the course of a set of linguistic exchanges, as creating a sort of local comprehension module 'on the fly', whose encapsulation-conditions are continually modified as the conversation continues. But what becomes of the idea that there is some subset of the total information available that the comprehension system can look at, if *any* item of information *could* have been salient?

It might be replied, however, that we are dealing here with a *briefly existing* encapsulated system, created out of the resources of a longer-lasting comprehension system by facts about the recent environment. *Given* the previous history of the conversation, then some items of information are much more accessible than others. So a search process that operates on principles of accessibility *can* only look at that information, and other information in the mind *cannot* influence the comprehension process. Granted, if the earlier facts about the conversation had been different, then other information *could have had* an influence on the comprehension of the sentence in question. But this doesn't alter the fact that, the previous history of the conversation having been what it was, that information *cannot* now have an influence.

Although there is a sense in which this reply works, the victory is a Pyrrhic one. For the resulting notion of modularity is highly problematic. Cognitive science, like any other science, is in the business, *inter alia*, of discovering and studying the properties of the set of *natural kinds* within its domain. And a natural kind, in order to be a worthwhile object of study, must have a certain sort of *stability*, or regular recurrence. In contrast, the state of a comprehension system that has undergone a specific conversational history, and hence that has a particular distribution of degrees of accessibility amongst its representations, is something that might exist just once in the history the universe. That particular combination of processing principles and accessibility (yielding the 'processing database' of an on-the-fly module) might never recur again.

If cognitive science is to attain the sort of generality that one expects of a science, it needs to carve its kinds at *recurring* joints. This requires us to think of the comprehension system as a *single* system over time, operating partly on principles of accessibility that help to make its operations information-frugal. So if we are to think of the comprehension system as a module, as the thesis of massive modularity will require, then we must think of it as an unencapsulated module (i.e. as a module only in the weak sense employed in Sections 3 and 4 of this chapter). And likewise, then, with Take the Best: instances of this, too, should be thought of as unencapsulated modules, which nevertheless are constructed so as to be suitably frugal in their computations.

7.3 Wide-Scope Versus Narrow-Scope Encapsulation

If encapsulation isn't a constraint on the modularity of a system, then the simple practical-reasoning system sketched in Carruthers (2002a) can count as modular. This takes as initial input whatever is currently the strongest desire, for P.[31] It then queries the various belief-generating modules, while also conducting a targeted search of long-term memory, looking for beliefs of the form Q ⊃ P. If it receives one as input, or if it finds one from its own search

---

[31] Note that *competition for resources* is another of the heuristics that may be widely used within our cognitive systems; see Sperber, 2005, and Chapter 2 below. In the present instance one might think of all activated desires as competing with one another for entry into the practical-reasoning system.

of memory, it consults a database of action schemata, to see if Q is something doable here and now. If it is, it goes ahead and does it. If it isn't, it initiates a further search for beliefs of the form R ⊃ Q, and so on. If it has gone more than n conditionals deep without success, or if it has searched for the right sort of conditional belief without finding one for more than some specified time t, then it stops and moves on to the next strongest desire.

Such a system would be frugal, both in the information that it uses, and in the complexity of its algorithms. But does it count as encapsulated? This isn't encapsulation as that notion would generally be understood, which requires there to be a limited module-specific database that gets consulted by the computational process in question. For here, on the contrary, the practical-reasoning system can search within the total set of the organism's beliefs, using structure-sensitive search rules. But for all that, there is *a* sense in which the system is encapsulated that is worth noticing.

Put as neutrally as possible, it can be said that the idea of an encapsulated system is the notion of a system whose internal operations *can't* be affected by *most or all* of the information held elsewhere in the mind. But there is a scope ambiguity here.[32] We can have the modal term 'can't' take narrow scope with respect to the quantifier, or we can have it take wide scope. In its narrow-scope form, an encapsulated system would be this: concerning most of the information held in the mind, the system in question *can't* be affected by *that* information in the course of its processing. Call this 'narrow-scope encapsulation'. In its wide-scope form, on the other hand, an encapsulated system would be this: the system is such that it *can't* be affected by *most* of the information held in the mind in the course of its processing. Call this 'wide-scope encapsulation'.

Narrow-scope encapsulation is the one that is taken for granted in the philosophical literature on modularity. We tend to think of encapsulation as requiring some determinate (and large) body of information, such that *that* information can't penetrate the internal operations of the module. However, it can be true that the operations of a module can't be affected by most of the information in a mind, without there being some determinate sub-division between the information that can affect the system and the information that can't. For as we have just seen, it can be the case that the system's algorithms are so set up that only a limited amount of information is ever consulted before the task is completed or aborted. Put it this way: a module can be a system that *must* only consider a small

---

[32] Modal terms like 'can' and 'can't' have wide scope if they govern the whole sentence in which they occur; they have narrow scope if they govern only a part. Compare: 'I can't kill everyone' (wide scope; equivalent to, 'It is impossible that I kill everyone') with, 'Everyone is such that I can't kill them' (narrow scope). The latter is equivalent to, 'I can't kill anyone.'

subset of the total information available. Whether it does this via encapsulation as traditionally understood (the narrow-scope variety), or via frugal search heuristics and stopping rules (wide-scope encapsulation), is inessential. The important thing is that the system should be *frugal*, both in the information that it uses and in the resources that it requires for processing that information.

The Fodorian argument from computational tractability, then, does warrant the claim that the mind should be constructed entirely out of systems that are *frugal*; but it doesn't warrant a claim of encapsulation, as traditionally under-stood (the narrow-scope variety). It does, however, warrant a non-standard encapsulation claim (the wide-scope version). And since we have reason to think that some, at least, of the systems that make up the mind will oper-ate through heuristic-guided searches over an extensive database (Gigerenzer et al., 1999), or by sending out queries to a wide range of other systems for information (Shanahan and Baars, 2005; see also Section 2 above), then we shouldn't insist that modules should be narrow-scope encapsulated, in the context of a defense of the massive modularity of mind.

7.4 Inaccessibility

While the argument from frugality fails to support the claim that the mind must consist entirely of systems that are encapsulated in the traditional (narrow-scope) sense, it does support the claim that the processing systems in question should have internal operations that are *inaccessible* elsewhere. Or so I shall now briefly argue by *reductio*, and by induction across current practices in AI.

Consider what it would be like if the internal operations of each system were accessible to all other systems. (This would be *complete* accessibility. Of course the notions of *accessibility* and *inaccessibility*, just like the notions of *encapsulation* and *lack of encapsulation*, admit of degrees.) In order to make use of information about those operations, those other systems would need to contain a model of them, or they would somehow need to be capable of simulating or replicating them. In order to use the information that a given processing system is currently undertaking such-and-such computations, the other systems would need to contain a representation (either explicit or implicit) of the algorithms in question. But this would defeat the purpose of dividing up processing into distinct sub-systems running different algorithms for different purposes, and would likely result in some sort of combinatorial explosion. At the very least, we should expect that *most* of those processing systems should have internal operations that are inaccessible to all others; and that *all* of the processing systems that make up the mind should have internal operations that are inaccessible to *most* others.

One very important exception to this generalization is as follows. We should expect that many mental modules will be composed out of other modules as parts; and likewise we should predict that many modules will share parts. For this is entailed by the hierarchical account of modular organization, discussed and defended in Section 3, and also by induction from biological systems generally.[33] Some of these component parts may feed their outputs directly and automatically to other systems. (Hence such components might be shared between two or more larger modules.) Or it might be the case that they can be queried independently by other systems. These would then be instances where some of the intermediate *stages* in the processing of the larger module would be available elsewhere, without the intermediate *processing* itself being so available. This is an important distinction. Inaccessibility is about the unavailability of the internal *processes* of a module to other systems. But this needn't mean that all of the *information* generated in the course of that processing is unavailable elsewhere. On the contrary, wherever a module is composed of sub-modules some of which are shared with others, we should predict that some of the information generated in the course of the processing of the larger containing-module should be made available to other systems.

The conclusion that the internal processing of most computational systems should be unavailable elsewhere is also supported inductively by current practices in AI, where researchers routinely assume that processing needs to be divided up amongst distinct systems running algorithms specialized for the particular tasks in question. These systems can talk to one another and query one another, but cannot access one another's internal operations. And yet they may be conducting guided searches over the same memory database. (Personal communication: Mike Anderson, John Horty, and Aaron Sloman.) That researchers attempting to build working cognitive systems have converged on some such architecture is evidence of its inevitability, and hence evidence that the human mind will be similarly organized.

Recall the argument from design, discussed at length in Section 3 of this chapter. It is a necessary condition for the incremental construction and modification of complex systems that they should be made up of systems of independent parts, which are in turn made up of such parts, and so on. This is a constraint that governs the organization of biological systems quite generally, and also the organization of complex computer programs. Each of the parts,

---

[33] The design of complex electronic control systems—such as those that are involved in the automatic management of telephone networks—suggests a similar conclusion. See Coward, 2001.

or modules, will have some particular function or set of functions to play in the operation of the whole, and will have an internal organization of sub-parts and processes suited to the execution of those roles. When the complex system in question is a mind, therefore, realized computationally in a hierarchically organized network of computational modules, we can predict that each of these modules will stand in function-specific input and/or output relations with some others, and each of these modules will execute some task-specific information-processing algorithm.

Each processing module will have its own job to do, in the course of which it may seek information from memory, query the outputs of certain other modules, and so on. But it shouldn't care what processing is being conducted in other computational modules meanwhile, except insofar as the outputs of that processing might be amongst the information it needs to do its own job. Each module should be concerned to carry out its own function, interacting with others as necessary to do so; and the overall system will operate properly when all the separate sub-systems operate properly; but individual modules shouldn't care *how* the other modules with which they are connected execute their tasks. Which is to say: the internal operations of those other systems should be inaccessible to them.

Moreover, if the internal operations of a system *were* accessible elsewhere, then this would violate the separate-modifiability constraint, which formed an important part of the argument from design. Recall that this is a constraint on the evolvability, or incremental construction and improvement, of complex systems. For if the internal operations of a system (e.g. the details of the algorithms being executed) were available elsewhere, then they couldn't be altered without some corresponding alteration being made in the system to which they are accessible. When the argument from design is applied to the special case of cognitive / computational systems, therefore, it strongly suggests that the internal processing conducted by each modular system should be inaccessible to the others. And the fact that when cognitive systems are designed, not by evolution but by AI researchers, they conform to the same principle strongly suggests that *inaccessibility* should be a universal property of computational modules.

This conclusion is then further confirmed when we add frugality-constraints into the picture. For if a given modular system had to know about the internal operations of some or all other systems, then in order to use that information it would have to be capable of calculating the meaning and significance of those operations. But this would vastly complicate its own computations, surely. For in addition to doing its own job it would, in significant measure, be replicating the computational tasks being undertaken elsewhere.

8 Conclusion

What emerges, then, is that there is a strong case for saying that the mind will consist of a great many different processing systems, which exist and operate to some degree independently of one another. Each of these systems will have a distinctive function, or set of functions; and each will have a distinct neural realization (albeit one that may be dispersed across a number of different brain regions). All of these systems will need to be *frugal* in their operations, hence being encapsulated in the wide-scope sense, at least (*some* modules will no doubt be encapsulated in the stronger narrow-scope sense). Moreover, the processing that takes place within each of these systems will generally be inaccessible elsewhere.[34] Only the results, or outputs, of that processing will be made available for use by other systems.

Thus construed, the thesis of massive modularity doesn't require that the mind should be composed of systems that are encapsulated in the traditional narrow-scope sense (although many might be). Nor need all of these systems be domain-specific in their input conditions (although most are likely to be). And while modules are function-specific, their algorithms needn't be—we might expect to see the same statistical packages re-used many times over in the brain in the service of different tasks, for example (Marcus, 2004). In addition, while many modules will be significantly innate, or genetically channeled, many will be constructed through some sort of (probably modular) learning process.[35]

I should stress, moreover, that there is nothing in these considerations to suggest that modules will be elegantly engineered atomic entities with simple and streamlined internal structures. On the contrary, evolution in general has to work with whatever is antecedently available, leading to the sorts of 'kludgy' architectures that look decidedly awkward in design terms (Clark, 1987), recruiting and cobbling together in quite inelegant ways resources that existed antecedently. (This is routine in biology, where the evolution of any new structure has to begin from what was already present. Thus the penguin's flippers, used for swimming, evolved from the wings that its ancestors once used for flight.)

---

[34] As we already noted above, the notions of 'encapsulation' and 'inaccessibility' admit of degrees. The processing within a given system may be *more* or *less* encapsulated from and inaccessible to other systems.

[35] Notice that these points render the thesis of massive mental modularity, as I understand it, immune to the anti-modularist arguments presented by Buller (2005) and others. For these not only assume that modules are encapsulated systems (in the traditional narrow-scope sense), but that they are in some important sense genetically pre-specified. I shall return to this latter point in Chapter 3, when discussing principles of brain organization and brain development.

We should, in addition, expect modules to have complex input and output connections with one another, sharing information, and often sharing parts. And for similar reasons, we should expect many modules and sub-modules to have multiple functions, passing on their outputs to a variety of other systems for different purposes. A glance at any of the now-familiar wiring diagrams for the visual cortex will give the flavor of what I have in mind. Consider Figure 1.3, for example, which is a partial map of the visual cortex of

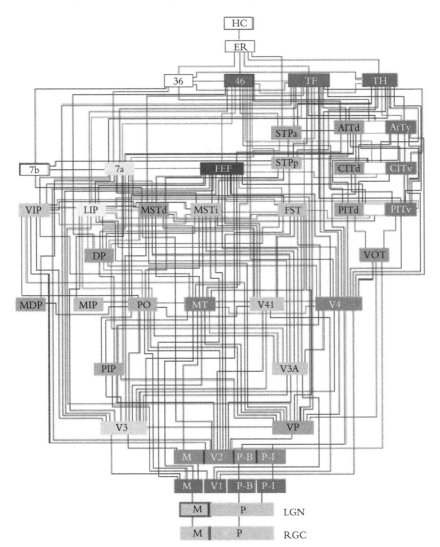

Figure 1.3. A map of the visual cortex of the macaque

a macaque. This gives us a useful model of what a modular mind might look like generally, I believe. Although many of the sub-systems are connected with multiple others, the connections are by no means general and indiscriminate. On the contrary, careful study of the map shows that each module is connected, on average, to just twenty-five percent of the other sub-systems (ten out of a total of about forty), with the maximum connectedness being fifty per cent (twenty out of forty), and the minimum being just five per cent (two out of forty). Few of these systems have direct connections outside the visual cortex. (This is consistent with the principle that sharing of parts should be mostly a local phenomenon, discussed in Section 3.)

Does such a thesis *deserve* the title of 'massive modularity', then? It is certainly a form of massive modularity in the everyday sense that we distinguished at the outset. And it retains many of the important features of Fodor-modularity. Moreover, it does seem that this is the notion of 'module' that is used pretty commonly in AI, if not so much in philosophy or psychology (McDermott, 2001). And it is pretty close to the sense in which 'modularity' is used by biologists (who also endorse a thesis of massive biological modularity; West-Eberhard, 2003). But however it is described, we have here a substantive and controversial claim about the basic architecture of the human mind; and it is one that is supported by powerful arguments.

In any complete defense of massively modular models of mind, so conceived, we must of course consider the various arguments *against* such models, particularly those deriving from the holistic and creative character of much of human thinking. This is a task that I shall undertake in later chapters. If those attempted rebuttals should prove to be successful, then we can conclude that the human mind will, indeed, be massively modular (in one good sense of the term 'module').

2

The Architecture of Animal Minds

My goals in this chapter are twofold. One is to flesh out and defend the major premise of the argument from animals that we articulated in Chapter 1.4 in support of massive modularity. That argument went something like this: the minds of non-human animals are massively modular in their organization; evolution is characteristically conservative, preserving and modifying existing structures rather than starting afresh; hence we can expect that the human mind, also, should be organized along massively modular lines. I argued in Chapter 1.5 that it is appropriate to extend evolutionary thinking to the human mind. In which case the argument sketched above should be convincing provided that its first premise (the modularity of animal minds) can be adequately established. That is one goal of the present chapter.

My second goal is to develop a quite specific picture—or 'flow chart'—of the likely organization of animal minds, on the assumption that much of this will have been preserved in the architecture of our own minds. So I shall start to build up a 'boxology' of the different types of modular system and their modes of interconnection. This will provide the foundations for our theorizing to follow. In Chapter 3 I shall discuss some of the new 'boxes' that are likely to have been added in the course of the evolutionary transition to the human mind. And then in the chapters thereafter our task will be to show that those structures are adequate to explain the distinctive flexibility and adaptability of the human mind.

1 Invertebrate Psychology

In the present section I shall argue that perception / belief / desire / planning / motor-control architectures are of very ancient ancestry indeed, being present even in insects and spiders. So the sort of cognitive architecture depicted in

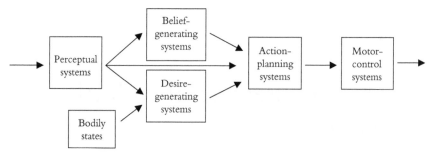

Figure 2.1. A perception / belief / desire / planning cognitive architecture

Figure 2.1 is likely to be shared by almost all animals that possess some sort of central nervous system. Note that my focus in the present section is on the overall architecture of animal minds, rather than on their massively modular sub-organization. So I shan't attempt to argue here that there are *multiple* belief-generating systems, *multiple* desire-generating systems, and *multiple* planning and motor-control systems. That will be the work of later sections.

According to the account depicted in Figure 2.1, a set of perceptual systems take information transduced from the environment to create pre-conceptual representations of some of the salient properties of, and relations amongst, items in that environment. These representations are then made available to a set of concept-involving belief-generating systems; and likewise (in conjunction with hormonal and other states of the body) to a set of desire-generating systems. The resulting beliefs and desires are in turn made available for the construction of plans. (Many of the latter are likely to be both partly conceptual and partly informed with perceptual content. They will often be highly indexical in character, yielding intentions like, 'I'll go through *that* gap to get over *there*'—hence the arrow from the perceptual box to the planning box in Figure 2.1.) And the plans are then used to control the detailed movements of the animal. (More on this in Section 2.)

1.1   *What does it take to be a Believer / Desirer?*

Some philosophers have placed very demanding conditions on what it takes to be a believer / desirer. Davidson (1975), for example, says: you need to be an interpreter of the speech and behavior of another minded organism. Only creatures that speak, and that both interpret and are subject to interpretation, count as genuinely thinking anything at all. And McDowell (1994) says: you need to exist in a space of reasons. Only creatures that are capable of appreciating the normative force of a reason for belief, or a reason for action, can count as *possessing* beliefs or *engaging* in intentional action. Likewise Searle

(1992) says: you need consciousness. Only creatures that have *conscious* beliefs and *conscious* desires can count as having beliefs or desires at all. On at least the first two of these accounts (and perhaps also the third, if the theory of consciousness defended in Carruthers, 2000, 2005, is correct) it seems unlikely that any animals besides ourselves will qualify as possessing beliefs and desires.

Such views seem to me quite ill-motivated; although I shall not pause to argue for this in any detail here. (For some further discussion, see Carruthers, 2004b.) The main point is that when science and philosophy come into conflict, it is generally the philosophers who should give way. For all that such non-empirically minded philosophers have to guide them is their 'intuitions'. And why should those count for much when set against the scientists' data and careful theorizing? Yet almost no one in the cognitive sciences takes at all seriously these demanding conditions on what to takes to be a believer / desirer. On the contrary, cognitive science is *rife* with attributions of beliefs and goals to non-human animals, as well as attributions of non-conscious beliefs and non-conscious goals to ourselves which wouldn't meet those demanding conditions either.

Other philosophers have placed quite minimal conditions on what it takes to be a believer / desirer. Dennett (1978, 1987), in particular, claims that all it really takes is that the system in question should be richly *interpretable as* possessing beliefs and desires. But almost any system—including the humble thermostat—*can* be so interpreted. We can, if we wish, adopt what Dennett calls *the intentional stance* towards the thermostat, interpreting its behavior as resulting from a desire to keep the temperature of the room above 70°F together with the belief that the temperature has fallen below 70, say. And there is, according to Dennett, no fact of the matter about whether it is right or wrong to adopt the intentional stance towards a given system. Rather, the issue is a pragmatic one. The intentional stance is *useful* to the extent that we can't easily explain the behavior of the system in other ways (adopting either of what Dennett calls *the physical stance* or *the design stance*). On this approach it is almost trivial that virtually all creatures—including insects—possess beliefs and desires, since the intentional stance is an undeniably useful one to adopt in respect of their behavior.

I propose to assume, on the contrary, that the architecture depicted in Figure 2.1 needs to be construed *realistically*. So there needs to be a real distinction between the non-conceptual or pre-conceptual perceptual states, on the one hand, and the concept-involving belief-states and desire-states, on the other. And the latter need to be genuinely distinct from one another in kind, each possessing their distinctive causal role (guiding and motivating action, respectively), and interacting with one another in the construction of plans. Moreover, these states must not only possess intentional contents but must, in addition, be both discrete, and structured in ways that reflect those contents. In addition, their detailed causal roles, too (the ways in which particular belief-states and particular desire-states interact) must be sensitive to those structural features. To be a believer / desirer therefore means possessing distinct content-bearing belief-states and desire-states that are discrete, structured, and causally efficacious in virtue of their structural properties. These are demanding conditions. But not *so* demanding that non-human animals can be ruled out as candidates immediately. Indeed I propose to argue, on the contrary, that many invertebrates actually satisfy these requirements.

Where does the list of properties of genuine belief / desire systems provided in the previous paragraph come from? Arguably they are implicit in our common-sense psychology (Ramsey et al., 1990; Davies, 1991, 1998; Frankish, 2004). We think that believing that it will rain here today is a distinct state from wanting it to rain today. And we think that on a given occasion it might be these states and not, for example, the desire to read a book (even if this is something that I also want at the time) that leads me to decide not to go out to water my new plants. And it is because those two states are both *about water*, in the right sort of way—in a way that enables them to fit together to lead to a decision—that my action is caused. Moreover, both states are composed out of distinct parts (RAIN, TODAY, HERE), and the processes of reasoning that lead to a decision are sensitive to these parts and their mode of combination. For example, believing that it will rain *there* today or that it will rain here *next week* is likely to lead to quite a different decision being taken.

Is it also a requirement on being a genuine believer / desirer that the animal in question should be capable, not just of reasoning and planning, but also of *instrumental* (in the sense of *causal*) reasoning and planning? A number of those who have written recently on the topic of animal rationality have assumed so (Dickinson and Balleine, 2000; Bermúdez, 2003). They have claimed that only creatures like rats, that are capable of identifying the causal consequences of their own actions, should be counted as having genuine beliefs and desires. But such claims have gone inadequately defended. For the authors have assumed (wrongly, as we shall see) that the only alternatives to forms of rationality that are instrumental in the strong causal sense are various kinds of associative conditioning, which needn't implicate a Figure 2.1 architecture. What they overlook are the myriad forms of *spatial* reasoning and *spatial* planning. And there are no principled reasons for denying that creatures capable of such forms of reasoning are believer / desirers, even if they aren't capable of *causal* belief and *causal* planning.

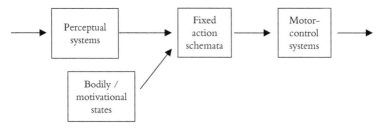

Figure 2.2. An architecture for fixed action patterns

1.2 Fixed Action Patterns

Not all cognitive scientists would agree that insects exemplify a belief / desire cognitive architecture. No doubt this is because *many* insect behaviors seem rather to be perceptually guided fixed action patterns, which can be triggered by both perceptual information and the creature's own bodily / motivational states. Such behaviors suggest an architecture of the sort depicted in Figure 2.2, rather than the one depicted in Figure 2.1.

We are all familiar with examples of the behavioral rigidity of insects. Consider the tick that sits immobile on its perch until it detects butyric acid vapor, whereupon it releases its hold (often enough falling onto the bodies of mammals passing below, whose skins emit such a vapor); and then when it detects warmth, it burrows. Or there are the caterpillars who follow the light to climb trees to find food, in whom the mechanism that enables them to do this is an extremely simple one: when more light enters one eye than the other, the legs on that side of its body move slower, causing the animal to turn towards the source of the light. When artificial lighting is provided at the bottom of the trees, the caterpillars climb downwards and subsequently starve to death. And when blinded in one eye, these animals will move constantly in circles.

Even apparently sophisticated and intelligent sequences of behavior can turn out, on closer investigation, to be surprisingly rigid. There is the well-known example of the Sphex wasp who leaves a paralyzed cricket in a burrow with her eggs so that her offspring will have something to feed on when they hatch. When she captures a cricket, she drags it to the entrance of the burrow, then leaves it outside for a moment while she enters, seemingly to check for intruders. However, if an interfering experimenter moves the cricket back a few inches while the wasp is inside, she repeats the sequence: dragging the insect to the burrow's entrance, then entering briefly once more alone. And this sequence can be made to 'loop' indefinitely many times over.

Or consider the Australian digger wasp that builds an elaborate tower-and-bell structure over the entrance of the burrow in which she lays her eggs (Gould and Gould, 1994). The purpose of the structure is to prevent a smaller species of parasitic wasp from laying *her* eggs in the same burrow. The bell is of such a size and hung at such an angle, and worked so smooth on the inside, that the smaller wasp cannot either reach far enough in, or gain enough purchase to enter. The female digger wasp builds the tower three of her own body-lengths high. If the tower is progressively buried while she builds, she will keep on building. But once she has finished the tower and started on the bell, the tower can be buried without her noticing—with disastrous results, since the bell will then be half on the ground, and consequently quite useless. Similarly, if a small hole is drilled in the neck of the tower, she seems to lack the resources to cope with a minor repair. Instead she builds *another* tower and bell structure, constructed on top of the hole.

In order to explain such behaviors, we don't need to attribute to the insect a belief / desire cognitive architecture. The digger wasp would seem to have an innately represented series of nested behavioral subroutines, with the whole sequence being triggered by its own bodily state (pregnancy). Each subroutine is guided in its details by perceptual input, and is finished by a simple stopping rule. But once any given stage is completed, there is no going back to make corrections or repairs. The wasp appears to have no conception of the overall goal of the sequence, nor any beliefs about the respective contributions made by the different elements. If this were the full extent of the flexibility of insect behavior, then there would be no warrant for believing that insects have minds that exemplify a belief / desire architecture.

1.3 A Simple Belief / Desire Psychology

From the fact that *much* insect behavior results from triggering of innately represented sequences of perceptually guided activity, however, it doesn't follow that *all* does. And it is surely no requirement on a creature qualifying as a believer / desirer that *all* of its behavior should result from interactions of belief-states with desire-states. Indeed, some of our own behaviors are triggered fixed action sequences—think of sneezing or coughing, for example, or of the universal human disgust reaction, which involves fixed movements of the lips and tongue seemingly designed to expel noxious substances from the mouth. So it remains a possibility that insects might be simple believer / desirers *as well as* possessing a set of triggerable innately represented action sequences. In effect, it remains a possibility that insects might exemplify the cognitive architecture depicted in Figure 2.1 *as well as* the architecture depicted in Figure 2.2. There would then be *dual* routes to the causation of an insect's behavior: a belief / desire route, and a triggered fixed action-pattern route. (The existence of dual routes to action will loom large once again in Section 2.) In what follows I shall argue that this is indeed the case, focusing on the minds of honey bees in particular.

Like many other insects, bees use a variety of navigation systems. One is dead reckoning (integrating a sequence of directions of motion with the velocity and time traveled in each direction, to produce a representation of one's current location in relation to the point of origin; Gallistel, 2000). This in turn requires that bees can learn the expected position of the sun in the sky at any given time of day, as measured by an internal clock of some sort. Another mechanism permits bees to recognize and navigate from landmarks, either distant or local (Collett and Collett, 2002). And some researchers have claimed that bees will, in addition, construct crude mental maps of their environment from which they can navigate. (The maps have to be crude because of the poor resolution of bee eyesight. But they may still contain the relative locations of salient landmarks, such as a large free-standing tree, a forest edge, or a lake shore.)

Gould (1986) reports, for example, that when trained to a particular food source and then carried from the hive in a dark box to a new release point, the bees will fly *directly* to the food, but only if there is a significant landmark in their vicinity when they are released. (Otherwise they fly off on the compass bearing that would previously have led from the hive to the food.) Other scientists have found it difficult to replicate these experiments directly, perhaps because bees have such a strong disposition to fly out on compass bearings to which they have been trained. But in a related experiment, Menzel et al. (2000) found that bees that had never foraged more than a few meters from the nest, but who were released at random points much further from it, were able to return home swiftly. They argue that this either indicates the existence of a map-like structure, built during the bees' initial orientation flights before they had begun foraging, or else the learned association of vectors-to-home with local landmarks.[1] But either way, they claim, the spatial representations in question are allocentric rather than egocentric in character.

More recently, Menzel et al. (2005) have provided strong evidence of the map-like organization of spatial memory in honey bees through the use of harmonic radar. The latter technology enabled them to track the flight-paths of individual bees. Bees that were just about to set out for a feeder to which

---

[1] A similar conclusion is supported by the experiments of Janzen (1971) with orchid bees. These bees forage exclusively from jungle orchids, and cover ranges of many kilometers in the course of their daily flights. Janzen captured a dozen such bees in their hive and transported them to randomly chosen release sites between fourteen and twenty-three kilometers from home. Seven of the twelve bees returned home on the day or their release (one returning at an average speed of more than five meters per second!), suggesting that they were capable of identifying landmarks that would give them a vector-to-home over a very large range indeed, even in the relatively featureless jungles in question.

they had been trained or recruited were captured and taken to random release points some distance from the hive. Initially, the bees then set out on the vector that they were about to fly out on when captured. This was followed by a looping orientation phase, once the bees realized that they were lost, followed by a straight flight, either to the hive, or to the feeder and then to the hive. The latter sequence (a flight straight to the feeder), in particular, would only be possible if the bees could calculate a new vector to a target from any arbitrary landmark that they know, which requires both a map-like organization to their memory, and the inferential resources to utilize it.

As is well known, honey bees dance to communicate information of various sorts to other bees. The main elements of the code have now been uncovered through patient investigation (Gould and Gould, 1988). They generally dance in a figure-of-eight pattern on a vertical surface in the dark inside the hive. The angle of movement through the center of the figure of eight, as measured from the vertical, corresponds to the angle from the expected direction of the sun for the time of day (e.g. a dance angled at $30°$ to the right of vertical at midday would represent $30°$ west of south, in the northern hemisphere). And the number of 'waggles' made through the center of the figure of eight provides a measure of distance. (Different bee species use different innately fixed measures of waggles-to-distance.)

Although basic bee motivations are, no doubt, innately fixed, the goals they adopt on particular occasions (e.g. whether or not to move from one foraging patch to another, whether to finish foraging and return to the hive, and whether or not to dance on reaching it) would appear to be influenced by a number of factors (Seeley, 1995). Bees are less likely to dance for dilute sources of food, for example; they are less likely to dance for the more distant of two sites of fixed value; and they are less likely to dance in the evening or when there is an approaching storm, when there is a significant chance that other bees might not be capable of completing a return trip. And careful experimentation has shown that bees scouting for a new nest site will weigh up a number of factors, including cavity volume, shape, size and direction of entrance, height above ground, dampness, draftiness, and distance away. Moreover, dancing scouts will sometimes take time out to observe the dances of others and check out their discoveries, making a comparative assessment and then dancing accordingly (Gould and Gould, 1988).

Bees don't just accept and act on any information that they are offered, either. On the contrary, they evaluate it along a number of dimensions. They check the nature and quality of the goal being offered (normally by sampling it, in the case of food). And they factor in the distance to the indicated site before deciding whether or not to fly out to it. Most strikingly, indeed, it has been suggested that bees might also integrate communicated information with the representations on their mental map, rejecting even rich sources of food that are being indicated to exist in the middle of a lake, for example.

Gould and Gould (1988) report experiments in which two groups of bees were trained to fly to weak sugar solutions equidistant from the hive, one on a boat in the middle of a lake, and the other on the lake shore. When both sugar solutions were increased dramatically, both sets of bees danced on returning to the hive. None of the receiving bees flew out across the lake, however (while plenty flew to the site on the lake shore). But this wasn't just a reluctance to fly over water. In experiments where the boat was moved progressively closer and closer to the far lake shore, more and more receiving bees were prepared to fly to it. These experiments went unreplicated for many years, but Srinivasan and colleagues have now fortuitously established the identical result, in the course of experiments designed to test how bees measure the distances that they travel (Tautz et al., 2004).

How should these various bee capacities be explained? Plainly the processes in question can't be associative ones, and these forms of bee learning aren't conditioned responses to stimuli. This is because many of the behaviors that we have described are undertaken after just a single exposure to a given stimulus, without any history of reward. Thus a foraging bee that has discovered a new source of nectar for itself, and loaded its stomach, will turn and fly directly towards the hive on a vector that it may never have flown before. And as we saw in Chapter 1.6, the computations that underlie such an ability can't be mere associative changes within a distributed connectionist network of any sort.

Might the bee behaviors be explained through the existence of some sort of 'subsumption architecture' (Brooks, 1986)? That is, instead of having a central belief / desire architecture of the sort depicted in Figure 2.1, might bees have a suite of input-to-output modular systems, one for each different type of behavior? This suggestion is wildly implausible. For (depending on how one counts behaviors) there would have to be at least five of these input-to-output modules (perhaps dozens, if each different 'goal' amounts to a different behavior), each of which would have to duplicate the costly computational processes undertaken by the others. There would have to be a scouting-from-the-hive module, a returning-to-the-hive module, a deciding-to-dance-and-dancing module, a returning-to-food-source module, and a perception-of-dance-and-flying-to-food-source module. Within each of these systems essentially the same computations of direction and distance information would have to be undertaken.

It might be objected that I have accepted, in Chapter 1, that natural selection often operates by copying sets of genes (and hence the structures that they build), before the new structure is turned to the service of a novel function. So why couldn't that have happened here? Why couldn't a single complex input-to-output module have evolved first (for navigating back to the hive, say), which was then copied and adapted to underpin other forms of behavior (such as dancing)? And didn't I allow in Chapter 1, too, that such copying could often be adaptive by ensuring robustness of function?

I have two things to say in reply. The first is that duplication of structure is only likely to occur in cases where there are two similar tasks that need to be undertaken at the same time (or within the same brief time-frame). For in such cases the need for parallel processing (and hence duplication) is clear. In instances where the structure in question is only needed at different times, in contrast, it will generally be more cost-effective to adapt it so that it can be utilized in the service of two distinct tasks. And notice that no bee ever needs to navigate to a previously discovered food source *and* read the dance of another bee at once; nor will it ever need to generate its own dance while reading the dance of another; and so on and so forth. So utilizing one and the same mental map (as well as one and the same direction-calculating mechanism, etc.) in the service of all of these forms of behavior is what we should predict.

The second thing I want to do is to stress, again, the resource costs associated with large brains. Recall from Chapter 1 that brains eat up energy at eight times the rate of the rest of the body in proportion to mass. And recall, too, that any increase in size will be accompanied by a significant increase in signaling time. Yet the Brooksian account mooted above amounts to the claim that the bee's brain might be five times larger than it needs to be! For within *each* of these input-to-output modules there will have to be a system that can learn the orientation of the sun for the time of day; a system that can construct and store a mental map; a system that can recognize and match perceptual cues of landmarks onto representations in its mental map; a system that can estimate distance traveled from visual flow; a system that can do dead reckoning; and so on and so forth. (Remember, the idea is that none of these systems can share resources with each other.)

The only remotely plausible interpretation of the data, then, is that honey bees have a suite of information-generating systems that construct represent-ations of the relative directions and distances between a variety of substances and properties and the hive, as well as a number of goal-generating systems taking as inputs body states and a variety of kinds of contextual information, and generating a current goal as output. (Note that this then satisfies the two criteria laid down by Bennett (1964) for a languageless creature to possess beliefs. One is that the creature should be capable of learning. And the other is that the belief-states should be sensitive to different kinds of evidence.)

These goal states can then interact with the information states within one or more practical-reasoning systems (probably more: see Section 7) to create a potentially unique behavior, never before seen in the life of that particular bee. It appears, indeed, that bees exemplify the architecture depicted in Figure 2.1. In which case, there can be minds that are capable of just a few dozen types of desire, and that are capable of just a few thousand types of belief.[2]

1.4 Structure-Dependent Inference

Recall, however, that the conditions on being a genuine believer / desirer that we laid down earlier included not just a distinction between information states and goal states, but also that these states should interact with one another to determine behavior in ways that are sensitive to their compositional structures. On the face of it this condition is also satisfied. For if one and the same item of directional information can be drawn on both to guide a bee in search of nectar and to guide the same bee returning to the hive, then it would seem that the bee must be capable of something resembling the following pair of practical inferences (using BEL to represent belief, DES to represent desire, MOVE to represent action—normally flight, but also walking for short distances—and square brackets to represent contents).

(1) BEL [nectar is 200 meters from the hive, at 30° west of the sun]
  BEL [here is at the hive]
  DES [nectar]
  MOVE [200 meters at 30° west of the sun]

(2) BEL [nectar is 200 meters from the hive, at 30° west of the sun]
  BEL [here is at nectar]
  DES [hive]
  MOVE [200 meters at 210° west of the sun]

These are inferences in which the conclusions depend upon structural relations amongst the premises.[3]

---

[2] The bee's capacity for representing spatial relations is by no means unlimited. There is probably an upper limit on distances that can be represented. And discriminations of direction are relatively crude (at least, by comparison with the almost pin-point accuracy of the Tunisian desert ant; see Wehner and Srinivasan, 1981). However, bees are capable of forming a limited range of beliefs of other sorts, too. They come to believe that certain odors and colors signal nectar or pollen, for example (Gould and Gould, 1988). And they can both learn and generalize to new cases an abstract modality-independent rule of the form, 'Turn right if the stimulus in the second chamber is the same as in the first, turn left if the stimulus in the second chamber is different from that in the first' (Giurfa et al., 2001).

[3] Note that I have characterized the contents of the bee's beliefs in terms of our familiar human concepts. But of course I am not committed to the view that bees have the concept METER, let alone 200 METERS. Rather, what will figure in the bee's beliefs will be a representation that is approximately

Is there some way of specifying in general terms the practical inference rule that is at work here, however (in a way that might be coded into a simple computer program)? Indeed there is. The rule might be something like the following: BEL [here is at G; F is m meters from G at $n°$ from the sun], DES [F], $\rightarrow$ MOVE [m meters at $n°$ from the sun]. This would require the insertion of an extra premise into argument (2) above, rotating the order of items in the first premise and adding an extra $180°$, transforming it into the form, BEL [hive is 200 meters from nectar at $210°$ from the sun]. And the rule for this inferential step would be: when *here* corresponds to the first position in the directional premise rather than the second, switch the ordering of those positions and add $180°$ to the direction indicated before extracting the conclusion.

It might be suggested that we have moved too swiftly, however. For perhaps there needn't be a representation of the goal substance built explicitly into the structure of the directional information-state. To see why this might be so, notice that bees don't represent what it is that lies in the direction indicated as part of the content of their dance; and nor do observers acquire that information from the dance itself. Rather, dancing bees *display* the value on offer by carrying it; and observing bees know what is on offer by sampling some of what the dancing bee is carrying. So it might be said that what really happens is this. An observing bee samples some of the dancing bee's load, and discovers that it is nectar, say. This keys the observer into its fly-in-the-direction-indicated subroutine. The bee computes the necessary information from the details of the dance, and flies off towards the indicated spot. If it is lucky, it then discovers nectar-bearing flowers when it gets there and begins to forage. But at no point do the contents of goal-states and the contents of the information-states need to interact with one another.

An initial reply to this objection would be that although the presence of nectar isn't explicitly represented in the content of the dance, it *does* need to be represented in the content of both the dancer's and the observer's belief-states. For recall that bees don't dance even for a rich source of nectar that is too far away (Gould and Gould, 1988). It therefore appears that the distance information needs to be integrated with the substance information in determining the decision to dance. Equally, observers ignore dances indicating even rich sources of nectar if the indicated distances are too great. So again, it seems that the distance information derived from the dance needs to be integrated with the value information before a decision can be reached.

---

extensionally equivalent to our concept 200 METERS, deriving from measures of visual flow. And something similar then goes for concepts like SUN, HIVE, and so forth.

A skeptic might be unconvinced. For might there not be two independent motivational factors that influence a recruiter's dancing subroutine? And likewise might there not be two different factors that influence a recruitee's fly-in-the-direction-indicated subroutine? The discovery of a rich source of nectar by a foraging bee might set its motivation to dance at a high level; but each unit of distance covered on its return trip might ratchet up a motivation *not* to dance. The result would be that foragers don't dance to indicate even rich sources of nectar that are too far away, but not because the nectar information is ever integrated with the distance information in a single representational state. Likewise a bee sampling some of a dancing bee's load might have its motivation to fly in the direction indicated set at a high level if the nectar is sufficiently rich. But when the distance indicated in the dance is great, this would have the effect of increasing its motivation *not* to fly in that direction, and to observe another dancing bee instead. Again, representations of distance and of nectar don't need to be combined with one another in a single belief-state.

There may be some merit in one or other of these suggestions. For as we shall see in Section 5.2, most desire-determining modules are likely to operate by integrating together a number of sources of information in order to create a given desire, such as the honeybee's desire to dance. But there are still a number of problems with the suggestion that goal information and spatial information are never integrated together in the same belief-state. One is that it makes it difficult to explain what happens in the simplest case: that of a foraging bee returning to a newly discovered foraging site once it has been unloaded at the hive. When such a bee has been unloaded of its nectar, presumably the seek-nectar goal becomes active once again. And on the skeptical interpretation sketched above, this would then be supposed to activate its fly-in-the-direction-indicated subroutine. But in which direction? For the bee isn't here reading the indications of another, but recovering directional information from long-term memory. But presumably not just *any* direction information—rather, a direction in which there is nectar. This makes it look as if the active representation, DES [nectar], needs to call up from memory a representation of the form, BEL [nectar is 200 meters from the hive at 210° west of the sun]. And then the content of the desire-state would need to interact with the content of the belief-state to select the behavior, MOVE [200 meters at 210° west of the sun].

Behavior observed and experimentally manipulated by Seeley (1995) also makes the skeptical interpretation hard to sustain. Consider a group of bees that had been foraging at a particular site which became depleted near the day's end. The next morning they don't all automatically return to the site. But nor do they allow themselves to be recruited immediately to other sites, either.

Rather, a few of them return to check their depleted site periodically, and the rest hang around on the dance floor observing the dances of other bees. Only when they encounter a dance that indicates nectar at their previous site (e.g. because the flowers in question have now opened with the morning sun, or because the experimenter has refilled the feeder with sugar solution) do they begin foraging again.

We can't explain this behavior in the skeptical manner indicated above. Not only do we have to ascribe to the bees a belief that there is a nectar source at a given location (where nectar is the object of a current goal), but we seemingly also have to ascribe to them a representation of *time*. That is, the waiting bees seem to be in a state like, BEL [nectar *was* 200 meters from the hive at 210° west of the sun].[4] And then observing a dance of a nectar-bearing bee that carries the content [200 meters from the hive at 210° west of the sun] causes them to update their BEL representation to the present tense, leading them to fly out once again to forage. (For further evidence that bees can represent time, see Section 3.2 below.)

From this discussion we can conclude, I believe, that not only do bees have distinct information states and goal states, but that such states interact with one other in ways that are sensitive to their contents in determining behavior. In which case bees really do exemplify the belief / desire architecture depicted in Figure 2.1, construed realistically.

1.5 The Generality Constraint

One final worry remains, however. Do the belief- and desire-states in question satisfy what Evans (1983) calls 'the Generality Constraint'? This is a very plausible constraint on genuine (i.e. compositionally structured) concept possession. It tells us that any concept possessed by a thinker must be capable of combining appropriately with any other concept possessed by the same thinker. If you can think that *a is F* and you can think that *b is G*, then you must also be capable of thinking that *a is G* and that *b is F*. For these latter thoughts are built out of the very same components as the former ones, only combined together with one another differently.

Now, bees can represent the spatial relationships between nectar and hive, and between pollen and hive; but are they capable of representing the spatial relationships between nectar and pollen? Are bees capable of thoughts of the

---

[4] Note that representations of direction of this sort need to be adjusted for the time of day. In fact, bees must continually update their representations of direction throughout the day. If they first learn that a nectar source is 30° west of the sun at midday, then an hour later they will need to update this to represent the nectar as 20° west of the sun, say; and so on.

form: BEL [nectar is 200 meters north of pollen]? And although scouting bees can represent the relations between different potential nest sites and the existing colony, are they capable of representing the relations between those nest sites themselves? Are bees capable of thoughts of the form: BEL [cavity A is 200 meters north of cavity B]? If not, it may be said, then bees can't be counted as genuine concept-users; and so they can't qualify as genuine believer / desirers, either.

It is possible that these particular examples aren't a problem. Foragers returning to a nectar site to find it almost depleted might fly directly to any previously discovered foraging site that is nearby; including one containing pollen rather than nectar, if pollen is in sufficient demand back at the hive. And if a bee that is just setting out to visit cavity A is captured and released in the vicinity of cavity B (which it also knows), then it is likely that it will be capable of flying directly to its destination. But there will, almost certainly, be other relationships that are never explicitly represented. It is doubtful, for example, that any bee will ever explicitly represent the relations between a foraging site, on the one hand, and the brood chamber, on the other. This is because, since bees navigate within the hive in the dark, they are unlikely to use solar-based vectors to do so. Hence it is doubtful whether any bee will ever form an explicit thought of the form: BEL [nectar is 200 meters north of the brood chamber].

Such examples aren't really a problem for the Generality Constraint, however. From the fact that bees never form beliefs of a certain kind, it doesn't follow that they *can't*. (Or at least, this doesn't follow in such a way as to undermine the claim that their beliefs are compositionally structured. I shall return to this point shortly.) One possibility is just that bees are only ever *interested in* (or have any use for) the relationships amongst various foraging and nesting sites and the hive, and not between those places and regions located within the hive itself. But the same sort of thing is equally true of human beings. Just as there are some spatial relationships that might be implicit in a bee's spatial representations, but never explicitly believed; so there are some things implicit in our beliefs about the world, but never explicitly entertained, either, because they are of no interest or use. My beliefs, for example, collectively entail that *mountains are less easy to eat than rocks.* (I could at least pound up a rock into powder, which I might then have some chance of swallowing.) But until finding myself in need of a philosophical example, this isn't something that I would ever have bothered to think. Likewise with the bees. The difference may just be that bees don't do philosophy.

Suppose, however, that bees lack the inferential resources to integrate information contained in the maps that they use when navigating by the sun, and the spatial relationships that they exploit when navigating within the hive itself. Hence suppose that, given the limitations on the bees' inferential abilities, a bee is actually *incapable* of forming a representation like: BEL [nectar is 200 meters north of the brood chamber]. Even this fact wouldn't give us any reason to claim that bees don't really employ compositionally structured belief-states, however, which they integrate with a variety of kinds of desire-state in such a way as to select an appropriate behavior. And in particular, the fact that the bees lack the ability to draw inferences freely and promiscuously amongst their belief-states shouldn't exclude them from having any belief-states at all. Which is to say: such facts about the bees' limitations would give us no reason for denying that bees possess a simple form of belief / desire psychology.

Many philosophers have given the Generality Constraint a much stronger interpretation than I have here, however. (For a recent example, see Camp, forthcoming.) They take as their paradigm the human capacity to generate new thoughts from their component parts *creatively*, in a way that far outstrips the set of thoughts that we could ever arrive at by inference on the basis of our experience. If I can think that the lion is eating the antelope, for example, then I can easily form from those components the (false) thought that the antelope is eating the lion. But surely no animal will ever entertain such a thought; and we might reasonably doubt whether an animal could even be *capable* of it, just as a bee might actually be incapable of arriving at the thought that nectar is north of the brood chamber. And this would then be presented as a reason for denying that animals are genuine concept-users, and hence as a reason for denying that animals possess beliefs or desires, either.

Granted, we humans are unique in the creativity and flexibility of our thought processes. As we shall see at length in Chapter 5, there are two closely connected facts about human beings that underlie this uniqueness. One is that we have the capacity to generate novel thoughts at will, freely combining and recombining their conceptual components in any way that we please. The other is that we are capable of taking the attitude of *supposing* towards the thought-contents thereby created, drawing further inferences from them. I can suppose that the antelope is eating the lion as part of an episode of pretending, for example, or when storytelling. Or I might suppose that there exist some tiny negatively charged particles in the course of scientific theorizing. But these capacities have to do with the ways in which thoughts can be caused to exist, and with the attitudes that we can take towards thoughts once they do exist (*supposing*, as well as believing and desiring). They have nothing to do with the sorts of *contents* or *component structures* that our thoughts possess. And hence they shouldn't have any bearing on whether or not we are prepared to ascribe concepts (the components of thoughts) to animals.

Let me put the point like this: from the fact that a bee lacks any mechanism that could ever cause it to go into a state with the content [nectar is 200 meters north of the brood chamber] it doesn't follow that the bee lacks compositionally structured thoughts. The Generality Constraint, if it is to be defensible, should be seen as a *metaphysical* constraint on genuine compositional structure, not as a constraint on the causal processes that serve to generate thoughts. If a bee is to be genuinely capable of a belief with the content [nectar is 200 meters north of the hive], then that thought must consist of components that can occur in other combinations within other thoughts. (And indeed, we have already seen that this is so.) In particular, it must possess the concepts, NECTAR, 200 METERS, NORTH, and THE HIVE (or sufficiently close analogs thereof). And the separability of these components then requires that it be *metaphysically* possible (given that the bee also has the concept, BROOD CHAMBER) for it to think a thought with the content [nectar is 200 meters north of the brood chamber]. But it doesn't follow that the tokening of that thought should be *causally* possible, given the other factors that are involved in the ways that the bee's cognitive system actually works.

Our conclusion stands, therefore: bees possess a simple form of belief / desire psychology. The evidence shows that their minds contain discrete representational states of each of these types, which possess a component structure, and which interact with one another in simple patterns of inference in the light of their structures.

1.6 Simple Planning

For instances of simple forms of advance planning in invertebrates, I turn from bees to jumping spiders. In the wild, jumping spiders display a number of remarkable hunting behaviors (Wilcox and Jackson, 1998). They typically don't build webs, but rather hunt their prey, including other spiders. They use a variety of 'smokescreen' tactics when approaching another spider across its web—sometimes only moving during a gust of wind, when its footsteps will be less easy to detect; sometimes using an irregular gait, which will make its footsteps seem like mere noise; sometimes setting the web into violent motion, during which, again, its footsteps won't be detectable. It might be possible to dismiss such tactics as mere fixed action-patterns. But jumping spiders will also make detours of up to one meter in length to gain access to prey, sometimes initially traveling away from their target in order better to approach it (Tarsitano and Jackson, 1994). And it is these navigation abilities that provide the best evidence of planning, in fact.

Tarsitano and Jackson (1997) tested jumping spiders in a laboratory setting. Each spider was positioned on top of a pole, from which it could view potential prey on one of two platforms at about the same height. These platforms were suspended from two different complex tree-like structures, each of which had a unique base. The spiders had to climb down from their pole in order to reach these structures, and from that time until the very end of the hunt their prey would be obscured from view on one of the two platforms above. Remarkably, the spiders succeeded in these tasks, sometimes traveling away from their prey on reaching the base of their pole in order to reach the correct trunk to begin their climb, and sometimes traveling past the incorrect trunk in order to reach the correct one. It appears that the spiders must have mapped out a possible route to their prey during observation from the top of their pole, and were then able to recall that route thereafter, correctly identifying the various elements of the route (especially the correct trunk to climb) when seen from the very different perspectives involved during travel.

Tarsitano and Andrew (1998) presented jumping spiders with a somewhat different challenge. The spiders were again positioned on top of an observation pole from which they could observe a prey item suspended from supports straight ahead of them. But in this case the spiders were presented with three different set-ups. In all three conditions there were two support poles, one to their right and one to their left, which they could only reach by climbing down from their observation tower and traveling some distance from the base. But in one condition both poles afforded a route to the prey; whereas in the other two conditions there was a gap in the sequence of beams that led to the prey (in the one case on the left, in the other on the right). The spiders were videotaped during their observation phase, so that their direction and extent of gaze could be analyzed thereafter.

The results were striking. In the cases where both poles led to the prey, the spiders showed no preference: they headed left or right from the base of their tower with equal frequency. But when one of the two potential routes was incomplete, the spiders displayed a marked preference for the other, complete, route. Analysis of the spiders' observation-behavior before setting out showed that they scanned along the routes away from the prey, returning their attention to the prey whenever they detected a gap. Hence they rapidly came to concentrate their attention on the complete route, tracing it with their eyes in reverse order (from finish to start) until they located the support pole that they would need to climb.

Taken together, these experiments demonstrate that jumping spiders plan their routes to their prey in advance. They scan the physical layout in search of a continuous path that will take them to the desired spot. They can recall that layout once identified. And they can use it appropriately to inform their current direction of movement, mapping the structures detected during the observation phase onto their later perceptions of those same structures seen from the different spatial perspectives involved during their journey.

1.7 Summing up: Simple Minds

From the fact that the minds of bees exemplify a perception / belief / desire architecture of the sort depicted in Figure 2.1, it doesn't follow that the minds of *all* animals exemplify such an architecture, of course. And from the fact that jumping spiders are capable of planning their sequences of action in advance, it of course doesn't follow that all animals can do the same. But it would surely be quite extraordinary if belief / desire / planning architectures weren't extremely common in the animal world, given that they are present in at least some species of invertebrate. For many different kinds of animal need to be capable of navigating through complex terrain; and many would stand to benefit from a capacity to plan their routes in advance. In which case it seems highly likely that perception / belief / desire / planning architectures will be present in all birds and mammals, at least, as well as in many other vertebrates and invertebrates. Or so I propose to assume in what follows.

2 Dual Visual Systems in Mammals (and others)

Vision is obviously modular, in the weak sense of 'module' articulated and defended in Chapter 1. It is a functionally (and anatomically) distinct processing system of the mind, whose properties can vary independently of other systems, and whose operations can be effected independently of most other systems. Its internal structure is substantially innate. And its processing is function-specific, deploying a variety of frugal heuristics, as well as being inaccessible elsewhere.[5]

It is well known, moreover, that the visual system contains multiple sub-modules with specific functions, which operate independently of one another to a significant degree, and which have complex input and output connections with others. Thus there are systems concerned with the processing of color information, systems concerned with the processing of movement, systems concerned with processing faces, and so on (see Figure 1.3). What is much *less* well known, however, is that there are actually two functionally distinct overall visual systems, one of which is located primarily in the temporal lobes and is

---

[5] Note that the facts that visual processing is heavily influenced by the nature of the task, the direction of attention, and background knowledge and expectations needn't stand in the way of the modular status of the visual system. For we aren't requiring that modules should be encapsulated in the traditional narrow-scope sense.

concerned with object recognition, memory formation, and action planning, and the other of which is located in the parietal lobes and is concerned with the on-line visual guidance of movement (Milner and Goodale, 1995; Jacob and Jeannerod, 2003; Glover, 2004).[6]

While much of the evidence for the existence of these two systems comes from humans, there are homologous brain structures in all mammals, at least, and similar dissociations can be detected in other mammals. (Moreover, there is evidence of a similar two-systems divergence in respect of other perceptual systems besides vision.) I shall first describe the dual visual systems hypothesis itself. I shall then briefly review some of the evidence that supports it, as well as developing some implications that will be of importance in our later discussions. The main focus of this section is architectural. Taking modularity for granted, it will develop a specific picture of the ways in which perceptual systems sub-divide to interface with conceptual (belief / desire / planning) systems on the one hand, and with action-control systems on the other.

2.1 The Dual Visual Systems Hypothesis

One visual system is located ventrally in the brain, in the two temporal lobes, and the other is located dorsally, in the two parietal lobes. Each receives its main input from the primary visual projection area, V_1, at the back of the brain; which in turn receives its input from the retina via the lateral geniculate nucleus in the thalamus. The parietal-lobe system, however, also receives a separate stream of input from the retina via the superior colliculus in the midbrain. (In fact this sub-cortical pathway alone is as large as the whole of the auditory nerve!) There are homologous brain systems in all mammals, and precursors of them exist in all vertebrates (Milner and Goodale, 1995).

The outputs of the temporal-lobe system are 'globally broadcast' (in the sense of Baars, 1988) to a wide range of conceptual consumer systems. In humans its outputs are characteristically conscious, and those outputs are available to inform object recognition and categorization, as well as for desire-formation and the generation of emotion. They are used to form medium and long-term memories, and are also available to inform action-planning in relation to the perceived environment ('I'll go *that* way and pick up *that*'). Moreover, the temporal-lobe system utilizes allocentric ('object centered') spatial representations, representing the spatial relationships amongst the objects

---

[6] There are some differences between the views of the authors cited that aren't relevant for my purposes. In addition, Rizzolatti and Gallese (2003) argue that there really exist *three*, rather than two, visual systems. But the data that they present are consistent with their third 'ventro-dorsal' system being a common sub-component of the other two, I think, mediating interactions between them. (Note that on the account of modularity presented in Chapter 1, modules can share parts.) See Section 2.3 below.

perceived, as well as their relation to the perceiver. In addition, its operations are comparatively slow.

The outputs of the parietal-lobe system, in contrast, aren't available for object recognition or memory formation; nor are they conscious. Rather, they are used in the on-line control of movement, serving to guide the detailed execution of the action schemata that have been selected by the planning systems. The parietal-lobe system utilizes egocentric spatial representations, representing objects in body-centered and limb-centered coordinates, without representing their relations to one another. Its operations are significantly faster than those of the temporal-lobe system, and it has a memory window of just two seconds.

The two-systems arrangement can be seen depicted in Figure 2.3. Note that the upper level corresponds pretty closely to the perception / belief / desire / planning architecture depicted in Figure 2.1. This is perception as common sense conceives of it. What is novel (from the perspective of common sense) is the addition of the lower level for guiding the detailed execution of our actions. Notice, too, that I have included an arrow from the desire systems to the action-schemata box. This is to provide for the dual routes to action that we deemed necessary in our discussion of invertebrates in Section 1. Hence, while action schemata can be selected via some sort of planning process, they can also be activated directly by motivational states without the intervention of any belief, giving rise to the fixed (but perceptually guided) action-patterns

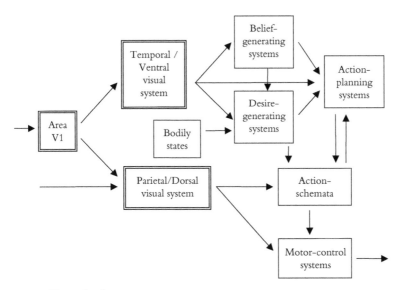

Figure 2.3. Two visual systems

characteristic of some innate animal behaviors. Note, in addition, that I have included an arrow between the belief systems box and the desire systems box. This is because (as we shall see in Section 5) it is likely that the systems that generate motivation receive input not only from perception, but also from belief.

The basic perception / belief / desire / planning architecture depicted in Figure 2.1 needs to be made significantly more complex, then—at least in the case of mammals, and at least in connection with visual perception.[7] For there are really *two* kinds of perception: perception that informs belief, desire, and planning, on the one hand, and perception that provides on-line guidance of movement, on the other. One further point should be emphasized here, however, since it will prove to be of some importance in Section 7. This is that the parietal-lobe visual system probably isn't unitary, either—not just in the sense that it contains within it a number of sub-modules (as does the temporal-lobe system, of course), but in the sense that it is really a *collection* of semi-independent functionally distinct modules (Milner and Goodale, 1995). Each of these systems might control the movement of a different limb or a different organ (e.g. the hand or the eyes). And some might be specialized for particular types of behavior (e.g. grasping a moving object, which requires cooperative movements of both hand and eyes).

Seen in evolutionary and cognitive-engineering terms, it makes perfectly good sense that the tasks of sensorimotor control, on the one hand, and the generation of percepts to provide the basis for conceptualized thought, on the other, should be devolved to distinct perceptual systems. For our motor responses to a changed or changing environment need to be provided extremely fast (think here of hand-to-hand fighting, of throwing a projectile at a moving animal, or of running at full speed over uneven terrain). And they need to operate from a set of body-centered spatial coordinates, providing highly specific information about the relative positions of the hand and object-to-be-grasped, for example, that will never be exactly the same twice. But such responses do not, in general, require much in the way of conceptualization.

Once a decision has been made to throw a rock at a rabbit, it doesn't much matter that it is a *rabbit* that one is throwing at (nor that it is a rock that one is throwing, come to that). One just needs to track the motion of a particular three-dimensional shape through space, and project forward to its likely future position. Similarly, once the decision has been made to pick a

---

[7] Actually, similar dissociations between judgment-guidance and action-guidance exist in other sense-modalities. Paralleling the phenomenon of blindsight in the visual system (see Section 2.2), there are also cases of 'deaf-hearing' and 'insensate touch', at least. See Michel and Peronnet, 1980; Paillard et al., 1983; Rossetti et al., 1995.

particular berry ('*That* one is ripe'), it doesn't much matter that it is a *berry* that one is picking. One just needs to guide the fingers to frame the outline of a particular three-dimensional object without crushing.

Thinking, in contrast, doesn't need to be so fast. We think in order to plan for the medium or longer term ('I will throw at *that* rabbit', 'I will pick *that* berry', and so on). And then, having thought, it is best to act without it. (It is a familiar point from the psychology of sport—long known previously to Japanese Zen masters—that thinking while acting has a detrimental effect on skilled performance.) Moreover, conceptualized perception must employ allocentric (object-centered) spatial coordinates for purposes of object-recognition and planning; and it is likely, in any case, to be a slower business, since there are always indefinitely many different concepts that one *could* bring to bear on any given input. So choices have to be made, and principles of relevance deployed.

2.2 The Evidence Supporting Dual Visual Systems

The two-visual-systems hypothesis is supported by multiple lines of evidence, each of which is far more extensive than can possibly be surveyed here. (For details, see Milner and Goodale, 1995; Jacob and Jeannerod, 2003; Glover, 2004.) One is physiological. Neurophysiologists tracing out the main anatomical nerve-pathways in the brain have long realized that there are two substantially distinct streams of connectivity spreading out from the primary visual projection area V1. One of these travels up the back of the cortex through the parietal lobes towards the motor-control areas that stretch in a band across the top of the cortex (the dorsal / parietal stream). The other travels forwards around the sides of the cortex through the temporal lobes towards the 'association' areas that are linked to conceptualization, memory, and language.

Another line of evidence derives from the behavioral dissociations that result from local brain damage to the two systems. One of these is 'blindsight', which is now well-established after more than two decades of investigation and critique (Weiskrantz, 1986, 1997). Humans and other primates who have had portions of area V1 damaged *judge* that they see nothing in the corresponding area of their visual field. But the data show that they are capable of at least simple kinds of unconscious perceptual discrimination. For example, subjects can accurately trace the movement of a light across a screen in the blind portion of their visual field, entirely by guesswork, professing that they are aware of nothing. And Marcel (1998) has shown that blindsight patients are capable of reaching out and grasping objects on their blind sides with something like eighty or ninety per cent of normal accuracy, and of catching a ball thrown towards them from their blind side, again without conscious awareness. (The usual experimental controls were in place to ensure that subjects didn't move their eyes during the task, thereby obtaining visual information in their receptive field.)

Similar phenomena have been demonstrated in other primates. A monkey with one half of area V1 missing can be trained, first, to press a button following a warning tone if a light does *not* illuminate on a screen presented to her sighted field. When a light or a bright moving stimulus is then presented to her blind field, she presses for 'not seen', thus indicating that she lacks awareness of the stimulus—and this despite it being one that she can be shown to discriminate in other ways, such as in her reaching behavior (Cowie and Stoerig, 1995; Stoerig and Cowie, 1997). Likewise the blindsighted chimpanzee Helen (Humphrey, 1986), who had the whole of her primary visual cortical area V1 surgically removed, was incapable of recognizing and identifying objects by sight. (For example, if she were to pick up a small object she would first have to put it into her mouth in order to determine whether it was a nut or a stone.) Once she became used to her condition, however, she could pick up seeds from the floor with precise and accurate finger grip. She could snatch out of the air with her hand a fly going past in front of her head. And she could move across the room relatively normally, avoiding obstacles in her path.

Although these phenomena are highly counter-intuitive to common sense, they aren't especially surprising when seen from the perspective of neurophysiology. For as we noted above, there are substantial projections from the retina to parietal cortex independently of V1. So even with cortical area V1 completely removed, significant amounts of visual information should be available in parietal cortex for the control of movement.[8]

Similar data emerge where people suffer brain damage restricted to temporal cortex. One such syndrome is *visual form agnosia*, which results from damage localized to both temporal lobes, leaving area V1 and the parietal lobes intact. (Visual form agnosia is normally caused by carbon monoxide poisoning, for reasons that aren't fully understood.) Such patients can't recognize objects or shapes, and may be capable of little conscious visual experience; but their sensorimotor abilities remain largely intact. One particular patient—D.F.—has now been examined in considerable detail (Goodale et al., 1991, 1994a, 1994b; Milner et al., 1991; Carey et al., 1996). While D.F. is severely agnosic, she isn't completely blind. Her capacities to perceive colors and textures are almost completely preserved. (Why just these sub-modules in her temporal cortex

---

[8] How, then, does such information enable patients, not only to point and grasp appropriately, but also to answer questions, for example concerning the orientation of a grating? Milner and Goodale (1995) suggest that such patients may be influenced by subtle behavioral and motor-programming cues of which they lack conscious awareness, e.g. to begin tracing out the line of orientation of the grating with a hand or with the eyes.

should have been spared isn't known.) As a result, she can sometimes guess the identity of a presented object—recognizing a banana, say, from its yellow color and the distinctive texture of its surface. But she is unable to perceive the shape of the banana (whether straight or curved, say); nor its orientation (upright or horizontal; pointing towards her or away).

Yet many of D.F's sensorimotor abilities are close to normal. She would be able to reach out and grasp the banana, orienting her hand and wrist appropriately for its position and orientation, and using a normal and appropriate finger grip. And in one famous episode, an experimenter held up a pencil in his hand and asked D.F. if she could tell him what it was. She replied, 'Here, let me have a look', and reached out smoothly and unhesitatingly to take it from him, placing her thumb and forefinger precisely in position to grasp it—despite having no conscious awareness of its shape, orientation, location, or identity (Ramachandran and Blakeslee, 1998).

Under experimental conditions it turns out that while D.F. is at chance when identifying the orientation of a broad line, she is almost normal when posting a letter through a similarly shaped slot oriented at random angles. In the same way, although she is at chance when trying to discriminate between rectangular blocks of very different sizes, her reaching and grasping behaviors when asked to pick up such a block are virtually indistinguishable from those of normal controls. It is very hard to make sense of these data without supposing that the sensorimotor perceptual system is functionally and anatomically distinct from the object-recognition system.

The converse condition to visual form agnosia is also found, sometimes called *Bálint-Holmes syndrome*. This is caused by damage to the parietal lobes (either to one lobe alone, in which case the syndrome is displayed in respect of contra-lesional space; or to both, in which case the deficit is global). Patients with this syndrome can have difficulty in moving their eyes towards a target; they can be very poor at moving their hands in the direction of a target; they often can't orient their hand correctly to pass it through a variably oriented letter-box slot; and they are poor at reaching out and grasping objects (Ratcliff and Davies-Jones, 1972; Perenin and Vighetto, 1988). Yet in all such cases patients can give good verbal reports of the identity, position, and orientation of objects within their visual field. So once again it is hard to make sense of these data except by supposing that the conceptualizing perceptual system in the temporal lobes is functionally independent of the sensorimotor one.

But how is it that Bálint-Holmes subjects are able to grasp objects *at all*, if the relevant sensorimotor systems are destroyed? The answer is that perceptual information from the conceptualizing temporal-lobe system can also be used to drive motor behavior, activating action schemata that are executed in a crude and not very fine-grained way (see Figure 2.3). The evidence for this claim consists of two parts (Goodale et al., 1994a). First, when normal subjects reach towards a remembered object that they can no longer see following a delay of two seconds or more, the details of their reaching and grasping behavior show a quite different profile from normal. Secondly, when patient D.F. is asked to reach towards a remembered object following a delay of more than two seconds, her abilities collapse completely, suggesting that the sensorimotor system that is still intact in her case is only capable of responding to the here-and-now. The suggestion, then, is that conscious perceptual information can be used to generate motor commands from memory in normal subjects; and this same information may be accessed by Bálint-Holmes subjects in whom more fine-grained sensorimotor information isn't available.

Another line of evidence supporting the two-visual-systems hypothesis comes from the study of normal subjects, where there is now a wealth of relevant data (Milner and Goodale, 1995; Jacob and Jeannerod, 2003; Glover, 2004). Here let me mention just a couple of highlights from this research. One concerns visual illusions. Conscious perception is subject to a number of well known illusions, such as the famous Müller-Lyer illusion of size, which leads us to see an arrow-tailed line as longer than an arrow-headed one, even when we know that there is really no difference. But action-guidance isn't subject to these illusions. People reaching out to position the finger and thumb of their hand at either end of the line (as if it were a pencil to be picked up by the two ends) will *not* make their grasping movement any wider for the arrow-tailed line.

This point has been demonstrated by Aglioti et al. (1995) who actually used a somewhat different illusion in their experiments, having to do with the way perceptions of size are influenced by the size of surrounding objects. This is the Titchener illusion, in which a circle surrounded by larger circles will appear smaller than a circle of the same size surrounded by smaller ones (see Figure 2.4), and where circles of different sizes can be made to appear the same size by surrounding them with further circles that are also different (larger for the larger circle and smaller for the smaller circle). Subjects were asked to reach out and grasp one of two target circular chips, reaching for the left if the chips appeared equal in size and reaching to the right if they appeared different. (It was thus an elegant feature of the experiment that the very same action by which subjects manifested awareness of the illusion *also* displayed insensitivity to it in the details of its motor trajectory.) Subjects were unable to perceive their own hands while reaching, thus eliminating visual feedback from the degree of 'match' between finger aperture and the chip being grasped. Their grip-aperture was monitored and recorded while reaching. By this criterion,

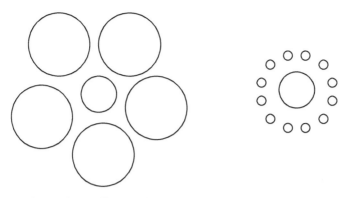

Figure 2.4. The Titchener illusion of size

subjects weren't at all sensitive to the illusion, although in all cases their reaching *choices* treated discs that were actually different as the same, and discs that were actually the same as different.

Another set of experiments has demonstrated that people can make motor adjustments to changes that they aren't consciously aware of, which occur during a saccadic eye movement just as they begin to act. In these experiments a target can be moved unpredictably, by an amount equivalent to ten per cent of the reaching distance (Bridgeman et al., 1981; Hansen and Skavenski, 1985; Goodale et al., 1986). Subjects responded to the changes smoothly and efficiently, pointing just as accurately and just as swiftly to moved as to unmoved targets. But at no time were they aware of any movement. Even when asked to guess after each trial whether or not movement in the target had occurred, subjects performed at chance. In contrast, when the displacement was made large enough for conscious awareness, the movements of the hand and arm became considerably slower and less accurate.

2.3 Back-Projecting Pathways within the Visual Systems

As described thus far, and as depicted in Figure 2.3, one might think that the ventral and dorsal visual systems are entirely feed-forward in character, and also that they are entirely independent of one another (post-V1, that is). But each of these suggestions is highly misleading. In fact, both systems contain very substantial back-projecting neural pathways. And they are, moreover, significantly connected with one another via an area of ventro-dorsal cortex, which is probably best thought of as a common functional *component* of each.[9]

---

[9] Specifically, the areas in question are the superior temporal sulcus and area FP in the rostral part of the inferior parietal lobule. These are strongly interconnected with each other, and also with area F5 in pre-motor cortex (Rizzolatti, 2005).

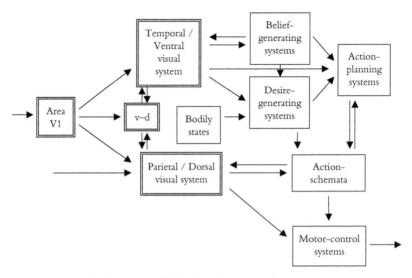

Figure 2.5. Two visual systems with back-projecting pathways

This more complex arrangement is depicted in Figure 2.5 (in which 'v-d' stands for 'ventro-dorsal'). In the present section I shall say something about the functions of this additional complexity, since it will prove to be important later.

The functions of the back-projecting pathways in the ventral stream are now quite well understood. They are used to direct *attention* of various sorts towards aspects of incoming information, and they are involved in object-recognition and classification. They are likewise involved in the generation of visual imagery (Kosslyn, 1994). In fact many of the conceptual modules should probably be thought of as containing recognitional 'front ends', which attempt to match a set of perceptual templates for their proprietary concepts against the perceptual input. These templates are used to project object and event schemata back through the ventral stream (perhaps even as far as V1), attempting to generate a match with visual input. They are used, in effect, to 'query' the perceptual input, helping to resolve the interpretation of degraded or ambiguous input, as well as playing an important role in the recognition process.[10]

---

[10] It turns out that even bees use top-down processing in their visual systems. Srinivasan and colleagues first tried to train bees to discriminate between two partially occluded patterns, without success, despite lengthy training. They then (successfully) trained a different set of bees to distinguish those patterns when un-occluded, before returning them to the original task. Now the bees were able to learn to discriminate the patterns without difficulty—just as occurs with humans, when the patterns were familiar, they 'popped out' of the partially occluded display. See Zhang and Srinivasan (1994).

Moreover, the patterns of neural activity created earlier-on in the ventral stream by the activation of these back-projecting pathways are then processed in the normal 'feed-forward' manner by the visual system, just as if the corresponding object or event were being perceived. So these very same back-projecting pathways used in object-recognition are also implicated in visual imagery. A visual template for an apple, for example, can be projected back through the ventral system, generating activity that is then processed in the usual way, giving rise to a conscious experience *as of perceiving* an apple (albeit fainter and less determinate).

It is important to realize that these claims need involve no commitment to the so-called 'Picture Theory' of visual imagery (extensively criticized by Pylyshyn, 2003), although that theory is also defended in some form in Kosslyn (1994). Claiming that visualizing is like seeing need involve no commitment to the 'pictorial' character of either. All that I really need to claim for my purposes here and later in this book—and what is now well established—is that visual imagery utilizes the resources and mechanisms of the visual system. And this results in the global broadcast of conscious images to a wide range of conceptual modules, in exactly the way that conscious visual percepts are so broadcast.

Extensive back-projecting pathways similar to those in the ventral stream also exist in the dorsal visual system. These exist to help monitor and fine-tune the on-line guidance of action (Wolpert and Flanagan, 2001). And they probably aid the various action-guiding modules in the dorsal stream to interact and cooperate with one another. But there is also evidence that they play an important role in the deliberate *transformation* and *movement* of conscious visual images, perhaps via the systems in ventro-dorsal cortex that are shared between the ventral and dorsal visual streams, and that also house part of the 'mirror-neuron system'. Let me briefly elaborate.

Kosslyn (1994) argues on the basis of a variety of (mostly behavioral) data that motor cortex and pre-motor cortex are active whenever subjects transform visual images—for example, when they are rotating an imagined figure. The idea is that subjects will get their image to rotate by activating a motor schema for an act of rotation linked to the imagined figure. In effect, the idea is that we get the image to rotate by imagining ourselves *acting* in such a way as to *cause* the imagined object to rotate. This claim has been further confirmed by later research.

For example, Ganis et al. (2000) find that interfering with the activity of motor cortex via direct electrical stimulation has a significant effect on response times for people engaged in imagery-rotation tasks. Similarly, Turnbull et al. (1997) report that people with lesions in ventro-dorsal cortex have problems in recognizing objects that seem to require transformations of imagery, such as recognizing an object seen from an unusual perspective. And Kosslyn et al. (2001) report the results of a brain imaging study in which subjects watched an object being rotated either by hand or by a machine, before undertaking a mental-rotation task involving a similar sort of object. They found that primary motor cortex was active only in the first ('by hand') condition; but that pre-motor cortex was activated in both conditions—suggesting that motor-schema planning of some sort lies at the bottom of all imagery transformation. (See also Richter et al., 2000; Lamm et al., 2001.)

It is very natural to link these findings to the discovery of the so-called 'mirror-neuron system' in monkeys and humans (Gallese et al., 1996; Rizzolatti et al., 2000). For this system is partly located in a region of ventro-dorsal cortex containing neural systems that appear to be shared by both the ventral and dorsal visual streams. There are neurons within the mirror system that fire *either* when the monkey perceives someone executing a quite specific movement (for example, grasping a piece of food with the whole hand) *or* when the monkey executes just such an action for itself (Gallese et al., 2002). Much of the discussion of the likely function of these neurons has been about their possible role in subserving our understanding of the goals and actions of others (e.g. Gallese and Goldman, 1998).[11] But they are equally well positioned to map our own intended or imagined movements into visual representations of movement.

One function for such mappings—namely in the control of action—is well understood (Wolpert and Ghahramani, 2000; Wolpert et al., 2003). When a motor schema is activated, not only are commands sent to the muscles necessary to control the intended action, but an 'efference copy' is at the same time created and used to generate a representation of the perceptions (both proprioceptive and visual) that are to be predicted as resulting from the execution of that motor schema, together with its further effects. (This probably requires that there should exist one or more separate 'emulator systems' which take efference copies as input and are capable of generating predictions about the likely future positions of the limbs and body, perhaps utilizing some sort of model of the kinematics of the body; Grush, 2004.) The predicted sequence is then compared with the actual sensory input received, and the detailed further execution of that action (or its replacement by another one) is determined accordingly.

---

[11] Csibra (2005) makes an important conceptual point against this interpretation. This is that, since some of the mirror-neurons in question will fire when the monkey observes someone grasping a piece of food with the hand, but *not* when observing someone make an otherwise-identical movement that doesn't involve food, those neurons must *already* be receiving input from neural systems that 'understand' that the one action, but not the other, has the obtaining of food as its goal.

Consider the action of grasping the handle of a coffee pot, lifting, and pouring a cup of coffee, for example. An abstract action schema for the action is activated, and rendered successively more determinate in the light of perceptual input. Motor commands are then issued, and an efference copy is projected back through parietal cortex to systems that generate predictions of the ways that the intended action should *feel* (the proprioceptive perceptions that are to be expected) and of the ways that the resulting changes in the world should *look*. These are matched against the incoming perceptual data. If discrepancies are found (for example, the pot is heavier than expected, or the coffee begins to pour closer to the edge of the cup than expected) then the motor program is adjusted accordingly.

In addition to the function sketched above, in Section 8 I shall elaborate an important further function for the back-projecting mappings between motor schemata and perceptual representations, in the form of mental rehearsals of intended action. These constitute the basis, I shall argue, for a whole new kind of practical reasoning, which may have emerged for the first time at some point in the primate lineage.

3 Multiple Belief-Generating Modules

In the present section I shall be arguing that animal minds contain *multiple* learning modules for generating information from environmental input. (Hence the 'belief-generating systems' box in Figures 2.3 and 2.5 contains *many* distinct processing systems.) There is space here only to provide the barest sketch of some of the evidence, mentioning a few salient highlights from an immense body of research. For further elaboration and detailed discussion of the examples that follow, together with many others, see Gallistel (1980, 1990), Gould and Gould (1994), Tomasello and Call (1997), and Hauser (2000).

3.1 Navigation

Considering just the one domain of spatial navigation, a number of different innately structured learning mechanisms are required. Many animals possess a mechanism for learning the solar ephemeris—that is to say, the position of the sun in the sky for the time of day, as measured by an internal clock of some sort. In the case of bees this mechanism—like the human language faculty—appears to have an innate 'universal grammar'. All bees in the northern hemisphere are born knowing that the sun is in the east in the morning, and in the west in the afternoon (Dyer and Dickinson, 1994). Thereafter they have to learn the sun's precise trajectory through experience. But this learning gives rise to expectations that go well beyond anything that they have ever experienced. So bees tricked into foraging at night-time, for example, demonstrate in their dances and their interpretation of dances that they believe that the sun is due north at midnight (Gould and Gould, 1988). Bees (and many other navigating animals) also have a mechanism for figuring out the actual position of the sun from the polarization of light in the sky (crucial for navigating on often-overcast days in Europe).

Many animals have another mechanism for learning, by dead reckoning, where they are in relation to a point of origin (the hive, say). And in this case it is 'visual flow' that seems to be used as the measure of distance traveled, at least in the case of bees (Srinivasan et al., 2000). Consider the Tunisian desert ant, which is spectacularly talented in this respect. It leaves its nest (a small hole in the ground) and travels many meters across the featureless desert terrain, following a complex zigzag pattern in search of food. When it finds a dead cricket, say, it bites off a chunk and heads *straight* for home (not retracing its original search path), to within a degree or two of accuracy (see Figure 2.6). When it gets within a few centimeters of where its hole should be, it breaks off its journey into a zigzag search pattern once again. We know that the ant isn't following scent trails or navigating via landmarks, since if it is lifted up just as it turns for home and carried in a dark box hundreds of meters across the desert, and is then released on a fresh patch of desert marked out in a checker-box pattern for measurement purposes by the scientists, it will travel in a straight line at a steady speed to within a few centimeters of where its hole *should* be, if it had been traveling from its original turning point (Wehner and Srinivasan, 1981).

What the ant is doing (and what many other animals are capable of doing likewise, including human infants)[12] is keeping a running tally of the direction

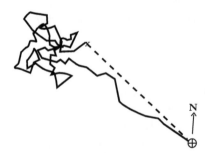

Figure 2.6. Ant navigation

[12] See Landau et al. (1984), who conducted a series of experiments with a congenitally blind 31 month-old child, demonstrating that she, like the desert ant, was doing path-integration (dead

and distance of home, computed from the distance traveled in each direction, together with the angle of each turn. (This is *dead reckoning*, used by mariners at sea to compute their position, too.) This is a learning mechanism that begins its computations afresh each time the animal embarks on a new journey, often covering ground never before traveled. So it obviously can't be an associative conditioning mechanism of any sort. And it is plainly distinct from the mechanism that computes compass directions, and the mechanism that computes distance traveled from visual flow. Indeed, it presupposes those mechanisms, receiving their outputs as its primary input.

Other animals navigate by using the Earth's magnetic field, or by using the moon or the stars. Night-migrating birds study the sky at night when they are chicks in the nest, for example, thereby extracting a representation of the center of rotation of the stars in the night sky. In the case of chicks raised in the northern hemisphere, this can lead to the identification of Polaris, which for the past few hundred years happens to have been positioned near the center of rotation. But the learning task isn't just to recognize Polaris, for a migrating bird will often need to navigate while Polaris is hidden behind clouds. (And in any case, birds raised in the southern hemisphere solve essentially the same learning task, although there is no star that happens to be positioned at the center of the sky's rotation.) When the chicks later leave the nest, they use this information to guide them when flying south (in fall in the northern hemisphere) and again when flying north (in spring in the northern hemisphere) (Able and Bingham, 1987). And the representations in question are learned, not innate, as can be demonstrated by rearing chicks in a planetarium where they observe an artificially generated center of night-sky rotation (Emlen, 1969).

Similarly, many kinds of animal will construct mental maps of their environment which they use when navigating; and they update the properties of the map through observation without conditioning (Gould and Gould, 1994). Many animals can adopt the shortest route to a target (e.g. a source of food), guided by landmarks and covering ground never before traveled. This warrants ascribing to the animals a mental map of their environment. But they will also update the properties of the map on an on-going basis.

Food-caching birds, for example, can recall the positions of many hundreds or thousands of hidden seeds after some months; but they generally won't return to a cache location that they have previously emptied (Gallistel, 1990). Similarly, rats can be allowed to explore a maze on one day, finding a food

reckoning). A variety of experimental controls showed that she was computing the direction and distance of a target object from the information gained during her own travels between objects, integrating the angles of her turns with the distances traveled in each direction.

reward in both a small dark room and a large white one. Next day they are given food in a (distinct) large white room, and shocked in a small dark one. When replaced back in the maze a day later they go straight to the white room and avoid the dark one (Gould and Gould, 1994). Having learned that dark rooms might deliver a shock, they have updated their representation of the properties of the maze accordingly. Likewise, western scrub jays will update the representations on their map of cached foods, and behave accordingly, once they learn independently of the different decay rates of different types of food. Thereafter they access the faster-decaying caches first, and don't bother to access those caches at all once the point of decay has been passed (Clayton et al., 2002, 2004).

Just as dead reckoning requires the integration of two types of information (direction and speed), so the construction of a mental map also requires that two different types of information should be integrated into a single representation—geometric and object-property information, in particular. A map is a representation of the geometry of a space, and generally has the relations amongst landmarks, together with the properties of those landmarks, also represented. There is evidence that there are two distinct systems charged with computing these two sorts of information, which operate independently of one another. And the system that constructs geometric representations is insensitive to other sorts of information.

The evidence derives from a series of experiments conducted by Cheng (1986). Rats were allowed to explore a symmetrical rectangular container, and were shown the location of some food hidden in one corner. In each of the experiments the box contained other vivid landmark cues of various sorts, which rats are perfectly well capable of learning in other circumstances. Thus one wall might be distinctively patterned, or heavily scented. But when the rats were removed from the containers, disoriented, and placed back into them once again, they ignored all those cues and relied exclusively upon the geometry of the space for purposes of reorientation. Hence they searched equally often in the geometrically equivalent corners, and so only succeeded in the task on fifty per cent of occasions.[13]

It seems that when disoriented, and when there is no directional beacon available by which to reorient (such as a distant hill, or the position of the sun), rats will draw *exclusively* on the information provided by their geometric module for purposes of reorientation. This makes good ecological sense, since in the natural environment the geometry is almost always unique, long-lasting,

---

[13] Young children, too, will perform in just such a manner when disoriented in a small room (Hermer and Spelke, 1994, 1996). These data will loom large in our discussions in Chapter 4.

and asymmetrical, whereas local landmarks will vary significantly with time—a tree may lose its leaves, for example, and the scents that mark its base will tend to alter.

In each of these cases—learning the sun's azimuth, computing a direction from the position of the sun, estimating speed of travel, doing dead reckoning, learning the center of rotation of the night sky, computing a direction from the position of a constellation, constructing a representation of the geometry of an environment, and constructing a mental map—it is overwhelmingly plausible that there are *distinct* learning mechanisms involved. For the computational resources necessary to engage in these varied sorts of learning are surely quite different. Anyone who thinks that there could be a *single* learning mechanism, running a single set of algorithms, that is capable of all these distinct tasks is hereby challenged to build one.

3.2 Number, Time, and Rate

There is now widespread agreement that the minds of animals (and of human babies) contain a numerosity module, capable of constructing approximate representations of number across sensory modalities and across categories of thing (events, objects, etc.) (Gallistel, 1990; Dehaene, 1997; Butterworth, 1999; Flombaum et al., 2005). The representations in question are *only* approximate, however, and are subject to Weber's law: the closer two numbers are together, and the larger those numbers are, the more likely it is that errors will be made. So 7 and 5 are harder to distinguish from one another than are 13 and 5; and 13 and 11 are harder to distinguish from one another than are 7 and 5.

Pigeons and rats can be trained to make their responses dependent upon number. They can learn, for example, that in order to receive a reward they have to press one lever 50 times before they press another one. Their response to the first lever will approximate to 50. (Adult humans, too, can access the mechanism that enables the animals to do this. If you are asked to tap 50 times with your hand as fast as you can—too fast to count—your actual performance is likely to show very similar error-bars to that of the rat.) And a variety of data demonstrate that it is number that the animals are tracking, rather than some other property (Gallistel, 1990).

Especially striking experimental evidence is provided by Church and Meck (1984). They placed rats in a cage with two levers, and trained them to respond by pressing the left lever if either two tones were played or two lights flashed, and to press the right lever if four tones were played or four lights flashed. They then presented the rats with cross-modal stimuli: either one tone paired with one flash of light (two events in total) or two tones paired with two flashes (four events in total). The rats immediately generalized on the basis of number: in the first of these circumstances they responded by pressing the left-hand lever, and in the second they responded by pressing the right-hand lever.[14]

A variety of kinds of evidence suggests that animals are capable of representing the time of day of an occurrence, as measured by their internal circadian clock, with an accuracy of plus-or-minus three minutes (Gallistel, 1990). And the animals demonstrate in their behavior that they are genuinely *representing* the time of occurrence, rather than having their behavior caused at that time directly by some process linked into their circadian rhythms, since they can behave *flexibly* with respect to that time. Indeed, it seems that all memory in animals is mandatorily linked to a time (and place) of occurrence, and that these are the basic coordinates used in the retrieval of learned information (Gallistel, 1990).

Consider, for example, the experiments reported by Koltermann (1974), conducted with bees. Each experiment was done with an individual bee, to rule out the effects of bee communication. All the training was done in a single day. The bees were allowed to feed continuously from a beaker, returning at approximately five-minute intervals throughout the day. But each hour, for a period of three bee visits (normally about fifteen minutes), the beaker was paired with a particular odor, or a particular color. Next day there was again food in the beaker, except during five minute test periods that occurred every half hour. During the test period the bee was presented with two empty beakers, one paired with the original odor or color, and the other paired with a different odor or color. The bees never showed any interest in the beaker paired with the novel odor or color. But they repeatedly visited the beaker paired with the familiar odor or color (landing, entering it, finding no food, flying around, then landing and entering once more). And they did so with more than double the intensity at times coinciding with the times at which they had previously experienced the food and the odor or color paired together. Hence the bees were able to recall, not just the pairing of an odor or color with the presence of food in the beaker, but the times of day (in this experiment, within a half-hour window) at which the pairing had occurred.

Virtually all animals represent times of day. But only some animals—including rats and pigeons, but not insects—represent temporal *intervals*. (A temporal interval is the time that elapses between two events, rather than a period that

---

[14] Note how striking and counter-intuitive this result is from the perspective of associationist learning theory (see Section 4 below). The rat had been trained to press the left lever when presented with two tones, and also to press the left lever when presented with two flashes of light; but when presented with both sets of stimuli together, instead of the action of pressing the left lever being especially strongly determined (as one might expect), the rats pressed the right-hand lever instead.

occupies a fixed interval of the day.) And it is plain that the mechanism that computes intervals (at least when those intervals are five minutes or shorter in duration) must be distinct from the circadian clock-system, if the latter is only accurate to plus-or-minus three minutes. In the laboratory, rats and pigeons on a fixed-interval reward schedule will time their rate of responding to a crescendo that coincides roughly with the time at which the next reward will become available. (In these schedules, a reward is made available at a fixed interval from the time when the animal last harvested a reward, but only a proportion of the trials are actually rewarded. The data are then taken from the unrewarded trials.)

To see the importance of representations of intervals in nature, consider the hermit hummingbird of Costa Rica (Gill, 1988). It feeds from sequences of flowers of known location (a 'trapline'). Once a flower has been emptied of nectar, there is an interval of time before it can next be harvested (different for different flowers and different times of day). If the bird returns to a given flower too soon, it may find nothing; and likewise if it returns after an interval that is too long it may find nothing, because the flower may already have been re-harvested by another bird. In addition, time spent feeding means fewer opportunities for mating. The male hummingbird spends much of each day displaying to attract females. If it is inefficient in the timing of its foraging visits, and consequently has to forage for longer periods to maintain its energy levels, then it will succeed in mating less often.

If animals can represent (approximate) number, and can represent temporal intervals, then they have the resources to represent *rates*—especially rates of availability of food from different foraging patches, or from different foraging activities. For a rate is a number per unit interval of time. And indeed, we know that many animals are extremely good at estimating rates. Thus a flock of ducks will distribute 1:1 or 1:2 in front of two feeders throwing food at rates of 1:1 or 1:2 within one minute of the onset of provisioning, during which time many ducks get no food at all and very few of them experience rewards from both sources (Harper, 1982). And similarly, if the feeders throw at an equal rate, but one of them is throwing chunks that are twice as large as those thrown by the other, the birds will again distribute themselves in a 1:2 ratio (albeit taking slightly longer to do so: within five or six minutes of the onset of provisioning).

But are animals capable of calculating and *representing* rates, as opposed to building stronger behavioral dispositions as a result of differential rates of reward (as Vaughan, 1985, suggests)? This would be the standard associationist explanation, in which it is assumed that the birds are *conditioned* to respond as they do by the variable rewards that they receive. The trouble with this explanation, however, is that when the ducks were able to distribute themselves in a 1:2 ratio in response to two feeders throwing at rates in the ratio of 1:2, they did so in just one minute. During this time only fifty per cent of the ducks received a reward from either patch, and few if any received rewards from both. So the animals must have distributed themselves as they did on the basis of *observation* of the relative rates of provisioning (together with observation of the number of birds already positioned at each patch, of course, since otherwise they would all have congregated in front of the higher-rate provisioner), rather than on the basis of conditioning.

Similar results have been demonstrated in the laboratory. Both pigeons and rats on a variable reward schedule from two different alcoves will match their behavior to the changing rates of reward. There is a lever in each alcove, each set on a random reward schedule of a given probability—in such a way that if the lever is pressed in one alcove there is a probability of 0.2, say, that the animal will receive a reward, whereas if the lever is pressed in the other alcove there is a probability of 0.7 of receiving a reward. But these probabilities themselves change randomly. So after ten minutes on the above schedule, for example, the probabilities might shift to one of 0.8 in the first alcove and 0.4 in the second. It turns out that the animals respond to these changes *very* rapidly, closely tracking the random variations in the immediately preceding rates (Dreyfus, 1991; Mark and Gallistel, 1994). They certainly aren't averaging over previous reinforcements, as associationist models would predict. On the contrary, the animals' performance comes very close to that of an ideal Bayesian reasoner (Gallistel et al., 2001). And the only model that can predict the animals' behavior is one that assumes that they are capable of calculating the ratio of the two most recent intervals between rewards from the two alcoves (Gallistel, 2000; Gallistel and Gibbon, 2001).

3.3 Foraging and Nature

The abilities surveyed above come together with others in animal foraging behavior. For in order to forage or hunt effectively, an animal must be able to estimate the relative rates of food availability at the various locations that it can access. But of course it must also be able to do very much more than this. First of all, an animal needs to know *what* to eat, and it needs to adjust its consumption of different types of food to meet all its nutritional needs. (It turns out that even predatory insects will adjust their hunting and feeding behavior differentially, if deprived of different types of nutrient. See Mayntz et al., 2005.)

In some cases this knowledge may be innate, but in many instances (especially amongst generalist feeders like rats, black bears, chimpanzees, and humans) it is learned. No doubt trial and error plays a part in such learning. But random trials of food can be dangerous, and can lead to death. In rats the primary learning mechanism is by odor-transfer, smelling the whiskers and breath of other rats. In the case of apes, in contrast, the main mechanism would appear to be observation of the feeding behavior of others, especially observation of maternal eating behavior prior to the weaning of the infant. Infant gorillas, for example, spend many months clinging to their mother or sitting on her lap, watching not only *what* she eats, but *how* she eats it (Byrne, 1995). For most of the plants eaten by mountain gorillas are protected by stings or sharp spines, and need to be handled with care.

Monkeys and apes have a problem that most other largely vegetarian species don't. They are for the most part only active in the day; they have relatively small body sizes; and they have simple stomachs. Other herbivores like deer, horses, and elephants can extract the nutrients that they need from poor-quality plant matter because they have a number of digestive specializations like multiple stomachs. Moreover, they forage for long periods, being nearly as active at night as in the day. Hence primates need to eat a wide range of types of food in order to achieve a balanced diet, often including fruits, leaves, fungi, bark, shoots, roots, insects, and the occasional small mammal. And many of these foods can be hard to find. Byrne and colleagues (1993), for example, were amazed at the subtle cues used by the baboons they studied in identifying some of their plant foods, such as the dry stem of an orchid bulb that is the same color as the dead grass with which it is intermingled. At the harshest times of year, the main foods needed by the baboons for survival are all either underground, or tiny and inconspicuous.

In consequence of their generalist diet, many monkeys and apes have extensive knowledge of the natural world around them. Besides knowing *what* they can eat, they know where their different food items can be found and in what quantities, how they can be located, and at what times of day and year they can be found. So they can integrate category concepts with representations of places, times, temporal intervals, and rates. They also understand the relationships amongst some living things, such as the relationship between a type of fruit and the type of plant that bears it. Menzel (1991) demonstrated this in an experimental study with Japanese macaque monkeys. In his three types of condition he hid either ripe akebi fruit (artificially ripened shortly before the start of its normal season), or chocolate, or (as a control) nothing along the side of a well-used monkey trail. When the monkeys found the chocolate, they searched on the ground around it for more. When the monkeys found the fruit, in contrast, they looked up into the nearby trees where akebi vines might be found, and they set out to visit and check nearby akebi-vine locations. They did none of these things in the control condition.

Finally, a chance observation fully documented by Byrne and Byrne (1988) suggests that chimpanzees understand that leopard cubs will one day grow up to be dangerous predators. At considerable risk to themselves, the males in the troupe managed to extract a leopard cub from the birth-cave where it was holed up with its mother, thereafter pummeling it to death. Given the obviousness of the risk to themselves (the females and juveniles in the group were all high off the ground in the trees while this was going on, screaming and showing fear-grins), there had to have been a clear point to it. And the only available suggestions are either that the chimpanzees were attempting to rid the area of a future predator, or that they were attempting to provide the female with a deterrent to continuing to live in the area. Since there would have been less dangerous ways of pursing the latter goal via a program of harassment, the former provides the most plausible interpretation.

3.4 Causation

In Section 1 I argued that animals don't need to be capable of genuinely *instrumental* (in the sense of causation-involving) reasoning in order to count as possessing beliefs and desires, or in order to be capable of planning. For the causation can be left implicit in the animal's own agency, rather than explicitly represented. And planning can be purely spatial / navigational in character. Nevertheless, some animals do seem to have beliefs about causation, as I shall now briefly argue.

Dickinson and colleagues have shown that rats are sensitive to the degree of causal efficacy of their own actions (Dickinson and Charnock, 1985; Dickinson and Shanks, 1995). In particular, the rat's rate of action drops (just as a human agent's will do) as the degree of causal connection between act and outcome falls. Moreover, if a rat has been trained to perform two distinct kinds of action to achieve two different types of food, and is then induced to have an aversion to one of these types, it will immediately cease performing the action that would deliver it (Adams and Dickinson, 1981). This suggests that the rats know that one type of action causes the presence of one type of food, and the other causes the presence of the other.

It even turns out that rats display exactly the same *illusions* of causality as do humans (Dickinson and Shanks, 1995). The set-up in these experiments is that the probability of an event occurring (e.g. a figure appearing on a TV monitor, for the humans) or a reward being delivered (for the rats) is actually made independent of the action to be performed (pressing the space bar, or pressing a lever), while sometimes occurring in a way that happens to be temporally paired with that action. If (but only if) the unpaired outcomes are signaled in some way (by a coincident sound, say), then both rats and humans continue to believe (and to behave) as if the connection between act and outcome were a causal one.

Chimpanzees display a remarkable knowledge of the causal contingencies amongst events, and utilize a variety of tools in the wild (Tomasello and Call, 1997). They use stones in combination as a hammer and anvil on which to crack nuts. They throw stones and swing sticks aggressively. And they use both stout sticks (for puncturing) and flexible fronds (for extracting) when hunting for termites (Sanz et al., 2004). Moreover, in captivity they have piled boxes and used poles to reach desired out-of-reach objects, they have positioned poles as ladders with which to climb fences and walls, and much more. At the very least, chimpanzees are adept at tracking and predicting the causal relationships amongst observable events, and at perceiving some of the causal affordances of familiar types of object.

It is doubtful, however, just how *deep* chimpanzees' understanding of causality is. In particular, Povinelli (2000) has conducted a series of detailed experimental studies designed to test how well his young captive chimpanzees understand the causal properties of objects (e.g. that a rake can be used to pull small objects towards them when it has its prong side up, but not when it has its prong side down, when the small objects slip between the prongs), and to what extent they conceptualize causal processes in terms of hidden forces and causes. The results were largely negative, and he concludes that while chimpanzees are excellent at tracking causal contingencies amongst events, they lack theories of the underlying properties and processes involved. Some have critiqued this work, however, partly on methodological grounds (Hauser, 2001; Whiten, 2001), so its conclusions should be treated with caution.

In addition to the evidence from extant species of non-human primate, the stone-tool-making abilities of earlier species of hominid indicate a sophisticated grasp of fracture dynamics and the properties of stone materials. Making stone tools isn't easy. Besides considerable hand and eye coordination and upper-body strength, it requires complex causal judgment. This is demonstrated from the testimony of practiced contemporary stone-knappers, who have replicated some of the more sophisticated tools from the hominid tool-kit (Pelegrin, 1993). Since stone-knapping uses a reductive technology (starting from a larger stone and reducing it to the required shape), utilizing variable and unpredictable materials, it cannot be routinized in the way that (presumably) nest-building by weaver birds and dam-building by beavers can be. Stone-knappers have to hold in mind the desired shape and plan two or more strikes ahead in order to work towards it using erratically behaving materials (Pelegrin, 1993; Mithen, 1996). And in order to do so, they have to think about the ways in which physical forces will interact with the shapes and properties of the materials involved.

3.5 Social Cognition

It seems likely that all social mammals can recognize other individuals within their social group, and can distinguish kin from non-kin, including elephants (Moss, 1988), lions (Packer, 1994), dolphins (Connor et al., 1992), and all primates (Tomasello and Call, 1997). In primates, at least, it seems that kin are identified via a more-or-less reliable heuristic: individuals who grow up together and continue to associate together are kin. This is the interpretation that is commonly given by primatologists, and it has been confirmed experimentally by Welker et al. (1987) who raised macaques in artificially composed groups containing both genetic kin and non-kin. When the groups were later merged, the main determinant of kin-like behaviors was whether or not the individuals in question had been raised together.[15]

Likewise it is likely that all social mammals—but especially primates—are adept at reading the behavior of other individuals. All such animals have species-specific behavioral displays of various sorts, especially those that are expressive of emotion. Thus there will be displays of anger, fear, and of invitations to mate. Such displays are highly predictive of what the animal is likely to do next, at least in a given social or environmental context (such as the presence of a predator). And other members of the species are adept at reading them, and can respond appropriately. Moreover, all social animals are capable of learning how other individuals in the group are likely to behave towards them in particular circumstances, such as being approached while food is being consumed.

Consider Menzel's (1974) studies with chimpanzees, for example. (These will also figure in a later discussion, in Section 8.) On a series of occasions Menzel hid food somewhere within a one-acre enclosure, sometimes allowing just one of the group of chimpanzees to observe the location while the others were locked up. All the chimpanzees were then released into the enclosure as a group. The other chimpanzees rapidly came to be able to identify the individual who knew the location, from cues such as level of excitement and

---

[15] The same kin-recognition heuristic turns out to be responsible for some human attitudes and behaviors, as well. Thus the main determinant of sexual revulsion at the idea of sex with your sibling is whether or not the two of you were raised together in the same household. Siblings raised apart—but who know that they are siblings—tend to feel no such revulsion. Whereas unrelated individuals raised together—even when they know that they are unrelated—rarely form sexual liaisons with each other. (This is why the children of kibbutzim rarely marry; Shepher, 1983.) This is the Westermarck hypothesis, confirmed by a range of data (Fessler and Navarrete, 2004).

purposefulness of stride. And from that individual's direction of travel they could sometimes predict where the food might be found, on some occasions even arriving there first.

Tomasello and Call (1997) argue that where primates stand out from other social mammals is in their ability to understand third-party relationships. One aspect of this is that primates not only know their own kin-relationship and dominance-relationship to other individuals in the group, but they also know who is kin to whom, and who is dominant or subservient to whom. Moreover, they understand a good deal about how the individuals in such relationships are likely to behave towards one another. These facts make the primate social world very much more difficult to negotiate than the social worlds of other social mammals, by many orders of complexity.

These abilities are nicely illustrated by a call play-back study conducted with baboons by Cheney and Seyfarth (1999). The experimenters exposed a number of pairs of unrelated females to three sorts of auditory stimulus. In each case what the females heard was a recording of an agonistic exchange between two individuals (the threat-grunts of a dominant combined with the screams of a subordinate). But in the first condition one of the two individuals was related to one of the females and the other was related to the other; in the second condition only one of the individuals was so related; and in the third condition neither was related. What the experimenters predicted was: (a) that the females should pay much more attention (both to each other, and to the fight) when the sounds that they heard emanated from their two relatives; (b) that in the case where only one relative was involved in the fight, the female whose relative it was should look in the direction of the fight, whereas the other female should look in her direction; (c) when neither relative was involved, neither female should pay much attention; and (d) when both their relatives were involved in the fight, the females' own behavior towards each other should change, but not otherwise. These predictions were borne out by the results.

Most primates—and especially chimpanzees—are adept at forming strategic alliances. Sometimes these work to the individuals' immediate mutual benefit. But sometimes they seem to display reciprocal altruism, working to the benefit of one but not the other in the short term, with reciprocal aid rendered to the other on a later occasion (Tomasello and Call, 1997). Chimpanzees will also coordinate hunts together, with seeming understanding of the roles of the respective participants (Boesch, 2002). And the male chimpanzees in a group will sometimes embark on a border raid on another group, moving quietly and in coordinated fashion through the forest before attacking and killing some of the males in the other group, winning some of its females (Byrne, 1995).

Many primates—and again, especially chimpanzees—are adept at recruiting allies and forming coalitions for a variety of purposes. Sometimes these are for defense, sometimes to gain access to mates or to food, sometimes to overturn an existing dominance hierarchy. Indeed, de Waal (1982) famously argues on the basis of his and others' observations that chimpanzee social life contains all of the main elements of human political life. And in the same spirit, many primatologists have suggested that apes display sophisticated forms of 'Machiavellian intelligence' (Byrne and Whiten, 1988, 1997).

In order to count as genuinely Machiavellian in their abilities, however, chimpanzees would have to be capable of thinking, not just about the likely behavior of others and about the interventions that might alter and manipulate that behavior, but about the mental states behind the behavior. A true politician understands what his rivals *want*, what they *believe* about their circumstances and the beliefs and goals of others, and what they *intend* to do. Many of the contributors to Byrne and Whiten (1988) make just such claims on behalf of chimpanzees. They claim that chimpanzees possess 'a theory of mind' or (to use the language I prefer), that they are 'mind-readers'.[16]

Part of the evidence for chimpanzee mind-reading comes from their seeming use of tactical deception. For to deceive someone is to induce them to hold a false belief. And you can only do this intentionally if you know what beliefs are (and that they can be either true or false), and know something about how they can be caused. Consider the following example, described by Menzel (1974) from his food-hiding experiments. When one of the females—Belle—knew the location of the food, the alpha male would follow her until he could identify where the food was hidden. Then he would push her aside, sometimes biting and kicking her, and take all of the food for himself. Belle tried a number of strategies to circumvent him (such as sitting near the food waiting for him to wander off), but with little success. But on a number of occasions what she hit upon doing was this. She marched off in the wrong direction and started to dig. When the male pushed her aside as usual and took over the digging for himself, she doubled back quickly to where the food was really hidden while he was preoccupied, and was thus able to retrieve and consume it.

It has been disputed whether examples of this sort genuinely require a mind-reading explanation, however. And in most such cases weaker explanations in terms of knowledge of behavioral rules can be provided instead. In this instance, Belle might not have been trying to get the male to *believe* that the

---

[16] It is disputed to what extent a capacity to understand the minds of others depends upon a theory. Some think that it might rather be grounded in a capacity to *simulate*, or in the operations of a distinctive processing module. See many of the papers in Carruthers and Smith (1996). So the term 'theory of mind' is tendentious to describe this capacity, in a way that 'mind-reading' is not.

food was buried in the wrong location. She might merely have foreseen that, if she were to start digging there, then he would push her aside and take over. And she could have known that while he was digging he would be unlikely to follow her when she traveled to the true location of the food. Both of these things she could have learned on the basis of previous experiences, from dealing with him and with others. But neither requires her to be capable of attributing mental states to him.

When the mind-reading capacities of chimpanzees and other apes have been subjected to careful experimental investigation, for the most part the results have not been encouraging. Povinelli (2000), for example, reports a series of experiments in which his young chimpanzees were first taught to beg for food from one of two experimenters. They were then tested in conditions where one of the experimenters had her eyes covered, or was looking at the ceiling, or had a bucket over her head. The chimpanzees tended to beg indiscriminately in these circumstances, suggesting that they failed to know that seeing is necessary for believing in these conditions; or suggesting that they didn't understand the connection between eye-direction and perception.

As we noted earlier, Povinelli's work has been criticized on methodological grounds by some primatologists; hence we need to be cautious in relying upon it. And others have claimed to have greater success in discovering mind-reading in chimpanzees in more naturalistic experimental settings (Hare et al., 2000). Now, however, I think that the jury is still out on the mind-reading abilities of chimpanzees and other apes. But what everyone surely agrees upon is that chimps are at least very smart *behaviorists* (Smith, 1996). They are extremely good at identifying types of behavior, at learning connections amongst types of behavior, and at predicting the consequences of a given type of behavior in a given set of circumstances.

3.6 Conclusion: Multiple Learning Modules

As advertised at the start of this section, my conclusion is that animal minds contain *multiple* modules for extracting information from the environment and for generating new beliefs. There are systems for judging directions, for judging both the time of day and temporal intervals, for judging velocity, for doing dead reckoning, for constructing and drawing inferences from mental maps, for estimating number, for calculating the rates at which events occur (especially provisioning events, but also events of other kinds), for learning about and identifying living kinds, for extracting causal information from sequences of events, for learning about social relationships, and for drawing inferences about likely behavior. In each of these cases the structure of the learning problem is quite distinct from the structures of the others, presenting the learner with unique computational challenges. It is highly implausible that there might be just one learning system (or even a few) that can accomplish all these (and many other) learning tasks that animals routinely face. And it is even less plausible that such a system might be an associationist one, building and weakening the strengths of connections amongst representations.

4 The Case Against General Learning

Someone might concede the existence of multiple learning modules whilst *also* insisting that there exists such a thing as *general* learning. And in particular, it might be said that, alongside the various specialized learning mechanisms described in Section 3, animal minds also contain a general-purpose associative learning mechanism, of the sort that is routinely assumed by many people to underlie conditioning behavior. This mechanism pairs and builds associations amongst stimuli and resulting rewards.[17] But in fact Gallistel (1990, 2000) argues convincingly that even conditioning—the very heartland of associationist general-purpose learning theory—is better explained in terms of the computational operation of a specialist rate-estimating module, whose parameters have been shaped by evolution for its role in foraging. Here I shall briefly review some of the highlights from an extensive and thoroughly worked out set of data and arguments.

We have already mentioned one significant problem for associationist learning theory in Section 3.2. There we noted that animals in conditioning experiments where they are required to respond to randomly changing rates of reward are able to track changes in the rate of reward about as closely as it is theoretically possible to do. If the pigeons and rats in question were ideal Bayesian probability-calculators they couldn't do much better! This is *very* puzzling from an associationist perspective, since on any such account it ought to take significant time to build and to weaken the associations between each of the two alcoves in question and reward. But of course it makes perfectly good sense if what the animals are really doing is calculating and comparing the changes in the relative rates of resource-availability in the two alcoves, as Gallistel's model claims.

---

[17] This isn't the only possible candidate for a general learning mechanism, of course. But it is the one that is assumed by many people to be operative in non-human animals. As we shall see in Chapter 6, some developmental psychologists believe that there is also a quite different sort of general learning—or 'scientific theorizing'—mechanism present in the minds of human infants.

Another problem for the associationist account of conditioning is that it predicts that increasing the amount of *delay* in the presentation of the reward, following the initiation of the stimulus to which the animal is responding (e.g. the illumination of a light), should always retard learning. If a reward is only available after the light has been illuminated for 30 seconds, say, then this should make it harder for the animal to associate the light with the reward than if the latter is available after an illumination of just 5 seconds. And indeed, this is the case under some experimental conditions—specifically, if the intervals between trials (e.g. one illumination of the light and the next) is kept fixed. But if the inter-trial intervals are increased in the same proportions, then increasing the delay between stimulus and reward has *no* effect on learning (Gallistel and Gibbon, 2001).

For example, suppose that in the brief-delay condition the sequence is: light for 5 seconds; reward available; rest for 10 seconds; light for 5 seconds; reward available; rest for 10 seconds; and so on. And suppose that in the long-delay condition the sequence is: light for 30 seconds; reward available; rest for 60 seconds; light for 30 seconds; reward available; rest for 60 seconds; and so on. In these circumstances it won't take the animal any more trials to learn the behavior in the long-delay condition than it does in the brief-delay condition, because the *ratio* of stimulus presentation to background conditions remains fixed. This result is predicted by Gallistel's computational model, but is extremely puzzling from the standpoint of an associationist.

Other well-established conditioning phenomena are equally problematic for associationist learning theory. Thus the number of reinforcements that are necessary for an animal to acquire the intended behavior is actually unaffected by mixing *un*reinforced trials into the learning process. For example, one set of animals might be trained on a 1:1 schedule: these animals receive a reward every time that they respond when the stimulus is present. But another set of animals might be trained on a 10:1 schedule: here the animals only receive a reward once in every 10 trials that they respond when the stimulus is present. Still it will, on average, take both sets of animals the same number of rewarded trials to acquire the behavior. It will take the second set of animals *longer* to acquire the behavior, of course. If it takes both sets of animals 40 rewarded trials to acquire the behavior, then the first set will learn it in 40 trials, whereas the second set will take 400. But the number of *reinforcements* to acquisition is the same. Again this is extremely puzzling from the standpoint of an associationist. One would expect that all those times when the stimulus *isn't* paired with a reward ought to *weaken* the association between stimulus and reward, and hence make learning the intended behavior harder. But it doesn't, just as Gallistel's model predicts.

Something similar is true of the *extinction* of a learned behavior, which happens once the stimulus ceases to be paired with any reward. Whether the animal was trained on a 1:1 schedule or a 10:1 schedule, it will take the same number of missed reinforcements for the animal to lose the behavior, once the behavior ceases to be rewarded. Note: it won't take the same number of unreinforced *trials* (in fact it will take 10 times as many on the 10:1 schedule). Rather it will take the same number of trials on which the animal *would* have been rewarded during the learning phase of the experiment. So to stick with the same numbers above, if it takes the animal 40 rewarded trials on a 1:1 schedule to learn the behavior, it might take it 40 unreinforced trials to lose the behavior again. And if it takes the animal 400 trials to learn the behavior on a 10:1 schedule, it will take it 400 unreinforced trials to extinguish the behavior. But in each case it takes only 40 *missed reinforcements* to lose the behavior. This, too, is extremely puzzling from the perspective of an associationist: one would expect that it would be the *absolute* number of unreinforced trials that would be effective in extinguishing an established association between stimulus and reinforcement.

The computational model worked out by Gallistel and colleagues is able to explain the data outlined above, and more (Gallistel, 1990, 2000, 2003; Gallistel and Gibbon, 2001, 2002; Gallistel et al., 2001). It is also able to unify within a single predictive framework learning phenomena that are treated as quite distinct within associationist models (Gallistel, forthcoming). On this account, what the animals are really doing is calculating the relative rate of reward when the conditioning stimuli are present as against the rate of reward when those stimuli are absent. In effect, the animals are learning the extent to which the stimulus *predicts* a reward, and this can only be done by comparing the rate of stimulus-reward pairings with the rate of reward in background conditions. And the timescale invariance of such properties is the key to explaining the phenomena above.

For example, as mentioned above, increasing the amount of time that the stimulus has to be present before a reward is available has no effect on learning (provided that the inter-trial intervals are increased in proportion). The reason for this is that the extent to which the stimulus predicts the presence of a reward depends upon the ratio of stimulus presence to background conditions (i.e. to the inter-trial intervals). And this remains exactly the same. When the light is illuminated for 5 seconds before a reward becomes available with the inter-trial interval being 10 seconds, this ratio is 1:2. And likewise when the light is illuminated for 30 seconds before a reward is available, with the inter-trial interval being 60 seconds, the ratio is also 1:2.

The explanation for the failure of partial reinforcement to make any difference to rates of learning is similar. Suppose that the training schedule is such that on each trial a light is illuminated for 5 seconds, followed by a 10 second inter-trial interval. An animal on a 1:1 reward schedule then (with a reward being available on every trial) will experience the light for half as much time as non-light for every time that a reward is available. But the same is true of an animal on a 40:1 reward schedule: it will have experienced the light, on average, for 200 seconds for every time that a reward becomes available, whereas it will have experienced non-light for 400 seconds per reward. And this is the very same 1:2 ratio.

The conditioning data make perfect sense, then, within the framework of a specialized computational rate-estimation module; whereas they appear extremely puzzling from the perspective of associationist general learning theory. In which case we have good reason to believe that there is no such thing as general learning (at least of this form—we will return to consider other alternatives in Chapters 3.2 and 6.3). On the contrary, learning is modularist through-and-through.

5 Multiple Motivational Modules

I have argued in Sections 3 and 4 that the informational / belief-creating side of animal cognitive architectures consists entirely of multiple belief-generating modules. I now propose to argue—albeit more briefly—that the same holds true of the motivational / desire-creating side of animal minds, too.

5.1 Against the Alternatives

How could it *fail* to be the case that animal minds contain multiple motivational modules? One extreme possibility would be to postulate that animals have just one (or perhaps a very few) intrinsic goals—to maximize inclusive fitness, say; or to maximize happiness or well-being. Perhaps all those desires that we *experience as* intrinsic ones—such as desires for food when hungry, or for sex when aroused—are really learned *instrumental* desires. Perhaps individuals only come to desire these things because they have learned that they will contribute towards their one-and-only ultimate goal.

This possibility can be ruled out almost a priori, on two distinct grounds. First, it attributes hugely implausible sophistication of a general-learning sort to the belief-generating systems of the mind. For in each case desires for particular things or events would have to be produced by learning or somehow reasoning that achieving the thing or event in question would contribute to the ultimate goal. Yet many of these desires appear in infants from a very young age, when there has been little opportunity for learning; and in many cases the connections with any supposed ultimate goal will be far from obvious.

To see the character of the second problem with the above suggestion, notice that from an evolutionary perspective the only remotely plausible candidate for an ultimate goal is inclusive fitness. For this is what evolutionary processes in general look at. And any other goal that one might care to postulate—well-being, say—would sometimes conflict with inclusive fitness, and hence would be selected against. (Think here, for example, of a mother bear abandoning her cubs at the smallest hint of a predator on the grounds that she is pursuing her own well-being.) But the reason why inclusive fitness *cannot* be the only ultimate goal, is that in many cases the question whether or not an action favors inclusive fitness just can't be discerned within the lifetime of a single individual. So it can't be learned by any *possible* general learning mechanism (Tooby et al., 2005).

Consider, for example, coalition-related punitive desires in primates. Sometimes when there has been a public fight of some sort between a member of group A and a member of group B, other members of the one group will thereafter attack or harass other members of the other (Tomasello and Call, 1997). The evolutionary gains from such behavior are far from obvious. In fact they might well be *tiny* and yet still have an impact on inclusive fitness in the long run, across many generations. But no learning mechanism could be expected to see this in the course of a single lifetime. What one would anticipate, then, is that the evolutionary process should fix in place a novel intrinsic motivation, in this case a desire for third-party coalition-based revenge.

How else might one deny that there are multiple desire-generating modules? Someone might concede that there are many evolutionarily fixed intrinsic desires, but deny that the processes that give rise to such desires in specific circumstances are computational in character, or involve any processing of information. Rather, it might be claimed that the processes that give rise to desires are entirely physio-chemical in nature. And there seems no doubt that such a claim contains at least a grain of truth. Thus in most female mammals the desire to mate is triggered directly by cyclical hormonal levels. And desires to eat or to drink might be thought to depend upon similar, but homeostatic, physio-chemical processes. But this can't be the *whole* story, surely. For the desire to mate in most *male* mammals isn't triggered by bodily state, but rather by visual or olfactory stimuli (especially of a sexually presenting female); and, even though triggered hormonally, females are often discriminating about the question *with whom* to mate. And likewise the desire for food in most predator species can surely be triggered by perception of a predating opportunity.[18]

In fact the most plausible model for the way in which intrinsic desires are usually generated is one that involves sensitivity to both bodily *and* informational factors of various sorts—although some cases might fall more at the bodily end of the spectrum, and some might be almost entirely informational. Let me illustrate the general model via consideration of a well-understood case: the system that gives rise to dancing-motivations in honey-bees.

5.2 A Model of a Desire Module

Each foraging bee is known to monitor and integrate two different sets of variables in order to establish the level of her motivation towards dancing when she returns to the hive, as well as how vigorously and for how long she should dance, if she dances at all (Seeley, 1995). One concerns the profitability of the food source that she has located. For this she has to notice the distance of the source from the hive, the sugar content of the nectar (if it is nectar that she is gathering), and the nectar abundance at the source (e.g. how large the patch of flowers is, and how widely dispersed the flowers are). Integrating these together gives her a measure of the profitability of her source, which she maps onto an innately known scale of profitability. (Even a naive forager on her very first foraging trip knows how to judge the profitability of a food source in a way that accords with the judgments of others.)

The second set of variables that the foraging bee is known to monitor concerns the context in which her foraging trip takes place. Here she has to observe the weather (whether or not it is windy or showery, and whether or not there is an approaching storm), and she has to observe the time of day (if it is late in the day then this will make her reluctant to dance). Moreover, she also has to estimate the colony's overall nectar influx. The latter she does by noticing how far she has to travel into the hive before she can find a food-storer bee to take her load, as well as how vigorously and energetically she is unloaded, and by how many food storers. (If the hive as a whole is successfully gathering large quantities of nectar, then she will have to travel further to find a food storer, who will be less excited to see her. If nectar is in short supply, on the other hand, then she will likely be met at the entrance by many excited food storers.)

---

[18] Think, too, of how the sight and/or smell of chocolate cake at the end of a meal can lift a person out of their previously replete state, and make them feel hungry once again.

Seeley (1995) describes what the bee is doing in integrating all these items of information as reaching a *decision* on whether or not to dance, and if so, how vigorously. But if this is what she is doing, then she certainly isn't taking a decision in pursuit of some further goal. The bee certainly isn't thinking about whether or not dancing would further her other aims. For the only possible candidate for such a goal would be that of maximizing the overall energetic intake of the hive (or something similar). Yet it is *hugely* implausible to suppose that the bee has any such goal. But then neither is she starting from an intrinsic desire to dance (of some fixed strength), and figuring out whether it is acceptable for her to satisfy that desire in the circumstances—we shouldn't see her as reaching a decision on the question, 'Shall I do what I want [dance]?'

Rather, the correct way to conceptualize what is happening is that the various calculations are taking place within a sub-system of the bee's mind whose function it is to determine a level of intrinsic motivation towards dancing. What those calculations do, is determine how much she *wants* to dance when she gets unloaded at the hive—the stronger this desire, the more likely she is to dance; and the stronger that desire above a certain threshold, the more vigorously she will waggle, and for longer. The desire to dance then interacts with her beliefs about the direction and distance of the food source to determine the orientation of her dance, and number of waggles that she should do through the center of its figure of eight.

I propose this as a model for what desire-generating modules should look like in general. They will have been designed to pull together information from various sources, and some at least of those sources will be belief-generating modules in their own right. (Thus the information about the distance to the nectar source will be a belief produced by the bee's dead-reckoning system; and the information about time of day will derive from her own body clock integrated with her beliefs about the solar ephemeris.) In many cases these desire-generating modules will also have been designed to respond to physico-chemical properties of the body, such as hormone levels or blood-sugar levels, or will be turned on by such properties. Different desire-generating modules will be sensitive to different sorts of environmental information, and to different bodily properties, with the weights assigned to these respective components varying significantly as well. (In the example above, almost all the factors are informational—although the bee's own degree of tiredness will have an impact on her motivation to dance, too.) But in each case the upshot is a novel, context-specific, intrinsic desire—something that the animal just finds itself wanting for its own sake.

Thus for example, the strength of a female squirrel's desire to mate with a particular male is likely to depend upon the operations of a mating-motivation module, which is keyed into activity by her own hormonal state but then also takes as input a variety of kinds of information. The latter might include comparisons of the male's appearance against some sort of mate-preference template, evaluating such factors as the bushiness of his tail and the thickness of his fur. And it might include information about how successful the male in question has been in chasing her through the trees, perhaps as compared with the other males known to her in the vicinity. Likewise, a mountain lion's desire to capture and kill a particular jackrabbit will depend upon the operations of a predation-motivation module, which is sensitive both to her own blood-sugar levels and to information concerning the type, size, and distance away of the prey item.

Consider also the disgust system in generalist feeders like rats and humans. It is well known that rats can be induced in a single trial to avoid a novel food substance by being made to feel ill many hours after eating it (sometimes by exposing the animal to X rays, sometimes by injecting it with an emetic; Gould and Gould, 1994). Presumably the rat feels something very much like disgust when it encounters the novel food again; for it now has an intrinsic desire not to eat it, and placing some of that food in its mouth induces a disgust reaction not unlike our own. The system that underpins such learning must store a medium-term record of whatever the rat eats, in case it should later become ill. Whenever it does subsequently become ill, a search must be conducted through the items in that record for the most likely culprit, which then becomes the object of disgust. But the mechanism doesn't attempt to record *all* properties of items ingested. On the contrary, it only records taste and smell. (You can't train rats to avoid eating a substance categorized by color, for example, although you can train them to do other things in response to color; Gould and Gould, 1994.)

5.3 Emotional Modules

Most theorists of emotion believe that there are a set of basic emotion systems (Ekman, 1992a, 1992b; Damasio, 1994, 2003; Lazarus, 1994; Levenson, 1994; Rolls, 1999). These include systems for producing anger, fear, joy, sadness, surprise, and disgust. These basic systems are innately structured and universal amongst all humans, and similar systems exist in many other species of animal. They each give rise to a distinctive suite of physiological changes, and come with an innately fixed set of display behaviors (which can nevertheless be modified or repressed). Thus the facial expressions characteristic of the basic emotions are similar across all cultures, and people in one culture can easily recognize these emotions in the faces of people from another (Ekman, 1992a, 1992b). And each comes with an abstractly described set of conditions that triggers the system into activity. Thus according to Lazarus (1994), for anger it is 'a demeaning offence against me or mine'; for fear it is 'an immediate, concrete, and overwhelming physical danger'; and so on.

These basic emotion systems come with a cognitive appraisal 'front end', whose contents are heavily learning-dependent (Ekman, 1992a, 1992b; Levenson, 1994). It may be that some stimuli are wired up to provoke a corresponding emotion innately. Thus sudden and very loud noises are likely to cause at least momentary fear, except in circumstances where one has become habituated to them. But most signs of danger have to be learned. A novice entering a jungle for the first time will be afraid at each sound and movement in the undergrowth; whereas the experienced hunter will have learned what are the indicators of genuine danger, and will respond (or fail to respond) accordingly. So the fear module should be thought of as a system that takes both percepts and beliefs as input, and that generates an intrinsic motivation—in this case, a desire to flee—as output. (Note that this fits the hypothesized structure of desire-creating modules generally, described in Section 5.2.)

The 'front end' of each emotion module is likely to have its own dedicated learning mechanism built into it, whose business it is to acquire an appropriate set of eliciting conditions for the emotion in question. In experiments conducted with rooks, for example, they were able to learn a new template for their predator-aversion mechanism from one-trial observation of the mobbing behavior of other rooks (Gould and Gould, 1994).[19] The novice rook was placed in a cage on one side of the laboratory, with an experienced rook in a cage on the opposite side. In between the two was a screen, with a stuffed owl on the side facing the experienced rook, and a target object of some sort on the side facing the novice. (In the initial experiments the target object was an innocent type of nectar-feeding bird; in later experiments other sorts of objects were inserted, including a bottle of laundry detergent!) When the experienced rook began to 'mob' what it could see (the owl), the novice would join in, targeting its mobbing behavior at what *it* could see. Thereafter the novice would mob whatever was the target object in the initial experiment (as seen from its own perspective), and would teach this behavior to other birds.

5.4 Social Motivations

Many animals have motivations that are directed towards other members of their species. Emotional attachments to mothers, for example, are very common; as are attachments to offspring. The mechanisms that identify

---

[19] I am unsure whether to describe this mechanism as the rook fear-system or the rook anger-system; or perhaps a combination of both.

one's mother can sometimes deploy very simple heuristics, as demonstrated by Lorenz's (1970) famous experiments with newly hatched ducklings. The ducklings would imprint on the first moving thing that they saw, including Lorenz himself. And likewise the mechanisms for identifying offspring can be extremely simple. For many birds the rule seems to be: 'If it is in my nest, it is mine.' This is what enables cuckoos and other parasitic egg-layers to be successful. Moreover, adults of some species of animal pair-bond with mates, sometimes for a season, but sometimes for life. (In the latter case, loss of a mate leads to emotional states bearing a significant resemblance to human grief.) In each of these cases the motivation system in question would seem to come with some sort of appraisal or input mechanism designed to turn it on, and a set of behaviors that the motivation is intended to control.

Social animals like primates will have a range of novel emotions and motivations related to their sociality. In species with an important dominance hierarchy, the desire to be high up in that hierarchy seems likely to be both innate and intrinsic. It is *possible* that the motivation in question is instrumental. Each animal might notice that being high up in the hierarchy leads to more food and better mating opportunities, and hence forms its desire for that reason. But this is likely to be one of those cases where evolution wouldn't leave the formation of the motivation to the vagaries of individual learning. For learning is costly; it takes time; and it is 'noisy' and subject to errors. The status-motivating mechanism, then, is likely to be an innate module that identifies the local dominance hierarchy and the individual's existing position within it, and which generates a desire to be higher in the rank.

What of the motivations involved in coalitions and alliances? In part these are likely to be exaptations of an existing attachment mechanism, especially in the case of long-term kin-based alliances. The input to this system would be relatively simple, relying upon the principle 'familiarity breeds attachment' (Tomasello and Call, 1997). But the output seems likely to be a complex set of intrinsic desires that one might loosely characterize as 'identification with the other'. Thus there will be intrinsic desires to groom kin, to support kin in conflicts with others, and so on. Short-term strategic coalitions, in contrast, may rely largely on instrumental motivations, if the individuals in question can see that the coalition works in their best interests. But even here, to the extent that anything resembling reciprocal altruism is involved, then there are likely to be corresponding intrinsic motivations.

It seems likely that the minds of primates contain systems for generating many other forms of intrinsic motivation as well. Thus de Waal (1996) makes out a strong case that primates experience an emotion similar to sympathy or compassion; that they sometimes feel something resembling guilt or shame;

and that they sometimes have desires for revenge, and for reconciliation. The precise details won't matter here for my purposes. Enough has been said, I think, to complete the main case: alongside multiple belief-generating modules, the minds of animals contain a great many desire-generating modules also.

6 Multiple Memory Systems

I have argued that the minds of non-human animals (and therefore the minds of human beings, too) contain multiple processing modules for generating novel information and for issuing in appropriate new motivations. But what of the storage of that information? What of memory? Does this, too, divide up along massively modular lines?

A prior question is what the main arguments supporting massive modularity imply about the organization of memory. Should those arguments lead us to expect that there will be multiple systems of memory alongside the multitudes of processing modules? Actually, this isn't so clear. The argument from design predicts that there should be distinct systems wherever there are distinct functions, but *information storage* might well count as just a single function, for these purposes. And likewise there is nothing in the argument from learning that predicts the existence of multiple memory modules. While the *extraction* of different kinds of information from the environment requires specialized learning systems, it isn't clear that the storage of that information once extracted should be similarly specialized. One might therefore envisage the existence of just a single memory store organized hierarchically by content type, which can be accessed by the various processing systems using a variety of content-specific search heuristics.

The argument from computational frugality, in contrast, might well suggest a modular organization of memory systems. The extreme slowness of signal propagation within and between neurons (about a million times slower than turn-of-the-century computers) might lead us to predict that information should be stored in a location physically close to wherever it is most likely to be needed. And there are two sorts of system within which the information produced by a given processing module is likely to be utilized thereafter. One is in the operations of that module itself. And the other is within the downstream modules to which the processing module in question normally passes its output. Since these downstream modules are likely to be as close to the source module as the constraints on overall organization permit (Cherniak et al., 2004), one might then predict that information produced by a given module should be stored within it or immediately adjacent to it, and that the other modules that need to make use of that information should do so by querying the module that produced it. This would make for the most efficient and frugal organization overall.

Consistent with this idea, I believe that some of the distinctions amongst kinds of memory that are most commonly drawn by cognitive scientists are best understood in terms of the principle that information should be stored where it is produced. I shall shortly begin elaborating on this idea, before turning to consider the (limited) evidence of domain-specific memory systems. While much of the data that I shall cite derives from experimental work with humans, it is generally assumed that the discoveries apply also to non-human animals, and there is considerable evidence to support such a view (Zola, 2003). One exception is so-called *episodic* memory, however, which remains controversial (Baddeley et al., 2002).

6.1 Types of Memory

Perhaps the deepest cut is between a variety of forms of *long-term* memory, on the one hand, and different kinds of *working* (short-term) memory, on the other. It is now well established that these are distinct. Patients with damage to the hippocampus suffer from more or less profound anterograde amnesia. They are unable to commit new information to memory (whether visual or verbal), they lack a capacity to learn to navigate a novel environment, and they fail to recognize people who work with them regularly. But their capacity to repeat back a string of digits such as a telephone number can be normal (Milner, 1966). And the same is true for those suffering from retrograde amnesia, who may be unable to recall anything from the time prior to their accident. Moreover, the converse syndrome also exists: there are patients who are incapable of repeating back more than a couple of digits, but whose capacity to learn, and to recall previously learned information, is unimpaired (Shallice and Warrington, 1970).

The best-known model of the human working memory system has been developed by Baddeley (1986), who postulates a short-term executive system controlling the operations of two sensory slave systems, one for manipulating visual images and one for phonological rehearsal. This model will be considered in Chapter 4.7, where it will be compared and contrasted with my own related account. At this point I just want to stress that these models are designed to account for the *conscious* processes that take place when someone undertakes a novel task, or reasons about a novel problem. For I shall claim that this working memory system isn't really a distinct module, but rather supervenes on the activity of a wide range of sensory and conceptual modules. And as we shall begin to see in Section 8 of this chapter, it is a system that is probably present in the other great apes, at least.

It seems highly likely that there are an immense number of additional working memory systems within the minds of both animals and humans. More specifically, there is likely to be at least one such system within each of the processing modules in the mind. This conclusion can be reached on the grounds of task analysis. For computational processes presuppose a capacity to bear in mind (to remember) an input representation while computations are being effected over it, as well as a capacity to sustain for short periods some of the intermediate representations produced, before the next stage in the computation can be undertaken. But it is also supported by experimental evidence, at least in respect of perceptual modules, where the working memory systems in question go under the names of 'iconic memory' (in the case of the visual system) and 'echoic memory' (in the case of the auditory system), with similar systems postulated for each of the other senses (Atkinson and Shiffrin, 1968).

While the existence of multiple forms of working memory is not so often stressed by researchers, there is general agreement that there are multiple kinds of long-term memory—albeit not so much agreement as to *which* kinds. Everyone accepts that there is a basic distinction between what are often called *explicit* (or *declarative*) and *implicit* (or *non-declarative*) forms of memory. Explicit memory would encompass such things as the knowledge that President Kennedy was assassinated, and memory images from my last summer vacation. Implicit memory would include such things as a capacity to tie one's shoelaces. And then within explicit memory, many believe that there is a distinction between a *semantic* long-term memory system containing knowledge of facts (that Kennedy was assassinated, that ducks are birds), and an *episodic* (or autobiographical) system containing knowledge of individual life-events. I shall discuss this division first, before turning to discuss the different forms of implicit memory.

One common view has been that the distinction between semantic and episodic memory is merely one of degree, with accumulations of episodes leading gradually to general (semantic) knowledge. But this empiricist account is now largely discredited. For one thing, many facts are learned following just a single exposure or report. But there is also the clinical evidence provided by Vargha-Khadem et al. (2002). They describe a number of patients who, despite being amnesic (in respect of event-memory) from an early age, have acquired normal semantic knowledge. Although they commonly forget the events of everyday life, they have acquired an extensive body of factual knowledge. This indicates that the formation and maintenance of semantic memories is independent of the operations of an episodic memory system.

The converse dissociation also exists (at least partially—I shall return to this point in a moment), in the form of semantic dementia (Hodges and Graham,

2002). Patients suffering from this syndrome show progressive loss of semantic knowledge. They not only lose the capacity to name and describe objects, but they also lose their understanding of the function of different classes of object. Thus one patient held a closed umbrella horizontally over his head during a rainstorm, poured orange juice onto his lasagna, and set the clocks in his house forward in time in the hopes that this would get him to his favorite restaurant earlier. But such patients typically retain broad autobiographical facts about their lives (where and when they were born, where they have lived, how many children they have, and so forth), and their event memories from the immediate and recent past are spared. Day-to-day memories are good, and such a patient might be able to relate accurately the events from a recent vacation in Australia (albeit with prominent word-finding difficulties). Interestingly, however, longer-term episodic memory in semantic dementia does seem to be damaged. In the reverse of the pattern characteristic of retrograde amnesia (and for reasons that aren't well understood), patients typically can't recall events prior to about three years before the onset of their illness.

Conway and Pleydell-Pierce (2000) develop a model of autobiographical memory as a distributed system in the brain, depending upon the operations of a number of distinct memory systems, including semantic memory and various forms of perception-based memory. According to this model it is predictable that brain damage that leaves semantic knowledge intact might nevertheless disrupt the cortical connections between these knowledge stores and the frontal lobes which issue cues for memory retrieval. This gives rise to the phenomenon of retrograde amnesia, in which episodic memories (especially recent episodic memories) are lost while other forms of memory are left intact. It is also predictable that damage to some of the systems underlying semantic knowledge (such as occurs in semantic dementia) might leave the operations of the remainder of the autobiographical memory system intact. (But why long-term autobiographical memories should be lost in semantic dementia remains mysterious.)

When episodic memories are formed, according to Conway and Pleydell-Pierce's model, representations occurring within perceptual modules are linked to one another and to conceptual knowledge schemes and then stored, with the component elements of the memory being stored in the locations where they were produced. Thereafter, cues that activate one element in this structure will be apt to bring the others to mind as well, with the resulting phenomenology (especially involving visual images) distinctive of autobiographical remembering. This model is partially supported by functional neuro-imaging studies showing that posterior neocortex (the visual area of the brain) is active during episodes of autobiographical remembering (Conway et al., 1999).

It is a widely held view that information is stored in the brain in the locations where it was originally represented (Mayes and Roberts, 2002); and this view applies especially to semantic and episodic forms of memory. But it is also known that the hippocampus plays a crucial role in the formation and retrieval, and *perhaps* also the storage, of both kinds of memory (Mayes and Roberts, 2002). For example, lesions in the hippocampus will selectively impair a rat's spatial memory (Ramos, 2000). And in humans, too, selective damage to the hippocampus prevents the formation of new explicit memories (Bechara et al., 1995). Moreover, Riedel et al. (1999) found that temporarily deactivating the hippocampus in rats prevented them from learning the layout of a water maze. It also prevented them from accessing knowledge of a previously learned maze, but only temporarily—when the hippocampus became active once again, they were able to utilize their knowledge of the layout.

It has been debated whether or not non-human animals are capable of episodic memory (Tulving, 1983; Aggleton and Pearce, 2002; Clayton et al., 2002). It is hard to tell whether an animal is capable of *reliving* a prior experience, with all of the imagery and emotional valence characteristic of human autobiographical memory. But there is at least powerful experimental evidence that animals are capable of storing the *what, where,* and *when* elements of episodic memory in a single representation. This is demonstrated by the careful series of experiments conducted with scrub jays by Clayton et al. (2002, 2004), already noted briefly in Section 3.1. Scrub jays in the wild cache their foods, and show remarkable long-term memory for food locations; they also rarely revisit a site that they have previously emptied. But so far this is consistent with the jays deploying a map-like representation on which food items are marked, with the map being updated when caches are emptied. No representations of time (or of the birds' own actions) need be remembered. This is what Clayton et al. set out to test.

Scrub jays much prefer mealworms to crickets, and they prefer mealworms and crickets to peanuts. They also show a strong preference to cache, recover, and eat foods that are still fresh. One group of birds were given training trials in which they learned both that mealworms are still fresh after four hours but thoroughly decayed after a day, and that crickets are still fresh after one day but decayed after four. (Another group of birds were used as a control.) The birds were then allowed to cache all three types of food, and were given the opportunity to access their caches four hours, one day, or four days later. If the birds not only represent what is cached where, but also *when* it was cached there, then they should show a preference to access the mealworm caches at four hours, ignoring those caches and accessing the cached crickets after a day, and ignoring the other sources of food and recovering the peanuts at four days. And this is just what they did. Moreover, they generalized what they had learned to other temporal intervals, behaving appropriately when tested on intervals of two days, three days, and five days.

It seems, then, that not only are there multiple forms of working memory, but that there are at least two varieties of long-term memory (explicit and implicit), and that explicit memory, in turn, sub-divides into semantic and episodic types. I shall discuss the further fractionation of semantic memory along domain-specific lines in Section 6.3. But first I shall review some of the varieties of implicit memory.

6.2 Forms of Implicit Memory

What do people mean when they talk about implicit memory? One of the leading researchers in the field, Schacter (1995), explains that implicit memory is revealed when and only when 'previous experiences facilitate performance on a task that does not require conscious or intentional recollection of those experiences.' But by this criterion many semantic memories, too, would count as implicit. I can know, for example, that the Battle of Hastings was fought in 1066 without being able to recall anything about the experiences via which I acquired this knowledge. Dienes and Perner (1999), in contrast, characterize the distinction by appeal to whether or not the information is carried by a proposition-like representation (an item of Mentalese), or whether it is implicit in a processing rule of some sort, instead. This is more plausible, but I doubt that it will cover motivational forms of implicit learning, to be discussed shortly. In fact it is probably a mistake to look for any single characterization of implicit memory. Rather, the term has been used to designate forms of acquired knowledge of very different types, as we shall see.

Retention of acquired skills and habits (both behavioral and cognitive) is one of the forms of implicit memory. And there is now robust evidence that this kind of memory dissociates from both semantic memory and epis-odic memory (Squire, 1992). Subjects suffering from retrograde amnesia may nevertheless retain previously acquired skills. And likewise people suffering from anterograde amnesia (who are incapable of learning new facts or forming new episodic memories) can still acquire new skills. Moreover, very different brain areas are implicated in skill acquisition from those that are involved in explicit learning. Skill learning is represented in the motor areas of the brain, in posterior frontal cortex (Karni, 1995). The storage and utilization of explicit knowledge, in contrast, utilizes the hippocampus in conjunction with anterior frontal cortex and the posterior and temporal lobes (Squire and Knowlton, 1995). Furthermore, Hikosaka et al. (2000) show how the pre-supplementary motor areas are implicated in the initial stages of skill acquisition, whereas the cerebellum and supplementary motor areas are active once the skill becomes well established.

Another form of implicit memory is priming. In one classic paradigm, people are given a list of words to study. Thereafter (following an interval whose length can be varied from experiment to experiment) they are given word stems and asked to utter the first completion of the stem that comes to mind—e.g. completing 'hor' to form 'horse'. Priming is then observed in the extent to which subjects tend to select a word-completion that is the same as one of the words studied in the previous list. The effect is robust, even when people have no explicit memory of the word having been on the list (Schacter and Buckner, 1998). Moreover, so-called 'levels of processing' manipulations that have an effect on explicit recall (such as having subjects judge the category of thing named by each word when studying the initial list) have no effect on priming, in most cases (Schacter, 1995).

In fact, different forms of priming can be distinguished—perceptual and conceptual. Word-stem completion is a perceptual task; whereas an otherwise-similar experimental setup in which subjects have quickly to offer an example of a presented category (e.g. saying 'duck' when presented with 'bird') is a conceptual task. Perceptual priming is specific to a given sense modality, and doesn't transfer across modalities. Thus when someone has *listened* to a list of words before completing a visual version of the stem-completion task, priming will not occur. And perceptual-priming effects can be influenced by minor factors within a given sense modality, too, such as changing the style of font in which the words / word-stems are written. Conceptual priming, in contrast, is modality independent, and is enhanced by 'deep' (semantic) processing of the items in the initial study phase (Hamman, 1990). It is thought that perceptual-priming effects are localized within the perceptual modules in question, whereas conceptual priming occurs within the so-called 'association areas' of the brain which deal with conceptual processing (Schacter, 1995).

One would expect that priming and skill memory should dissociate, given that they appear to utilize quite different regions of the brain (perceptual and association areas of the cortex in the case of priming, motor cortex in the case of knowledge of skills). And indeed they do (Salmon and Butters, 1995). Patients with Alzheimer's disease, who generally have damage to the ventral and posterior areas of the brain, show impairment of priming in word-stem completion tasks while displaying spared learning of new motor skills. In contrast, patients with Huntington's disease, which effects the motor system, show normal priming combined with impaired capacities to acquire new motor skills.

A third form of implicit memory that is frequently listed is classical conditioning (Squire, 1992). This is known, from work done with animals, to depend upon the amygdala (Cahill et al., 1995; Ledoux, 1996). Classical conditioning is independent of explicit memory, which depends instead upon the hippocampus, as we noted above. A double dissociation between the two forms of memory is described by Bechara et al. (1995). They tested three patients: one with damage localized to the amygdala, one with damage localized to the hippocampus, and one with damage to both regions. (They also used four normal controls.) All subjects were given a series of training trials in which they either looked at a colored slide or heard a tone. One of the four slides displayed, and one of the four tones, was always paired with a sudden unpleasant noise (a very loud boat horn). The subjects were later tested using the slides / tones alone, while their skin conductance was measured. They were also questioned about which colors / tones had been paired with the loud sound.

The patient with amygdala damage showed normal skin-conductance responses (indicative of emotion) to the sound of the horn during the initial training phase; but he failed to become conditioned to the color / tone that was paired with that sound. He could, however, clearly remember and report on the association. In contrast, the patient with hippocampal damage couldn't report which color or tone had been present when the horn sounded; but he showed a normal skin-conductance response when the conditioned stimulus was later presented. As expected, the patient with damage to both regions could neither remember the pairing between test items and the horn, nor did he acquire any conditioned skin-conductance response.

I argued in Section 4 that classical conditioning shouldn't properly be thought of as an associationist, non-cognitive, process. Rather, it involves the operations of one or more computational rate-estimation systems, working in conjunction with the motivational and emotional modules. And in Section 5 I argued that there are quite a number of the latter. These systems come with an 'appraisal' front-end, are capable of learning, and may also receive information generated by the belief-modules as input. It seems likely, then, that the amygdala plays a crucial part in the storage of information within a number of distinct emotional / motivational systems, where the information in question concerns the types of stimuli or circumstances that should issue in an emotional response.

However, the pre-frontal cortexes, too, form part of these emotional learning and response systems. This is nicely illustrated in an experiment by Bechara et al. (1997), undertaken with patients who had suffered damage to the pre-frontal lobes of the brain. (The same experiment again illustrates the dissociation between emotional learning and explicit knowledge.) Both patients and controls played a risky gambling game with four decks of cards. Turning a card yielded either a reward or a loss. Two of the decks were arranged to give a steady stream of small rewards and losses, leading to significant gains over time. The other two decks were set up to give occasional large rewards and large losses, leading to significant losses over time. But subjects weren't told which decks of cards were which. Their skin-conductance responses were measured, especially when they were just about to select a given card.

Normal subjects began to display anticipatory skin-conductance responses when they were about to turn over a card from one of the 'bad' decks *before* they had explicit knowledge of which decks were bad. It seems that their emotion systems had succeeded in learning the risky status of those decks, but that this knowledge wasn't accessible to the systems responsible for verbal report. Subjects with pre-frontal damage, in contrast, never displayed a skin-conductance response, even when they had finally figured out, and were able to say, which decks were good and which bad. But interestingly, this explicit knowledge had little impact on their actual choices—they tended to continue selecting from the 'bad' decks. (This point will loom large in Section 8, when we come to discuss Damasio's model of the role of emotion and emotional response in practical reasoning—see Damasio, 1994, 2003.)

It therefore seems that, in addition to two forms of explicit long-term memory (semantic and episodic), there are at least three varieties of implicit memory—there is memory for skills and habits, at least two different kinds of priming, and emotional / motivational memory. The latter, in turn, probably subdivides into a fair number of distinct varieties (one for each emotional or motivational module), in accordance with the general principle that information should be stored wherever it is generated and used.

6.3 Domain Specificity in Semantic Memory

Let me now return briefly to the case of semantic memory, examining evidence that this fractionates into a number of distinct memory systems.[20] In their extensive review of the extant clinical studies, Capitani et al. (2003) conclude that the data indicate at least that memory for animate living things, inanimate living things (e.g. fruits and vegetables), and artifacts / tools all dissociate from one another. They also conclude that there is significant evidence for the separate storage of knowledge of foodstuffs (whether living or processed), and body parts. Moreover, Mahon and Caramazza (2003) argue decisively that the hypothesis of domain-specific memory organization is the one best able

---

[20] Here the evidence is all drawn from studies done with humans. And we certainly shouldn't expect animal semantic memory systems to fractionate along the same lines as our own—for example, with a separate system devoted to knowledge of artifacts. Rather, we should expect the sub-divisions to correspond to domains that are evolutionarily significant for the species in question.

to account for the facts, contrasting it with a pair of non-domain-specific alternatives. And then in addition, besides reviewing and extending those arguments, Caramazza and Mahon (2005) review evidence that the category of conspecifics (other people) should be added to the list of dissociable memory domains.

There are thus brain-damaged patients who are impaired in their conceptual knowledge of animate living things, but normal in their knowledge of inanimate living things and non-living things. They will have difficulty naming different kinds of animal or demonstrating how those animals move, and will be unable to answer questions about their provenance and life history. But they show no comparable deficit for fruits and vegetables, or for artifacts. And conversely there are patients who are impaired in their conceptual knowledge of inanimate living things, while being normal in their knowledge of animals and artifacts. There are also patients whose knowledge of artifacts is differentially impaired. And there are patients who have lost the capacity to identify or state facts about famous people while other memories are intact, and while displaying no deficits in face perception as such.

In addition to showing how semantic memory fractionates along domain-specific lines, Caramazza and Mahon (2005) review evidence that each of these domain-specific systems in turn divides into a strictly conceptual 'central' memory store, and a more perceptually based, modality-specific, sub-system. Thus people can be poor at visual recognition of living things as compared with their recognition of non-living things, although their conceptual knowledge of the two domains is equivalent. And someone can be poor at recognizing faces but not visually presented objects, as well as the reverse: poor at recognizing objects but not faces.

There is also functional brain-imaging data that supports the conclusions reached above. Thus Chao et al. (1999) found that distinct regions of temporal cortex were active when subjects perceived, named, or thought about tools from when they engaged in similar activities concerning animals. And many other studies have reached similar conclusions—although not always unam-biguously, it should be stressed. (As always, real science is messy and difficult.) For a review, see Martin and Chao (2001).

If the principle that information should be stored where it is produced holds good in general (and applies to all forms of semantic memory in particular), then the thesis of massive mental modularity generates a clear empirical prediction. This is that there should exist a distinct and potentially dissociable semantic memory system in connection with each central / conceptual module. So in every case where a modularity theorist postulates the existence of a conceptual module (e.g. for mind-reading, or for reasoning about social norms—see Chapter 3), the prediction will be that there should be brain-damaged individuals who are impaired in their semantic knowledge of this one domain alone (as well as others who are damaged in other domains but not in this one). This prediction is consistent with the data that has been collected so far, as we have seen. But plainly there is much more clinical work here waiting to be done. Patient populations need to be located and investigated in ways that are guided by hypotheses about likely modular organization.

6.4 Rounding up

The evidence thus suggests that there are many different types of memory, many of which, in turn, fractionate into numerous sub-varieties. (See Figure 2.7.)[21] Thus there is a conscious working-memory system which utilizes the resources

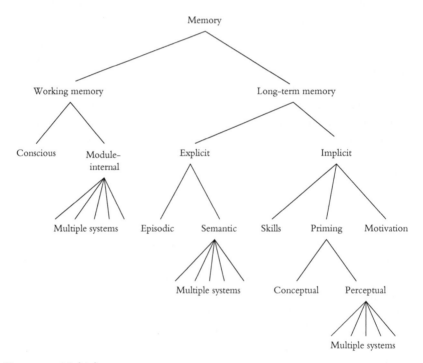

Figure 2.7. Multiple memory systems

[21] Note that only those memory systems are depicted for which evidence has been provided in the present section. In fact there is also evidence that within episodic memory, *recollection* and *recognition* involve distinct processes (Yonelinas, 2002); and as we saw in Chapter 1.3, each skill is likely to be realized in a distinct control system. Moreover, given that there are multiple motivational modules, we should expect there to be multiple forms of motivational memory, if the principle that information is stored where it is utilized holds good.

of a number of other processing systems, as well as numerous working-memory systems within those processing systems themselves, including the various perceptual modules. There are two basic forms of explicit long-term memory (episodic and semantic), the latter of which further fractionates along domain-specific lines. And then there are three or more forms of implicit memory—memory for skills and habits, a number of kinds of priming-memory located within the various perceptual and conceptual systems, and a variety of forms of emotional memory. Moreover, with the exception of the episodic memory system and the conscious working-memory system (which are relatively 'global' in their locations), each of these systems seems to be positioned in or near the areas of the brain where the corresponding forms of processing are effected. There is thus good reason to think that memory, like processing, is a massively modular phenomenon.

7 The Fragmentation of Action-Control

I have argued that there are multiple belief-modules, multiple desire-modules, and multiple memory systems in the minds of most animals, and certainly in the minds of our great-ape ancestors. In the present section and the one following I turn to the systems that determine action, considering whether they, too, divide up along modular lines.

7.1 Two Models of Practical Reason

How do beliefs and desires collectively determine action? One model is sketched in Carruthers (2002a, 2004a). On this account, there is a single practical-reasoning system. The various desire-generating modules compete with one another for access to this system. When the strongest desire wins out, and is received as input by practical reason, then the latter sets to work querying memory, querying the belief-generating modules, and accessing a motor-schema database in an attempt to find a way for that desire to be satisfied.

In a little more detail, as we saw in Chapter 1.7, the system is envisaged to work like this. It takes as input whatever is the currently strongest desire, for P. It then initiates a search for beliefs of the form, $Q \supset P$, cueing a search of memory for beliefs of this form and/or keying into action a suite of belief-forming modules to attempt to generate beliefs of this form. When it receives one, it checks a motor-schema database to see whether Q is something for which an existing motor schema exists. And if so, it initiates a search of the contents of current perception to see if the circumstances required to bring about Q are actual (i.e. to see, not only whether Q is something doable, but doable here and now). If so, it goes ahead and does it. If not, it initiates a further search for beliefs of the form, $R \supset Q$, and so on. Perhaps the system also has a simple stopping rule: if you have to go more than n number of conditionals deep, stop and move on to the next strongest desire.

My main goal in putting forward this model was to demonstrate that practical reasoning (or simple forms of practical reasoning, at least) can be implemented in computationally tractable ways. And I was concerned to show, in particular, that it needn't involve anything as computationally infeasible as calculations of expected utility across all of the animal's existing desires and beliefs. The idea was to allow *competition* between desires to absorb much of the computational cost, and then to utilize heuristics for searching memory systems that are organized along content-addressable lines, together with the parallel operations of a set of belief-generating modules, to absorb the rest.

One problem with this model is its sequential nature, however. In particular, the achievability of lower-ranking goals is only ever explored, on this account, once the currently highest-ranking desire has been deemed not satisfiable in present circumstances. But in many cases this is likely to lead to significant delays, and consequent lost opportunities. We would surely expect, in contrast, that *achievability* should be one of the factors that enters into the competition for the control of action. So we should expect that *all* of the animal's currently active desires (that is to say, the current outputs of the animal's motivation-generating modules) should be used to initiate searches, in parallel, for the means necessary for them to be satisfied, in something like the manner sketched above. The overall decision might then be made on a 'first come first served' basis; or there might be more complex algorithms that delay action somewhat when the race for achievability is won by a goal that is significantly less desirable than another, to give the stronger desire a chance to find a means to its own realization.

Gallistel (1980) develops a model of this latter sort. On this account there are motivational systems that control a range of types of behavior (e.g. mating, or foraging). Each of these can be decomposed into two sub-systems. One takes input from perception, stored knowledge, and bodily states (e.g. hormonal levels) and generates a motivational state. (These are the desire-generating systems described in Section 6 above.) And the other starts from the desire in question and attempts to recruit action schemata, perceptual information, belief-generating systems, and stored knowledge (beliefs) in such a way as to satisfy the desire. All of these systems are simultaneously in competition with one another to control the behavior of the organism. And the main point is that there is supposed to be a separate action-controlling module for each distinct type of motivational state. This module will have a range of action schemata that it looks at, and the addresses of particular types of stored information and/or information-generating modules that it should consult.[22]

If the model sketched by Carruthers (2002a, 2004a) is correct, then while the mind as a whole might be massively modular, the process of action-selection won't be. On the contrary, there will be a single system (a single module) that conducts this task. If the model outlined by Gallistel (1980) is correct, on the other hand, then the mind is massively modular all the way through, from input (perception), through belief-formation and desire-formation, to output (action-selection and motor-control).[23] A number of considerations suggest that Gallistel's model is actually the correct one.

7.2 The Case for Multiple Action-Controlling Systems

One point in favor of Gallistel's multiple-systems account has already been mentioned. The single-system model looks as though it would introduce a serious computational bottleneck, whereas multiple systems operating in parallel would be a great deal swifter and more efficient. Another consideration in the same general vein is this. On the single-system model there can be no constraints on the belief-modules from which information should be requested, or on the memory locations at which information should be searched for. And there should likewise be no constraints on the actions that can be performed in the service of any given goal. For the whole of the action-schemata database will need to be available to the practical-reason system to search. This wouldn't necessarily mean that such a system would be computationally intractable, since it might deploy a range of both innately fixed and learned heuristics to simplify its search strategies. But it does appear that the internal organization of the system would have to be quite complex to compensate.

On the multiple-systems account, in contrast, the different sub-systems can come with built-in restrictions on the modules to query and locations to search, as well as having a restricted set of action schemata available to them. (Such restrictions might either be innate or result from previous learning.)

---

[22] Someone *might* regard the *set* of action-controlling modules as the functional equivalent of an overall practical-reasoning module, and hence describe it as such. But it is really just a set of distinct modules that compete with one another. There are no more-general resources available to the overall 'system' that would want to make us call it a module in its own right—with the one exception, perhaps, of any algorithms that might be employed to determine the winner of the competition.

[23] Although our main focus is on action-selection here, it is worth noting that many researchers have proposed that motor-control systems, too—which are designed to control the detailed execution of selected actions on-line—are also divided up along massively modular lines. See Jacobs et al. (1991); Milner and Goodale (1995); Ghahramani and Wolpert (1997); Wolpert and Kawato (1998); Haruno et al. (2001).

The set of such action-selection systems operating in parallel would then look to be significantly faster and more computationally efficient (albeit somewhat less flexible) than the alternative single system. And the empirical evidence supporting the multiple-systems account turns on just this point, having to do with the inflexibility that animals display in the sorts of information that they can bring to bear in the service of their desires, and in the sorts of action that they can learn to execute in pursuit of those goals.

Consider the latter point first. Many animal motivational systems are quite restricted in the sorts of action schemata that they can recruit. There is the well-known point that you can't train a dog to retreat from food in order to obtain it—the hunger-desire seems to make the 'approach it' action schema mandatory. Likewise it is almost impossible to teach rats to jump to obtain food, while it is easy to get them to press a lever to obtain food; and conversely it is almost impossible to teach them to press a lever to avoid a shock, but easy to get them to jump to avoid a shock (Gould and Gould, 1994). Thus the desire to obtain food can only recruit action schemata that involve approaching and/or manipulating with the forepaws; whereas the desire to avoid something unpleasant happening beneath them can only recruit action schemata that involve leaping. And as Gould and Gould (1994) point out, this makes good ecological sense. In their natural environment rats obtain food by approaching it and manipulating it; and they avoid danger by leaping with their powerful hind legs.

Something similar holds true of pigeons. They can't be trained *not* to peck a key when it illuminates just before food is delivered nearby, even when the wiring is such that pecking the key *prevents* the delivery of food (Gould and Gould, 1994). And while it is easy to train them to peck at a key to obtain food, it is impossible to train them to hop to obtain food. Likewise, while it is easy to train them to hop to avoid a shock, it is impossible to train them to peck at a key to avoid shock. (Researchers who thought that they had succeeded in the latter training task were surprised to see, when opening up the box to observe the bird's actual behavior, that it was flapping its wings vigorously whenever it was about to be shocked, hitting the key with its wings; Gallistel, 1980.) And once again these restrictions on the action schemata that different desires can recruit make good ecological sense. Pigeons in their natural environment hop and fly to avoid danger, and peck to obtain seeds and other foods.

There are similar sorts of restrictions on the information that animals can be taught to utilize in pursuit of their goals. A hungry rat will utilize odor information in pursuit of food, but can't easily be taught to respond to colors or sounds. Pigeons, in contrast, can swiftly learn to utilize visual cues such as colors when searching for food, but can't be taught to respond to odors or sounds. When the pigeon's goal is to avoid a shock, on the other hand, it can easily learn to respond to sound as a cue. Again these restrictions make ecological sense, as Gould and Gould (1994) point out. Rats are nocturnal scavengers, and in their natural environment will rarely need to rely on visual or auditory cues to recognize food. Likewise the seeds that pigeons eat rarely have odors and never make sounds. But the dangers that pigeons face will often be associated with sounds.

Gallistel's model would appear to be warranted, therefore. There are different action-selection modules associated with different types of motivation. Each such system looks at a restricted database of action schemata that it can utilize, with the selection varying with the circumstances. (And these action schemata in turn, when activated, attempt to recruit more basic action schemata depending on the circumstances, and so on down through an action-control hierarchy of increasing fineness of grain.) And each such system has a restricted set of memory locations and/or belief-generating modules that it can access for information that it can use in pursuit of its goal—although if Gallistel (1980) is correct in claiming that spatial and temporal information is a mandatory aspect of *all* information storage, then all action-selecting modules will have at least *these* forms of information available to them.

7.3 Acting Without Thinking

There is another important factor in the generation of actions amongst mammals and birds that needs to be mentioned, which Gallistel (1980) calls 'the principle of autonomous build-up of action-specific potentiation'. Consider actions that are normally only performed as components of a larger action schema and in the service of another goal, such as running (in rats) or pouncing (in cats). Normally rats run when exploring a novel environment or in search of food; and cats pounce in the course of predatory behavior. But when these sorts of actions have not been performed for some time, there is a build-up of an intrinsic disposition to do so—in effect, creating a novel intrinsic desire.

Thus rats can, of course, learn to work by running on a wheel in order to obtain water or food. But equally they will learn, if they are prevented from running, to drink in order to run. And a cat that hasn't pounced for some time will work with considerable resourcefulness at patterns of action that finally yield something to pounce upon. Likewise Lorenz (1950) describes the case of a starling that had been caged for some weeks, and which had thus been unable to hunt. When released from its cage it exhibited the entire sequence of actions in its insect-hunting behavior. But there were no insects present, and the bird itself was fully fed.

The result is that many animals—and especially monkeys and apes—will spend significant amounts of time engaged in seemingly aimless mixing of behavioral fragments. We often describe this as 'play', although it is common in adult animals as well as in infants. One function might be to keep the actions themselves fine-tuned and efficiently performed, in readiness for their co-option into the service of a biologically important goal. But Schiller (1957) suggests another function, based on his analysis of the problem-solving abilities of the apes studied by Köhler (1927). This is that the jumbling of action components can create novel combinations, which can sometimes generate a reward of some sort. The latter can then stabilize the new combination in the animal's behavioral repertoire.

It is also worth noting that simple kinds of creative action are actually quite widespread in the animal kingdom, in the form of so-called 'Protean' erratic behavior (Driver and Humphries, 1988; Miller, 1997). Let me briefly elaborate. When a moth is hit by bat ultrasound (signaling a predator's approach) it will start to loop and tumble in a fashion that seems genuinely random and is wholly unpredictable; and this is actually a much more effective evasion technique than mere passive tumbling or a predictable (but faster) straight flight away (Roeder and Treat, 1961; Roeder, 1962; May, 1991). Such randomized escape behaviors are extremely common in the animal kingdom, and for good reason. For the best way to make your behavior unpredictable to a predator is somehow to make it genuinely unpredictable, period. It was for just this reason that submarine commanders in World War II would throw dice to determine the timings and directions of their zigzag travel paths, to make themselves unpredictable to submarine-hunting surface vessels.

Although animal actions are normally selected in the service of a current goal, therefore, through simple forms of planning, most animals also have ways of activating sequences of action schemata that *aren't* determined by prior thought and planning (but that aren't *fixed* action schemata, either, of the sort discussed in Section 1.2). Sometimes an action schema will be activated simply because it has been left dormant for a while. And sometimes (especially in the service of an escape goal) sequences of action schemata of a certain class will be activated in an unplanned fashion through some sort of randomizing process. These facts will prove to be of some importance for the account of distinctively human creativity of thought and action that I shall outline in Chapter 5.

8 Mental Rehearsal and Practical Reason

This section will have to be a little more speculative than the others. It draws on evidence of the role of mental rehearsal in human practical reasoning to suggest that the main elements of the arrangement are likely to be present in the other great apes and earlier forms of hominid. And it presents some behavioral evidence that supports this interpretation.

8.1 Self-Monitoring Models

According to the model of human practical reasoning provided by Damasio (1994), such reasoning proceeds, for the most part, through our monitoring our own emotional / bodily reactions to our thoughts concerning the options being considered. When making decisions we reason about our options and imagine various scenarios, of course. But the crucial component involves responding emotionally to those scenarios, monitoring these responses, and then using them to determine our decisions. (All emotional states come entrained with a suite of distinctive bodily changes, of course—such as the increases in heart-rate and breathing-rate characteristic of the 'fight or flight' response—and some theorists regard these as the very essence of what emotions are; Prinz, 2004.) For Damasio's frontally damaged patients can generally *reason* perfectly well on practical matters, making sensible considered judgments about what ought to be done, and when. But they fail to act on those judgments; and their lives as practical agents are a terrible mess. In Damasio's view, what has gone wrong is something to do with the somasensory self-monitoring system.[24]

A somewhat different account is presented by Schroeder (2004). (See also Rolls, 1999, for a related theory.) According to Schroeder, what we monitor isn't our *somatic* responses to our emotional and motivational states, but rather the pleasure and/or displeasure that is occasioned by such states. He argues that the basic determinants of desire satisfaction and desire frustration (which he identifies with the traditional psychological properties of *reward* and *punishment* respectively) are unconscious, and realized in activity deep amongst the more ancient parts of the brain. (Specifically, in the ventral tegmental area and the pars compacta of the substantia nigra within the mid-brain.) But these states are *represented* in the frontal cortex, in an area that appears to be the neural seat of pleasure and displeasure. (Specifically, in activity within the

---

[24] It is important to note that Damasio thinks that in addition to the monitoring of actual bodily responses, the practical-reasoning system can often operate in a swifter 'as if' mode, responding to *predicted* bodily responses before actual responses occur, or even if their occurrence is too fleeting to be detected. For the most part I shall ignore this further elaboration of Damasio's position in what follows, in order to simplify the discussion.

perigenual region of anterior cingulate cortex.) And it is these hedonic states that we monitor when making decisions.

For my purposes it doesn't matter much which of these two accounts is endorsed. For both are agreed that the basic determinants of motivation are unconscious and realized in ancient parts of the brain. And both are agreed that these motivational states have effects that are represented and monitored in the frontal cortices, which is the seat of so-called 'executive functions' (Passingham, 1993; Geary, 2005). Whether what is monitored are hedonic states of pleasure and displeasure, representing states of desire satisfaction and frustration, or rather a wider set of bodily responses to satisfaction and frustration (or both), essentially the same sort of self-monitoring decision-making architecture would seem to be involved.

Here is how we might flesh out these accounts a bit within a massively modularist framework. We can suppose (as I have been arguing in this chapter) that there are a whole suite of belief-generating and desire-generating modular systems. And the latter, in particular, have been designed to take both perceptual and conceptual inputs of various sorts, perhaps combining those with knowledge stored in module-specific databases, in order to generate appropriate motivational states of varying strengths. Then consider a case where I have some goal, for P, and am considering whether or not to perform some action, Q, in pursuit of that goal. If the supposition, *that I do* Q, can somehow be 'globally broadcast' (see below), then it will be received as input by the various desire-generating systems, and they will be keyed into action. Hence if doing Q is itself something desirable, then an appropriate desire will be generated, conditional on the original supposition. But by being globally broadcast, the supposition that I do Q will also be taken as input by the various belief-forming modules. Some of these may generate further predictions of the form, $Q \supset R$. In which case R, too, can in turn be taken as input by the desire-forming modules, issuing in positive or negative (or neutral) motivational states, again still conditional on the supposition that I do Q. What we have to do next is monitor our somatic / emotional / hedonic responses to the imagined outcomes. And some sort of mechanism must then operate to sum across these various responses, either diminishing or extinguishing the attractiveness of the original goal, or strengthening it still further.

Notice that this sort of process of mental rehearsal and self-monitoring has the resources necessary to overcome one of the inflexibilities present in animal decision-making that we reviewed in Section 6.2, enabling information relevant to a given goal to be accessed that wouldn't otherwise be available. Consider, for example, a rat in a conditioning experiment. On some occasions in the past when the rat has pressed a lever, food has been delivered; but on most occasions pressing the lever has got the rat nothing. In fact those successful actions occurred when a bell had sounded shortly before the lever-press; but this information isn't available in the service of the rat's desire for food. When the rat is hungry, information about food odors is accessed (but in the circumstances no such information is available that is of any use), as is information about previously successful actions—in this case, pressing the lever; but information about colors and sounds is never looked for.

So there the rat is in the conditioning box, with a problem: it has no idea *when* to press the lever. So the rat's only real option is to keep on pressing at random. But suppose that it had the capacity mentally to *rehearse* the action of pressing the bar, and were to try this out a few times. On one such occasion the rat's rehearsal occurs shortly after the bell has rung. This rehearsal is globally broadcast to all central / conceptual systems (not just those that would normally be recruited by hunger), including some that contain the information that bar-pressings paired with a ringing bell have yielded food in the past. This information is activated and used to generate an image of food for global broadcasting. This is made available to the hunger motivational system, which responds as if to a reward. If the rat could now utilize its awareness of that response, cranking up the attractiveness of pressing the bar right now to the point of doing it, then it would be successful in getting the food delivered: problem solved.

Notice that the way in which mental rehearsal introduces additional flexibility isn't by means of constructing some sort of novel *lingua franca* that enables previously isolated systems to talk to one another. Rather, by utilizing the global broadcast of perceptual information to all belief-generating and desire-generating modules, mental rehearsal is able to co-opt the resources of those modules sequentially. The globally broadcast image of a bar-press combined with the sound of a bell are taken as input by some system that can generate the prediction that in this case food would be made available for eating. (This is a system that couldn't previously be accessed in the service of the desire to eat, and still can't, in any direct manner.) That in turn generates a rehearsed image which, when taken as input by a desire-module, results in a motivational reaction. The latter, when sensed, raises the desirability of pressing the bar to the point where the action gets performed. None of this requires cross-module talking that couldn't already happen before.

How plausible is it that some such system as this might exist in non-human animals? I shall discuss in Sections 8.2 and 8.3 some behavioral data from apes and earlier species of hominid that are quite naturally interpreted in this light. Let me first stress here, however, that virtually all of the *components* of the mental rehearsal and self-monitoring systems described by Damasio (1994), Rolls (1999), and Schroeder (2004) are, almost certainly, present in other animals besides ourselves. Recall from Section 2.3 our account of the functions of the back-projecting neural pathways in the two visual systems that are used in humans to generate visual images. Those pathways in the ventral / temporal visual system are there to help with object-recognition and categorization (Kosslyn, 1994). And the corresponding pathways in the dorsal / parietal system are there to help fine-tune the on-line guidance of action (Wolpert and Ghahramani, 2000; Wolpert et al., 2003). Since a great many animals are capable of sophisticated object-recognition, and since many are capable of skilled action, we should expect that the very same back-projecting pathways will be present. (As indeed they are.)

Let me focus, here, on the back-projecting pathways in the dorsal / parietal system, since it is these that are crucially implicated in mental rehearsal of action. They can be used to underpin two different kinds of mental rehearsal, with distinct functions. One of these is unconscious and the other is conscious (at least in the sense of being globally broadcast; Baars, 1988, 1997).[25] Consider the unconscious kind first. This occurs internally within the dorsal / parietal visual system, when efferent copies of activated motor schemata are projected back to meet and match the incoming perceptual information while the movement is being executed. Failures of match will allow the agent to respond extremely swiftly to changes in the expected conditions and/or the expected trajectory of the action, as when the object towards which one is reaching is moved (Castiello et al., 1991; Milner and Goodale, 1995). Many, many, species of animal will deploy their visual system in just such a way.

The second form of rehearsal occurs when the projection back from an activated motor schema is used to generate a visual image of the action within the ventral / temporal visual pathway, perhaps via the ventro-dorsal bridge between the two systems (see Figure 2.5). (Alternatively, the efferent copy of the motor schema can be sent elsewhere to generate a proprioceptive / motor image for global broadcasting.) This image, if it is sufficiently vivid, will then be globally broadcast by the ventral system in the manner of a conscious perception, and will be taken as input by the full suite of belief-generating and desire-generating modules. Some of those belief-generating modules may predict further consequences flowing from the action, and these can then be added to the image using the back-projecting pathways within the

---

[25] According to the account of consciousness developed by Carruthers (2000, 2005), global broadcasting of perceptual information is necessary but not sufficient for phenomenal consciousness. This point is irrelevant for present purposes, however.

ventral / temporal system.[26] And some of the desire-generating modules may produce an emotional / motivational reaction to the unfolding scenario being envisaged. This reaction will produce a suite of physiological and hedonic changes of various sorts, many of which will be detected by the somasensory systems. (See Figure 2.8.)

It seems plain that all of the main elements needed for this second—more sophisticated—form of mental rehearsal are present in primates, at least. For we know that they can make the requisite mappings between action and perception, through the 'mirror neuron' system (Rizzolatti et al., 2000; Gallese et al., 2002). And primates surely possess well-developed somasensory systems. The only real questions are whether primates utilize mental rehearsal for purposes of decision-making, and whether they have the necessary mechanisms for summing across their detected somasensory and/or hedonic responses. Before we turn to that question, however, it is worth noticing that the mental rehearsal and global broadcast of intended actions will create a sort of virtual, multiple-system-involving, working-memory system, very similar in character to that discussed in Section 6.1 above. So if primates, too, utilize mental rehearsal, then working memory is unlikely to be restricted to humans.

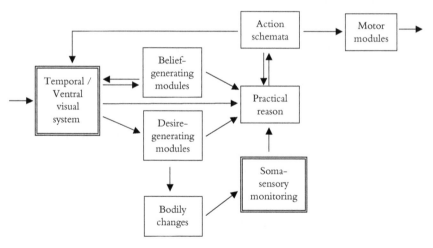

Figure 2.8. Mental rehearsal and somasensory monitoring

---

[26] Note that this means that many of the processes involved in the generation and transformation of images will be *inferential* in character, utilizing knowledge and resources from outside the visual system itself, just as Pylyshyn (2003) argues. But this is perfectly consistent with the claim that those images themselves are realized in the mechanisms of the visual system, and are globally broadcast in the manner normal for the products of that system.

8.2 *Step One: Simple Mental Rehearsal*

Recall Belle, the chimpanzee from Section 3.5 who was a frequent subject in Menzel's (1974) food-hiding experiments. And consider a case where she stops and sits down some distance before reaching the food. Why does she do this? The obvious answer is that she knows that once she reaches the location of the food the male will attack her, push her aside, and take the food for himself; and she doesn't want those things to happen. But we can dig a little deeper and ask how these items of knowledge, and these desires, come to be activated in the first place if her mind is organized along modular lines. For at the outset of the sequence, presumably, only Belle's desire for the food was activated, which was able to access her knowledge of the food's location and recruit an action schema (walking) necessary to get her to that location. And at that stage neither the presence of the male, nor her previous beatings, need have been at all salient.

Our question can be answered if we suppose that Belle was capable of at least a simple form of mental rehearsal. Suppose that when activating her walking-to-the-location-of-the-food-and-uncovering-it action schema, she used it to generate a visual and/or motor image of herself doing just those things. This image was globally broadcast. When taken as input by her motivational systems, it created a feeling of satisfaction at the thought of herself consuming the food. But the same image was also taken as input by her belief-generating systems, one of which came up with the prediction, based on past experience, that the male would follow her, attack her, and take the food for himself. These elements were added to her image, and the result was again globally broadcast. When taken as input by her desire-generating systems, this caused her to feel fear at the thought of the attack, and disappointment at the loss of the food. She sensed these emotional states in herself, and that was sufficient to abort the action-sequence on which she had initially embarked. So she ceased to approach the food, and sat down instead.

A similar rehearsal-based explanation can be given of instances of medium-term planning in chimpanzees. Consider the chimpanzees of the Congo basin, for example, who have been videotaped making regular visits to a number of termite mounds over a wide area (Sanz et al., 2004; see also Mulcahy and Call, 2006). In order to harvest from subterranean nests they use two kinds of tool in combination: a strong stick to puncture the mound, and then a frond to dip for termites through the hole that they have made. (Above-ground nests can be harvested using just a dipping-frond and a twig to open up the termite holes.) Chimpanzees were never observed to arrive at a subterranean nest without the requisite tools, unless there was already a puncturing-stick at the site. (Dipping-fronds decay too quickly to be left at a site and reused on a later visit. These were always carried on arrival.) But puncturing-sticks are always constructed from the same type of tree, and frequently the closest tree of that type was tens of meters away through the forest, from which point the termite mound wasn't visible. So we can be confident that these are instances of advance planning.

How is such planning cognitively realized? A plausible account can be given in terms that involve mental rehearsal. When the chimpanzee's desire to eat termites is activated,[27] a search of memory is conducted for appropriate locations, and for information on the timing of recent visits. One of the nearest not-recently-visited locations is selected, and the animal sets off towards it. As the chimpanzee travels, she activates (for purposes of rehearsal only) the motor schemata for the various action-sequences that are needed to reach termites in a subterranean nest, including the act of approaching the nest and puncturing it. This is transformed into a visual and/or motor image and globally broadcast, reminding her that she needs to have a puncturing-stick in her hand. This creates a novel sub-goal (to carry such a stick), which in turn initiates a search for the information and motor schemata necessary to achieve it. Since she doesn't recall leaving a puncturing-stick at the nest site, but does recall the location of a nearby tree of the appropriate type, she now adjusts her direction of travel towards that.

In both of the examples described above, the role of mental rehearsal is to recruit existing items of knowledge, as well as the operations of the complete range of belief-generating and desire-generating mechanisms, in the service of a goal. By mentally rehearsing the action already decided upon and either about to be or currently being undertaken, and transforming it into an image that is globally broadcast to all belief-generating and motivation-generating systems, new beliefs and new emotional reactions are activated. This can either lead to the abandonment of the initial action (in the case of Belle), or to the addition of novel, not initially planned-for, actions (making a detour to collect a puncturing-stick).

8.3 Step Two: Creative Mental Rehearsal

Each of the examples above involves what one might think of as an *analytic* use of practical reason. The animal reasons backwards from a goal in search

---

[27] How does this happen? Plausibly this, too, involves mental rehearsal. (After all, there need be nothing in the context to remind her of termites and elicit a desire, since the nearest nest may be some kilometers away.) Think how we ourselves decide what to seek out to eat when hungry when there is no food visible. We imagine ourselves eating a number of things and substances that we have eaten in the past, and monitor our bodily / appetitive / hedonic reaction to each (watering mouth, and so on), while at the same time recalling information about accessibility.

of actions that might be sufficient to achieve that goal. (Compare the sort of planning undertaken by jumping spiders, discussed in Section 1.) In the first of the above examples (Belle), an initial means of achieving the goal is discovered, on a second pass through using mental rehearsal, to be *in*sufficient. And in the second example, mental rehearsal is used to turn a one-step plan ('Go to dig up termites') into a two-step one ('First get a puncturing stick'). But many practical problems can't be solved in such a manner. Often there is no obvious way of working back from the goal to something that one can do here-and-now to achieve it. Indeed, this was precisely Belle's problem. She needed to reason 'synthetically' or creatively.

How, then, did she eventually hit upon her successful solution (going to dig in the wrong place)? I suggest that the best available explanation is that she used mental rehearsal creatively—not activating action schemata already decided upon (as in the examples in Section 8.2), but trying out some related actions via mental rehearsal, to explore where they might lead. In fact, having abandoned her original plan, Belle may have mentally rehearsed going to dig in another, foodless, spot. (Where this idea might come from will be discussed in a moment.) When this new action schema is activated for purposes of rehearsal, the schema's normal outcome (action) needs to be suppressed, of course. Rather, it gets transformed into an image of herself walking to a particular spot from her current location, and beginning to dig. This image is globally broadcast in the manner of perception generally, and received as input by her belief-generating and desire-generating modules. One of these comes up with the prediction that the male will follow her and push her aside when she begins to dig, taking over the digging himself.

This information in turn is used to generate an appropriate image for global broadcasting, using the feedback connections from conceptual forms of representation to perceptual ones (normally used in object-recognition and in the activation of episodic memories; Kosslyn, 1994). Another module, receiving this new input, then comes up with the prediction that the male will be preoccupied while digging, and will no longer be likely to follow her. (One of the behavioral generalizations that she is already likely to have learned is that busy individuals seldom interfere with what others are doing.) This serves to create a new imagined standpoint (herself having just been pushed aside, with the male busily digging nearby) from which, when she reactivates the original desired action schema (walking from the new standpoint to where the food really is, digging it up, and consuming it), she no longer foresees any undesirable consequences. So she now has a workable plan, which she sets about implementing.

In this sort of 'synthetic' practical reasoning, then, how should we imagine that the choices get made amongst further action schemata to activate, once the initial mentally rehearsed action is predicted to end unsuccessfully? My guess is that the choice is partly, but by no means completely, random. It might surely be influenced by similarities with the initial (now rejected) schema—so instead of walking to dig *here* she rehearses walking to dig *there*. And it might also be a function of salience in the current physical and motivational context—so she might rehearse climbing a particular palm tree because it is salient in her field of vision (this wouldn't get her any advantage, of course), or she might rehearse attacking the male because her initial rehearsal, which ends in the prediction that he will push her aside, generates anger towards him (again this is likely to get her nothing).

The suggestion, in effect, is that creative generation of action schemata gets driven by associative processes of one sort or another. Schemata that are *similar to* the failed one are activated and rehearsed (e.g. walking to dig, but in a different spot); schemata that share conceptual components with salient beliefs about her environment (e.g. TREE) are activated and rehearsed; and further schemata that are primed by her current motivational state (in addition to consuming the food) are rehearsed (attacking the male out of anger). The process is one in which the outputs of various belief-generating and desire-generating modules are in a sort of associative competition with one another to activate and rehearse related action schemata. And there is no reason to think that the processes involved—simple as they are—shouldn't be computationally tractable.

It is tempting to suppose that the creative mental rehearsal of action schemata might build upon and adapt either the principle of autonomous build-up of action potentiation or the capacity for 'Protean' action-generation, which were discussed in Section 7.3. As we noted, many animals will perform actions and action-fragments in seemingly random combination, sometimes hitting upon useful novel combinations. And many will combine actions in random sequences when fleeing from a predator. When the capacity for mental *rehearsal* of action emerges in evolution, these dispositions might be harnessed and altered in such a way as to allow the animal to generate and try out in imagination novel combinations of action that are either random, or are in one way or another primed by the context.

Notice that creative mental rehearsal has the resources to solve the other aspect of animal inflexibility of action identified in Section 7.2. (The failure to recruit relevant beliefs can be solved through *un*creative rehearsal, as we saw in Section 8.1.) This is that particular goals normally have a restricted range of action schemata that they can recruit and activate. Consider a rat in an experimental setup where it has learned that the sound of a bell predicts that a painful shock will be applied to its feet shortly thereafter. So when the bell rings the rat jumps, but this doesn't get it away from the floor for long enough to avoid the shock. Sometimes (by accident, perhaps) the rat has pressed a lever shortly after the bell has rung, and a shock *hasn't* been delivered. But the rat's pain-avoiding goal only looks at a restricted repertoire of potential actions, and pressing a lever with its forepaws isn't on the list.

But now suppose that the rat were to have the power of creative generation and rehearsal of action schemata. So there it is when the bell rings, desperately casting around for something to do to avoid the pain. (It knows that jumping doesn't work.) The rat activates and rehearses action schemata from its repertoire of potential actions at random, or primed by prominent features of its situation. Since the lever is salient in an otherwise featureless cage, perhaps this might lead it to rehearse the action of bar-pressing (often used in the past to obtain food). A visual or motor image of this action is globally broadcast, and one of the rat's belief-generating modules generates the prediction that no shock will be delivered. When taken as input by the motivational modules, this causes it to feel relief, and in consequence it presses the bar. Again, problem solved.[28]

Note, too, that the synthetic mode of operation of practical reason comes with somasensory monitoring of bodily / emotional / hedonic reactions to envisaged actions, and requires some mechanism in place for fixing the eventual level of motivation in the light of that monitoring. I claim that when we get to this stage, there *is* good reason to think of the set of action-controlling modules as collectively constituting an overarching practical-reasoning module. For there is now more than just competition amongst the components. Rather, there are general mechanisms for adjusting motivation levels up or down in the light of somasensory information resulting from mentally rehearsed action schemata. And creative activation of action schemata means that any such schema is now potentially recruitable in the service of a given goal.

---

[28] As previously, it should be stressed that the extra flexibility that would be introduced here doesn't result from any new *lingua franca* that enables previously isolated modules to communicate. Rather, mental rehearsal recruits existing channels of communication to generate a motivation to perform an action that is within the rat's repertoire (a bar-press) where no motivation would have existed previously.

8.4 Hominid Mental Rehearsal

I believe that my mental-rehearsal-based explanation of creative—or 'insight-ful'—behaviors in chimpanzees and other apes is a plausible one.[29] It is even more plausible that some earlier species of hominid were capable of this sort of mildly creative practical reasoning. The stone-tool making abilities of earlier hominids has already been mentioned in Section 3.4, where they were cited as evidence of the sophisticated causal knowledge and understanding that such hominids possessed. Here I want to use these abilities to argue also for the 'synthetic', or creative, planning capacities of those earlier species.

A number of authors have stressed the cognitive difficulties involved in making the symmetrical hand-axes and blades that were being produced by members of *Homo ergaster* from about 1.4 million years ago (Gowlett, 1984; Pelegrin, 1993; Mithen, 1996, 2002; Schlanger, 1996; Wynn, 2000). Many of these items possess a fine three-dimensional symmetry that was plainly intended (Wynn, 2000). And it is often the case that hand-axes from the same assemblage or from the same region conform to a similar pattern. So it is evident that their makers started out with a clear idea of the intended product, and that in some sense planning was involved. Moreover, we now know quite a lot about how hand-axes were made, both from the testimony of contemporary knappers who have succeeded in reproducing them (Pelegrin, 1993), and from processes of painstaking reconstruction in those rare instances where a completed hand-axe has been found together with the waste-flakes left over from its manufacture (Schlanger, 1996).

What we know is that it is impossible to produce such an artifact by reasoning purely 'analytically'. Even if the whole production process is well-practiced and familiar, there is generally no way to work back from the desired finished product to what one should do first (nor to what one should do at many of the intermediate stages, either). For the stone cores from which the production process starts are always to some degree unique in shape, size, and the details of their material composition; hence each core presents a unique challenge.

---

[29] If the explanation is correct, then it predicts that chimpanzees shouldn't display the sorts of inflexibility of action that are found in other mammals and birds (or not nearly so much). For as we saw in Sections 8.1 and 8.3, an animal with the power of creative mental rehearsal should be capable of recruiting any belief that it has, and any action schema in its repertoire, in the service of a given goal. I believe that there are presently no data to enable us to say whether or not this prediction is correct (personal communication: Dick Byrne, Randy Gallistel, Juan Carlos Gomez, Daniel Povinelli, Peter Smith, and Andy Whiten). But the *absence* of such data is at least suggestive, given how intensively chimpanzees have been studied.

Even an experienced knapper must pause at a number of different stages in the production process to visualize the next goal (such as the preparation of a small ledge, or 'striking platform', which can be used to dislodge a larger flake from the core), and he has to try out in imagination various potential strikes, or sequences of strike, that might achieve that goal.

In effect, the stone-knapper must continually be entertaining thoughts of the form, 'Suppose I struck it *there* like *that*; or suppose I struck it *here* instead, like *this*.'[30] He will thus be rehearsing a number of different action schemata and monitoring the predicted results, sometimes then rotating his visual image of the resulting core to see what it would look like from the other side (Wynn, 2000). So we can conclude, then, that at least some limited capacity for creative thought would have been present in the minds of our hominid ancestors, prior to the evolution of *Homo sapiens*. Specifically, our ancestors had the capacity to 'try out' a number of different action schemata in visual imagination, hence making those supposed actions available as input to the full range of belief-generating, desire-generating, and action-selecting systems, and thus recruiting the activity of those systems into the service of the intended goal.

9 Conclusion

I have argued that animal minds are massively modular in their organization. Basic forms of perception / belief / desire / planning / motor-control psychology have been around for many, many, millions of years, and are possessed even by some invertebrates. Many animals have modularly organized perceptual systems, including a basic division between systems that subserve conceptual thought and those that subserve on-line guidance of action. And all such animals have multiple belief-generating systems, desire-generating systems, memory systems, and action-selecting systems (as well as multiple movement-controlling systems, too). Moreover, at least some other animals (including perhaps some or all primates, but at least including earlier species of hominid) are capable of engaging in *cycles* of module-based cognitive activity. They can mentally rehearse potential actions, and monitor and make further use of the cognitive and motivational results.

---

[30] Let me stress that I don't mean to imply, here, that such thoughts must be entertained in natural language. On the contrary, as we will see in more detail in Chapter 5, I believe that creative thought is possible in the absence of language, even if it is greatly enhanced and extended by the presence of language. Rather, the thoughts in question will be realized in mental rehearsals of actions from the agent's repertoire.

The main argument for the massively modular organization of animal minds takes the form of an inference to the best explanation of the behavioral data. Animals display quite a remarkable range of abilities for learning, and for forming adaptive desires. It isn't remotely plausible that all of these abilities should be underpinned by some sort of general associative conditioning device. (Moreover, the fact that some animals excel in just some of these tasks, whereas others don't, counts directly against such a suggestion.) Indeed, the evidence suggests that even conditioning behaviors are better explained as resulting from the operations of a specialized rate-estimation module, working in conjunction with different goals and action schemata. And given that the computational demands of the learning / acquisition tasks are very different in different cases, it is highly plausible that there should be *different* acquisition devices specialized for the distinct tasks. (And even in those cases where a number of different learning tasks might each be subserved by a similar sort of statistical learning mechanism, then—provided that those tasks are sometimes faced simultaneously—the argument from design of Chapter 1 suggests that we should expect *multiple* such devices to exist, one for each adaptively different acquisition problem. I shall return to this point in Chapter 3.2.)

Given that animal minds are organized along massively modular lines, then normal biological reasoning should lead us to expect that massively modular architectures will be preserved in the minds of members of *Homo sapiens*, too. And we now have some specific suggestions about what that core architecture should look like (see Figures 2.5 and 2.8), together with a range of likely belief-generating and desire-generating modules contained within it. In Chapter 3 I shall consider some further modules that appear to have been added to that pre-existing architecture in the course of the transition to contemporary *Homo sapiens* from the last common ancestor of ourselves and the other great apes. Then in the remaining chapters of the book our challenge will be to show how distinctively flexible and creative human cognition can arise out of the operations of, and interactions between, those components.

3

Modules of the Human Mind

In this chapter I shall consider some of the modules that may have been added (or lost) in the transition from the minds of our great-ape common-ancestors to ourselves. I will argue that there have been multiple additions. So what is distinctive of the human mind isn't just a single new module. Nor is it just an increase in general-learning capacity resulting from enlargements in brain size, or the addition of some sort of a-modular general-purpose problem solver. Without making very firm claims as to the details, I shall sketch some of the likely new modules, and the ways in which they fit into the overall architecture of cognition inherited from other animals. Our task in the chapters that follow will be to show how distinctively flexible and creative human cognition can emerge out of the operations of such a massively modular mind.

The chief goals of this chapter, then, are similar to those of Chapter 2. One is to complete the argument for the massively modular organization of the human mind, begun in Chapter 1 and continued through Chapter 2. The other is to extend our sketch of the functional organization of mammalian and great-ape minds to include some of the likely new human components. But in the present chapter the balance will be somewhat different. I take it that the main case for massive modularity has now been made (in Chapters 1 and 2), and should be accepted unless there are convincing arguments to the contrary. (Some of these arguments will be considered in Section 1 of the present chapter.) Our more important task is to outline the materials that we have to work with when explaining the distinctive flexibility of the human mind. (The latter will form the topic of Chapters 4 through 7.)

Concerning some of these novel human components—e.g. the language faculty, or the mind-reading faculty—there now exist *immense* bodies of literature. I can't attempt anything like a full review and discussion here, but will say just enough to subserve my present purposes. Nor shall I try very hard to argue that these capacities are realized in mental modules, attempting to convince those who believe otherwise. For given the framework laid out in Chapters 1 and 2, this should be our default assumption, to be accepted in the absence of convincing arguments to the contrary.

1 Against the 'One Major New Adaptation' Hypothesis

Human minds seem quite remarkably different from the minds of non-human animals, and even from the minds of our nearest cousins, the other great apes (chimpanzees, gorillas, and orangutans). Most theorists have tended to focus on just one innate human faculty in order to explain the difference. For example, they have appealed to our capacity for language (Bickerton, 1990, 1995), or to our capacity for mind-reading and social cognition (Dunbar, 2000), or to our capacity for imitation and cultural learning (Tomasello, 1999). In one way, this can seem like a laudable preference for simplicity: don't look for multiple strands of explanation when one will do. But actually, appeals to simplicity should cut little ice in the biological realm. On the contrary, we should expect biological systems to be messy and complicated, full of exaptations and smart kludges. And in any case, the resulting accounts are singularly implausible. I shall say a little about each of these proposals in turn.

1.1 Just One Adaptation? A Preliminary Discussion

If language is held to be the one crucial difference between ourselves and other animals, then the distinctive human capacities for mind-reading, for causal reasoning, and for imitative learning all have to be explained in terms of language. But language can't be *sufficient* for mind-reading, at any rate (even when combined with forms of learning shared with other animals), since autistic people can have normal linguistic ability while retaining a deficit in mind-reading. Nor does it appear to be necessary, since even severe aphasia can leave mind-reading abilities (as well as causal reasoning abilities) fully intact (Varley, 1998, 2002).[1] And it is even less likely that language should be responsible for our imitative abilities.

---

[1] Might language nevertheless be *developmentally* necessary for mind-reading? There are no data that speak directly to this topic. For in many cases of long-term absence of language, such as Genie (Curtiss, 1977), development is abnormal in many other ways too, resulting from general abuse. And although deaf children who learn language late tend to be delayed on mind-reading tasks, this is consistent with a view that sees the interpretation of speech as a powerful, and strongly motivating, mind-reading challenge, helping to strengthen the development of the latter without being *necessary* for its development (Siegal and Surian, 2006). Moreover, the excellent non-linguistic communicative abilities (e.g. through pantomime) of deaf people who lack any language beyond their own invented form of

Likewise if mind-reading is taken to be basic, then the human language faculty has to result from some combination of mind-reading and forms of learning that we share with our great-ape cousins. But the autistic case tells strongly against this hypothesis also, since autistic people can develop normal language abilities (in respect of everything but pragmatics), while retaining a mind-reading deficit. Moreover, there is now an immense body of data and theory suggesting that language is a relatively autonomous and partially innate faculty of the mind (Pinker, 1994).

Similar points tell against the suggestion that imitative ability might be the one crucial distinguishing mark of the human mind. If this were so, then the human capacities for language, for 'deep' causal reasoning, and for mind-reading, would all have to be explicable in terms of imitation. But none of these suggestions is remotely plausible. The idea that language might result from imitation combined with forms of learning held in common with animals ought surely to have died with Skinner, for example (Chomsky, 1959; Pinker, 1994).

In addition to being intrinsically implausible, the 'one new adaptation' account is inconsistent with the conclusion of the arguments from complexity and from learning, outlined in Chapter 1. (It probably conflicts with the argument from computational frugality, too, which was also outlined in that chapter. For there are just too many different tasks that such a system would have to perform.) We should expect that there are *multiple* cognitive adaptations distinguishing us from the other great apes, just as there are multiple physical ones (opposable thumbs, upright gait, hairlessness, sweat glands, increased brain size, decreased gut size, concealed ovulation, and menopause, to name but a few).

One argument used in support of the 'one new adaptation' hypothesis is that there hasn't been enough *time* for multiple mental modules to evolve in the 5–7 million years that have elapsed since our ancestral line divided from that of the other great apes (Tomasello, 1999). But it is left quite unclear why more time should be required for the evolution of cognitive than for physiological differences, which are myriad, as we have just noted. On the contrary, there are some additional factors that might speed the evolution of multiple cognitive differences—such as statistical reasoning packages that can be copied many times and put to work in the service of distinct capacities in different domains (Marcus, 2004), or the evolution of new cognitive adaptations by runaway sexual selection amongst hominids capable of mind-reading (Miller, 2000).

'home sign' is strong evidence that at least many of the elements of mind-reading can develop normally in the absence of language (Schaller, 1991; Goldin-Meadow and Zheng, 1998).

Another argument used, is that there aren't enough genetic differences between ourselves and chimpanzees to code the details of a whole new suite of mental modules. And at this point the claim that we share 98.5 percent of our genes with chimpanzees is often deployed (Churchland and Sejnowski, 1992; Elman et al., 1996). But this argument makes multiple errors. One is the assumption that massive modularists need to be committed to the discredited 'blueprint model' of the way in which genes code for biological structure. One the contrary, massive modularists can embrace fully the 'recipe model', which stresses that genes only ever operate in complex developmental interactions with their environments. And there is no question of us needing to claim that the position of each neuron, dendrite, and synaptic connection needs to be separately coded for, or anything so absurd. On the contrary, as Marcus (2004) demonstrates, a relatively small number of genes can be used to build whole new banks of neurons, with novel patterns of connectivity.

In any case the figure of 98.5 percent probably vastly underestimates the genetic differences between ourselves and chimpanzees. One reason is that even when genes are indistinguishable, they can be spliced differently in different species during the process of transcription. Indeed, recent research suggests that a significant source of diversity amongst mammals lies in species-specific alternative splicings of genetic sequences (Pan et al., 2005). Another reason for doubt is that the figure of 98.5 percent only includes base-pair substitutions. When insertions and deletions are also included, the differences between humans and chimpanzees are much more significant, yielding a figure closer to 87 percent in common (Anzai et al., 2003). And most importantly, the quoted figure only concerns protein-coding genes. But we now know that much of the DNA previously regarded as 'junk' is actually involved in *regulating* the gene-expression of particular genes or sets of genes. And when one looks specifically at sequences of DNA known to be involved in gene regulation, what emerges is that the differences between chimpanzees and humans are of the order of 15 percent (Ebersberger et al., 2002). So there is no question but that there are plenty of materials, here, with which to explain the existence of multiple species-unique mental modules in humans.

Other lines of reasoning in the same general spirit as the 'one major adaptation' argument are a bit more nuanced, suggesting that perhaps *some* distinctive capacities evolved piecemeal over the first five million years of human evolution, including increased social capacities, increased abilities to understand physical objects (especially the fracture-dynamics of rocks), and an increased ability to learn about the living world. But such people point to the immense stasis that exists in the fossil record until very recently—with stone-tool designs remaining virtually unchanged for hundreds of thousands of years, but with an explosion of change, and in human creative and symbolic abilities, around 40,000 years ago. They therefore argue that there was perhaps a single catastrophic evolutionary event that underlies all other unique aspects of our cognition (Bickerton, 1990, 1995). It seems increasingly likely, however, that the Upper Paleolithic 'revolution' is actually an artifact of the much greater concentration of archeological research in Europe than in Africa, as well as poor preservation and of the effects of small and dispersed populations (McBrearty and Brooks, 2000; Shennan, 2001). I shall return to develop this point further in Chapter 5.1, in the context of a discussion of the evolution of creativity.

1.2   Uniquely Human

What then *are* the cognitive differences between ourselves and our nearest relatives? Arguably humans are unique in possessing the following mental capacities. (At the very least, we are unique in the depth and sophistication of these capacities.) Whether each of them involves a distinct mental module, or whether some can be fully explained in terms of others, is a matter for discussion, both here and in later chapters. (Note, however, that even the partial list of capacities given below is too extensive for all items to be discussed.)

1. A folk-physics capacity, enabling 'deeper' causal reasoning about physical phenomena than may be available to chimpanzees (at least, if Povinelli, 2000, is right about the latter). (See Section 2 of this chapter.)

2. A folk-biology capacity, involving a weak form of biological essentialism and also enabling 'deeper' causal reasoning and inductive generalizations concerning living organisms. (See Section 2.)

3. A mind-reading capacity, enabling us to attribute mental states to other people, and to predict their likely actions in the light of their beliefs and goals. Whether there is a separate self-monitoring faculty for attributing mental states to oneself, or whether self-attributions result merely from focusing one's mind-reading abilities upon oneself, is open to debate. (See Sections 2 and 3.)

4. A language capacity, involving capacities both to learn and to utilize language. In its mature state it probably divides into production and comprehension sub-systems, perhaps linked to a database of knowledge of grammatical and phonological rules. (See Section 4.)

5. A sophisticated imitation ability, perhaps underpinned, in whole or in part, by some aspects of mind-reading (in particular, the capacity to attribute goals and intentions) and by some aspects of folk-physics (which enables us to distinguish relevant from irrelevant aspects of someone's action targeted on a physical object). (See Section 5.)

6. A capacity to acquire complex skills through practice, of the sort involved in piano playing or kayak building. This capacity presumably involves or presupposes the capacity to imitate the actions of another, as well as to convert linguistic instructions into an appropriate sequence of actions. It also presupposes a capacity to take one's own acquisition of a skill as a goal, if one engages in practice *in order to* acquire it. Whether the capacity to build complex 'action modules' is distinctively human or merely exploits a capacity already present in animals is open to debate.

7. Some motivational systems designed to underpin and to guide social learning, including desires to model one's behavior on that of peers, and desires to model one's behavior on that of the most successful. (What is learned, here, might include norms—in the sense of #10 below—but will also include much that isn't properly normative.) (See Section 6.)

8. Some motivational systems designed to underpin and promote successful social interaction, including perhaps a system that figures out what might enhance one's social status, and makes one want it; as well as direct desires for the high regard of members of one's social group. (See Section 6.)

9. Systems for generating personal attachments to kin, to friends, and to mates. (Arguably that latter isn't really a distinct adaptation, if romantic love is just a combination of personal attachment and lust, as some argue; see Prinz, 2004.)

10. Normative capacities, containing components specialized for learning the social norms that are operative in one's society, for generating intrinsic (non-instrumental) motivation to comply with those norms, and for generating a range of emotions in case of norm non-compliance (guilt, in one's own case; anger and desires to punish, in the case of other people). (See Section 7.)

11. A disposition to gossip, and an interest in the actions and personal lives of others in one's social group.

12. A capacity to reason about social exchanges (and especially to detect those who have cheated in an exchange), and to generate appropriate motivations to do one's bit in a social exchange. (Whether this is a distinct capacity, or is just an aspect of the operations of a wider normative capacity, is up for debate.) (See Section 7.)

13. A sense of humor, and a disposition to tease, to tell jokes, and to play tricks.

14. An interest in stories, and a disposition to invent and transmit such stories.

15. A capacity for music; a sense of rhythm; and a disposition to dance and to sing.

16. A capacity for exact numerical cognition concerning numbers larger than four. This builds on animal and infant capacities for approximate large-number cognition, and for tracking exact small numbers (Hauser and Spelke, 2005).

17. A capacity to entertain suppositions, used in counter-factual and hypothetical thinking (and also in mind-reading). This capacity is the main element involved in the species-unique pretend play displayed by human children of eighteen months and older. And arguably the function of pretend play is precisely to develop and practice the capacity to suppose. (These points will be extensively developed in Chapter 5.) Whether this capacity is underpinned by a distinct module, or rather reduces to a combination of mental rehearsal (which is shared with other animals) and language, is up for debate.

18. A capacity to think creatively, generating novel ideas, novel hypotheses, and novel solutions to problems. (See Chapter 5.)

19. A capacity for similarity-based and analogical thinking and reasoning, manifesting itself in metaphor, but also in our tendency to use one domain (when familiar and well-understood) as a model for the operations of a less-familiar system, drawing often-appropriate inferences about the latter. (Whether this reduces to our capacity for language, and the ways in which language is deployed in 'inner speech', is up for debate; see Chapter 5.)

20. A capacity to make inferences to the best explanation in general, and to reason scientifically, in particular. This capacity is arguably quite ancient, being required for successful tracking of prey when hunting, as we shall see in Chapter 6. It surely presupposes suppositional and creative capacities, but also requires an ability to select between hypotheses on grounds of simplicity, consistency, explanatory power, and so forth.

21. An indefinitely flexible capacity for practical reasoning. When we reason practically, our reasoning can involve normative beliefs ('I ought to do X'), evaluative beliefs ('It would be good to do X'), or desiderative beliefs ('I want to do X'). And there seem to be no limits on the kinds of considerations that can be introduced into one's practical reasoning, and that can influence its outcome. (This will be discussed in Chapter 7.)

22. A capacity, not just to reason theoretically and practically in intelligent and flexible ways, but also to reflect upon, and to modify, one's own reasoning practices. The study of logic can make a big difference, for

example, just as the adoption of an explicit scientific methodology can have a significant effect on one's practice. (See Chapter 4.)

It will be the task of this and the following chapters to consider how some of these distinctively human capacities should best be explained.[2] But the chances that they might all be manifestations of some single uniquely human cognitive ability strike me as vanishingly small.

1.3 Did the Brain Merely get Bigger?

Someone might concede that there are a great many distinctively human cognitive capacities, while denying that there are very many distinctive human cognitive *adaptations*—claiming that the capacities in question are a by-product of massively increased brain sizes in humans (Gould, 1991). In one variant of this idea, increased brain size may have been driven by selection for one particular cognitive function, as defenders of the 'Machiavellian intelligence' hypothesis have proposed (Byrne and Whiten, 1988, 1997; Dunbar, 2000). On this view, it was heavy selection for *social* intelligence that produced dramatic increases in brain sizes, leading to increases in intelligence in other domains as well. In another variant of the same idea, it was selection for *general* intelligence that produced bigger brains, with the resulting 'spare' cortical tissue thereafter being co-opted for a variety of different purposes (Finlay et al., 2001).

In defending these ideas (and in attacking massive modularity), some have claimed that there are constraints on the ways that brains develop, resulting from the control and timing of neural cell differentiation during development. This means that brains have to get bigger or smaller as whole units (Finlay et al., 2001; Ridley, 2004); and it means that when absolute brain size increases, the relative size of the neocortex also increases. The claim, in effect, is that brains aren't subject to *mosaic* (piecemeal) evolution. And the main evidence adduced is that comparative study of the brains of different species of animal shows that (when adjustments are made for absolute brain size) the same relative dimensions amongst the various structures making up those brains are conserved across species.

There are at least two significant problems with this argument. One is that it assumes a naive identification between the extent of a given cognitive competence and the size of the brain regions underlying that competence. It

---

[2] As I remarked above, there are too many distinctively human capacities for us to attempt an explanation of all. Our focus will be on those that are likely to be the products of novel and distinct modules, on those that generate architectural novelties that will be important for our later discussions, and (beginning in Chapter 4) on those that (like scientific reasoning) might be thought to present a special *challenge* to massively modular accounts of the human mind.

seems just as likely, in contrast, that increases in a cognitive competence might result from detailed changes in the neural wiring underlying it. For often a novel competence might require a new or changed set of algorithms to be run, rather than increases in general-processing power or greater memory. So it is consistent with the overall size and dimensions of the brain evolving as a unit, that there might nevertheless be a great many cognitive adaptations (resulting from micro-changes in neural wiring within different brain areas), just as most massive modularists suppose.[3]

The second significant problem with the argument is that a variety of methodological criticisms can be made of the data collected and the inferences drawn from them (Barton, 2001). Chief amongst these is that Finlay et al. (2001) examined only gross morphological structures in the brain when collecting their comparative data, without regard to function. When the comparisons involve brain regions individuated by presumed function, in contrast, then extensive differences in the relative sizes of those regions emerge across species (Barton and Harvey, 2000; Clark et al., 2001; de Winter and Oxnard, 2001). For example, Huffman et al. (1999) show that the relative sizes of different function-specific areas of somasensory cortex in a number of species of mammal are *very* different from one another, depending on that species' behavioral specializations.

It appears, therefore, that brains *are* significantly subject to mosaic evolution when their components are individuated in terms of function—as of course they must be, if what we are considering is whether there are a great many distinct, separately evolved, cognitive adaptations. Consistent with this conclusion, there is evidence that many function-specific areas in the human brain are significantly larger than one would predict from the overall size of the cortex alone (Geary, 2005). Thus pre-frontal cortex, for example (the seat of so-called 'executive function') is about ten percent larger than expected (Holloway, 2002). Moreover, a number of specialized areas within the pre-frontal cortex have become differently organized and proportionately much larger in humans. These include the anterior cingulate, and specific areas of left and right dorsolateral pre-frontal cortex (Semendeferi et al., 2001; Koechlin et al., 2003).

Suppose that these problems with the claims of Finlay et al. (2001) are set to one side, however. So suppose that the hominid brain really did increase in size as a unit, perhaps driven by the demands of Machiavellian intelligence. Does it follow from this that massive modularity is false? Not at all. For recall

---

[3] And indeed, Striedter (2004) describes many cases in which the detailed wiring of different brain regions has altered in the course of evolution, independent of any change in size. See also Geary (2005).

from Chapter 2 that the minds of non-human animals are massively modular in their organization. Surely there isn't any reason to think that an overall increase in the size of the brain would sweep all of that organization away. On the contrary, on the naive assumption that increases in size lead to increases in processing power, what one would expect is that each of those pre-existing modules would be considerably deepened and enhanced. And indeed, it does appear that many of the cognitive faculties that are distinctive of the human mind have precursors in the cognition of non-human animals. Thus it could plausibly be claimed that the human folk-physics module is a deepening of the module for causal reasoning in rats and other mammals; that the human folk-biology module is a deepening of the foraging module in apes and monkeys; that the human folk-psychology, or 'mind-reading', module is a deepening of the module in apes that underpins their sophisticated social cognition; and so on and so forth. (I shall return to this idea in Section 2.)

1.4 What happens when Brains get Bigger?

Not only are the 'laws of brain-size evolution' *consistent* with massive modularity, but they also give the latter some independent support. Striedter (2004) reviews a wide range of comparative and evolutionary data, and is able to extract a number of robust generalizations about what happens to brains when their absolute size increases, within a certain lineage (see also Geary, 2005). One is that larger brains become significantly more modular in their organization. This is because, as the total number of neurons increases, the density of dendrite connectivity amongst neurons significantly *decreases*. (This is, no doubt, partly because of the energetic costs associated with building and maintaining neural connections—Aiello and Wheeler, 1995; and partly because of the constraints imposed by slow speeds of signal propagation within and between neurons, already noted in Chapter 1.3.) The result is that neurons tend to maintain more of their local connections, while giving up a greater proportion of their long-distance ones, resulting in an architecture that appears significantly more modular.[4]

Another (related) generalization described by Striedter (2004) is that an increase in the size in a given brain region tends to be accompanied by increases in functional differentiation amongst its sub-regions. And this generalization

---

[4] Whether increasingly modular *brain* organization translates straightforwardly into increasingly modular *cognitive* organization is of course another matter. But there is at least a powerful *ad hominem* argument here, against those who argue that increasing brain size would lead to increases in *general* intelligence. And although it was taken to be a truism in philosophy of mind in the 1960s and 70s that cognitive functions needn't map in any systematic way onto brain regions or connected systems of brain regions, in fact everything that we have learned since then suggests that they do.

holds good, not only for local brain regions, but also for the brain as a whole. In particular, the lateralization of brain functions increases as the overall size of the brain goes up, no doubt because of the costs of maintaining neural connections between the two hemispheres.

What we should predict, then, as a result of the fourfold increase in brain size that occurred through the evolution of hominids, is that the brains (and presumably the minds) of humans became much *more* modular—containing many more functionally distinct processing systems—than the brains of our great-ape ancestors. Since I have previously argued in Chapter 2 that the minds of apes and other non-human animals are already massively modular in organization, this is likely to mean that the transition to *Homo sapiens* will have seen the addition of many new mind / brain adaptations.

Should the resulting systems count as *adaptations*, however? Aren't they rather side-effects of some general *Bauplan* governing increases in brain size? Initially, perhaps, some of them may have been. But *ex*aptation is actually a form of *ad*aptation. Where systems are shaped and maintained by natural selection they can count as adaptations, even if the processes through which they initially arose weren't targeted on them in particular. (The penguin's 'wings' are an adaptation for swimming, although they are exapted from limbs once designed for flight.) And such shaping and maintaining is likely to apply to most of the brain systems underlying the human mind, since cognition is just too important for survival and reproduction for it to be otherwise. However, this isn't strictly an issue that I need to take a stand on. For recall from Chapter 1 that it isn't built into the notion of a *module* that modules should be adaptations. And yet my overall goal, of course, is to defend the thesis of massive mental modularity.

There is one other 'law of brain evolution' described by Striedter (2004) that is worth mentioning here, since it bears on the explanation of item 6 in our list of distinctively human capacities in Section 1.2. This is that as the size of one brain region increases relative to another, the extent of the neural projections from the larger to the smaller also increases. The result is that the relatively enlarged human neocortex has culminated in unusually extensive projections from the neocortex to the motor neurons in the medulla and spinal chord. This may give us a partial explanation of our species' impressive abilities for fine-grained motor control, not only involving movements of the hands, but also the lips, tongue, and respiratory system necessary for the control of speech.

1.5 Neural Proliferation and Pruning

I have replied to the argument that the 'laws of brain evolution' rule out massive modularity. Buller (2005) claims that massive mental modularity is inconsistent with what is known about the processes of brain *development*, however. He suggests that we can, on the contrary, see just a single novel adaptation underlying human uniqueness. This is the process of neural over-proliferation, and subsequent pruning in response to experience, that sculpts our brain organization during the course of development.

Let me review some of the pertinent facts, following Webb et al. (2001). Almost all of the neurons that the brain will ever contain are produced before birth, during the first seven months of development. These continue to grow connections and build synapses with one another for the first two years after birth, with the maximum total number of brain synapses occurring at around two years of age. Thereafter there are two major periods of 'pruning', during which both neurons and their synapses are lost in response to patterned experience (or rather, caused by the lack of it). One occurs in the third and fourth years of life, followed by a 'plateau' through the childhood years, after which there is another period of pruning in early adolescence. Around forty percent of the neurons created in the first seven months of life die by the time that children reach adulthood, and likewise the same percentage of the total synapses present at two years of age are lost by the age of sixteen. The process of pruning itself appears to obey the old adage, 'use it or lose it.' Neural connections that aren't functional, or that are rarely used, are lost, whereas those that are frequently employed are retained.

Are these facts inconsistent with, or otherwise problematic for, the thesis of massive mental modularity, as Buller (2005) alleges? By no means. First of all, it is important to stress that the initial placement of neuronal connections in the brain isn't at all random. On the contrary, neurons migrate to their eventual positions within the brain, and send out their axons to quite specific locations, guided by a range of chemical gradients and other forms of signaling (Korsching, 1993; Thoenen, 1995). So the initial organization of the cortex certainly isn't some sort of equipotent set of neural connections that is then sculpted into shape entirely by experience, as Buller contrives to suggest. On the contrary, a number of recent interventionist studies have found that the brains of animals will develop normally up to the time of birth, at least, in the absence of any relevant experience whatsoever (relevant to the formation of the brain regions under study, that is) (Miyashita-Lin et al., 1999; Verhage et al., 2000; Molnar et al., 2002).

In fact it seems likely that the subsequent role of experience in brain development (in the first instance, at least) is to add precision to the inherently vague and noisy chemical signaling systems that guide the placement of initial synaptic connections, on a highly local basis. Since neurons that perform the same function are generally arranged together in banks, by making the eventual placement of synaptic connections both activity-dependent and competitive, the brain can ensure that boundaries between systems are drawn much more precisely than would otherwise happen.

A second point is that a significant amount of the neural sculpting that takes place, at least within some systems, is produced by endogenously produced signals, rather than by experience of the environment. In early visual cortex in mammals, for example, neurons are organized into sequences of columns corresponding to each of the two eyes. It has long been known that depriving cats of post-natal visual experience disrupts the formation of these columns (Hubel and Wiesel, 1970). But it is now known that these ocular dominance columns develop in stages, the first of which is guided by spontaneous neural activity produced by the two retinas prior to birth. The basic structure of the cortical circuits is laid down in advance of any externally produced visual experience (Katz et al., 2000). And we now know that something similar is true in connection with the face-recognition system, likewise (Bednar, 2003).

Moreover, a great deal of the role of experience in sculpting brain circuits isn't well characterized as a form of *learning* on the basis of experience, as Buller (2005) himself acknowledges. Indeed, Katz and Shatz (1996) argue that much of the later role of experience is best seen as an extension of the work of the earlier endogenously produced stimuli, namely *preparing* cortical circuits to engage in learning. For in many cases all that is required is *some experience or other*, or experience of some very general (module-specific) type, such as face-like shapes, or object boundaries. What a cortical circuit requires, in order for its neural components to be 'pruned' appropriately, is experience of the general type that falls within its intended domain. At this early stage the system isn't so much learning in response to experience, as using that experience to distinguish itself functionally from surrounding modules.

None of this is to deny, of course, that experience and learning can cause neuronal changes of various sorts to occur, some of which involve alterations in the local wiring patterns within cortical circuits. Indeed, we are beginning to discover how learning can trigger cascades of gene expression within particular groups of neurons, causing new dendrites to grow and new synapses to be formed (Ridley, 2003; Marcus, 2004). But even where this is appropriately thought of as the formation of a new brain system or the reconfiguring of an old one (as opposed to the laying down a specific memory, for example), it turns out that it isn't inconsistent with massive modularity. For remember that the thesis of massive mental modularity, as I am understanding it, doesn't require modules to be genetically pre-specified. And it is still possible for the resulting system to count as an adaptation. For natural selection can rely on the presence of reliably recurring features of the environment (such as the presence of face-shaped stimuli) when selecting for particular developmental programs (Griffiths and Gray, 2001; West-Eberhard, 2003; Barrett, 2006). Moreover, I have argued in any case (in Chapter 1.3) that some modules are a product of experience and learning, without their modular status thereby being compromised.

I conclude, then, that the processes by means of which brains develop and form their cortical circuits are fully consistent with massive mental modularity, just as we earlier found for the processes through which brains evolve.[5]

1.6 A Place for g?

I have argued against the idea that there is just one major cognitive adaptation separating humans from other animals. And I have argued that neither the 'laws of brain evolution' nor the 'laws of brain development' are inconsistent with massive modularity. But what place can a massively modular model of the human mind find for general intelligence, or g? At the very least, even if it is granted that there are many other uniquely human cognitive adaptations, the existence of an important g factor might be thought to be inconsistent with *massive* modularity. For what is *general* intelligence, if not an *a*-modular property of the mind? Alternatively, it might be claimed that general intelligence alone is sufficient to explain all of the cognitive differences between humans and other animals; in which case this would be another variant on the 'one major new adaptation' hypothesis.

Evidence for the existence of a g factor, and of both its significant heritability and strong correlation with many other measures of practical success, is now quite robust (Hernstein and Murray, 1994; Gordon, 1997; Gottfredson, 1997; Jensen, 1998; Geary, 2005). So any acceptable model of the mind must find a way to accommodate it somehow. But how is this to be done within the framework of a massively modular account? The existence of g is by no means an insuperable problem for massive modularity, however, as I shall now try to show, contrasting my explanation with that of other massive modularists.

The most attractive approach would be to say that g somehow supervenes on the total set of mental modules, as I shall show in due course. But one variant of this idea is suggested by Cosmides and Tooby (2002), who argue

---

[5] Note, too, that the plasticity that brains can display in response to damage, especially when young, is no argument against massive modularity, either (contra Elman et al., 1996). For quite apart from the point that modularity, in my sense, doesn't entail innateness, the same plasticity is equally true of the development of other aspects of the body (Samuels, 1998; Marcus, 2004). Thus if a cell that would ordinarily become an eye cell, for example, is transplanted into the stomach early enough in development, then it will turn into a stomach cell. The body in general has a remarkable degree of flexibility and capacity for self-repair during development.

that general intelligence results from the total set of modules being bundled together in the right way, along with the addition of some sort of 'scope syntax'. They point out that humans are unique in having come to occupy a *cognitive niche*, acquiring and utilizing large amounts of contingent information about the physical, biological, and social worlds. The result, the authors think, is a domain-general *scope syntax* governing mental representations, which makes the manipulation of such information useful and tractable. But they run together a number of different capacities under this idea, some of which we share with even quite simple animals.

One is that information needs to be tagged for origin, and for the times and places of its validity. But we saw in Chapter 2 that if Gallistel (1990) is right, *all* stored information is tagged for time and place; and many animals can represent the times and/or temporal intervals during which an event can be expected to occur. Another thing that Cosmides and Tooby describe as 'scope syntax' is the capacity to embed propositions within attitude-descriptions, as in, 'John *believes that* the mushrooms are edible.' This may well be a uniquely human capacity; but it isn't the basis of general intelligence, as we will see in our discussion later in this chapter and again in Chapter 4. And yet another thing that Cosmides and Tooby have in mind is the capacity to entertain *suppositions*, and to keep track of the scope of suppositions in processes of further reasoning. This is certainly important, and it has an important part to play in the explanation of general intelligence, as we shall see in Chapter 5; but as we also saw in Chapter 2.8, it is unlikely to be uniquely human.

Another approach that a massive modularity theorist might be tempted to take would be to claim that g results from some kind of global property of the brain, such as the speed of neural transmission. The idea would be that, while the mind is wholly composed of a great many modules, in individuals with high g all of those modules operate more swiftly and efficiently because the underlying brain systems are all of them faster in their operation. But there is direct evidence against the 'speedy brain' theory of general intelligence, in fact, since the genes that effect speed of neural transmission only explain a small part of reaction-time differences and don't correlate very well with g (Posthuma et al., 2001). Neither do direct measures of nerve conduction velocity correlate very well with g (Vernon et al., 2000).[6]

The speedy brain hypothesis is also successfully criticized by Kanazawa (2004), who points out that it predicts that g should co-vary with success in

---

[6] Speed of inspection time is another matter: this does correlate moderately well with g (Nettlebeck, 2001). But this is a cognitive not a neural measure, and is thought by some to be a function of the ability to focus *attention* effectively (Geary, 2005). And this in turn is a crucial component in the global broadcasting of perceptual information that will figure largely in my own account.

module-based thinking. Kanazawa argues, on the contrary, that there is plenty of evidence that success in evolutionarily ancient, module-involving, domains (such as social cognition or mate selection) is independent of g; and conversely that the domains within which g correlates significantly with success are all of them evolutionarily novel ones (such as sitting examinations or building a successful career as a lawyer). He argues that the reason why g correlates so well with so many measures of successful cognition is that the vast majority of problems that we face in the contemporary world are evolutionarily novel, and that g itself is an adaptation to such novelty.

Kanazawa (2004) therefore defends a different approach. He argues that g should be identified with a distinct module of the mind, which was selected for in evolution in order to deal with evolutionarily novel adaptive problems. If true, this would explain the datum that g can be low while other module-based forms of cognition can be normal (see above). And conversely, it would also explain the datum that at least some aspects of g can be high in individuals in whom (some) other forms of module-based thinking are damaged or absent (Scheuffgen et al., 2000).

But this approach faces important problems of its own. For if a modular g-system were to explain the sorts of success that smart people enjoy in the modern world, then it would have to be capable of (at least) the following: (a) generating novel ideas, hypotheses, and potential solutions to problems, (b) evaluating those ideas, and reasoning to the best explanation of the phenomena that pose the problem, (c) searching for stored information, and recruiting the activity of other modules to serve its own processing needs, and (d) seizing control of the activity of the whole organism in order to implement the solutions arrived at. It is very hard indeed to see how there could be any single modular system with all of these properties, nor how the internal operations of that system could be computationally tractable. It is also very hard to see how such a system could have evolved through natural selection *ab initio*.

Geary (2005), too, develops a theory of g within a framework that is modularist (albeit not massively so), and argues that it is an adaptation to the complexity and unpredictability of human life (especially social life). On his account g is a complex system, involving a set of attentional mechanisms directed by the executive systems in the frontal lobes of the brain which orchestrate the global broadcasting of perceptual and other information. It also involves a working-memory system that utilizes the globally broadcast, conscious, information, and that can rehearse and develop imaginary scenarios for purposes of problem-solving. And what is especially important, on Geary's account, is the ability of the executive system to utilize and control the contents of working memory effectively in the service of current goals.

As we shall see in Chapter 4, this account has many points of contact with my own. I, too, will claim that distinctively human 'general' intelligence involves mental rehearsal and the global broadcast of perceptual and quasi-perceptual (imagistic) information, as well as the representation and development of imaginary scenarios. But Geary tells us nothing about where novel ideas and imaginings of future events and actions are supposed to come from (see Chapter 5); nor does he say much about how they are evaluated (see Chapter 6). Nor is he as explicit as I will be about how the g-system is *realized in* the operations and interactions of a large set of modules, many of which are shared with other animals, but some of which are uniquely human (see Chapters 4 through 7).

My own suggestion is that g is a special sort of *interaction effect* of existing modular systems, together with some evolutionarily novel dispositions and tendencies. One aspect of this idea will be sketched in Chapter 4. This is that a pre-existing capacity for action-rehearsal utilizes the resources of the human language-production module to broadcast representations of sentences globally to the full range of central / conceptual modular systems, initiating cycles of inner speech. Other aspects—especially an enhanced capacity for the creative generation of new ideas, and inferences to the best explanation to select amongst those ideas—will be outlined and discussed in Chapters 5 and 6.

On the account that I shall defend, then, general-purpose thinking will turn out to be realized in both the operations of, and (more importantly) a distinctive mode of interaction of, a large set of modules. And there is no reason why the properties governing such interactions shouldn't be significantly heritable. So we should predict that the well-functioning of the 'general intelligence system' (that is to say, high g) might vary independently of variations in the underlying modules themselves, to a significant extent. It will be especially easy to understand how g might be low while the underlying modules are normal. But we should also predict that the system might continue to function pretty well (at least in some contexts) despite damage to one or more of the underlying modules (but not nearly so well, crucially, in the case of damage to the language modules).

A good theory of g should explain why high g correlates with success in the modern world, of course, and also why it correlates with performance across a wide range of domains, including the spatial, arithmetic, and linguistic components of standardized tests. But by the time we have finished it will be plain why these facts should be so. For the modular interactions that constitute general-purpose thinking, on my account, are also constitutive of what is often called 'System 2' thinking and reasoning (Evans and Over, 1996), as we shall see in Chapters 4 through 7. And this is the sort of thinking that is primarily tested in intelligence tests, and that is also critical for complex problem solving (Stanovich, 1999). Moreover, if the dispositions underlying these modular interactions are significantly heritable, as we can suppose, then we can explain why g itself should be both heritable and relatively constant through the lifespan.

2 Physics, Biology, Psychology, and Statistics

I have argued against the 'one major new adaptation' hypothesis, and defended massive modularity against a number of related challenges. In the present section I shall briefly review some of the (extensive) literature on the development of human folk physics, folk biology, and folk psychology. These are three of the modules that are candidates to be distinctive of the human mind. (Then since both the architecture and architectural connections of the folk-psychology module will be important for our later discussions, it will receive more extensive treatment in Section 3 following.) I shall also briefly address the question whether our capacities in these areas are the result of some sort of domain-general statistical reasoning or theorizing ability.

2.1 Domain-Specific Development

The pioneering developmental work of Piaget through the middle part of the twentieth century was largely *domain-general* in character (Piaget, 1927, 1936; Piaget and Inhelder, 1948, 1966). Cognitive development was seen as unfolding in sequence across a broad front of abilities, following an internal logic that was for the most part content-independent. But the result of almost all developmental theorizing since that time has been not only to date the acquisition of the various abilities much earlier in development, but to emphasize the *domain-specific* character of child development. Children's acquisition of various cognitive capacities is now seen as following very different trajectories in the various domains, each of which has a timetable and internal logic of its own. While this doesn't directly entail modularity (even in our weak sense of 'module'), it does imply that the mechanisms involved in the acquisition of these abilities are at least partially distinct from one another. And when combined with the general *expectation* of modularity warranted by the arguments of Chapters 1 and 2, it gives us good reason to think that the human acquisition and utilization of each of these abilities is served by a distinct module.[7]

---

[7] See also Geary (2005) for a useful review of the evidence supporting distinct modules in the domains of physics, biology, and psychology. And see Martin and Weisberg (2003) for evidence that

The science of child development has been revolutionized over the last quarter-century, partly by increasingly clever and sophisticated experimental techniques for use with toddlers and pre-schoolers, partly by the invention of the looking-time paradigm now used extensively with infants to probe their beliefs and expectations. The former have enabled scientists to explore the understandings of young children in the domains of physics, biology, psychology, number, and many others. The latter have enabled scientists to discover precursors (at least) of these understandings in infants.

In the physical domain, for example, researchers have now charted how infants' knowledge and expectations emerge through the first few months of life (Baillargeon et al., 1995; Spelke et al., 1995). Infants as young as three months are surprised if a moving object that disappears behind a screen is later revealed in a position that it could only have reached by passing through a barrier; and they are surprised if an unsupported object doesn't fall. Similarly, by three months of age infants expect an object to move when it is struck by another; and by six months of age they understand that the amount of displacement of the stationary object is a function of the size of the moving one; and so on and so forth.

Likewise in the psychological domain infants display a precocious understanding, if not quite *so* precocious. Until recently the consensus amongst most researchers was that mind-reading abilities emerge through the first four or five years of development, undergoing extensive conceptual / theoretical change in the process (Wellman, 1990; Perner, 1991). Before the age of one year infants can distinguish between agents and non-agents, and are surprised if an agent doesn't take the most rational route to an apparent goal (Gergely et al., 1995; Johnson, 2005). By the age of eighteen months they understand that people will choose items that they prefer, rather than items that the *infant* prefers (Repacholi and Gopnik, 1997), and they share attention with caregivers and take account of others' eye-direction. And then by the age of around four years children come to understand that what people do depends upon their beliefs, desires, and perceptions, and they know both that beliefs can be false and that perceptions can be misleading (Wellman, 1990).

This developmental sequence has often been conceptualized as a transition from an early form of *goal psychology*, through a more sophisticated but still non-representational *goal and perception psychology*, culminating in a mature *belief / desire psychology*. And while this transition is often hypothesized to result from a process of infant theorizing (Wellman, 1990; Gopnik and Meltzoff,

different brain regions are activated when the same stimuli (movements of triangular shapes on a screen) are interpreted in social terms, as opposed to being seen as mere mechanical motion.

1997), it is equally consistent with a process of modular unfolding and growth, or as resulting from the operations of a domain-specific specialized learning mechanism (Baron-Cohen, 1995; Siegal and Surian, 2006).

It has always been possible, however, that younger children's failures at false-belief tasks are mere failures of *performance*, masking an underlying competence that emerges much earlier (Fodor, 1992). And evidence supporting this interpretation has begun to accumulate. Even two-year-old children are sensitive to the state of knowledge or ignorance of a caregiver (O'Neill, 1996). And young children can engage in simple forms of deceit, which seems to require that they possess the concept of false belief (Chandler et al., 1989; Hala et al., 1991). For to deceive someone is to induce them to hold a false belief. Moreover, the use of measures such as initial eye direction and unreflective swift action (rather than the usual verbal report) also suggest that children of age three or younger can appreciate that other people have false beliefs (Clements and Perner, 1994). Even more strikingly, the extension of the non-verbal looking-time paradigm from the domain of folk physics to the domain of mind-reading has found that even fifteen-month-old infants are sensitive to the false belief of another (Onishi and Baillargeon, 2005).

These and other data are pulled together by Birch and Bloom (2004) into a theoretical framework that they call 'the curse of knowledge'. (See also Leslie and Polizzi, 1998, for a related idea.) Granted, young children are poor at describing their own previous false beliefs, and at attributing false beliefs to other people. But then so, too, are adults—albeit to a smaller degree. In the adult literature the tendency to misattribute false beliefs to one's earlier self is called 'hindsight bias'. And adults, too, can often fail to take account of the false belief of another, especially when task demands are high (Keysar et al., 2003). According to Birch and Bloom, it is always difficult for us to make allowances for the lesser knowledge of another person, or of our own previous selves, setting aside our own better-informed perspective—which is likely to be especially salient to us, of course. What changes in development is just that older children and adults increasingly acquire the ability to set aside their own knowledge, allowing their underlying competence with the notions of ignorance and false belief to manifest itself. And this competence is present at a very young age.

Whatever the precise developmental timetable, virtually all researchers now accept that the developmental pathways involved in infants' emerging understandings of physics and of psychology are at least partially distinct. Each follows a distinctive trajectory, and issues in a set of implicit principles that characterize the domain in question, with greater or lesser accuracy.[8] Most strikingly, indeed, there is evidence that young infants see the domains of agents and physical objects as actually disjoint, in such a way that agents aren't subject to the same laws that apply to physical objects. Specifically, five-month-old infants show no surprise when an agent undergoes discontinuous motion, whereas they *are* surprised if a non-agent undergoes discontinuous motion (Kuhlmeier et al., 2004). This leads Bloom (2004) to think that people's common-sense belief in the non-physical nature of minds (so-called 'Cartesian dualism') is very deep-seated indeed, having its origins in early infancy.

2.2 Does Biology Emerge from Psychology?

Our capacities for reasoning about physics and psychology are early emerging ones, then; and they appear to develop independently of each other. This is at least consistent with the idea that our mature competencies in these domains are realized in distinct modules, and also with the claim that the systems charged with developing those competencies are modular learning mechanisms. Some have argued, however, that our capacity for reasoning about living things (our folk biology) is comparatively late developing—emerging sometime between the ages of seven and ten—and that it is based, initially, upon our common-sense psychology (Carey, 1985). The evidence for the latter claim consists in a set of experimental studies suggesting that younger children tend to reason about living kinds by analogy with humans, treating human beings as archetypal living things.

As Atran (2002a) points out, however, these experiments were all conducted with urban and suburban children in the developed countries of the west (mostly the United States). Such children have minimal contact with the natural world, beyond what they see in books and nature programs. Such children are, you might say, extremely 'biologically deprived'. And when the relevant studies are conducted with children drawn from cultures like the forest-dwelling Mayan people of the Yukatek region of Mexico, the picture that emerges is really quite different. They show no bias in favor of humans as exemplars of living beings, and their inductive projections of properties across species barriers are appropriate for those creatures' degrees of relatedness.

These data, together with a wealth of comparative anthropological evidence, lead Atran (1998, 2002a) to argue that humans possess an innately structured

---

[8] Interestingly, amongst adolescents and adults it appears that our innate naive physics is distinctly *Aristotelian* in character, rather than Newtonian (McCloskey, 1983).

living-kind learning mechanism (a module, in our weak sense).[9] The mechanism takes for granted that living kinds should be arranged into hierarchically organized mutually exclusive groupings, from sub-species ('Siamese cat'), through species ('lion'), families ('feline'), to kingdoms ('animal'). And it also assumes that members of each species should have an underlying nature or 'essence' which explains their manifest properties and aspects of their life cycle, and which grounds more or less reliable inductive inferences to the properties of groups that are more or less closely related within the hierarchy. While this learning mechanism works to impose a similar sort of organized structure on people's beliefs about living kinds across cultures, of course a great deal of local learning also takes place. But it is learning that is focused and guided by a dedicated learning mechanism.

2.3 Theorizing Theory and Bayes Nets

Some researchers concede that humans possess innate domain-specific knowledge of various sorts, as well as domain-specific attention biases, but argue that the processes that elaborate that knowledge from infancy onwards are domain-general in character. So the different trajectories of development in differing domains can be explained in terms of differences in the nature and timing of the various starting points (the initial bodies of domain-specific knowledge in question) together with differences in the accessibility of data, while denying that different learning mechanisms are involved. Gopnik and Meltzoff (1997) argue, in particular, that the processes of knowledge-development in the various domains (physics, biology, psychology, and so on) are general-purpose processes of theorizing, closely akin to the scientific theorizing of human adults. Their claim is that human infants are little scientists, revising, transforming, and building from their initial theories in the light of data received, in much the same manner that scientists will revise, transform, and build theories in the light of their observations and experimental results.

This claim will be examined and criticized in Chapter 6.3, in the context of our discussion of the cognitive basis of distinctively human scientific thinking and reasoning abilities. Here I shall briefly discuss a somewhat weaker

---

[9] Certainly it is true that humans living in hunter-gatherer communities today are *exceptionally* skilled at extracting resources from the ecologies within which they live. See Kaplan et al. (2000). It is also true that the brain mechanisms that store information pertaining to living kinds are doubly dissociable from the mechanisms that store information about artifact kinds, as we noted in Chapter 2.6. Indeed, within the domain of living kinds, it is possible to find deficits caused by selective brain damage just to knowledge of animal kinds, leaving knowledge of plants, fruits, and vegetables intact, or vice versa. See Capitani et al. (2003) for an extensive review of the evidence. So given the assumption that knowledge is stored where it is processed, there would appear to be two distinct processing modules for dealing with the biological domain, rather than just one.

hypothesis put forward more recently by Gopnik and colleagues (Gopnik and Glymour, 2002; Gopnik and Schulz, 2004). This is that the minds of human infants contain a powerful statistical reasoning mechanism, of the sort lately formalized computationally in *causal Bayes nets* (Glymour and Cooper, 1999; Pearl, 2000). These computational packages can take data about the conditional probabilities of events, together with data about the effects of causal interventions in sequences of those events, to extract the underlying causal processes at work in the domain in question. So the suggestion is that human infants take their observations of the physical, biological, and social worlds—together with the results of their own probings of those worlds—to extract the underlying causal structure of each domain, using some sort of Bayes learning net.

It is possible that these suggestions are correct (although the *very* early ages of acquisition of infants' competence in the domains of physics and psychology seem to me to count against them). And if correct, they would explain the striking fact that in each of the domains of physics and psychology, at least, the knowledge and understanding of chimpanzees seems remarkably *shallow* in comparison with our own—if Povinelli's (2000) characterization of the former is accurate, that is. It seems that while chimpanzees are extremely adept at tracing surface regularities and conditional probabilities, they lack any theories of the underlying mechanisms (whether physical or mental) that are involved. This fact would be neatly explained if what had emerged in the course of the six million years of evolution separating the two species was some much more powerful Bayes learning net, which when set to work on the knowledge already available to chimpanzees in these domains could extract the latter's underlying causal structures.[10]

Recall from Chapter 1, however, that it is one thing to claim that a learning mechanism is domain-general in the algorithms that it employs, and quite another to claim that it is *functionally* domain-general, with one and the same mechanism being put to work in the service of many different learning tasks. And the arguments of Chapter 1 suggest that the latter is unlikely. Rather, as often happens in biology generally (Marcus, 2004), we should expect the genes responsible for building the learning mechanism in question to have been copied and used to construct a number of different instances of that type of mechanism, adapted for different tasks. What we should expect, then,

---

[10] The acquisition of human folk-biology appears to follow a different model, however. For here there is evidence that it is the naming practices of adults that play a crucial role in children's acquisition of kind-concepts, rather than Bayesian inference across patterns of conditional dependence. See Xu, 2002.

is that there are a number of different causal Bayes nets, taking domain-specific inputs and delivering contrasting theories of the differing domains. For learning in each of these domains will have to be taking place at the same time.

Dissociation evidence is needed to differentiate between these two hypotheses. The hypothesis that there exists just a single Bayes learning net predicts that there should occur syndromes in which the starting points of development are normal, but in which both folk physics and folk psychology either don't develop further at all, or only do so haltingly and with considerable delay. (This would be because of selective damage to the learning net in question.) I know of no evidence that any such syndrome exists. The hypothesis that there exist two or more function-specific learning nets, in contrast, predicts that there should occur syndromes in which the starting points of development are normal (remember, both hypotheses claim that development starts from a base of innate domain-specific knowledge), but in which folk physics develops normally while folk psychology remains stagnant, or vice versa. Is there evidence of such a dissociation?

One well-known finding is that autistic children have severe difficulties in mind-reading while being normal in their reasoning about physical events (Baron-Cohen, 1995). This would be strong evidence of special-purpose learning mechanisms in the two domains *if* we could be confident that the two starting-points for development in these two domains are intact in autism. Here evidence is scanty, unfortunately. For although we know that infants have the capacity to identify intentional agents, and to attribute simple goals to such agents (Gergely et al., 1995; Johnson, 2005), such capacities haven't been tested in young autistic children. (The reason is that autism is rarely diagnosed before the third year of life.) But it does seem that older autistic children have difficulties in attending to and identifying socially generated stimuli like speech (Ceponiene et al., 2003), as well as the patterns that are characteristic of human movement (in the form of moving point light displays; Blake et al., 2003). So it seems likely that autism isn't *simply* a developmental disorder, but that the starting point is different from normal too. This is consistent with there being just a single Bayes learning net, which is intact in autism.

Although the case of autism doesn't provide direct support for the hypothesis that the learning mechanisms underlying the acquisition of folk physics and folk psychology are distinct from one another, the case of Down syndrome does. Down syndrome people are relatively normal in their mind-reading abilities, despite having severe *general* learning difficulties (Baron-Cohen et al., 1985). This suggests that the learning mechanism that enables them to acquire their ability to reason about the mental states of other people isn't a general-purpose one. Similar support is provided by the case of Williams syndrome. Williams syndrome children are relatively normal—indeed, precocious—in their social and linguistic abilities, despite having severe difficulties in the domains of physical and spatial cognition, and despite having severe general learning disabilities (Bellugi et al., 2000).

Even if children's acquisition of folk physics and folk psychology results from the operations of some sort of causal Bayes net, then (as Gopnik and Shultz, 2004, suggest), there are reasons of both a theoretical and an empirical sort for believing that there are two or more such learning mechanisms, rather than just one. But it also remains possible that the mechanisms in question aren't just function-specific, but also operate using algorithms that are specialized for their respective task demands. And the evidence of *very* early acquisition of both physical and psychological understanding reviewed in Section 2.1 above gives us some reason to think that this is so.

3 Mind-Reading and Mental Architecture

I propose to assume in what follows, then, that human competences in the domains of physics, biology, and psychology are realized in special-purpose learning modules. This is what the arguments of Chapters 1 and 2 would lead us to expect; and it is both consistent with, and to some degree supported by, the existing evidence. In the present section I shall say rather more about the psychology module, and the way in which it fits into the overall architecture of the mind. For this is a topic that will prove to be of some importance for later chapters.

3.1 Nichols and Stich's Model of Mind-Reading

The best worked-out and best defended model of the internal architecture of the mind-reading module and its interactions with other components of the mind is provided by Nichols and Stich (2003). Their diagram representing that model is reproduced here as Figure 3.1. Notice that it is embedded within a standard belief / desire / practical-reasoning architecture, of the sort adopted (in its modularized form) in Chapter 2. Nichols and Stich don't themselves use the language of 'modularity' in connection with their model. But this is because they interpret that language pretty strictly, along the lines of Fodor (1983). Given the weak construal of modularity defended in Chapter 1, in contrast, it seems perfectly appropriate to regard the components in their model that are specific to mind-reading as constituting a module with modular sub-components.

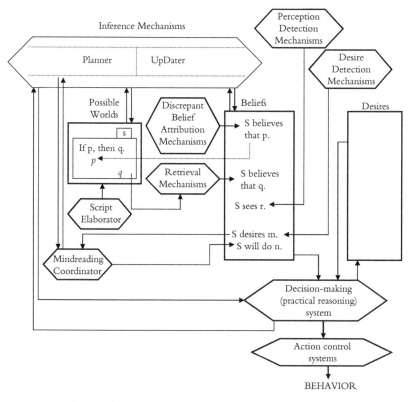

Figure 3.1. Nichols and Stich's model of mind-reading

The mind-reading module then contains: a mechanism (or mechanisms) for attributing desires and goals to other people; a mechanism for attributing perceptual states to people; a mechanism for attributing beliefs to other people when those beliefs are discrepant with one's own (otherwise our own beliefs are used by default); and a coordinating system that receives the outputs of the other three, and both provides inputs to and queries other systems as needed. (Nichols and Stich's diagram also contains a separate 'retrieval mechanism'; but no evidence is provided for its distinctness. It seems to me better to roll this up into the coordinating system.)

It may be that each of the different attribution mechanisms grows or comes on-line at a different stage of development—first the goal-attribution module in the first year of life, giving a form of simple desire-psychology; then the perception-attribution mechanism in the second year of life, giving a desire-perception-psychology; and finally the discrepant belief-attribution mechanism in the third year of life, yielding a full representational theory of mind (Wellman, 1990). Or it may be that each is present from an early age, and that what changes is just the range of tasks within which they can participate (Birch and Bloom, 2004; Onishi and Baillargeon, 2005). Each of these components in turn has significant internal structure, sometimes including separate sub-components, innately structured learning mechanisms, and socially acquired information of various sorts.

The mind-reading module operates in close conjunction with the subject's own planning and inferential systems, utilizing a capacity for hypothetical / suppositional reasoning, which Nichols and Stich (2003) label the 'possible worlds box'. (The latter will loom large again in our discussions in Chapter 5, when we come to consider both pretend play and creative thinking more generally.) In order to figure out what *else* someone is likely to believe, who has been attributed the discrepant-belief that P, the mind-reading coordinator places the supposition that P in the possible worlds box, where it is worked on and elaborated by the subject's own inferential systems (see Figure 3.1). The results of those inferences—say the proposition Q—are then taken by the coordinating system and attributed to the other person. Likewise, in order to figure out what someone will do who desires that M and who believes that P, the mind-reading coordinator sets the subject's own planning and inferential systems to work on those as suppositions, before attributing the results to the other person—'S will do N.'

Notice that this model includes elements of both 'theory-theory' and 'simulationist' accounts of our mind-reading capacities (Davies and Stone, 1995; Carruthers and Smith, 1996). For the mind-reading module contains a structured body of knowledge about minds and their workings, some of which is explicit, and some of which may be implicit within the processing algorithms that it runs, just as theory-theorists maintain. But at the same time the mind-reading module uses the subject's own inferential and planning capacities, taken 'off-line' to operate on suppositional input, hence *simulating* the likely reasoning of the target person. This eclectic mix is one of the model's strengths, enabling it to draw support from the evidence adduced in favor of both theory-theory and simulationist approaches.[11]

3.2 Are there Separate Self-Awareness Systems?

Nichols and Stich (2003) offer a very plausible account of the basis for our attributions of mental states to other people, then, and of our capacity to predict

---

[11] It is important to distinguish, however, between theory-theory as an account of the end-state of mind-reading development, and what might be called 'theor*izing*-theory', which is the view that the end state is reached by a process of reasoning akin to scientific theorizing. It is only the former that Nichols and Stich (2003) are committed to—and rightly so, in my view (see Chapter 6.3).

their likely behavior. But what of attributions of mental states to ourselves? Here they defend the view that there are two (or more) distinct self-monitoring mechanisms, one (at least) for monitoring and providing self-knowledge of our own experiential states, and one for monitoring and providing self-knowledge of our own propositional attitudes. These mechanisms are held to be distinct from one another, and also from the mind-reading system that deals with the mental states of other people.

In defending this view, however, they take their opponent to maintain that attributing mental states to oneself is entirely theoretical in nature, resulting from interpretation of one's own overt behavior, and only that behavior. This is, of course, absurd. But a monolithic form of theory-theory isn't actually their only or most plausible opponent. A number of us have defended a hybrid view, according to which our knowledge of our own *experiences* is semi-immediate and recognitional, whereas our knowledge of our own propositional *attitudes* is theoretical (Carruthers, 2005). And the first part of this view, at least, is one to which Nichols and Stich themselves should have been led, since the existence of a separate perception-monitoring mechanism is wholly unnecessary, even on their own account.

To see this, one just has to notice that the overall mind-reading faculty (as described above) must be capable of receiving perceptual inputs. More specifically, the perception-detection mechanism must receive such inputs. For it will need to receive a percept representing the relations that obtain between the target subject and his environment, for example, on which it then needs to effect various computations (e.g. tracking the subject's line of sight) to figure out what the subject is perceiving. And likewise the desire-detecting mechanism will need access to perceptual input concerning the target subject's facial expressions and movements, in order to figure out what it is that the subject wants. (The most plausible way of developing this idea would be to adopt some variant of Baars' (1988, 1997) global broadcasting model, according to which perceptual states—when conscious—are globally broadcast to a whole suite of consumer systems for drawing inferences, for forming beliefs, for forming memories, for planning, and so on. For included amongst these consumer systems for perceptual states would be the mind-reading module, or some of its 'front end' elements.) But then if the mind-reading mechanism is already receiving the subject's own perceptual states as input, it will be trivially easy for it to self-ascribe experiences. The existence of a separate perception self-monitoring mechanism is wholly unnecessary.

Notice, however, that in one sense the detection of one's own experiential (and imagistic) states will be 'theoretical', on this alternative account, since it will involve the very same information-rich mechanism that is involved in the attribution of such states to other people. But the process of detection will be trivial, requiring only the classification of the perceptual inputs to the system as such. (Some of us who have written on this topic have talked about recognitional applications of theoretically embedded concepts, in this connection; Carruthers, 2000.) What we would have here is an information-rich mechanism for ascribing mental states to other people that is also capable of self-ascribing experiences on the basis of the perceptual states that are available to it as input.

Now consider the self-ascription of propositional attitudes, on this alternative account (which assumes that there is no self-monitoring mechanism separate from the mind-reading faculty, remember). It is important to notice that the evidence available to the mind-reading faculty will include both visual imagery and 'inner speech'. For the data suggest that these phenomena utilize the very same mechanisms as do vision and speech-perception respectively (Paulescu et al., 1993; Kosslyn, 1994; Shergill et al., 2002). In which case they, too, should be available as inputs to the mind-reading faculty. (Moreover, as we shall see in Chapter 5, there is good reason to think that it is images resulting from action rehearsals of various sorts that *realize* the possible worlds box described in Nichols and Stich's model.) This then provides us with the materials to flesh-out what Nichols and Stich (2003) describe as the 'mystery version' of the theory-theory account of self-awareness (namely, that there is a special source of information exploited in reading one's own mind in addition to one's own behavior). And it also serves to undermine a great many of their arguments in support of the propositional self-monitoring mechanism.

For example, on the present view it should come as no surprise that high-functioning autistic subjects are able to solve certain meta-memory tasks, such as describing how they set about remembering a sequence of numbers (Farrant et al., 1999). For memory tasks of this sort routinely involve manipulations of visual images and/or items in inner speech (Baddeley, 1986). And these should be reportable just as easily as are manipulations of numerals on paper, or one's own verbal utterances. There is no support for a separate self-monitoring mechanism to be had here.

It is important to note, too, that verbalization of a propositional attitude (whether overtly or in inner speech) is unlikely to require higher-order knowledge that one *has* that attitude. In order to express my belief that today is Monday, I don't *first* have to believe *of* myself that I believe that today is Monday. Rather, the occurrent belief that today is Monday just has to be taken as input by the language faculty and encoded into a suitable linguistic format. So the fact that people are highly reliable in *expressing* their occurrent thoughts in experimental 'think aloud' protocols (Ericsson and Simon, 1993) does nothing to support the idea of a self-monitoring mechanism, as Nichols and Stich (2003) allege. For there isn't any reason to believe that people who are engaged in a 'think aloud' task have any access to their own thoughts independent of and prior to the expression of those thoughts in speech.

3.3 Confabulating and Theorizing

Not only are there no good reasons for believing in a separate self-monitoring mechanism, but there is powerful evidence that we do actually attribute beliefs and goals to ourselves as a result of swift and unconscious *self-interpretation*, much of the time. More than half a century of research in social psychology has uncovered a wealth of evidence that many of our beliefs about the thought-processes that cause our own behavior are actually *confabulated* (Festinger, 1957; Bem, 1967, 1972; Wicklund and Brehm, 1976; Nisbett and Wilson, 1977; Eagly and Chaiken, 1993. See Gazzaniga, 1998, and Wilson, 2002, for reviews.) Far from having direct access to our own reasoning and decision-making processes, what we actually do in many cases is interpret our own behavior, ascribing mental states to ourselves in much the same sort of way that we might ascribe them to another person. And where the true causes of behavior are obscure to common-sense psychology, such self-attributions will frequently be false. But we aren't aware that what we are doing is confabulating. For we tend to operate with a simplified model of the mind, according to which our own thought processes are transparent to us.

Consider one of the examples of confabulation described by Gazzaniga (1998). A split-brain patient gets up and begins to walk across the room because the instruction, 'Walk!' is flashed on a screen in his left visual field (hence being available only to the right hemisphere). But when asked what he is doing, the left hemisphere responds, 'I want to get a drink from the fridge.' (In most people the left hemisphere houses both the language centers, which answer the question, and also the main elements of the mind-reading faculty, which generates the self-interpretation.) Although the explanation is plainly confabulated, the patient isn't aware that this is so. On the contrary, he takes himself to be acting as he does *because* he is *aware* of a desire for a drink. Yet the causes of his action were actually first-order ones having nothing to do with thirst: he got up to walk because he comprehended a written instruction to do so, delivered by a person of some authority (the experimenter).

I don't mean to be claiming, of course, that our self-interpretative processes are entirely epiphenomenal, and have no effect on our behavior. On the contrary, the higher-order interpretative narratives that we weave for ourselves can constrain us and guide us in various ways. (Indeed, this is one of the insights that is developed by 'dual process' models of human reasoning and decision-making, to be discussed extensively in Chapter 4 and thereafter.) One constraint is provided by the desire to act consistently with the self-image that we have constructed. I would be prepared to bet, for example, that having formulated his confabulated explanation, Gazzaniga's patient did indeed go to the fridge to get a drink. Since he thinks that this is what he wants, this is what he would probably do; and the explanation becomes self-fulfilling. My point is just that much *less* of our behavior may actually be caused by conscious thought-processes than we are intuitively inclined to believe. And more importantly, in the present context, we have good reason to think that our access to our own propositional attitudes is self-interpretative, except in cases where those attitudes receive expression in visual imagery or inner speech. (Recall that these latter states will be globally broadcast, and will thus be received as input by the mind-reading mechanism.)

3.4 Two Models of the Psychology Module

It might be objected that we have moved too hastily from the evidence that humans *sometimes* confabulate when explaining their own behavior, to the claim that intra-modular reasoning and decision-making processes (i.e. those that aren't globally broadcast) will *generally* be inaccessible to, and uninfluenced by, higher-order thought. And indeed, such a move is too hasty. There are two different models of the way in which our psychology faculty is embedded into the architecture of the mind, and connected with other systems, which carry different implications on just this point. It is worth briefly sketching these models, and articulating some reasons for preferring one to the other of them. For this will prove to be of some importance in later chapters.

On one model, the psychology faculty only has direct access to perceptual (and to quasi-perceptual, e.g. to imagistic or emotional) states. This is the account that has been implicitly assumed up to now, and is the one represented in Figure 3.2. The explanation is the standard one given in the cognitive science literature, namely that the module in question evolved for purposes of predicting and explaining (and hence also manipulating) the behavior of other people (Byrne and Whiten, 1988, 1997). This required it to have access to perceptual input. The directing of this faculty upon oneself to explain one's own behavior, in contrast, is a secondary phenomenon, not under independent selection. Hence, while the psychology faculty might have access to stored information (e.g. about someone's previous actions) when constructing its representations, and while it can query other processing systems for information in the course of its operations, it has no access to the inferential *processes* that generate that information. Nor does it routinely monitor the outputs of those other systems on an on-going basis. I shall continue to call this account,

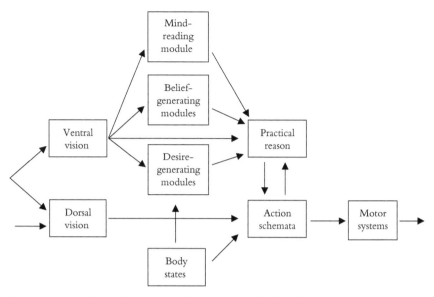

Figure 3.2. A mind with an outwardly focused psychology faculty

'the mind-reading model', since it conceives the function of the faculty in question to be that of attributing mental states to others (and only derivatively to oneself).

It needn't be claimed that the mind-reading faculty has *no* access to the inferential processes that take place within the subject, of course. But that access will be limited to processes that in one way or another implicate sensory representations. For example, if some of our thinking is conducted consciously in imaged natural-language sentences, in 'inner speech', as I shall claim in Chapter 4, then those processes of thinking will be both conscious and available to the mind-reading faculty, issuing in higher-order thoughts about those processes. Indeed, the mind-reading model can mesh successfully with 'dual process' theories of human cognition (also to be discussed in Chapter 4), and with accounts like that of Dennett (1991), according to which there is a level of language-dependent mentality (Dennett's 'Joycean machine') which is imbued with higher-order thinking. For these processes, involving states that are quasi-perceptual in character, can be made available to the mind-reading module in just the same way that perceptual contents are.

But didn't we concede in Chapter 1.2 that the mind-reading system might often need to operate by querying other belief-generating systems for inform-ation, as well as conducting searches of memory? And doesn't that require the mind-reading system to have access to the outputs of those other systems?

In which case it should be capable of self-attributing those outputs without needing to engage in any sort of process of self-interpretation. In reply we need to distinguish between the capacity to *query* belief-generating systems for information, and the routine monitoring and representation of the outputs of those systems to subserve immediate self-attributions of current belief and judgment. It is very plausible that the mind-reading faculty should have the former capacity, for the reasons presented in Chapter 1.2. But this gives us no reason to think that it should routinely monitor the outputs of the various belief-generating systems, irrespective of context. (AI is replete with systems that can query one another for information when executing their own tasks, for example, but which have no access to the reasoning processes that go on within those other systems, and which make no attempt to monitor and represent the outputs of those systems on a routine basis.)

The alternative model—which might as well be called 'the self-monitoring model'—claims that at least one of the functions of the psychology faculty is to monitor, to intervene in, and to correct where necessary, the subject's own reasoning processes.[12] This then requires, of course, that the module in question should have *access to* those processes, representing the activity and/or outputs of the systems in question on a routine basis, as depicted in Figure 3.3. This alternative model might be framed in terms of one of two distinct evolutionary explanations. On the one hand it might be claimed that self-monitoring is an *additional* function of the psychology faculty, that either evolved on the back of a prior mind-reading ability, or that co-evolved simultaneously with it (this seems to be the position of Shallice, 1988). Or it might be claimed, in contrast, that self-monitoring is the *primary* evolutionary function of a psychology faculty—in which case we could expect to find higher-order thought in creatures that as yet lack any capacity to attribute mental states to others (this seems to be the position of Smith et al., 2003).[13]

The self-monitoring model needn't claim that the psychology faculty has complete and infallible access to all inferential processes within the subject, of course. So the model can be made consistent with the confabulation evidence reviewed in Section 3.3. (However, we are still owed a story about *which* reasoning processes are available to the self-monitoring system

---

[12] Nichols and Stich (2003) present a special case of this sort of view, claiming that there are actually two distinct systems involved—one for mind-reading and one for self-monitoring.

[13] It counts against this latter hypothesis, I think, that young children can attribute mental states to other people some while before they are capable of reflecting on and attributing such states to themselves (Gopnik, 1993; Flavell et al., 1995). Moreover, Smith et al. (2003) focus on uncertainty monitoring. But as I show in Carruthers (2005), this can take place *without* any capacity to attribute mental states to oneself.

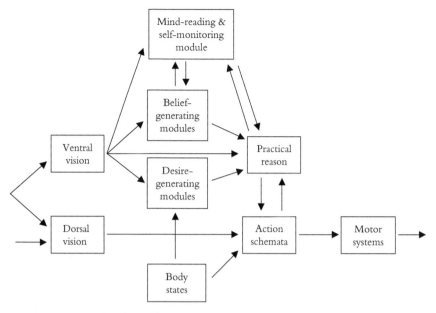

Figure 3.3. A mind with a self-monitoring faculty

and which aren't. This isn't going to be a trivial thing to provide. I shall return to this point in a moment.) But the model will claim that *many more* human cognitive processes are non-inferentially available to higher-order thought—being self-attributable without self-interpretation—than would be allowed by the mind-reading model.

3.5 Adjudicating the Two Models

The contrast between the mind-reading and self-monitoring models is a large issue for cognitive science to address, of course, and it cannot be discussed adequately here. But it is still worth articulating briefly why the mind-reading model is much the more plausible of the two. One point is that the self-monitoring model doesn't seem capable of explaining, in anything other than an ad hoc way, the frequent *failures* of self-monitoring, as revealed in the extensive social-psychology data on confabulation. If the mind-reading faculty had the power to monitor the outputs of belief-generating systems and the practical-reasoning system, then why is it that the self-attribution process should go awry in just the ways that it does?

What seems to hold true of the cases represented in the confabulation literature is that they fit one of two patterns. Either the thoughts that are really driving people's behavior in the experimental circumstances are ones that would be surprising to common-sense psychology (hence some other explanation needs to be confabulated). Or there is a plausible but false common-sense explanation, which is then mis-attributed. (For examples, that people choosing amongst what are actually identical items should have a tendency to select from the right hand side of the array falls into the first category; and that people should enjoy a game less if they are paid to participate in it falls into the second. See Wegner, 2002, and Wilson, 2002, for discussion and references.) This patterning in the confabulation data suggests that people are engaging in self-interpretation in all cases.

A second point is this: in the case of mind-reading, we have a highly developed competence with obvious adaptive significance. Human beings are quite remarkably good at attributing mental states to others (and to themselves), and hence at engaging in the sorts of manipulative and/or cooperative behaviors whose success depends upon those attributions being accurate. And everyone agrees that this competence is part of the natural endowment of any normally developing human being. In contrast, it is far from clear that we possess any very useful competence in the domain of self-monitoring. Of course we are good at *attributing* mental states to ourselves (absent the confabulation cases), but for a mind-reading theorist this is just a matter of our turning our mind-reading abilities upon ourselves. What is in question is whether we have the sort of highly developed capacity to monitor, troubleshoot, intervene in, and improve upon our own modular reasoning processes on-line, in the way that the self-monitoring model requires.

There is little reason to think that we possess any such natural competence. Indeed, naive subjects are quite remarkably poor at distinguishing good sequences of reasoning from bad ones, or at fixing up the latter to make them better (Kahneman et al., 1982; Piattelli-Palmarini, 1994). And insofar as people have any such capacity, it only emerges late in development, not until late childhood or early adolescence (Pillow, 2002; Moshman, 2004). This isn't to say that naive subjects are bad *at reasoning*, of course. For many (if not all) of our first-order information-generating systems will have been under selection pressure for speed and reliability. And moreover, some of the heuristic reasoning processes that people employ turn out to be quite remarkably successful (Gigerenzer et al., 1999). Rather, it is to say that naive subjects are bad at reasoning *about reasoning*—at identifying mistakes in reasoning, at theorizing about standards of good reasoning, and at improving their own and others' reasoning. Yet this is the sort of competence that the self-monitoring model predicts we should have.

One of the defining features of advanced human civilizations, in fact, is that they contain socially transmitted bodies of belief about the ways in which one *should* reason. And these bodies of belief need to be laboriously acquired through processes of formal education. (Examples would include the canons of experimental method in science, developed piecemeal over the last five centuries or so, and standards of logic and rhetoric, stretching back at least to ancient Greece; neither is easily acquired.) Insofar as we have any competence in evaluating and improving reasoning, therefore, this isn't a *natural* competence, but a socially transmitted one. And the result is that two *sorts* of reasoning systems need to be postulated to explain human performance, as we shall see more fully in Chapter 4—a set of swift and unconscious reasoning modules, on the one hand, and laborious conscious reasoning in accordance with believed normative standards, on the other. And the latter, utilizing globally broadcast sentences in 'inner speech', as well as other forms of imagery, requires only a mind-reading system that has access to perceptual input.

It might be objected that self-monitoring can be undertaken for purposes other than the imposition of correct normative standards of reasoning. Indeed, aren't cognitive science and AI rife with postulated mechanisms that monitor whether tasks have been completed, whether the output of some process matches what was expected, and so forth? And didn't the practical-reasoning system described in Chapter 2.8 involve the self-monitoring of bodily / emotional reactions to envisaged outcomes? All this is quite true, but irrelevant. For the sort of monitoring that is in question in the present section is monitoring that issues in higher-order thoughts—that is to say, thoughts that are explicitly *about* our first-order thoughts and beliefs, as generated by our conceptual modules. The sorts of self-monitoring processes just described, in contrast, can all be realized without subjects having the capacity to attribute mental states to themselves at all.

Monitoring whether some cognitive task has been completed can just mean having some mechanism that is sensitive to whether or not the system has generated an output. This needn't require that the mechanism in question should have the conceptual resources to self-attribute that output. Likewise for a process that matches the output of a module against some previously generated template or expectation. And monitoring of *bodily* reactions is a first-order perceptual process, rather than a higher-order one.

I think that we can set the self-monitoring model of self-knowledge of propositional attitudes a dilemma, then. Insofar as we have any reason to believe that something like self-monitoring occurs, then this is either monitoring that doesn't really require any capacity for higher-order thought, or it does require such a capacity, but operates on globally broadcast perceptual or quasi-perceptual items (visual images, rehearsals of natural language sentences in 'inner speech', and so on). And yet the latter sort of monitoring is fully explicable from the perspective of the mind-reading model, according to which the mind-reading faculty is focused 'outwards', via access to the outputs of the perceptual modules. Hence we have no reason to think that the architecture of our cognition is as the self-monitoring model claims, or as Figure 3.3 depicts.

4 Language in Mind

There is now an *immense* body of literature on language acquisition, language production, language comprehension, and the cognitive faculties underlying each, much of it directly or indirectly influenced by the work of Chomsky (1957, 1965, 1975, 1986, 1995). A significant portion of this literature is reviewed by Pinker (1994), who makes out a powerful case supporting the existence of an innately structured language module. (See also Siegal and Surian, 2006, who also review evidence for the distinctness of the language and mind-reading modules.) I cannot hope to discuss more than a tiny part of the evidence here. But nor do I need to for my purposes. For in the light of the arguments of Chapters 1 and 2, the modularity of core aspects of the language faculty (as with core aspects of mind-reading) should now be our default hypothesis. I shall confine myself to laying out some of the assumptions that I shall need in Chapter 4.

Influenced partly by the evidence provided by different forms of aphasia (specifically, production aphasia and comprehension aphasia), but also by other considerations, Chomsky (1995) suggests that the language faculty divides into three main components. There is a language *production* (or output) system, a language *comprehension* (or input) system, and a knowledge base of grammatical and phonological rules that underlies the operations of each. (See Figure 3.4.) The language production system receives its input from the various central / conceptual modules, as well as from practical reason; and it makes its output available to the motor control systems, issuing in speech, Sign, or writing. The language comprehension system, in contrast, receives its input from the perceptual systems (primarily hearing and vision) and makes its output available to the various central / conceptual modules. Let me say just a little more about the operations of each.

Along with most standard accounts of speech production, I shall assume that the process of language production often begins with a message-to-be-communicated (Levelt, 1989)[14]—although in Chapters 4 and 5 I shall defend

---

[14] The obvious challenge that arises here is to explain how this message-to-be-communicated gets selected from amongst the multitude of thoughts that might be active in one's mind at any one time,

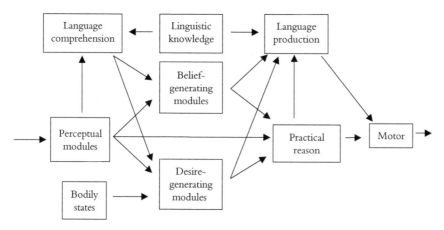

Figure 3.4. The place of language in the mind

a couple of important modifications to the idea. This message will generally be a thought produced by one of the conceptual modules, or by practical reason, formulated in some structured representational code (a sentence of Mentalese). The language production sub-system will take this representation and draw on lexical, syntactic, and phonological knowledge to formulate a description of the sentence-to-be uttered. This description might initially be modality-neutral; or it might at the same time be an abstract motor schema, encoding the instructions necessary to begin speaking, Signing, or writing.

As for how the comprehension sub-system makes its output available to the various central / conceptual modules, one plausible suggestion is that this output takes the form of so-called 'mental models'—that is, non-sentential, quasi-imagistic, representations of the salient features of a situation being thought about (Johnson-Laird, 1983). For it is now well-established that mental models play an indispensable role in discourse comprehension. (See Harris, 2000, for reviews.) When listening to speech, what people do is draw on their knowledge of syntax, the lexicon, and so on to construct a mental model of the situation being described, which they can then use to underpin further inferences. The reason why this may work is that mental models, being perception-like, are already in the right *form* to be taken as input by the suite of central / conceptual modules. For of course those modules would originally have been built to handle perceptual inputs, prior to the evolution of the language faculty.

without us having to postulate anything so anti-modularist as some sort of 'central executive system'. I take this challenge to be of-a-piece with that of explaining creative action-selection in general. I shall return to this topic at some length in Chapter 5.

Just as was the case with the mind-reading system considered in Section 3, both the production and comprehension sub-systems of the language module are likely to interact with other modules in the course of their normal operation. In fact, both are likely to interact heavily with the mind-reading system itself. (Indeed, Gomez, 1998, makes out a powerful case that language and mind-reading co-evolved, with advances in either one setting up an evolutionary 'arms race' to encourage advances in the other.) For the process of language comprehension will often need recourse to beliefs about the speaker's intentions and background assumptions, especially (but not only) when the language used is metaphorical, or in some other way 'non-literal' (Sperber and Wilson, 1995). Likewise in the process of speech production, we need to deploy our mind-reading ability in figuring out the probable effects of a given utterance on our audience. (As we shall see in Chapter 4, such predictions are likely to be made by mentally rehearsing utterances before they get made.)

5 Imitation and Cultural Accumulation

In this section I shall discuss the human ability to acquire novel behaviors through imitation, and the ways in which this ability makes possible much of the flowering of material culture that is so distinctive of our species, and that has played such an important part in our success.

5.1 Imitation

Human beings may be unique in their capacity to imitate the actions of others; and they are at least uniquely proficient at it. Members of other species of primate are capable of learning from one another, and can develop local cultural traditions of a limited sort. Famously, the technique of washing sweet potatoes in water to remove their covering of sand was invented by one Japanese macaque and spread (albeit very slowly) through most of the rest of the troupe (Kawai, 1965). And local chimpanzee populations vary in such behavior as the use of stones to crack nuts and the use of sticks to probe for termites, but in such a way that the explanation for those variations is unlikely to be either ecological or genetic (McGrew, 1992; Wrangham et al., 1994). Yet Tomasello (1999) argues, nevertheless, that it isn't probable that these behavioral traditions result from imitation in the fullest sense. Let me explain.

A number of different forms of social learning can be distinguished. The simplest is often called 'stimulus enhancement'. If you are frequently in the vicinity of someone who uses a stone as an anvil on which to crack nuts, then you, too, will have ready access to the necessary materials. And then even if you make no observations of the other's behavior at all, this makes it more likely that you will learn the behavior for yourself through trial and error. Also pretty simple is the acquisition of novel goals through observation of others. If you see your mother consuming termites and consequently try eating some yourself that happen to be easily available—finding that you like them—then you are likely to attempt to get more of them for yourself, both then and in the future.

Rather more sophisticated is what Tomasello (1999) calls 'emulation learning'. By observing someone using a stone as an anvil, and noticing the results, you can come to know of the causal affordances of such stones, even if you haven't analyzed the details of the behavior in question. Or by observing your mother roll a log and then eat the insects underneath, you can learn that insects are often found beneath fallen logs, and hence start looking in such places yourself. There is no doubt that chimpanzees are excellent social learners in each of the above senses.

More sophisticated still, is what Byrne (1995) calls 'program level imitation'. Here one analyzes a complex behavior into its component parts and sequences. Byrne (1995) describes a number of examples of the food-processing behavior of mountain gorillas, and argues that they must be acquired in something like this way. (The behaviors almost certainly aren't innate.) The edible portions of the plants that mountain gorillas eat—such as the pith contained within the hard casing of mountain celery—can generally only be extracted after considerable processing; and many of the plants themselves are defended by spines or stings, as are nettles. In order to process such foods, complex sequences of action are required. The sequences involved seem to be learned by infant gorillas from observation of their mothers, but not all the details of the behavior are copied. And Byrne (1995) argues that some sort of statistical parsing of the action sequences, together with observation of the consequences of each, might be sufficient for this sort of learning. This requires infant gorillas to be capable of categorizing movement types, but they don't yet have to be representing, and figuring out, the intentions of the actor.

By around the age of eighteen months, in contrast, human infants will copy actions by imitating the agent's intention. Thus if infants see an adult trying to pull apart two components of an unfamiliar object, then they will replicate the (successful) target action themselves, irrespective of whether or not the adult ever succeeds (Meltzoff, 1995). And when infants watch two sequences of action with interesting results, one of which is signaled as intentional (by the actor saying, 'There!' on completing it) but the other of which is signaled as accidental (by the actor saying, 'Oops!'), they are much more likely to imitate the former (Carpenter et al., 1998). This meshes nicely with the data noted in

Section 2, which suggests that infants are capable of identifying and reasoning from an agent's apparent goals (Gergely et al., 1995; Gergely and Csibra, 2003).

True imitation, of which human beings (and perhaps only human beings) are manifestly capable, requires the deployment of a number of distinct abilities. One is to identify the overall goal of the target behavior, interpreting the behavior in question as performed with the intention of achieving that goal. Another is to parse a complex behavior into its component parts, understanding the result in terms of goal / sub-goal structures. And yet another is to discriminate the relevant from the irrelevant, both in the details of the actions themselves, and in their effects. Each of these abilities might be underpinned by a distinct module—a nascent mind-reading module, for intention attribution; a statistical parser of a sort that might be shared with gorillas; and one or more causal-reasoning modules, which might or might not be shared with other animals.

Whether the unique human propensity for imitation results from the addition of one or more new modules to the repertoire of the other great apes (perhaps the mind-reading module, or perhaps a deeper causal-reasoning module), or rather from a novel disposition to utilize a set of existing modules in a new way (perhaps by adding a disposition to take the acquisition of novel behaviors as an explicit goal), seems to me an open question at this point. But undoubtedly the 'mirror neuron' system that we saw in Chapter 2.8 serves to underlie the human (and perhaps great ape) capacity for mental rehearsal of actions also plays an important role in our capacity to imitate actions (Hurley and Chater, 2005). For it is this that enables us to map the perceived movements of another person into a motor schema of our own.

5.2 Cultural Accumulation

Although the cognitive differences underlying the enhanced imitative abilities of humans over the other great apes may be fairly small, the effects have been dramatic, as Richerson and Boyd (2005) emphasize. For successive *accumulations* in material culture become possible as a result, leading eventually to the invention of such things as digital computers and the internet. Innovations introduced by one individual (whether arrived at by accident or through creative problem solving) can be reliably learned by others and spread through the local population, setting up a base from which yet further innovations can be made and disbursed. The result can be something like a ratchet effect, with each generation building on the achievements of previous ones.

It seems to me very doubtful whether imitative abilities *alone* can account for the dramatic accumulations of material culture that have taken place over the last 200,000 years, however. For cultural accumulation can only occur where the rate of successful innovations is relatively high in comparison with the error rate, or the rate at which errors are introduced during the copying process (Boyd and Richerson, 1985; Shennan, 2001). It is therefore important to the explanation of run-away cultural accumulation, I think, both that humans should be capable of creative problem solving and that they should be capable of sophisticated causal understanding of the properties of their material products. The former is necessary to ensure that the rate of innovation is relatively high, and the latter is necessary to ensure that the error rate is low. (If you understand *why* something is made in a certain way, then you are less likely to introduce changes for the worse when learning how to make it for yourself.)

Adding language into the mix, too, must surely have had a significant impact, in two distinct ways. First, language makes it possible to supplement mere practical demonstrations with some explicit teaching—such as pointing out to the novice the crucial stages in the process, explaining the important properties of the device, and/or providing an abstract description of the construction process which can be used to guide learning. Secondly, language is of course used to transmit bodies of belief, through testimony. Hence part of what can be accumulated within a culture are socially transmitted bodies of belief about matters that are highly relevant to material culture, such as where to obtain stones of a certain sort for tool making, or where to obtain the beetle larvae needed to manufacture poisons, or the best time of year at which to sow wild corn, and so on and so forth.

It remains the case, however, that without the capacity for imitation there would be no significant material culture. This is because it is extremely hard to learn any complex behavior through verbal instruction alone. Such behaviors need to be demonstrated to be acquired. So it does seem appropriate to regard our imitation capacities as a crucial *necessary* condition for the success of our species, even if not to consider them *sufficient* (as Tomasello, 1999, appears to suggest). I also want to stress here, however, that there are important components of culture that can't be explained in terms of imitative capacities at all. For much of what makes different cultures distinctive, and can sometimes explain their differential success, consists in patterns of social organization and the rules by which they operate. In short, much of culture is *normative* rather than material or merely behavioral. And the acquisition and transmission of norms requires a different set of explanatory primitives, as we shall see in Section 7.[15]

---

[15] This point is often missed by those who write on these topics. Indeed, people frequently fail to draw any distinction between (a) the mechanisms needed to acquire *beliefs* from others (and to

5.3 *Adaptations to Culture and Cultural Evolution*

Once cultural accumulation became a reliable part of the human phenotype, a new set of evolutionary forces was released, and humans and culture began to *co-evolve*. Amongst the most famous examples of an interaction between human genes and human culture is the evolution of the genes that confer lactose tolerance after normal weaning (Durham, 1991). These genes are common in human populations with a substantial history of dairy production, but only as a function of latitude. The advantage doesn't derive from consumption of dairy products as such, since cheese and yoghurt can make such products digestible in a way that raw milk normally isn't. Rather, the advantage derives from the role that milk plays in the manufacture of vitamin D, of crucial significance for those living at high latitudes, whose exposure to direct sunlight is small. (The Eskimo, in contrast, eat foods that are already rich in vitamin D.)

This is an example where a cultural practice—milk drinking, together with the beliefs and behavior necessary to sustain it—co-evolved with a physiological adaptation. But there is every reason to think that cultural practices may have co-evolved with *cognitive* adaptations, too. The most important examples are probably ones where the development of cultural accumulation *as such* co-evolved with cognitive adaptations to culture. Given the vital importance of culture to human fitness, we should expect to see the appearance of adaptations that make cultural practices easier to learn, and that direct the learner towards practices that are more likely to be successful. In the former (ease of learning) category it may well be the case that there has been selection for enhanced belief-acquisition, skill-acquisition, and norm-acquisition systems. (The last of these will be discussed in Section 7.) And in the latter (directed learning) category, a number of novel motivational modules seem to have resulted, as we shall see in Section 6.

The existence of cultural accumulation also means that there will be differences in the adaptiveness of different human groups, as such. As a result, natural selection acting on the human group becomes an important factor in human evolution, as a number of theorists have argued (Boyd and Richerson, 1985; Sober and Wilson, 1998; Richerson and Boyd, 2005; Wilson, 2006). The result can be selection either for the genes prevalent in a given group, or for the cultural practices of that group, or both.

---

pass them on), (b) the mechanisms necessary to acquire and transmit behavioral *skills*, and (c) the mechanisms required for the acquisition and maintenance of social *norms*. All three are almost certainly distinct from each other. Here, as elsewhere, it is easy to make the task of explaining distinctively human cognition look simpler than it really is by failing to draw relevant distinctions.

6 Human Motivational Modules

In this section I shall discuss some of the motivational modules that seem likely to have been added to the human mind in the course of our evolution. The point of the discussion is to flesh-out our picture of the massively modular mind, not to add any architectural novelties. Since not much in later chapters will turn on the details, my discussion will be brisk.

6.1 Mating and Sexual Selection

A significant portion of the evolutionary psychology research undertaken over the last couple of decades has been about mating behavior and mating motivations, concerning which there is now a huge literature, and about which much is now known. (For reviews, see Buss, 1999, and Barrett et al., 2002.) A good deal of this research has been guided by hypotheses deriving from evolutionary theory, combined with the facts of human biology.

In common with most other mammals, women's lifetime reproductive potential is limited, whereas men's reproductive potential is limited only by the number of available partners. One would therefore expect women to be more choosy about when and with whom they should have sex. And indeed, men cross-culturally show a much greater willingness to engage in casual or short-term mating; and when women do engage in short-term mating they tend to use it either as a strategy for ending an existing long-term relationship, or as a way of obtaining 'better genes' while remaining within a long-term partnership (Buss, 1999).[16]

Similarly, women's fertility is highly correlated with age, whereas in men the correlation is much weaker. (Indeed women, almost uniquely amongst mammals, undergo menopause some twenty years before the end of their natural life cycle, at which point they become completely infertile.) But at the same time (and again uniquely amongst mammals) women's monthly time of ovulation is largely concealed; so there are few direct cues of female fertility. One would therefore expect men to have evolved a mating-motivation system that is sensitive, *inter alia*, to cues that correlate with age, and hence with

---

[16] Strikingly, and in support of the latter point, the number of extra-pair couplings of women in long-term relationships varies across the menstrual cycle. The number of such couplings is higher during their time of peak fertility, whereas the number of couplings they have with their long-term partner remains constant (Baker and Bellis, 1995). Moreover, symmetrical males are more likely to be taken as extra-pair partners (Gangestad and Thornhill, 1997); and ovulating women prefer the smell of a T-shirt worn by a symmetrical male to one worn by an a-symmetrical male (Thornhill and Gangestad, 1999). (Symmetry is a reliable indicator of genetic quality along a number of dimensions; see Campbell, 2002.)

fertility.[17] And indeed, the features that men find physically attractive in women cross-culturally (such as clear firm skin, lithe body, relatively slim waist, and so on) are good indicators of age. Women, in contrast, are much less interested in physical features that correlate with age, and are much more interested in indicators of status and resources, especially (but not only) when choosing a long-term mate (Ellis, 1992; Buss, 1994, 1999; Campbell, 2002).

At the same time, the uniquely long period of infant and childhood dependency amongst humans has necessitated a mating system based on pair-bonding, just as exists in some other mammalian species and amongst many species of birds. This means that women's motivations towards long-term mating are heavily influenced, not only by the male's resources, but also by signs of long-term commitment (such as expressions of love and costly gifts), as well as by indicators that the male may make a good husband and father, such as either generalized kindliness or kindliness towards children in particular. Indeed, Miller (2000) argues that female mate choice (and similar mate choices exercised by men—see below) is likely to have been an important factor in selecting for traits such as kindliness and sympathy.

Given a breeding system based largely on pair-bonding, then men, too, need to be extremely choosy in selecting a long-term mate. For time invested in supporting one woman and helping to provision and care for her children is time that cannot be devoted to another; while also restricting opportunities for short-term mating. Men should therefore be interested in much more than just youthfulness and beauty. They, too, should be interested in signs of long-term commitment, and in indicators (such as kindliness) that the woman will make a good mother. And they should be especially interested in the sexual fidelity of their partners. For as the old adage has it, 'maternity is always certain, paternity never so.' A woman is never in danger of unwittingly investing in children that aren't her own, whereas men are always faced with such a risk. The result is a sexual jealousy motivational system that is especially potent in men (Wilson and Daly, 1992).

While men and women differ in many of the factors that influence their choice of a mate, it is important to emphasize that they also agree on a great deal. It has already been mentioned that both sexes rate kindliness and commitment highly in a potential long-term mate; and in each case the evolutionary explanation is likely to be the same. But both sexes also

---

[17] Let me emphasize two points here. One is that men's preference isn't likely to be for youth *as such*, but rather for perceptible factors that correlate with youth, such as smooth skin. The other is that this will only be one motivational factor amongst many in men's mating decisions, as will become clear as our discussion continues. Buller (2005) goes astray on both of these points in the course of his critique of (what he thinks of as) the evolutionary psychology theory of mate preference.

rate intelligence very highly (Buss, 1994). The probable explanation is that intelligence (in the sense of resourcefulness and problem solving ability) is highly correlated with long-term reproductive success. This is pretty obvious in connection with hunter-gatherer males (see Chapter 6.2). But it is equally true for women: the reproductive success of hunter-gatherer women today is much more influenced by their resourcefulness than by their fertility; and many women don't succeed in raising even a single child to adulthood, despite giving birth to many children (Hrdy, 1999). Moreover, both sexes value a sense of humor very highly (Buss, 1994). Miller (2000) speculates that a sense of humor (together with the positive emotions to which it gives rise) may result from sexual selection for what is, after all, an honest indicator of intelligence—you have to be smart to be funny: it can't easily be faked (prior to the advent of scriptwriters, at least).

The structure of the various motivational systems that are concerned with human mating behavior seem likely to conform to the general model of a desire-generating module outlined in Chapter 2.5. These will be systems that are designed to respond to both perceptual cues (such as the shape of a woman's figure, or the symmetry of a face) and to bodily ones (such as hormone levels at a certain stage in a woman's menstrual cycle). But they are also designed to integrate these cues with stored information of various sorts, concerning both the person's previous behavior (whether kindly, funny, and so on) and the agent's own value in the mating market, to deliver a certain strength of intrinsic motivation towards mating.

What is different about humans, of course, is the extent to which we can develop theories about the factors that influence our choices—both our own and other people's. Hence women might often articulate that one of their reasons for marrying a particular man is that he is wealthy, or prestigious. This makes it look as if her decision is a calculated one, designed to secure resources for herself and her offspring. And sometimes, no doubt, it is. But there is also likely to be a motivational module at work, which operates unconsciously and delivers a motivation towards partnership that is intrinsic. This is evidenced by the fact that women are still attracted by rich and prestigious men even when (as often happens in our contemporary era) they themselves are independently wealthy and have no intention of having children (Ellis, 1992).

It is one thing to say that there are motivational modules involved in mating decisions, however, and another thing to say how many. On one account, there might be a single module that integrates all the various factors (appearance, humor, kindliness, status, and so on) and delivers a certain degree of attraction. On another account, there might be a number of distinct modules involved—one that delivers a certain level of physical attraction, one that delivers a certain degree of liking on the basis of one or more characteristics (humor, kindliness), and one that finds indicators of status (such as wealth and prestige) attractive. Since we already know that there are systems delivering the latter two sets of motivations, independently of mating decisions, the many-modules hypothesis is the most parsimonious. (Of course we find humor attractive in our same-sex friends, for example; and most of us want status for ourselves.) But it is still possible that the mating-motivation system takes inputs from these other modules, rather than leaving them to operate independently.

6.2 Parenting and Kin Selection

Some human adaptations directed at parenting have already been discussed in Chapter 1.5, in the context of our defense of evolutionary psychology. Recall that biological reasoning leads to the predictions that (a) high-fitness women should want sons, whereas low-fitness women should want daughters; (b) parents (mothers especially) should invest differentially in their children depending on such factors as the child's health, together with the mother's health, age, and access to resources; and (c) parents should be reluctant to invest in children that are not their own. And recall, too, that these predictions are confirmed (Daly and Wilson, 1988, 1995, 1998; Gaulins and Robbins, 1989; Mann, 1992; Bereczkei and Dunbar, 1997; Hrdy, 1999; Campbell, 2002). These points should now be viewed through the lens of the general model of motivation-creating modules that we adopted in Chapter 2.5.

Moreover, if Hamilton's (1964) theory of kin selection applies to humans, we should expect people to be more generous to kin than to non-kin, and that their preparedness to aid kin should be proportional to the degree of relatedness involved (although of course the resulting adaptation won't be a uniquely human one). These predictions are now amply confirmed by a wide array of data, ranging from anthropological studies of hunter-gatherer tribes, through patterns of homicide and bequests of wealth in contemporary societies, to experimental studies showing that people will bear more pain to aid kin than to aid non-kin. (See Buss, 1999; Barrett et al., 2002, for reviews.) Here, too, we should expect that there will be a cognitive mechanism that takes beliefs about degrees of relatedness as input, and delivers a motivation to assist as output. But of course this motivation will be one amongst many, including motivations to act to benefit oneself. So the relationship between degrees of relatedness and the actual issuing of aid will be by no means deterministic.

Especially interesting in this connection is the possible relationship between grandparental motivations to assist grandchildren, on the one hand (which are markedly stronger amongst grandmothers, as well as varying with paternal certainty; Euler and Weitzel, 1996), and female menopause, on the other. The very existence of menopause seems initially like a biological anomaly: why continue to exist at all if you have no chance of reproducing? It can perhaps be partially explained by noticing that there is little point in a woman giving birth just before she dies, since in hunter-gatherer communities the chances of an infant surviving without its mother are extremely slim (Hrdy, 1999). But this is unlikely to be the whole explanation. For since women's fertility falls off sharply before menopause, a woman dying at the age of menopause is unlikely to have given birth to an infant very recently anyway; and the chances of her children's survival without her rise sharply as they get older. What many have suggested, therefore, is that there has been selection to extend women's lifespans to enable them to invest in their grandchildren (Boyd and Silk, 1997; Buss, 1999; Barrett et al., 2002). This is certainly consistent with data from Hawkes et al. (1997) and elsewhere, indicating that grandmothers (and to a lesser degree grandfathers) in hunter-gatherer communities have a powerful impact on the health and growth of their grandchildren.

6.3 Social Motivations

Human beings engage in many different forms of cooperative and helping behavior towards those who are non-kin; and there must presumably be some distinctive kinds of motivation that underlie these behaviors. Notably, humans form friendships and are strongly motivated to help their friends irrespective of any expectation of a return (Tooby and Cosmides, 1996). Humans cooperate in larger groups and exchange favors with unrelated individuals, such as sharing their food obtained from hunting. And humans also display a willingness to help strangers, in many circumstances. It is unclear to what extent the motivations involved are uniquely human, however. For as we noted in Chapter 2.5, other apes sometimes make alliances with non-kin, and show behavior that seemingly demonstrates compassion for unrelated individuals (de Waal, 1996).

Since Trivers (1971), it has been known that a willingness to engage in reciprocal altruism can evolve, under the right conditions—that is, in circumstances where the participants are known to one another and interact frequently, and where there often exist situations in which the costs to the giver are small in relation to the benefits to the receiver. Since these conditions are satisfied in hunter-gatherer groups, some have suggested that they laid the foundations for the evolution of a module concerned with reciprocal exchange (Cosmides and Tooby, 1992). This system will be charged with keeping track of previous exchanges and of who owes what to whom; it will detect those who cheat in an exchange and provide the motivation to punish cheaters; and it will motivate the individual both to enter into exchanges in the first place and to contribute what they owe to others. These claims are very plausible, and have some empirical support (Cosmides and Tooby, 1992; Fiddick et al., 2000; Stone et al., 2002). Since the system in question deals with relations and motivations that are *normative*, however, further discussion will be deferred to Section 7.

The reciprocal exchange system is likely to be distinct from the system charged with building and maintaining friendships. For the psychology of friendship is quite different from the psychology of social contracts, as Cosmides and Tooby (1996) point out. We seek out and take pleasure in the company of our friends for its own sake. And we are prepared to help our friends when needed without thought of reciprocation. However, it may be that the underlying evolutionary pressure was a sort of reciprocal altruism, nevertheless. For those who have friends are more likely to receive important support when help is needed, in such a way that in the long term (and on the whole) each party benefits.

In addition, it should be noted that it is possible for practices to look a lot like forms of reciprocal exchange when they really aren't, and where the underlying explanation needs to be sought in a distinct set of motivations. Consider the widespread practice of food-sharing amongst hunter-gatherers (Barrett et al., 2002). Since the food most commonly shared is meat from large game, it is natural to think that some kind of reciprocal altruism is at work. For large game hunting is always highly variable in its results, and even the best hunters will often be unsuccessful. If meat is widely shared, however, then these hills and valleys of success can be smoothed out, and everyone will benefit. The trouble with this explanation, though, is that hunting skill is also highly variable, and the best hunters end up with significantly *less* meat in the long run because of the practice of food sharing.

Hawkes (1991, 1993) argues extensively that the motive behind food sharing is actually *status*—it is a form of 'showing off' undertaken by successful males (see also Bliege-Bird and Bird, 1997). This provides them with a larger pool of potential allies, as well as increasing their mating opportunities. For the data suggest that successful hunters father more children than do others (many of them outside of marriage), and that their children are more likely to survive to reproductive age, probably because of the additional support provided by the community to the children of high-status individuals (Hill and Kaplan, 1988).

These data (together with a wealth of similar evidence in the same vein), when combined with the data on mate choice reviewed in Section 6.1, should lead us to expect that there will be a distinct motivational system concerned with status as such. For indicators of high status are valued in both long-term and short-term potential mates (Ellis, 1992). We also know that they are valued more highly by females than by males; and that there are the expected inverse sex differences in the degree to which status is desired for oneself. (That is, men want to achieve status more strongly than do women; Buss, 1999; Campbell, 2002; Deaner, 2006.) Moreover, it does appear that desires for things indicative of high status are often intrinsic ones, and are independent of considerations of utility.[18]

The status module, then, will be a system designed to monitor the social environment to learn what are the reliable indicators of high social status in one's society, and to generate intrinsic motivations towards obtaining some of those things (especially where those things are attainable by the agent, given the agent's circumstances and abilities). Since status is useful to women as well as men, this module should be operative in both sexes. But since status is not *as* useful to women (it isn't ranked nearly so highly in men's desiderata for a mate, for example), the module should operate much more powerfully in men. These predictions are consistent with the data, I believe (Ellis, 1992; Buss, 1999; Campbell, 2002).

Such an account enables us to explain the otherwise bewildering variety of intrinsic desires that people can have, since almost anything can become culturally designated as an indicator of status. Moreover, it can also enable us to explain some of the variations in intrinsic motivations *within* a given society, if we suppose that part of what the status module is designed to do is locate a 'niche' within which the individual can be successful in achieving status. Partly, no doubt, by monitoring one's initial successes, and partly by monitoring the strengths and weaknesses of competitors, we gradually chart a path for ourselves. Some find themselves with intrinsic desires for sporting prowess; some find themselves wanting to perfect and exercise some skill, such as playing a musical instrument or manufacturing jewelry; and some want to tell stories, or to tell jokes.

6.4 Emotional Modules

We have already noted in Section 6.1 that, as a pair-bonding species, humans are susceptible to the emotion of jealousy. This emotion comes in two forms: sexual jealousy, whose object is another person having sexual relations with one's mate; and emotional jealousy, whose object is another person usurping

---

[18] Consider wealth, for example. This is often desired on instrumental grounds, because of the other things that it can get us (although note that these 'other things' are often, themselves, mere indicators of status, such as a flashy car or a large house on a hill). But wealth is also wanted for its own sake. And in misers it is desired *only* for its own sake. This is initially puzzling: for of what use is money if you do nothing with it? But the puzzle disappears when we remind ourselves that wealth is itself an indicator of high status.

the love and attention of one's mate. Both forms of jealousy are felt by both men and women. But predictably, men tend to feel sexual jealousy more strongly, whereas women tend to feel emotional jealousy to a greater degree (Buss, 1994). Whether these emotions are uniquely human, however, is doubtful. For it is quite possible that they are manifestations of emotions that are common to many other pair-bonding species.

Humans are subject to a wide range of other social emotions, including shame (whose object is an action or event that might decrease one's social standing), guilt (whose object is a normative transgression made by oneself), indignation (whose object is the normative transgressions of other people), and moral disgust (whose object is a distinctively moral transgression). Some of these will crop up again in Section 7, when we discuss normative modules in general. Here I propose just to comment briefly on the question whether there is a distinct module for moral disgust, or rather whether the different varieties of disgust (at foods, at bodily fluids, sexual disgust, moral disgust, and so on) are all socialized *extensions* of a single core food-based disgust system, as Rozin et al. (2000) argue.

There is no research that bears directly on this question at present. But there *is* research demonstrating that sexual disgust, at least, is a system separate from the others. Fessler and Navarrete (2003) asked women to complete copies of the disgust-sampling questionnaire designed by Haidt et al. (1994), which is now widely used in research on this topic. It covers all the main categories of disgust elicitor, presenting subjects with descriptions of disgusting items and activities of various kinds, and asking them to rate how disgusted they feel at the thought of those items / activities. At the end of the questionnaire the women were asked to record various personal details about themselves, included in which was the date of their last period. What the authors found was that women's degree of sexual disgust (and only their sexual disgust) rose and fell with their menstrual cycle; and in particular, that women felt most disgusted at disgusting sexual activities during their time of peak fertility. This makes good evolutionary sense given that it is at times of peak fertility that women should be most discriminating about their sexual choices, and given that the function of disgust is to make a given choice less likely. But the important point for our purposes is that it shows that there is a sexual-disgust system in women that is at least partially distinct from the systems that generate other forms of disgust.

6.5 Motivations that Aid Learning

Human beings are an information-gathering and information-using species: we occupy what Cosmides and Tooby (2002) describe as an 'informational niche'. Much of our success as a species depends upon our capacity to learn swiftly about the properties and affordances of novel environments, using both our own observations and the testimony of others. But we also make extensive use of technology; and this, too, requires both factual information and know-how, much of which must be learned from others. Moreover, our capacity to act successfully within social groups depends upon knowledge of the other members of the group, their mental states and other properties, and the rules and customs by which the group (and different sub-sets within the group) operates. Given all this, one might predict that there should be some distinctive kinds of motivation that are targeted specifically on the acquisition of information in general, and on the acquisition of information from other people in particular.[19]

One obvious example of such a motivation is *curiosity*. To be curious about something is to *want to know more* about it—and to want to know, not for some pragmatic purpose or other, but for its own sake. It is therefore likely that there is a distinct module designed to generate the intrinsic goal of *knowing more*, in various contexts (that is, in contexts of manifest ignorance, of various sorts). But whether this system is unique to humans is open to doubt. For of course many other species of animal exhibit curiosity as well. We are, unquestionably, intensely *more* curious than any other species. But whether this results from an enhanced curiosity-generating system, or rather from the operations of a homologous system existing in the context of a suite of enhanced learning mechanisms, is open to question. For after all, if there is a lot more that you are *capable* of learning, then you will have a lot more opportunities to be curious.

Another suggestion that has been made in this area is that humans have an innate drive to seek causal *explanations* of the phenomena that they observe (Gopnik, 1998). This *is* very likely to be uniquely human—at least if Povinelli (2000) is right that we are the only species capable of reasoning about the underlying mechanisms behind observable phenomena. Gopnik (1998) likens explanation to orgasm: when you are successful in finding an explanation for something, you experience a rush of pleasure that is unrelated to any further goals that you might have (like orgasm). This is a very plausible idea. And it can be held independently, I think, of Gopnik's own view that children and infants operate in the manner of little scientists, proposing, testing,

---

[19] And not *only* motivations, of course, but also systems of a cognitive / doxastic sort. In Chapter 6.6, for example, I shall discuss some properties of the mechanism charged with deciding whether or not to believe what others tell us. The existence of a cultural / informational niche in which many of our beliefs are acquired from the testimony of other people, but in which those people are often to some degree 'Machiavellian' in their motivations, gives rise to a crucial new adaptive problem: whose testimony should I accept?

and developing novel explanatory theories (see Chapter 6.3). One could rather think, as I do, that children's basic explanatory frameworks in various domains are either innate (emerging under maturational constraints) or constructed by means of dedicated domain-specific learning mechanisms, while also accepting that children and adults are intrinsically motivated to *use* those frameworks in generating explanations.

Much of what humans learn they learn from other people, of course— whether by copying their behavior or by believing what others tell them. In effect, much human learning is culturally mediated. And this sets up a novel adaptive problem for learners: whom to learn *from*. One strategy is to imitate / adopt the beliefs of the majority in your community. Mathematical modeling demonstrates that this is adaptive in a wide range of circumstances (Henrich and Boyd, 1998). For individual learning is difficult, error prone, and costly; whereas if the community is a stable one, its beliefs and practices are likely to be adaptive on the whole. This leads Richerson and Boyd (2005) to the claim that there should be a species-unique motivational mechanism in humans that makes us *desire to conform*. (Or rather, the mechanism will compute the most frequent variants of behavior and belief in one's environment, and deliver a desire *to behave / believe like that*.) And indeed, there are a whole raft of experiments and data in social psychology that demonstrate people's desire to conform, and its powerful effects on behavior (Myers, 1993).

Another strategy that one can adopt is to imitate / adopt the beliefs of those who are most successful. Here, too, mathematical modeling shows that there are many circumstances in which the strategy can be adaptive (Boyd and Richerson, 1985). And this prompts Henrich and Gil-White (2001) to argue that we have evolved a species-unique motivational mechanism that makes us want *to resemble the prestigious*. We attempt to get close to those who are prestigious, and we try to learn from them, and to model our behavior on theirs (even to the point of purchasing a type of undergarment merely because Michael Jordan is said to wear them). This gives rise to a social dynamic in which those of us who grant prestige to others allow them certain privileges, in return for which they allow us to get close enough to learn from them. And here, too, there is an extensive body of experimental literature supporting the claim that we have a strong tendency to want to be similar to those who are prestigious (Rogers, 1995; Henrich and Gil-White, 2001).

Henrich and Gil-White (2001) argue that there is an important (and often overlooked) distinction amongst kinds of social status, between *dominance* and *prestige*. Dominance is based upon force. Many primate species have dominance hierarchies, and recognize a form of social status determined by dominance rank. Prestige, in contrast, is freely conferred. People become prestigious when sufficiently many others in the community come to recognize their superior knowledge and/or skills. It seems plain that status based upon prestige is a uniquely human phenomenon, and that the resulting human-specific motivational mechanisms are an adaptation to our cultural and informational niche.

Human societies include both dominance-based and prestige-based forms of social organization (Krackle, 1979). But in hunter-gatherer communities, prestige-based forms of leadership are the norm (Boehm, 1999). This is because such communities are mostly organized along *fission–fusion* lines, consisting of smaller groups of individuals who live and move together for a while, embedded within a larger tribal group that meets together for ceremonial occasions, and from within which spouses are sought (Barrett et al., 2002). Since membership in these smaller groupings is fluid, it is hard for any dominance hierarchy to remain stable for very long—for if someone attempts to rule the group in a way that isn't based upon persuasion and respect, the others can simply leave. (Or more likely: the others can band together to ridicule, ostracize, or execute an overly dominant leader; Boehm, 1999.) It therefore makes perfectly good sense that an elaborate form of prestige-psychology should have evolved, in the way that Henrich and Gil-White (2001) claim.

7 Normative Reasoning and Motivation

In the present section I shall consider whether there are distinctively human modules concerned with norms and normative motivation. Although to some degree speculative, our conclusions will be vital to the account that I shall sketch in Chapter 7 of the distinctive forms that are taken by human practical reasoning.

7.1 The Ubiquity of Norms

Norms—in the sense to be discussed here—are social rules specifying what people (or certain people, or certain people in certain circumstances) *must*, or *must not*, or *may* do. They should be distinguished from *laws*, which are rules embedded in formal institutions, and which are backed by institutionalized punishment. Breaches of norms, in contrast, are punished informally by such social mechanisms as disapproval, ostracization, gossip, and sometimes individual or collective violence. Moreover (and very importantly) people for the most part are *intrinsically* (not instrumentally, or not *only* instrumentally) motivated to comply with social norms. The phenomenology of norms and norm compliance is that they strike people as possessing a certain intrinsic 'to be doneness'. As most moral philosophers from Kant onwards have emphasized, *moral* norms, at any rate, are apprehended in the form of 'categorical imperatives'—they tell us what must or mustn't be done irrespective of the consequences or our own personal interests. To put it differently, we *internalize* a set of norms, in such a way that they seem to us to form part of the very fabric of the world, and in such a way that we have some intrinsic motivation to comply with them (Edel and Edel, 2000; Joyce, 2001).[20]

Norms in this sense are a human universal: all human communities have them, and all human communities have a lot of them (Brown, 1991). And in most communities norms extend well beyond the domains that we (in the liberal West, at least) would consider to be ethics. On the contrary, norms enter into the fabric of almost every facet of life, covering such matters as with whom and how and when to have sex, or how to dress, or how to prepare and consume food, or how to deal with the dead, and so on and so forth. Most communities draw no clear distinction between such rules and those governing such matters as killing, stealing, and breach of contract: all are seen as equally objective and obviously-to-be-complied-with. (This isn't to say, of course, that they always *are* complied with. For people also have many other sources of motivation that can lead them to break a norm. But when they do so, they characteristically feel guilt.) Moreover, norms appear to be a uniquely human phenomenon. For although many ape communities have systems of rules that are enforced by violence within dominance hierarchies, there is no evidence that the motivations to comply with those rules are anything other than instrumental ones.

Although people are intrinsically motivated to comply with the norms that they have internalized, breaches of those norms are also enforced by the community, in three main ways: loss of social esteem, ostracization, and physical violence. Then since human communities are characteristically imbued with a great many norms, norm compliance becomes a crucial adaptive problem for the individual. For punishment by the community will generally have a significant impact on your individual fitness. If your social status drops as a result of breaches of social norms, then there are many ways in which this is likely to lower your fitness, ranging from fewer mating opportunities to fewer allies. If you are ostracized by the community, likewise, then there will be many ways in which both you and the members of your family will

---

[20] Some experimental evidence that our motivations to comply with, and to enforce, norms are intrinsic in character will be considered in Section 7.4. But phenomenologically, this is certainly the way it seems. See also the 'moral dumbfounding' experiments conducted by Haidt (2001), which demonstrate that people's emotional reaction to a normative transgression is often prior to, and more fundamental than, anything that they can offer in the way of an instrumentalist rationale.

suffer. (Note that the most extreme form of ostracism is banishment, which in hunter-gatherer communities is likely to result in death.) And physical violence against you, too, is obviously very likely to have a negative impact on your fitness. All this sets up a powerful selective pressure for a norm-based psychology which will make norm compliance more reliable. And here, as so often in cognitive evolution, nature's solution has been (in part) to give us motivations to comply with the norms of our community that are intrinsic, rather than leaving it up to the vagaries of individual reasoning.

Why do norms exist in the first place? Because communities that can act cohesively out-compete communities that can't, whether the competition is direct (e.g. in warfare) or indirect (building up a resource-base and the wherewithal to increase population size). So this is likely to be a prime example of gene–culture co-evolution, where the selective mechanism is a form of group selection (Boyd and Richerson, 1992; Sober and Wilson, 1998; Wilson et al., 2000; Sripada, 2005). The adaptive solution to the problem of collective action is rule-based punishment. And punishment becomes even more effective when backed by *meta*-punishment—we not only disapprove of those who break the rules, but we disapprove of those who fail to disapprove of those who break the rules (Boyd and Richerson, 1992; Sripada, 2005). And the adaptive solution for individuals in groups governed by punishment-backed norms is to develop a norm-psychology which both assists in learning the community norms and provides an intrinsic motivation to comply with them. Such a psychology will be sketched in Section 7.3 (following Sripada and Stich, 2006).

7.2 Experimental and Developmental Evidence

What is the evidence that humans possess some sort of deontic (norm-based) reasoning module? One line of argument starts from the observation that human adults are much better at reasoning that involves deontic conditionals than at parallel reasoning involving indicative conditionals (Cheng and Holyoak, 1985; Cosmides, 1989). For example, people are much better at spotting violations of a rule of the form, 'If you perform action *A*, then you must first meet condition *P*', than they are at recognizing circumstances that would falsify an indicative conditional having an otherwise similar form, 'If you perform action *A*, then you first have property *P*.'

Numerous experimental studies have now been undertaken, carefully controlling for possible confounding factors, and devising pairs of experiments that differ only in the target property: that one condition requires subjects to look for someone cheating on a deontic rule, whereas the other doesn't (Cosmides and Tooby, 1992; Gigerenzer and Hug, 1992). Indeed, some of these experiments pair conditions in which subjects consider the very same deontic rules, but in one condition they are cued to adopt the perspective of someone looking for cheaters, whereas in the other they aren't. Subjects prove to be much better at detecting people *cheating* on a rule than at detecting mere rule violations.[21]

In addition to these studies with normal adults, Stone et al. (2002) report a series of experiments with a particular brain-damaged man, whose performance was compared with other brain-damaged controls. Relative to the controls, this person proved to be very poor at reasoning about social contracts, deontic rules, and the detection of cheaters. In contrast, his capacity to solve structurally parallel tasks concerning risks and dangers was preserved. Stone et al. (2002) conclude, very reasonably, that this is evidence of a separate system designed to make inferences about obligations and permissions within social contracts, and to detect those who cheat on a social contract.

There is also plenty of evidence that a capacity to reason about rules and obligations is an early emerging one, cross-culturally (Cummins, 1996; Harris and Núñez, 1996; Núñez and Harris, 1998; Harris et al., 2001). Three-year-old and four-year-old children are highly reliable at identifying cases where someone has broken a rule; and they are also very good at distinguishing between intentional and accidental non-compliance (categorizing only the former as 'naughty'). Moreover, they do this not only in connection with rules imposed by an authority (e.g. a parent or teacher), but also when reasoning about agreements negotiated between children themselves. And as one might expect, deontic *concepts* are acquired even earlier still. Psycholinguistic research shows that children as young as two years of age can make appropriate uses of modal terms like 'have to' and 'must' (Shatz and Wilcox, 1991).

Of course it doesn't *follow* from these data that human children have an innate module specialized for deontic reasoning, as Harris (2000) points out. For permissions and obligations are very salient in children's lives, from an early age. They might be learning how to reason about them through some sort of inductive, general-learning, process. But this possibility is unlikely, given: (a) the difficulties of reducing deontic conditionals to any other form of conditional, and hence the difficulty of seeing how deontic concepts could be other than innate; together with (b) the general case in support of specialized learning systems made out in Chapters 1 and 2; and (c) given also the evidence from normal and brain-damaged adults reviewed briefly above. Moreover, even if

---

[21] Sperber et al. (1995) claim to challenge these results, and provide an alternative explanation grounded in Relevance Theory (Sperber and Wilson, 1995). But as Fiddick et al. (2000) point out, this explanation only works for indicative conditionals; and they provide yet further experimental evidence in support of their claim of a special adaptation for deontic reasoning. To this Sperber and Girotto (2002) reply in turn. Here, as so often in this book, I am forced to skate over issues that are actually very complicated.

children could learn by induction how to *reason* deontically, there is no obvious way for them to learn inductively how to respond *emotionally* to rule violations in appropriate ways. But from as early as they start to use deontic terms, children become indignant if another child reneges on an agreement, say, or tries to gain an unfair advantage by breaking a rule that the first child has obeyed.

7.3 Normative Modules 1: Norm Acquisition and Motivation

In the light of points such as these (the immense adaptive significance of norms and norm-compliance for individuals, the intrinsic motivation that attaches to norms, the plausible case that can be made for co-evolution of cognition and culture in this domain, together with the evidence of early and better reasoning with deontic conditionals) Sripada and Stich (2006) propose a very plausible psychological model of the normative faculty. It consists of four main components: an acquisition mechanism; a norms database; a reasoning system; and a motivational system. Let me discuss each of these briefly in turn.

The job of the acquisition mechanism is to scan the social environment so as to figure out the norms that are operative therein. Some of this work might seem to be pretty straightforward, based upon explicit instruction from parents and other members of the community. But even here, actually, there will be considerable work for the leaning mechanism to do. For if a parent says, 'You mustn't hurt your little sister', it is by no means obvious what underlying norm should be extracted. Is it: 'Don't hurt someone weaker than yourself'? or, 'Don't hurt a girl'? or, 'Don't hurt a family member'? or, 'Don't hurt anybody'? or, 'Don't hurt anyone unless provoked'?, or what? In other cases the mechanism might draw inferences from the emotional reactions of caregivers and others to observed (or described) actions. And myths and exemplary stories might play an important role too.[22]

Once a set of norms has been acquired, and stored in the norms database, then a set of inferential mechanisms has to be alert for circumstances in which a given norm might apply. If I have stored the norm, 'I mustn't hurt someone weaker than myself', then I shall have to be on the lookout for circumstances in which this might happen. And plainly this requires the normative module to interact with other systems, such as one that might estimate people's relative strengths. But if norms are stored in the form, not of explicit rules, but rather

---

[22] Moreover, although Sripada and Stich (2006) don't say anything about this, the acquisition mechanism must somehow figure out which rules in the community are worthy of being *moralized*. For not all social rules get internalized, and have intrinsic motivation attached to them. Many rules are learned, but left as merely instrumental ones. ('I must clean my teeth before bed if I don't want to get told off.') It is an open empirical question how children go about figuring out which rules should be which. But figure it out they do.

of paradigm cases or exemplars (as Sripada and Stich, 2006, indicate that they might be), then the reasoning involved will have to be of a rather different kind. I shall have to be on the lookout for circumstances that are relevantly similar to one of my stored moral paradigms, and then figure out what action would be required of me if I am to act in the sort of way exemplified.

Most importantly, though, what the normative module does is attach intrinsic motivation to the rules stored in its database. So when the inferential system accesses a stored norm, and figures out that in order to comply with that norm I must perform some action A, it produces in me in consequence an intrinsic desire to A. (Of course, as already noted above, this desire has to compete with others for the control of my behavior. So in any particular case I might or might not perform the action A.) And it does this whether or not I *also* have *extrinsic* reasons to A—such as fear of ostracism. But not only does the system produce an intrinsic desire that I should A, it also produces an emotion of *guilt* in case I do not. And it produces anger or indignation if I learn of someone else in such circumstances who fails to A, as well as if I learn of someone who fails to be angry or indignant at such a failure. Such emotions lead me to think less well of such a person, to shun their company, and in extreme cases to attack them.

The point that I most want to emphasize here, however—which will prove to be especially important in Chapter 7—is that there is a sense in which the norms module *straddles the belief / desire divide*. It acquires and stores a set of *beliefs* (albeit beliefs of an unusual—deontic—form). But it also creates in me the desire that I and others should act as those beliefs describe. This means, I think, that whatever theoretical / doxastic inferential resources I have available to me can be applied to the contents of the norms database; but the results will at the same time have motivational force. So whatever sources of flexibility there are on the doxastic side of the mind can give rise to a similar degree of flexibility in motivation. This will, I think, go a long way towards explaining the distinctive creativity and flexibility of human practical-reasoning abilities.

7.4 Normative Modules 2: Fairness and Reciprocity

As described thus far, the norms module is, in a sense, *content free*. For no constraints have been placed on the rules that can be stored in the norms database, internalized, and hence become associated with an intrinsic source of motivation. But as Sripada and Stich (2006) note, while there is immense variation in the norms that are operative across societies, there are also some universals. And in particular, all societies have norms of fairness and reciprocity, and rules against arbitrary killing and harming of members of the community. Whether this represents the operations of some sort of distinct social contracts module (Cosmides and Tooby, 1992), or whether it results from some innate structuring within the wider norms module, is an open question.[23]

A great deal of research has been conducted by experimental economists in recent decades, concerning the ways in which people behave in various cooperative / competitive games. These games are generally played for real money. In some conditions they are played just once; sometimes they are iterated. Most often they are played anonymously, sometimes not. One absolutely robust finding, however, is that no one behaves as rational (selfish) 'economic man' would prescribe (Thaler, 1992). On the contrary, people are motivated by considerations of fairness and reciprocity, even when they stand to gain nothing by doing so, and even when their actions will remain anonymous. And some of this research has now been replicated cross-culturally, with similar results (Henrich et al., 2004).

Consider just a single example: the Ultimatum game. This has two players, and is generally played anonymously. One player is given a sum of money (say $10) and told that they must offer some portion of that money to the other player. If the other player accepts the offer, then each of them will keep their proportions. If the other player rejects the offer, however, then neither player will get anything. 'Economic man' would make the smallest offer possible, reasoning like this: 'Even with this small offer, the recipient is still better off; and he knows that if he rejects my offer, he will get nothing; so the only rational course is for him to accept it, and the rational course for me is not to offer any more.' No one at all behaves like this however! In the US the average offer is about $4.50, and offers significantly smaller than this are often rejected. And likewise in the fifteen small-scale societies around the world studied by Henrich et al. (2004), most offers range between $2.50 and $5.50; and again, low offers are often rejected.

It seems that people all round the globe are intrinsically motivated by considerations of fairness, and intrinsically motivated to punish those who act unfairly. And people are prepared to bear significant costs to exercise these motivations. For note that if you reject an offer of $3, say, on the grounds that it is too low, then you are both punishing the other (he loses $7), and accepting a real cost to yourself in order to do so (you lose the $3). Moreover, it turns out that people are prepared to accept significant costs in order to punish (anonymously) those who fail to cooperate in a collective-action game where all stand to gain by acting together, but where a free-rider can gain

---

[23] Haidt and Joseph (2007) argue that the diversity of moral beliefs and practices amongst human cultures can be explained in terms of the interactions of five moral modules, each with its own phylogenetic history: social-perceptual abilities related to harm / suffering, reciprocity / fairness, ingroup / outgroup, hierarchy / duty, and purity/ pollution.

even more (Fehr and Gachter, 2002). It seems that the motivation to punish collective-action norm violations is an intrinsic one, too.

These results are intriguing. They confirm that people's motivations to comply with, and to punish violators of, at least some norms are intrinsic ones. But when set alongside the evidence that hunter-gatherer societies are generally egalitarian in structure, and governed by prestige rather than by dominance (Boehm, 1999; Barrett et al., 2002), they suggest that some sub-set of norms concerned with fairness and reciprocity might be part of the natural human endowment.[24]

8 Conclusion

This chapter has completed my case in support of the massively modular organization of the human mind. We have seen that it is unlikely that the modular architecture of primate minds has somehow been swept away in the evolutionary transition from our great-ape common-ancestors to ourselves. Nor is there any reason to think that what has been added to that architecture is just more processing power resulting from a bigger brain, or just one or a few new cognitive adaptations. On the contrary, the evidence suggests that there have been many new modules added to make up the human mind, and we have sketched some of the likely contenders, together with the ways in which they are probably embedded into the pre-existing belief / desire / practical-reasoning architecture. The important ones to carry forward into the discussion to follow are (a) a mind-reading faculty, which is unlikely to have a separate self-monitoring component; (b) a language faculty, containing both input and output sub-components; and (c) one or more modules for dealing with social norms, with both a belief-like component and a motivational component.

We are now ready to embark on the defensive part of the present project. My goal henceforward is to reply to the main challenges to the thesis of massively modular organization. Most of these have to do with the seemingly unlimited creativity and flexibility of the human mind. And the challenge is: *how could a massively modular mind be like **that***? Outlining and answering the various strands in this challenge will now occupy us through the remaining four chapters of this book.

---

[24] These norms may have evolved from a much more limited set of quasi-normative rules and expectations concerned with fairness that are present in monkeys and other apes. See Brosnan and de Waal (2003), who show that capuchins who observe another monkey being given a greater food reward for equal work will thereafter refuse to cooperate with the human experimenter who short-changed them.

4

Modularity and Flexibility: The First Steps

Is there any special puzzle or problem about developing an acceptable form of massively modular conception of the human mind, given the relatively weak construal of 'module' that we have adopted? Why would anyone think that the mind *shouldn't* be modular, in that weak sense? Some have argued that the mind *cannot* be massively modular, of course (Fodor, 2000); but they have employed a much more demanding notion of modularity, according to which modules have to be encapsulated in their processing. Once we retreat to the weaker notion of modularity articulated and defended in Chapter 1, then it is far from obvious that these arguments should retain their force. So is there any particular challenge remaining for massive modularity theorists to answer?

In Section 1 I shall articulate a number of such challenges. Thereafter (in this chapter and the chapters following) I shall discuss how those challenges should best be met. I shall be arguing in the present chapter that mental rehearsal of action (especially speech action) plays a crucial role in linking together and combining the outputs of some other central / conceptual modules, and in facilitating cycles of language-dependent activity, in so-called 'inner speech'. That role also makes possible a new *form* of language-based thinking and reasoning, I shall argue, realized in the operations of an underlying set of conceptual modules. If these accounts can be made to work, then the result should be highly attractive to massive modularists. For it is widely agreed that language is itself a module consisting of further sub-modules, as we saw in Chapter 3. In which case it might be the addition of a language module to the mix of modules that make up the human mind that is responsible for much of the latter's characteristic flexibility.

I believe, then—and will argue herein—that natural language has an important role to play in the distinctive flexibility of the massively modular human mind. But the thesis is, of course, an empirical one. And it should be acknowledged that most of the evidence required to support it just hasn't been looked for or collected. (Some alleged evidence will be considered in Section 4.) But even if my conclusion were merely that it is causally (as opposed to logically) *possible* that language should play such a role, this would still be a result of significant interest and importance. For most of the people who reject massively modular models of the human mind do so because they can't see how minds with the flexibility of ours could *possibly* be modular in organization. I aim to show them how. One goal of this chapter, then, is to answer a 'How possibly?' question: how could the human mind *possibly* be composed of a massive array of modules? But I shall also hope to show that the proposed account of the role of language in cognition is, moreover, a *plausible* one, worthy of both further theoretical development and experimental investigation.

1 The Challenges

Recall that the thesis of massive modularity articulated and defended in Chapter 1 has the following form. The mind consists of a great many distinct processing systems (roughly one for each evolutionarily stable function or capacity, plus many others constructed through learning). The properties of these systems can vary independently of one another, their operations can be separately affected by other factors, and many of them can be damaged or destroyed without completely undermining the functionality of the whole arrangement.

We should also expect that there will be a good deal of variation in the degree of connectedness amongst modules. (See Figure 1.3.) For which other systems a module can receive input from, and where it will make its outputs available, will be a function of the processing task undertaken by the module in question, as well as the processing tasks undertaken by the others with which it is connected. But it almost certainly isn't the case that every module will be connected up with every other, since such connections will be costly to build and maintain, and since the addition of each such connection will make processing significantly less frugal. Roughly, there should only be connections where there really *need* to be connections (Coward, 2001).

As we also stressed in Chapter 1, the processing undertaken by mental modules will need to be frugal in terms of time and resources. They will all of them thus be encapsulated in the wide-scope sense distinguished in Chapter 1, although many might also be encapsulated in the stronger narrow-scope sense. (This means that *all* modules should have internal processes that require them to consult only a small subset of the total information available in the mind in the course of their processing, but some will also be restricted in the *kinds* of information that they can look at—i.e. they will have a module-specific data-base.) And it will be very rare indeed that one module should have any access to the internal processes of another (as opposed to the outputs of one or more of the sub-modules contained within that other). Rather, other modules will at most have access to the results of that processing. So in addition to being wide-scope encapsulated, the internal processing of all modules should be *inaccessible* to most (if not all) other systems.[1]

1.1 Massive Modularity and Common Sense

This form of massive modularity hypothesis predicts, then, that the mind decomposes into far *more* components than would generally be recognized, either by common-sense psychology or by regular (non-evolutionary) cognitive psychology. So part of the task before us is to articulate an architecture that can make sense of this. We need to say enough about the various modules and their mode of connectivity, either to explain how the common-sense picture can nevertheless be broadly correct in its outline framework; or to explain how the common-sense account can be so successful while being radically wrong.

This can be considered our first challenge. But meeting it is a straightforward matter. For I have suggested in Chapter 2 that the massive modularity thesis is best developed within the framework of a perception / belief / desire / planning / motor-control psychology. And then the basic architecture postulated by common sense will actually be correct. (Percepts give rise to beliefs and serve to inform practical reasoning; beliefs and desires interact in practical reasoning to create intentions and actions; percepts guide the execution of those actions.) Common sense's only failing will be that it doesn't postulate *enough* perceptual mechanisms, nor nearly *enough* mechanisms for producing new beliefs, new desires, and new actions. Compare Figures 4.1 and 4.2, in this regard. One difference between them is that in Figure 4.2 the visual system has been bifurcated, in accordance with the 'two visual systems' hypothesis of Milner and Goodale (1995). Another is that in place of some sort of unified theoretical reasoning system, there are now *multiple* reasoning systems for generating beliefs (and desires) in different domains. In addition, there are now multiple (and competing) decision-making systems,[2] and multiple motor-control systems.

---

[1] Recall that inaccessibility and encapsulation are matters of degree. The conclusion of Chapter 1 was that the mind should be constructed out of a great many modular systems that have internal processes that are *largely* inaccessible and (wide-scope) encapsulated.

[2] Recall from Chapter 2.8, however, that the precursor architecture does allow for a sort of *virtual* unified practical-reason system, utilizing mental rehearsal and somasensory monitoring. This isn't represented in Figure 4.2. See Figure 2.8.

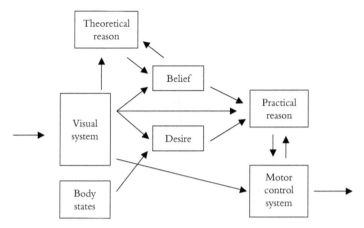

Figure 4.1. The common-sense mind

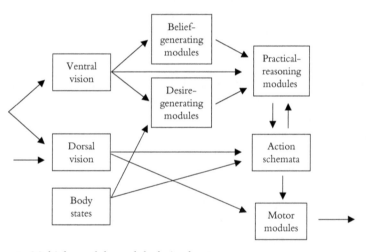

Figure 4.2. Multiple modules and dual visual systems

There is a different sort of objection to massive modularity that can be raised from the perspective of common sense, however. This is that it doesn't *feel* to us, on the inside, as if our minds were composed of massively many modules acting both sequentially and in parallel. On the contrary, we have the impression that the mind is diaphanous, or transparent to itself, with everything that happens within it occurring in a single unified arena containing conscious experience, conscious thought, and conscious decision-making. This is the intuition to which Locke (1690) gave voice when he wrote that there could be nothing within the mind that the mind itself was unaware of. And I suspect that it, or a close descendent of it, lies at the root of a great deal of the resistance to massive modularity amongst philosophers and (to a much lesser extent) amongst cognitive scientists. Despite the fact that almost everyone now accepts the existence of unconscious mental states and processes, the picture of a diaphanous mind nevertheless maintains its grip on us, only now confined to so-called 'central cognition' or to 'personal' (as opposed to 'sub-personal') mentality.

As we saw briefly in Chapter 3.3, the human mind-reading module operates with a simplified model of the mind and its operations, included in which is the idea that the mind is transparent to itself. This is probably why the notion of unconscious perceptual states was so hard for people to accept, and met with such vigorous resistance, when proposed by Weiskrantz and colleagues (Sanders et al., 1974; Weiskrantz, 1980, 1986). And it also explains why the thesis of massive mental modularity should seem so counter-intuitive. Since the basic model employed by the mind-reading module is very likely innate (to some significant degree) it is to be expected that the intuition of a diaphanous mind would prove robust and hard to get rid of. In this respect it is similar to the intuition that it is more probable that Linda (who did voluntary work for civil rights groups and feminist organizations while at college) is now a bank teller *and* a feminist than it is that she is just a bank teller—despite the fact that it is impossible for a conjunction to be more probable than one of its conjuncts (Kahneman et al., 1982).[3]

Those of us defending massive modularity face an uphill struggle, therefore. Just as logicians and probability theorists have to labor to get people to set aside some of their intuitions of validity and probability; and just as physicists have to work to get physics students to overcome their Aristotelian intuitions about motion (McCloskey, 1983); so massive modularists face a similar hurdle. One part of this involves convincing people that the human mind-reading faculty deploys a greatly simplified model of the mind's operations, which works perfectly well for purposes of everyday prediction and explanation, but which lacks any scientific standing (as I argued in Chapter 3.3). This has been amply demonstrated by cognitive scientists in recent decades. (See Gazzaniga, 1998, and Wilson, 2002, for recent reviews.) But note that even with conviction assured, the intuition of a diaphanous mind will be apt to reassert itself whenever we aren't paying attention. Keeping our intuitions under control

[3] Note, however, that there is a (small) element of truth in the idea of a diaphanous mind. This is that globally broadcast perceptual and imagistic states are made available to the mind-reading faculty for immediate recognition. And likewise, both mentally rehearsed actions and sentences in 'inner speech' can utilize the same global broadcasting architecture. So there is, after all, a sort of virtual central system within which experiences and thought-contents are transparently available for self-ascription and report. (See Carruthers, 2005, for discussion.) But not much of the actual work of the mind goes on within this arena.

can take constant effort. The other part of a defense of massive modularity—in addition to laying out the evidence in its support (as I have done in Chapters 1, 2, and 3)—is to show that the account can explain everything that it needs to. That is the task of the remainder of this book.

There is, of course, yet another source of resistance to massive modularity, that is so endemic that it almost deserves to be counted as part of 'common sense'. This is that the heavy dose of innateness that is part and parcel of the massive modularity thesis is inconsistent with the empiricist conception of the mind as a 'blank slate'. This picture has dominated western intellectual life since the Enlightenment, and continues to be almost a religious orthodoxy in the humanities and social sciences, and to a lesser extent in some areas of psychology. (Again Locke, 1690, serves as an early exemplar, and is generally credited as the first to introduce the metaphor of the mind as initially a blank slate, waiting to be written upon by experience.) And it is a picture that is closely intertwined with a set of 'progressive' ethical and political attitudes, to the point where denial of the orthodoxy is felt by many to be morally threatening, if not outright morally reprehensible.

The scientific case that supports an account of the mind as possessing a rich innate structure seems to me to be overwhelming, as I have argued in Chapters 1, 2, and 3. (See also Carruthers et al., 2005, 2006, and that planned for 2007.) And the remainder of this book is designed to reply to the main intellectual challenges to such an account. But the *moral* objections will have to pass unanswered. Replying to them would require quite a different sort of book. And that book has, in any case, already been written—see Pinker (2002), who does a masterful job of identifying the various political and emotional currents underlying blank-slate psychology, while at the same time disarming them of intellectual credibility.

1.2 Massive Modularity and Flexibility

Should massive modularity theorists predict that there will be limitations on the degree of *flexibility* of the human mind, and its resulting behavior? A number of different kinds of flexibility and inflexibility can, and should, be distinguished. One kind of flexibility is flexibility of *action*. As we saw in Chapter 2.7, the minds of many animals are inflexible in the following sense: particular types of desire can only be paired with certain kinds of belief, and not others; and particular types of desire can only recruit certain kinds of action schema, and not others. But as we saw in Chapter 2.8, this sort of inflexibility can be overcome by minds that have a capacity for the mental rehearsal and subsequent global broadcasting of action schemata. The human mind undoubtedly has such a capacity, as do probably the minds of other species of ape and earlier species of hominid.[4] But such a capacity doesn't by any means compromise the massively modular status of the mind; on the contrary, it recruits the activity of existing modules to subserve the task of action selection.

All this will loom large again in Chapter 5, when we discuss the distinctive *creativity* of the human mind. But it is worth noting at this stage that there are independent reasons to think that feedback loops of various sorts are the right place to look for sources of creativity and flexibility. (I owe this observation to Chris Pyne.) For consider what happens in video feedback (Crutchfield, 1984). If you direct a video camera at a blank television screen, in circumstances where the camera is wired up so that its output will be displayed on that very screen, then all sorts of interesting things start to happen. Rich patterns of color and shape tend to result from the continual cycling of the feedback loop alone, without the injection of any initial content, and without design. So, too, perhaps in the human mind, once it begins its cycles of mental rehearsal.

Another kind of flexibility is that a mind (and the behavior in which it results) might be more or less *context-sensitive*; and yet another is that it might be more or less *stimulus-bound*. (Other forms of flexibility will be distinguished shortly.) The minds of insects seem inflexible in both of these sorts of ways. A wasp might continue with the same kind of behavior (building a nest to protect her eggs, say) in the same kind of situation (pregnancy) irrespective of the context in which the activity is taking place, such as the presence of a human experimenter who makes holes in the mud tube of the nest, or who buries the nest in sand. (See Gould and Gould, 1994, on the Australian digger wasp.) Likewise an insect might always behave in the same way when presented with the same stimulus, irrespective of circumstances.

It is obvious that human minds aren't inflexible in either of the above senses, however. One of our most distinctive properties is the way in which we can adapt (not always, but at least sometimes) to changed circumstances, and think and behave in a context-sensitive manner. And likewise our thought processes plainly aren't inflexible in the stimulus-bound sense, either. On the contrary, we routinely entertain thoughts, and whole sequences of thought, that bear no relation to our current physical or social circumstances. I shall discuss in turn the alleged challenges to a thesis of massive modularity raised by these forms of flexibility.

[4] Geary (2005), too, emphasizes the importance of mental rehearsal in explaining distinctively human problem-solving abilities. But he thinks that a capacity for mental rehearsal is restricted to humans. I think, on the contrary, that it is present in other apes, but greatly enhanced in humans. See Chapter 5 for further discussion.

1.3 Context-Flexibility

I don't believe that the context-sensitive form of flexibility raises any particular problem for a massively modular conception of the human mind. For there are a number of distinct but mutually compatible strategies that a massive modularist can adopt in seeking to explain our distinctive context-flexibility. In order for us to see this clearly, however, it is necessary to distinguish between two different *forms* of context-flexibility. One way for an organism to be context-flexible is for it to pick up on the information in the environment that is relevant to its current goals, and to modify its behavior accordingly. This would lead us to expect that different organisms with the same goals in the same circumstances should behave similarly. But another way in which organisms can be context-flexible is where different individuals are apt to pick up on and respond to different aspects of the context, leading those individuals to behave *differently* in the *same* circumstances. (Human beings are context-flexible in both of these senses, of course.)

When context-flexibility is construed in the first of the above ways, it should be obvious that it raises no special problems for massively modular conceptions of mind. Quite the contrary. For the greater the number of modules that exist, and that are operating in parallel, the more features of the environment / context the agent can pick up upon and respond to. And so we can, in effect, turn the objection on its head. A monolithic mind containing just one general-purpose processing and inferential system (if such a thing can really be envisaged) would surely be a mind that could only pick up on one item of information at a time, or that would at least be limited in the flexibility that it displayed in relation to features of context.

If there is a problem for massive modularity arising out of the context-sensitivity of the human mind, then, this must be a problem in respect of context-flexibility of the second sort, pertaining especially to differences *between* individuals. And it is easy to see how the objection might go. For shouldn't we expect the outcome of the operations of the same set of modules (especially if innate) to be the same whenever presented with the same input? There are, however, at least three different, but mutually consistent, sorts of response that a massive modularity theorist can make.

1.4 Three Ways to be Context Sensitive

One way of reconciling massive modularity with the context-sensitive character of the human mind (in both of the above senses) is proposed by Sperber (2005). He argues convincingly that the operations of the mind as a whole should be characterized by various kinds of *competition* amongst modules. Modules will compete with one another for a variety of forms of resource, both physical (such as increased blood-flow to one region of the brain rather than another) and cognitive. Amongst the latter might be included competition for various forms of working memory, and for a variety of kinds of attention. Moreover, where a module can receive input from a number of other systems (in the way that we described for the practical-reasoning modules in Chapter 2.8), then there might be competition amongst those systems to have their outputs received and processed as input by the module in question.

On this approach the context-sensitivity of a massively modular mind might be expected to arise in something like the following manner, then. Different modules are cued by different features of the environment—social, physical, animal, vegetable, etc.—and at various levels of abstractness (e.g. suddenly moving stimuli and loud noises versus cheater detection). All, when activated, compete with one another for resources, and to get their outputs entry into downstream inferential and decision-making systems. But how this competition pans out in any given case might often be highly sensitive to the details of the context (both environmental and cognitive), and also to the learning history of the person in question. Certainly there should be no hint of any crude environmental determinism here.

A second proposal for dealing with the context-sensitivity issue comes from Barrett (2005). He elaborates and discusses what he calls 'the enzyme account' of modularity. The idea is to model the operations of modules on the way in which enzymes build proteins within cells. There are many different kinds of enzyme within a cell. Each has a characteristic shape, and floats around waiting to meet a protein that matches that shape. When it finds one, it builds a new protein of a characteristic sort and pushes the result back out into the soup of chemicals within the cell once again. Translated into cognitive terms, the idea is that there might be a whole host of specialist processing devices ('modules') all focused on a common 'bulletin board' of representations. Whenever a device comes across a representation that 'fits' its input condition it gets turned on, and it then performs some set of transformations on that representation before placing the results back on the bulletin board for other devices to pick up on.

One can thus envisage a cascade of inferences and transformations taking place (with some modules looking for representations that possess increasingly abstract tags placed there by other modules, and so forth), but without there being any architectural constraints on the flow of information through the system. And the result would be processing that is highly context-sensitive, but resulting from the independent operations of a set of enzyme-like modules, whose collective output depends partly on happenstance.

This proposal fits nicely with the 'global broadcasting' model of perceptual consciousness put forward by Baars (1988, 1997), in support of which there is robust empirical evidence (Baars, 2002, 2003; Dehaene and Naccache, 2001; Dehaene et al., 2001, 2003; Baars et al., 2003; Kreiman et al., 2003).[5] We can think of the enzyme model as an account of how the various conceptual modules continually scan the contents of globally broadcast states, searching for ones that trigger their input conditions. Indeed, we can think of it as a model of how the conceptualization of perceptual states takes place, given that the concepts in question are deployed by specialist modules of one sort or another.

The enzyme model looks plausible as an account of how perception gets conceptualized by modular processes, then. But it might seem singularly *im*plausible as an account of how more abstract modules operate, such as the social contracts / cheater detection system (Cosmides and Tooby, 1992). For *cheat* isn't a perceptual category. In which case, for the account to work, it might appear that we would need to postulate multiple global broadcasting systems, some dealing with perceptual contents, and some with more abstract conceptual ones. Yet there is no independent evidence that the latter exist.

I doubt that this is a serious problem for the enzyme model, however. Granted, *cheat* isn't a perceptual category. But why shouldn't that concept nevertheless become attached to a perceptually represented and globally broadcast item? In effect, what would be globally broadcast would be a perceptual item conjoined with the thought, *that is a cheat*, where the indexical 'that' refers to the perceived person in question. This combination could be made available to a wide range of consumer systems (enzyme-like modules), some of which might be searching for the content *cheat* in order for their processing to be turned on.[6]

The enzyme model doesn't just provide us with an account of the conceptualization of perception, however. It also suggests how module-generated predictions based on current perception can also be made globally accessible, utilizing the back-projecting neural pathways present in all perceptual systems to create visual and other forms of imagery, which can then be globally broadcast in turn. Suppose, for example, that I see a ball flying towards a glass window, from which my physics module predicts that the window will shatter.

---

[5] In saying that there exists robust evidence of global broadcasting, I don't mean to say that there is evidence supporting global broadcasting as a proposed reductive account of phenomenal consciousness. For it may well be the case that mammalian brains all share a global broadcasting architecture in respect of a privileged set of perceptual states; and it may well be the case that those states are in fact phenomenally conscious in humans; but they might not be phenomenally conscious *because* they are globally broadcast; indeed, on my own account, they aren't (Carruthers, 2000, 2005).

[6] Such a model provides us with a natural way to think of the operations of the natural-language comprehension system, indeed. That system operates on perceptual input to deliver a conceptual output of the message being communicated. But the latter isn't detached and independent of the initial percepts. On the contrary, the phenomenology of speech perception is that one *hears* the meaning of the words being uttered, as well as hearing the sounds—pitch and tone of voice and so forth—that constitute the utterance.

This prediction can then be displayed in the form of a visual image prior to the event occurring. This makes that prediction widely accessible to the full range of central / conceptual systems, many of which wouldn't normally have received the physics module's output directly. These systems can then generate yet further inferences or emotional reactions that might prepare me for action (running from the scene, perhaps, if I was the hitter).

At a much more basic level than either the competition-for-resources or the enzyme-model responses to the problem of context-flexibility, however, it should be emphasized that many modules are *learning* systems, and that many other modules are in the business of *building* modular systems from the contingencies of environmental interactions. So overall flexibility of behavior—both in response to variations in the natural and social environment, and co-varying with the different learning histories of different individuals—is precisely what a massive modularist should predict. (And in addition, of course, there will be innate differences between different individuals concerning the properties of their respective learning modules, yielding yet further differences in behavior.) Let me elaborate.

As we emphasized in Chapters 2 and 3, many of the modular systems that constitute the minds of both animals and humans are designed to extract information of some specific sort from the environment. The multiple systems involved in spatial navigation are designed to extract information about the spatial relationships between the agent and other things, and amongst those things themselves, for example. (Likewise the human language faculty is designed to extract information about the meanings of utterances spoken by members of the agent's local community.) How a creature will navigate will then be sensitive to the spatial context in which it has done its learning, and in which it now finds itself. (Likewise the language that a person speaks will be sensitive to the linguistic context in which that person has been immersed.)

Not only do humans have what Fessler (2006) calls 'information-rich' learning modules of the above sort, but they also have information-*poor* learning systems, as we saw in Chapter 3. A number of investigators have demonstrated that humans have a variety of dispositions that aid in the learning of culture-specific information, where what is to be learned can't be second-guessed by the evolutionary process (Richerson and Boyd, 2005). People have a disposition to observe and to copy those who are prestigious, together with an associated emotion system that generates admiration (Henrich and Gil-White, 2001). And they have a disposition to observe and copy slightly older / more experienced peers who are similar to themselves along some relevant dimension. Moreover, they have a disposition to observe, learn, and attach intrinsic motivation to the norms that are current in their community (Sripada and Stich, 2006).

These dispositions, together with the background capacities underlying imitation with which they interact, make possible the development of rich technological and normative cultures. And again, a massive modularist should predict that the configuration of any given individual's mind will be sensitive to the context of the surrounding culture, with wide variations in outcome (even within a single culture) depending upon the happenstance of details of the individual's learning history, and on variations in learning strategy.

In addition to acquiring *knowledge* from the surrounding culture, of course, humans also acquire a range of behavioral skills, from stone-tool knapping, through cooking, to kayak building, to reading and writing. In each of these cases it is plausible to claim that what are being assembled during the learning process are behavioral modules, which can be held constant when yet other behavioral modules are acquired, and whose properties can vary, and can be influenced, independently of the others. Into the process of assembly will go observation, practice, sometimes explicit instruction, and feedback of various kinds. And again the result will be a behavioral repertoire that is highly context-sensitive, and that will vary with the individual's physical and cultural environment, as well as with the details of their idiosyncratic learning history.

In summary of this sub-section, then, I believe that massive modularity theorists have a number of resources with which to explain the distinctive context-sensitivity of human cognitive processes and behavior. Context-sensitivity doesn't present an especially difficult challenge for the thesis of massive modularity to meet.

1.5 The Stimulus-Free Mind

In contrast to context-flexibility, the stimulus-free nature of much human mental activity does pose more of a problem for massively modular conceptions of mind (as it does for anti-modular accounts as well; the problem is by no means unique to modularity theory). But here, too, we can distinguish between two different forms of stimulus independence. One of these is relatively straightforward to explain, and will be tackled in Section 2. The other is much harder, and will be deferred to the closing sections of Chapter 5, when we complete our discussion of creativity.

One challenge is to explain how a network of belief-generating modules and desire-generating modules can be arranged into an architecture in such a way that the behavior of the whole system can often be free of environmental input. Somehow we will have to provide for the overall system to be *self-stimulating*, or at least *self-sustaining*, in its operations.

Recall how human thought-processes can be radically independent of current circumstances. I can get into a day-dream and spend minutes or hours reliving events from my past, or fantasizing about my next vacation. Or I can be sitting immobile at my desk thinking about what I should say during an annual appraisal interview with my boss some weeks in the future. These obvious facts might appear to present something of a problem, because the basic model sketched in Chapters 2 and 3 is a *feed-forward* one (see Figure 4.2). External stimuli are processed by the perceptual systems, and the resulting percepts are made available to a range of belief-forming and desire-forming modules; the ensuing mental states are made available to practical reasoning, which issues in an act or in an intention to act. It is initially hard to see what scope there can be for these systems to operate in the absence of, or independently of, any sort of perceptual stimulus.

Many neural systems contain back-projecting neural pathways of various sorts, of course. This is certainly true of the visual system, where there are pathways projecting all the way back to the primary cortical projection area V_1. These are used to direct attention and to 'query' degraded or ambiguous input; and they are also the basis of visual imagery, as we saw in Chapter 2.2 (Kosslyn, 1994). Moreover, humans (and other apes) have a capacity for mental rehearsal of action schemata, which takes a representation near the 'output' end of the mind (in motor control) and uses it to build a quasi-perceptual representation of the intended action, which can then be globally broadcast and received as input by the full suite of central / conceptual modules, as we saw in Chapter 2.8. Showing how these elements can be utilized and combined to give rise to the distinctive stimulus-independence of human thought will be one of the tasks of the present chapter, to be undertaken in later sections.

There is another way of characterizing the stimulus-free character of the human mind which is much more deeply challenging, however. This is the property that was at issue in the famous debate between Chomsky (1959) and Skinner, which Chomsky (1975) has since taken to describing as 'the creative aspect of language use', or 'CALU'. Confronted with one and the same external stimulus (a painting hanging on a wall), there are no end of things that one could intelligibly say. One might say, 'Dutch', or, 'It is hanging too low', or, 'It clashes with the wallpaper', and so on, and so on, without limit. Each of these responses might be perfectly *appropriate* in the context, but without being under stimulus control. How is this possible?

Some aspects of this problem reduce to the problem of explaining the context-sensitive character of human thought and behavior (discussed in Section 1.4), and can be handled accordingly. Thus it is certainly to be expected that different people, with their different and idiosyncratic learning histories, might respond differently to one and the same stimulus. And even for the same person at different times, one might expect that the competition between modules to get their outputs entry into the language production system might pan out differently, depending upon different motivational and contextual saliencies. But it is very doubtful that the creative aspect of language use can be exhaustively explained in either of these ways.

It should be stressed, however, that the creative aspect of language use isn't just a problem for massive modularists. On the contrary, it is a problem for everyone. And Chomsky (1975) has even suggested that the problem may be so hard that its solution is *cognitively closed* to us, in the same sort of way that an explanation of gravitational phenomena is cognitively closed to a rat. It will therefore be a large 'plus mark' in favor of massively modular approaches to cognition if they can enable us to make some progress with the problem. I shall return to this topic towards the end of Chapter 5.

1.6 Flexibility of Content

Should massive modularity theorists expect that there will be limitations on the flexibility with which concepts (the components of thought contents) can be combined? (Call this 'content-inflexibility'.) I believe that the answer to this question is 'Yes'. There are two reasons for this. The first is that we surely shouldn't expect that every system will be connected up with every other. (See Figure 1.3 and the surrounding discussion in Chapter 1.) The flowchart of information through the mind to the point of decision-making should place some restrictions on which concepts can be combined with which, and when. So if one concept can be proprietary to one conceptual module and another to another, then these might be two concepts that can never get combined into a single thought. This will be because the modules that initially generate tokens of those concepts lack any connection with one another, direct or indirect.

This problem would certainly be mitigated if there were some sort of domain-general formal logic module, as we speculated in Chapter 1.2 that there might be. For this would be capable of taking any (small) set of beliefs produced by any given subset of modules and deducing some of the simpler logical consequences from those beliefs. So it ought, in particular, to be capable of taking any belief P and any belief Q, and combining them to form the cross-modular thought, P *and* Q. For this requires only a simple step of conjunction-introduction. Likewise if there should turn out to be a module capable of calculating the statistical dependencies amongst arbitrary pairs of properties, then it would be capable of generating a proposition of the form, $P \supset Q$, for any P and any Q.

Notice, however, that neither of these proposals would make it possible for two module-specific concepts to be combined within a single *atomic* (as opposed to molecular or quantified) proposition. For example, if the output of some sort of geometric module were the belief that a target object is in a corner with a long wall on the left and a short wall on the right, and the output of some kind of object-property module were that the target is near a red wall, then there might still be no way for these two beliefs to be combined into the single integrated representation, THE OBJECT IS IN A CORNER WITH A LONG WALL ON THE LEFT AND A SHORT *RED* WALL ON THE RIGHT, even if the short wall *is* a red wall. The best that the logic-module would be able to get us is the thought, THE OBJECT IS IN A CORNER WITH A LONG WALL ON THE LEFT AND A SHORT WALL ON THE RIGHT *AND* THE OBJECT IS NEAR A RED WALL.

Without knowing the details of the flowchart of modular connectivity in the mind, however, it is hard to generate specific predictions from the claim that a massively modular mind should display content-inflexibility, except in obvious cases. Thus we can predict that contents concerning surface boundaries produced early in the visual system, for example, shouldn't be combinable with thoughts about the stars, nor about other people's beliefs.[7] But as for which concepts might fail to be combinable with which other concepts, this is impossible to predict without knowing the connectivity of the conceptual belief-generating modules in question.

The second reason for expecting that a massively modular mind should be to some degree content-inflexible is as follows. Even if two concepts can be combined somewhere for one purpose, it doesn't follow that they can be so combined for another, or that the system that is operative in the latter context can access the combined representation. So for concreteness (and in line with the evidence briefly reviewed in Chapter 2.3), suppose that the representation produced by the geometric module, THE OBJECT IS IN A CORNER WITH A LONG WALL ON THE LEFT AND A SHORT WALL ON THE RIGHT, and the representation produced by the object-property module, THE OBJECT IS NEAR A RED WALL, are routinely passed to a map-creating system, which builds the integrated representation, THE OBJECT IS IN A CORNER WITH A LONG WALL ON THE LEFT AND A SHORT *RED* WALL ON THE RIGHT. But under conditions of disorientation (when the goal is to find out where I am when I am lost), the latter representation isn't accessed. Rather, the reorientation goal mandates a search for geometric information alone, pulling up the geometric representation, THE OBJECT IS IN A CORNER WITH A LONG WALL ON THE LEFT AND A SHORT WALL ON THE RIGHT.

---

[7] Of course one can, downstream of the visual system, come to conceptualize something *as* a boundary of a surface, and then go on to wonder whether the stars have boundaries like that. But this is another matter. Here one re-represents, in fully conceptual format, a content similar to one that had elsewhere been deployed within the visual system. This isn't the same as saying that the latter content has been extracted and combined with a thought about the stars.

In such circumstances there might be no way for the content-integrated representation, containing RED, to have any effect on behavior. So the organism would display a sort of content-inflexibility here, but only in conditions of disorientation, not absolutely. In principle it might be possible to solve this problem via mental rehearsal. For example, if one were mentally to rehearse going towards the red wall, then the geometric system could perhaps kick in with the actual location of the object. But in any given case such rehearsals might lie outside the normal repertoire of agents, with their acquired strategies and heuristics for generating useful rehearsals. It might just never occur to people to rehearse turning towards red, for example.

In this sort of case, too, however, it is hard to generate specific predictions without knowing the identities of the modules that make their outputs available to the practical-reasoning systems, and the manner in which the latter operate. But we do at least have some reason to think that the example of local content-inflexibility just sketched is real enough, since it is displayed in the behavior of rats and young children. This evidence will be extensively discussed in Section 4.

Even if the prediction of content-inflexibility is vague and unspecific, however, it still creates a significant problem for the thesis of massive mental modularity. For, in contrast to that prediction, humans would appear to be capable of freely combining concepts across the boundaries of all central / conceptual modules. This is manifest to ordinary introspection. I can be thinking about thoughts one moment, horses the next, and then a landslide the next; and I can then wonder what led me to think about thoughts, horses, and falling stones—thereby combining into a single thought concepts drawn from the domains of folk-psychology, folk-biology, and folk-physics. And likewise for any set of conceptual modules that you care to mention. How is this possible, unless there is some a-modular central arena in which the contents of conceptual modules can be received and recombined, further inferences drawn from the results, and so forth? This is yet another challenge to massive modularity.

It might be replied that I have, over the previous two chapters, committed myself to the existence of just such a central arena, namely the practical-reasoning system (see Figure 4.2). I have suggested that this system is capable of receiving any desire and any belief as input. So why shouldn't it be this system that has the power to combine and recombine concepts drawn from disparate domains? For it can at least *receive* all of those concepts amongst its inputs. But in the first place, practical reason actually consists of many different desire-specific modules, as we saw in Chapter 2.7. And even though mental rehearsal and self-monitoring can transform the collective operation of these modules into a more-unified overarching practical-reasoning system (as we saw in Chapter 2.8), this couldn't help with the first problem of content integration outlined above (where two modules are isolated from one another absolutely); and it might not be sufficient to solve the second, either, as we have just seen.

Moreover, task-analysis of the requirements of practical reason (at least of the sort found in non-human animals) suggests that the combinatorial and inferential powers of the practical-reason system should be quite severely restricted.[8] While practical reason can receive any desire and any belief as input, it should have no capacity to conjoin and integrate the contents of such states, except where the beliefs in question are conditional in form—in which case it might have the power to collapse $P \supset Q$ and $Q \supset R$ to form the conditional $P \supset R$, thus 'conjoining' the propositions P and R together in a single thought for the first time. Nor should it have the capacity to draw many inferences from the propositions it receives, except in so far as it executes the practical reasoning equivalent of *modus ponens* (namely: *I want R, P ⊃ R, P is something that I can do, so I'll do P*).

It might be claimed, of course, that precisely what happened in the evolutionary transition from our great-ape ancestors to ourselves was that the practical-reasoning system underwent a transformation into a general content-conjoiner and inference engine. But such a proposal remains mysterious in the absence of (a) a more detailed task-analysis of the functions that such a transformed practical-reasoning faculty might be expected to perform, and of (b) some account of the evolutionary pressures that would have led such changes to occur. And as it stands, the proposal seems inconsistent with the complex and hedged-about 'one function / one module' generalization that emerged from our discussions in Chapter 1.

1.7 Flexibility of Reasoning Process

I have argued that a massively modular model of the human mind might lead us to predict (falsely, of course—hence our problem) that there are some constraints on the mind's capacity to conjoin and combine concepts drawn from different modular systems. Let me now argue that the same model should lead us to expect that there might be severe limits on the kinds of reasoning

---

[8] And even though human practical reasoning is by no means restricted in the manner in which thought-contents can be combined and conjoined, this doesn't solve our problem. For generating intentions and actions from beliefs and desires is one task, combining and drawing other sorts of inferences from thought-contents is quite another. So the argument from design, articulated in Chapter 1, should lead us to predict that there should be distinct systems for these distinct tasks. At the very least we are owed an account of how a simple practical-reasoning system could evolve into some sort of universal content-conjoiner. The topic of human practical reasoning will be further pursued in Chapter 7.

and decision-making *process* in which humans can engage. This will give rise to yet another challenge for a thesis of massive modularity to overcome. But first I need to provide a little background, in order that the argument can be set up.

If we accept that there is one overarching decision-making / practical-reasoning system (albeit made up out of multiple sub-modules), then this will be a point at which 'everything comes together.' The decision-making system is the point of maximum convergence of information, since the outputs of the various belief-modules and desire-modules should all be made available to this system. (Indeed, all may be competing to have their outputs received as inputs to it; see Section 1.1 of this chapter.) There will therefore be maximum demands on the computational resources of the practical-reasoning system. If its computations are to be tractable, and executable in real time (sometimes in fractions of a second), we might expect it to deploy a number of heuristics, or 'quick and dirty' short-cuts, in order to ease the computational load, and to render practical reason's task more frugal in terms of time and resources.[9]

As it turns out, this is an idea that has been explored with remarkable success by Gigerenzer and colleagues (1999). They propose and examine a range of decision-making heuristics of a simple sort, pitting them against a number of much more sophisticated competitors such as multiple regression and Bayes' rule. It turns out that under a variety of test conditions (both real-world and simulated) such simple heuristics are almost as reliable as their fancier competitors, and are much more frugal in terms of time and computational resources. However, there are also predictable kinds of circumstance in which such heuristics will go wrong (Kahneman et al., 1982).

I postulate that three different *kinds* of heuristic should be employed. First, there should be heuristics governing *how long* one should search for information and reason about the alternatives before taking a decision. The mate-choice heuristics explored by Gigerenzer et al. (1999) would be an example. Secondly, there should be heuristics governing what sorts of information one should seek out and rely on in a given choice situation. For example, a variety of data suggest that when animals are disoriented they employ a set of nested heuristics for deciding in which direction to travel to reach their target. And for many species of animal, including rats and human children, those heuristics are organized in the following sequence: (1) seek a directional beacon (e.g. the

---

[9] Notice that we certainly should *not* expect practical reason to be performing calculations of maximum expected utility, integrating measures of the degree of desirability of all goals with measures of the likelihood of all foreseeable ways of achieving them. Although philosophers and economists routinely assume that maximizing expected utility is a normative constraint on human practical reasoning, this is plainly a mistake, provided that one accepts the traditional principle that '*ought* implies *can*.' See Gigerenzer et al., 1999.

sun, or a distant landmark such as a familiar line of hills); (2) if no beacon is available, look to the geometrical properties of the local environment and seek a match with geometric memory; (3) if no geometric match is found, seek a recognizable local landmark and attempt to locate its position on a mental map (Shusterman and Spelke, 2005).[10]

The second of the above heuristics concerns the type of information that one should search for in order to reach a given decision; the first concerns how long one should search before reaching a decision (or abandoning the task). To see a place for a third type of heuristic, recall that in apes the practical-reasoning system will also have a capacity for mental rehearsal of action, feeding a sensory (normally visual) representation of the action-to-be-considered back through the various belief- and desire-generating modules as input, and monitoring one's bodily / emotional reactions to the results. The obvious type of heuristic to expect here would concern which of the action-schemata in one's action database to activate in a mental rehearsal. Heuristics such as 'Take the Last' (i.e. activate the action-representation that was used last in connection with a decision-problem of this type) explored by Gigerenzer et al. (1999) could naturally be adapted to serve in this third kind of role.

While it is now well-established that humans do use a variety of decision-making heuristics (Kahneman et al., 1982; Gigerenzer et al., 1999), just as a massive modularity thesis might predict, it is equally obvious that human beings aren't limited to, nor strongly constrained by, those heuristics. Courses in logic, or in probability theory, or in scientific method really can make a difference to the ways in which people think and reason, at least when they reason reflectively. By acquiring beliefs about the ways in which we *should* reason, it is possible for us to change the ways in which we *do* reason, at least some of the time. This gives rise to yet another challenge for a thesis of massive mental modularity to answer. How can the operations of a range of inferential modules be overridden by our explicit beliefs about norms of reasoning? By what mechanism can the latter pre-empt or control the former?

1.8 More Challenges: Creativity, Science, and Practical Reason

We have discovered, then, three different forms of flexibility that look problematic from the perspective of a massively modular conception of the human mind: stimulus-independence, flexibility of content, and flexibility of reasoning and decision-making processes. None of these challenges presents a problem of *principle* for massive modularity, of course, of the sort that Fodor (2000) attempts

---

[10] In other species of animal, including monkeys and chickens, the ordering of (2) and (3) appears to be reversed (Vallortigara et al., 1990; Gouteux et al., 2001). I shall return to this point in Section 4.

to defend. Rather, they are just that: *challenges*. We are challenged to explain how humans manage to attain the flexibility of thought and reasoning that they manifestly possess, supposing that the thesis of massive modularity is true. Answering these flexibility-challenges will form the topic of the remaining sections of present chapter.

In addition to the flexibility-challenges to massively modular accounts of the human mind, of course, there will remain the problem of explaining the distinctive *creativity* of human thought processes. This is manifested in childhood pretend play, in story telling and fantasy, in metaphor, and in science. There is a sense in which creativity might perhaps be thought of as a sub-species of content flexibility, since in all these different domains creativity can manifest itself in the formulation of novel thoughts, not plausibly produced by the routine (module-dependent) processing of perceptual input. However, creative content-generation raises problems of its own, as we shall see. Accordingly, it will be given separate treatment in Chapter 5.

While scientific thought and reasoning may depend in part upon our creative abilities, they involve much else besides. Indeed, they provide a significant challenge for *any* account of the mind to explain, whether modularist or anti-modularist. Although disagreeing about almost everything else, for example, Pinker (1997) and Fodor (2000) are united in thinking that the capacity for scientific reasoning is a genuinely *hard* problem for any scientific account of the mind to explain, to be likened to the so-called 'hard problem' of consciousness (Chalmers, 1996). This is a challenge that I shall return to in Chapter 6. It will be an important point in favor of modular models of the human mind if they can demonstrate progress towards meeting it.

Finally, there remains the problem of explaining distinctively human practical reasoning. There seem to be no limitations on the kinds of consideration that can enter into such reasoning, and new strategies for practical reasoning can be learned. Once again there is a sense in which this can be seen as a sub-species of the various flexibility-challenges to massive modularity that are under consideration in the present chapter; and both creativity and (I shall argue) science-like reasoning are presupposed. But here, too, it will turn out that there are distinctive problems to be addressed by a massively modular account. Further discussion of this topic will therefore be deferred to Chapter 7.

2 Stimulus Independence and Inner Speech

Recall from Chapter 2.8 that one of the precursor systems within pre-hominid forms of cognition was a capacity for mental rehearsal of action. This sub-divides into two parts: a capacity for creative generation of action schemata when problem solving; and a capacity to map those action schemata onto an appropriate perceptual representation of the action, so that a representation of the action being contemplated can be received as input by the various central / conceptual modules in such a way that its consequences (both physical and social) can be calculated. I shall first discuss how such a capacity may be deployed in visual and other forms of imagery, before turning to its more-novel manifestation in 'inner speech'. Thereafter I shall devote some time to discussing a third category of stimulus-independent cognition (one that is independent of *current* stimuli, at any rate), namely episodic memory.

2.1 Imagined Actions and Sequences of Imagery

Recall the example of Belle from Chapter 2.8, who was faced with a problem. Each time she went to retrieve some hidden food whose location she had been shown, the alpha male would follow her and push her aside as soon as she began digging, seizing the food for himself. And recall, too, how she may have been able to hit upon her solution. Mentally rehearsing her initial intention (to go to the food), she imagines failure, and feels disappointment. So she activates and mentally rehearses some of the other actions available to her, from one of which (digging elsewhere) she is able to envisage circumstances (the male's preoccupation) in which she can imagine obtaining and eating the food. This gives her a novel two-step plan which she implements successfully.

This is a sequence of cognitive activity that is prompted by an external stimulus, perhaps (e.g. the opening of the enclosure in which the chimpanzee knows the location of some food), but which thereafter proceeds in large degree independently of external stimuli. And in humans, with their much-increased conceptual resources and much-increased capacity for reasoning and prediction, we might expect that such sequences of planning by mental rehearsal should become considerably more frequent and extensive. And indeed, human subjects can spend extended periods of time physically inactive, trying out in imagination a variety of scenarios for solving some problem or for achieving some goal. This is one aspect, at least, of the stimulus-independence of human cognitive processes.

In order to go further in the direction of stimulus-independence, we need only suppose that humans have acquired the disposition to activate action schemata that are much more loosely connected to, and/or less controlled by, external stimuli. (As we shall see in Chapter 5, such a disposition may be an effect—and perhaps the proper function—of childhood pretend play.) The shape of a passing cloud, a phrase overheard on the bus, or a note in a diary can all prompt one to engage in extended periods of action-schemata rehearsal, sometimes in the service of medium- or long-term planning, sometimes serving as mere fantasy. And all of this can take place wordlessly, in sequences of visual and other images generated by feedback loops from activated action schemata. Each image in the series is taken as input by the various central / conceptual modules, which generate further predictions and emotional reactions. And this can serve as an internally generated stimulus for the activation of yet another action schema, which gives rise to yet another sequence of images, and so forth.

2.2 Inner Speech

Speech, of course, is a form of action. So one would expect that the precursor capacity for action rehearsal would carry over into this new domain. In which case there should be a capacity for creative generation of speech schemata (i.e. representations of possible utterances in a code appropriate for receipt by the motor systems), and a capacity to map those representations into a sensory modality (normally hearing), so that they can be globally broadcast and received as input by the conceptual modules. Indeed, we can predict, I think, that there would have been *special* pressure for the development of such feedback / rehearsal loops in the course of the evolution of language. Let me elaborate.

There are two main accounts of the original functions of language, and of the evolutionary pressures that led to its development. (Another will be mentioned later.) One is that language was for mutually beneficial exchange of adaptive information, in which case its evolution is to be explained in the same general way as the evolution of reciprocal altruism (Pinker, 1994; Sober and Wilson, 1998). Language was (and is) a way of transferring information from one person to another that is almost cost-free for the donor, but which can bring huge benefits to the receiver. If I have seen a poisonous snake wriggling into your hut, then telling you about it costs me only a few moments of my time and a few extra breaths; whereas it may save you your life.[11]

The other main proposal is that language evolved initially for social functions. Language was for *gossip* (Dunbar, 1996), which served sometimes to maintain and strengthen alliances and personal relationships, sometimes to manipulate other people; as well as functioning as a powerful mechanism of social control. According to Dunbar, gossip is a way of *grooming* other people, enabling humans to maintain personal relationships in larger groups than those existing in any other primate species. But it would also, and very rapidly, have become

---

[11] If you are my rival, of course, then telling you about the snake *will* have a significant cost—it will be the cost of foregoing an opportunity to get rid of a rival. The example shows that the costs and benefits of exchanging information will be by no means always easy to calculate.

a mechanism for achieving many other social ends, from wooing a mate to deceiving a rival (Miller, 2000). And it is also the primary means of enforcing social norms (Sripada, 2005). If someone has broken a social norm, then gossiping about it can lower their social standing, leading in extreme cases to social exclusion.

It may well be the case that *each* of these accounts is correct, and that language served *both* informative *and* social functions from the very beginning. But even if language started out in just one of these ways, it would rapidly have become co-opted for the other. As soon as you can inform people of things then you can start using language both to maintain alliances and to deceive and manipulate people, provided you are socially smart (as our hominid ancestors no doubt were). And as soon as you have a language that is rich enough to gossip about a variety of kinds of social activity, then you will have a language that is rich enough to exchange other forms of information as well.

The important point for my purposes, however, is this. Whichever of the above accounts is correct, there would have been intense pressure for the development of mechanisms of mental rehearsal of speech, leading to the sort of architecture depicted in Figure 4.3. Rehearsal provides a plausible mechanism for how one can come to predict the likely consequences of saying, 'There is a black mamba in your hut', for example, thereby discerning that this is an utterance worth making. For this would enable the mind-reading system to receive as input a representation of that utterance being made, and to generate the prediction that you will either stay out of your hut or enter it armed with a stick. And likewise mental rehearsal of an utterance would

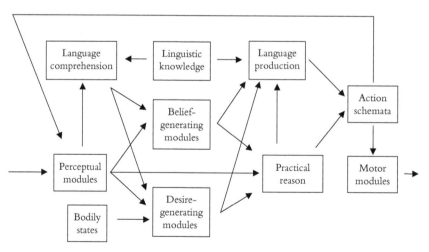

Figure 4.3. Mental rehearsal of speech

explain how one can come to predict the consequences of saying to a potential mate, 'Your eyes are like sapphires'—again discerning that this might be an utterance worth making—thus enabling the mind-reading system to generate the prediction that it would cause her to be pleased, and to be more receptive of one's advances.

Note that in each of these cases it is the mind-reading system that is one of the crucial consumer-systems for the mentally rehearsed utterance. Gomez (1998) makes a very plausible case that there would have been a sort of evolutionary 'arms race' in the development of both language and mind-reading, with advances in either one putting extra pressure on the development of the other. Moreover, Sperber and Wilson (2002) argue that there is a distinct sub-module of the mind-reading faculty devoted to communication, and to the calculations of *relevance* that underpin successful communication. (Consistent with this idea, Happé and Loth, 2002, show that children make allowances for the false belief of another in communicative contexts before they are capable of solving false-belief tasks of the regular sort.) So it may be that in modern humans there is a distinctive form of speech rehearsal that utilizes only a feedback loop to this specialized system, which one can deploy swiftly and unconsciously in the course of much regular communication, only resorting to full-blown conscious rehearsal where wider cognitive effects need to be predicted.

With a language faculty in place, together with a sophisticated capacity for mental rehearsal of linguistic utterances, then all that would have been needed was the evolution of a disposition to generate utterances *outside of* any communicative context. All that had to happen, in effect, was to take an existing network and use it more often. We would then get the cycles of 'inner speech' that are such a characteristic feature of human waking life (Hurlburt, 1990, 1993).[12] Such a cycle will begin with a mentally rehearsed utterance, perhaps primed by something recently seen or heard. That utterance is then globally broadcast by the auditory system and received as input by the language comprehension system. The latter generates from it a propositional representation—perhaps building

---

[12] Subjects in Hurlburt's studies wore headphones during the course of the day, through which they heard, at various intervals, a randomly generated series of bleeps. They were instructed that when they heard a bleep they were immediately to 'freeze' what was passing through their consciousness at that exact moment and then make a note of it, before elaborating on it later in a follow-up interview. Although frequency varied widely, all normal (as opposed to schizophrenic) subjects reported experiencing inner speech on some occasions—with the minimum being 7% of occasions sampled, and the maximum being 80%. Most subjects reported inner speech on more than half of the occasions sampled. (The majority of subjects also reported the occurrence of visual images and emotional feelings—on between 0% and 50% of occasions sampled in each case.) Think about it: more than half of the total set of moments that go to make up someone's conscious waking life is occupied with inner speech—that is well nigh continuous!

from it a mental model that might be imagistically expressed—and makes that available to all the various central / conceptual modules, including emotional and desire-generating systems. These then process that proposition as input, drawing inferences and generating emotional reactions, as appropriate. The result is a new cognitive context for the generation of yet another mentally rehearsed utterance, and so on.

What we have, then, is an explanation of the stimulus-independence of so much of human thought and behavior. For the initial utterance-rehearsals needn't be caused in any very direct way by stimuli impinging from outside. And once the cycle of inner speech has started, it can continue under its own momentum, with rehearsed utterances causing cognitive activity, which either causes further utterances directly, or changes the cognitive / emotional landscape against which another utterance can be generated and rehearsed.

2.3 A Problem: The Unlimited Character of Language

So far so good. But isn't there the following important difference between mental rehearsal of actions generally and mental rehearsal of utterances? In the case of physical actions, one can imagine that there might be a finite database of action schemata. And then the process of rehearsal can begin with the activation of one of these existing schemata, perhaps primed by features of the perceptual context, or activated by a heuristic like 'Take the Last'. But in the case of language there can't be a finite database of *utterance* schemata, since there is no end to the number of utterances that any competent speaker is capable of. So in this case the schemata will have to consist of utterance *components*—mostly words and phrases, but perhaps also some frequently used sentences, such as, 'What should I do next?' or, 'What am I doing wrong?' So the process of utterance rehearsal can't always begin with the activation of an existing utterance-schema. Rather, it looks as if a thought-to-be-uttered will often *first* have to be formulated, after which the utterance can be built by the language-production system combining and activating the appropriate sequence of action schemata.

This is, indeed, a significant difference between speech-actions and (some) others. (I shall return to consider some exceptions in a moment.) But there are a number of things that can be said in reply. One is that even if we confine ourselves to the standard speech-production model (Levelt, 1989)—in which utterance-generation always begins with a thought-to-be-uttered—we can still explain the stimulus-independence of much of human cognition. Granted, the initial utterance in a cycle of inner speech might be caused in a feed-forward manner by conceptual modules operating on perceptual input and competing to make their outputs available to the language production system. But as we shall see in Section 5, the language system may have the power to combine some of these into a single utterance, whose content will therefore be different from the content of any single thought currently being entertained. And one might expect that when an utterance is rehearsed (even one that is a direct encoding of an existing thought) a whole new set of inferences and emotional reactions might result once that thought has been globally broadcast and received as input by the full range of conceptual modules. In which case, even if the first utterance-rehearsal in a cycle of inner speech is stimulus-dependent, the cycle will rapidly take on a life of its own, including utterance-rehearsals that are quite remote in content from the original stimulus.[13]

It is also important to realize that there are domains besides that of language where we have an unlimited (potentially infinite) behavioral repertoire. Think of music and dance, for example. In each of these cases performers will have a repertoire of basic actions that they can perform. (A chord or sequence of chords played on the piano, for instance.) But there is no end to the ways in which these can be combined and recombined to make further actions of the same general type. Quite how such creative abilities are to be explained is the subject of the next chapter. But one might think that new combinations might sometimes be tried out randomly, constrained by the current context and previously performed actions, or perhaps guided by abstract resemblances to previous successful combinations. Someone improvising on the piano, for example, might at a given point select the next chord to be played at random, constrained only by whatever musical conventions are being held in place. Or they might select a chord similar to one that served well in a similar musical context recently, only in a different key.

2.4 Imagination and Episodic Memory

Thus far in this section I have focused on the way in which activations of action schemata can generate sequences of imagery, most commonly visual or auditory. But imagery surely isn't caused *only* by feedback from activated action schemata. Think how the scent of a particular flower might evoke a vivid visual image of my lover's face, or of how mention of Paris in the springtime might call up an image of us walking hand in hand through Saint Germain in the sunshine. It doesn't seem at all plausible that either of these images should be caused by an activated action schema (and in the first case, it isn't

---

[13] Another thing that can be said is that utterance generation and rehearsal may result from thoughts that are only weakly related to the initial stimuli, or that utilize heuristics for generating sentences that don't encode *any* prior thought. These ideas will be discussed extensively in Chapter 5, in the context of my treatment of creativity.

even clear what the relevant schema would be: surely there is no such thing as the looking-at-my-lover's-face action schema). And yet each is only loosely connected with the initial stimulus, and might give rise to a train of emotional reactions, images, and further episodic memories that could eventually take me a *long* way away from the initial stimulus.

There is reason to think that there are at least two distinct routes to the causation of a visual image, in fact (see Figure 4.4). One is the action-schema rehearsal route, discussed earlier in this section. This is argued by Kosslyn (1994) to be a mechanism through which we rotate and transform images—we do so by first imagining the movements that might cause such a transformation. But another is the concept-activation route, deploying back-projecting neural pathways from temporal cortex to visual area V1, for example. These are used in normal perception to query ambiguous or degraded input, helping in the process of object-recognition (Kosslyn, 1994). In normal vision multiple concepts might be partially activated by a given visual input, and these would then be used to generate images, in an attempt to determine a 'best match'. But this same system can also be deployed 'off-line', creating images that are unrelated to current visual stimuli.

What happens when an episodic memory is formed is that a number of different things get bound together (Baddeley et al., 2002). Aspects of current experience, together with emotional reactions and beliefs about current circumstances or likely consequences—realized in different brain systems and produced by a variety of modules—get linked together and stored. Thereafter, activation of any part of this complex can serve also to activate the remainder. Perhaps perception of something similar to the imagistic aspect of the memory serves to evoke the surrounding beliefs and emotions; or perhaps a remark containing some of the crucial concepts (PARIS, SPRINGTIME) serves to evoke both the relevant beliefs and to reactivate the relevant image or sequence of images.

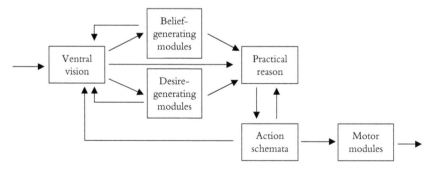

Figure 4.4. Two types of route to the generation of visual imagery

When an episode is recalled, imagery (normally visual) of the original scene will be evoked. These images are then processed by the visual system in the usual way—perhaps being elaborated and 'filled out' in the light of the subject's background beliefs and expectations—and made available to the conceptual modules once again. These in turn can generate further beliefs and further elaborations of the image, which may be stored as part of the episodic memory thereafter. (This is how memories can be elaborated and 'constructed' over time with each revisiting.)

Humans have, of course, come to enjoy evoking episodic memories for their own sake, and for the sake of the emotional reactions and rewards that come with them. Hence we have developed a variety of methods for calling up memories in ourselves and others, from the social sharing of memories in speech, through diaries, snapshots, videos, and other sorts of memorabilia. And to some extent then, episodic remembering is 'stimulus bound'. But oftentimes an aspect of the episodic memory—perhaps an element in the image that gets generated, or perhaps one of the reactivated beliefs about the circumstances—can activate yet another episodic memory, and so on. The result can be a chain of remembering that continues for some time, most of the contents of which can be unrelated to current stimuli.

Although humans now evoke memories for their own sake, that was presumably not their original function. Much more likely is that by recalling details of a previous event, one can learn something of relevance to current goals. By recalling what happened on a previous occasion of the present sort, I may be better able to figure out what I should do in the circumstances. And by recalling previous occasions in which I have interacted with someone, I may be helped in deciding whether or not to trust him now. And so on. The important point for our purposes, however, is that there is no reason to think that episodic memories are responsible for the distinctive creativity of the human mind, which will form the topic of the next chapter. For that role, the generation of action schemata seems a much more likely possibility.

2.5 Rounding up

In summary of this section, then, the stimulus-independence of human cognitive processes can be explained in two rather different ways. One is in terms of the operations of a basic capacity that we share with (some) animals, namely the capacity for mental rehearsal of action. This capacity is greatly extended by our increased, distinctively human, conceptual and knowledge-generating capacities; and especially by the development of human language, which makes possible cycles of linguistic activity in inner speech. And the other part of the explanation is in terms of episodic memory (perhaps also shared with animals;

Morris, 2002; Clayton et al., 2002), where the retrieval process gives rise to images of various sorts, which can in turn spark further episodic memories, and so on. Since all of the systems involved in both of the above sorts of process can be modules (in our weak sense of that term), there is no threat here to massively modular conceptions of the human mind.

3 Language as Content-Integrator

The hypothesis that I now want to explore and defend through the next three sections of this chapter is that natural language may be what enables us to solve the problem of content-flexibility. Versions of this hypothesis have been previously proposed by Carruthers (1996, 1998a, 2002a), by Mithen (1996), and by Spelke and colleagues (Hermer and Spelke, 1996; Hermer-Vazquez et al., 1999). I shall now sketch the thesis itself, showing how it addresses the problem of content-flexibility, before discussing (in Section 4) the experimental evidence that is alleged to support a limited version of it. In Section 5 I shall consider some alternatives and challenges. And then in Section 6 I shall turn to the problem of flexibility of reasoning-process, showing how natural language might play an important part in addressing this, as well. Section 7 will then be devoted to some clarifications and comparisons with other related proposals.

Recall from Chapter 3 that the likely shape of a language faculty, and its position within the architecture of the mind, is as depicted in Figure 3.4. It consists of distinct comprehension and production sub-systems, each of which can draw on a common database of phonological and syntactic rules, a common lexicon, and so forth. The function of the comprehension sub-system is to receive and analyze representations of natural language sentences (whether spoken, written, or signed) and—working in conjunction with other systems, both attentional and inferential—to build from that input a representation of the intended message. The latter is made available to the various belief-generating and desire-generating modules, which then get to work on that propositional content (presumably expressed in some sort of compositionally structured Mentalese or 'language of thought'),[14] evaluating or drawing further inferences, as appropriate.

---

[14] As we saw in Chapter 3.4, one plausible suggestion is that the output of the comprehension sub-system is in the form of so-called 'mental models'—that is, non-sentential, quasi-imagistic, representations of the salient features of a situation being thought about (Johnson-Laird, 1983). But because mental models are compositionally structured, they nevertheless count as tokens of Mentalese. See the discussion in Chapter 1.6.

The function of the production sub-system, in contrast, is to receive input from the various central / conceptual modules (belief-generating modules, desire-generating modules, and the practical-reasoning modules), encoding the propositional content received from those systems into a representation of a natural language sentence, which can then be passed to the motor systems for expression in speech, writing, or Sign. The inputs to the language production module will be in the form of some sort of Mentalese (not necessarily the same format or code for each of the various modules in question), and the outputs will be Mentalese representations of the phonology of natural language sentences. (Representations of natural language syntax will be utilized in the interim, helping with the mapping from input to output.)

The production sub-system is ideally *positioned*, then, to conjoin contents from all of the various central / conceptual modules, since it receives input from each of them, and since it has the capacity to convert that input into a representation of a natural language sentence. But two questions immediately arise. The first is *why* the language faculty should have acquired the capacity to *conjoin* and *integrate* contents, as opposed to expressing each sequentially. The second is *how* the conjoining process is supposed to be effected.

The first of these questions is relatively easy to answer. For *speed* of utterance is one of the important design-considerations constraining the evolution of the language faculty. Whatever the precise adaptive forces that shaped the evolution of language—whether it was the mutually adaptive exchange of information (Pinker, 1994), gossip and social manipulation (Dunbar, 1996), or perhaps even sexual display (Miller, 2000)—it will be true that the faster you can frame a thought or sequence of thoughts into language and express it, the better. And certainly the speed of language production is really quite remarkably fast. (This was one of the considerations that led Fodor, 1983, to argue for the modular nature of the language faculty.) In which case, whenever the production system receives two propositional representations from different conceptual modules concerning the same event, object, or circumstance, there would have been considerable utility in being able to express those propositions in a single sentence, rather than in two separate ones.

For example, suppose that the subject is charged with describing the location of an object in a rectangular room with one colored wall. And suppose that there are distinct geometric and object-property modules that respectively deliver the Mentalese representations, THE TOY IS IN A CORNER WITH A LONG WALL ON THE LEFT AND A SHORT WALL ON THE RIGHT, and, THE TOY IS NEAR A RED WALL. Then instead of having to utter two sentences separately, 'The toy is in a corner with a long wall on the left and a short wall on the right', and, 'The toy is near a red wall', the subject can just say, much more succinctly (and hence much more swiftly), 'The toy is in a corner with a long wall on the left and a short *red* wall on the right.'

As for how this conjoining is supposed to take place, a reasonable hypothesis is that the abstract and recursive nature of natural language syntax is one crucial determinant. Two points are suggestive of how sentences deriving from two or more distinct modules might be combined into a single module-integrative one. The first is that natural language syntax allows for multiple embedding of adjectives and phrases. Thus one can have, 'The toy is in a corner with the *long* wall on the left', 'The toy is in a corner with the *long straight* wall on the left', 'The toy is in a corner with the *long straight white* wall on the left', and so on. So there are already 'slots' into which additional adjectives—such as 'red'—can be inserted.

The second point is that the reference of terms like 'the wall', 'the toy', and so on will need to be secured by some sort of indexing to the contents of current perception or recent memory. (This will be necessary when fixing the interpretation of a pronoun in an exchange of sentences with someone, for example.)[15] In which case it looks as though it wouldn't be too complex a matter for the language production system to take two sentences sharing a number of references like this, and to combine them into one sentence by inserting adjectives from one into open adjective-slots in the other. The language faculty just has to take the two sentences, 'The toy$_1$ is in a corner with a long wall$_1$ on the left and a short wall$_2$ on the right', and, 'The toy$_1$ is near a red wall$_2$' and use them to generate the sentence, 'The toy is in a corner with a long wall on the left and a short red wall on the right.'

Notice that the integrative role of the language module, on this account, depends upon it having the capacity for certain kinds of inference. Specifically, it must be capable of taking two sentences in so-called 'Logical Form' (LF), constructed from the outputs of two distinct conceptual modules, and of combining them appropriately into a single LF representation. But it might be felt that such a claim is highly implausible, and that it is in conflict with the views of most contemporary linguists. I don't believe that either of these claims is correct, however.

It is important to see that what is in question is *not* the existence of a general-purpose inference engine located within the language faculty. For

---

[15] Consider an exchange in which someone says to me, 'The toy belongs to Mary.' My language comprehension system has to figure out (in cooperation with other systems, no doubt) the intended referents of both 'The toy' and 'Mary' in the context. If the thought that I then formulate as the basis for my reply has the content, *Mary plays with the toy often*, then my language production system will have to index the phrases 'Mary' and 'The toy' in such a way as to display their co-reference with the equivalent phrases in the original utterance, in order that it can be determined that it is appropriate for me to say in response, '*She* plays with *it* often', with pronouns substituted in place of the original noun phrases.

indeed, such a claim is not only intrinsically unbelievable (as well as being inconsistent with the 'one function / one module' generalization of Chapter 1), but certainly wouldn't be believed by any working linguist. However, just about every linguist *does* think (with the possible exception of Fodor and those closely influenced by Fodor) that *some* inferences are valid, and are known to be valid, purely in virtue of our linguistic competence. Most linguists believe, for example, that the inference from, 'John ran quickly', to, 'John ran' is endorsed in virtue of semantic competence (Parsons, 1990); and many would claim that such competence is embodied in the language faculty. In contemporary parlance, this amounts to saying that the inference is made by the language module transforming sentences of LF.

Admittedly, on some approaches to natural language semantics the sorts of powers and transformations envisaged at the semantic level aren't plausibly attributed to the language faculty, but would rather belong to some centralized (and pretty powerful) thought capability. This is especially true of semantics done in the tradition of Montague (1974), which presupposes a capacity to abstract arbitrarily complex concepts by deletion of components from complete thoughts, replacing those components with variables. But there are also forms of semantic theory that are much more closely integrated with Chomskian approaches to syntax, as articulated by Higginbotham (1985). Just such an account is worked out by Pietroski (2005), according to which the basic format of semantic inference is that of covert quantification over events together with conjunction introduction and reduction. Thus on this sort of approach, 'John ran quickly', really has the form, $\exists e$ *(e is a running & e is by John & e is quick)*. And then the inference to, 'John ran' is just a simple instance of conjunction elimination. On such an account, then, it is far from implausible that certain limited forms of inference (notably conjunction introduction and conjunction elimination, among others) should be handled internally within the language faculty, in transformations of LF sentences.

4 The Reorientation Data

I have suggested that if the mind were massively modular, then we should expect there to be some limits on the ways in which concepts can be combined and integrated with one another. (This prediction will be strengthened still further by some of the considerations to be adduced in Section 5.) Yet we have reason to think that there are no such limits on the flexibility of the human mind. So we have a problem: how can such flexibility of content arise in a massively modular mind? I have been suggesting that there are reasons of a general sort for thinking that it is the language production module that performs such a role, initially in the service of speech efficiency. But Spelke and colleagues have claimed to find direct evidence in support of just this conclusion, at least in one limited domain (Hermer and Spelke, 1996; Hermer-Vazquez et al., 1999; Shusterman and Spelke, 2005). The present section will examine and discuss their argument.

4.1 The Data

The story begins with an earlier discovery of a geometrical module in rats (Cheng, 1986), already briefly discussed in Chapter 2.3. A rat disoriented in a rectangular space will rely exclusively upon geometric information when attempting to reorient itself. When its task is to search for food that it had previously seen hidden in one of the corners, it will search equally often in the geometrically equivalent corners, ignoring all other cues. One of the walls can be distinctively patterned, or distinctively scented; but the rat ignores these cues (which it is nevertheless perfectly capable of using when searching in other circumstances), and relies only upon the geometry of the space.[16] Rats therefore fail in the task roughly fifty percent of the time.

Now admittedly, it doesn't follow from these data that rats *cannot* integrate geometric with object-property information; nor does it follow that they *don't* sometimes do so for other purposes. For all that the data show, it may be that there are links between the geometric module and the object-property module, which can lead to thoughts in other circumstances that combine concepts from both domains. But the data do at least show that in conditions of disorientation, it is only geometric information that is relied upon by the practical-reasoning system when the latter seeks to know the location of a desired target.

It should also be noted, similarly, that the finding that some other species (notably chickens and monkeys) *can* solve these sorts of reorientation tasks (Vallortigara et al., 1990; Gouteux et al., 2001) doesn't demonstrate that the members of these species are *integrating* geometric and landmark information. For the tasks can be solved by accessing the two types of information *sequentially*, first using object-property information (e.g. the location of the one red wall) to reorient, before using geometric information to guide the final stages of search. The difference between monkeys and rats may lie, not in their

---

[16] This makes perfectly good ecological / evolutionary sense. For in the rat's natural environment, overall geometrical symmetries in the landscape are extremely rare, and geometrical properties generally change only slowly with time; whereas object-properties of color, scent-markings, and so on will change with the weather and seasons. So a strong preference to orient by geometrical properties rather than by object-properties is just what one might predict.

powers of conjoining module-specific information, but rather in the heuristic rules that their practical-reasoning systems deploy when searching for a target object in conditions of disorientation. The monkeys may deploy the rule, 'When disoriented (and there is no directional beacon available, like a distant line of hills or the position of the sun), seek for a familiar landmark object first, and then use the local geometry', whereas the rats may use the converse ordering, 'When disoriented (and there is no directional beacon available), use the local geometry first, and then seek for familiar objects.' Indeed, this is the most parsimonious explanation of the data.[17]

Hermer and Spelke (1996) made the startling discovery that young human children are like rats, rather than like monkeys, in this respect. The child is led into a rectangular room consisting of three white walls and one red wall, and is shown a toy being hidden in one of the corners. The child is then blindfolded and turned around until disoriented. Then the blindfold is removed, and the child is instructed to find the toy. Provided that the room is small enough that the child isn't cued to treat the red wall as a directional beacon (Leamonth et al., 2001; Shusterman and Spelke, 2005), then the child behaves just as a rat would: searching equally often in either of the two geometrically equivalent corners, and ignoring the information provided by the one red wall.

Human adults can solve these tasks, as can children older than about six or seven years. Hermer and Spelke (1996) examined the factors that predict success. It turns out that a capacity to succeed in these tasks isn't directly correlated with age, non-verbal IQ, verbal working-memory capacity, vocabulary size, or comprehension of spatial vocabulary. The only significant predictor of success in these tasks that could be discovered was the spontaneous use of spatial vocabulary conjoined with object-properties (e.g. 'It is left of the red one'). And in a follow-up study Shusterman and Spelke (2005) demonstrated that the connection is a causal one. Children who are given training in the use of 'left' and 'right', and who succeed in mastering the meanings of those terms, are much more likely to succeed when tested in a version of the reorientation task a week later.

Hermer-Vazquez et al. (1999) showed, further, that the performance of adults in the reorientation tasks is severely disrupted by occupying the resources

---

[17] It is tempting to seek an adaptationist explanation of these species differences. Open-country dwellers such as rats and pre-linguistic humans may have an innate predisposition to rely only on geometric information when disoriented because such information alone will almost always provide a unique solution (given that rectangular rooms don't normally occur in nature!). Forest dwellers such as chickens and monkeys, in contrast, will have an innate predisposition to seek for landmark information first, only using geometric information to navigate in relation to a known landmark, because geometric information is of limited usefulness in a forest—the geometry is just too complex to be useful in individuating a place in the absence of a landmark such as a well-known fruit tree.

of the language production module. If subjects are required to 'shadow' speech while undertaking the tasks (repeating out loud what they hear someone saying through a pair of headphones), then their performance collapses to that of younger children and rats—they, too, rely exclusively on geometric information, ignoring the information provided by the red wall. If subjects are required to 'shadow' a complex rhythm, in contrast (tapping out with their hand the rhythm played to them through their headphones), their performance isn't disrupted. So the conclusion from this, together with the childhood studies, is that it is natural language (specifically spatial language) that enables older children and adults to succeed in orientation tasks requiring them to utilize both geometric and object-property information.

4.2 Explaining the Data

So far so good. The data are quite convincing in demonstrating that it is rehearsals of natural language sentences that somehow enable older humans to solve these reorientation tasks. But do they show that the role of language is to enable the conjoining of geometric with object-property information, thus integrating the outputs of two distinct conceptual modules? Unfortunately, they do not. One salient fact is this. If the attention of younger children is drawn explicitly to the significance of the red wall (e.g. by the experimenter saying, 'Look, I'm hiding the toy by the *red* wall'), then they will succeed, despite lacking productive use of the language of 'left' and 'right' (Shusterman and Spelke, 2005). By pragmatically informing young children of the importance of the red wall, they can be cued to reorient to the red wall first, thereafter utilizing geometric information to complete their search, and following the same successful ordering of the task as do monkeys and chickens. And this (rather than a module-integrating function) may be the role that language plays in enabling older children and adults to solve the reorientation tasks, too.

Another salient fact is that adults report on the basis of introspection that the kind of sentence they rehearse when solving these tasks is, 'It is left of the red wall', rather than the more unwieldy, 'It is in the corner with a long wall on the left and a short red wall on the right.' But the former (as opposed to the latter) don't encode geometric information. The description, 'left of the red wall', combines *spatial* information with object-property information (as does, '*near* the red wall', of course). But it doesn't combine *geometric* information with object-property information; a sentence of the more unwieldy sort would be needed for that. So the role of language in enabling adult success can't be that it enables people to combine the outputs of a geometric module and an object-property module (either for the first time, or in circumstances in which such contents wouldn't otherwise be combined).

I suggest that the existing data are best explained as follows. Young children entering a reorientation task might well try out for themselves, as an aid to solving it, the natural language description, 'It is near the red wall.' But they would easily see that such a description doesn't carry adequate information, since it doesn't tell them *where* in relation to the red wall the object is. (Of course *they* don't know that they have a geometrical module, and that if they could only get themselves oriented towards red, that module would deliver the solution for them.) And they therefore discard it (i.e. make no attempt to rehearse it). But if the experimenter tells them, in effect, to look for the object near the red wall, then they rehearse the relevant sentence, and this enables them to succeed, overriding their natural disposition to rely upon geometric information first. Adults and older children, in contrast, who possess the language of 'left' and 'right', can try out the description, 'It is left of / right of the red wall', and will see that this encodes all of the information that they need to enable a solution.[18] They can then rehearse it (provided that their language production module isn't preoccupied with concurrent speech-shadowing), and can then use that sentence to guide their search-behavior once the blindfold is removed.

But how, exactly, does mental rehearsal of a sentence guide search behavior? How does it lead to the determination of a novel action (orienting towards the red wall)? The best explanation parallels the one that we sketched in Chapter 2.8 for the role of mental rehearsal in practical reasoning generally. By mentally rehearsing, 'It is left of the red wall', the content of that sentence is extracted by the language comprehension system and globally broadcast to belief-generating and desire-generating modules, and to practical reason. The latter, on accepting a representation of the target object as being to the left of the red wall, can easily put together an action schema for the retrieval of the object. When this in turn is mentally rehearsed, an image of the subject successfully retrieving the target object is generated and broadcast, which when received by the motivational systems causes the subject to feel some satisfaction. And this in turn ratchets up the desirability of executing the action schema in question.

Although the existing data don't support the view that it is language that enables the outputs of a geometric module and an object-property module to be combined, it is important to see that they *do* nevertheless demonstrate a significant cognitive role for natural language in these tasks. For it is the rehearsal

---

[18] How does language enable people to succeed when the target object is placed in one of the other two corners? For (since there are *three* white walls), the description, 'Left of the white wall' doesn't uniquely identify a place. But in fact the *short* white wall is the only pragmatically salient white wall. For if the target object had been placed in either of the corners where a long white wall adjoins the red one, then the position could have been identified by means of the description, 'Left of red' or, 'Right of red'; and subjects know this.

of natural language sentences that enables human subjects to overcome their natural disposition to reorient on the basis of geometric information first. In effect, the role of natural language, here, is best assimilated to the way in which language enables flexibility of reasoning *process* (rather than content-flexibility), to be discussed in Section 6. And this is still an important result.

Moreover, I hypothesize that it ought to be fairly easy to devise a version of the reorientation tasks in which language *would* enable people to succeed by combining geometric information with object-property information. For notice that, when the tasks are conducted in a rectangular room, there is no single lexical item that means, 'corner with a long wall on the left and a short wall on the right'. The descriptor, 'left of the red wall' is therefore a great deal more convenient to use. But suppose that the shape of the room were, not rectangular, but rather rhomboid, in the form of a squashed parallelogram. Then two of the geometrically equivalent corners would be acute-angled, and two would be obtuse. And then the description, 'It is in the acute corner near red' would contain not only all the information necessary for success, but would do so in an acceptably compact form. And such a description *does* combine geometric with object-property information. We might predict that at least some adults would deploy such a sentence to enable them to succeed in the tasks. And we might predict that young children who don't yet have the vocabulary of 'left' and 'right', but who are given training with the terms 'acute' and 'obtuse' (or more accessibly, perhaps, with the phrases 'pointy corner' and 'wide corner'), might thereby be enabled to succeed.

5 Alternative Theories of Content Flexibility

Although the existing experimental data don't directly support a content-integration account of the cognitive role of language, it seems highly likely that such data could be obtained with the right experimental manipulation. And I have argued that there are in any case general theoretical reasons for taking seriously the idea that it is language that enables us to combine the outputs of some different belief-modules. (Recall that a great deal of content-integration will already be taking place by virtue of the wiring connections that exist between some belief modules and some other belief modules.) Now in the present section I shall consider two alternatives to the account of content-integration sketched in Section 3. One is that the module doing the work of content-integration isn't the language faculty, but rather the mind-reading system. The other is that there might be a special-purpose content-integrating mechanism downstream of the central / conceptual modules, positioned between them and the practical-reasoning system. In the course of this discussion yet further reasons for taking seriously the content-integration role of language will emerge.

5.1 Meta-Module or Language Module?

Atran (2002b) presents the following challenge to the above account: Why should we think that it is language that does inter-modular integration, rather than some sort of meta-representational faculty—a theory of mind mechanism (ToMM) or a mind-reading mechanism? Atran agrees with the modularist framework adopted here; and he agrees that domain-general flexible cognition somehow has to be built out of modular components. But he sees nothing yet to discriminate between my proposal and the idea previously advanced by Sperber (1996) that it is the mind-reading module that has the power to combine the outputs of all the others.

As we saw in Chapter 1, it is perfectly plausible that some modular systems might routinely exploit the resources of other systems independently of language, querying those systems for needed information. And this will surely be the case for a mind-reading mechanism. Indeed, just such an account of the operations of the mind-reading faculty has recently been offered, and ably elaborated and defended, by Nichols and Stich (2003), as we saw in Chapter 3.3. So I fully accept that the system in question can access some of the contents generated by these other systems, no matter whether they be concerned with mates, financial institutions, falling stones, or whatever. The point is just that the mind-reading system itself should be incapable of drawing any further inferences from these contents, except those mandated by its own inferential principles.

So the mind-reading module will be able to go from, 'John has *seen* Mary with a basket of red tomatoes', to, 'John probably *knows* that Mary has a basket of red tomatoes' (in virtue of the mind-reading principle, 'seeing leads to knowing'). But the mind-reading system itself won't be able to infer, 'John knows that Mary has some *ripe* tomatoes.' To get that inference, it will have to send out a query elsewhere, and get the response, 'Red tomatoes are ripe', or the response, 'Mary has a basket of red tomatoes ⊃ Mary has a basket of ripe tomatoes', and then rely on the mind-reading principle, 'People know the obvious consequences of other things that they know.'

The main point here is one of task-analysis, combined with the form of 'one function / one module' generalization defended in Chapter 1. Attributing mental states to other people on the basis of behavioral cues, and/or predicting people's behavior from mental states previously attributed to them, is what the mind-reading system is primarily about. Combining concepts and propositions, and drawing arbitrary inferences from them, would seem to be a distinct set of functions entirely. In which case we should expect that the latter functions will be carried out in one or more distinct modules. For there is no reason to think that they will come 'for free' with mind-reading functions. In contrast, there *is* good reason to think that the content-combining functions *will* come for free with the language module, given the constraint of speed of sentence-production.

Another (related) difficulty for the Sperber / Atran proposal is to explain why their proposed meta-representational inter-modular architecture should have evolved. For the main business of the mind-reading faculty is presumably to predict and explain the behavior of conspecifics. This capacity would only have required the construction of inter-modular thoughts if others were *already* entertaining such thoughts. Otherwise attributions of module-specific thoughts alone would have done perfectly well. (The same point is valid, of course, even if the primary purpose of the mind-reading faculty were the introspective ascription of thoughts to oneself. For there would only be a point in self-ascribing an inter-modular thought to oneself if one were already capable of entertaining such a thought, prior to the operations of the mind-reading faculty.)

In the case of language, in contrast, the demands of swift and efficient communication would have created a significant selection pressure for inter-modular integration, allowing the outputs of distinct central modules concerning the same object or event to be combined into a single spoken sentence. So instead of saying separately, 'The object is near a short wall', and, 'The object is near a red wall', one can say much more succinctly, 'The object is near a short red wall' (given that the short wall in question *is* the red wall, of course).

It might be replied that the pressure for the mind-reading system to integrate contents across modules could have come, not from the demands of predicting and explaining the behavior of oneself and others, but rather from the benefits that such integration can bring for other areas of activity (such as solving the reorientation problem). This is possible. After all, it is common enough in biology that a system initially selected for one purpose will be co-opted and used for another. And it might be claimed that the mind-reading system would be ideally placed to play the integrative role, receiving information from all the other central modules, and providing outputs to practical reasoning.

But actually, it is hard to see how one could get from here to anything resembling the full flexibility of human cognition. For there is no reason to suppose that the mind-reading system would have been set up in such a way as to provide its output *as input to* the other central modules (as opposed to *querying* those modules for needed information). In which case there would be no scope for *cycles* of reasoning activity, with the mind-reading system combining the outputs from central modules and then feeding the conjoined content back to them, harnessing their resources for purposes of further reasoning. In contrast, since language is both an output *and* an input module, it is well positioned for just this role, as I argued in Section 3.

In conclusion of this sub-section, then, I claim (on both general theoretical and evolutionary grounds) that language is a much more plausible candidate for integrating the contents of other central modules than is the mind-reading system.[19]

5.2 *A Special-Purpose Content-Integrator?*

Each of the proposals considered so far maintains that content-integration is carried out by systems that initially evolved for other purposes (communication, in the case of language; explanation and prediction of other people's actions, in the case of mind-reading). The obvious competitor hypothesis is that content-integration is undertaken by a special-purpose module of the mind that was designed to do just that: integrate contents. This system would have to be located downstream of the various central / conceptual modules, from which it would receive its input. And it would need to make its output available to the language production system, and perhaps also to practical reason (see Figure 4.5).

It might be said that this model has an advantage over my language-based one. This is that language production can here operate entirely along classical lines. The language production system will receive a complete integrated thought of some sort—THE TOY IS IN AN ACUTE-ANGLED CORNER NEAR A RED WALL, as it might be—and it will encode that thought into speech. No inferences will need to be drawn, and no content-conjoining needs to take place within the language faculty. It is doubtful, however, whether this is a

---

[19] In addition, suppose we were satisfied that the dual-task data collected by Spelke and colleagues (Hermer-Vazquez et al., 1999) are about content *integration* rather than content *sequencing*; or suppose that we could successfully obtain such data. That would then support my own proposal quite strongly, when matched against the Sperber / Atran one. For if subjects fail at the task in the speech-shadowing condition (but not in the rhythm-shadowing condition) because they cannot then integrate geometrical and landmark information, it is very hard to see how it can be a disruption to mind-reading that is responsible for this failure. For there is no reason to think that shadowing of speech should involve the resources of the mind-reading module. Admittedly, a good case can be made for saying that normal speech comprehension and production will implicate a sub-system (at least) of the mind-reading module—where that sub-system is charged with figuring out the conditions for *relevance* in communication (Sperber and Wilson, 2002). So normal instances of speaking and comprehending would surely disrupt any other concomitant task that involves mind-reading (and so any task requiring inter-modular integration, on the hypothesis that it is the mind-reading module that performs this role). But there is no reason to think that this should be true of speech *shadowing*. For in this case there is no requirement of comprehension, and no attempt at communication.

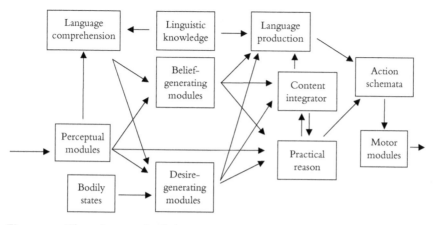

Figure 4.5. The existence of a distinct content integrator

very powerful consideration in support of the model. For if many linguists are already inclined to believe, on other grounds, that the language faculty has limited inferential abilities, and is capable of combining words and phrases about the same subject matter, then we shall already have all the materials necessary for the language-based account of content-integration to operate.

If we are to believe in a special-purpose content-integrator, moreover, then we had better be provided with some account of the evolutionary pressures that might have led to its existence. What could these have been? Not the demands of swift and efficient communication, presumably, since these would have been much more likely to give rise to the minor alterations in the language-production system required for it to take on the content-integration role, as we saw in Section 3. Nor, I think, can the existence of a content-integrator be explained by the benefits that might accrue to intra-modular processing, deriving from integrating the outputs of two or more modules that both feed their output into a given (third) module. For this would have created pressure for an adaptation in that latter module itself, rather than for the creation of a whole new system to perform the task.

The explanation of content integration via language that we provided in Section 3 had to do with speed of communication of thoughts deriving from distinct modular systems. And then it might be said that pressures of speed, not on communication, but rather on practical reasoning, might have given rise to a special-purpose content-integrator. For in that case, instead of having to receive two or more distinct thoughts in sequence, the practical-reason system could receive just a single integrated thought. But this would have required a corresponding increase in the complexity of the algorithms being operated by the practical-reason system. In fact, it would have had to develop some way of 'looking into' an atomic proposition to discern and utilize its distinctive integrated content. And besides the obvious costs in terms of computational complexity, these operations would also take up additional time, of course; so there is unlikely to have been any overall gain in speed.

It seems to me, then, that the costs of feeding integrated contents to the practical-reason system would have more than outweighed any benefits. In the case of language, in contrast, the initial pressure for changes in the systems that consume the newly integrated linguistic contents would have lain outside the head of the speaker, in the language comprehension systems of his or her interlocutors. One can easily imagine a sort of evolutionary 'arms race' taking place, here, in which the benefits deriving from increases in speed of communication drive small changes in the language production system, enabling distinct sentences to be integrated with one another before utterance, with corresponding pressure on the language comprehension system to upgrade itself as a result.

The only other way that I can imagine the idea of a distinct content-integration module being fleshed out would be to postulate that this is actually the work of a logic module, of the sort that Sperber (1996) has suggested might exist. This would be a module that responds just to the *forms* of the propositions that it receives as input, looking for opportunities to derive some logical consequences from them. So if the module receives two representations, P, and, IF P THEN Q, as input then it generates the consequence, Q, as output; and so forth.

There may well be such a logic module. Certainly the capacity to derive some of the simpler logical consequences of what you believe would be a useful capacity to have. But it can't do the work required of it in the present context, as we noted in Section 1.6. This is obviously the case if the system in question deals only in propositional logic, since such logics treat propositions as 'atoms', whose contents can get *combined* with one another (e.g. by conjunction introduction) but never *integrated*. And even if the system implements some sort of predicate logic with identity, this still doesn't have the resources to effect the sort of inference required. In the simplest case, we want to be able to integrate the contents of two propositions like, THAT₁ IS A SHORT WALL, and, THAT₁ IS A RED WALL, to form the representation, THAT₁ IS A SHORT RED WALL. But predicate logic doesn't have the resources to construct complex predicates like, 'short red wall'. This seems much more likely to be the work of a language faculty, whose business is precisely to build up complex sentences and phrases from their parts.

There is one final consideration that counts against the existence of any sort of special-purpose content-integrator, and in favor of our language-based account. This arises out of the following fact. There is nothing to guarantee that the outputs of all belief-generating modules possess the same representational format; and it seems quite likely, indeed, that those outputs *aren't* all in the same format. For example, the output of the geometrical module might be in some analog quasi-spatial, quasi-perceptual, format; whereas the output of the object-property system might have a digitalized sentence-like format. So the evolution of a content-conjoiner module would at the same time have had to be the evolution of a system that can interface with systems that employ a variety of representational formats. This means that there would have to have been some especially strong pressure for the existence of such a module.

Something similar is true of the language system, of course. It too, on the production side, would need to be capable of receiving input from all the different belief-generating and desire-generating modules, whose outputs might differ from one another in their representational format. But this doesn't set any special puzzle for a content-integrating account of the role of language, since interfacing with conceptual modules is something that a language faculty would need to do anyway. And it would be natural language itself that would provide the 'common format' in which the outputs of the different conceptual modules could be integrated. We don't need to postulate any extra selection pressure on the language faculty to enable it to integrate the contents that it encodes; the abstract and recursive nature of natural-language syntax will see to that. Whereas, in contrast, we *do* need to postulate an extra-strong selection pressure for the existence of a content-conjoining system, to enable it to interface with central modules.

In the case of language, there exist plausible accounts of the adaptive forces that might have led to its evolution, as we have seen. And some of these accounts postulate that the evolutionary process might have been gradual and incremental, precisely in respect of the number of other systems with which the language faculty can interface. (Dunbar, 1996, for example, supposes that language was initially for communication of *social* information. So presumably, on this account, the interfaces with the various social modules—mind-reading, cheater-detection, and so forth—would have been built first; with interfaces to other systems only being added later.) But what would have been the selection pressure for a special-purpose content-integrator? As we saw earlier, it is very hard to discern one.

5.3 *Conclusion of Sections 3, 4, and 5*

I have sketched an account of the way in which a language module might be responsible for the seemingly unlimited content-flexibility of the human mind, and I have contrasted this account with alternatives. While the experimental evidence that has been alleged to support such an account currently falls short of doing so, it seems quite likely that this lacuna can be filled. And there are a number of general considerations that support the proposal over the available competitors.

6 Inner Speech and the Flexibility of Reasoning

Thus far we have sketched modularist, language-based, explanations of both the stimulus-independence of so much of human cognition and the content-flexibility of human thought. But what of the flexibility of human reasoning *processes*—the acquisition and maintenance of new patterns of thinking, and new rules of reasoning? Can this be explained within the framework outlined above? I believe that it can. But first I need to explain and elaborate the so-called 'two systems' account of human reasoning processes.

6.1 Two Reasoning Systems and Mental Rehearsal

Virtually all of the scientists who study human reasoning and the pervasive fallacies that so often occur in human reasoning have converged on some or other version of a two-systems theory (Evans and Over, 1996; Stanovich, 1999; Kahneman, 2002). System 1 is really a *collection* of systems, arranged in parallel. These systems are supposed, for the most part, to be universal (common to all members of the species), to be evolutionarily ancient, and to operate swiftly and unconsciously. Moreover, their processing algorithms are either immutable, or subject to their own idiosyncratic trajectory of learning and change—at any rate, explicit instruction has little impact on their operations. In the context of the present discussion, then, they can be identified with the set of central / conceptual modules.

System 2, in contrast, is supposed to operate linearly (rather than in parallel), and to be slower and characteristically conscious in its operations. But it can override or pre-empt the results of System 1. And its algorithms are much more mutable, and are more easily influenced by explicit teaching of various sorts. System 2 is also much more subject to individual variation. Thus Stanovich (1999) shows that variability in success in the various standard reasoning tasks (which are thought to require the operation of System 2) correlates highly with IQ, and hence also with *g*. And even when IQ is factored out, it correlates highly with certain measures of variable cognitive *style* (such as a disposition to be reflective, and a capacity to distance oneself from one's own intuitive views).

As I have already remarked, within the context of massively modular models of the human mind we can identify the parallel System 1 processes with the operations of a set of central / conceptual modules. And we can then understand System 2 as supervening on the activity of those systems, realized in cycles of mentally rehearsed action in general, and inner speech in particular. We will return to consider in some detail how such cycles can give rise to novel beliefs and novel actions in Chapters 6.7 and 7.4 respectively. But for the moment it should be noted that speech is an *activity*, of course. And like any other activity, sequences of action can be learned and practiced, and can improve as a result of explicit instruction. And one can also reflect on those sequences, and form beliefs about their appropriateness. Let me elaborate.

Consider a simple action like lifting an object from the floor and placing it on a table-high surface. There is a more or less intuitive and natural sequence of actions that most people will perform in a case of this sort. One will approach the object, bending from the waist (perhaps with some bending of the knees, depending on how high the graspable surface of the object rides above the floor), grab it with arms fairly straight, and then lift by straightening one's back while at the same time bending one's arms at the elbow. This works very effectively in a wide range of situations. But as many people now know, it can be a recipe for back-injury when the object to be lifted is heavy, or when many lighter objects have to be lifted in a repetitive sequence. In such cases, the proper sequence of action is to approach the object, go almost into a squatting position in front of it, bending one's knees fully while keeping one's back straight, grasping the object with arms bent at the elbow, and then lifting by straightening one's knees while keeping one's arms fairly immobile.

This novel sequence of action can of course be learned by imitation, or as a result of explicit verbal instruction; and it can be practiced until it becomes smooth and natural—indeed, *habitual*. And it is possible to reflect on it or alternatives to it, in the sort of way that physical trainers and athletes often do—debating, either externally with others or inwardly with oneself, which sequence of act-components would best realize one's overall goals. And having debated, and reached a conclusion, it is possible to train oneself to act accordingly.

Likewise then, suppose that I am faced with a version of the Wason card-selection task, and am asked which of the four cards I should turn over to tell whether or not the target statement, 'If P then Q', is true.[20] Like so many other

---

[20] In these now-famous experiments, subjects are confronted with four cards on which propositions are inscribed, of the form: $P, \sim P, Q, \sim Q$. They are told that on the back of each of the $P / \sim P$ cards will be inscribed either Q or $\sim$ Q; and that on the back of each of the $Q / \sim Q$ cards will be inscribed either P or $\sim P$; and that these four cards correspond to the truth-value combinations of P and Q in the envisaged situation. And their task is to decide which of the four cards they need to turn over to decide whether or not the statement, 'If P then Q' is true.

people, I turn over just the *P* card, relying on my swift-and-intuitive System 1 cognitive processes. But then I take a course in propositional logic, in which the instructor informs me that a conditional is only false in the case where the antecedent is true and the consequent false. 'Remember', the instructor might say, 'in order to evaluate the truth of a conditional you need to look for a case where the antecedent is true and the consequent false.' Then, when faced with a Wason selection task on some later occasion, I take a moment to reflect, ask myself (in inner speech), 'What do I have to do in order to evaluate a conditional?' The global broadcast of the content of this question enables me to recall what I was told, and hence I correctly turn over both the *P* and *not-Q* cards. And of course it is possible to reflect on *patterns* of sentences used in reasoning, too, trying to develop rules by means of which to reason better, as logicians and scientific methodologists have traditionally done.

Consider, in addition, how we might explain the main elements of cognitive style that correlate so well with success in difficult (System-2-involving) reasoning tasks (Stanovich, 1999). The disposition to be reflective before giving an answer or reaching a decision maps nicely into our model. This will be the disposition to engage in explicit conscious thinking in inner speech or other forms of imagery before responding. And the capacity to distance oneself from one's own intuitive views, too, finds a ready explanation on our model. For this can be identified with a readiness to entertain alternative suppositions, formulated and mentally rehearsed in inner speech or other forms of imagery. And that each of these elements of cognitive style should correlate with success in the sort of reasoning that requires access to learned rules is exactly what would be predicted, on our account.[21]

The proposal being made here, then, is that in addition to a set of swift and unconscious modular thinking and reasoning processes (System 1), humans also engage in a kind of reasoning that is slower (realized in *cycles* of System 1 activity), that is conscious (by virtue of the global broadcasting of sensory representations of utterances in inner speech and other action rehearsals), and that is to a significant degree language-based. The latter (System 2) is realized in sequences of action-schema activations (often rehearsals of natural language

---

[21] An interesting further prediction is that people who are introverted should be disproportionately successful at difficult System-2-involving tasks, and should thus be over-represented in populations of gifted individuals. (I owe this observation to Chris Pyne.) For introverts have a well known tendency to be both self-stimulating and introspective (presumably occupying their time in cycles of visual imagery and inner speech). And indeed, a recent survey of research on this topic finds that introverts are to be found significantly more often amongst gifted students in comparison to control populations (Sak, 2004).

utterances), with the sequences taking place (sometimes) in accordance with learned rules and inferential procedures.

6.2 System 2 as Mental Rehearsal: For and Against

We will explore this proposal in greater detail in future chapters. But some additional support for it can be found in the extended defense of the 'think aloud' protocol for research into human cognitive processing mounted by Ericsson and Simon (1993). They argue that in connection with a wide range of cognitive tasks (most of which we would now categorize as 'System 2'), reliable evidence of how people actually solve these problems can be gathered by requiring subjects to 'think out loud', in overt speech, while they tackle them. They emphasize that it is crucial not to ask people to comment on, or describe, how they are solving the problem. For provision of such a meta-commentary will demonstrably interfere with the normal performance of the task in question, and will thus provide unreliable evidence of how such tasks are normally undertaken. But if subjects are encouraged to 'speak their thoughts', then the thoughts that they articulate will actually map nicely onto one or another of the various *possible* ways of solving the problem, as gleaned from task-analysis. And the resulting account will also be supported by other indirect measures, such as the length of time that the task takes.

These facts are easily and neatly explained if what people are doing when they attempt to solve problems in a System 2 manner (or at least when they tackle the sorts of System 2 problems tested by Ericsson and Simon) is that they engage in cycles of verbal rehearsal in inner speech. For then all that the think-aloud protocol does is remove the inhibitory process that would normally prevent the activated motor schemas, which are used to generate the sentences of inner speech, from emerging in overt action.

There is also a natural *objection* to the proposal being made here, however. For I am suggesting both that System 2 processes play an important role in explaining individual variations in *g*, and that such processes are realized in mental rehearsals of action, including mental rehearsals of speech action, in 'inner speech'. These claims would seem to imply that people whose language system is damaged or destroyed should always perform poorly on standard psychometric tests. But some aphasics can show spared performance in such tests (Kertesz, 1988; Varley, 1998). And likewise, there are sub-populations of children with Specific Language Impairment (SLI) whose general intelligence is within the normal range (van der Lely, 2005). Let me reply to these points separately.

It is very doubtful whether my proposal concerning the role of language in System 2 processes entails that children with SLI should have lower IQs than normal. This is because the deficits involved (within the relevant sub-population, at least) are relatively subtle ones. Children in this group make frequent errors in their use of actives and passives, in agreement, and in tense. They might say, for example, 'He fall to the ground', rather than, 'He fell to the ground.' But it is quite unclear why this should lead to any failures in the child's own reasoning. (It certainly shouldn't interfere with the content-conjoining role of language outlined in Section 3.) For when the child mentally rehearses such a sentence when problem solving, there will generally be ample cues to enable the child's language comprehension system to extract a past-tensed thought from the present-tensed rehearsed sentence. If there are any effects here, they will be subtle time-to-completion ones, which wouldn't show up in an IQ score.

As for IQ in aphasia, there are two points to stress. One is that my view is *not* that System 2 reasoning per se is language-dependent. Rather, it is that System 2 is dependent on mental rehearsals generally, with language-rehearsal being just one (very important) form amongst others. And the second point is that *verbal* psychometric tests, of course, cannot even be administered to aphasics. So it might be the case that the reasoning underlying successful performance in *those* tests is verbally mediated. And the fact that an aphasic subject can have preserved abilities to reason with Raven's Matrices, for example, or in tasks that require pictures to be ordered to make a coherent narrative, should not be surprising, on my view. For the relevant rehearsals can be conducted in visual imagery rather than speech.

6.3 *Thinking as Acting*

Notice that the account sketched here has the resources to explain our common-sense belief that thinking is often an *activity*, and is something that we *do* (being at least partly under our intentional control), rather than something that merely *happens* within us (Frankish, 2004).[22] This belief might initially seem to be problematic in the context of a massively modular conception of the human mind. For if the mind consists entirely of modular special-purpose

[22] I should stress that I don't mean to be claiming that *all* conscious thinking results from the activation and rehearsal of action schemata. On the contrary, some visual images (e.g. of a window shattering from an impending impact) are produced from the output of our belief modules, utilizing the back-projecting neural pathways in the visual system that are also used in object-recognition (Kosslyn, 1994). And visual and other images can also be passively evoked when an episodic memory gets activated by some cue. What I shall claim in Chapter 5, however, is that all *creative* thinking results from the activation of action schemata. So all conscious thinking that is *creative* is a form of acting.

systems (each of which just goes ahead and does its own processing-job automatically), and if all thinking has to be realized in the operations of such systems, then how *could* thinking be active rather than passive? But now the solution to this puzzle is easy to see, if System 2 thinking consists largely in sequences of action-rehearsal (including utterance-rehearsals). For these are a species of *action*—not to be assimilated to consciously planned activities undertaken to achieve certain goals in the light of one's beliefs, perhaps; but at least similar to routine bodily movements and sequences of movement like stretching, driving a car over a familiar route, or stepping around an obstacle in one's path.

Since System 2 thinking is a species of acting, thinking *skills* can be acquired via any of the variety of mechanisms through which behavioral skills are normally learned. One such mechanism is explicit instruction. People can *tell* me what actions and sequences of action to perform in the service of a given goal. As noted above, a logic teacher can tell me what steps to take in order to evaluate the truth of a conditional, just as an experienced kayak maker might tell a novice how to prepare and shape the materials for use in the frame. And in both cases the beliefs thus acquired can be recalled at the point of need, and used to guide novel instances of the activity in question (evaluating a conditional, building a kayak).

Another way of acquiring skills, of course, is imitation. Many complex skills are learned through forms of apprenticeship in which both explicit instruction and trial-and-error learning may play some role, but in which novices also spend extended periods of time working alongside, and observing and imitating, experienced practitioners. Where the skills in question are thinking skills, this can only happen when the teacher chooses to 'think aloud' for the benefit of the novice. Much of what happens in scientific lab meetings should perhaps be seen in this light, where problems are reasoned through publicly in the presence of undergraduate and graduate research assistants. And likewise, many college lecturers see themselves not only as imparting information to their students, but also as *exemplifying* in their lectures the patterns of thinking and reasoning that the students are to acquire. Certainly I have always looked at my own lecturing in this way, as providing my students with an example of how one might think through a problem. I intend them to imitate the forms, if not the contents, of my thinking.

Whatever the mode of their initial acquisition, thinking skills, like all other skills, can become smoother, swifter, and less error-prone with practice. Much of what takes place in mathematics classrooms can be understood in this light. Through rote learning of their times-tables, children acquire and gradually render habitual a series of action-sequences. And when learning how to do addition sums and division sums, they acquire behavioral procedures that are initially slow and halting, and are conducted overtly (often on paper), but which with time and practice can become both habitual and internalized, in inner speech or sequences of visual imagery.[23]

The present account of many forms of conscious thinking—in terms of the activation, rehearsal, and global broadcast of action schemata—can also mesh nicely with our best accounts of *disorders* of thinking, such as frequently occur in schizophrenia (Frith, 1992; Campbell, 1999). Patients with schizophrenia often complain that their thoughts are not their own. On the contrary, they claim, their thoughts are being *inserted* into their minds by members of an alien race, or by government agents, say. And likewise they often claim that their overt actions are not their own, either. A patient might complain, for example, that when he picks up a comb and runs it through his hair, it is not he who controls his hand but some outside force. This commonality between delusions of thought-insertion and delusions of behavior-control is easily explained given an account of (System 2) thinking as a species of acting.

According to Frith et al. (2000), part of what has gone wrong in patients with schizophrenia involves damage to the system that utilizes efferent copies of motor commands to construct a sensory representation of the intended outcome, normally used for purposes of comparison, self-monitoring, and self-correction. Because of this, schizophrenics don't feel that their own actions (including the thought-actions that issue in inner speech and sequences of visual and other imagery) are their own, even though they are intentional, and even though the outcomes are the ones that were intended. And just as this explanation predicts, it turns out that schizophrenic patients are incapable of using *mental practice* to improve performance through internally generated feedback, and they can't make swift corrections to their behavior in the light of sensory feedback, either (Frith et al., 2000). And also as predicted, they have

---

[23] Evidence consistent with these suggestions is presented by Spelke and Tsivkin (2001), who conducted three bilingual arithmetic training experiments. In one, bilingual Russian–English college students were taught new numerical operations; in another, they were taught new arithmetic equations; and in the third, they were taught new geographical and historical facts involving both numerical and non-numerical information. After learning a set of items in each of their two languages, subjects were tested for knowledge of those items in both languages, as well as tested on new problems. In all three studies subjects retrieved information about exact numbers more effectively in the language in which they were trained on that information, and they solved trained problems more effectively than new ones. In contrast, subjects retrieved information about approximate numbers and about non-numerical (geographical or historical) facts with equal ease in their two languages, and their training on approximate number facts generalized to new facts of the same type. These results suggest that one or another natural language is implicated in thought about exact numbers, but not when representing approximate numerosity (a capacity shared with other animals).

difficulty in distinguishing between experiences (such as a tickle on their hand) that are self-produced and those that are other-produced.

6.4 Norms for Thinking

Recall from Chapter 3.7 that one of the likely modules that is specific to the human mind is a system for learning, storing, and reasoning with *norms*, as well as for generating intrinsic motivations towards compliance with them. Most norms are rules governing behavior. They tell us what we must, must not, or are permitted to *do*. Hence if System 2 thinking is a species of behaving, as I have been arguing that it is, then it is easy to understand how the very same normative system can come to govern much of human thinking and reasoning as well. As a result, there will be at least three different *kinds* of ways in which System 2 thinking / behaving can be motivated. Two have already been mentioned above. One is that the activation of a particular goal habitually calls up a certain action-sequence in its own service. Another is that the subject believes that a certain action or sequence of actions is a reliable way of achieving a given goal. But now the third is that the subject believes that a certain type of action is mandated / required (or forbidden) in the context, and thus feels intrinsically motivated to think / behave in the appropriate way.

Consistent with this prediction, people do seem to be intrinsically motivated to entertain or to avoid certain types of thought or sequence of thought. Thus if someone finds himself thinking that P and thinking that $P \supset Q$, then he will feel *compelled*, in consequence, to think that Q. And if someone finds herself thinking that P and also thinking that $\sim P$, then she will feel herself *obligated* to eliminate one or other of those two thoughts. (And in circumstances where a contradiction isn't easily eradicated—such as arguably occurs in classical electrodynamics (see Frisch, 2005)—people will take steps to ensure that the contradiction doesn't very often surface in consciousness, but rather remains, for the most part, covert. This may be because contradictory thoughts, like normative breaches generally, make us feel uncomfortable.) The explanation is that the norms module has acquired a rule requiring sequences of thought / action that take the form of *modus ponens*, as well as a rule requiring the avoidance of contradiction, and is generating intrinsic motivations accordingly.

The action-theory of System 2 thinking, combined with a norms module for constraining and guiding action, can thus explain how so much of our conscious thinking should take place in a sea of normative beliefs, or should seem to occur within what some have called 'the space of reasons' (McDowell, 1994). But it is important to distinguish the account being advanced here from the often-defended—but in my view radically mistaken—claims that norms of reasoning are *constitutive* of thinking as an activity, and that correct ascriptions of thoughts to people are constrained and partly constituted by norms of rationality (Davidson, 1973; Dennett, 1987; McDowell, 1994; and many other philosophical writers). It is worth spending a few paragraphs to explain the difference.

On my account it is *beliefs about* norms, rather than norms themselves, that do the explanatory work. Representations involving modal concepts like MUST or MUSTN'T are stored in a special-purpose belief-box, attached to a reasoning system that is continually on the lookout for circumstances that might lead to a match with the non-normative content of those representations. When one is found, the system generates an intrinsic motivation towards performing the action described by that content (in the case of 'must'), or against acting (in the case of 'must not'). Whether the represented norms are *true* or *correct* is quite another matter. And the resulting account is fully consistent with a naturalistic, purely causal, account of thinking and believing.

According to the account endorsed by some philosophers, in contrast, the very notions of *thought* and *belief* are themselves intrinsically normative. Thinking itself is said to be an inherently *rational* process, such that any deviations from ideals of rationality make it more difficult for us to conceive of the agent as a thinker at all. And attributions of thought to an agent have to be constrained by the rational norms (such as 'avoid inconsistency') that govern all thinking.[24] In consequence, such philosophers can't offer a fully naturalistic account of what thought itself *is*. Davidson (1970) thus maintains that while each *token* thought is a physical state of the brain which has causes and effects, thoughts themselves (as types) play no causal role in the world. (This is his so-called 'anomalous monism'.) And likewise Dennett (1987) maintains that beliefs and thoughts have no reality independent of our practices of thought-ascription, in which we adopt what Dennett calls 'the intentional stance' for purposes of predictive convenience.

I am not wanting to claim that beliefs about norms of reasoning play no role whatever in our attributions of thoughts to others, of course. Quite the contrary. For the way in which we generally go about attributing to someone the thoughts that they will arrive at by reasoning from a given starting point is to utilize *our own* reasoning processes in a partial 'simulation' of the reasoning of the other person, as we suggested in Chapter 3.3. And then if our own System 2 reasoning involves beliefs about norms of reasoning, the outcome

---

[24] For a particularly elegant and powerful critique of this sort of view, see Cherniak (1986). See also Nichols and Stich (2003).

will be a function of what we take those norms to be. But to reiterate, it is our beliefs about norms of reason, not norms themselves, that are to some degree constitutive of our practices of thought-ascription. And thoughts themselves can be fully naturalistic entities that are *not* normatively constituted.

7 What the Thesis is and Isn't

The picture that I have been developing in this chapter is that a number of the kinds of flexibility that are distinctive of human thought processes can be partially explained by supposing that those processes are conducted in inner speech, recruiting both the resources of the language module and the resources of a wide range of central / conceptual modules (as well as the motor-control modules used to build and streamline increasingly sophisticated action schemata). In the present section I shall attempt to clarify these ideas further, by contrasting them with others with which they might naturally be confused, and by comparing them with some other familiar models.

7.1 Thinking in Language?

According to the views that I have been developing, natural language has important cognitive functions (in addition to its obvious communicative ones). And one might gloss this by saying that some of our thinking is conducted in rehearsals of natural language sentences. But does this really mean that some System 2 processes are conducted *in* language, and/or that natural language sentences serve as the *vehicles* for our System 2 thoughts? And if so, can these ideas actually be made sense of? For there are familiar and devastating objections to the claim that we (English people) think in English (Jackendoff, 1997; Pinker, 1997; Pylyshyn, 2003).[25]

For example, one objection is that English sentences are almost always radically incomplete encodings of the intended thought. If someone says, 'The fridge is empty', they will have some particular standard of emptiness, and some particular fridge, in mind. (Do they mean that there isn't enough in the fridge to make a meal, so that the statement might count as true even though the fridge contains some lettuce leaves and a bottle of milk? Do they mean that the fridge is now ready for cleaning, in which case what they say will be false if it contains bottles of milk, but true if it contains only crumbs of bread and

---

[25] We might also enquire how, in more detail, we are to explain how new beliefs can be arrived at in such a manner. But this question will be deferred to Chapter 6. For it is intimately connected with the question of how abductive / scientific reasoning is to be explained, as we shall see.

cheese? Or do they intend a standard consistent with the fact that it now *has* been cleaned, in which case the statement is false if the fridge contains even crumbs? Moreover, which fridge is intended as the referent of '*the* fridge'?) The intended standards and referents will have to be gathered, by inference, from the context. Since attaching a specific content to the sentence, 'The fridge is empty', requires thought, that sentence cannot by itself carry the content of the thought that it communicates.

In fact it would be highly misleading to express the view that I am developing by saying that natural language sentences are the *vehicles* of System 2 thinking. For, first of all, there aren't actually any sentences of English contained in the human mind / brain. Rather, there are (Mentalese) *representations of* English sentences, and it is these representations that do (or are involved in doing) the real work. Secondly, one should in any case say that natural language sentences (or rather representations thereof) are *implicated in* System 2 thought processes, or are essential *components of* those processes, rather than that they are the *vehicles* of those processes. Let me elaborate on each of these points.

My hypothesis is that some human thought processes involve rehearsals of natural language utterances. And for a native English speaker, of course, these will be rehearsals of sentences of English, each consisting in an activated action schema that contains a representation of the sentence in question. This action schema is used to generate a representation of what it would be like to hear (or see, in the case of Sign) the corresponding utterance. And this quasi-perceptual imagistic representation is globally broadcast and made available *inter alia* to the language comprehension system, which attaches a content to it and makes that content (as expressed in some sort of Mentalese representation, perhaps in the form of a mental model) available to the suite of central / conceptual modules. Nothing in this story requires us to talk about *sentences* of English figuring in cognition, as opposed to *representations of* English sentences. Nor does it presuppose that the computations that underlie our basic thought processes are defined over such representations.

But how can these representations of natural language utterances be constitutive of *thinking*? In answering this, it will help to introduce a simple convention. Let us use single quote marks to designate representations of natural language sentences, and line brackets to designate all other Mentalese expressions. And then imagine a case where what gets rehearsed is a representation of the natural language sentence 'P', and where the Mentalese sentence that gets constructed by the comprehension system on receipt of the representation 'P', is |Q|. (Since there is no guarantee that the comprehension process will issue in a Mentalese representation with the same content as was used to construct the natural language sentence in the first place, it is safest—here and elsewhere—to consider examples where it doesn't.) And let us suppose for simplicity that |Q| has the content *that Q*.

Now according to a number of the hypotheses sketched above, the pairing <'P', |Q|> has further consequences in cognition—and not just *any* consequences, but those that are distinctive of thinking. One way in which this might be the case is if the representation |Q| is one that can *only* be formed (either absolutely, or in context) via the construction of an appropriate natural language sentence, as 'module-integration' accounts of the role of natural language in cognition suggest (Hermer-Vazquez et al., 1999; Carruthers, 2002a). The sentence 'P' is constructed by combining and integrating a number of other sentences—'R' and 'S', say—individually produced from the outputs of a pair of conceptual modules. When 'P' is mentally rehearsed the comprehension system extracts from it the Mentalese representation |Q|, which can then (especially if it takes the form of a mental model) be globally broadcast for all the different central modules to get to work upon, provided that any aspect of it meets their input-conditions. The result might be further thought-contents that would never have been entertained otherwise.

Another way in which pairing <'P', |Q|> might have consequences that are distinctive of thinking is if it is only by virtue of articulating the sentence 'P' in auditory imagination, and hence making its content available to the various inference-systems that exist downstream of perception and consume its products, that the subject comes to believe |Q| (i.e. comes to believe *that Q*) for the first time. (See Chapter 6.7.) The process of articulating 'P' leads to |Q| being evaluated and accepted, in a way that would not—as a matter of fact and given the circumstances—have happened otherwise. In such a case it seems perfectly sensible to say that the act of articulating 'P' is part of the process of *thinking* that leads to the generation of a new belief (the belief *that Q*).

Yet another way in which the pairing <'P', |Q|> might have consequences distinctive of thinking can be derived from the account of the dual systems of reasoning discussed in Section 6. If the agent has learned, through training, explicit instruction, or imitation, to engage in those speech / action sequences in which sentences of type Φ should always be followed by sentences of type Ψ (where 'P' belongs to type Φ and 'R' belongs to type Ψ), then the pairing <'P', |Q|> will lead to some further pairing of the form <'R', |S|> . In which case the process that leads the subject to entertain the thought *that S* will be one that constitutively involves representations of natural language sentences (in this case, representations of the sentences 'P' and 'R').[26]

---

[26] The rules governing such action-sequences may sometimes be highly abstract, as are the rules of formal logic. But there is no objection to the proposal to be raised from this direction. For even bees

7.2 Weak Whorfianism?

Many philosophers and social scientists throughout the twentieth century maintained that language is the medium of all human conceptual thinking. Most often this claim has been associated with a radical empiricism about the mind, according to which virtually all human concepts and ways of thinking, and indeed many aspects of the very structure of the human mind itself, are acquired by young children from adults when they learn their native language. And it has been held that these concepts and structures will differ widely depending upon the conceptual resources and structures of the natural language in question. This mind-structuring and social-relativist view of language is still dominant in the social sciences, following the writings early in the last century of the amateur linguist Whorf (many of whose papers are collected together in his 1956). Indeed, Pinker (1994) refers to it disparagingly as 'the Standard Social Science Model' of the mind.

My views should be distinguished sharply from those of the Standard Social Science Model, of course. I maintain, on the contrary, that most of our concepts, and many of our forms of thinking and learning, are independent of, and prior to, natural language. And I maintain that much of the architecture of both human and animal minds is innately fixed, and that the mind contains many innately structured learning mechanisms. In recent decades a weaker set of Whorfian views have been explored by cognitive scientists, however. According to such views natural language doesn't *create*, but rather *sculpts* or *shapes* human cognitive process. For example, acquisition of Yucatec (as opposed to English)—in which plurals are rarely marked and many more nouns are treated grammatically as substance-terms like 'mud' and 'water'—is said to lead subjects to see similarities amongst objects on the basis of material composition rather than shape (Lucy and Gaskins, 2001). And children brought up speaking Korean (as opposed to English)—in which verbs are highly inflected and massive noun ellipsis is permissible in informal speech—are said to be much weaker at categorization tasks, but much better at means–ends tasks such as using a rake to pull a distant object towards them (Gopnik et al., 1996; Gopnik, 2001).

The basic idea behind weak Whorfianism can be expressed in terms of Slobin's (1987) idea of 'thinking for speaking'. If your language requires you to describe spatial relationships in terms of compass directions, for example, then you will continually need to pay attention to, and compute, geocentric

---

can learn to generate actions in accordance with the abstract rule, 'Turn right in the second chamber if it is marked in the same way as the first, turn left in the second chamber if it is marked differently from the first.' They can generalize to new forms of marking (such as new combinations of color), and also generalize across sense modalities—trained on colors, they can generalize to instances of the rule involving odors. See Giurfa et al., 2001.

spatial relations; whereas if descriptions in terms of 'left' and 'right' are the norm, then geocentric relations will barely need to be noticed. This might be expected to have an impact on the efficiency with which one set of relations is processed relative to the other, and on the ease with which they are remembered (Levinson, 1996). Likewise in respect of motion events: if you speak a language, like English, that employs an extensive and often-used vocabulary for *manner* of motion ('walk', 'stride', 'saunter', 'hop', 'skip', 'run', 'jog', 'sprint', etc.), then you will continually need to pay attention to, and encode, such properties. In languages like Spanish and Greek, in contrast, manner of motion is conveyed in an auxiliary clause ('He went into the room *at a run*'), and it often goes unexpressed altogether. One might then predict that speakers of such languages should be both slower at recognizing, and poorer at remembering, manner of motion (Slobin, 1996). This claim has been subjected to careful experimental scrutiny by Papafragou et al. (2002), however, who are unable to discover any such effects.

Levinson's claims for the effects of spatial language on spatial cognition have also been subject to a lively controversy (Levinson, 1996, 2003; Li and Gleitman, 2002; Levinson et al., 2002; Li et al., 2005). Let me pull out just one strand from this debate for brief discussion. Levinson (1996) had tested Tenejapan Mayans—who employ no terms meaning *left* and *right*—on a spatial reversal task. They were confronted with an array of four items on a desk in front of them, and told to remember the spatial ordering of three of the items. They were then rotated through 180° and walked to another table, where they were handed the three items and told to 'make them the same.' As predicted, the Mayans employed geocentric rather than egocentric coordinates when complying with the instruction, just as the hypothesis of 'thinking for speaking' would predict.

In the course of their critique, however, Li and Gleitman (2002) point out that the task is plainly ambiguous. The instruction, 'make them the same', can mean, 'lay them out similarly in respect of geocentric space', or it can mean, 'lay them out similarly in respect of egocentric space.' (And indeed, Westerners who are given these tasks will notice the ambiguity and ask for clarification.) Li et al. (2005) therefore reason that Levinson's results might reflect, not an effect of language upon thought, but rather an effect of language upon language. Since the instruction is ambiguous, subjects are presented with the problem of disambiguating it before they can respond appropriately. And since geocentric descriptions are overwhelmingly more likely in the society to which the Mayans belong, they might naturally assume that the instruction is intended geocentrically, and act accordingly. It doesn't follow that they would have had any particular difficulty in solving the task in an egocentric fashion if cued accordingly. And for all that the experiment shows, they might routinely deploy egocentric concepts in the course of their daily lives (if not in their daily speech).

To test this, Li et al. (2005) devised a series of unambiguous spatial tasks that admit of only a single correct solution. In one of these, for example, the subjects had to match a card containing two differently sized circles to one of four cards of a similar sort, but variously oriented. Once they were familiar with the task, they were allowed to study the card at one table before being rotated 180° and walked to a second table where four cards were laid out for them to match against. But they did this under one of two conditions. In one, the card was covered and carried to the other table while they watched without its orientation relative to the Earth being changed. (This is the geocentric condition.) In the other, the card was placed in their hands and covered before they turned around through 180° to face the other table. (This is the egocentric condition.) Contrary to Levinson's predictions, the subjects did just as well or better in the egocentric condition. And when the task demands were significantly increased (as when Li et al. had subjects recall and trace out one particular path through a maze under two conditions similar to those described above), the Mayan subjects actually did significantly better in the egocentric condition (80% correct versus 35% correct).

In an earlier presentation of some of the views defended in this chapter I was concessive about the powers of different natural languages to sculpt cognition differently during development, as weak Whorfian accounts of the role of language in cognition maintain (Carruthers, 2002a). However, there is no particular *need* for me to be concessive towards the 'language sculpts cognition' approach. Each set of data will have to be examined on a case-by-case basis, of course. And at the moment the jury is still out on the question whether language sculpts cognition to any significant degree. But certainly the weak forms in which this thesis is currently being pursued are consistent with the strong modularism adopted in the present book, and also with my main theses. But no such weak Whorfian claims are supported or entailed by my views. And the empirical data are still subject to a variety of interpretations. Accordingly, this topic will now be dropped for the remainder of our discussions. It has been mentioned here only in order to contrast it with the cognitive functions of language to which I am committed (i.e. the functions of stimulus-independence, content-flexibility, and flexibility of reasoning process).

7.3 Vygotsky and Dennett

In the present section I shall contrast my views with those of Vygotsky (1961) and Dennett (1991), who each present proposals that are significantly (and in my view, unacceptably) stronger than my own.

At around the same time that Whorf was writing, Vygotsky was developing his ideas on the interrelations between language and thought, both in the course of child development and in mature human cognition. These remained largely unknown in the West until his book *Thought and Language* was first published in English (Vygotsky, 1961). This attracted significant attention, and a number of further works were translated through the 1970s and 1980s (Vygotsky, 1971, 1978; Wertsch, 1981, 1985). And some of Vygotsky's claims have obvious points of contact, as well as elements of contrast, with my own.

One of Vygotsky's ideas concerns the ways in which language deployed by adults can *scaffold* children's development, yielding what he calls a 'zone of proximal development'. He argues that what children can achieve alone and unaided isn't a true reflection of their understanding. Rather, we also need to consider what they can do when scaffolded by the instructions and suggestions of a supportive adult. And such scaffolding not only enables children to achieve with others what they would be incapable of achieving alone, but also plays a causal role in enabling children to acquire new skills and abilities. Relatedly, Vygotsky focuses on the overt speech of children, arguing that it plays an important role in problem solving, partly by serving to focus their attention and partly through repetition and rehearsal of adult guidance. And this role doesn't cease when children stop accompanying their activities with overt monologues, but just disappears inwards. He argues that in older children and adults *inner* (sub-vocal) speech serves many of the same functions.

Several of these ideas have been picked up by later investigators. For example, the self-directed verbalizations of young children during problem solving activities have been studied. One finding is that children tend to verbalize more when tasks are more difficult, and that children who verbalize more often are more successful in their problem solving (Diaz and Berk, 1992). The thesis that language plays such scaffolding roles in human cognition isn't (or shouldn't be) controversial. But in Vygotsky's own work it goes along with a conception of the mind as socially constructed, developing in plastic ways in interactions with elements of the surrounding culture, guided and supported by adult members of that culture.

These stronger views—like the similar constructionist views of Whorf (1956)—are inconsistent with the thesis of massive mental modularity being defended in this book, at least if interpreted in any robust form. But a restricted version of them can survive as an account of the development of System 2 thinking and reasoning. For as we have seen, such thinking is to a significant extent dependent upon inner speech, which both supervenes on and recruits the activity of underlying modules. And as we have also seen, many of the patterns of activity that take place within System 2 are learned from others (via both instruction and imitation), as well as being guided by socially acquired norms of reasoning.

Let us turn now to Dennett (1991). He famously argues that human cognitive powers were utterly transformed following the appearance of natural language, as the mind became colonized by *memes* (ideas, or concepts, which are transmitted, retained and selected in a manner supposedly analogous to genes; see Dawkins, 1976). Prior to the evolution of language, on this picture, the mind was a bundle of distributed connectionist processors. These conferred on early hominids some degree of flexibility and intelligence, but were quite limited in their computational powers. The arrival of language then meant that a whole new—serial and compositionally structured—cognitive architecture could be programmed into the system.

This is what Dennett calls the *Joycean machine* (named after James Joyce's 'stream of consciousness' writing). The idea is that there is a highest-level processor that runs on a stream of natural-language representations, utilizing learned connections between ideas, and patterns of reasoning acquired in and through the acquisition of linguistic memes. On this account, then, the concept-wielding mind is a kind of social construction, brought into existence through the absorption of memes from the surrounding culture. And on this view, the conceptual mind is both dependent upon, and constitutively involves, natural language.[27]

Here, too, there is much that I can agree with, as well as disagree with. Of course I can agree that cycles of inner speech both sustain and partially constitute our System 2 thought processes. And I can also agree that much of the activity of System 2 depends upon beliefs and norms of rationality that have been acquired from the surrounding culture, and that System 2 operations exemplify patterns of activity that have been learned from other people, either by instruction or imitation. But I shall also claim that most concepts and structured thought processes are independent of language, involved in the operations of numerous System 1 modules. And even the role of socially acquired memes, within System 2, should look quite different when seen through the lens of massive modularity. Or so I shall now briefly argue.

Like most others who use the notion of a 'meme' as an explanatory construct, Dennett (1991) thinks of memes as passively acquired items of cultural

---

[27] Admittedly, what Dennett will actually *say* is that animals and pre-linguistic hominids are capable of conceptual thought, and engage in much intelligent thinking. But this is because he is not (in my sense) a realist about thoughts. (See Chapter 2.1.) On the contrary, he thinks that there is nothing more to thinking than engaging in behavior that is *interpretable as* thinking. Yet he commits himself to saying that it is only with the advent of natural language that you get a kind of thinking that involves discrete, structured, semantically evaluable, causally effective states—that is, thoughts *realistically construed*.

information. But as Sperber (2000) points out, very little cultural learning is a mere matter of absorbing and retaining information. On the contrary, most socially communicated information needs to be *reconstructed* through processes of (module-based) inference of various sorts. And this means that the transmission process will be heavily biased by the underlying modular architecture. These ideas are especially nicely illustrated in the work of Boyer (2001), who shows that the seeming cacophony of religious ideas in the myriad religions of the world are actually organized around the central modular domains of psychology, living beings, non-living physical things (e.g. mountains), and artifacts. Almost all religious beliefs concern things that are drawn from one or other of these domains, but with properties that violate some of the central assumptions of the module in question (for example, a stone statue that can listen to prayers). Such beliefs thereby combine maximum memorability (from the violated expectation) with maximum inferential potential (from the normal operations of the module in question).

7.4 Clark and Jackendoff

By way of yet further clarification, in the present section I shall consider some views of the role of language in cognition that are significantly weaker than those that I have been defending.

Clark (1998) draws attention to the many ways in which natural language is used to scaffold human cognition, defending a conception of language as a cognitive *tool*. (Chomsky, too, has argued for an account of this sort. See his 1975, ch. 2.) Such instrumental uses of language range from the writing of shopping lists and post-it notes, to the mental rehearsal of remembered instructions and mnemonics, to the performance of complex arithmetic calculations on pieces of paper. According to this view—which Clark labels 'the supra-communicative conception of language'—certain *extended* processes of thinking and reasoning constitutively involve natural language. The idea is that language gets used, not just for communication, but also to augment human cognitive powers (especially by enhancing memory).

Thus by writing an idea down, for example, I can off-load the demands on memory, presenting myself with an object of further leisured reflection. And by performing arithmetic calculations on a piece of paper, I may be able to handle computational tasks that would otherwise be too much for me (and my working memory). In similar fashion, the suggestion is that *inner* speech serves to enhance memory, since it is now well-established that the powers of human memory systems can be greatly extended by association (Baddeley, 1990). Inner speech may thus facilitate complex trains of reasoning, by enabling us to hold their component parts in mind in a way that would otherwise be impossible (Varley, 1998).

Notice that on this supra-communicative account, the involvement of language in thought only arises when we focus on a process of thinking or reasoning *extended over time*. So far as any given individual (token) thought goes, the account can (and does) buy into the standard conception of language as a mere input–output device. It maintains that there is a neural episode that carries the content of the thought in question, where an episode of that type can exist in the absence of any natural language sentence and can have a causal role distinctive of the thought, but which in the case in question causes the production of a natural language representation. This representation can then have further benefits for the system of the sort that Clark explores (off-loading or enhancing memory).

According to the account of the cognitive role of language presented in this chapter and the one following, in contrast, a particular tokening of an inner sentence is (sometimes) an inseparable part of the mental episode that carries the content of the thought-token in question. So there is often no neural or mental event at the time that can exist distinct from that sentence, which can occupy a causal role distinctive of that sort of thought, and which carries the content in question; and so language is actually involved in (certain types of) cognition, even when our focus is on individual (token) acts of thinking.

Jackendoff (1996, 1997), likewise, puts forward an account of the role of language in cognition that is weaker than that being defended in this book. (See also Carruthers, 1996, for presentation and defense of some similar ideas.) He suggests, in particular, that inner speech serves to focus our conscious *attention* on our thoughts and thought processes. As a result, two sorts of further cognitive effect tend to ensue. One is that the thought or thought process in question is subjected to more detailed processing, by virtue of being 'anchored' in working memory through expression in inner speech. This might lead, for example, to the development of a more comprehensive plan of action, or to the generation of further thoughts that are consequences of the one under consideration. The other effect is that the thought or thought process becomes available to meta-cognitive awareness, enabling it to be questioned, criticized, and improved.

These proposed cognitive roles for language are quite plausible, and are fully consistent with the ideas presented in the present chapter. I have suggested that the mechanism by means of which inner speech achieves a focusing of attention upon thought is via the global broadcast of sensory representations of natural language utterances. And many of the further effects of those broadcasts result from the contents of the utterances in question being received as input by the myriad conceptual modules, creating cycles of modular processing. (Jackendoff, too, presents his ideas within a modularist framework, albeit one that isn't quite so massively so.) And likewise I have suggested that, because speech is a form of action, inner speech can enable our thought processes to become subject to norms of rationality and truth.

The ideas that I am defending go further than this, however. Both here and in Chapter 5 I suggest that language can enable thought-contents to be formulated for the very first time, and/or be entertained in circumstances where they would not otherwise occur. In the present chapter I have argued that language plays a role in conjoining otherwise disjoint module-produced concepts. And in the chapter following I shall argue that it plays a role in the creative generation of wholly novel thoughts, too. In addition, I have argued that sequences of sentences in inner speech occur as they do not *just* because of the way in which modular processes get to work on the contents of each (as Jackendoff, 1997, suggests). Rather, because speech is an activity, speech-sequences of a given type can be learned as an acquired skill, through instruction or imitation.

7.5 Baddeley's Working Memory

In this section I shall compare and contrast the model of human cognitive architecture sketched in the present chapter with the account of the working-memory system developed over a number of years by Baddeley and colleagues (Baddeley and Hitch, 1974; Baddeley, 1986, 1990, 1993; Gathercole and Baddeley, 1993). Both theories postulate short-term working-memory systems intimately linked to such cognitive functions as planning, reasoning, and conscious awareness; and both assign a role to imagistic representations of language within the systems described.

Baddeley has proposed that the working-memory system consists of a central executive and two specialized slave-systems, the *visuo-spatial sketchpad* and the *phonological loop*. The relationships between them are represented in Figure 4.6 (adapted from Gathercole and Baddeley, 1993). The central executive controls the flow of information within the system as a whole, and is charged with such functions as action-planning, retrieval of information from long-term memory, and conscious control of action. The executive also allocates inputs to the visuo-spatial sketchpad and phonological loop, which are employed for spatial reasoning tasks and language-related tasks respectively. Since the central executive must presumably have access to linguistic knowledge, if it is to be able to generate linguistic inputs to the phonological loop, this model could easily be presented in such a way as to resemble fairly closely the model represented earlier in Figures 4.3 and 4.4.

Figure 4.6. Working memory

One difference from my model concerns the special-purpose nature of the phonological loop. In particular, Baddeley seems to think of it as *essentially* a phonological system. In contrast, my model proposes that we can, in principle, entertain linguistically formulated thoughts through the imaginative use of any language-related sense-modality. In normal individuals, no doubt, such thinking involves auditory, or perhaps articulatory (kinesthetic) imagination (or both). But in the case of those whose only native language is some form of Sign, my account predicts that their linguistic thinking will involve the manipulation of *visual* (or kinesthetic) images. And perhaps some ordinary thinkers, too, sometimes employ visual images (in this case of written language) in their language-based thinking.

One empirical prediction of my model, then, is that exactly the sorts of interference-effects that have been used to explore the properties of the phonological loop in normal subjects would be found in the visual (or perhaps the kinesthetic, gestural) modality for deaf subjects whose native language is a form of Sign. Another prediction is that aphasics or other brain-damaged patients who have lost the phonological component of working memory should be able to recover their capacity for language-based thinking by employing the resources of some other form of imagination—either kinesthetic, developing an articulatory loop, or visual, manipulating images of written sentences. For according to my model, the exact form in which linguistic information is represented in language-based thinking is plastic, and may vary from individual to individual, and within individuals over time.

Another difference between Baddeley's model of working memory, on the one hand, and my massively modular model of System 2 processes, on the other, concerns the *function* of the phonological loop—its causal role in the activity of the cognitive system as a whole. In Baddeley's account the phonological loop is employed *only* for language-based tasks—that is, only for tasks that are explicitly *about* language, or explicitly *involve* language. Thus the phonological loop is said to be involved in such tasks as memorizing sequences of letters, vocabulary acquisition, reading development, and language comprehension. But there is no suggestion that it is also involved in the planning of action, or in other forms of reasoning about the world (rather than about language). These tasks are allotted, rather, to the central executive.[28]

In my own model, in contrast, the phonological loop (and/or its equivalent in other sense-modalities) is involved in many forms of conscious thinking and reasoning about the world. Recall that my hypothesis is that some of our occurrent thoughts are formulated in the form of images of natural language sentences, which are then globally broadcast to a wide range of inferential systems. (See Figure 4.3.) By virtue of such broadcasting our cognitive system is able to gain access to some of its own processes of thinking, in such a way as to render them conscious.[29] And cycles of sentence production and global broadcasting make possible System 2 thinking and reasoning. The function of the phonological loop is thus much more than just to enable the mind to engage in language-involving processing tasks. It is also to enable the overall system to gain access to its own occurrent thoughts, thus facilitating cycles of such thought, as well as the sort of indefinite self-improvement that comes with self-awareness and System 2 thinking and reasoning.

I do have to concede, of course, that there is also a need for something resembling Baddeley's central executive within my own account. For *something* must be responsible for selecting and manipulating the imaged sentences in the phonological loop, which therefore become the system's conscious occurrent thoughts (in virtue of the reflexive availability of the contents of the loop). And likewise something must be responsible for selecting and manipulating the visual images in the visuo-spatial sketchpad, which are similarly globally broadcast. But on my account, the system in question is a sort of *virtual* executive, involving the interactions of many different belief-generating systems and action-selecting systems. It isn't itself a distinct isolable system. Thus competition between modules to present their outputs as input to the language system might play a role. And as we shall see in Chapter 5, associations amongst related concepts will also be important. My hope would be that an account along the lines of the one being developed here could eventually be seen as a workable *realization* of Baddeley's model within a massively modular mental architecture.

[28] In fact Gathercole and Baddeley note in passing, following Hitch (1980), that the phonological loop may be implicated in mental arithmetic; see their 1993, p.234. But nothing further is made of this point. For evidence supporting such a view, see Spelke and Tsivkin (2001).

[29] This is true whether one endorses a *first*-order account of what makes mental events conscious (Baars, 1988, 1997; Tye, 1995, 2000) or whether one endorses a *higher*-order account (Carruthers, 2000, 2005). According to the former, conscious status is a matter of the availability of the mental events in question to systems charged with belief-formation and practical reasoning—and this is what global broadcasting achieves. But according to the latter, consciousness is a matter of availability to higher-order thought, giving us *awareness of* our thoughts. And this, too, is achieved by global broadcasting. For one of the systems to which imagistic events will be broadcast is a mind-reading faculty capable of higher-order thoughts about those events. See Chapter 3.3.

8 Conclusion

In this chapter I have articulated the main challenges that a thesis of massive mental modularity must face (albeit with 'module' taken in the weak sense defended and adopted in Chapter 1). I have distinguished several different ways in which human thought and behavior might be said to be distinctively *flexible*. And our task has been to show how these forms of flexibility can be accommodated and explained within a massively modular model of the human mind. Some of these challenges have proven relatively easy to meet—at least, on the assumption that representations of natural language sentences play a constitutive role in human cognitive processes. (These are the objections from context-flexibility, from stimulus-independence, from content-flexibility, and from the flexibility of human reasoning processes.) Other challenges are harder, and will be confronted in the chapters that follow.

5

Creative Cognition in a Modular Mind

In the present chapter I shall continue in my attempt to show how a mind that is massively modular in its organization might nevertheless have all of the properties of flexibility displayed by our human minds. My focus will be on the creative and innovative capacities of the human mind, in particular.

But what *is* creativity? Although it would be foolish to attempt a definition, some elucidatory remarks might help to orient our discussion. Creativity, as I shall understand it, is constituted (at least in part) by a capacity to combine ideas in novel ways in abstraction from any immediate environmental stimulation. And it will normally manifest itself in new types of behavior, going beyond mere reapplications of established scripts or action-patterns. So anyone who is imagining how things could be other than they are (and other than they can be predicted to be) will be thinking creatively. Whereas someone who thinks, *the cat is vomiting purple liquid*, in the presence of a cat doing just that, will not be, even if they have never before entertained a thought with that content. And a creature adopting a novel solution to an environmental problem may be acting creatively, whereas one that is merely applying an old solution in new circumstances (e.g. dipping for ants with one sort of stick rather than another) will not be. Note, however, that applications of the predicate 'creative' will admit of degrees, of course. An individual person or creature, or a given type of animal, can be more or less creative by engaging to a greater or lesser extent in creative thought-processes and creative behaviors.

My hypothesis is that the basic capacity for a form of creativity evolved just once, probably at some point in the great-ape / hominid lineage. (I am open to the suggestion that the capacity in question may be even more ancient still.) And my view is that this capacity consists in an ability for the creative generation of action schemata during problem solving. (I call this 'the creative-action theory' of creativity.) The later flowering of human creativity in art, in science, in pretend play, and in storytelling and fantasy are all exaptations of that original basic ability that we share with our seemingly uncreative great-ape / hominid cousins, combining it with other faculties of the mind (especially language and mind-reading), and adding one or two further elements of a relatively minor sort.

This idea will be developed in Section 2 of the present chapter, and thereafter defended and contrasted with alternative hypotheses. I shall begin in Section 1, however, with discussion of a number of potential constraints on theorizing about human creativity.

1 Introduction: Constraints on Theorizing

In addition to the core desideratum of explaining our capacity for creative thought, are there any other constraints on an acceptable modularist account of creativity? Two have been proposed. One is that such an account should be capable of explaining the sudden explosion of creativity that took place amongst humans in the Upper Paleolithic (Mithen, 1996; Carruthers, 2002b). The other is that it should be capable of explaining the connection between adult creativity and childhood pretend play (Carruthers, 2002b). I shall discuss these in turn, before turning to introduce some others.

1.1 The 'Creative Explosion' of the Upper Paleolithic

In previous work on this subject (Carruthers, 2002b) I took it to be a constraint on theorizing about human creativity that we should be capable of explaining the 'creative explosion' (sometimes called the 'cultural big bang') that took place in the Upper Paleolithic, a mere 40,000 years or so ago. From this time onwards we find evidence of much more elaborate stone tools, of the carving of statuettes, of cave painting, of the manufacture of beads and other bodily ornaments, of ceremonial burial of the dead, and much else besides. I no longer think, however, that this is an appropriate constraint. The creative explosion may correspond to no significant cognitive change at all, but might merely be the combined product of increasing population densities, together with a long-standing research-focus on Europe by archaeologists. (Note that there *were no* members of *Homo sapiens* in Europe prior to about 40,000 years ago.) Let me elaborate on each of these points in turn.

There are some impressive demonstrations of the ways in which population density can play a critical role in the maintenance, preservation, and accumulation of cultural innovations—where such innovations are often the fruits of individual or collective creativity, of course (Carvalli-Sforza and Feldman,

1981; Shennan, 2000, 2001). A number of assumptions are made in these models, the parameters of which can then be varied in order to run a variety of computer simulations. One is that innovations need to be copied from other people in order to be preserved down the generations; another is that innovations can be improved, with innovation being added to existing innovation; and yet another is that errors can occur in the copying process, with errors being introduced at a certain rate. Now the important point is that if innovations are to be preserved or improved, then people need to have access to good models. This is where population density starts to matter. Under reasonable assumptions about the values of the various parameters, it turns out that highly dispersed populations can actually *lose* cultural inventions over time.

Henrich (2004) applies these ideas successfully to explain the puzzling case of Tasmania, where we know from archaeological records that the first aboriginal settlers had an elaborate technology when they reached Tasmania via a land-bridge. (The land-bridge then disappeared some 8,000 years ago.) But by the time Tasmania was discovered by Western explorers the inhabitants had lost almost all of the elements of their original technology, and were employing stone tools only a little more sophisticated than those that had been used by *Homo erectus* many hundreds of thousands of years earlier, and not much more sophisticated than the tool-use of chimpanzees. (Note that in other respects, however—e.g. in their social lives—these aboriginal Tasmanians were just as smart and sophisticated as any other human group.)

It is easy to imagine, then, that with low population densities of *Homo sapiens* in Africa through the period 150,000 to 50,000 years ago (on some views dropping to a total of just 10,000 individuals around 70,000 years ago; Ambrose, 1998; Lahr and Foley, 1998), few technological innovations lasted for long enough for there to be a significant chance of them being preserved in the archaeological record. The humans throughout this time might have been just as individually creative as those living in Europe during the Upper Paleolithic. (And as we will see in Chapter 6, tracking of prey requires creative thought; but it will leave no trace in the archaeological record.) It might merely be that, with dispersed populations, there was little cultural accumulation, and hence little to preserve.

The other reason for skepticism about the so-called 'creative explosion' is that, for historical reasons, much the majority of the archaeological effort over the last two centuries has been focused upon Europe. So what looks like an explosion of culture may actually be an artifact of sampling bias. And when the African data are reviewed carefully, what emerges is a pattern of gradual change—with the direct ancestors of *Homo sapiens* diverging from an earlier species called *Homo helmei* some 300,000 years ago (in all probability the common ancestor of ourselves and the Neanderthals); and with the modern behavioral repertoire emerging gradually from that point onwards. There are blades, grindstones, and pigments from 280 thousand years ago (ka); points from 250 ka; shell-fishing and long-distance exchange from 140 ka; fishing from 110 ka; bone tools, barbed points, mining, incised notes, and burial of the dead from 100 ka; beads from 60 ka; and images from 50 ka (McBrearty and Brooks, 2000).

I am no longer convinced, then, that there is any creative explosion for an evolutionary psychologist to explain. In which case we don't have to come up with an account of the cognitive structures underlying creativity such that some small, but crucial, innovation in those structures could have evolved in parallel—amongst dispersed human populations living in very different environments—through either sexual or cultural selection as late as 50,000 years ago (by which time modern humans were already spread across much of the globe). Rather, those structures can have evolved via regular survival-selection gradually over the period 300 ka to 100 ka, before modern humans began their dispersal out of Africa.[1]

In my 2002b I also suggested, however, that it is a constraint on theorizing about human creativity that we should be capable of explaining the connection between pretend play in childhood and creative thinking and reasoning more generally. And this is a constraint that I still want to endorse.

1.2 Pretend Play

In addition to our remarkable learning capacities, linguistic abilities, mind-reading capacity, and creativity, another salient species-specific fact about human beings is that the young of our species engage extensively in *pretend play* in infancy and childhood. From the age of about eighteen months all normal children, in all human cultures, start to do something that appears very odd indeed (when viewed from an external perspective, at least)—they begin to pretend. They engage in imaginary conversations with make-believe characters (talking to a doll; inventing an imaginary companion) and they pretend to be engaging in a wide variety of adult or fictional activities (talking into a banana as if it were a telephone; pretending to cook and eat mud pies; pretending to be a bird or an airplane). The young of no other species of creature on earth behaves like this in natural circumstances—not even the other great

---

[1] I don't mean, here, to be ruling out appeals to sexual or cultural selection in the explanation of human creativity. Indeed, while I shall make little use of the idea in what follows, I believe that accounts in terms of sexual selection might be especially plausible in this domain (Miller, 2000). My point is just that accounts of our creative capacities aren't constrained by the supposed evolution of those capacities in parallel in dispersed and largely separated human populations.

apes (although adult hand-reared and language-trained chimps have sometimes been observed to engage in activities that look very much *like* pretence, at least; Jolly, 1999).

It is hard to believe that these two species-specific properties—adult creativity and childhood pretend play—aren't intimately connected with one another, although it is true that they aren't often discussed together.[2] I shall argue in a moment that the two capacities can be seen as sharing essentially the same cognitive basis, insofar as both involve exercises of imagination. It will then be plausible to claim that adult creativity in thought and action is what childhood pretence *is for*. That is to say, it will appear likely that the function of pretence is to practice and enhance the kind of creativity that acquires so much significance in our adult lives.

(This shouldn't be taken as a claim about children's intentions, of course—they aren't *trying* to turn themselves into creative adults. Rather, it should be seen as a (tentative) claim about evolutionary and developmental *function*. The idea is that children are predisposed to engage in pretend play because this disposition helped their ancestors, when children, to grow up to become creative adults, which in turn caused the genes responsible for that disposition to become general in the population.)

Although this suggestion needs to be worked out (a task to which I shall return in Section 2), it does at least receive some preliminary support from comparative biology. For the young of all mammalian species engage in just the kinds of play that serve to practice, and are tailored towards enhancing, their distinctive adult behaviors. (And recall that on the account defended in Chapter 4, much conscious thinking is itself a form of behaving.) Thus kittens of all species of cat will engage in the sort of play-stalking, play-jumping, and play-biting that will later be used when hunting; young male deer will take part in the kind of head-butting that will later be used in the competition for mates in the rut; the young of many prey species like gazelle engage in play-leaping and play-running of just the sort needed to escape from predators; and so on and so forth (Smith, 1982; Bekoff and Byers, 1998). By analogy, then, if we ask what human *pretend* play is for, the answer will be: its function is to practice for the kind of imaginative thinking that will later manifest itself in the creative activities of adults.

The connection between the two forms of behavior, arguably, is that each involves essentially the same cognitive underpinnings—namely, a capacity to

---

[2] For example, the Cambridge *Handbook of Creativity* (Sternberg, 1999) contains no references to pretence and only two references to play within its 400-plus densely packed pages, despite the presence of a whole section of papers devoted to the evolutionary and developmental origins of human creativity.

generate, and to reason with, novel suppositions or *imaginary scenarios*. When pretending, what a child has to do is to *suppose* that something is the case (that the banana is a telephone; that the doll is alive), and then think and act within the scope of that supposition (Perner, 1991; Jarrold et al., 1994; Harris, 2000; Nichols and Stich, 2003).[3] Similarly, when adults are engaged in the construction of a new theory, or are seeking a novel solution to a practical problem, or are composing a tune, they have to think: 'Suppose it were the case that P', or, 'Suppose I did it like *this*', or, 'Suppose it sounded like *so*.' Given these commonalities, it does then seem plausible that the young of our species should engage in supposition-for-fun in childhood in order that they may be better able to suppose-for-real when they reach adulthood.

After a fallow period extending through much of the twentieth century, there is now an extensive psychological literature on the subject of human creativity. (See, for example, Langley et al., 1987; Sternberg, 1988, 1999; Boden, 1992, 1994; Finke et al., 1992; Smith et al., 1995; Amabile, 1996.) Much of this has concentrated on what might be called 'successful creativity' or 'influential creativity', studied by examining the lives and circumstances of famous innovators in the arts, sciences, and business worlds. As a consequence, those taking this approach tend to emphasize such factors as 'extensive background knowledge or training' and 'high levels of intrinsic motivation' in their analyses of creativity. For these qualities are shared almost universally by those who have succeeded in making a significant contribution to their chosen field of activity.

My interest, however, is in the universal cognitive underpinnings of normal (often mundane) human creativity, rather than in the qualities of character, motivation, and prior knowledge of those who excel in this respect. (Boden, 1992, labels what interests me 'psychological creativity', distinguishing it from what she calls the 'historical creativity' of those who stand out by introducing noteworthy innovations.) And here the two most important factors—whose relevance is acknowledged by all parties—are some sort of capacity to generate new ideas, on the one hand (e.g. by noticing a novel analogy), together with abilities to see and to develop the significance of those ideas, on the other. These factors are certainly accorded a fundamental role in one of the influential psychological accounts that is explicitly designed as a theory of universal cognitive creativity, the so-called 'geneplore' (for 'generate and

---

[3] Leslie (1987) argues, in contrast, that what children need is the capacity to *meta-represent* their own representational states, hence 'decoupling' them from their normal connections with belief and action. See Jarrold et al. (1994) and Nichols and Stich (2003) for critiques of this view.

explore') model of creativity developed by Finke and colleagues (Finke et al., 1992; Finke, 1995; Ward et al., 1999).

According to Finke, creative cognition involves two distinct stages. First, there is the generation of a novel hypothesis or idea—which at this stage is merely *entertained* rather than believed or endorsed—and then there is the exploration of that idea, developing it and working out its consequences, before finally accepting it or putting it into practice. This two-stage account maps remarkably smoothly onto our best accounts of pretend play. An episode of pretence will begin with an initial supposition or imagined scenario—that the banana is a telephone; that the teddy bears are having a tea party; and so on. The child then acts as if that supposition were true, following familiar scripts and/or drawing inferences appropriate to its truth in the light of her background knowledge—making dialing movements, say, or setting out the tea cups and saucers (Harris, 2000; Nichols and Stich, 2003). Often, too, yet further suppositions will be introduced into the play episode, serving to elaborate and extend the pretence—for example, supposing that Grandma has answered the phone-call and hence beginning to talk to her; or supposing that there is cake to set out with the tea as well.

I shall take it as a tentative constraint on theorizing about human creativity, then, that both adult creative thought and activity, on the one hand, and pretend play, on the other, have essentially the same cognitive basis. This resides in a capacity to generate and reason with *suppositions*. The main question before us is what sort of cognitive architecture serves to realize this capacity. I shall begin to address this question in Section 2.

1.3 Creativity of Action

Thus far in the discussion I have tacitly assumed that all forms of creativity have, at their basis, creativity of *thought*. But how plausible is this? Can't there be creative *actions* that aren't preceded by creative thoughts? Consider a jazz musician who improvises a series of variations on a musical theme.[4] Or consider a dancer who extemporizes a sequence of movements that she may never have made before (and may never make again). These are undoubtedly kinds of creativity. But they seem to be forms of creativity of *action*, rather than creativity of thought. For the novel movements appear to be made 'on-line',

---

[4] In the course of his extensive discussion of jazz improvisation, Berliner (1994) outlines a number of different strategies and heuristics that jazz improvisers will adopt to guide and frame their performance. But beyond that, the particular notes and phrases that they play on any given occasion will often strike them with the force of discovery. They are often surprised by their own playing, which seems to them to have a life of its own. I shall return to this point shortly.

sometimes extremely swiftly, and without prior reflection or planning—or at least, without prior *conscious* reflection or planning.

Someone might pick up on this last concession to argue that jazz and dance improvisation *do* involve planning—only the thoughts in question occur unconsciously, immediately prior to the execution of the movements in question. Such a view seems to me implausible, however, for a number of reasons. One has to do with the *fineness of grain* that can be present in skilled improvisation. Someone executing a novel sequence of notes on the saxophone, for example, or a novel sequence of bodily movements in a dance, doesn't *just* play those notes, or make those movements. For these might, indeed, be actions that the agent has names and/or concepts for ('E flat, followed by F, followed by C flat', or, 'up a fourth, down a fifth', and so on). But the agent will also choose a precise length for each note, or a precise speed for each movement, for which there is no name (and probably no concept). Likewise the agent will add a precise timbre to the playing of the note, or a precise articulation to the movement. Although intentional, these aren't actions that can plausibly be fully captured in any sort of propositional / conceptual description.

In fact there is a strong case for saying that skilled action-control has a *non-conceptual* (or at least an *analog*) aspect, just as perceptual contents are partly non-conceptual or analog in nature. A percept of the precise shades of red in a rose-petal has a fineness of grain that escapes any conceptual description that one might attempt to impose on it, and that is prior to the application of any concept (Carruthers, 2000; Kelly, 2001; Gunther, 2003). Likewise a precise movement or sequence of movements, too, has just such a fineness of grain and partially non-conceptual character. In which case skilled creative action can't be fully explained in terms of the creativity of thought. For even if there are (unconscious) conceptual thoughts that precede the action, they can by no means fully determine it; and hence there must at least be an *element* of the creativity displayed by the agent that doesn't reduce to conceptual creativity.

It might be replied that creative action can always be underlain by creative thoughts that are indexical in form. So a dancer's thought that precedes and explains a novel set of movements might take the form, 'I shall move my arms *thus* while moving my legs *so*.' But what, on this account, would fix the intentional content of the two indexicals '*thus*' and '*so*'? Since the thought precedes the action, those indexicals can't be grounded in a *perception* of the movement in question, in the way that the indexical in a thought like, 'I shall pick up *that* apple', can be grounded in an analog / non-conceptual percept of the object seen. So the only remaining possibility is that the contents of the indexicals in a movement-determining thought are given imagistically. Hence when the dancer thinks, 'I shall move my arms *thus*', the content of '*thus*' will be given by a proprioceptive or visual image of a particular set of fine-grained movements of the arms.

It is implausible that every creative action should be preceded by some such creative thought, however. For consider just how *fast* creative actions can be. A jazz improviser can be playing at full speed, piecing together and recombining previously rehearsed phrases and patterns, when he suddenly finds himself playing a sequence of notes that he has never played before, and which surprises him (Berliner, 1994). For example, Charlie Parker was famous for being able to play his improvised solos at amazing speed—some of them at speeds of 400 beats per minute (Owens, 1995). Most of us would have trouble even beating our feet to such a tempo. And even though his solos were mostly composed out of arrangements and rearrangements of formulaic fragments—ranging from two or three note patterns to clusters of a dozen notes—it is difficult to believe that there was time in which to form a conceptually driven but fully detailed imagistic representation of each such fragment in advance of activating the motor schema for it.

Moreover it is, on reflection, problematic to allow that image-involving indexical thoughts might occur during improvisation without being conscious. For if these images are to help explain the intentional character of the resulting actions, then it looks as though they need to feed into some sort of evaluative process. And the only model that we have for that, at the moment, is some or other version of the global broadcasting account defended by Baars (1988, 2002) and others (Dehaene and Naccache, 2001). Yet there is every reason to think that globally broadcast events are coextensive with consciousness.[5]

Even if we were to concede the above point, however, and were to allow that every creative action is preceded by a creative indexical thought, it remains the case that creative act-generation can't be reduced to creative thought-generation. For recall the evidence discussed in Chapter 2.2, to the effect that the movement and manipulation of visual (and other) images is driven by activating a corresponding set of action schemata. If this is the case, then in order to form a visual image representing a particular set of movements of my arms, I *first* have to activate and rehearse a motor schema that codes for just those movements. So the basic form of creativity, here, must consist in the creative generation of an action schema. And then given that action schemata

---

[5] This isn't yet to endorse the global broadcasting theory of consciousness, I should stress. For it remains possible to maintain, as I do, that it is some particular *aspect* of global broadcasting that renders experiences conscious. In particular, it is possible to claim that it is the availability of a perceptual content to the mind-reading system (achieved by global broadcasting) that renders that percept conscious, by conferring on it a higher-order, self-referring, intentional content. See Carruthers, 2000, 2005.

can be produced creatively in the absence of any prior creative thought, there is no reason why they shouldn't be used to initiate movements directly, too, without first being used to generate imagistic representations of the actions involved. No doubt the latter often happens, when there is time. But there isn't any reason why it should always happen so.

Let me now return to the point noted in passing above, that jazz improvisers are often surprised by their own products. This is direct evidence in support of the view being proposed here, that actions can be creative without prior creative thought. For surprise is the emotion that we feel when something *unexpected* happens. But the expectations in question don't have to be consciously entertained. On the contrary, events can be most surprising when they violate tacit expectations that it would never have occurred to us to formulate consciously otherwise. So when a jazz improviser is surprised by the sequence of notes that he hears himself play, this is evidence that he didn't have a prior expectation that he would play just those notes (whether conscious or unconscious). At the very least it follows that the creative thought that is alleged to precede the action must occur within some sub-system that is cut off from access to globally broadcast perceptions (in this case, of sound). But that would require a major modification in the basic architecture that we have suggested for the mind, according to which *all* central / conceptual systems have access to perceptual input.

I suggest that it is a constraint on any adequate account of creativity, then, that it should at least find a separate place for creativity of action in addition to the creativity of thought. (That is, if it doesn't actually reduce the latter to the former, as I shall propose to do.)

1.4 How Many Kinds of Creativity?

I have concluded that the creativity of action can't be reduced to the creativity of thought. But how plausible is it that there should be two distinct and independent sources of creativity—one for action, and one for thought? Although possible in principle, any such view assumes a heavy explanatory burden. For we would need to tell two distinct evolutionary stories about the emergence of these two forms of creativity, and we would need to describe two distinct cognitive mechanisms underlying them. It is therefore preferable to explain the creativity of thought in terms of the creativity of action, if we can. Although this seems initially unpromising—indeed, mysterious: for how do new *actions* create novel *thoughts?*—I believe that it is defensible, and arises naturally out of some of the ideas introduced in Chapter 4. And a view of just this sort will be elaborated and defended in the present chapter.

I shall suggest, in fact, that all creativity reduces to the creative generation of action schemata. Sometimes these schemas are used to bring about novel actions directly. But sometimes they are use to generate visual or other images, which are globally broadcast in the manner of perceptual states generally (Baars, 1988, 1997), and received as input by the myriad conceptual modules. (See Figure 2.8.) And in the special case where the action schema that gets created is a linguistic one, its mental rehearsal results in a sentence in 'inner speech', which when processed by the language comprehension system will present a novel propositional thought to the various conceptual modules for further processing. (See Figure 4.3.)

It might be objected that there is only a 'heavy explanatory burden' imposed on the view that there are two or more distinct sources of creativity if we think of creativity as being some sort of *process* (like sentence parsing). But why can't creativity be a *property* or *manner* that a whole variety of events and processes could instantiate? Why can't creativity be more like *stealth* or *haste*? There is no temptation to think that there must be a single system or capacity underlying haste. On the contrary, almost any activity or cognitive process can be conducted in haste, utilizing just the resources that are normally involved in that activity or process itself. Might it not be so with creativity?

It seems to me plain, however, that creativity can't be just a *manner* in which familiar events or processes are conducted, precisely because creativity involves the introduction of *novelty*. So it makes sense to ask at what point or points within cognition novelty can be introduced. And for each such 'point' that is proposed, it looks as though some sort of evolutionary explanation can be demanded. We shall return to this topic in Section 5, when we examine a competing thought-based account of creativity in more detail.

In addition to reducing our explanatory burden by half, the view that all creativity reduces to the creative generation of action schemata has other virtues too, as we shall see in more detail later. It enables us to envision how creativity might evolve quite easily by exapting and utilizing mechanisms that were already in place for other purposes. (Any 'thought first' account, in contrast, will face difficulties on this front, as we shall see in Section 5.) We have already proposed, in Chapter 2.8, that a limited capacity for creative mental rehearsal of action is present in other great apes and earlier forms of hominid. And we also noted, in Chapter 2.7, that something very like creative action is present in many species of birds and mammals, through what Gallistel (1980) calls 'the principle of autonomous build-up of action-specific potentiation'. This leads animals to recombine and execute the elements of their behavioral repertoires in random or semi-random fashion, whenever those components have lain dormant for sufficient time. Indeed, we also noted that simple forms of creative action are actually quite widespread in the animal kingdom, in the form of protean, genuinely unpredictable, sequences of behavior (Driver and Humphries, 1988; Miller, 1997). Such behavior is especially common when a prey animal is attempting to escape from a predator.

There is good reason to think, then, that a capacity for unplanned action-schema activation is quite widespread amongst animals, leading to novel sequences of action that aren't preceded and caused by any novel thought. In contrast, there is no evidence that I know of that non-human animals besides the great apes have any capacity for creative thinking. So it will be much more plausible to explain how distinctively human forms of creativity can grow from simpler forms of creativity of action, than to pursue any sort of 'thought first' account.

1.5 Modularity and Computational Tractability

A final constraint on acceptable explanations of human creativity comes straight out of the arguments of Chapter 1, together with the overall project of this book. One aspect of this constraint should be obvious. For if our goal is to defend a massively modular conception of the human mind, then we should require that any explanation of human creativity must be consistent with massive modularity. But it should be equally obvious that creative thinking cannot be an *encapsulated* process (in the familiar narrow-scope sense), since precisely what it can involve is the bringing together of disparate items of information or disparate ideas. So our account of creative thinking will somehow have to utilize *un*encapsulated modular processes, but ones that are nevertheless computationally feasible for minds like ours. This is our challenge, and the task on which I shall shortly embark.

1.6 What the Constraints on Explanation Aren't

I should emphasize that it *isn't* a constraint on modularist explanations of creativity that they should be capable of explaining (let alone predicting) the particular creative thoughts that individual people entertain on specific occasions. There are a couple of reasons for this. One is that, for all that anyone knows, the processes that produce creative thoughts may be partly random or chaotic in nature. In which case no explanation of a thought produced by such a process can be forthcoming. The most that it will be possible to hope for is an account of the cognitive architecture within which the randomizing process is embedded, together with the other factors that influence its operations.

The second reason why it would be unreasonable to demand an explanation for specific creative thoughts is this. It seems likely that the processes that generate creative thoughts are heavily content-dependent in the following sense: they may be highly sensitive to the particular beliefs and learning history of the agent, as well as to the specific cognitive context in which the creative thought is produced (such as the thoughts that had been active shortly before, the perceptual contents recently caused by the detailed environment of the agent, and so forth). In which case it may be practically impossible for us to know all of this in enough detail to lay out an explanation, even if all the cognitive processes involved in creativity are deterministic ones.

Our goal should be to locate the processes responsible for creativity within the overall architecture of the human mind, and to say just enough about the ways in which such a system might operate to demonstrate that human creativity is at least consistent with the thesis of massively modular mental organization. And to the extent that the resulting account is deemed plausible, then to that extent we can claim additional support for massive modularity. For creativity is a problem for everyone, of course, and not just for massive modularists. If the thesis of massive modularity can help us to make progress with it, then that is a further feather in the cap of those of us who defend such a belief.

2 The Creative-Action Theory of Creativity

The hypothesis to be considered and defended here is that the ultimate cognitive basis of creative supposition lies in the creative generation of action schemata. Notice, to begin with, that mental rehearsal of action is itself a limited form of supposition, even when the action schema that gets rehearsed *isn't* generated creatively. Consider the ape who pauses before executing her default schema, *going to dig up the food*. (She knows that the food is there; she knows how to get to that spot; and she knows how to dig. So as we saw in Chapter 2.8, her practical-reasoning system, activated by her desire for the food, can easily put together the two-step action-plan, *approach the food and then dig*, from information provided by other modules.) Rehearsing that schema she generates the prediction, 'The male will push me aside and take the food for himself', based upon past experience. This leads her to feel disappointment, and hence to abandon her original plan.

The point to notice here is that the action-rehearsal in question is the functional equivalent of entertaining the supposition, 'What if I were to go to that spot and begin digging?' It is an idea that isn't yet believed (of course the ape doesn't believe that she *is* in that spot digging, nor does she yet believe that she *will* go to that spot to dig). And although she *wants* to get the food, and had just formed the *intention* of going to dig it up, the causal role of the rehearsal differs from that of desire (it isn't provided as input to practical reason, but rather to belief-generating and desire-generating modules), and also from the role of intention (the rehearsal isn't used to initiate an action). So it is a fourth sort of intentional state, distinct from believing, desiring, and intending.

I suggested in Chapter 2.8 that when Belle engages in *creative* rehearsals (eventually hitting upon the plan of digging in the wrong spot), they are in various ways belief-driven and actual-motivational-state-driven. She tries activating action schemata *similar to* the original, abandoned, one ('Suppose I dug, but over *there*'); she tries activating schemata that share conceptual components with some of her salient beliefs about current circumstances ('Suppose I climbed that palm tree'); and she tries activating schemata motivated by her emotional state ('Suppose I attacked the male').[6] I now want to suggest that the main difference introduced by suppositional reasoning in childhood (especially in pretend play) lies here: in the ways in which an initial supposition is generated. What the child is capable of doing is selecting an action schema for mental rehearsal that *isn't* amongst the most epistemically or motivationally salient. And the crucial new hominid adaptation is the mechanism that makes this possible, as I shall now explain.

2.1 Pretence and Embedded Supposition

A child sees a banana, activating the mental representation, BANANA. But the banana is somewhat similar in shape to a telephone handset; so the representation, TELEPHONE, is also (albeit more weakly) activated. So far, we might suppose, this doesn't introduce anything different from what might happen in the mind of an ape.[7] But now the crucial difference is that *each* of these representations might be used to activate related action schemata—peeling the banana and eating it; making a telephone call to Grandma. And each of these schemata is mentally rehearsed. But the child isn't hungry, so the imagined eating of the banana generates no emotional rewards. Talking to Grandma on the telephone, on the other hand, is just what the child likes to do; and imagining doing it is emotionally rewarding. (I shall discuss how these rewards

---

[6] Notice that I have been forced to cast in *propositional* format, for purposes of communication in writing, the suppositions that Belle entertains by activating various action schemata. This is, of course, misleading. Her action schemata will in each case be more or less abstract motor representations of an action, which are used to generate partly non-conceptual images of that action, and which are only awkwardly described in natural language.

[7] Few—if any—apes will have the concept *telephone*, of course. My point is just that we might expect that other concepts, that apply to things that are *similar to* the target object, will be weakly activated in apes as well as in humans. So when the ape sees a coconut, not only COCONUT but perhaps also BALL and APPLE will be activated, to some smaller degree. I shall return to this point shortly.

arise in a moment, drawing on the work of Damasio and others.) The child therefore decides to act-out the telephone-call schema; and her motives for doing so are just the same as the motives for undertaking *any* mentally rehearsed action from which rewards are envisaged, I shall argue.

But of course the child doesn't believe that by lifting up the banana and dialing she will actually get to talk to Grandma; and she isn't disappointed when she doesn't really hear Grandma's voice. Why not? How does the suppositional nature of a mentally rehearsed action schema get transformed into a suppositional *action sequence*? Consider the difference between the ape's problem-solving-oriented mental rehearsal and the child's. Although the ape mentally rehearses an action schema that she doesn't yet intend or believe will take place, it is a schema that is grounded in *beliefs* about her current circumstances. Thus the ape *believes* that there is food hidden in a particular location within the enclosure, and *believes* that the alpha male will follow her when she re-enters the enclosure. And when she rehearses going straight to dig where the food actually is, and generates the prediction that the male will push her aside and take the food, this is a further consequence (conditional upon the rehearsed sequence in question) that she comes to *believe*.

In order for this to work, all subsequent belief-like representations that occur downstream of the imagined action-sequence must somehow be 'tagged' as conditional upon the initial supposition, and hence as not to be believed outright. These tags must be passed on transitively from one informational state to another, in such a way that representations that are generated by inference from an initially tagged belief-like state will in turn be so tagged. And since new supposed action schemata can be activated within the scope of an existing supposition, it must be possible for new tags to be added, with each one serving to preserve a link to the supposition on which the state to which it is attached depends.

Recall that once the original plan has been abandoned, Belle eventually rehearses digging in a new location. The resulting belief-like state, THE MALE WILL FOLLOW AND PUSH ME ASIDE, then has to be tagged as conditional upon that initial supposition (the mentally rehearsed action). But when the ape then rehearses walking from that imagined new location to the real location of the food and beginning to dig, and generates the prediction, THE MALE WON'T FOLLOW ME, this new belief-like representation has to be doubly-tagged—once to carry its dependence upon the new imagined action, and again to carry its dependence upon the original imagined action as well.[8]

---

[8] It may be helpful to think of this on the model of the ways in which dependencies upon earlier suppositions are presented within formal proof-systems. In some such systems the dependencies are

While the ape's suppositions (imagined actions) are grounded in its beliefs about current circumstances, the child's mental rehearsal of the action schema of making a telephone call to Grandma, in contrast, *isn't* grounded in an initial belief that the banana in question really is a telephone. The mechanism that artificially boosts the weakly activated representation, TELEPHONE (or that uses that representation to activate action schemata that are suggested by the affordances of telephones), must also be one that tags all subsequent representations as mere suppositions, not to be believed outright. Thus when the child activates the action schema of dialing in order to call Grandma on *that telephone*, and generates the prediction that talking to Grandma will result, the child *doesn't* come to believe that activating the schema in question will actually result in talking to Grandma; and that is why, when the child subsequently acts out her pretence, she isn't disappointed when she doesn't really hear Grandma's voice.

The belief-like states that are generated in a mentally rehearsed pretence will then be doubly-tagged from the start—once to display their dependence on an imagined action-sequence, and once to display their dependence upon the weakly activated concept / suppositional belief-like state that is used to generate the initial action rehearsal. And in the subsequent acting-out of the pretend sequence, each of the child's action-representations remains tagged to the initial belief-like supposition. Note, however, that on this account the initiating representation, TELEPHONE, is itself only very weakly belief-like. For while it is used in the process that activates the action schema of telephoning Grandma, it cannot (I am supposing) be taken directly as input by other inferential mechanisms. It is only when the weakly activated concept TELEPHONE is 'boosted' and used to activate telephone-related action schemata, that the feedback loop via mental imagery makes it available as input to the various belief-generating conceptual modules *indirectly*.

Why am I insisting that what initiates an episode of pretence isn't a fully-fledged thought? Why can't it be the (creatively generated) thought, *The banana is a telephone*, that is the initial supposition that frames and guides the pretence? The reason is that this would then commit us to a 'thought-first' account of creativity, and would require us to postulate some way in which such thoughts can be 'broadcast' to the consumer systems that utilize them and draw inferences from them. It is simpler and more plausible to suppose that

displayed by numbers written alongside the proposition in question, which refer to the line-numbers on which that proposition depends (Lemmon, 1965; Mates, 1965). In other systems line-brackets might be drawn down the side of the page to enclose the proposition, visibly displaying the sets of suppositions on which it depends for support (Simpson, 1988). I am suggesting that something similar to these processes occurs within the minds of apes and humans. See Harris (2000) for a parallel suggestion.

a weakly activated concept (in this case, TELEPHONE) can prime conceptually related action schemata, and that the disposition that underlies pretence is one that 'boosts' and mentally rehearses such schemata, resulting in their global broadcast in the manner of perceptual representations generally. I shall return to the contrast between 'action-based' and 'thought-first' accounts of creativity in Section 5 of this chapter.

Notice that according to the present proposal, the basis of pretence, and hence the basis of creativity generally, is *associative* in character (albeit later supplemented by learned action-sequences and learned rules and heuristics of various sorts—see below). For it is action schemata that are *primed* in various ways by the current context or by the contents of immediately prior thoughts that get activated and rehearsed. One way of modeling this would be to assume that concepts like TELEPHONE and BANANA are stored along with a set of semantic primitives of various sorts, some of which (such as CURVED) are shared by more than one such concept. Then when BANANA is activated, these semantic primitives will also be activated, leading to weak or partial activation of any other concepts (like TELEPHONE) with which they are connected. The disposition that underlies pretend play, then, would consist in a willingness to activate and rehearse some of the action schemata that are in turn primed by, or that are affordances of, the resulting weakly activated concepts.[9]

In Chapters 1 and 2 I set my face against associative accounts of cognition in general, and argued in support of computational approaches. Yet I believe that there is a place for associationism within theories of *creative* cognition in particular. The associative processes that Hume (1739) and other empiricists have assumed to be properties of cognition generally are actually only relevant when accounting for *creative* cognitive processes, and may be unique to humans. For while the concepts of monkeys and apes, too, will be weakly co-activated when their shared semantic primitives are co-activated, this plays no further significant role in their cognitive lives, I suggest. Associations amongst concepts are only really useful when you need some way of generating novel thoughts or novel behaviors that can't be arrived at computationally, or on the basis of salient facts in your environment. Hume was right that the conscious and creative aspect of the human mind is, to an important degree, governed by associations. But he was wrong to assume that this holds for minds in general.

[9] It might seem that the explanation offered in this paragraph commits me to some or other version of a classical ('definitional') or neoclassical theory of concepts. But this isn't so. One reason is that prototype theories of concepts, too, will postulate semantic primitives of the sort that I appeal to. But another reason is that even if concepts lack semantic structure, they can still have *psychological* structures that don't play any role in fixing reference or other semantic properties, but which have other sorts of psychological effects (such as co-priming). See Laurence and Margolis, 1999.

2.2 Pretence and Motivation[10]

How do motivational states factor into this account? There are two things that need to be explained. The first is how *imagined* action can generate *real* action. And the second is why children ever act-out their pretence overtly, externalizing their play fantasies. Why don't they keep it all in their heads? Moreover, since pretend actions of one sort (talking to Grandma) are nevertheless real actions of another (holding a banana in one's hand and talking), we need to find some real—not imaginary—desires that they satisfy, or else the behavior in question will remain mysterious within the framework of a belief / desire psychology.

Let us begin with the question of how action-rehearsals lead to action. Recall from Chapter 2.8 the model put forward by Damasio (1994) and others (e.g. Rolls, 1999), which finds a crucial role for somasensory monitoring. (See Figure 2.8.) The account proceeds like this. When Belle imagines herself walking to the location of the food and digging, this representation is globally broadcast to desire-generating and emotion-generating modules as well as to belief-generating ones; and the tagged belief-like consequences of that initial representation are also made available to her motivational systems. So when the prediction is generated that the male will push her aside and take the food, this causes her to feel *disappointment*, resulting from the frustration of her (real) desire to eat the food, and it perhaps also causes her to feel *anger*. Likewise when she subsequently imagines herself digging up and consuming the food while the male is occupied elsewhere, this causes her to feel *satisfaction*, resulting from the representation of a state that would fulfill her desire to eat the food.

Notice that the emotions generated are *real* ones, on this account—albeit *fainter* than normal, perhaps reflecting the relative faintness and instability of imagined experience as against real experience. (As many teenage boys will know, actually looking at a picture of a naked woman is much more sexually arousing than merely *imagining* a naked woman.) So our hypothesis should be this. While the belief-like states that are produced by the belief-generating modules when they receive an imagined action as input are tagged to reflect their dependency on something that is a mere supposition, the same isn't true of the motivational products of imagination (or not in the same way, at any rate). The emotional and motivational products of an imagined action are real ones, not motivation-*like*, and so it might seem that no tagging needs to take place.

But now we have a problem. If it is real anger against the male that is caused by the mentally rehearsed action of digging up the food, then why does this

---

[10] For more extensive discussion of this topic, see Carruthers, 2006b.

lead her to try out an alternative action schema, rather than attacking the male here and now in retaliation? And if it is real satisfaction that she feels when she later imagines herself eating the food, why doesn't this lead her to abandon all pursuit of the food, since her hunger has now been satisfied? It is here that we see the role of somasensory monitoring, on Damasio's account; and also the need for something *like* tagging of motivational states to display their dependence upon imagined scenarios.

According to Damasio (1994), the feelings that are caused by our emotional reactions to imagined phenomena involve physiological changes of various sorts, which we detect in ourselves via somasensory monitoring (see also Prinz, 2004). We become aware of the physiological changes characteristic of sexual arousal, or the increased heart-rate and breathing-rate characteristic of anger, or the extra salivation characteristic of eating a desired food, and so on.[11] And we use our awareness of these changes to make corresponding adjustments in the desirability of the initial imagined action. So there is a kind of 'tagging' going on here too; but it has a somewhat different functional role. While the emotions produced by an imagined action are real ones, they need to be tagged as being dependent upon the execution of that action, so that our motivation to perform the action can be adjusted up or down (depending upon whether the emotional valence is positive or negative).

So here is how the sequence might go. First, Belle imagines herself walking straight to the food and digging it up. But this generates the prediction that she will be pushed aside, which causes her disappointment. Her awareness of this feeling causes a reduction in her motivation to go straight to the food, to such an extent that she temporarily abandons that plan. She then tries out some alternative scenarios, one of which is that she should go and dig elsewhere. This leads to a number of further predictions, and to the further embedded imagination of herself walking back to where the food really is while the male continues to dig in the wrong spot. She is able to imagine herself consuming the food, and feels satisfaction at the result. Her awareness of this feeling leads to an increase in her motivation to perform each of the imagined actions on which it depends. And those, consequently, are what she does.

---

[11] An interesting variant on these ideas is defended by Schroeder (2004), as we noted in Chapter 2.8. He argues that the crucial elements in somasensory monitoring are *pleasure* and *displeasure*, which are conscious signals representing that the envisaged action is rewarding or punishing. Reviewing a wide range of evidence provided by cognitive neuroscience, he argues that the basic determinants of reward and punishment are unconscious, but that these generate signals elsewhere in the brain representing that our desires are being satisfied (in the case of pleasure) or frustrated (in the case of displeasure). So on this account it isn't somasensory monitoring of physiological changes generally, but monitoring of pleasure and displeasure in particular, that is the crucial determinant in decision making.

We are now in a position to explain why children engage in pretend play. We only need to suppose that the above system continues to operate unchanged once the novel disposition appears at some point during hominid evolution mentally to rehearse action schemata that are only loosely suggested by the context (and that aren't grounded in beliefs). The sight of the banana causes the representation, TELEPHONE, to be weakly activated via the same sort of associative process that operates in apes. This in turn causes the child mentally to rehearse the action of calling Grandma, utilizing the affordances of telephones. And since talking to Grandma is something that she loves to do, she feels satisfaction as a result. Her awareness of this feeling consequently boosts her motivation to perform the envisaged action schema. And since that motivation is unopposed by any negative emotion, it may be sufficient to motivate her to begin executing the entire sequence of calling and talking to Grandma—all suppositional on *that* (banana) being a telephone.

Of course, beginning to execute an action schema is one thing, and continuing with it through to the end is quite another. Why doesn't the child stop as soon as she realizes that she isn't going to hear Grandma's voice, or as soon as she fails to hear a real ringing tone once she has executed the sequence of movements characteristic of dialing? Well, one of the consequences of representing herself as dialing Grandma might be that she *imagines* herself hearing Grandma's voice as a result. But even if she goes straight into talking, since what she is doing is executing the action schema *talking to Grandma on the telephone*, she will represent her own movements, and her own speech-acts, under that description (tagged for their suppositional status, of course). So her perceptions of her own actions will be globally broadcast and taken as input by her motivational systems under the description *talking to Grandma*. (I shall return to discuss how this happens in Section 2.4.) And since this is something that the child loves to do, we should expect her to experience real satisfaction as a result.

But why does the child actually act, picking up the banana and pretending to dial? Why doesn't she keep the whole sequence in her head? Why is pretending better than imagining? There are two replies. One is that the standard mode of operation of mental rehearsal of action schemata is this: once positive emotions are detected from the envisaged action and/or its predicted consequences, then a real action should ensue. (Think again of Belle.) So it will require additional sophistication and control *not* to externalize one's fantasies. But the other reply is that imagination is hard work. It requires persistent effort and concentration to keep a complex sequence of images in mind with sufficient vividness to generate a sustained emotional response. If the sequence is externalized in pretend play, in contrast, then perception of one's own actions will automatically take up most of the load. So we should expect that young children will find pretence to be a good deal easier and more rewarding than fantasy.

On my account, then, it is the very same sort of motivational system that leads to the execution of creatively generated action schemata during problem solving, on the one hand, and that leads to episodes of pretend play, on the other. The novel hominid disposition that is both responsible for pretend play, and that is further strengthened by engaging in rewarding episodes of pretend play, is just the disposition mentally to rehearse action schemata independently of any current project or practical concern.

It should be emphasized that the *goals* of action will be different in the two cases, however. When the ape acts on her action schema and starts to dig in the wrong place, what she is intending to do is get and consume (really consume) the food. In contrast, when the child picks up the banana and starts to make dialing movements, her goal is *not* to talk to Grandma, but rather to *pretend* to talk to Grandma. Or perhaps better (since the child might as yet lack the concept of pretence), we can say that she has the goal of talking to Grandma *conditional on the supposition that the banana is a telephone*. Everything that the child does within the episode of pretence remains tagged to the supposition-like status of the initial representation TELEPHONE that grounds it. But the motivational rewards of the episode are real, and they are the very same rewards that would accrue from really talking to Grandma (albeit weaker, perhaps).

It will help to introduce a little technical terminology at this point. Let us say that the child's enactment of talking to Grandma *quasi-satisfies* her actual desire to talk to Grandma. Since she doesn't believe outright that she is talking to Grandma, her desire isn't really and fully satisfied. But by representing what she is doing *as* talking to Grandma she is able to generate many of the same feelings and positive emotions as would be derived from the real thing. Although *she* isn't fooled by her pretence into thinking that she is actually talking to Grandma, her emotional systems *are* so fooled, and respond accordingly.

2.3 Varieties of Motivation in Pretence

The account sketched above will also fit many other instances of pretence rather nicely. Consider a little boy pretending to be a cowboy. If he finds cowboys and their activities admirable, then when he skips along as if he were riding a horse while yelling, 'Yee-hah!', he will be representing himself to be something admirable. And he might be expected to find the whole sequence emotionally rewarding as a result. Likewise in the case of a little girl playing with dolls who is pretending to bathe a baby: if she finds mothers and mothering activities admirable or otherwise attractive, then by representing what she is doing *as* the actions of a mother bathing her baby, she might be expected to experience a reward. Indeed, it is an appealing feature of this account that we can explain the *patterning* that we see in childhood pretence. For the most part, children pretend to be or to do things that they admire, want, or otherwise find attractive. The explanation is that by representing themselves *as* being or doing something wanted, they will experience some sort of quasi-satisfaction of their desires.

Thus far the examples of pretence that I have considered have involved the emotions of *love* (for Grandma) or *admiration* (for cowboys and mothers), or some close analog thereof. By pretending to talk to Grandma the child represents herself as talking with a loved person, which is something that she enjoys doing. And by pretending to be a cowboy the child represents himself to be something that he finds admirable, which is why he does it. But these aren't the only sorts of emotion that can motivate pretence. Consider the child who is talking with her imaginary friend who lives in a tree in her yard. Here the motivational rewards derived are those that are distinctive of intimate conversation in general. By representing her own speech acts under the description, TALKING TO MY INVISIBLE FRIEND WENDY, she fools her emotional systems into responding much as they would if she were conversing with a real friend.

Or consider the child who pretends to be a dead cat (Nichols and Stich, 2003). If we suppose, as seems reasonable, that he *doesn't* find dead cats to be admirable, then the question is, 'Why?' My guess is that it is important to this particular example that it should occur in a social context. (And indeed, Nichols and Stich report that the child in question began by drawing his audience's attention, first of all saying, 'Look, I'm a dead cat', before lying motionless on his back with his tongue hanging out and his arms and legs stiff and straight.) Casting around for something to do, the child may have hit upon the sentence, 'I am a dead cat.' (I shall return to such uses of language in Section 3.) Assembling and mentally rehearsing an appropriate (in)action schema, he predicts that his audience will find it funny. Since this is something that he wants, he goes ahead and does it.

Suppositions can also interact with the emotion and motivation systems in more complex ways to generate rewarding pretence. For example, think of a child playing at hide and seek, who is pretending that his father is a monster who is coming to eat him. Representing himself in this light, the child might experience fear, which would normally be an inducement to cease the activity. But at the same time he knows that he is only pretending, and that he is not really about to be eaten. So he retains an important element of control over his fear. For at any moment, by reminding himself that this is only a game, and that no one is really going to hurt him, he can close down the pretend inputs to his emotion systems, hence shutting down or modulating their response. And this might (in a different way) be pleasurable.[12]

The core of the idea is just this, then: when a pretend action schema is mentally rehearsed, it is globally broadcast and made available to the whole suite of emotional and motivational modules, which might respond in various ways, some of which are directly rewarding. But in some instances, however, the emotional rewards can be more indirect. And likewise when a child acts-out a pretence: by representing what she is doing *as* an action of a certain pretend sort, her emotional and motivational modules respond appropriately to that pretend input, generating direct or indirect emotional rewards.

2.4 Pretence and Mind-Reading

It is crucial to the above account that the child should be capable of seeing her own actions of holding a banana and making dialing movements *as* the action of dialing to talk to Grandma on a telephone. For otherwise there will be nothing rewarding about the sequence. There is surely nothing enjoyable about holding a banana and poking at it *as such*. And hence pretence surely implicates at least a limited capacity for mind-reading. More specifically, the mind-reading system, on receiving perceptual input of various sorts concerning the child's movements and speech, has to be capable of interpreting those movements *as* the actions of dialing and talking to Grandma. This requires a capacity to classify actions as such, and to interpret them as directed towards a particular goal. Fortunately, there is good reason to think that infants in their second year possess just such capacities (Johnson, 2005).

Recall from Chapter 2.2 that the dorsal / parietal visual system (and its equivalent in other sense modalities), which initially generates perceptual representations of mentally rehearsed action schemata, is *non-conceptual* in character. Only when those representations are mapped into the ventral / temporal visual system (or equivalent) via the ventro-dorsal bridge do they acquire a conceptualized content. Likewise, then, when the child actually acts during an

---

[12] There is a long-standing puzzle about how it is possible for us to take pleasure in negative emotional responses to theatre, literature, or music, of course, as well as to pretence (Levinson, 1997). And while some writers do seek to explain this pleasure in terms of *control*, in something like the manner sketched in the text (Eaton, 1982; Morreall, 1985), this is only one possibility amongst others. Another idea consistent with those being developed in the present chapter would be that the pleasure that we take in negative emotional responses to horror or tragedy results from thinking ourselves to be in various ways *admirable* for being susceptible to those emotions, or for being able to control those emotions (Levinson, 1982; Feagin, 1983); and likewise in the case of fearful or terrible pretence.

episode of pretence—the perceptual expectations that are generated via the dorsal / parietal system are initially unconceptualized ones; as are the perceptions of the child's own movements that are entering the ventral / temporal system from outside. So it is by no means automatic that those percepts should acquire the content, *dialing on a telephone to talk to Grandma*, rather than the content, *poking at a banana*. But without the former content being attached and globally broadcast to the motivational systems, no rewards will be experienced.

Might the mind-reading system have privileged access to the contents of the child's own intentions / action schemata that generate and guide her movements? If so, then there would be no need for *interpretation* of perceptual input concerning those movements. Rather, the content derived from the intention could be automatically attached to the relevant percepts for global broadcast. However, we saw in Chapter 3.3 that the mind-reading system is unlikely to have any such access. (And as we shall see further in Section 4, the supposition that it doesn't will enable us to explain the absence of pretend play in autism.) While the mind-reading system might be able to query some of the belief-generating modules in the course of its operations, it won't be able to monitor their output on a regular basis. And it is quite likely that the mind-reading system won't be able to receive any information from the action selection and control systems at all. So it will have no other option but to engage in interpretation.

What information would the mind-reading system have available to it in setting about its task of interpreting the child's own movements during pretence? Like all other belief-generating systems, it will be receiving its perceptual inputs 'tagged' for the pretend or suppositional status of the action. So this will be a crucial cue for the mind-reading system, telling it to set to work to interpret the perceived action *as* suppositional, searching for a content to attach to it that can make sense of it. But many other cues are also likely to be available, including any visual images that are also evoked (such as an image of Grandma's face, generated when the concept GRANDMA is activated along with some of the affordances of telephones), or any words or phrases uttered or mentally rehearsed (such as, 'Call Grandma', caused by the activated action schema).

2.5 Pretending, Talking, and Imitating

Notice that the hominid disposition that we have postulated to exist—and the pretend play in which it eventuates—isn't fundamentally dependent upon natural language. Although the central example that I have been discussing throughout—using a banana as a pretend telephone to talk to Grandma—involves the use of language, this is accidental. An exactly parallel account could be provided for forms of pretence that don't involve language. For example, a child sees a chair, which weakly activates his concept BUS DRIVER (since bus drivers also sit in chairs). This in turn activates the motor schemata for some of the movements involved in driving a bus, which are mentally rehearsed and the resulting images globally broadcast. If the child finds bus drivers admirable, he may experience an emotional reward, hence motivating him to execute the entire sequence—sitting in the chair and making movements as if turning a steering wheel, and so forth.

Notice that this example involves action schemata that didn't previously exist within the child's repertoire, however. (Presumably he has never actually driven a vehicle of any sort.) While this aspect, too, is accidental—think of a child pretending to eat, or pretending to drink—it is worth asking how it is possible. Plainly, a capacity to imitate actions is presupposed. But this in itself isn't a problem, since we know that even quite young children are adept at imitation (Meltzoff, 1995). The question is how the child gets from seeing the chair to imitating the actions of a bus driver. Here is how the sequence might go: seeing the chair, the child is reminded of buses and bus driving, activating an episodic or semantic memory of some sort, which is used to construct an image of the appropriate sequence of movements. The child might then be independently motivated to copy those movements. Or the representations of those movements might be projected through the mirror neuron system to prime the appropriate sequences of action schemata. These are then activated and rehearsed, leading the child to feel a reward for representing himself to be doing something desired or admired. And that then leads him to act as represented.

Many forms of pretend play are like this. Many kinds of pretence presuppose a capacity to imitate some activity for which the child doesn't antecedently possess an action schema. Such a schema must first be constructed, either from memory or from observation. A child who pretends to drive a bus must first assemble a representation of the motor sequences used in driving—turning the start key, depressing the accelerator, turning the steering wheel, and so forth—before copying those sequences. And even more complex, a child who is to pretend to *be* a bus must first map some of the parts of the bus onto himself, or some of the movements of parts of the bus onto movements of parts of himself—for example, moving his arms in circles to represent the motion of the bus's wheels.

My focus in this chapter is human creativity of thought and action. So when I come to discuss the evolutionary and developmental function of pretence in Section 4, my main focus will be on the ways that pretence serves to encourage and enhance our ability to generate and entertain creative suppositions. But it is equally true that pretence serves to practice and enhance our imitative abilities, and this might plausibly be counted amongst its functions (Bodgan, 2005).

It is important to emphasize, however, that by no means every case in which a novel action schema is assembled will result from copying of a pre-existing exemplar of some sort. On the contrary, just as a monkey or ape might try out novel sequences of action by combining elements from its repertoire when problem solving (either at random, or perhaps primed by various features of the context), so, too, might a child try out novel sequences of action during pretence. Consider the little girl who is pretending to bathe her baby (her doll). She knows that the faucets need to be turned on to put water in the bath, and she knows that the baby needs to be placed in the bath; and each of these actions might already exist in her repertoire. But she might have no inkling of the proper sequence. So at random, or because her doll is already in her hands, she places it in the pretend bath before pretending to turn the faucets. This is a sequence of movements that she might never have performed before. Instances of pretend play will surely be rife with such cases.

2.6 Imagining What can't be Done

My thesis is that it is the creative activation of action schemata that lies at the basis of all creative thought, action, and imagery. We have just seen that this sometimes requires a novel action schema to be constructed via imitation. But more problematic, it might be felt, is the creative generation of images of things that are actually *impossible*, for which one couldn't possibly possess an action schema. For example, during a dull faculty meeting I might imagine everyone in the room but myself floating up and becoming attached to the ceiling. Or I might imagine the Eiffel Tower collapsing sideways into the Seine. How can I generate such an image at all, if creative imagery requires the prior activation of an action schema? For I surely can't cause any such thing to happen. (And nor can anyone else, so I can't construct such an action schema by imitation, either.)

One aspect of this problem is relatively easy to deal with. For whenever a conceptual / propositional description of the impossible event has first been constructed, then the feedback connections within the ventral / temporal visual system (or their equivalent in other sense modalities), which are generally used in the course of object recognition (Kosslyn, 1994), can be used to construct an image of the event described. Just such a conceptual description might be derived from hearing or reading the sentences produced by another person. (As you read the words in the previous paragraph you doubtless formed appropriate imagery of people moving up to the ceiling or of the Eiffel Tower falling over, utilizing this route.) But it might also be derived from a self-generated sentence, too. And as we shall see in Section 3, these can be produced creatively and rehearsed without first formulating a creative thought. So on seeing the Eiffel Tower I might think, in inner speech, 'What if it fell over?' And the content thereby expressed, once decoded by the language comprehension system, could be used as the basis for generating an image of the Eiffel Tower falling over.

There are surely many cases that don't fit this model, however. On seeing the Eiffel Tower (or on seeing a picture of it, or on imagining it) I might surely form an image of it collapsing *without* first formulating a description of such an event in language. How, then, does this happen, given that I don't have any relevant action schema that I could creatively activate and rehearse? In order to answer this question we need to remind ourselves, again, that the dorsal / parietal visual system that generates imagery from action schemata utilizes only non-conceptual representations. So the Eiffel Tower couldn't be represented *as such* within it. How, then, would it be represented? Presumably by means of an indexical tag, of the sort explored at length by Pylyshyn (2003) in his account of the operations of the visual system. And both the inputs and the outputs of the dorsal / parietal and the ventral / temporal visual systems would surely need to be linked to one another by means of such indexicals. Let me elaborate.

Suppose that, on seeing a cup of water on the desk before me, I form and mentally rehearse a conceptualized plan with the content, *I'll pick up that cup.* This intention is grounded in contents deriving from the conceptualizing ventral / temporal system. So how is it able to communicate with the dorsal / parietal system to create an image of the appropriate action, given that the latter system doesn't know anything about cups as such (nor about *picking up*, for that matter, categorized in that way)? The answer is that it first has to be converted into a non-conceptual motor schema with a content of the sort, *I'll [picking-up motor schema] that*, where the indexical in question retains its links back to the relevant item in the conceptual thought, and also to the relevant indexically marked percept in the ventral / temporal visual system. This schema is then used to drive the construction of an appropriate image through the dorsal / parietal system, which when passed across to the ventral / temporal system yields a concept-imbued image of picking up the cup, as such, by virtue of the indexical tags shared between the two systems.

With this sketch of an account in place, it is now possible to explain how one might creatively form and transform images of events that couldn't be produced by any action. When someone sees the Eiffel Tower (or has an image of the Eiffel Tower evoked somehow) an abstract motor schema with the content, *pushing over a tower*, might be primed. (After all, children spend much of their early play time pushing over toy towers of one sort or another, so one might expect the priming effect here to be fairly strong.) This is activated by the creative mechanism, and the indexical term THAT (referring to the Eiffel Tower) is inserted in place of the quantified phrase to yield the motor plan, I PUSH OVER THAT. This is now projected back through the dorsal / parietal system (which has no knowledge of the Eiffel Tower or its properties, remember) to create an image, which when received, processed, and conceptualized by the ventral / temporal system yields an image of the Eiffel Tower, as such, falling sideways. (And falling into the Seine, given the right initial orientation of the action plan.)

2.7 Wrapping Up

I shall be arguing in Section 4 that one of the main evolutionary functions of pretend play is to enhance and develop creative suppositional thinking. So the first of the desiderata set out in Section 1 will eventually be satisfied. But what of the *tractability* constraint? It should be obvious, I think, that this isn't a problem for the account sketched so far. For the processes involved in the creative generation of action schemata are broadly associative ones, rather than computational in character. It is such things as the similarity in shape between a banana and a telephone handset that lead to the representation, TELEPHONE, being weakly activated. That representation, in turn (via the operations of some sort of uniquely human 'boosting mechanism'), activates all conceptually related action schemata (or perhaps just some of them at random, or selected as a result of other salient conceptual or motivational components). And thereafter all of the inferential processes that take place are intra-modular ones, which are—by hypothesis—suitably computationally frugal.

Although pretence as such doesn't require language, I shall argue in Section 3 that children's capacities for pretence are greatly enhanced as soon as language, and a capacity for mental rehearsal of speech, are put into place. And just as the function of pretence is to enhance creative generation of action schemata, so is it also to enhance the creative (practical-concern-independent) generation of *speech* action schemata. All this will require some explaining, however.

3   Creativity and Inner Speech

My thesis is that the ultimate basis of all forms of creativity lies in the creative generation of action schemata, and that such creativity begins during infancy in the form of pretend play. Now speech, of course, is an action (as is Signing). So we should expect that the same mechanisms that prime and activate novel action schemata will operate in the case of language too. Recall how the similarity in shape between a banana and a telephone handset will prime and weakly activate the concept TELEPHONE. Then not only will the latter prime some of the action schemata suggested by the affordances of telephones, but so will it also prime *speech* act schemata that contain the *word* 'telephone'. Hence the child might activate and rehearse (in inner speech) the schema for uttering the words, 'That is a telephone', or (since the concept GRANDMA will also be primed by the priming of TELEPHONE) the words, 'Grandma talks on the telephone', might be assembled. Such sentences, globally broadcast by the auditory system (or visual system, in the case of Sign), will be processed by the language comprehension module, and a propositional content extracted and likewise broadcast to the entire suite of belief-generating modules and motivational modules, which respond accordingly. The result might be a desire to talk to Grandma on *that*, hence issuing in an episode of pretend play.

Some of the other examples that we have discussed might also be initiated by the creative generation of a speech act schema. The initial step is to generate the *sentence* (either overtly, or silently in 'inner speech'), 'I am a cowboy', or, 'I have an invisible friend called "Wendy".' (How this might happen will be discussed in a moment.) This is received by the language comprehension system, and the content of the sentence—*I am a cowboy*, in the first of the above examples—gets extracted. Since this content isn't generated by a belief-creating module, but rather from mental rehearsal of an action schema, it gets flagged as a supposition before being received as input by the belief-generating and desire-generating modules. The latter then set to work drawing inferences from it, such as, I RIDE HORSES, and generating emotional reactions.

If the child finds cowboys and their activities to be admirable, then when the representation, I AM A COWBOY, is received by the motivational modules, he will experience some sort of glow of satisfaction. Likewise if the suppositionally flagged representation, I RIDE HORSES, is used to construct a motor schema of the child riding a horse (legs bowed and apart, one hand holding reigns, the other holding a whip), which is then used to generate an image of the child riding a horse. The resulting image is received by the motivational modules, and if the child finds not only cowboys but also the horse-riding activities of cowboys to be admirable, then a positive emotional reaction will be the result. And the same sorts of mechanisms described in Section 2 will then provide the child with a motive to enact the mentally rehearsed action schema. Moreover, the full execution of the action schema will be sustained by the motivational rewards that the child receives by representing what he is doing under the description, I AM A COWBOY RIDING A HORSE (which is the most abstract specification of the relevant action schema).

A similar story can be told for the child who pretends to be a bus or a steam-train. Initially the sentence, 'I am a steam-train', is constructed and rehearsed. The language-comprehension system extracts the Mentalese representation, I AM A STEAM-TRAIN, which is flagged as a supposition and received as input by the various conceptual modules. Some of these access the information that steam-trains have wheels, that they go, 'Chuff, chuff, chuff', that when the driver pulls the chord they go, 'Whooo, whooo', and so forth. Now by this time the child will have learned that pretend play is rewarding. So a new goal may be generated: *I want to act as a steam-train acts*, or perhaps, *I want to pretend to be a steam-train*. The child then sets to work seeking analogies between a steam-train and himself (e.g., if his arms moved in circles with elbows bent, then they might resemble wheels in motion), and assembling an appropriate motor schema from the various elements. And this is then enacted as above.

3.1 Selecting What to Say

Some forms of pretence begin with an episode of inner speech, on this account—an act of mentally rehearsing a linguistic-utterance action-schema. But where do such utterance action schemata come from? How do they get assembled and selected from amongst the unlimitedly many things that the child *could* say to herself? Sometimes such utterance rehearsals will be sparked or primed by elements of the child's context, whether external or cognitive, just as with other action rehearsals generally. Thus the utterance, 'I talk to Grandma on the telephone', might be primed by the sight of a banana, or by a mental image of a banana caused from some other source (hearing the word, say). But sometimes sentences might be formulated and rehearsed that *aren't* in any way sparked by the context. And then the question is how this can happen.

Recall that the capacity for mental rehearsal of speech is a manifestation of the more-general capacity for mental rehearsal of action. We suggested in Chapter 4 that this capacity might be deployed so as to help people to know which utterances might be worth making, enabling them to predict the likely effects of those utterances on others. But *this* mechanism can't be the one that is operative in the case of solitary play not primed by the context, since the child isn't then in the business of *telling* anyone anything. So what explains why the child should rehearse an utterance schema at all, in such circumstances? And how does the child go about selecting an appropriate utterance to rehearse?

I think that this isn't necessarily such a difficult problem. For suppose that the child has learned, through pretend play not involving language or from observing the example of others, that pretend play is rewarding. Then when looking for something to play in the absence of any existing suggestion or idea, the child just has to search amongst possible fillers for the sentence schemata, 'I am a....' [cowboy, nurse, and so on], 'I am Φing' [riding a horse, bathing a baby, and so on], or, 'I have....' [an invisible friend, wings, and so on]. And various search heuristics can then be imagined. The child might attempt to recall some admirable things, activities, or types of people. She might attempt to recall a role that she has played, or observed others play, in the past. Or she could search under a more abstract description, such as, 'things that I could pretend to be, do, or have that would be in some way surprising, remarkable, or funny'. (I would guess that the dead cat role-play was hit upon using some variety of this last heuristic.) Or, finally, possible fillers for these sentence schemata might be selected at random.

Which sub-system is it that conducts the search amongst possible completions of these sentence schemata, however, and that executes the various search heuristics? For it surely isn't plausible that this should be a conscious, whole-person, activity. Recall from Chapter 2.7 that the human mind (like the minds of other animals) will contain multiple practical-reasoning modules, each concerned with a specific type of motivation. Some of these modules will be innate, while others will have been constructed by some sort of learning mechanism. Each will search for the types of information relevant to its proprietary goal, and will attempt to recruit certain types of action schemata in the service of that goal. Some of these search locations will be innately specified, too, but some, no doubt, will be learned. And it will be just such a practical-reasoning module that is operative, I suggest, when the goal in question is pretend play.

3.2 What Does Language Add?

What difference does language make to the creative thought, play, and behavior of young children? First and foremost, heuristics for sentence selection like those indicated above give the child a way of generating new thoughts for consideration, leading to new episodes of pretence, independently of any prior environmental or cognitive priming. This might be expected greatly to extend the range and variety of types of play that we see, enabling children to amuse themselves even in conditions of minimal stimulation, without external props. And in so doing, of course, the child will be practicing and developing heuristics for fruitful creative sentence production, some of which might then be adapted in the service of other goals.

Moreover, once the child's language system is operative, then language won't only have a contribution to make in initiating a new pretence, of course. For mental rehearsals of speech can be used to supplement or extend an episode of pretence at any point, as well as forming a constitutive part of the pretend-episode action schema, in many cases. (A child who is playing with her doll and pretending to bath a baby needs to talk to the baby, too, since this is what parents characteristically do.) Thus a child pretending to hold a tea party with her dolls might at some point think to herself, in mentally rehearsed speech, 'Now where is teddy? I'm sure teddy would like to join us', and get up to get teddy from her bed; after which the game continues with an extra player. And so on and so forth. One might expect that the pretend play of a child capable of speech would be greatly extended and enhanced.

In addition, language probably helps to guide the playing child through scripts that may be familiar but hard to remember. A child who is pretending to be a diner in a restaurant has to recall, rehearse, and execute the sequence of events involved—entering, being shown to a table, receiving a menu from the waiter, listening to the waiter's mention of any daily 'specials', ordering, eating, calling for the check, paying, and leaving. This isn't an easy task. We know that in general young children will verbalize when task demands are great, verbalizing more as task demands increase, and that those who verbalize more tend to be better at problem solving (Diaz and Berk, 1992). By articulating, rehearsing in language, and globally broadcasting each item in the evolving script as it arrives, the child can focus and recruit attention and action on the task in hand. But note that this isn't, as such, a creative use of language. It is rather a way in which language can help to support a creative activity.

3.3 Language in Play and in Testimony

When the child rehearses the sentence, 'Teddy would like to join us', she doesn't really believe any such thing, of course. The prior existence of a system for mental rehearsal of action can perhaps explain why, when she mentally rehearses that utterance in inner speech, she doesn't thereby come to believe that she has really *said* anything. But how are we to explain why the *content* of that item of inner speech should be insulated from issuing in belief, and in particular from belief in the truth of that content? Doesn't this have to be a distinct adaptation? Perhaps so, but it is one that would need to have been in place already, serving at least two distinct functions. One is the speech-rehearsal role discussed earlier. If people are mentally to rehearse utterances in advance of making them in order to predict their effects, the contents of those utterances will need to be flagged in such a way as to prevent them from issuing in unconditional belief. But the second function is the role of sentence-contents in sophisticated testimony, as I shall now briefly explain.

When language was first used for purposes of testimony, one might imagine that the content of an interpreted utterance was fed straight to various inferential systems in the manner of a new belief, giving rise to a suite of additional beliefs (belief in that content itself, belief in the predictable consequences of the truth of that content, and so forth). But there would very soon have been intense pressure for the utterances of others to be monitored for truthfulness before being believed (if this hadn't already been a pressure from the outset). Other people sometimes want to deceive, and they are sometimes in no better position to know something than you are.

Monitoring for truthfulness would have required passing the content of the heard sentence to various inferential systems, checking that content for consistency with one's existing beliefs, and checking its predictable consequences for such consistency. And in more sophisticated versions, one can imaging checking not just for *consistency* but for *plausibility*. (See Chapter 6.6.) Moreover, once these systems are in place, so that the content of an utterance can be entertained and evaluated without the subject yet having any disposition to believe it, one can understand how practices of storytelling can become established, and be enjoyable. For the contents in question would still engage with the motivational systems, just as they do with the various inferential systems. In listening to a story one elaborates a mental model, or mental scenario, consistent with the content of the story; and one responds emotionally to that scenario (Harris, 2000).

3.4 An Empirical Prediction

I have been arguing that some kinds of creativity involve language, in the form of mental rehearsals of speech-act schemata, in inner speech. But some kinds don't involve language, consisting of mental rehearsals of other forms of activity, as when the child rehearses making prodding movements at the banana under the description, DIALING ON A TELEPHONE. But *all* forms of creativity involve either action itself, or mental rehearsals of one sort of action or another, on this account. And herein lies a potential objection. For it might be said that there can surely be forms of creativity that don't involve language, and that don't appear to involve either action or action-rehearsal either. Might not a composer manipulate sounds in auditory imagination without using natural language to direct the process, for example, and without imagining himself playing or singing the sounds either (nor writing them down on a score sheet)?

I postulate that such a thing is only possible as a result of over-learning from imagined playing / singing. As is familiar, well-practiced activities can be undertaken without awareness. Someone walking through the forest will make adjustments for the unevenness of the path, and step over tree roots and so on, without awareness—perhaps focused entirely on the beauty of his surroundings. And a practiced car driver will make many movements in the course of driving—adjusting pressure on the accelerator pedal to control the speed of the car, braking for a corner, or indicating for a turn—again without awareness that he is making them. Likewise, then, I postulate that it may be possible to *rehearse* such actions below the level of awareness. All that one would be aware of would be the results of such rehearsals—the globally broadcast images of sequences of sound, for example.

What motivates these claims? First, there are the data presented by Kosslyn (1994) and others—and discussed in Chapter 2.2—that activated action schemata, in the form of motor imagery, are what drive *manipulations* or *intentional changes* in one's visual (and presumably other) imagery. And secondly, the alternative routes to the generation of imagery, namely episodic memory and conceptual projections back down into the perceptual systems (normally used in the process of object-recognition), seem inadequate to the task, in the present context. It is obvious that novel images of sound can't result from episodic memory, since by hypothesis the sequences in question haven't been heard before. And the other alternative would require the composer to have a detailed *conceptual*/propositional representation of the tune being invented in advance of imagining it, using that propositional representation to drive the imaginative process. This seems intrinsically implausible, and only pushes the question of the origins of creativity back a step. In contrast, we already have good reason to think that action schemata can be creatively generated.

These ideas lead to a straightforward empirical prediction (but not necessarily one that is easy to test). I postulate that no one could be a composer who was neither capable of playing an instrument nor of singing (nor perhaps of writing music, to rule out the possibility that the creative process involves *visual* images of notes on a stave, created by manipulations of motor images of the writing process). I know of no counter-example to this hypothesis.

3.5 *Language as Creator of Novel Thoughts*

Let me stress something about the sort of role that language is playing on this account. This is that in those instances of creative pretence that start from a supposition formulated in natural language, language isn't just serving to augment memory, or anything of that sort. In discussions of the role of language in cognition, some have conceded that it plays *some* role—boosting short-term memory, perhaps, and in general serving as a 'scaffold' for thought—but without introducing anything fundamentally new (Jackendoff, 1996, 1997; Clark, 1998; Varley, 1998, 2002). On my account, in contrast, language serves to introduce some propositional contents into the cognitive system for the very first time, and in a way that would not have been possible otherwise.[13]

Consider the child who begins an episode of pretence by entertaining and rehearsing the sentence, 'I am a cowboy', thereby introducing the suppositional content, *I am a cowboy*, into his mind for what might be the first time. This sentence is *not* generated in what is generally reckoned to be the standard way (Levelt, 1989), beginning with a thought formulated in Mentalese, and then recruiting lexical items and syntactic and phonological knowledge to express that thought in English. Rather, it begins with the child trying out a heuristic for the creative generation of action schemata, completing the sentence-frame, 'I am a...', with a word for an admirable object (in this case, 'cowboy'), perhaps selected at random. Only when this sentence is mentally rehearsed and understood by the language comprehension system, and presented to the various central / conceptual modules, is the content, *I am a cowboy*, thereby entertained.

I argued in Chapter 4.3 that we are only required to make a *small* modification in the standard model of speech production in order for us to explain how language can serve to integrate some thought contents, deriving from different modules, for what might be the first time. The modification being proposed here is more radical, but should still be acceptable, if not wholly uncontroversial. The claim is that action schemata for items of speech can be assembled in the absence of any prior thought-content for them to encode, but rather for purposes of supposition. We can *try out* saying things, either out loud or to ourselves in inner speech, using various heuristics for the generation of such sentences, without previously entertaining in thought the contents of the things that we say. New contents are thereby created, which might go well beyond anything that could ever have been generated as output by our central / conceptual modular systems, whether singly or in combination. Herein lies a good deal of the distinctive creativity of the human mind. (But by no means all of it—remember that speech is just one action amongst others, from my perspective.)

It is, moreover, our capacity for creative assembly of speech action schemata that explains why human thought is fully subject to Evans's (1982) 'Generality Constraint' (discussed in Chapter 2.1). Because I am capable of assembling and recombining the speech actions that would produce each of the component words and phrases, I can frame any sentence allowed by the grammar of my

---

[13] Consistent with this suggestion, Schooler and Melcher (1995) found that shadowing of speech interfered with subjects' capacities to solve an 'insight task' (which requires creative thinking), but not with subjects' capacities to solve an 'analytic task' (which doesn't). Such interference experiments could be much more widely used as a test of some of the ideas being developed in this book.

language. And I can do this without first having to entertain the thought thereby expressed. I can thus rehearse in inner (or outer) speech sentences like, 'The number seven is red', or, 'The number seven has an electric charge that is greater than that of a perfect square', and can subsequently (once these sentences have been processed by my language comprehension system) thereby come to entertain the thoughts, *The number seven is red*, and, *The number seven has an electric charge that is greater than that of a perfect square*. These aren't, of course, thoughts that could ever have been produced by my conceptual modules, whether singly or in combination.

It is thus true of human beings that for any concepts F and a that they possess, they can entertain the thought that Fa; and likewise, for any concepts a, R, and b that they possess, they can entertain the thought that aRb. But this capacity is parasitic upon our linguistic abilities, and on our capacity to activate and recombine the act-schema components of speech actions for purposes of supposition. This makes it all the more obvious that the Generality Constraint is far too restrictive as an account of what it takes for an organism to be a genuine concept user, or to entertain genuine thoughts. (At least this is so when the Generality Constraint is interpreted in its causal form, which requires that it should be *causally* possible for thinkers to entertain any permutation of concepts that they possess. Recall from Chapter 2.1 that there is an innocent metaphysical version of the constraint, which is entailed by the claim that the creature's thoughts are compositionally structured.)

4 Autism and the Evolutionary Functions of Pretence

I have sketched an account of the cognitive underpinnings of creative pretence that begins from a prior capacity for mental rehearsal of action schemata. By being globally broadcast, such rehearsals recruit the operations of a suite of belief-generating and motivation-generating modules for purposes of problem solving. And the additional adaptation that leads to pretend play is a disposition to rehearse action schemata that aren't grounded in beliefs about the child's current circumstances. All of this seems computationally feasible, making fast and frugal use of the mind's existing resources. I shall now return to the question of the evolutionary function of the disposition to pretend.

4.1 The Function of Pretence

Given the cognitive similarities between childhood pretend play and adult creative thinking and reasoning, it seems very plausible that what the former is *for* is to practice and develop the latter. Just as the kinds of play displayed by the young of most species of animal appear to have been selected-for to practice some of the crucial adult behaviors of the organism, so too has pretend play been selected-for to practice creative thinking, which is a distinctively human phenotypic character. (Or it is distinctively human in the *degree* to which it characterizes human life, at least.) But what, more precisely, is it that it is being practiced? And what might we predict would be the developmental consequences of failure to engage in pretend play?

One obvious thought is that pretend play might be designed to encourage us to engage in creative thinking *more often*. Although I have been taking for granted that apes have a *capacity* for creative generation of action schemata when problem solving, they don't appear to exercise this capacity a whole lot. We can suppose that action schemata are only rehearsed when there is an urgent need to do so; and that only those action schemata that are salient in the context, or are somehow cued by aspects of the context, get activated. But human creative thinking is a great deal more common than this, and it can range much more widely. We spend much of our waking lives entertaining ideas that aren't factually based, building imaginary scenarios of one sort or another. And many of these scenarios aren't remotely related to current circumstances.

One likely function of pretend play, then, is to get us used to rehearsing action schemata that are sparked by more-or-less remote similarities with aspects of the environment or the previous cognitive context, much as the child's episode of pretending to telephone Grandma is sparked by the similarity in shape between the banana and a telephone handset. This would lead us to entertain a much *wider* range of imagined scenarios, and also to engage in mental rehearsal much more often. And our prediction should be that someone who is deprived of opportunities for pretend play during childhood will be relatively impoverished in their creative problem-solving abilities as an adult. They might rehearse some of the more obvious possibilities, but they should be comparatively uncreative in the strategies that they consider and attempt.

Recall, also, the hypothesized role of natural language in pretend play. By mentally rehearsing sentences in inner or outer speech whose contents bear no relation to the facts ('I am a cowboy', 'I am a steam-train', 'I am a dead cat', 'I have an invisible friend'), children may be led to engage in episodes of pretence that wouldn't have occurred to them otherwise, and they reap emotional rewards for doing so. Hence another likely function of childhood pretence is to get us used to rehearsing sentences whose contents bear little or no relation to current circumstances, and independently of any communicative intention. And our prediction should be that someone deprived of opportunities for pretend play during childhood should engage in this sort of inner speech much less often.

I also suggested, moreover, that language would play further supplementary roles in childhood pretend play. Language is used as an intrinsic part of many of the play sequences (pretending to talk to Grandma on the telephone; talking with an imaginary friend; talking while pretending to bathe a baby; etc.). Language may help the child to recall and follow familiar scripts. And language is also used to introduce additional assumptions into the pretence ('Here comes Teddy to join the party'; etc.). Once again this will practice the child in non-assertoric uses of language (activating utterance schemata that aren't expressive of belief). And the child will also gain practice at using language *appropriately* and *fruitfully* within the scope of an assumption (in this case, within a game of pretence).

4.2 Predictions for Autism

Our account therefore generates the following predictions: someone deprived of pretend play as a child should show impoverished problem-solving abilities when older; and someone deprived of pretend play should also engage rather less in inner speech as an adult. Both predictions are borne out by data from people with autism. (Admittedly, the data are only robust in respect of the first prediction; in respect of the second, there exists only one small-scale study.) For it is well known that one of the main diagnostic criteria for autism is the absence of pretend play (Wulff, 1985). And, just as predicted, older autistic people have well-documented problems of executive function (Russell, 1998). In particular, they tend to display a certain rigidity and perseverance in their approach to problem solving, sticking with failing strategies instead of casting around creatively for novel ones.

Moreover, one small-scale study has been conducted with three high-functioning autistic men that used the introspection-sampling method devised by Hurlbert (Hurlbert et al., 1994; for the original studies with normal and schizophrenic people, see Hurlbert, 1990, 1993). None of the three reported any inner speech, consistent with the account of the function of pretend play sketched above. Now, this might just be an accident of small sampling. But given that *all* normal people engage in inner speech some of the time, and that most are found to engage in inner speech on more than fifty percent of occasions sampled (Hurlbert, 1990), it looks as though there might be something genuine going on here that needs explaining. The explanation comes readily to hand if one of the functions of childhood pretend play is to encourage people mentally to rehearse utterances that aren't intended for communication.

We have provided an account of childhood pretence that brings out quite clearly the cognitive similarities with adult creative cognition, then; and our suggestions about the evolutionary / developmental function of pretence seem to be borne out in the case of autism. But it may be a further advantage of the account if it can explain *why* autistic children don't engage in pretend play in the first place. To that I now turn.

4.3 Explaining the Absence of Pretence in Autism

One important fact that should be emphasized in this context is that autistic children *can* pretend when prompted to do so, but they appear to lack any motivation for, or interest in, pretending—they say that they can't see the point (Lewis and Boucher, 1988; Jarrold et al., 1993). Admittedly, autistic children are also somewhat less good at pretending than are normal children. For example, when prompted to do or to be as many things as they can think of in the space of a minute, the autistic children generate significantly fewer pretend episodes than do normal controls. But this is exactly what should be predicted if part of the function of pretence is to practice the creative process. For then if autistic children haven't engaged very much in pretence before, we should expect them to be much less creative at it.

If we make two further assumptions about the nature of autism, then I think we can explain why it is that autistic children *don't* pretend while they nevertheless retain the *capacity* for pretence. One is that autism at least *involves* a mind-reading deficit of some sort. This is now well established (Baron-Cohen, 1995), although it remains controversial whether it is problems with mind-reading that lie at the very basis of the syndrome (Russell, 1998; Hobson, 2002). The second assumption is that autism involves some systematic delay or deficit in *all* of the main elements of mind-reading, not just in those aspects of it that deal with belief / desire psychology. This second assumption will require some explanation. Most developmental psychologists believe that mind-reading emerges in stages. Infants have the capacity to identify intentional agents, and to attribute simple goals to such agents (Gergely et al., 1995; Johnson, 2005). Two-year-old children understand some aspects of perception and desire, but still lack the capacity to solve false-belief tasks (Repacholi and Gopnik, 1997). Then four-year-old children have a fully representational understanding of mind—they know that beliefs are representational states that can *partially* represent a fact or situation, or that can *mis*represent it (Wellman, 1990).

We might think of this developmental process either in terms of the gradual unfolding over time of a single mind-reading system, or in terms of the different component parts of the mind-reading system developing at different times, perhaps with each emerging part being triggered into growth and/or activity by the input provided by the previous one (Baron-Cohen and Swettenham, 1996). (As massive modularists, we should perhaps prefer the latter hypothesis. See also Nichols and Stich, 2003.) But either way, we could think of the autistic deficit as involving a significant developmental delay to the early-developing system, which then cascades through the delayed / damaged development of the later-developing systems or components of the overall mind-reading system.

The evidence relevant to our second assumption isn't unequivocal. What is *very* well established is that older autistic children have significant problems with the later-developing aspects of mind-reading, especially false-belief tasks and the like (Baron-Cohen, 1995). But since language tends to develop late in autistic children (if at all), and since autism isn't often diagnosed until after the age of three, little testing has been done with young autistic children. However, when older autistic children are tested on the simplest tasks, they do seem to continue to have difficulties in attending to and identifying socially generated stimuli like speech (Ceponiene et al., 2003), as well as the patterns that are characteristic of human movement (in the form of moving point light displays; Blake et al., 2003).

In addition, there is also a good deal of clinical evidence that young autistic children have difficulties with the agency aspects of mind-reading. They are said to treat other people as *objects* rather than agents, for example—sitting on an adult as if she were a piece of furniture, leading an adult by the hand and then pushing the hand in the desired direction, seemingly treating it as a useful *tool* like a stepladder or a broom, and so on. Moreover, the very fact that there is a significant language delay amongst even high-functioning autistic children is evidence that goal-attribution and intention-attribution are delayed in such children. (The majority of autistic children never acquire language at all.) For Bloom (2002) argues convincingly that word learning depends crucially on a capacity to read the referential intentions of speakers (and also on other more general abilities that aren't damaged in autism).

Suppose, then, that our two assumptions are granted. What might be predicted concerning the pretend behavior of autistic children? Well first, we would predict that they should retain the *capacity* for pretence. For there is nothing in our account of the latter that seems to require mind-reading abilities. But we would also predict, I think, that autistic children might find it difficult to derive the normal motivational rewards from pretend activity, and that they might therefore not engage in such activities much or at all. For recall why the child from our earlier example finds pretending to be a cowboy rewarding. By representing the movements that he is making and the sounds that he is uttering *as* those of a cowboy riding a horse, he is representing himself to be something that he finds admirable; and this is emotionally rewarding. But if autistic children have difficulty in understanding and representing actions and agency, then they might have difficulty representing what they are doing in such a way; and hence they would derive no emotional reward from it.

Let me work through this example in just a little more detail by way of emphasizing the point. An autistic boy might well know quite a bit about cowboys and what they do; and he, like many little boys, might find the idea of being a cowboy attractive. If prompted to suppose that he *is* a cowboy, then, he should have no difficulty in assembling an appropriate motor schema and acting upon it (just as we find to be the case; Lewis and Boucher, 1988). So he skips along with the *intention* of being a cowboy riding a horse (conditional upon the assumption that he is a cowboy, of course). So far, there are no problems on the output / behavioral side. But in order to derive pleasure from what he is doing, the representation of himself *as a cowboy* has to be received as input by the motivational systems. And this requires the mind-reading system to be capable of 'seeing' his own movements in that light.

More strictly: the boy's mind-reading system, receiving visual, auditory, and proprioceptive input concerning his own movements and sounds, has to be able to interpret them *as* the movements and sounds of a cowboy riding a horse. (This is actually a kind of 'seeing as' not unlike seeing a cloud *as* a dragon, say.) The way in which this might work could be along the lines of the 'enzyme model' of modularity discussed by Barrett (2005), which was outlined in Chapter 4.1. Perhaps the boy's mind-reading system needs to 'tag' the perceptions of his own movements with the conceptual representation, COWBOY RIDING A HORSE, in such a way that the result is then globally broadcast to all the central / conceptual modules, including the motivational ones. But if attributions of agency and interpretations of action are slow and awkward (or otherwise difficult) for the autistic child, then we might expect this to be problematic. And to the extent that the child has difficulties with action-attribution, then he won't be able to reap the motivational rewards of his own behavior.

5 A Contrasting Theory of Pretence and Creativity

In the present section I shall compare and contrast the account of creativity and pretence sketched above with the best-worked-out alternative model of pretence on the market today. This is the account provided by Nichols and Stich (2003), which will also serve (under one interpretation, at least) as an exemplar of 'thought-first' theories of creativity (to be contrasted with my own 'action-based' theory).

5.1 Nichols and Stich's Model

Nichols and Stich (2003) argue that in order to explain the phenomenon of pretence, we need to postulate the existence of a 'possible worlds box', distinct from the 'belief box' and 'desire box'. This is a working memory system in which representations of alternative possible worlds are held, being elaborated through interactions with the subject's beliefs and belief-generating inferential systems. They also postulate the existence of a 'script elaborator', which has the function of introducing extra suppositions into the course of an episode of pretence (as when the child who is pretending to telephone Grandma pretends that Grandma has answered, and has asked her about school). But since they actually think that the script elaborator creates the initial supposition, too, which begins an episode of pretence, it would be better to call it the 'supposition generator'.

Taken in one way, there is no inconsistency between these proposals and the model sketched earlier in this chapter. Indeed, the latter could be seen as a more-detailed account of how the possible worlds box and the supposition generator are implemented. Suppositions would be created via the activation and mental rehearsal of action schemata (including sentences of 'inner speech'). And the tagging of motivational and belief-like states for their dependency on the relevant globally broadcast suppositions, when those states are generated by the central / conceptual modules receiving act-schemata rehearsals as input, could be seen as an implementation of Nichols and Stich's possible worlds box and its interactions with inferential systems.

Read in this first (weak) way, the possible worlds box and supposition generator are mere relabelings of the capacity to hold in mind and reason with a hypothetical scenario, and the capacity to create such scenarios in the first place. If this is how the account is intended, then it isn't a competitor with the one sketched earlier in this chapter. There is some reason to think that Nichols and Stich don't merely intend their model in this weak way, however. For they postulate links between the possible worlds box and some, but not all, other systems. (See Figure 5.1.) Thus they suggest that the possible worlds box can interact with a set of inference systems, but not directly with motivational (desire-generating) systems. And they suggest (by omission) that the supposition generator is connected only to the possible worlds box, receiving no inputs from motor-control systems, and having no connections with perceptual systems.

We can read Nichols and Stich's account more robustly and realistically, then—taking their box-and-arrow diagrams to postulate a set of distinct interacting systems, not just as labels for a set of capacities. And read in this

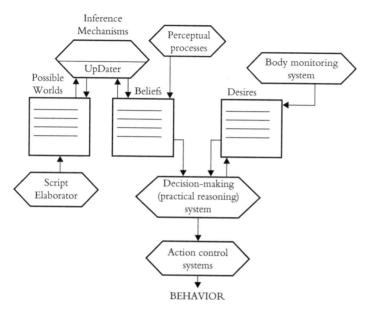

Figure 5.1. Nichols and Stich's account of pretence

way, the account really is in direct competition with my own. Whether or not Nichols and Stich themselves intend their account in this stronger way, I propose to evaluate it in that light. For only in that case is there a competitor hypothesis on the table for us to consider.[14]

5.2 Suppositions and Motivation

One distinctive feature of the Nichols and Stich model is that the possible worlds box has no connections to the motivational, desire-generating, systems. While the possible worlds box provides input to the suite of inferential systems that generate beliefs, it provides no input to the desire box, nor to the systems that create emotions.

One immediate question to arise, then, is how Nichols and Stich are to explain *why* people engage in pretence. In the account presented in Section 3 above, pretence was said to generate motivational rewards of various sorts, through representing oneself *as* being or doing what one *wants* to be or do. But this requires suppositional states to be taken as input by the motivational and emotion-generating systems. What Nichols and Stich actually say is that

---

[14] For more detailed development of the criticisms of Nichols and Stich's (2003) account of pretence that I sketch here, as well as for critical discussion of Currie and Ravenscroft (2002), see Carruthers (2006b).

pretenders have the desire 'to behave in a way that is similar to the way some character or object behaves in the possible world whose description is contained in the possible worlds box' (2003, p.37). They suggest that some sort of generic desire of this sort is innate, and is what explains the activity of pretending.

One problem with this suggestion is that the proposed desire appears to be much too broad. Surely I don't have the desire to behave in the way that *any* agent or thing represented in my possible worlds box behaves. When I entertain the supposition that the Supreme Court may repeal *Roe versus Wade*, I feel no impulse to behave in the manner of a Supreme Court Justice. And when Galileo entertained the supposition that the Earth moves round the Sun, I doubt whether he felt any impulse to move around in circles himself. So some way will have to be found to restrict the scope of the pretence-motivating desire—it will only be the desire to behave in a manner similar to the way that *some* of the things that I represent in my possible worlds box would behave. But it is hard to see how one might generate a definite hypothesis from this vague proposal.

Another (related) problem with Nichols and Stich's idea is that it can't explain the *patterning* that we see in children's pretence. As I noted earlier, for the most part children pretend to do or to be things that they find in some way admirable. This is readily explained if the reason why they do them is that, by representing themselves *as* doing / being something admirable while they act, they quasi-satisfy the underlying desires, and hence reap emotional rewards from so doing. But this isn't an account that is available to Nichols and Stich, if they maintain that suppositions aren't taken as input by the motivational systems.

Moreover (and again relatedly), this component of Nichols and Stich's model seems straightforwardly incorrect unless (implausibly) it is restricted in such a way as to be an account of the role of motivation in pretence *only*, and not its role in suppositional reasoning more generally. For as we all know, suppositions *do* engage with motivational and emotional systems. If I suppose that my boss might evaluate my performance negatively, for example, I can feel depressed or angry as a result. The account provided in Section 3, in contrast, is able to take full advantage of Damasio's (1994) model of suppositional reasoning, and of the way in which suppositions generate emotional reactions that can then be monitored, leading to adjustments in motivation towards (or against) the supposed scenario.

Nichols and Stich could, however, alter their account in such a way as to answer the above objections. (Indeed, in his recent writing Nichols acknowledges that suppositions interact with emotion systems; see his 2004 and forthcoming.) They could include additional arrows in their model from the possible worlds box to the desires box and to the systems whose function it is to generate desires and emotions. And they could embrace an emotional-rewards account of the reasons why children pretend, modeled closely on the account sketched in Sections 2 and 3 above. This would still leave them with a theory that is in competition with my own, differing over the format of the supposition generator, in particular.

5.3 *Thought-Based Versus Action-Based Creativity*

The main remaining difference between Nichols and Stich's model and my own, is that on their account the supposition generator is purely propositional, and has no connections either with motor-control systems or with perceptual systems. What the supposition generator does is generate a fully conceptual, propositional, representation of a supposed possibility. For example, it creates a thought (in suppositional mode) with the content, *The banana is a telephone*. This thought is then received as input by the various belief-generating and (we can now allow) desire-generating inferential systems. At no point in this process do perceptual images need to be produced.

According to the account articulated in Sections 2 and 3, in contrast, the concept TELEPHONE is weakly activated by virtue of the similarity between the banana in question and a telephone handset. The 'boosting mechanism' that is the adaptation responsible for pretend play then uses this as the basis on which to activate some related action schemata (perhaps especially those that can be described as 'affordances' of telephones). These are mentally rehearsed, using feedback loops from motor-control systems to the visual system (and other perceptual systems) to create sequences of images that are (in the manner of perceptual states generally) globally broadcast and taken as input by a whole suite of belief-generating and desire-generating inferential systems. (See Figure 2.8.) So on this account the initial supposition is an action schema, and it needs to give rise to imagistic states in order to receive further elaboration within the 'possible worlds box'.

My own account appeals to processes that we already have reason to believe in, then. There are good reasons to think that perceptual and quasi-perceptual (imagistic) states are globally broadcast to a wide range of inferential systems for forming memories, for creating new beliefs and emotions, and for practical reasoning (Baars, 1988, 1997, 2002, 2003; Dehaene and Naccache, 2001; Dehaene et al., 2001, 2003; Baars et al., 2003; Kreiman et al., 2003). And there is good reason to think that motor schemata can be used to create and transform visual images (Kosslyn, 1994; Turnbull et al., 1997; Ganis et al., 2000; Richter et al., 2000; Kosslyn et al., 2001; Lamm et al., 2001). And there are also good reasons, I claim, for thinking that a limited capacity to reason with suppositions in the form of mental rehearsals of potential actions might have long pre-dated the evolution of human beings. What humans have in addition is a disposition to engage in childhood pretence. There would therefore only have needed to be a *small* evolutionary benefit accruing from pretence, in order for the novel disposition to generate suppositions that aren't so directly related to the actual environment to emerge. For all of the basic connections and systems would already have been in place in our great-ape / hominid ancestors.

A thought-first account, in contrast, can't similarly build on the existence of known systems and processes. The supposition generator would somehow have to be built *ab initio*, as would a specialized propositional working-memory system (a 'possible worlds box'). And input and output connections would need to be constructed from the possible worlds box to each of the belief-generating and desire-generating systems with which it is to interact. For there is no reason to think that any of this would already have been in existence, waiting to be co-opted into the service of creative thinking when the latter began to make its appearance.

This has two implications for the evolution of our capacity for supposition in general, and for pretend play, in particular. One is that there would then need to have been some very significant selection pressure at work. For evolution would need to build a whole new cognitive system, with myriad input and output links to other systems. And the other implication is that it therefore becomes difficult to tell a sensible story about piecemeal evolvability. Does the supposition generator get connected up to other inferential systems one by one, for example? If so, how?

Notice, too, that it isn't enough just to build connections between the possible worlds box and other systems, since there would also have to be corresponding adaptations within each of the inferential systems to which the possible worlds box feeds its representations. The adaptation would be: when you receive input from the possible worlds box, you *only* pass your output back to that box, not onwards as a belief to any other system with which you may be connected; or if you do pass it on, you pass it on tagged so as not to be believed. Something like this is necessary to explain how inferential systems that get to work on a supposition don't issue in beliefs.

This makes it even more difficult to see how the possible worlds box could have evolved. Granted, it is of considerable use to be able to engage in conditional and suppositional reasoning. But how could such a capacity ever get started, on the model under consideration here? For in the absence of the adaptations to each of the receiver systems, serving to insulate suppositions from issuing in belief and action, the creation of a possible worlds box would have been disastrous. The only option that I can see would be that the possible worlds box evolved in conjunction with the required corresponding adaptation in its consumer systems one at a time. That box first emerged linked to just one inferential system, where that system also happened to be altered in such a way as to pass on any subsequent output tagged so as not to be believed. And then this adaptation was copied into each of the other inferential systems as new input-connections were built to them.

The account sketched in Sections 2 and 3 above, in contrast, builds upon the cognitive architecture defended in Chapter 2.8, according to which the mind already contains a capacity for *action* rehearsal.[15] Motor schemata can be activated in suppositional mode, for the purpose of testing the consequences of actions. Here I think one can get a handle on how such a system might evolve, because one can see the significance and usefulness of adapting just a single inference system in such a way that, when an act-rehearsal is received as input, the output of the inference is limited in its effects. Consider, for example, imagining that I strike one stone with another, or imagining that I make a specific type of movement within someone else's sight. And with that system in place, it would only have required small changes to begin the *creative* generation and rehearsal of action schemata.

By the same token, the action-based account sketched in Sections 2 and 3 can help us to bridge the divide between ourselves and other animals. For virtually all of the systems implicated in action-based creativity would long have pre-existed human beings. This is true for associative partial activations amongst concepts, for the mental rehearsal of action schemata—generating imagery of the actions being undertaken or under consideration—and for the global broadcast of some of the images so generated. Granted, humans are, in many ways, rather special. But it is surely a huge plus-mark in favor of a theory if it can explain (as the action-based theory of creativity surely can) how that specialness emerged against a backdrop of animal capacities, which collectively provided most of the main elements of the ensuing human-specific system.

Perhaps there are further things that could be said on behalf of Nichols and Stich's (2003) model, at this point (interpreted as a thought-first account). But it should be clear that their theory faces problems and challenges that don't exist on my own account, which for the most part utilizes pre-existing systems and pre-existing connections amongst systems. Other things being equal, then, the action-based theory should be preferred.

---

[15] And note, too, that we argued in Section 1 that there is a kind of creative action-generation that can't be reduced to thought-generation. (Recall on-line improvisation in jazz.) Given that we need to believe in creative act-generation in any case, it is surely profligate to believe in a separate capacity for creative thought-generation as well, if we can reasonably avoid doing so.

6 Creativity and Metaphor

I have been arguing that the cognitive basis of human creativity lies in a capacity for creative generation and rehearsal of action schemata—some aspects of which are prior to language, and some aspects of which are dependent upon language. Some people have proposed, however, that the human cognitive system contains a pre-linguistic capacity to map one domain onto another, giving rise to metaphorical conceptual schemes; and that this is a large part of the explanation of our distinctive creativity. (As we shall see in Chapter 6, metaphor and analogy play a big role in science generally, and in scientific innovation in particular.)

For example, the domain of debate and argument can be mapped onto the domain of warfare, giving rise to an elaborate system of concepts summarized by the slogan, 'Argument is war' (Lakoff and Johnson, 1980). And it is suggested that such conceptual schemes are non-linguistic in character, receiving expression *in* metaphorical language, rather than being reflections *of* it. So on such an account the basic mechanism of inter-modular integration and creative content-generation will be this domain-general structure-mapping capability, rather than anything involving motor control or natural language.

The fact that there exists a correlation between cross-domain conceptual mapping and metaphorical language is one thing, however; the question of the direction of causation here is quite another. It might be possible to claim that such conceptual mappings begin initially with the integrative and creative functions of language. Or so, at least, I shall argue.

For these purposes it is important to distinguish between live metaphors and dead ones. Live metaphors are fresh creations and strike us (if they are effective) with the force of insight. Dead metaphors are once-live metaphors that have been used so commonly that it takes hardly any effort to process them, and their metaphorical status is barely discerned. For notice that the metaphorical conceptual systems studied by Lakoff and Johnson (1980, 1999) and others are dead ones, enshrined in common patterns of speech. If someone says, for example, 'Don't worry; I'm on top of the situation', we probably won't even notice that a metaphor has been used. And it is very doubtful whether the spatial meaning of 'on top of' needs to be accessed in order to understand it.

In reply it might be denied that the live / dead distinction can carry much weight, on the grounds that all dead metaphors are still 'live' for children who hear them for the first time. But actually, it is far from clear that children have to understand and process these dead metaphors *as* metaphors. If a mother says to a child, 'Don't worry, Daddy is on top of the situation', how does the child understand her? One possibility is that it is just like a case of *ambiguity*, as when she says, 'Daddy is sitting on the bank, fishing', at a stage when the child understands bank-with-money but not bank-of-river. The child first accesses the familiar meaning, and realizes that it can't be what is meant. So he hunts around for the intended meaning in the context, and on finding it, opens a separate 'bank' file to which that meaning is attached. Thereafter there are two separate lexical entries for 'bank'. Likewise, then, with 'on top of'. The child realizes that something spatial can't be what is meant, and hunts around for what is intended in the circumstances, figuring out that it means something like, 'is dealing with successfully'. That then gets attached to 'on top of' as a separate lexical entry. At no time is a metaphor processed and understood as such.

Dead metaphors express conceptual systems that were once built creatively, but which are now acquired and used in the manner of regular, non-metaphorical, concepts. So the real question is whether the capacity to create, and to understand, *live* metaphors is independent of, and/or more basic than, the creative capacities discussed thus far. And in particular, the question is whether humans possess some general pre-linguistic structure-mapping capability that can map one concept or domain onto another, and then use the structure of the one to generate novel inferences and/or predictions concerning the other. If there were such a capacity, then this would be an alternative cognitive basis for an important (and distinctively human) form of creativity.

I am not convinced that we need to postulate a form of creativity distinct from those already proposed in earlier sections of this chapter in order to explain our capacity for metaphorical thought, however. A novel metaphor can be initiated in essentially the same sort of way that we envisaged for the analogy between a banana and a telephone handset, resulting from their similarity in shape. All we have to suppose is that when one concept is activated, so will any other concept be (weakly) activated that is similar to it, either in terms of its input-conditions, or in terms of its structure and elements. Hence someone observing an argument between two people (prior to the 'argument is war' metaphor becoming entrenched), and in whom the concept ARGUMENT is fully active, might also on occasion have their WAR concept weakly activated in the circumstances. For the argument in question (like a war) might manifest anger or hatred, and each participant is trying to get the other to concede that he is wrong.

So far this seems very much like the case of the child whose concept TELEPHONE is activated somewhat, by virtue of the similarity in shape between a banana and a telephone handset. But instead of activating related motor schemata, issuing in an episode of pretend play, the co-activation of the two concepts (one fully, one weakly) is used as the basis for entertaining the supposition, either silently or in publicly rehearsed language, 'Argument is war.' This utterance is received by the comprehension sub-system, which globally broadcasts its content to a wide range of central / conceptual modules that set to work drawing inferences from it. Thus if argument is war, then the two sides in an argument will *attack one another* just as they do in war; and one side might try to *overwhelm the other's defenses*, just as happens in war; and so on. These further inferences are explored and evaluated within the scope of the initial supposition; and many of them can find a true interpretation.

Generalizing from this example, then, one might propose that a live metaphor is first created when some sort of structural correspondence or similarity between two phenomena leads to at least weak co-activation of the concepts applying to each. The resulting metaphorical thought is formulated in language by the suppositional system, and fed back as input to the various modular inferential systems. Consequences that are evaluated as true or useful are retained, and the rest discarded. (For example, the playing child is likely to discard from its game the inference, 'If the banana is a telephone, then it won't squish if I squeeze it.') This account presupposes no domain-integrating capacity beyond the language-dependent aspect of the supposer-system.

In terms of such an account it is easy enough to see how culturally entrenched dead metaphors might become established. Wherever two domains are structurally alike in some significant respect, this is likely to lead to weak co-activation of the corresponding concepts on at least some occasions, and hence people will sometimes entertain the supposition that the one domain (or an aspect of the one domain) *is* the other. If there are enough structural similarities between the two domains for the one to serve as a viable partial model of the other (as in the case of, 'Argument is war') then the corresponding modes of speech are likely to become entrenched. Hence we now talk of 'overwhelming someone's defenses', and 'attacking someone's premises', and so forth without giving it a second thought.

Some additional support for these proposals is provided by Shanahan and Baars (2005). They review a variety of computer models of metaphor and of analogical reasoning, concluding that the most psychologically plausible of these models is LISA, developed by Hummel and Holyoak (1997, 2003). And they argue that the structure and operations of LISA map nicely onto a global broadcasting architecture. For a limited number of propositional structures are held in a working memory system at any one time in such a way as to be globally broadcast to a wide range of conceptual systems operating in parallel, which can draw inferences from those propositions. And this proposal, in turn, maps nicely onto those made in the present chapter, provided that we are allowed two further assumptions. One is that global broadcasting always involves sensory / imagistic states (including inner speech). I know of no evidence inconsistent with this assumption, and it is supported by the best-known model of the working memory system (Baddeley, 1986, 1993). And the other is that it is the creative activation of motor schemata (including speech schemata) that issues in such states.

In conclusion of this section, then, I claim that we can explain the deeply metaphorical character of much of our language and speech consistently with my main hypothesis, without having to suppose that people possess some sort of language-independent domain-general structure-mapping capability. And nor does the human capacity to see and to reason with analogies require any such capacity.

7 Scaling up: Creativity in Adulthood

I have argued that creative cognition is ultimately grounded in the creative generation and mental rehearsal of action schemata. I have suggested that such rehearsals can figure in an explanation of the species-specific activity of childhood pretend play. And I have suggested that the function of pretence may be to practice both inner speech and creative content-generation generally. But how, more exactly, is the latter supposed to work? I have sketched how a combination of associative concept-priming and learned heuristics might serve to explain the creativity involved in childhood pretence. But what of creative thought in adulthood? What, for example, of the generation of explanatory hypotheses in science and in ordinary life?

Any attempt at a detailed answer to these questions must fall well beyond the scope of this book. Recall that my goals are twofold. The first is to answer a 'How possibly?' challenge to massive modularity. The second is to say enough about the various elements of the account to make it seem plausible that flexible human cognition should be realized in the interactions of a massive set of modules—or plausible enough, at any rate, for the idea to be worthy of further investigation. My sketch of the very simplest form of creative human cognition, in childhood pretence, might already be sufficient for the first goal. In pursuit of the second, however, something more probably needs to be said before we can have confidence that the results will 'scale up' to more complex forms of adult cognition.

7.1 Creative Hypothesis Generation

Recall, from Chapter 4, the distinction between System 1 and System 2 reasoning processes. One of the System 2 problem-solving strategies that most of us learn (presumably internalizing a successful public strategy of seeking aid from other people) is to formulate *questions* for ourselves in inner speech. ('What am I going to do now?'; 'Where are my car keys?'; 'How can that have happened?'; etc.) These have the function of recruiting into service the network of belief-generating modules, and of directing searches for stored information. Sometimes the information that we need isn't actually available within the mind, however, but can be searched for externally. Yet sometimes we know that there is no direct route to obtaining it, frequently because the information that we want concerns some event in the past. In such cases we often need to seek, and to propose and evaluate, some possible *explanations* of the data that we have available to us in the present. And our question, at this point in our discussion of creativity, is where these proposed explanations are to come from.

In some cases there is a strictly limited list of potential explanations, and hypothesis generation is therefore routine. Suppose, for example, that I have heard a rumor that my wife is having an affair with a colleague at her workplace. I confront her with the allegation, and she denies it. Here there are only two candidate explanations of her denial: either she is telling the truth, and she isn't having an affair; or she is lying, and she is. Nothing creative is required to generate these candidate explanations. I just need to access my knowledge that assertions of fact are either intended to be truthful, or intended to deceive.[16]

Suppose that I raise the question of the explanation of the rumor itself, however. One possibility is that one of my wife's co-workers observed her and her lover in a passionate embrace, and then told others about it, who in turn told yet others, and so on. Another possibility is that someone started just such a sequence of reports with a malicious lie—never really having seen my wife and her colleague embracing; and there might then be a whole range of candidate explanations for such a lie, in turn. Yet another possibility is that the initial report was intended as a joke of some sort, which was misheard or misinterpreted. And yet another possibility is that, as in a game of 'Chinese Whispers', an initially innocent report of some event involving my wife and her co-worker gradually got transformed in the course of each telling into a report of an infidelity.

---

[16] Deciding which of the two is the *better* explanation, in contrast, is another matter entirely—this can't be routinized, and may set me off on an open-ended investigation. The cognitive basis of so-called *inference to the best explanation*, or *abductive inference*, will be discussed in Chapter 6.

There seems to be no obvious way of closing off the list of candidate explanations, here. For there are no end of things which, if they *were* true, might explain the existence of a rumor. (For example, God might have intervened directly—for reasons best known to himself—to create in someone the false memory of having seen my wife and her co-worker in an embrace.) So one problem for us is to explain how we manage to limit ourselves (in general and on the whole) to a set of hypotheses that are *plausible*.

Note that the first three of the above explanations of the rumor are grounded in true generalizations of one sort or another. People who say that P often do so because they have observed that P. People who say that P are often lying. And people who say that P in jest are sometimes misinterpreted. So one obvious strategy in seeking an explanation of an event (in this case, a series of reports of an infidelity) is to look for a generalization that, if it were applicable in this case, would subsume it or otherwise imply it. So in the present case the obvious heuristic strategy is to conduct a search for generalizations about *infidelity* or generalizations about *reports* and/or *rumors*. And provided that memory is organized into networks of content-related files, this should be tractable.

The fourth of the above explanations, in contrast, relies upon a different strategy. It requires noticing a *similarity* between a rumor and a game of Chinese Whispers, insofar as each involves a repetition of the same statement from person to person in a series. For (given this similarity) if a message can become garbled in the one case, then presumably it can likewise become garbled in the other. This illustrates a strategy for successful explanation-generation that is very common in everyday life and (especially) in science—namely, that you should look for some phenomenon that is *similar to* the target to be explained, and then try creating explanations based upon that.

Notice that this *similarity heuristic* for generating explanations it itself very much like the processes we saw to be at work in creating the suppositions that frame an episode of pretend play, such as the similarity in shape between a banana and a telephone, or the similarity in appearance between a doll and a (small!) person. So our suggestion that the function of pretend play may be to practice the child for adult creative thinking is hereby strengthened. What the child is building, through its play, is a disposition to activate thoughts that are grounded in an initial similarity, and then to think and reason within the scope of those suppositions.

This is just one example, of course. No doubt an analysis of others would uncover yet other heuristics for constructing explanations. And no doubt some of these aren't employed generally, but are restricted to (or prioritized within) particular domains. One that often works well in the biological domain, for instance, is the *design heuristic*. When seeking an hypothesis to explain some biological capacity, what one does when using this heuristic is to ask oneself, 'How would I go about *designing* a system with that capacity?' This utilizes a different way of thinking (practical reason rather than theoretical reason), which can often prove fruitful. And what I suggest is that part of what we are doing in the transition from childhood to adulthood is building up a set of heuristics and strategies for creating explanatory hypotheses.

In the very hardest cases—such as will often occur in science—I suggest that what happens is that the circle of search gets increasingly wide, as previous failures to find an adequate explanation push one to try ever more distant and seemingly implausible ideas. In such cases one attempts to find similarities across disparate domains, as when hypothesizing that light might be a *wave*, for example. This is, no doubt, one of the reasons why the timescales for success in science are so long in comparison with everyday cognition. (Often decades, and sometimes centuries, of investigation elapse before an adequate explanation is found; Nersessian, 2002.) These are topics that we shall return to in Chapter 6.

7.2 *The Creative Aspect of Language Use*

Can the ideas sketched in this chapter be extended to explain what Chomsky (1975) calls 'the creative aspect of language use' (CALU)? This is our capacity to generate novel sentences (either in conversation with others or in inner speech) that are relevant in the context without in any sense being determined by it. Chomsky himself thinks that an explanation for the CALU might lie forever outside our cognitive grasp, being too complex and difficult for our limited minds to entertain. It would obviously be a huge plus-mark on the side of massive modularity in general, and the creative-action theory of creativity in particular, if it should enable us to make some progress on this topic. But plainly it won't help merely to postulate a CALU module (as Baker, forthcoming, tentatively does), unless we can explain how that module operates and interacts with others. (On this, Baker is skeptical, and sides with Chomsky.)

Part of my reply to this challenge takes the same form as the disclaimer I made in Section 1.6. Quite plausibly, the detailed processes underlying creative language use are to some degree random or chaotic in character. Certainly they will be *highly* sensitive to myriad aspects of a given speaker's circumstances, learning history, and current and recent psychological states. So we should no more expect to find explanations or predictions of fine-grained aspects of language use than we can expect to find explanations and predictions of fine-grained aspects of the course of a hurricane. No one thinks that it is reasonable to demand that meteorology should ever be able to explain or predict the precise wind speed and direction at a precise spot (e.g. 64 meters due north of the Washington Monument) at a precise time (when the clock begins to strike noon). Nor should meteorologists be required to explain or predict exactly how many raindrops will fall into a given rainfall collection device within a precisely delineated time-period (the first 32 seconds following midday, for example). For we all recognize that there are just too many variables relevant to such phenomena, most of which we can never have access to. But for all that, no one thinks that meteorological phenomena are inherently mysterious. Nor need we thereby be prevented from having good theories of hurricane formation in general, as well as a capacity to make broad predictions.

Likewise, then, in the case of language use. Cognitive science shouldn't be required to explain why someone utters one sentence rather than another at a given moment, or to predict what they will say next. Nor should it be counted as any sort of failure that it doesn't. Rather, what we might reasonably demand is a general account of the mechanisms underlying creative language use, and of the various factors that can influence their operation. This might be sufficient for us to achieve an *understanding* of creative language use (at least in the sense of rendering it unmysterious), in something like the way that meteorologists can understand the various factors that determine the formation and general trajectory of a hurricane.

I have to admit, however, that I can't really provide even this. It would require a book in its own right, the writing of which would require bodies of expertise in linguistics and cognitive science that I simply don't possess. The most that I can realistically hope for is to gesture in the directions in which an understanding of creative language use should be sought, which might be sufficient to justify an expectation of future understanding, as well as warranting continued confidence in the viability of a massively modular approach to cognition. What I shall say is somewhat comparable, in fact, to the suggestion that the formation of hurricanes probably has something to do with local increases in ocean surface temperatures—true and fruitful, perhaps, but hardly deserving of being called an explanation by itself.

One important point to notice is that all uses of language are actions, whether overt (as when one converses with another person or muses aloud in soliloquy) or covert (involving mental rehearsal in inner speech). As such, they are subject to the same range of explanations as any other form of action. And recall from Chapter 2.7 that there are multiple action-control modules associated with different types of motivation, each of which searches in a specific set of locations for information relevant to the satisfaction of that motivation, and each of which attempts to recruit a (limited) range of action schemata in the service of the same type of goal. In that earlier discussion my emphasis was on a variety of innate constraints amongst different species of animal on the sorts of information sought for in the service of different sorts of goal, and on the kinds of action schema that can be recruited to those goals. But it is also very plausible that these modules for action control should be capable of various forms of learning. Indeed, a natural construal of the results of animal conditioning experiments is that a given action-control module can learn, not only what factors (such as the illumination of a light) predict that achievement of the goal in question is possible (and to what extent), but also which action schemata should be recruited in the service of that goal in the circumstances. Thus a rat might learn that it should try pressing one lever with its forepaws rather than another when a given cue is present, for example.

Now notice that all types of human goal are such that they can sometimes be furthered by linguistic activity. Whether you want to strengthen a friendship, woo a mate, protect a child, obtain food, secure material resources, solve an engineering problem, or find your way home, on at least some occasions saying something to someone can help you to get what you want. What we should expect, then, is that each action-controlling module in adult humans should have built up an extensive body of information about the sorts of utterance schemata that can usefully be activated in the service of the goal in question. Thus if you want to make someone like you, one way of doing it is to say something flattering. And if you want to find your way to somewhere, one way of achieving it is to ask someone who knows. And so on and so forth. Then just as the various action-control systems compete with one another to gain control of other sorts of behavior (as we saw in Chapter 2), so they also compete with one another for access to the resources of the language production system. Herein lies one of the likely roots of the unpredictability, in detail, of linguistic behavior.

Recall, too, that processes of action production will generally proceed from an abstract—often highly schematic—representation of the behavior in question, through progressively more concrete and fine-grained implementations of that schema (guided partly by details of the context), until issuing finally in a fully detailed behavior. Suppose, for example, that I am thirsty, and that I form the intention of having a drink. Then depending on the circumstances in which I find myself and what there is to hand (and perhaps my knowledge of what there is in the fridge), I might form the plan of carrying *this* empty glass to the kitchen to get water from the faucet. But I then have to pick the glass up with one hand or the other, and with one sort of grip or another; I have to choose a precise route to the kitchen; and I have to reach to turn the faucet with one hand while holding out the glass with the other, monitoring the level of the water as it rises. And so on. At each stage choices amongst more-detailed motor schemata have to be made, often influenced by their relative ease of implementation (e.g. there is already an empty glass on the desk before me), but sometimes selected at random.

Likewise, I suggest, when speech is recruited to the service of some goal, such as strengthening a friendship. On seeing an old friend again for the first time, I might form the intention of saying something flattering. This is a highly non-specific utterance schema, which then needs to be made progressively more precise, influenced by features of the context (does her hair look recently done? do her clothes look new? and so forth), as well as by background knowledge of my friend's beliefs and values, and perhaps also utilizing mental rehearsal of some of my options to pull in the inferential resources of my mind-reading module. Here, too, at each stage choices need to be made, from the general (should I comment on her clothes or her seeming youthfulness?) to the precise (should I use an active or a passive sentence? should I use this word or that?), partly influenced by similar factors to those noted earlier. But language production is also constrained and partly guided by considerations of relevance, in the technical sense of Sperber and Wilson (1995). That is to say, speakers have the standing goal of achieving significant cognitive effects in the other, while at the same time minimizing the processing effort required from the audience for those effects to be achieved.

This way of seeing speech as a form of action suggests a perspective on sentence production that is even further away from the standard model (Levelt, 1989), which begins with a conceptual representation of the message-to-be-communicated. Often, no doubt, speech production is like this, when one's goal is simply testimony (telling someone that P, for some particular P). But often it isn't. Often the starting point is a specification of a kind of utterance (saying something flattering), which then needs to be made more precise. In such cases the content communicated might be the end-point of the process of speech production, rather than the beginning. And even many cases of normal conversation that *look* as though they might fit the standard model (I tell someone what I did at the weekend; she tells me what she plans to do tomorrow evening), probably don't really do so. For the actual information exchanged is often incidental to the activity, which is really governed by such goals as keeping a conversation going (finding *something* to say), being pleasant to an acquaintance, or whatever.

The processes that govern the assembly and rehearsal of speech-act schemata in *inner* speech, on the other hand, are to a significant degree different, as emerged earlier in this chapter. For what is practiced and developed in childhood pretend play is a disposition to assemble, activate, and rehearse action schemata (including speech-act schemata) that are only loosely connected to the context, or to current goals. In consequence, during much of our waking lives as adults our conscious minds are occupied with sequences of visual images and sentences of inner speech, whose production is partly associative in character. One rehearsed sentence, when globally broadcast and taken as input by the full range of informational and motivational modules, gives rise to a novel cognitive context that can spark the formulation and rehearsal of a very different sentence, in accordance with a variety of acquired sentence-generating heuristics.

Not all inner speech is generated associatively, of course. For sometimes what get rehearsed are candidate sentences intended for public utterance, which are being 'tested out' before being utilized in the service of some goal. On other occasions the sequences instantiate some set of acquired behavioral skills, as when one engages in mental arithmetic. And on yet other occasions inner speech *is* organized and generated in the service of a goal, much as outer speech often is, as when one consciously *thinks through* (in inner speech) to the solution of some practical or theoretical problem. For amongst the skills that most adults have acquired (partly through formal education) are a set of heuristics and dispositions for verbalizing the crucial stages in problem solving.

All this amounts to just the barest sketch of an explanation of the creative aspect of language use, of course. But I hope that I have said enough, both to indicate the general directions in which deeper explanations should be sought, and also to make it seem plausible that those explanations should be looked for within the context of a massively modular account of the architecture of the mind.

8 Conclusion

In this chapter I have tried to show how creative thinking could be realized in a massively modular mind, utilizing some relatively simple dispositions (such as the one deployed in pretend play to 'boost' a weakly activated concept into an activated and rehearsed action schema) together with some simple additional components (such as heuristics for generating sentences for global broadcasting in inner speech). The story that I have told has woven together an hypothesis about the evolutionary and developmental functions of childhood pretence with a sketch of the cognitive mechanisms that are deployed when pretending, especially the creative activation and rehearsal of novel action schemata. And so far as I can tell, there is nothing here that requires us to retreat from our postulation of a massively modular mental architecture.

6

The Cognitive Basis of Science

The human capacity for science has led to the most amazing accomplishments. It has enabled us to transform the world in which we live, often (although by no means always) for the better. We now have earthquake-resistant high-rise buildings, genetically engineered crops, carbon-fiber and stainless steel, motor cars and airplanes, heart-transplants and penicillin, telephones and television, and laptop computers and the internet. And our capacity for science has enabled us to understand much about the underlying structure of the world within us and around us. We now have successful theories of sub-atomic particles and processes, chemical elements and chemical bonding, the structure of DNA and the processes of embryogenesis, the physiology of human and animal bodies, the evolution of living species through natural selection, continental drift and the creation of mountain ranges, nuclear fission and the processes that govern the expansion and extinction of stars and galaxies, as well as theories of the age of the universe itself and the rate at which it is expanding.

Some have claimed that our capacity for science is itself one of the last remaining deep scientific mysteries, comparable to both the origin of the universe and the physical basis of consciousness in its recalcitrance to human understanding (Pinker, 1997). Others have argued that there are principled reasons why our capacity for science, and for 'abductive' reasoning more generally, cannot receive an explanation within the current (or probable future) framework of cognitive psychology. They have urged that we should give up on attempting to make any progress with the problem for the foreseeable future (Fodor, 2000). And it seems *especially* problematic to understand how a capacity for science can exist in a mind that is massively modular in character, given that in the course of scientific thinking anything can in principle connect with anything else, as we shall see in Section 1.

In the present chapter I shall take up this challenge, sketching in outline how the human capacity for science can be realized in the interactions of sets of specialized modules. (Here, as elsewhere in this book, I hope to provide just enough detail to convince readers that a 'How possibly?' question has been answered successfully, while also trying to convince them that the outcome should be thought *plausible* as well.) The account will utilize many of the elements already defended in Chapters 4 and 5, such as a capacity for creative action-generation in general, and for speech-generation in particular; the use of language to integrate contents across modules; learned abstract sentence-transition skills; and the use of cycles of inner (and outer) speech to broadcast thought-contents as input to the suite of conceptual modules, where further inferences can be drawn. But some new elements will also be added. If the resulting account is successful, then we shan't *only* have answered a 'How possibly?' challenge to the thesis of massive modularity, but we shall have provided that thesis with some independent support, by showing how it can help us to make progress with issues that many have regarded as intractable.

1 What does it take to be a Scientist?

By way of background to the discussions that are to follow, in the present section I shall describe some of the main ingredients of the overall scientific process in a very general way, dividing them roughly into *cognitive* elements, *motivational* elements, and *social* elements.

1.1 Cognitive Ingredients of Science

On one view, the goal of science is to discover the causal *laws* that govern the natural world; and the essential activity of scientists consists in the postulation and testing of *theories*, followed by the application of those theories to the phenomena in question (Nagel, 1961; Hempel, 1966). On a contrasting view, science constructs and elaborates a set of *models* of a range of phenomena in the natural world, and then attempts to develop and *apply* those models with increasing accuracy (Cartwright, 1983; Giere, 1992). But either way, science generates principles that are *nomic*, in the sense of characterizing how things *have to* happen (if everything else is held constant), and in supporting subjunctives and counterfactuals about what would happen, or wouldn't have happened, if certain other things were to happen, or hadn't happened.

   Crucial to the activity of science, then, is the provision of theories and/or models to explain the events, processes, and regularities observed in nature. Often these explanations are couched in terms of underlying mechanisms that haven't been observed, and that may be difficult to observe; and sometimes they are given in terms of mechanisms that aren't observable at all. More generally, a scientific explanation will usually postulate entities and/or properties that aren't manifest in the data being explained, and that may be unfamiliar—where perhaps the only reason for believing in those things is that if they did exist, then they would explain the phenomena that puzzle us.

Science also employs a set of tacit principles for choosing *between* competing theories or models—that is, for making an *inference to the best explanation* of the data to be explained. The most plausible account of this is that contained within the principles employed for *good* explanation are enough constraints to allow one to rank more than one explanation in terms of comparative goodness. While no one any longer thinks that it is possible to codify these principles, it is generally agreed that the good-making properties of a theory include the following features:[1]

- *accuracy* (predicting all or most of the data to be explained, and explaining away the rest);
- *simplicity* (being expressible as economically as possible, with the fewest commitments to distinct kinds of fact and process);
- *consistency* (internal to the theory or model);
- *coherence* (with surrounding beliefs and theories, meshing well with those surroundings, or at least being consistent with them);
- *fruitfulness* (making new predictions and suggesting new lines of enquiry); and
- *explanatory scope* (unifying a diverse range of data).

(See Newton-Smith, 1981.)

Under extreme idealization, the scientific process can be seen as breaking down into three distinct stages. First, there is hypothesis generation, in which one or more theories or models are proposed that might explain the target phenomenon in question. Secondly, there is testing, in which the implications of those theories are worked out and either matched against the existing data, or used as the basis on which to search for new data that will discriminate between them, either by further observation or through experimental testing. And then thirdly, there is inference to the best explanation, in which the best

---

[1] Does the uncodifiability of the principles of abduction employed in science cause a problem for computational theories of cognition? For wouldn't the latter require us to specify a precise *algorithm* according to which abductive inferences can be computed? In fact there is no real problem here, for two distinct reasons. One is that according to the explanation that I shall advance in Section 6, abductive inferences emerge out of partly competitive, heuristic governed, interactions between a number of distinct processes (each of which could be algorithmic). The other is that there are individual differences between different scientists in the weights that they attach to the distinct factors. And since science is a heavily social phenomenon (as we shall see shortly) it might be impossible to codify the principles on which *science* proceeds, even if the thinking of each individual scientist were fully algorithmic in character.

of the proposals is accepted (at least tentatively) as correct, as judged by the criteria listed above.[2]

In the context of massively modular models of mind it is important to stress that each of the first and third of the above stages will frequently involve thinking that crosses modular and scientific domains. In formulating hypotheses to explain some set of data, scientists often draw upon analogies with phenomena that are better understood, as when light gets compared to the propagation of waves through water. And when deciding whether or not to accept an hypothesis, any belief, drawn from any domain, can in principle be relevant. As Fodor remarks, 'in principle, our botany constrains our astronomy, if only we could think of ways to make them connect' (1983, p. 105). We will return to these points repeatedly in the sections that follow.

1.2 The Thirst for Knowledge

It is often remarked that we are an *information-hungry* species. Like many other animals, we are inherently curious. But our desire for information goes much, much, deeper than that. We poke and prod at systems that we want to learn about, observing the effects; and in general we target interventions into the world around us in such a way as to extract information from it. But we also take knowledge and truth as explicit goals.

It is our mind-reading capacity that makes it possible for us to take knowledge as a goal. For knowledge is a mental state of a particular sort, and mental-state concepts are embedded in, and are dependent upon, such a capacity, as we saw briefly in Chapter 3. Truth, however, is another matter. For sentences as well as beliefs can be true. So it would be possible for a language-user to take truth as a goal even if she lacked mental-state concepts altogether. Indeed, one way in which autistic people can bootstrap their way into a limited understanding of mind is by modeling *belief* on *assertion* (Wellman et al., 2002). But either way, it seems likely that the capacities to take knowledge and truth as goals are uniquely human, if other species not only lack language, but also any mind-reading capacity (Povinelli, 2000).

It is debatable to what extent science depends upon taking knowledge and/or truth as *intrinsic* or *ultimate* goals. Papineau (2000) makes a plausible case that such goals are, like hunger and the desire for sex, part of our innate endowment. But some have emphasized such competing goals as social prestige, and the winning of major prizes (Kitcher, 2002). And there is no doubt that many scientists pursue their work because (at least in part) they

---

[2] Note the similarities, here, with the 'Geneplore' models of creativity that we discussed in Chapter 5, in which the sequence is: generate, explore, adopt and/or implement (Finke et al., 1992).

hope that the results might have beneficial effects—e.g. curing some disease, or leading to a new item of technology. (Of course it can be the case that knowledge is *both* an intrinsic *and* an instrumental goal, just as one can seek sex both for its own sake and in order to have a child.) Since these debates won't matter very much to what follows, I shan't pursue them. But for what it is worth, my own guess is that the shape of science, as a social institution, would look *very* different if we didn't ever take knowledge as an intrinsic goal.

1.3 Social Ingredients

While some lay-people entertain romantic images of the scientist as a lonely individual, working for a lifetime alone with test tubes in a damp basement or a drafty garret, in fact science is, and always has been, an intensely social enterprise. For most of the last century at least, scientific work has been conducted in teams, involving frequent discussion and debate; and most scientific publications have had multiple authors. But even in the early days of modern science, researchers such as Galileo and Newton engaged in extensive correspondence and debate with other investigators.

Equally important, almost all of the background knowledge and skills with which a scientist approaches some novel problem will have been socially acquired, through reading, imitation, and explicit teaching and training. Each generation of scientists builds on the achievements of previous ones, as is the case with cultural products generally (Richerson and Boyd, 2004). Young scientists spend extensive periods of time studying the work of previous scientists. And for the most part scientists undergo extensive apprenticeships and training. Some of this training, it should be stressed, is of a cognitive sort. Budding scientists are required to take courses in advanced mathematics and statistics, for example, as well as training in the physical skills and procedures required in the laboratory.

Much of the surrounding context of scientific work is culturally provided too, from university salaries and research grants, though printing presses and libraries, to the equipment and materials needed to conduct the work. These facts, together with the training element, mean that science isn't just a social *activity*—it is a social *institution*.

1.4 The Age of Science

Given the above sketch of the ingredients of normal scientific activity, it is plain that there can be no science 'module'. Indeed, scientific activity seems to be the very archetype of a whole-person, System 2, activity (as opposed to being the product of some specialized *part* of the person). Science is for the most part slow, conscious, and explicit; and much of it is conducted in the public domain, in the form of conversations, debates, and written exchanges of results and theories. As a result, searching for a science module would be quite the wrong strategy for massive modularists to take. Rather, our task is to show how science can somehow result from the overall operations of a massively modular mind.

One view would see science as grounded entirely in System 2 processes that have been acquired from the surrounding culture—with the exception, perhaps, of the creative aspect, which can be allowed to be either associative, or random, or both. (Dennett, 1991, seems to endorse a view of this sort.) The rules for working out the implications of a given hypothesis, and for devising experiments, might be culturally acquired; as might be the criteria for judging that one particular theory is the best of those available. And then since massive modularity is consistent with the 'two reasoning systems' hypothesis (as we saw in Chapter 4), such an account of science would be *consistent* with massive modularity. But the modularity of the mind wouldn't play much of a role in the resulting explanation.

This sort of account would naturally go along with a view of science as a restricted historical phenomenon, being localized (until recently) to the cultures of western Europe and their descendents during the last five hundred years. It would emphasize the culturally local character of analytic thinking in general, as inherited from the ancient Greeks (Nisbett, 2003). And it would draw attention to the existence, in Europe in the sixteenth and seventeenth centuries, of a class of moneyed gentlemen, who had the resources and leisure to pursue their intellectual interests, and who both enjoyed and cultivated an atmosphere of free enquiry. Moreover, a crucial intellectual advance during this time was the invention of the controlled experiment, and more generally the spread and establishment of the idea that one should look for evidence to discriminate between competing theories.

There is, no doubt, an element of truth in this picture. But it requires us to draw a sharp line between science, on the one hand, and technology and invention, on the other. For on the latter fronts we see a relatively continuous and cumulative set of advances from the invention of agriculture some 12,000 years ago through to the present day, with many of those advances being distributed across different civilizations around the globe. There may be good historical reasons why the pace of change and accumulation quickened especially fast in post-Medieval Europe (Diamond, 1997), but it is doubtful whether a shift to a whole new culturally transmitted style of thinking was amongst them.

It is unlikely, moreover, that the distinction between science and technology can bear very much weight, in this context. For many new inventions result from theorizing about the ways in which things will behave when combined in some specific manner. It may *sometimes* be the case that a novel item of technology can be hit upon by mere trial and error, with no understanding of the properties of the materials used, or of the law-like regularities in nature that are thereby exploited. But even then, the result will be, not just a new invention of some sort, but a new bit of knowledge of a law-like regularity—namely, the normal functioning of the type of device in question.

Rather than pursing the issue in this way, however, I propose to argue directly against the view of science as a late cultural invention by showing that most of the cognitive and many of the cultural ingredients are universally present amongst hunter-gatherers, manifested especially in their tracking of prey when hunting. If this is so, then the cognitive capacities that are involved in scientific activity are of very ancient ancestry—probably no less ancient than *Homo sapiens* itself.

2 The Hunter as Scientist

I shall argue that the same set of cognitive capacities that are employed in science are employed much more broadly, and especially in hunting and tracking prey. It may therefore be the case that any novel ingredients (beyond the modules that we share with animals, and those distinctively human modules that were outlined and discussed in Chapter 3) were directly selected for.

If there *were* intense selection pressure for successful hunting and tracking, however, then shouldn't the arguments of Chapter 1 lead us to predict that the result would have been a dedicated module to do the job? In which case we surely shouldn't expect an examination of the cognitive processes involved in hunting to shed much light on the processes involved in science. But whether there can be a module to undertake a given task depends, of course, on both the pre-existing cognitive architecture and the nature of the task. And as we shall see, the demands of tracking, like the demands of science, don't easily allow for the process to become modularized. For in both of these domains creative thinking is required. And not only the development, but also the evaluation, of the resulting hypotheses requires utilizing the inferential resources of the full range of conceptual modules. As we shall see, tracking (like science) is, and perhaps can only be, a whole-person, System 2, activity.

2.1 *The Hunter-Gatherer as Natural Historian*

Is there any evidence that hunter-gatherer communities engage in activities that resemble science? It is now a familiar and well-established fact that hunter-gatherers have an immense and sophisticated understanding of the natural world around them. They have extensive knowledge of the plant and animal species in their environments—their kinds, life-cycles, and characteristic behaviors—that goes well beyond what is necessary for survival (Atran, 1990, 1999; Mithen, 1990, 1996). But it might be claimed that the cognitive basis for acquiring this sort of knowledge is mere inductive generalization from observed facts. It might be said that hunter-gatherers don't really have to engage in anything like genuine theorizing or model-building in order to gain such knowledge. And nor (except in their magic) do they seem to rely on inferences concerning the unobserved. So it might be claimed, on the contrary, that mere careful observation of the environment, combined with enumerative induction, is sufficient to explain everything that they know.[3]

In fact this appearance is deceptive, and at least some of the knowledge possessed by hunter-gatherers concerns facts that they haven't directly observed, but which they know by means of inference to the best explanation of signs that they can see and interpret (Mithen, 2002). For example, the !Xõ hunter-gatherers of the Kalahari are able to understand some of the nocturnal calls of jackals as a result of studying their spoor the next day and deducing their likely activities; and they have extensive knowledge of the lives of nocturnal animals derived from the study of their tracks, some of which has only recently been confirmed by orthodox science (Liebenberg, 1990). But it is the reasoning in which hunters will engage when tracking an animal that displays the clearest parallels with reasoning in science. Or so I shall now argue, following Liebenberg (1990).

2.2 The Art of Tracking

It is true, but by no means obvious at first glance, that tracking will always have played a vital role amongst human hunter-gatherer communities. This isn't especially because tracking is necessary to locate a quarry. For while this is important in many contexts and for many types of game, it isn't nearly so significant when hunting herd animals such as wildebeest. It is rather because, until the invention of the modern rifle, it would always have been rare for a hunter to bring an animal down immediately with an arrow or a spear. (And while hunting in large groups may have made it more likely that the target animal could be brought down under a volley of missiles, it would have made it much *less* likely that the hunters would ever have got close enough to launch them in the first place.)

---

[3] On an old-fashioned *inductivist* conception of science, then, it is plain that hunter-gatherers will already count as scientists. But I am setting the criterion for science and scientific reasoning considerably higher, to include inference to the best (unobserved and/or unobservable) explanation of the data (whether that data is itself observed or arrived at through enumerative induction).

In consequence, much of the skill involved in hunting consists in tracking a wounded animal, sometimes for a period of days. (Even the very simplest form of hunting—namely, running an animal down—requires tracking. For almost all kinds of prey animal can swiftly sprint out of sight, except in the most open country, and need to be tracked rapidly by a runner before they have the opportunity to rest.)[4] For example, the !Xõ will generally hunt in groups of between two and four men, using barbed arrows that have been treated with a poison obtained from the larvae of a particular species of beetle. An initial shot will rarely prove fatal immediately, and the poison can take between six and forty-eight hours to take effect, depending on the nature of the wound and the size of the animal. So a wounded animal may need to be tracked for considerable periods before it can be killed.

As Liebenberg (1990) remarks, it is difficult for a city-dweller to appreciate the subtlety of the signs that can be seen and interpreted by an experienced tracker. Except in ideal conditions (e.g. firm sand or a thin layer of soft snow) a mere capacity to recognize and follow an animal's spoor will be by no means sufficient to find it. Rather, a tracker will need to draw inferences from the precise manner in which a pebble has been disturbed, say, or from the way that a blade of grass has been bent or broken; and in doing so he will have to utilize his knowledge of the anatomy, detailed behavior, and patterns of movement of a wide variety of animals.[5] Moreover, in particularly difficult and stony conditions (or in order to save time during a pursuit) trackers will need to draw on their background knowledge of the circumstances, the geography of the area, and the normal behavior and likely needs of the animal in question to make educated guesses concerning its likely path of travel.

Most strikingly for our purposes, successful hunters will often need to develop speculative hypotheses concerning the likely causes of the few signs available to them, and concerning the likely future behavior of the animal; and these hypotheses are subjected to extensive debate and further empirical testing by the hunters concerned. When examined in detail these activities look a great deal like science, as Liebenberg (1990) argues. First, there is the invention of one or more hypotheses (often requiring considerable imagination) concerning the unobserved (and now unobservable) causes of the observed signs, and

---

[4] Many different species of animal—including even cheetahs!—can be hunted in this way given the right sort of open country. Under the heat of an African midday sun our combined special adaptations of hairlessness and sweat glands give us a decisive advantage in any long-distance race. Provided that the animal can be kept on the move, with no opportunity to rest, it eventually becomes so exhausted that it can be approached close enough to be clubbed or speared to death. See Liebenberg (forthcoming b).

[5] I use the masculine pronoun for hunters throughout. This is because hunting has always been an almost exclusively male activity, at least until very recently.

the circumstances in which they may have been made. These hypotheses are then examined and discussed for their accuracy, coherence with background knowledge, and explanatory and predictive power.[6] One of them may emerge out of this debate as the most plausible, and this can then be acted upon by the hunters, who at the same time search for further signs that might confirm or count against it. In the course of a single hunt one can see the birth, development, and death of a number of different 'research programs' in a manner that is at least partly reminiscent of theory-change in science (Lakatos, 1970).

2.3 Tracking: Art or Science?

How powerful are these analogies between the cognitive processes involved in tracking, on the one hand, and those that underlie science, on the other? There might seem to be one very significant *dis*analogy between the two. This is that the primary goal of tracking isn't an understanding of some general set of processes or mechanisms in nature, but rather the killing and eating of a particular animal. And although knowledge and understanding may be sought in pursuit of this goal, it is knowledge of the past and future movements of a particular prey animal, and an understanding of the causal mechanisms that produced a particular set of natural signs that is looked for, in the first instance. (Of course the hunters may *also* hope to obtain general knowledge that will be of relevance to future hunts.)

This disanalogy might be thought sufficient to undermine any claim to the effect that tracking *is* a science: if tracking doesn't share the same universal and epistemic aims of science, then it shouldn't be classed as one. Even if this point were granted, however (and I shall argue in a moment that it shouldn't be), it would be perfectly possible that the cognitive processes that are involved in tracking and in science should be broadly speaking the same. So we could still claim that the basic cognitive processes involved in each are roughly identical, albeit deployed in the service of different kinds of end. Indeed, just such a claim is supported by the anthropological data.

First of all, it is plain that tracking, like science, frequently involves inferences from the observed to the unobserved, and often from the observed to the unobservable as well. Thus a tracker may draw inferences concerning the effects that a certain sort of movement by a particular kind of animal would have on a certain kind of terrain (which may never actually have been observed

---

[6] I haven't been able to find from my reading any direct evidence that trackers will also place weight upon the relative *simplicity* and internal *consistency* of the competing hypotheses. But I would be prepared to bet a very great deal that they do. For these are, arguably, epistemic values that govern large areas of cognition in addition to hypothesis selection and testing (Chater, 1999).

previously, and may be practically unobservable to hunter-gatherers if the animal in question is nocturnal). Or a tracker may draw inferences concerning the movements of a particular animal (namely the one that he had previously shot and is now tracking) that are now unobservable even in principle, since those movements are in the past. Compare this with the way that a scientist might draw inferences concerning the nature of a previously unobserved and practically unobservable entity (e.g. the structure of DNA molecules before the invention of the electron microscope), or concerning the nature of particles that are too small to be observable, by means of an inference to the best explanation of a set of broadly observational data.

Secondly, it is plausible that the patterns of inference engaged in within the two domains of tracking and science are isomorphic with one another. In each case inferences to the best explanation of the observed data will be made, where the investigators are looking for explanations that will be simple, consistent, explanatory of the observational data, coherent with background beliefs, maximal in explanatory scope (relevant to the aims of the enquiry, at least), as well as fruitful in guiding future patterns of investigation. And in each case, too, imaginative / creative thinking has a significant—nay, crucial—role to play in the generation of novel hypotheses.

Let me say something more about the role of creative thinking in tracking and in science. It is now very widely accepted that inductivist methodologies have only a limited part to play in science. Noticing and generalizing from observed patterns can't carry you very far in the understanding of nature. Rather, scientists need to propose *hypotheses* (whether involving theories or models) concerning the underlying processes that produce those patterns. And generating such hypotheses can't be routinized. Rather, it will involve the imaginative postulation of a possible mechanism—guided and constrained by background knowledge, perhaps, but not determined by it. Similarly, a hunter may face a range of novel observational data that need interpreting. He has to propose a hypothesis concerning the likely causes of that data—where again, the hypothesis will be guided and constrained by knowledge of the circumstances, the season, the behavior of different species of animal, and so on, but isn't by any means determined by such knowledge. Rather, generating such hypotheses requires creative imagination, just as in science.

A final point of analogy between tracking and science is that both would appear to be whole-person activities, often conducted in the public domain. This has already been emphasized in the case of science. But tracking, too, is mostly conducted in small groups, with much explicit discussion and debate taking place amongst the hunters (Liebenberg, 1990). The benefits are similar in both cases. Since hypothesis-generation isn't easy, it can be helpful to have more than one person attempting to do it. And people with differing background experiences and knowledge are more likely to come up with fruitful analogies and explanations, and are more likely to see the implications of a novel hypothesis.[7] Furthermore, weak hypotheses are much more easily criticized by others than by the inventors of those hypotheses themselves.

I have been arguing that science and tracking are at least closely *analogous* activities. But even the alleged difference in overall aim (which might be thought to prevent tracking from *being* a kind of science) can be challenged, as Liebenberg (forthcoming a) points out. For many contemporary scientists have as their main goal some practical change in the world, as opposed to pure knowledge and understanding. (Think of someone looking for a cure for a disease, or experimenting with different types of building material.) And many hunters are interested in understanding the natural world around them for its own sake, and have knowledge that *far* outstrips anything that would ever be helpful in a hunt (in so far as this can be predicted—in hunting, as in science, it is very difficult to say in advance what might one day turn out to be relevant to what).

These various continuities between tracking and science seem to me sufficient to warrant at least the following claim: that anyone having a capacity for sophisticated tracking will also have the basic cognitive wherewithal to engage in science. The differences will merely be (1) some differences of *belief* (including methodological beliefs about appropriate experimental methods, say); and (2) some relatively trivial differences in inferential practices at the System 2 level (such as some of the dispositions involved in doing long-division sums, or in solving differential equations). In which case we can assert that the cognitive processes of hunter-gatherers and modern scientists are pretty closely continuous with one another, and that what was required for the initiation of the scientific revolution, therefore, were mostly extrinsic changes of one sort or another.

2.4 Science and Adaptation

If I am right that most of the basic cognitive abilities that figure in science are present and functioning amongst hunter-gatherers, then it is likely that those abilities are as ancient as *Homo sapiens*. Now it doesn't immediately follow from this that those abilities are innate, of course. For it may be that broadly

---

[7] In his micro-studies of the scientific reasoning that occurs in public during lab-meetings across a number of different research laboratories, Dunbar (2002) finds that the labs that contain people drawn from a variety of cross-disciplinary research backgrounds are more likely to be the ones that make genuinely ground-breaking discoveries.

scientific patterns of thinking and reasoning were an early 'System 2' cultural invention, passed on through the generations by imitation and overt teaching, and surviving in almost all extant human societies because of their evident utility. But this suggestion is highly implausible.

It is very hard to see how the principles of inference to the best explanation, in particular, could be other than substantially innate (Carruthers, 1992). For they certainly aren't explicitly taught, at least in hunter–gatherer societies.[8] While nascent trackers may acquire much of their background knowledge of animals and animal behavior by hearsay from adults and peers, very little overt teaching of tracking itself takes place. Rather, young boys will practice their observational and reasoning skills for themselves, first by following and interpreting the tracks of insects, lizards, small rodents, and birds around the vicinity of the campsite, and then in tracking and catching small animals for the pot (Liebenberg, 1990). They will, it is true, have many opportunities to listen to accounts of hunts undertaken by the adult members of the group, since these are often reported in detail around the campfire. So there are, in principle, opportunities for learning by imitation. But in fact, without at least a reasonably secure grasp of the principles of inference to the best explanation, it is hard to see how such stories could even be so much as *understood*. For of course those principles are never explicitly articulated; yet they will be needed to make sense of the decisions reported in the stories; and any attempt to uncover them by inference would need to rely upon the very principles of abductive reasoning that are in question.

It seems likely that hunting-by-tracking only fully entered the repertoire of the hominid lineage some 120,000 years ago, with the first appearance of anatomically modern, language-using, humans in Southern Africa, as Liebenberg (1990) suggests. And it may then be the case that the cognitive adaptations necessary to support scientific thinking and reasoning are not only innate, but were selected for precisely because of their important role in hunting.[9] Indeed,

---

[8] Nor are they taught to younger school-age children in our own society. Yet experimental tests suggest that children's reasoning and problem-solving is almost fully in accord with those principles, at least once the tests are conducted within an appropriate scientific-realist framework (Koslowski, 1996; Koslowski and Thompson, 2002). This is in striking contrast to many other areas of cognition, where naive performance is at variance with our best normative principles (see Evans and Over, 1996, and Stein, 1996, for reviews).

[9] Does this proposal predict that men should be much better than women at abductive inference? Not necessarily, since sexually selected traits are normally possessed initially by both sexes, as a result of the genetic correlation between the sexes (Miller, 2000). Then provided that abductive inference soon came to be useful to women as well, it would thereafter have been *retained* by both sexes. And certainly the reproductive success of hunter-gatherer women today is determined much more by their own resourcefulness than by fertility (Hrdy, 1999). Consistent with this suggestion, evidence of intrinsic sex differences in scientific abilities is slight (Spelke, 2005).

Liebenberg speculates that it may have been the *lack* of any sophisticated track-ing abilities that led to the near-extinction of the Neanderthals in Europe some 40,000 years ago. At this time the dramatic rise in world temperatures would have meant that they could no longer survive by their traditional method of hunting by simple tracking-in-snow through the long winter months, and then surviving through the brief summers on dried meats, scavenging, and gathering.

Note, however, that if the cognitive abilities involved in science are an adaptation, then evidence from contemporary hunter-gatherers suggests that the selective force at work would have been sexual rather than 'natural'. For almost all hunter-gatherer tribes that have been studied by anthropologists are highly egalitarian in organization, with meat from successful hunts being shared equally amongst all family groups (Boehm, 1999). If this were the case amongst ancestral groups too, then successful hunting wouldn't have improved the survival-chances of the hunter or his offspring directly. Nevertheless, successful hunters are highly respected. And there is evidence, both that they father significantly more children than do other men, and (somewhat more puzzling) that their children have a greater chance of surviving to reproductive age (presumably because their importance to the group is recognized by others; Boyd and Silk, 1997).

Whether or not scientific / tracking abilities are an adaptation, and if so, which elements of them were selected for and for what, is entirely moot at this point, however. One possibility is that those abilities are indeed an adaptation, but were selected for, not for their contributions to successful tracking, but for their role in theory-formation during infancy. To this idea we now turn.

3 The Child as Scientist?

The orthodox position in cognitive science over the last two decades has been that many of our cognitive capacities are subserved by bodies of belief or knowledge, constituting so-called 'folk theories' of the domains in question. These include our capacity to attribute mental states to ourselves and others (i.e. the capacity to 'mind-read'), and the capacity to explain and predict many of the behaviors of middle-sized physical objects. In themselves, such claims are consistent with the bodies of knowledge in question being substantially innate, emerging during normal development through a process of maturation rather than learning. Indeed, those claims are also consistent with a processing-module perspective in which the principles of folk 'theory' are merely implicit, and built into the processing rules of the module in question. But a number of developmental psychologists have gone further in suggesting that these theories are developed in childhood through a process of theorizing analogous to scientific theorizing (e.g. Carey, 1985; Wellman, 1990). This theorizing-theory approach has been developed and defended most explicitly by Gopnik and Melzoff (1997), and it is on their account that I shall focus my critique.

3.1 The Absence of External Supports

One of the main objections to a theorizing-theory account is that it ignores the extent to which scientific activity needs to be supported by external resources.[10] As we noted in Section 1, scientists don't, and never have, worked alone, but constantly engage in discussion, cooperation, and mutual criticism with peers. If there is one thing that we have learned over the last thirty years of historically oriented studies of science, it is that the positivist–empiricist image of the lone investigator, gathering all data and constructing and testing hypotheses by him- or her-self, is a highly misleading abstraction. Why should it be so different in childhood, if the cognitive processes involved are essentially the same?

I should emphasize that this point doesn't at all depend upon any sort of 'social constructivist' account of science, of the sort that Gopnik and Melzoff find so rebarbative (and rightly so, in my view). It is highly controversial that scientific change is to be explained, to any significant extent, by the operation of wider social and political forces, in the way that the social constructivists claim (Bloor, 1976; Rorty, 1979; Latour and Woolgar, 1986; Shapin, 1994). But it is, now, utterly truistic that science is a social process in at least the minimal sense that it progresses through the varied social interactions of scientists themselves—cooperating, communicating, criticizing—and through their reliance on a variety of external socially provided props and aids, such as books, paper, writing instruments, different kinds of scientific apparatus, and (now) calculators, computers, and the internet (Giere, 2002). And this truism is sufficient to cause a real problem for the 'child as scientist' account of development.

One sort of response would be to claim that children don't *need* external props, because they have vastly better memories than adult scientists. But this is simply not credible; for it isn't true that children's event-memories are better than those of adults.[11] And in any case it isn't true that science depends upon external factors *only* because of limitations of memory. On the

[10] See Stich and Nichols (1998), Foucher et al. (2002), and Harris (2002a) for development of a range of alternative criticisms.

[11] Admittedly the evidence here is confined to verbally expressible memories; so it could in principle be claimed that children have vastly better *non-conscious* memories than adults do. But there isn't any uncontentious evidence for this.

contrary, individual limitations of rationality, insight, and creativity all play an equally important part. For scientific discussion is often needed to point out the fallacies in an individual scientist's thinking; to show how well-known data can be explained by a familiar theory in ways that the originators hadn't realized; and to generate new theoretical ideas and proposals.[12]

Moreover, young children appear not to have any memory for their own previous mental processes (Flavell et al., 1995). And in particular, if they lack any concept of belief as a representational state (as many theorists maintain), then children under four cannot remember their own previous false beliefs, nor think about their own beliefs as such (Gopnik, 1993). Let us assume, for the moment, that this is so. Then the fact that younger children are incapable of thinking about their own previous mental states raises yet further problems for theorizing-theory. For while it may be *possible* to engage in science without any capacity for higher-order thinking—when revising a theory T one can think, '*These* events show that not-T', for example—in actual fact scientific theorizing is shot-through with higher-order thoughts. Scientists will think *about* their current or previous theories as such, wonder whether the data are sufficient to show them false, or true, and so on. It therefore looks as if a theorizing-theorist will have to claim that these higher-order thoughts are actually mere epiphenomena in relation to the real (first-order) cognitive processes underlying science. But this is hardly very plausible.

In Chapter 3.2 we noted that the traditional developmental story concerning mind-reading may be in error, however. In particular, there is evidence that infants as young as fifteen months are capable of appreciating, and reasoning appropriately about, the false beliefs of another person (Onishi and Baillargeon, 2005). From this perspective, young children's failures in traditional false-belief tasks are mere failures of performance, not reflecting an underlying lack of competence. If this were correct, then it might be thought to rescue the claim that infants may be theorizing in the manner of little scientists, routinely entertaining higher-order thoughts about their first-order beliefs and suppositions. But actually it doesn't do so.

There are two reasons for this. The first is that the best account that we have of the limitations on children's performance in false-belief tasks is that these limitations derive from the difficulties that they experience in distancing themselves from the perspective of another, and especially in setting aside their own beliefs (Birch and Bloom, 2004). This ought to make it equally

---

[12] And note that tracking, in contrast, *is* generally social and externally supported in just this sense—for as we have seen, hunters will characteristically work collaboratively in small groups, pooling their knowledge and memories, and engaging in extensive discussion and mutual criticism in the course of interpreting spoor and other natural signs.

hard for them to distance themselves from their own current theoretical beliefs (querying, doubting, and making alterations) in the manner required of scientists. And the second point is that, according to theorizing-theorists, 'theory of mind' is itself one of the theories that is supposed to be arrived at by scientific theorizing in infancy, no matter how early it is achieved. So *that* theorizing, at least, cannot involve higher-order thoughts.

Can these various differences between children and adults plausibly be explained in terms of differences of attention, motivation, or time, in the way that Gopnik and Melzoff try to argue? They cannot. For adult scientists certainly attend very closely to the relevant phenomena, they may be highly motivated to succeed in developing a successful theory, and they may be able to devote themselves full-time to doing so. But still they cannot manage without a whole variety of external resources, both social and non-social. And moreover *radical* (conceptually innovative) theory change in science (of the sort that Gopnik and Melzoff maintain occurs a number of times within the first few years of a child's life) is generally spread out over a very lengthy timescale indeed (often as much as a hundred years or more; Nersessian, 1992, 2002).

3.2 The Extent of the Data

According to Gopnik and Melzoff (1997), the main difference between child-hood theorizers and adult scientists lies in the extent and ease of availability of relevant data. In scientific enquiry, the relevant data are often hard to come by, and elaborate and expensive experiments and other information-gathering exercises may be needed to get it—perforce making scientific enquiry essentially social. But in childhood there are ample quantities of data easily available. Young children have plenty of opportunities to experiment with physical substances and their properties—knocking objects together, dropping or throwing them, pouring liquids, and mixing materials—when developing their naive physics. And they have plenty of opportunities to observe and probe other agents when developing their naive psychology as well. Moreover, since infants come into the world with a set of innate domain-specific theories, on Gopnik and Melzoff's account, they already possess theoretical frameworks that constrain possible hypotheses, determine relevant evidence, and so on.

This point, although valid as far as it goes, does not begin to address the real issue. If anything, the extent of the data available to the child is a further *problem* for the 'child as scientist' view, given the lack of external aids to memory, and the lack of any public process for sorting through and discussing the significance of the evidence. That plenty of data are *available* to an enquirer is irrelevant unless that data can be recalled, organized, and surveyed at the moment of need—namely, during theory testing or theory development.

Gopnik and Melzoff also make the point that much relevant data is actually presented to children by adults, in the form of linguistic utterances of one sort or another. Now, their idea isn't that adults *teach* the theories in question to children, thus putting the latter into the position of little science *students* rather than little scientists. For such a claim would be highly implausible—there is no real evidence that any such teaching actually takes place (and quite a bit of evidence that it doesn't). Their point is rather that adults make a range of new sorts of evidence available to the child in the form of their linguistic utterances, since those utterances are embedded in semantic frameworks that contain the target theories. Adult utterances may then provide crucial data for children, as they simultaneously elaborate their theories and struggle to learn the language of their parents.

This proposal does at least have the virtue of providing a social dimension to childhood development, hence in one sense narrowing the gap between children and adult scientists. But actually this social process is quite unlike any that an adult scientist will normally engage in. For scientists (as opposed to science students) are rarely in the position of hearing or engaging in discussions with those who have already mastered the theories that they themselves are still trying to develop. And in any case the proposal does little to address the fundamental problems of insufficient memory, bounded rationality, and limited creativity that children and adults both face, which the social and technological dimensions of science are largely designed to overcome.

3.3 Simple Theories?

Might it be that the scientific problems facing adults are very much more complex than those facing young children, and that this is the reason why children, but not adult scientists, can operate without much in the way of external support? This suggestion is hardly very plausible, either. Consider folk psychology, for example, of the sort attained by most normal children by four or five years of age (if not a great deal earlier). According to Gopnik and Melzoff (1997) themselves, this has a deep structure rivaling that of many scientific theories, involving the postulation of a range of kinds of causally effective internal state, together with a set of nomic principles (or 'laws') concerning the complex patterns of causation in which those states figure.[13] There is no reason at all to think that this theory should be easily arrived at. Indeed, it is a theory that many adult scientific psychologists have *denied*

---

[13] Even on the sort of mixed theory-theory / simulationist account of our mind-reading capacities that we endorsed in Chapter 3.3 (following Nichols and Stich, 2003), these are *information rich*, utilizing a variety of forms of innate and acquired information, just as theorizing-theorists like Gopnik and Melzoff have supposed.

(especially around the middle part of the twentieth century)—namely those who were behaviorists. It took a variety of sophisticated arguments, and the provision of a range of kinds of data, to convince most people that behaviorism should be rejected in favor of cognitivism.

So why is it that *no* children (excepting perhaps those who are autistic) ever pass through a stage in which they endorse some form of behaviorism? If cognitivism were really such an easy theory to frame and establish, then the puzzle would be that adult scientific psychologists had such difficulty in converging on it. And given that it *isn't* so easy, the puzzle is that all normal children *do* converge on it in the first four or five years of development (at least if they are supposed to get there by means of processes structurally similar to those that operate in science). Worse still, it isn't just normal children who succeed in acquiring folk psychology. So do children with Down syndrome and Williams syndrome, who in many other respects can be severely cognitively impaired, and whose general learning and theorizing abilities can be well below normal. The natural conclusion to draw, at this point, is that folk psychology is both theoretically difficult and *not* arrived at by a process of theorizing, but rather through some sort of modular and innately channeled process of development and learning.

3.4 Rounding up

I conclude that the child-as-scientist account is highly implausible. All the evidence that we have suggests that scientific thinking and reasoning are demanding whole-person activities, involving speech (both overt and inner), debate, and various other social and external supports. But very little of the evidence that we have suggests that childhood development in such domains as mind-reading or naive physics has this character. Two-year-old children don't ask questions about how minds work, nor debate with one another about whether reasons can cause actions independently of any desire, for example.

Admittedly, there is evidence that children who have older siblings acquire mind-reading abilities faster (Perner et al., 1994), and there is evidence that deaf children are delayed in mind-reading acquisition (Peterson and Siegal, 1999). These facts might be thought to suggest a role for social bootstrapping of one sort or another. But in fact they are equally well explained on a modularist account, since one might predict that the speed of development of a cognitive module would be a partial function of the amount of work that it is given to do. (Think of how children develop muscles, by way of analogy.) Children who have to compete with, and figure out how to outwit, an older sibling are likely to work harder at mind-reading than those who don't. And likewise, children who have lots of speech acts to interpret are likely to have to work harder at mind-reading than those who are deprived of others' speech.

It remains perfectly possible, however (as we noted in Chapter 3.2), that the minds of young children contain a number of statistical mechanisms for the extraction of causal structure from data, one of which is focused on the behaviors of middle-sized physical objects, one of which is focused on the behaviors of animate organisms (especially people), and so on. But as we saw, we should expect there to be a number of such structure-extracting mechanisms, rather than just one, operating in parallel. Each would be targeted on a particular domain, with internal operations that might have become tweaked somewhat to adapt it better for extracting the causal structure of that domain. And there is no reason to think that these mechanisms are available to assist the adult scientist—except indirectly, in so far as the thinking of scientists is dependent upon the operations of all of their cognitive modules.

4 System 2 Reasoning and Science

In this section I shall briefly argue that two of the three main elements of scientific enquiry—creative hypothesis generation, on the one hand, and exploration of the implications of an hypothesis, on the other—are explicable in terms of processes already discussed in Chapters 4 and 5, realized in mentally rehearsed cycles of inner (and outer) speech and visual imagery, and utilizing learned rules and procedures. Then in Sections 5 and 6 I shall turn to the principles involved in abductive reasoning / inference to the best explanation.

I have nothing more to say about creative hypothesis generation at this point, beyond what has already been said in Chapter 5. But let me emphasize that the products are, in my view, explicit and consciously entertained. The hypotheses in question are derived from the rehearsal of action schemata (whether of speech or other forms of physical movement), and globally broadcast in the form of a visual image or an item of inner or outer speech. For example, to entertain the hypothesis of continental drift for the first time, a scientist might transform a visual image of the major landmasses of Earth in such a way that they move relative to one another; or the scientist might rehearse the sentence, 'Perhaps the various landmasses can move.' And these activated action schemata will be arrived at through the sorts of heuristic and associative processes canvassed in Chapter 5.

Such globally broadcast representations are flagged as suppositions, and taken as input by all the various belief-generating and motivation-generating modules. These modules set to work, where they can, drawing inferences from or further elaborating those representations. For example, the naive physics module, on receiving as input an image of two rigid surfaces floating on hot viscous liquid and starting to pull apart, might generate the prediction that the liquid will bubble upwards as the split develops, and then harden as it cools—hence arriving at the idea of the mid-Atlantic ridge. And where the globally broadcast state is a representation of a natural language sentence, some inferential work might also be done by the language faculty itself, if the idea mooted in Chapter 4—that the language faculty has limited inferential abilities of its own—is correct. The language faculty might play a role, for example, in inferences involving multiple embedded quantifiers.

Thus far the model consists of cycles of globally broadcast hypotheses and their globally broadcast implications or elaborations, separated by unconscious, System 1, intra-modular inferential processes. And these System 1 processes are no doubt vital in delivering the 'intuitions' that can play such a significant role in science and in determining the acceptability of a scientific theory. (Note that such intuitions can sometimes also lead us astray.)

A great deal of the reasoning that takes place in science, however, is surely System 2—involving learned rules of one sort or another, sometimes manipulated consciously. Data will be subjected to various statistical tests, for example, and inferences drawn accordingly. The procedures for setting up and conducting a controlled experiment may very well be prescribed within a given scientific discipline. And there are rules and conventions for presenting the results of such experiments, for example in the form of bar-graphs with error-bars. Indeed, as we have already emphasized in Section 1 of this chapter, much of the training of young scientists consists not just in teaching them *facts* (including previous and current theories, and generalized data), but in *training* them in inferential and experimental procedures. These procedures then need to be recalled and adhered to in the conduct of enquiry, in the manner of System 2 processes generally.

Aside from variations in background belief, almost all of the differences between hunter-gatherers and contemporary scientists will lie here, at the System 2 level. Both sets of thinkers will creatively generate explanatory hypotheses, rehearsing those hypotheses for global broadcast and subsequent System 1 elaboration and evaluation; and both sets will also, I suggest, deploy similar overall standards for inferring to the *best* explanation. However, the explicit (System 2) methodologies deployed by scientists will be much richer (including those mentioned in the previous paragraph). Yet this isn't to say that hunters tracking prey will have *no* beliefs about the proper way to conduct their enquiries, of course. On the contrary. And one good example is provided by the widespread practice amongst hunters of adopting the perspective of the animal, trying to figure out what one would do next if one was in the animal's situation (Liebenberg, 1990). This is a practice that is consciously and reflectively adopted and modulated, and it is one that proves remarkably successful.

I want to emphasize, however, that much of what constitutes the System 2 level of reasoning in science won't consist of explicit beliefs about methodology or acceptable inference, but rather in dispositions to execute sequences of action-schemata activation that instantiate certain abstractly characterizable types. Scientific thinking is a *skill*—or rather, it consists of nested sets of such skills. These are acquired in the manner of skills generally, through a combination of explicit instruction and practice, combined with imitation of the skills exemplified by those who are experts in the field. In most contemporary sciences, many of these skills are mathematical in character. But they also incorporate more general phenomena, including certain patterns of questioning and debate.

5 Fodor on Abductive Reason

I have argued that two of the three elements of scientific reasoning that we distinguished at the outset—namely, creative hypothesis-generation and inferences drawn from those hypotheses—are explicable within the framework of a massively modular model of the human mind. But what of the third element, namely inference to the truth of an hypothesis on the grounds that it provides the best explanation of the data (so-called 'inference to the best explanation' or 'abductive inference')? In the present section I shall address Fodor's (2000) arguments that a capacity for abductive inference can't be explained by either present or any foreseeable future cognitive psychology, let alone by any sort of massively modular account. Then in the section following I shall provide a positive sketch of a modularist explanation of abduction.

Fodor (2000) gives two distinct arguments in support of the alleged mysteriousness of abductive inference (although these aren't distinguished very clearly from one another in his text). One starts from factual claims about the forms that abductive inference can take in science; the other starts from normative claims about the conditions under which belief-formation in science is rational. I shall address these in turn.

5.1 Fodor's Factual Argument

Fodor's factual argument begins from the claim that in science, anything can be relevant to anything else. The point can be illustrated by a supposed connection between solar physics and Darwin's theory of natural selection. Shortly after the publication of *The Origin of Species* a leading physicist, Sir William Thompson, pointed out that Darwin just couldn't assume the long timescale required for gradual evolution, because the rate of cooling of the sun meant that the Earth would have been too hot for life to survive at such early dates. Now we realize that the Victorian physicists had too high a value for the rate at which the sun is cooling down because they were unaware of radioactive effects. But at the time this was taken as a serious problem for Darwinian theory—and rightly so, in the scientific context of the day.

It seems to follow from this that the mechanism of abductive inference can't be an encapsulated one (or at least, not in the strong, narrow-scope, sense of 'encapsulation' that we distinguished in Chapter 1). If an inference to the truth of a theory, on the grounds that the theory provides us with the best available explanation of the data, can be impacted by any one of the beliefs that we hold, then that inferential process can't be encapsulated—indeed, it can't be closed off from *any* of the beliefs that are held in the mind, let alone from *most* of them. And it does seem likely that, for any encapsulation-conditions on a faculty of inference to the best explanation that anyone might care to propose, we should be able to find some real episode from the history of science that violates those conditions.

Now so far there isn't any reason for a massive modularist to be concerned, given the weak notion of 'module' that is in play. And this remains true even if one wanted to claim that there is a single module that performs inferences to the best explanation—hence adding a distinct 'abductive reason box' to our flowchart of the architecture of a massively modular mind. (Fodor's factual argument will be even less of a problem for the sort of modularist view being developed in the present chapter, according to which abductive inferences are realized in cycles of activity of a wide range of central / conceptual modules.) For as we argued in Chapter 1.7, it is a mistake to think that all modules need to be encapsulated (in the narrow-scope sense). Rather, their processing can be rendered computationally tractable by other means, and especially through the use of a variety of fast and frugal heuristics.

Fodor (2000) seems to be aware of this lacuna in his argument, and devotes a short section to critiquing the use of heuristics to try to solve the problem of the unencapsulated character of scientific cognition. His main claim is that any such use of heuristics must generate a vicious regress. For how is it to be decided *which* heuristic to employ in a given circumstance? If this in turn is a heuristic matter, then there will have to be yet further heuristics to determine which of those higher-order heuristics should be applied; and so on, indefinitely. In which case the only alternative, Fodor thinks, is that the process that selects amongst first-order heuristics should be a *non*-heuristic one, and moreover one that is wholly unencapsulated in character. And as he says, no one has the least idea how to model such a system computationally.

This argument limps badly at both of its main steps, however. First of all, it is very doubtful whether the choice amongst the first-order heuristics that one might employ in a given circumstance must be made through the application of some higher-order heuristic (if it isn't to be made by some unencapsulated 'general reasoning system', that is). For why shouldn't each heuristic come with a sort of recognitional 'front end'? (See the discussion of Barrett's enzymatic conception of modules in Chapter 4.1.) This would contain a specification of the sorts of circumstances in which it is to be applied. Then we could imagine that heuristic systems, like conceptual systems generally, are continually searching amongst the contents of perception and the contents of working memory for the conditions that 'turn them on' and make them begin their work. And just as with conceptual recognition generally, we could imagine that many of the interactions between heuristic systems are competitive ones, with a number of different partially activated heuristic systems competing with one another to control the overall cognitive process in a given set of circumstances.

The second weakness in Fodor's argument is this. Even if we suppose that the initial choice amongst first-order heuristics has to be made via the application of a higher-order heuristic such as 'choose the heuristic that worked last time', it is quite unclear why any vicious regress would be generated. This is because we should expect there to be far *fewer* heuristics at the second-order level than there are at the first-order one; and there should be even fewer (if any) at the third-order level, concerning the choice of which second-order heuristic to apply. In particular, there will be no vicious regress if there is just *one* heuristic principle employed at one of these higher levels. Without a great deal more specification of the content of the various heuristics and their governing architecture, therefore, there is simply no argument here for a massive modularist to answer.

So far, then, there isn't any reason to think that inference to the best explanation can't be realized in cycles of modular activity, utilizing a variety of learned rules and heuristic processes. Indeed, many aspects of the actual conduct of scientific enquiry can fit quite naturally within such a picture. For norms governing public criticism and debate, peer review of research results before publication, and so on, are plausibly viewed as heuristics designed to circumvent (so far as possible) the inevitable limitations in the knowledge and rationality of each individual scientist. And often (as with the example of a physicist's objection to the theory of evolution by natural selection discussed earlier) the cooperation of a number of different minds might be required to bring to bear disparate information in the evaluation of a given hypothesis.

5.2 Fodor's Normative Argument

Fodor's descriptive argument against massive modularity is a failure, then. (And by the same token, so is his parallel argument for the pessimistic conclusion that we should give up on computational psychology—in respect of central processes of belief-fixation—for the foreseeable future.) His other, normative, argument comes in two slightly different forms. One starts from a version of Quine's (1953) claim that rational belief-confirmation is a holistic matter, depending upon *all* of a subject's existing beliefs. The other turns on the claim that abductive warrant for a new belief depends upon identifying properties such as simplicity and coherence with existing belief, which again depend upon one's total belief set. To each of these premises Fodor adds the seemingly anodyne descriptive claim that we do *sometimes* form beliefs in a rational manner when we reason abductively. And this warrants the conclusion that we must therefore possess doxastic / belief-forming mechanisms whose operations can, at least sometimes, depend upon all of the beliefs that we have.

Having got to this point, Fodor can then go straight to the pessimistic conclusion—he doesn't need to claim that (narrow-scope) encapsulation is the only way of rendering computations tractable, or to argue against heuristic-based models, because heuristic processes aren't going to help here. Heuristics of the sort we discussed in Chapter 1.7 are designed precisely to enable one to access *any* belief without having to access *all*. So if Fodor can establish that we have doxastic processes that access every one of our beliefs in the course of their operation, then he can get straight to the pessimistic conclusion—for no one has the least idea how this could be done in a way that would be computationally tractable. (Plainly an architecture of massively many modules wouldn't help us any, at this point.)

Let us initially consider the first (Quineian) version of Fodor's argument. One way of developing it, would be to identify ideally rational belief-confirmation with some or other variety of the Bayesian theory of rational belief acceptance (Kyburg, 1961; Kaplan, 1981). The claim would be that rational enquirers need to ascribe probabilities to each of their hypotheses in the light of the probabilities that they have assigned to their existing beliefs. Rational enquirers then need to update these probabilities as new evidence comes in, in ways that reflect their assessment both of the independent probability of the evidence and of its probability given the truth of the hypotheses. So the probability assigned to any particular hypothesis, at a given time, will depend upon the probability assignments made to each of the subject's other beliefs and hypotheses at that time.

When such an ideal of rationality is combined with the claim that people reasoning abductively do sometimes succeed in forming beliefs in ways that are rational, then the implication must be that people possess an ideal Bayesian reasoning *competence*. Although limitations on time, attention, memory, and so forth might often interfere in such a way as to undermine the rational status of our reasoning, if we do sometimes reason as the ideal of rationality requires (and don't do so accidentally), then we must possess an ideal abductive competence. (Compare the claim often made in linguistics, that speakers possess the underlying competence to use a particular grammatical system, even though their overt performance might often deviate from what such a grammar would require.)

The weak link in this first version of Fodor's normative argument comes in its initial premise, however. For it sets the standards on rationality a great deal too high. But perhaps it isn't quite right to suggest that this is the *only* weakness in the argument. For the second—descriptive—claim is also unwarranted if 'rational' is read in the demanding holistic sense. We really have no reason at all to believe that we ever form beliefs in ways that depend upon the totality of our existing beliefs. But in order to criticize the argument effectively, it is the first premise that needs to be attacked. Otherwise we shall be vulnerable to the incredulous question, 'Do you mean to say that we *never* form beliefs in a rationally warranted manner, then?' To reply, we need to argue that the standards on rational warrant are much lower than Fodor sets them. And this, I take it, is the whole point of the 'naturalized rationality' movement of recent decades. Let me elaborate.

Throughout much of the nineteenth and twentieth centuries research was focused on developing normative models of rationality that are, in various ways, *maximizing*. Systems of logic were created that would *guarantee* truth from truth; forms of probabilistic reasoning were developed that would match degrees of confidence to the objective probability of events; and accounts of rational decision-making were created that would maximize expected utility. But then in the latter half of the twentieth century it began to be noticed that actual human reasoning performance deviates systematically from these norms (Kahneman et al., 1982). Initially this was presented as evidence of systematic human *irrationality*. But some researchers began to realize that it was the norms themselves that were suspect, if they were intended as a guide to possible human behavior (Cherniak, 1986; Gigerenzer et al., 1999).

It is widely accepted that '*ought* implies *can*.' This seems entailed by the very action-guiding role of norms, indeed. For if norms are to *guide* action, then it must at least be *possible* to act in compliance with them. But the norms of 'maximizing' kinds of rationality serve to generate rules that it is impossible for finite and physically limited agents to comply with in realistic (useful and/or life-preserving) timescales. One might think, for example, that simple logic would entail the following norm: 'Before adopting any new belief, check that it is consistent with all your other beliefs.' For the avoidance of contradiction seems like an absolute constraint on rational belief-formation. But consistency-checking is demonstrably intractable if attempted on an exhaustive basis, as we saw in Chapter 1.7. So we have no option but to attempt something less: adopting heuristics for the avoidance of contradiction that will work *well enough* for our purposes, without guaranteeing that contradictions are never believed.

This motivates the perspective of *naturalized* rationality: what is rational for us depends upon our powers and limitations (Stein, 1996). If the norms with which we *should* comply have to be ones with which we *can* comply, then they cannot be the various maximizing principles that have been worked out by philosophers, logicians, and economists. And likewise, it can't be a requirement of rationality that we should attempt to make our adoption of any new belief sensitive to *all* of our existing beliefs, in the way that Fodor's Quineian argument supposes. Whatever the rational standard is, it will have to be something a very great deal less demanding than this. And then from the fact that we do sometimes form our beliefs in a rational way, it doesn't follow that we embody any sort of ideal reasoning competence—or at least, not one that it would be problematic to explain from the perspective of cognitive science in general, and massively modular accounts of the mind in particular.

The first version of Fodor's normative argument is a failure, then. The second version is initially much less demanding (or so it seems). It starts from the assertion that the rationality of an abductive inference can depend upon identifying such properties as the relative *simplicity* of a hypothesis, or the degree of *coherence* between a hypothesis and our existing beliefs. This seems undeniable, given our earlier discussion of the principles of inference to the best explanation employed by both scientists and hunter–trackers. And then equally uncontentious is the assertion that we are sometimes *correct* in believing that one theory is simpler than another (in a way that isn't just accidental), or that one theory coheres better with our other theories than does another. But what Fodor then needs to convince us of, if the argument for pessimism about the prospects for a cognitive science of central cognition is to go through, is that properties like simplicity can depend upon *all* the beliefs in one's belief set.[14]

But in fact we are presented with no reason whatever to believe such a claim; and on reflection it seems extremely doubtful. Why should we accept that the relative simplicity of competing theories of electromagnetism, for example, might be effected by the question whether my mother was born on a Monday or a Tuesday? There are really two different points here, of somewhat differing strength. First, how likely is it that a change of mind on the latter question might be enough by itself to reverse a judgment of the relative simplicity of two theories of electromagnetism? And secondly, how likely is it that the question of my mother's birthday has any impact at all on the degree of simplicity of those theories? I think the answer to both questions is, 'Not at all.' In which case we shouldn't be rationally required to consider the day of my mother's birth (and other matters of that ilk) when evaluating competing theories of electromagnetism.

Likewise in respect of a theory's coherence with existing belief: we are provided with no reason for thinking that the degree of coherence that a given hypothesis possesses can depend upon *all* of one's other beliefs. In deciding whether one theory of electromagnetism is better than another I am required to consider whether or not it coheres better with *related* beliefs and theories. But I am surely *not* required to consider whether or not it coheres with my belief that my mother was born on a Monday.

I suppose Fodor might respond that there is no way of knowing *in advance* which of one's beliefs might fail to cohere with a hypothesis. In which case, he might say, we have no option but to consider them all, if we are ever to make a warranted inference to the best explanation. But this just returns us to a point paralleling the one we made earlier about consistency-checking: since we *cannot* check whether a hypothesis coheres well with *all* of our existing beliefs, it can't be a rational requirement on us that we should perform any such check. Rather, something less demanding and more heuristic-like will have to suffice for the rationality of an abductive inference.

Fodor's arguments for the radically holistic nature of abductive inference are a failure, then. In which case we have been given no reason, yet, for thinking that such inferences can't be realized in the operations of a massively modular mind. But of course it is one thing to rebut an argument *against* such

---

[14] Note that this second version of Fodor's normative argument doesn't require him to claim that we are ideal reasoners, in either a performance or a competence sense. All he needs is that we have a cognitive mechanism that enables us to comply with *one element* of ideal rationality—namely, sometimes making warranted judgments of simplicity, coherence, and so on that are sensitive to one's total belief set.

a possibility; and it is quite another matter to show how such a thing can actually happen. To that positive task I now turn.

6 The Anatomy of Abduction

How should we attempt to account for our capacity for inference to the best explanation within the framework of a massively modular mind? In broad outline, there would seem to be just two possibilities. Either we can postulate the existence of a dedicated module to do the job; or we can claim that abductive inference is realized in the operations and interactions of existing modules. I shall discuss these options in turn.

6.1 An Abductive Inference Module?

We have accepted that scientific reasoning as a whole is a System 2 activity, involving the interactions of the full suite of conceptual modules. But this doesn't yet rule out the existence of a module for abductive inference. For it might be the case that it is creative hypothesis generation—in the form of mental rehearsals of utterances and other actions—together with the exploration of the implications of those hypotheses through modular processing together with learned rules and procedures, that renders scientific cognition overall as a whole-person-involving System 2 activity. So it remains possible that the cognitive products of those activities might be fed as input to a dedicated system—an abductive inference module—whose sole function is to perform inferences to the best explanation on those inputs. It might be claimed, moreover, that such a module was selected for in the course of hominid evolution as a result of its important role in hunting, especially in the tracking of wounded prey.

Although possible in principle, this hypothesis isn't a plausible one. This is because we surely need to minimize, so far as we can, the number and complexity of the specific adaptations that are required to make scientific reasoning possible. This isn't because appeals to simplicity are important in reasoning about biological systems generally. (On the contrary, there is very little reason to think that biological systems should be simple.) It is rather because the greater the number of adaptations that are needed to perform a given function, and the greater the complexity of their internal organization and mode of interconnection, the more unlikely it will be that there could have been any selection pressure in existence of the right kind, and for long enough, to fix them all into place. Yet we have already had to postulate one adaptation to render science possible, in the form of the dispositions that are responsible for pretend play in childhood, and ultimately for creative supposition-generation amongst adults. And on any view, the internal computations that would need to be undertaken by a supposed module for inference to the best explanation would have to be pretty subtle and sophisticated.

Moreover, it isn't easy to understand how a capacity for creative hypothesis-generation and a module for abductive inference could evolve in parallel together. For it looks as if the benefits of hypothesis-generation presuppose that there is *already* in place some capacity to select amongst hypotheses. What would be the point of evolving a capacity to generate explanatory hypotheses, if you had no way of deciding whether or not a hypothesis was good enough to believe? And conversely, it looks as if there would only be any point in having an abductive inference module if one *already* had the capacity for creative generation of hypotheses, for the module to make its selections amongst. For if you don't have a way of generating candidate hypotheses, then there could hardly be any point in having a module for selecting the *best* hypothesis, could there?

It would be preferable, therefore, if we could find a way to explain our capacity for inference to the best explanation in terms of capacities and dispositions that would already have been present, at the point when our capacity for creative supposition and the corresponding disposition to engage in childhood pretence first began to emerge. For in that case, when a capacity for creative hypothesis generation first began to manifest itself, there would already have been in place an ability to do something with the hypotheses that got produced.

Notice that, where the hypotheses in question are expressed in language, the problem of inferring to the best explanation reduces to the problem of deciding which of the candidate sentences to believe in the circumstances. And it may prove helpful to note, at this point, that the problem of deciding whether or not to believe new sentences would have been around from near the first evolution of the language faculty, probably from significantly before the first appearance of our fully human capacity for creative thinking. For one of the main things that language has always (or almost always) been for, presumably, is *testimony*. (Recall that on some accounts language evolved for purposes of sexual display, in the first instance, rather than for the exchange of information; see Miller, 2000.) People tell other people things, and then those others have to decide whether or not to believe what they are told.

I propose to examine what is involved in the acceptance of testimony, then, to see whether we can understand it in modularist terms—using that as some sort of prototype or basis for explaining how inference to the best explanation might come to operate in language-involving, System 2, thought. What I shall suggest, in fact, is that the principles involved in linguistic testimony and discourse interpretation might *become* a set of principles of inference to the best explanation once self-generated sentences start to be processed internally, in inner speech. And I shall suggest, too, that those principles could very well operate in ways that are computationally tractable.

6.2 Testimony

There are two broad models of testimony in the epistemological literature. One is a sort of reductive approach that dates back at least to Hume (1748), which claims that you should only believe an item of testimony if you have independent evidence of the reliability of testimony in general, and of this individual source in particular. This view has come in for sustained criticism in recent years, since it is psychologically extremely implausible. Children start believing what they are told from the start. Yet it is hard to accept that they are irrational in so doing. For if they didn't, then they would never learn the language of their parents, and they probably wouldn't live for very long, either.

This sort of critique motivates the contrary model, which claims that testimony is epistemologically basic, and that the default is just: 'Believe what you are told' (Coady, 1992; Burge, 1993; Owens, 2000). Extending this view just a little and turning it into a historical hypothesis, someone might propose that throughout the period of the evolution of language this default setting was the only rule in operation; and that it is only with the arrival of our capacity for creative thinking and inference to the best explanation that we acquired the power to be a bit more selective in the testimony that we accept. If this proposal were on the right lines, then it would undercut the suggestion that we can appeal to pre-existing features of testimony in explaining how our capacity for inference to the best explanation first arose, and in explaining how that capacity is now realized in a modular cognitive system. On the contrary, the order of explanation should be the other way around.

Luckily, this extended view isn't remotely plausible. On just about all accounts of the evolution of language, our mind-reading abilities would need to have been highly developed and pretty firmly in place before language could make its appearance (see, e.g., Origgi and Sperber, 2000). And on just about all views of human ancestry, many of the pressures on our evolution were social and/or competitive ones (Byrne and Whiten, 1988, 1997; Mithen, 1996). So for sure, from the outset of language-use people would have used language to manipulate and deceive as well as to inform. And in that case consumers of testimony would have needed, from the very start, to be discriminating about what testimony to accept. It might be correct to say that the *default* setting is acceptance. But it is still the case that utterances and circumstances will need to be monitored for clues indicating that a particular item of testimony should be rejected.

This thought receives some confirmation from recent studies of the role of testimony in child development, which have found that even quite young children can be discriminating about sources of testimony and the likely reliability of testimony (Harris, 2002a, 2002b). In particular, even very young children will reject items of testimony that conflict with what they already believe ('Fish live in trees', 'Cats bark'). Yet these same children will happily accept and reason with such statements if they are introduced with a 'let's pretend' voice-intonation, or in the context of storytelling. Moreover, it should be noted that these are pre-four-year-old children, who on some accounts as yet lack any explicit conception of false belief (Wellman, 1990), and who in any case cannot recall their own previous false beliefs (Gopnik, 1993). So the processes in question are likely to be automatic and unreflective ones.

It seems plausible, then, that the principles of testimony-acceptance are historically and developmentally prior to the principles of inference to the best explanation. Two questions arise. First, could the principles of testimony-acceptance be realized in ways that are both computationally tractable and explicable within a modularist framework? And secondly, might our principles of inference to the best explanation have been constructed out of those of testimony-acceptance, once internally generated sentences started to be created by the language-production system, mentally rehearsed, and then processed in something like the way that items of testimony are? I shall be suggesting that we should return positive answers to both of these questions.

6.3 The Cognitive Components of Testimony Evaluation

Although accuracy, consistency, and coherence of theories aren't quite the same thing, for our purposes they can be treated together. Subjects are less likely to accept a piece of testimony if what they are being told doesn't fit in with the data that they believe and/or their other theoretical beliefs, and/or if what they are told is internally inconsistent. How could one test for these properties within a modularist framework in computationally tractable ways?

Roughly speaking, a hypothesis is *accurate* to the extent that it entails the data that it is intended to explain (either on its own, or in conjunction with supplementary beliefs and theories). And a hypothesis is *inaccurate* to the extent that it either fails to entail some of the data that it should entail (i.e. that it is intended to explain), or if it entails statements that actually conflict with the data. There is nothing quite parallel to this in testimony-acceptance, since many items of testimony aren't intended to explain anything; hence there are no pre-existing bodies of belief ('the data') that they should entail. Nevertheless, the various conceptual modules can get to work drawing inferences from the content of an item of testimony. And to the extent that the conclusions are already believed, then one is given some reason to accept the truth of that content, hence coming to believe what one is told. So as soon as hypotheses begin to be self-generated for purposes of explanation, this same procedure could be followed; but in addition there will then be a *target* of explanation (a set of data to be explained). So one can actively get to work (using both System 1 and System 2 processes) to see if the hypothesis can be made to entail that data. And it doesn't appear that there should be anything computationally intractable here.

The internal consistency of a hypothesis or item of testimony can be tackled in a couple of complementary ways. One is by globally broadcasting its content to the full range of conceptual modules, since some of these may have limited powers of decomposition and inconsistency extraction. (And recall that we have argued that the language module, in particular, should have such powers.) The other is by setting to work using whatever learned System 2 processes are available for such a task, attempting in various ways to derive an explicit contradiction from the statement in question.

How do you check a statement for consistency with what you already believe, however? Do you need to access every single one of your beliefs, simultaneously or in sequence, for comparison? If so, then checking testimony for consistency with one's beliefs would be the very epitome of computational intractability! But actually, it looks as if one can get a fair approximation to what is required in computationally tractable form. Assuming that memory systems are organized along content-addressable lines, then one can do a search on the conceptual elements of the statement being evaluated. If the statement is, 'Buffaloes are dangerous', then one should do a search of one's buffalo-beliefs and a search of one's harmless-thing-beliefs to see if one can find a direct conflict. At the same time the sentence can be fed as input to the various conceptual modules, which will draw inferences from it, and those further conclusions can also provide the materials for further searches of memory.

Finally, what of *coherence* with existing belief? Is this a property that potential consumers of testimony could check for in ways that are computationally tractable? In so far as coherence differs from either accuracy or consistency, it seems to be a somewhat more nebulous property. People speak, for instance, of a theory 'fitting in with' or 'meshing with' our existing beliefs and theories. What does this amount to? One aspect of 'fitting in' occurs when two theories share the same or similar ontological presuppositions. Thus a thesis of mind–brain identity fits in with our theories of biology and physical causation in just such a way, whereas Cartesian dualism doesn't. But there are surely other aspects to coherence, albeit harder to characterize. For example, two theories 'fit' one another to the extent that we can imagine possible mechanisms that might underlie both, even if we don't know of any (Koslowski, 1996). Thus even prior to the discovery of DNA, evolutionary theory and genetic theory fitted in with one another for precisely this reason: people thought that there could well be a common physical mechanism underlying each.

Some aspects of coherence seem likely to have been employed for purposes of evaluating testimony prior to the emergence of our capacity for scientific reasoning. For whenever a proposition contains concepts that enable it to meet the input conditions for one of our domain-specific conceptual modules (folk physics, folk psychology, and so on), enabling that module to draw inferences from it, then that proposition is likely to share the basic ontology of our existing beliefs produced by that module. And this is, as we noted, one aspect of 'fitting'. (Moreover, this is trivially easy to test for: one just has to see if any of the conceptual modules get cued into activity when the proposition in question is globally broadcast by the language comprehension system.) And according to Boyer (2001), this is an important part of what leads people to accept new religious beliefs on the basis of testimony. For cross-cultural research shows that all such beliefs tend to fall into the domain of one or another of four main conceptual modules (while adding unexpected extra properties)—namely, non-living natural physical objects, artifacts, non-human living things, and persons/ minds.

Other aspects of coherence, in contrast, may well only emerge together with scientific thinking itself, in the form of an acquired (System 2) heuristic. Our preference for theories that seem likely to share common underlying mechanisms, in particular, seems most probably to result from the fact that one of the goals of modern science is to find *unity* in nature—seeking to find a common set of laws under which all natural phenomena can be subsumed, and seeking to understand how processes that are governed by some (higher-level) laws can be realized in processes that are governed by other (lower-level) ones.

When human beings first started producing new sentences creatively through their supposition generator, then, and began displaying those sentences to themselves in 'inner speech', there would already have been in place some of the processes necessary to evaluate those sentences for acceptability, treating them as if they were items of testimony. In particular, people would already have been capable of selecting amongst hypotheses on the grounds of accuracy, consistency, and (to some degree) coherence with existing belief. And the processes in question give every appearance of being computationally tractable ones.[15]

---

[15] Given the fallibility of our intuitions concerning computational tractability and intractability, however, it should be admitted that there is a promissory note issued here that I am myself unable to honor.

But what of simplicity, fecundity, and explanatory scope? These are crucial elements of inference to the best explanation. But would they play a role in testimony-evaluation prior to the beginnings of creative thinking and hypothesis-generation? Not directly, perhaps. It is hard to see a role for such principles when evaluating a statement like, 'Buffaloes are dangerous.' But I find it highly suggestive that on some influential accounts of discourse interpretation, principles of *relevance* play a central role (Sperber and Wilson, 1995). For the twin principles of relevance are *minimize processing effort* (which roughly amounts to the same as *seek simplicity*), and *maximize information generated* (which roughly corresponds to *seek a combination of fecundity and broad scope*).

The principle of relevance in communication amounts to something like this, then: other things being equal, *adopt the interpretation of the other person's utterance that is simplest and most informative.* And in default circumstances, or circumstances where the credibility of an informant isn't in question, the principle of relevance can then be formulated as a principle of testimony-acceptance, thus: *believe the interpretation of the other's utterance that is simplest and most informative.*

It is not so very hard to imagine, therefore, that in contexts where what is in question are self-generated sentences, this same principle might be co-opted to become: *believe the sentence that is simplest and most informative.* And then this, combined with the insistence on accuracy, consistency, and coherence, would give us all of the main elements of inference to the best explanation. A 'faculty' of inference to the best explanation could then be constructed 'for free' from principles already present and employed in linguistic communication and testimony.

6.4 The Tractability of Relevance

Is relevance maximization computationally tractable, however? As I understand it, the main practitioners of relevance theory don't think that subjects make explicit and direct computations of degrees of relevance (Sperber and Wilson, 1996). However, they do think that judgments of relevance might be made by a semi-independent sub-module of the folk-psychology faculty, which was selected for in human evolution because of its role in language comprehension (Sperber and Wilson, 2002). There are a number of aspects to this account that need to be discussed in turn.

Sperber and Wilson argue that the various modular systems out of which our cognition is constructed, together with the principles according to which they operate and interact, will have been honed by evolution to maximize relevance. For humans occupy what many people have described as an *informational niche*.

We seek out and store large quantities of information about our environments and social circumstances. Since both storage and maintenance of information are costly, there will have been a premium set on seeking out information that can be economically represented and that is likely to have significant cognitive effects. And since retrieval of information, too, is apt to be costly of both cognitive resources and time, it is important that salient information should be recoverable swiftly. We are therefore likely to have evolved procedures of attention and resource-allocation that maximize the amount of information that can be acquired and accessed with minimum processing effort; and it is likely that the algorithms now embedded in our various modular systems will be similarly directed towards achieving relevance.

The evolution of human systems of communication (primarily gesture and language) would have been governed by similar constraints. A communicative attempt of some sort can only be successful if its recipients attend to it, and take the time and make the effort to figure out its significance. Would-be communicators therefore need to ensure that their missives are *worth* attending to: in short, they need to ensure that their messages will be *relevant* to their audiences. And whatever may be true of the evolutionary background, the proposal that linguistic communication amongst humans today is governed by the goal of relevance (amongst speakers) and the presumption of relevance (amongst hearers) is one that has considerable explanatory power (Sperber and Wilson, 1995).

Let me focus on the standpoint of the hearer, here, since it is this that we need to exploit in understanding how self-directed 'inner speech' might be governed by principles of inference to the best explanation. In assessing relevance, do hearers have to represent all of the available interpretations of an utterance? And do they need to extract all of the information that can be inferred from those interpretations, calculating the degree of difficulty of their own computations as they go? If so, then it might well be the case that judgments of relevance are computationally intractable, for the purposes of a naturalistic cognitive science.

Sperber and Wilson (1996, 2002) argue that nothing of this sort needs to take place, however. Rather, subjects adopt a *satisficing* policy, governed by heuristics. They begin from the interpretation that is most *accessible* and/or *salient*, given the physical and conversational context. They then set their various computational systems to work in extracting information from that interpretation. If they achieve results that are relevant enough, they stop, assuming that this is the intended message. If they don't, then they move on to the next most accessible interpretation and set to work on that. In order for this procedure to be successful, subjects might need to monitor how *hard* they are having to work in extracting information from a given interpretation of a sentence. And they might need to monitor how *much* information they are extracting, where the extraction process is undertaken by a bunch of inferential processes that operate automatically (and for our purposes we can suppose: by the various modular systems to which the content of the sentence is presented as input). But at any rate, it doesn't appear that achieving judgments of relevance should be computationally intractable.

It would seem, then, that the hope that we expressed earlier may well turn out to be realized—not only can principles of inference to the best explanation be understood in terms of a prior set of principles of linguistic testimony and discourse interpretation, but those principles might very well be implemented in computationally tractable ways.

6.5 Spandrels Versus Functions

Does the above discussion suggest that our capacity for scientific thinking is a *spandrel*, however? Does it follow that such thinking is a mere by-product of other selected-for aspects of cognition (a modular language faculty, together with principles of testimony-acceptance and discourse-interpretation)? And then, if so, is it really believable that so much of what is distinctive of our cognition should be a mere by-product, especially when the adaptive consequences seem so vast? (Consider the rapid expansion of *Homo sapiens* around the globe in the course of a mere 100,000 years or so, and the astonishing expansion of science and technology in just the last 500 years, for examples.)

Certainly there is an element of happenstance in my proposed account. For there is no intrinsic connection between the evolution of language for the communication of module-specific contents and the appearance of distinctively human thinking. And it is (perhaps) fortunate that the principles deployed in interpretation of speech and the assessment of testimony should be capable of doing double-duty as principles of inference to the best explanation. (I shall challenge this point in a moment.) But there is nothing really surprising or remarkable about all of this. It is a routine finding in biology that items initially selected for one function should become co-opted and reused in the service of others.

In any case, however, there are a number of respects in which direct selection for aspects of scientific thinking will probably have played a role, on my account. Most obviously, the creative supposition-generator needed to be constructed from a prior ability for mental rehearsal of action schemata. Arguably such a mechanism could be built quite simply using materials that were already available (a capacity for mental rehearsal of action schemata, natural language structures, and patterns of semantic association and similarity). But the mechanism itself would have been new, as would have been the behavior (pretend play) that I hypothesize to have been selected for because of its role in helping to strengthen and fine-tune the disposition to think creatively.

In addition, it isn't enough that language should already have been *capable* of linking together and combining module-specific contents. There also needed to be a disposition for it to do this on a regular basis. Now admittedly, this may be partially explained by the evolutionary pressures on communication, since combining contents can lead to compression in their mode of expression. But still there needs to be a disposition to generate such sentences in auditory imagination on a regular basis (in 'inner speech'), and to take those sentences or their consequences to be candidates for belief, depending upon their effects. These dispositions would presumably need to have been selected for. (It is hard to imagine how they might be learned behaviors, or culturally transmitted ones.)

Before concluding this section, however, let me return briefly to a point that was conceded too swiftly above: that there isn't any intrinsic connection between principles of testimony-acceptance and principles of inference to the best explanation. For both would appear to be truth-directed, in fact, as well as being governed by similar pragmatic constraints of cognitive economy. In general, we only want to accept items of testimony that are true, just as we only want to accept theories if they are true, or at least if they advance us closer to the truth. And both internal inconsistency and conflict with existing belief would seem to be signs of falsehood in both testimony and theory-construction.

But what of the preference for simplicity and fecundity? Is there any connection between these as principles of interpretation and as principles of theory choice? Arguably the same goal underlies both domains: the need to maximize useful information. Other things being equal, we want *as much* information as possible (whether in communication or in science), but we want it in a form that is as *useful* as possible, presented in a format that enables us to draw conclusions as and when we need them.

6.6 Scientific thought without Language

Although I believe that language plays an important role in much scientific theorizing (and although language will loom large again in the section that follows), I want to emphasize that I don't believe that language is actually *necessary* for scientific thinking. As I have noted at various points already in this discussion, much scientific thinking can be conducted in the form of visual or other forms of mental imagery besides inner speech, albeit often framed by a sentential context. ('Perhaps the two continental plates are moving apart like *this* [image].') And stronger still, at least limited forms of scientific thought can take place in the absence of language altogether. Let me elaborate.

Varley (2002) conducted a series of tests of causal and scientific reasoning with SA, a deeply a-grammatic aphasic man. SA suffered extensive damage to his left hemisphere, as a result of which he is profoundly aphasic. His productive vocabulary is now confined to nouns only (together with a few adjectives—no verbs). And he is deeply impaired in both his production and comprehension of grammatical structure. Nevertheless, he retains capacities for mathematics (using pencil and paper), and he continues to be responsible for the family finances. And previous testing (Varley, 1998) had shown that he retains his mind-reading capabilities, as well as being adept at comprehending and communicating through gesture and pantomime.

In one set of tests, Varley (2002) confronted SA with a complex 'basket lifter' machine, all the working parts of which were visible, but which also contained many non-functional 'distractor' elements. SA was allowed to observe the machine in operation, and was then led out of the room while the machine was disabled at a couple of different points. When he was returned to the room and invited to explain why the machine was no longer functioning, SA had no difficulty in identifying the relevantly damaged parts (although his own poorly coordinated hand movements prevented him from fixing the machine for himself).

Now so far, perhaps, this isn't wholly remarkable. For one might explain SA's success in such a case in terms of the intra-modular operations of his folk-physics system, which is of course prior to and independent of language. But SA also proved adept at hypothesis generation, and at proposing plausible explanations of novel phenomena. He was shown pairs of 'before' and 'after' line-drawings (for example, of a baby crawling towards a brick wall, followed by the baby sitting beside the collapsed brick wall), and invited to provide explanations. (Three candidate explanations were requested in each case.) SA did very well in this test, generating plausible explanations for the novel phenomena he was presented with, and sometimes crossing domains in the answers that he provided. Thus one of his explanations for a tennis ball seemingly knocking down a building, for example, was 'dream'. (His answers were communicated through a combination of gesture, drawing, and single words or phrases.)

I emphasized in Chapter 5 that hypothesis generation is grounded in a pre-linguistic capacity for the creative rehearsal of action schemata. So it perhaps isn't surprising that this aspect of scientific thinking should sometimes be independent of language. But it might be felt that the explanation that I have offered of our capacity for abductive inference in the present chapter, in terms of prior principles of testimony acceptance and relevance, is much more heavily dependent upon language. In which case, how can I consistently claim (as the facts seem to show) that this aspect of science, too, can sometimes be conducted independently of language?

In fact, however, testimony isn't an exclusively linguistic phenomenon, even if it is paradigmatically so. For much can be purposefully communicated through pantomime and gesture. Schaller (1991), for example, describes the case of Ildefonso, who was a congenitally deaf Mexican man who had lived all his life without any exposure to any form of Sign. Ildefonso could nevertheless communicate complex sequences of events through pantomime, such as how he was stopped and searched at a border-crossing. So the same principles of testimony-acceptance that I appealed to in Section 6.3 ought also to be applicable when the self-generated and globally broadcast candidate explanations are imagistic in form, rather than formulated in inner speech.

And likewise, too (and by the same token), principles of relevance aren't exclusively linguistic, either, but are applicable to all forms of communication. Someone who is trying to communicate something through gesture, or through pantomime, needs to try to maximize both the quantity and quality of the information that he intends to get across, and with a minimum of processing effort. Moreover, his audience will make a presumption of relevance in interpreting him. So people should still have a preference for simplicity, accuracy, and fecundity when the candidate explanations are self-generated visual images, rather than self-generated sentences.

In conclusion, then, although I claim that a very great deal of scientific thinking and reasoning is conducted in language (or rather, in sequences of mental events within which representations of natural language sentences pay an important causal role—see Chapter 4.7), the basic principles of abductive inference deployed in such reasoning have a wider source, deriving from principles employed in testimony and in communication quite generally.

7 Two Kinds of System 2 Belief-Formation

In the present section I shall consider two alternative models of how a represented sentence of natural language, entertained in inner speech, can lead to a novel belief, or can at least become the functional equivalent of a novel belief. One is worked out in considerable detail by Frankish (2004). The other has been implicit in my discussion thus far. I shall argue that both of them can be correct, each being applicable in different types of case, and each being realizable in a massively modular mind.

7.1 From Abduction to Belief: The Simple Model

How does an inference to the best explanation of some body of data yield a belief in that explanation? The simplest account would involve a compilation of a number of different decision-heuristics, each of which might be applicable to a range of cases. We might suppose, for example, that there is some threshold in the degree to which a hypothesis provides a *good* explanation (composed somehow from its degrees of simplicity, accuracy, etc.—more on this in a moment) beyond which that hypothesis is automatically believed in the absence of any competitor. Since on many occasions in science it is hard to think up more than one hypothesis to explain the data, and since on many other everyday occasions we don't bother to think beyond a single working hypothesis, the application of such a belief-generating heuristic would be sufficient to explain our beliefs in these instances.

How would the measure of *degree of goodness* of an explanatory hypothesis be computed, for the purposes of this heuristic? This, too, could be a heuristic matter. For example, one heuristic might be: if all measures are to any degree positive, then the theory is *good enough* to warrant belief, in the absence of any competitor. Thus if the hypothesis is simpler than any alternative that comes to mind, if it explains at least some of the data without overtly conflicting with any of it, and if no inconsistencies (either internal, or with existing belief) are detected, then the hypothesis is automatically stored as a belief. This heuristic, too, might be sufficient to explain many of the actual cases in which people unreflectively make up their minds and form a new belief on abductive grounds, when no alternative hypotheses are in play.

But what of those cases where there are two or more competing hypotheses under consideration? Again there might be simple heuristics adequate to determine an outcome in many real cases. One candidate would be this: if one hypothesis is better than another along *any* dimension, then that hypothesis should be believed in the absence of any third competitor, provided that the second hypothesis *isn't* discernibly better along any dimension. Hence if both hypotheses fit the data, are consistent, are coherent with existing belief, and are of similar explanatory scope, but one is definitely simpler than the other (as measured by the ease with which we can generate some of its more immediate implications, for example), then that hypothesis gets to be believed. Or if both hypotheses are equally simple, consistent, and coherent, but one explains more of the data than the other, then the former gets to be believed. Or if both hypotheses fit the data, are consistent, and are equally simple, but only one shares the same basic ontology as our existing beliefs, then that theory gets to be believed. And so on.

While heuristics of these sorts might be sufficient to explain how we come to form our abductive beliefs in many cases, they plainly can't account for all. In particular, they can't cover those cases where there are two or more competing explanations in play, each of which is better than the other along some dimension of evaluation (for example: one is simpler, but the other has greater explanatory scope). Now, we might respond to this problem by proposing an elaborate system for assigning numerical weights to each evaluative dimension, which then get summed according to some algorithm to yield a decision. But two things militate against us taking this route. One is the difficulty that philosophers of science have experienced in attempting to articulate the criteria that guide our selection of scientific theories into any sort of general rule. The other is that a set of simple heuristics is surely preferable to a complex algorithm on grounds of both ease of evolutionary emergence and computational tractability. While neither of these considerations is necessarily decisive, they do give us some reason to consider an alternative sort of approach.

Even if the kinds of simple decision-heuristics that we have suggested can't account for all cases, however, it is worth noting that they do possess some other attractive features in addition to their simplicity. In particular, their modes of application would plainly admit of individual variation amongst subjects, and their application could be more or less cautious and reflective, depending on how much is at stake. For example, it is possible to work more or less hard at looking for alternative hypotheses to compete with the one that first springs to mind. And it is possible to work more or less hard (and more or less long) at considering the extent to which a given hypothesis can explain the data. Likewise, it is possible to work more or less hard and long at looking for inconsistencies with existing belief. And so on. So we might expect individual variation along these dimensions, as well as variations within the same subject at different times, tracking variations in the importance of the explanatory belief that is in question. All this is consistent with the finding of Stanovich (1999) that System 2 reasoning is highly variable between subjects, and is influenced by features of 'cognitive style', such as a disposition to reflect before making a decision.

7.2 Frankish on Supermind: The Meta-representational Model

The account of abductive belief-formation that we have just been considering can be entirely first-order in character. An hypothesis is entertained; if the data can be derived from it easily enough, and no competing hypothesis is in play, then the content of that hypothesis is stored as a belief, for example. No reflection *on* the hypothesis as such need be involved. And this remains true even when more than one hypothesis is being considered. A hunter examining a scuff-mark in the dust might think, 'Perhaps an antelope dragging a wounded leg made that mark; or perhaps it was made by a stone kicked up by a passing wildebeest.' No explicit reflection on these hypotheses *as hypotheses* need be involved. All of the hunter's thoughts, up to the point of forming a new belief ('The antelope made the mark'), can be first-order thoughts about the physical signs observed, and the animals or other phenomena that might have made them. Frankish (2004), in contrast, proposes an account of the System 1/System 2 contrast that lines up with the distinction between first-order and higher-order thought. So System 1 processes are purely first-order (except in the case where the System 1 system in question is the mind-reading faculty), whereas System 2 reasoning is always realized in processes that are partly second-order in character, involving (unconscious) thoughts about our own beliefs and hypotheses as such.

According to Frankish, there are two quite different *levels* of human mentality, with one serving to realize the operations of the other. He labels these 'mind' and 'supermind' respectively. One of these levels ('mind') is unreflective and unconscious in its operations; and for our purposes it can be identified with the processing contained within the set of central / conceptual modules.[16] The other ('supermind') is realized in cycles of activity of the first sort, with inner speech and visual imagery serving to broadcast contents for further modular processing; and its operations are reflective and conscious. Now so far Frankish's account is consistent with that being developed in this book. A difference emerges, however, in his explanation of how supermental activity gives rise to new decisions, or new beliefs. For Frankish, this is always a partly second-order, meta-representational, process, as I shall now explain.

Frankish (2004) argues that new beliefs arise from the entertaining of sentences in inner speech when (and only when) people take a decision to *commit themselves* to reasoning and acting in the future as if the sentences in question were true. Then provided that on suitable occasions in the future they recall these commitments, and want to execute them, and have the power to generate suitable further sentences or actions in such a way as to fulfill their

---

[16] Frankish himself operates on the assumption that System 1 thinking is realized in distributed connectionist networks, which contain no discrete, structured, representational states. But this isn't because he is committed to the view that distributed connectionism correctly characterizes System 1 processes. It is rather because he is interested in using his account of System 2 processes to defend our common-sense psychology against the threat of eliminativism posed by such a form of connectionism. So System 2 can contain discrete, content-bearing, compositionally structured, and causally effective states (sentences in inner speech), even if System 1 doesn't.

commitments, then each will be the functional equivalent of a new belief. From the point of view of the other sentences the person commits himself to, and the actions that he performs, it will be *just as if* he believed the proposition that the sentence expresses. But the underlying explanation will be different. What is really going on is that the person believes that he has made a commitment, wants to fulfill that commitment, and is then acting in accordance with that commitment.

Thus imagine a tracker who has been considering two competing hypotheses to explain a scuff-mark in the dust: either it was made by a wounded antelope going east, or it was made by a healthy wildebeest traveling north. After due deliberation, he *makes up his mind* that a wounded antelope made the mark, which for Frankish means that he has committed himself to thinking and reasoning in the future as if it were true. The tracker wants to capture the antelope, of course. If it were true that the antelope had been traveling east, then he would head off to the east in pursuit. He has committed himself to acting just as if it were true that the antelope is heading east, and wants to honor that commitment; so he sets off towards the east at a run. Here he behaves just as he would if he had simply *believed* that the scuff-mark was made by a wounded antelope heading east—it is, you might say, *virtually* as if he believed that. But the underlying explanation is that he believes that he has made a commitment, and wants to act in the way that he has committed himself to acting.

So on Frankish's account a System 2 'belief' is really a commitment to reason and act in the future on the assumption that a given sentence is true. Such beliefs are always meta-representational in content, therefore, containing a representation which is *about* the sentence to whose truth the person is committed. How plausible is such an account? When it is mapped into the framework of our massive modularity thesis, we should drop the talk of what *people* do, and talk instead in terms of the operations of component systems. So a System 2 sequence might begin when a representation of a natural language sentence, 'P', is generated by the language production system and mentally rehearsed, then being broadcast to all central / conceptual modules. That representation is received by the language comprehension system, in particular, and a semantic content is extracted. This may be different on some occasions from the original thought that gave rise to 'P'. So let us work with such a case: the comprehension system extracts the content (expressed in Mentalese) that Q. This content is also made available to the full range of central / conceptual systems, which get to work drawing inferences from it and evaluating it. And this is then supposed to issue in a commitment to think and reason in the future as if 'P' expressed a truth.

This account seems, on the face of it, to be much more elaborate than is necessary (at least as an account of all cases—I shall return to this point in Section 7.3). For if the upshot of the content Q being processed by the conceptual modules is that it is suitably consistent and coherent with the subject's other beliefs, as well as being sufficiently simple and informative, and is therefore accepted to be true, then one would expect the consequence to be simply that Q is stored as a belief. The sentence 'P' can drop out of the picture altogether.

Consider what happens in a normal case of putative testimony. Someone else utters the sentence 'P'. This is received, processed, and represented by the language comprehension system, and the content that Q is extracted as the intended message. This is made available to the various central / conceptual systems that check it for consistency and coherence with existing beliefs, and the mind-reading system gets to work trying to figure out if the speaker is being honest. One upshot can be that one or more of these systems finds reason to question the likely truth of Q, in which case it is either rejected outright, or a conversation of some sort ensures. But another is that Q meets whatever criteria are in operation as the threshold for the believability of an item of testimony, and Q is thereafter stored as one of the subject's beliefs. Here, too, the representation of the natural language sentence 'P' drops out of the process quite early on. Thereafter all the computations are focused on Q, and the upshot is a belief that Q, not a belief that the subject has committed himself to thinking and reasoning as if 'P' were true, as Frankish would have it.

It might be objected—and fairly so—that there is a big difference between entertaining a sentence that results from someone else's testimony, where there is plausibly a presumption in favor of truth, and entertaining a self-generated sentence, where there surely isn't such a presumption (or at least, not if the generative processes include more than just encodings of existing belief). In the case of testimony, the default is that the content of the utterance should be accepted (believed). So it makes sense that much of the process should be purely first-order (checking the content against existing belief), and that any higher-order components should concern such things as the veracity of the speaker. And the default sequence can therefore be: an utterance of 'P' leads to the content that Q, which leads to the belief that Q. Where the utterance of 'P' is self-generated, in inner speech, however, things surely can't work like this, since the generative processes in question can often be creative and/or associative ones.

We have already seen in Section 7.1, however, how there can be purely first-order heuristic processes that lead to belief from self-generated hypotheses. Granted, there can be no *default* acceptance of hypotheses that are entertained in inner speech. But the processes that evaluate those hypotheses, influenced by their relative simplicity, accuracy, and so forth, can all be first-order ones. So there is no argument to be had in support of Frankish's account here.

It might also be objected that if the sentence 'P' is of the module-integrating sort discussed in Chapter 4.3, then its content will have to be broken up (into R and S, say) before being presented to the conceptual modules. And then there is no longer any single proposition, here, to be stored as a belief. If something unified is to be believed, then the only option is to adopt the attitude of commitment to 'P' itself. But I think this objection fails at both stages. First, I have suggested that the language comprehension system may operate via the construction of quasi-perceptual mental models. If so, then there would be no need to break up the content of a module-integrating sentence, since that content could remain unified in the form of a model. (Perceptual contents, of course, are unified in the relevant sense.) But secondly, even if the sentence 'P' does itself have to be stored in order for belief to occur, it doesn't follow that Frankish's commitment-based account needs to be endorsed. Rather, the stored sentence could be a mere aid to memory, serving to pull up its content with it when needed. But it would then be the latter (or rather, its Mentalese bearer) that occupies all the roles appropriate for occurrent belief, without any need for higher-order attitudes.

It is important to notice that Frankish (2004) may very well be correct that mentally rehearsed sentences play an indispensable role in enabling us to keep track of our conscious reasoning processes. We might also need to appeal to them in explaining how conscious reasoning can be an active process, placed under our personal control. Indeed, these ideas are fully in line with those being developed in this book. But appeals to meta-representational commitments aren't thereby mandated. Rather, inner speech may enable us to gain conscious access to some of our thoughts. And the element of control may derive from our control of speech generation, together with our skills in creating sequences of utterances that conform to certain abstract types (such as valid inference). The results may be believed *simpliciter*, rather than taken as objects of higher-order commitment.

7.3 A Mixed-Character Account of Abductive Belief

Frankish's (2004) dual-level view seems unnecessarily complex as an account of all forms of System 2 abductive belief, then. For why shouldn't System 2 activity—realized in cycles of inner speech and other imagery—issue directly in a first-order belief, rather than in a higher-order commitment to reason and act as if a sentence were true? As we saw in Section 7.1, however, our heuristic-based first-order approach seems unlikely to be capable of accounting for all cases, either. A natural strategy to attempt, at this point, would be some combination of the two accounts, provided that we can find some principled way of marking out their respective domains.

Notice that Frankish's sort of account *is* very plausible in *some* cases. Consider a hunter–tracker who can't decide whether a particular scuff-mark in the dirt is most likely to have been made by a wounded antelope, or rather by a stone displaced by a wildebeest. There may be considerations that count on each side. But still he has to act, and do something, or the hunt will be over. And if time is short, then he might take a practical decision (albeit a tentative one) to *act as if* the scuff-mark had been made by the antelope, on the grounds that this suggests a potentially promising line of activity. ('If the antelope made that mark, then she will have been heading towards those bushes over there.') So the hunter commits himself (temporarily, for present purposes) to thinking and acting as if the hypothesis in question were true.

Likewise a scientist entertaining two different hypotheses might be unable, initially, to decide between them. One might be much the simpler and more elegant, whereas the other might fit the data rather better, for example. So he might then resolve to adopt one of them as his working hypothesis—committing himself to thinking, reasoning, and investigating on the assumption of its truth—albeit tentatively. And sometimes such a resolve might be made on pragmatic grounds, such as that the hypothesis chosen has been under-explored by others, or that it seems more likely to win the support of funding agencies.

The phenomenon that Frankish (2004) identifies as *supermental belief* is at one end of a spectrum of similar phenomena, in fact (as he himself points out). We can commit ourselves to thinking and acting as if a hypothesis were true for limited local purposes, as in the example of the hunter. Or we can commit ourselves more broadly to accepting the hypothesis for purposes of professional enquiry, as in the example of the scientist. Or we can commit ourselves *tout court*—resolving to think and act as if the proposition were true for *all* normal purposes. While Frankish restricts the phenomenon of supermental belief to the latter sort of case, it is actually the existence of the spectrum itself that is suggestive of a principled distinction between first-order and higher-order instances of System-2-caused belief. For in all of the latter cases it is the fact that a conflict between competing hypotheses isn't easily and swiftly resolved that motivates a decision to think and act as if just one of them were true.

So here is how a mixed-character account might be developed. In cases where there is just one explanatory hypothesis in play, that hypothesis will automatically get stored as a belief, provided that it meets some (individually variable) threshold of goodness. And likewise in cases where there are two or more hypotheses under consideration, but where one of them has all of the advantages, then that one will be believed. These are cases where the simple heuristic processes of abductive inference that we envisaged earlier can operate.

In cases where the heuristic processes don't yield a verdict between two hypotheses, however, then meta-level reflection is caused to ensue. The subject's conceptual modules cooperate to generate further considerations that might lead to an adjudication, either of a module-specific sort, or recalled from previous social learning. And the task is now one of practical reasoning, or practical decision-making, of the sort to be discussed shortly in Chapter 7. In effect the question becomes, 'Which of the candidate hypotheses *should* I accept?' The result might be a commitment to think and act as if one of the two hypotheses were true for some limited set of purposes, or it might be a commitment *tout court*. And there will be just as much individual variability in this process as there is in decision-making generally, with the nature and strength of the subject's goals, the character and strength of the individual's beliefs, as well as his degree of risk-aversion and so on, all having an influence on the outcome.

Notice, however, that the distinction between those abductive beliefs that are straightforwardly believed and those to whose truth we have committed ourselves needn't be a hard-and-fast one. For if the status of a hypothesis to which we are committed changes as further evidence comes in or is drawn to our attention, in such a way that it can now issue in a belief via the first-order heuristic route, then that is what is likely to happen. So a hypothesis that was once a *commitment* is now a belief *simpliciter*. Likewise a hypothesis that is initially believed outright can be moved to the status of a commitment if countervailing evidence or considerations are noticed, or drawn to the thinker's attention by other people.

8 Conclusion

I have proposed a three-component model of scientific reasoning: creative hypothesis-generation, inferences that explore the implications of a hypothesis or match a hypothesis to the data, and inferences to the best explanation / abductive inferences. Each of these components (singly and in conjunction) is very likely of ancient ancestry, dating from the first emergence of *Homo sapiens*. But quite how they were assembled by the evolutionary process is moot. I have argued that the selection pressure was unlikely to have been the benefits of theory-acquisition in infancy, and I have emphasized many significant disanalogies between scientific reasoning (which is generally of a

System 2 sort) and the learning processes undergone by infants. It is possible, in contrast, that the evolutionary pressures derived from the benefits to be gained through hunting via tracking, and/or through other sorts of abductive problem solving.

I have suggested that the implicational aspect of the three-component package is realized in a pair of complementary ways. One is the System 1 inferences undertaken by the suite of central / conceptual modules. The other consists in learned System 2 inferences, which are themselves realized in cyclical operations of those modules, involving inner speech and other imagery. And I have suggested that the creative hypothesis-generator is the one described in Chapter 5 as emerging out of the distinctively human capacity for pretend play in infancy.

As for inference to the best explanation, or abductive inference, I have argued that there is no reason of principle why it *shouldn't* be achieved in a massively modular mind. And I have sketched out how a capacity for such inference might be realized, piggybacking on processes that probably first emerged to deal with verbal and non-verbal testimony, and which involve measures of simplicity, accuracy, consistency, coherence with existing belief, fruitfulness, and explanatory scope. In straightforward cases such measures might issue directly in belief, utilizing a variety of simple decision heuristics. But in more complex cases, *practical* reason will enter the picture: we have to decide (on the evidence available and in the light of our goals) whether we *ought* to accept the hypothesis in question, committing ourselves to reasoning and acting in the future on the assumption of its truth.

All of this looks to be consistent with massive modularity, I have urged. And it also looks as if the processes involved should be suitably computationally tractable. Moreover, to the extent that any light has been thrown on our capacity for scientific and abductive reasoning in this chapter, our massively modular explanatory framework has been further confirmed.

7

Distinctively Human Practical Reason

In this chapter I shall discuss how a massive modularity theorist should explain the distinctive properties and flexibility of human practical reasoning. Most of the elements of my account have already been put into place in previous chapters, so our discussion can be (mercifully) brief.

1 The Challenges

In Chapter 2.8 I sketched a modularist account of how a limited form of creative practical reasoning might be present in other great apes, utilizing mental rehearsal. That account was then further extended in Chapter 5, in a way that enables us to explain how the practical reasoning of human beings can become much *more* creative and flexible. Action schemata (also including *speech* action schemata) are generated creatively and then rehearsed, relying upon partial activations of similarly structured concepts in a given context, and deploying a variety of innate and learned heuristics.

Utilizing this system, novel action schemas can be generated and rehearsed, or linguistic descriptions of proposed actions can be created and rehearsed, with the resulting states being globally broadcast and accessed by a whole suite of different inferential systems. These include both belief-generating and desire-generating systems, the latter of which respond to suppositional input much as they would respond to the equivalent perceptual input—by creating an emotional / motivational response. These responses are then monitored by the somasensory system, and motivation towards the envisaged action is adjusted up or down accordingly. There seems to be no particular limit, here, to the degree of flexibility of behavior that might result from cycles of operation of creatively generated action descriptions, utilizing the network depicted in Figure 2.8.

What isn't yet explained within this framework, however, is all of the *phenomenology* that is distinctive of human practical reasoning. Granted, such reasoning often does involve visual or other imagery of envisaged action possibilities, or inner dialogue about the possibilities for action that are open to us, combined with monitoring of our emotional reactions to those possible actions and their consequences. But it also often involves reflection on what it would be *good* to do or *bad* to do, or on what we *must* or *must not* do. And more generally, our practical reflection seems to involve consideration of the *reasons* for and against the various actions open to us. One of our main tasks in this chapter is to see how these aspects of practical reasoning should best be explained within our modularist framework.

Moreover, all that has been explained so far is reasoning about *means*, not reasoning about *ends*. Cycles of mental rehearsal begin with the supposition, 'Suppose I did Q', and adjust motivations and plans accordingly. Yet humans don't *just* reason in this fashion. We also reason about ends. One obvious thing that humans can do in the course of practical reasoning that hasn't yet been allowed for in the models sketched earlier, indeed, is to weigh one goal against another. It is easy to get a partial handle on how this might go, however. For when trying to adjudicate between the goal for P and the goal for G, I might mentally rehearse pursuing each, and engage in multiple cycles of rehearsal and reasoning, thereby enabling me to think in more detail about what getting each of them would involve, and about their further consequences. Such thinking would provide me with more detailed P-involving and G-involving scenarios to feed forward through my motivational systems, and by monitoring my own reactions I can find myself responding to one scenario more favorably than the other.

However, we also reason about whether one end is *better* or *more important* than another, about which ends *ought to be pursued* in a given context, and so forth. And it is hardly very plausible that all of this should really be covert reasoning about means, where the overarching end is happiness, or maximum desire-satisfaction, or something of the kind. (See the discussion of multiple motivation modules in Chapters 2.5 and 3.6.) How is such reasoning about ends to be provided for within a modular framework, without radically changing the powers of the practical-reasoning system as such?

I have argued in Chapters 4 through 6 that seemingly a-modular creative *theoretical* thinking might be constructed out of modular components with minimal further additions. On the proposed account, a modular language faculty serves to link together the outputs of various central / conceptual modules, and makes possible cycles of processing activity by making non-domain-specific linguistic contents available to the central modules once again, in 'inner speech'. And a computationally simple supposition generator is built out of a capacity for mental rehearsal of action. When utilizing the resources of the language faculty, this might generate new sentences in ways that pick up on weak similarities and analogies, past associations, and so on. And a sort of virtual faculty of inference to the best explanation can be constructed from principles involved in the assessment of linguistic testimony and the interpretation of speech, leading to a preference for internally generated sentences that are consistent, coherent, and fit the data, as well as being simple, fruitful, and unifying.

Might human practical reasoning, too, co-opt the resources of this language-involving reasoning system? One fact that is especially suggestive, in this regard, is our tendency to convert desiderative contents into seemingly descriptive ones. Thus instead of simply *expressing* a desire for some object or situation ('If only P!', or 'Would that P were the case!'), we tend to say (and think) that P would be *good*, that P is *important*, that *I want* P, or whatever. Instead of expressing desires in sentences with the same kind of world-to-mind direction of fit of desires themselves, we use indicative sentences with the sort of mind-to-world direction of fit appropriate for belief. One plausible explanation of this otherwise-puzzling tendency—and one of the main hypotheses to be explored in this chapter—is that by enabling motivational states to be re-represented as theoretical ones, it enables those states to be reasoned with using the resources of the language-involving theoretical-reasoning system.

Another possibility would be this. Suppose that I have two active goals in the present context, for P and for G. I can form from these the quasi-descriptive thoughts (in language), 'Getting P would be good', and, 'Getting G would be good.' I might then already have a stored belief that enables me to adjudicate between them, of the form, 'Getting P-type things is better than getting G-type things.' Or I might believe things from which I can infer something that adjudicates between them. (Such beliefs might be acquired by testimony from others, inculcated by moral teaching, or learned from previous experience.) This would then lead me to focus exclusively on the thought that getting P would be good. Imagining P and monitoring my own reaction, the desire for P is reactivated and now presented to practical reasoning as the only candidate for action. The search for ways of achieving P can then go on as before. Here the effects of theoretical thinking on practical reasoning would be by way of manipulating *attention*.

It appears that a massive modularist should have no difficulty in explaining the distinctive flexibility and creativity of human practical reasoning, then. And some progress can be made in explaining the distinctive forms and phenomenology of such reasoning. (This topic will be pursued further in Sections 2 and 3 below.) But a more direct challenge to the architecture of belief and desire that I have been using throughout this book has been mounted by a number of philosophers in recent years (Dancy, 1993, 2000; Parfit, 1997,

2001; Scanlon, 1998). These philosophers claim that evaluative beliefs about reasons for action, and evaluative reasoning, can yield both intentions and actions without the intervention of any desire or other motivational state. This is a radical challenge to belief / desire psychology, as well as to any massively modular account (such as my own) that presupposes such a psychology. This will be considered in Section 5, following a discussion of the role of intentions in practical reasoning in Section 4.

2 Normative Modules Again

In the previous section I sketched answers to some of the challenges facing a massive modularity theorist who seeks to account for distinctively human practical reasoning. But other possibilities remain to be explored. One of these is that theoretical thinking about *norms* can lead to the creation of a new desire. This will be taken up in the present section.

As we saw in Chapter 3.7, a number of the modules postulated by evolutionary psychologists (and to some degree confirmed by later experimental work) are concerned with normative issues. Thinking about permissions, obligations, and prohibitions develops very early in young children, for example (Cummins, 1996; Núñez and Harris, 1998).[1] Moreover, children understand these notions, not just in so far as they pertain to themselves (in which case one might have postulated some sort of direct connection to the motivational system or the will), but also as applying to third parties. It seems inevitable, then, that we should think of the module in question as delivering *beliefs about* obligations and prohibitions. But these would be beliefs that would be frequently accompanied by the associated desires; and presumably the whole system would have been designed in this way (Sripada and Stich, 2006). So when I believe that I am obliged to do something, I generally have an intrinsic desire to do that thing in consequence. When I believe that I am forbidden from doing something, I generally have an accompanying desire *not* to do that thing, and feel *guilt* if I do. And when I believe that someone else has done something forbidden, I might become angry and have a desire to exclude that person socially in the future.

Similar points hold in connection with the social-contracts system—or 'cheater detection module'—proposed and investigated by Cosmides and Tooby (1992; Fiddick et al., 2000; Stone et al., 2002). This, too, seems designed

---

[1] Núñez and Harris don't believe in an obligations module themselves. But if massively modular models of mind are taken for granted (as I am doing here, of course) then their work is quite naturally seen as providing support for the existence of such a module.

as a belief-generating module, which operates not just in the first person, but also in the third person and from the perspective of another (Gigerenzer and Hug, 1992). Its job is to reason about social contracts in terms of cost / benefit structures, and in terms of who owes what to whom; one central concept of the system being that of a *cheat*—someone who takes the benefit in an exchange without paying the cost. And here, too, it only really makes sense that such a system should evolve, if it were to co-evolve with adaptations on the desiderative side of the mind, in such a way that one generally has an intrinsic *desire* to do one's bit in an agreed exchange, as well as a desire to punish or avoid those who have cheated on a contract (whether with oneself or with others).

From a modularist perspective it seems likely, then, that we have one or more modules designed for normative issues, which can straddle the belief / desire divide.[2] It might be that such modular systems pre-existed the language module, or co-evolved with it, or both. But the selection pressures that led to the evolution of these systems would surely have been long-standing. We know that exchange and trading networks pre-existed the appearance of modern *Homo sapiens* (McBrearty and Brooks, 2000), and we also know that earlier hominids led complex social lives, in which the coordination of plans and activities would have been crucial (Mithen, 1996). Indeed, as Gibbard (1990) emphasizes, it is problems of interpersonal coordination that create the main pressure for systems of normative thinking and speaking to evolve.

Moral beliefs form one sub-class of normative belief, of course. And a variety of accounts are possible of the relationship between moral thinking and the sorts of modular systems envisaged above. On one view, for example, morality might have an independent source, being grounded in our natural feelings of *sympathy* when constrained by considerations of consistency (Singer, 1979). On another view, morality might be what you get when you combine an idea drawn from one of the above normative modules—that of *fairness* in an exchange—with thinking about the general systems of rules that should regulate human conduct (Rawls, 1972). And on yet another view, morality may result when more general normative thinking is combined with a certain distinctive sort of *affect* (Nichols, 2002). Moreover, once conducted in language, of course, or in cycles of linguistically formulated 'inner speech', such thinking would be capable of uniting concepts across modular domains, as well as generating novel norms for consideration and evaluation through the activity of the suppositional system.

---

[2] I am leaving it open whether the social-contracts system is a sub-module within a larger obligations / prohibitions system, or whether there are two distinct modules here dealing with closely related types of content.

I should emphasize that the ideas sketched here are consistent with a variety of positions concerning the nature of moral belief itself. Some such account as this ought to be acceptable to those who defend a sort of quasi-realism, or covert expressivism, about moral discourse, say (Gibbard, 1990; Blackburn, 1993). But it ought also to be acceptable to those who think that morality is more properly cognitive in character, and who perhaps see moral truths as *constructions*, grounded in the idea of a set of rules that no one could reasonably reject who shared the aim of free and unforced general agreement, for example (Rawls, 1972, 1980; Scanlon, 1982, 1998).

3 Theoretical Reasoning About Desires and Goods

The proposals on the table so far, then, are twofold. The first is that there is a flexible and creative theoretical-reasoning system built out of modular components. And the second is that there are one or more modules for generating normative beliefs, which can interact in complex ways with the theoretical-reasoning system, and which also tend to generate the corresponding desires. So in these respects, at least, our theoretical thinking can become practical.

This cannot, by any means, be the whole story, however. For it isn't just in respect of moral matters, or with regard to obligations and prohibitions more generally, that we are capable of practical reasoning of an unlimitedly flexible and creative sort. We can also reason in the same kind of flexible and creative way concerning things that we *want*. How is this to be accommodated within a modularist perspective?

3.1 The Problem of Descriptive Goals

Let us return to the suggestion briefly mooted towards the end of Section 1. This is that one way in which language might be implicated in an enhanced (but basically still modular) practical-reasoning faculty could result from our disposition to express desires and intentions in descriptive form. This would enable them to be processed in the manner of theoretical beliefs, hence harnessing the resources of the language-involving theoretical-reasoning system. Thus instead of just thinking longingly of some desired state of affairs, P, we are often disposed to think in descriptive mode, 'I want P', or, 'Getting P would be good.' These thoughts are then in the right format to be treated by a flexible and creative theoretical-reasoning faculty. (See Gibbard, 1990 ch. 5, for a related proposal.)

One significant problem for such an account, however, is the following. Systems of theoretical reasoning will be constructed so that *conviction* is transferred from premises through to conclusions. If we start from initial propositions that we believe to be true, and reason theoretically, then the result will be a further proposition in whose truth we have some tendency to believe (provided that we have no independent reason *not* to believe it, of course). Now, the proposal under consideration here is that we can further expand the powers of our practical-reasoning system by being disposed to convert motivational propositions into descriptive / theoretical ones, thereby harnessing the non-domain-specific powers of our *theoretical-reasoning system*. But how are we to guarantee that transfer of *conviction* in an argument involving such covertly desiderative propositions will also deliver a transfer of *motivation*?

Suppose that I start from a desire for some state of affairs, P. I then transform this into the descriptive statement, 'P is good', reason with it theoretically, and derive a further conclusion that I then have some disposition to believe, Q IS GOOD. But what then ensures that I translate this new descriptive belief back into a desire for Q? Without such a 'translation', the augmenting of the practical-reasoning module by the resources of theoretical reason would be without any practical pay-off.[3]

It looks, then, as if the proposal for the use of non-domain-specific theoretical reasoning to augment the powers of our practical-reasoning system might require a corresponding adaptation within the latter. Namely, whenever practical reason receives a descriptive / evaluative, but covertly desiderative, belief as input, it should generate the corresponding desire, and reason accordingly. While such an adaptation is no doubt possible, it would require a complex and messy interface between the two systems. For some way would have to be devised for identifying, from amongst the wider class of descriptive propositions, those that are covertly desiderative in content. Given the extensive range of evaluative predicates humans employ, this would be by no means easy. Moreover, such complexity would partly undermine the attractiveness of the original proposal, which was to explain how human practical reasoning could attain its distinctive inferential flexibility by co-opting resources that were already available.

---

[3] Am I warranted in writing of *the* practical reason module? For didn't I argue in Chapter 2.7 that there are multiple such modules? Recall from Chapter 1 that a module can have other modules as parts, however. And as we saw in Chapter 2.8, the practical-reasoning system that got constructed at some point within the great ape / hominid lineage is constructed out of multiple motivation-specific practical reason modules, combined with mental rehearsal, somasensory monitoring, and mechanisms to adjust motivation up or down accordingly.

3.2 Desiring to do What is Best

More plausible, and more minimal, might be the following. We can postulate that an adaptation subsequent to the appearance of theoretically augmented practical reason is an innate desire to do what one judges that it would be *best* to do. For in that case, when I conclude my theoretical reasoning about value with the belief that, all things considered, doing Q would be best, then this would create in me the corresponding desire to bring about Q.

Does this suggestion sit poorly with the claim that practical reason (like other forms of reason) is a satisficing process, rather than an optimizing one, however? Not at all. For the idea is *not* that some mechanism has evolved that can (at least sometimes) ferret out and identify what is genuinely the *best* solution to practical problems, working through all possible ways of solving those problems and exhaustively calculating their various costs and benefits. Rather, the claim is that when someone reaches the conclusion that a given option would be the best *of those that he has considered*, utilizing whatever satisficing and/or heuristic comparison procedures and stopping rules he actually employed, then he is disposed to *desire* that option as a result. The *judgment* that an option is best can be arrived at by whatever quick-and-dirty methods you like. My point is just that such judgments can have practical force provided that people have an innate disposition to desire what they judge that it would be best to do.

We would still need a story about how such a desire could be selected for, however. So we need a story about how the use of theoretical reason to augment practical reason would have some advantages in the absence of such a desire, and yet still more advantages *with* such a desire. Telling such a story isn't trivial, by any means. But we have already made a start on it, in fact, through some of the proposals sketched in earlier sections.

Consider the attention-manipulating use of theoretical reason, for example. One might expect that the effect of such attention manipulation would be less than perfect. For often the original competing desire may remain salient, and hence continue to intrude in the process of practical reasoning. If our judgments of what is better than what are generally reliable (aligning themselves with goals of greater adaptive significance), then there might be pressure for the theoretical system to have yet more influence on the practical one. An obvious way to do that would be to fix in place an innate desire to do what one judges to be the best.

Note that some such proposal can be rendered independently plausible through its capacity to handle the traditional philosophical problem of weakness of will. Sometimes we judge that, all things considered, it would be best to do Q, but we then go and do P instead. How is this possible? The answer comes readily to hand if a judgment of what it would be best to do is a mere belief, albeit one that is innately liable to generate a corresponding desire. For sometimes this tendency might fail; or the desire created might be of insufficient strength to defeat the desire for P in the competition to control the resources of the practical-reasoning system.

3.3 From the Good to the Obligatory

There is another way in which theoretical reasoning about goods might become practical. As we noted in Section 2, a number of belief-forming modules would seem to have—associated with them or built into them—connections to desire, in such a way that certain kinds of normative belief will generally give rise to a corresponding desire. It is possible, therefore, that as our theoretical-reasoning abilities become enriched through the addition of language and language-based creative thinking, thereafter some of the theoretical reasoning that results could at the same time become covertly practical, piggybacking on existing connections between belief-forming modules and desire. To see how this can happen, we need to draw a distinction between the *actual* and *proper* domains of a module (Sperber, 1996).

The *proper* domain of a module is the task or tasks for which the system in question was designed or evolved. But the *actual* domain is the set of concepts / conditions that happen to meet the modular system's input conditions. For example, the proper domain of the system in human males that generates sexual desire from visual inputs would presumably have been the presence of a sexually receptive female. But the actual domain now includes drawings, paintings, photographs, videos, and much else besides.

In the case of the obligations / prohibitions module, the proper domain would have been the task of learning, conforming to, enforcing, and exploiting the norms that are prevalent in one's society or social group. But the actual domain might be much wider. So it could be that language enables us to feed additional creative or inter-modular contents to the obligations / prohibitions module, in such a way as to generate a desire out of a theoretical belief where none existed previously. Specifically, if we were disposed to convert evaluative statements of what it would be *good* to do into statements of what one *must* do, what one is *obliged* to do, or of what one *should* do, then this would meet the input conditions of the obligations / prohibitions module in such a way as to generate the appropriate desire. And surely we do have just such a disposition. When reasoning about what it would be good for me to do, and reaching the conclusion that doing P would be best, it is entirely natural to frame such a conclusion in the format, 'So that's what I *must* do, then', or in the thought, 'So that's what I *should* do.'

A disposition of this sort would have the same sort of evolutionary rationale as the previous proposal concerning a desire to do what one judges best. For if our theoretical reasoning about value is reliable enough in evolutionary terms, then one might expect pressure for an evolved disposition to convert judgments of what it would be *good* to do or *best* to do into judgments of what one *must* do. This would enable it to harness the motivational powers of the normative-reasoning system, in such a way—again—that our theoretical reasoning can become practical. And it would be the functional equivalent of a disposition to desire what one judges to be best.

It begins to look, then, as if much that is distinctive of human practical reasoning might be explicable in modular terms. Such reasoning can happen via cycles of mental rehearsal and self-monitoring, and through a disposition to cast practical issues in theoretical language, hence harnessing the powers of our theoretical-reasoning abilities (which I have argued are themselves constituted out of a suite of interacting modules). This would require the evolution of a further disposition, either to desire what one judges to be best, or to convert theoretical judgments of value into judgments of what one *must* do or *is obliged* to do—hence piggybacking on the simultaneous theoretical / practical functions of a normative-reasoning module—or both.

4 Two Kinds of Practical Reasoning and Intention

There is an important strand in our practical lives to which I have thus far devoted insufficient attention. This is the role of *intentions* in coordinating and structuring our activities, both over time in our own lives and in our interactions with other people. This role has been emphasized especially by Bratman (1987, 1999), who argues not only that intentions aren't reducible to complexes of belief and desire, but that they are inherently normative in character. What I shall argue is that Bratman conflates two distinct *kinds* of intention. One is a simple variety that we share with other great apes, at least. The other is a more complex form that is, indeed, imbued with beliefs about norms, and that is probably distinctively human. But this more complex variety might well be reducible to suitable sets of beliefs, desires, and intentions of the simpler sort (in which case it isn't *qua* normative that intentions are irreducible).

4.1 Simple Intention

Often when we reason about what to do, the opportunity for action isn't yet at hand. Hence the conclusion of deliberation cannot be an action, but is rather an *intention* to act in a particular way in the future, when the right time or the right circumstance arises. For example, I might, in the morning, spend some time thinking about what to do that evening. After considering the merits of various possibilities I might decide to stay in with a movie that I have been thinking about renting for some weeks; and I might therefore form the intention of stopping by the Blockbuster store on my way home. I might then not think about the matter again for the rest of the day, until I get off my bus near my home. At that point something might remind me of my plan, and I then take a detour from my normal route in order to visit the store.

As Bratman (1987) argues in connection with similar cases, my desire to watch a movie needn't be active at the time when I take my detour. All that need happen is that I recall my plan of stopping to get a movie from the store and this, together with my knowledge of the store's location relative to my present position, determines the direction in which I set off walking from the bus stop. Nor can my intention be equated with a *desire* to stop at the store for a movie. (Nor with the *belief* that I *will* stop at the store, of course.) For such a desire would be in competition with my other desires to control my behavior, such as my desire to get home as quickly as possible. But what is distinctive of intentions, in contrast, is that they *trump* or *pre-empt* any competing desires, in normal circumstances—that is to say, unless some change in circumstances makes me decide to re-evaluate my original plan. (For example: my wife calls me on my cell phone to tell me that we have been offered free tickets to see *Othello* that evening.)

The cognitive architecture of belief, desire, and intention is depicted in Figure 7.1. I have used boxes in the regular way to represent processing systems, but ovals have been deployed to represent stored states. It seems most plausible to think of intentions as stored action schemata, of greater or lesser degrees of conceptualization and abstractness. (And by an 'action schema' I mean a state whose functional role is to initiate and organize some action or sequence of actions, guided by perceptual input.) Just as the output of a belief-generating module is an active item of information (an active belief), which can be either used immediately or stored in memory; so the output of the practical-reasoning system is an activated action schema, which can be either implemented immediately—if the conditions are right—or stored in what I would guess would be a distinctive form of memory for later reactivation.

As Bratman (1987) emphasizes, the *point* of intentions is to enable us to coordinate activities over time, given that we are creatures with limited reasoning abilities, and given that the amount of time we have for practical reflection is generally pretty restricted. Without intentions, we would continually be having to reason about what to do afresh every time that we act—reviewing our goals, the options open to us, and our beliefs about possible means to the realization of our goals. The computational burden would be enormous.

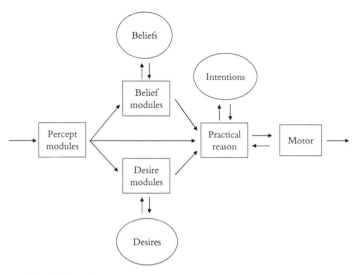

Figure 7.1. Stored intention

By forming intentions, in contrast, we can *settle* some aspects of our practical lives, in such a way that our intentions and plans are thereafter taken as fixed points in our reasoning, constraining our options unless something unexpected happens that forces us to reconsider them. We can then focus our attention and limited cognitive resources on filling in the gaps in plans already decided upon.

Thus conceived of, there seems no particular reason to think that intentions will be a peculiarly human phenomenon. For other species of ape, at least, face similar problems of cross-temporal and interpersonal coordination. Recall one of the examples from Sanz et al. (2004): chimpanzees who visit a site at which there are underground termite nests never arrive there without an appropriate puncturing stick, unless such a stick had already been left behind on a previous visit. It seems plausible that the chimp might have formed an intention rather similar to the one that I form about detouring to visit a Blockbuster store on my way home: 'When I get near to the site I will detour into the forest to collect an appropriately stout stick.' And this intention, when reactivated as the chimp nears the site, will determine its direction of travel without the animal having to repeat its earlier reasoning about the means necessary for securing termites from an underground nest, and without its desire for termites having to be reactivated, either.[4]

---

[4] Indeed, when the chimp navigates from one place to another—in this case heading for a particular set of termite nests—it seems unlikely that the desire that originally determined its direction of travel would need to be continually active. Rather, once the decision to head towards that spot has been taken, the chimp's movements are guided by an active intention or action-plan. The desire to eat termites impacts the initial decision, but thereafter can remain dormant.

4.2 Intentions as Commitments

Intentions of the sort discussed above are purely first-order phenomena, since the only thoughts that need to be involved in their formation and execution are thoughts about the things desired, and thoughts about the contingencies of the world. Nor are such intentions normative in character. For people executing such intentions don't have to consider themselves *required* to act in the way that they do. However, human beings do also form states of intention that are intrinsically normative (at least in the sense of involving beliefs *about* norms)[5] and that require a capacity for higher-order thought. For there is a kind of 'making up of mind' that is a *commitment* to perform a given action at a certain point in the future, where a commitment is a state possessing both of the above properties (Frankish, 2004). This is easiest to see in the case of explicit, publicly announced, intentions.

Suppose that I announce to my family before leaving for work in the morning that I intend to get the six o'clock bus home in the evening. As a result, others may make plans that in one way or another depend upon me fulfilling my intention. Knowing this, I have a new source of motivation, which can give rise to a sort of 'virtual' intention quite apart from whether my simple intention to travel on the six o'clock bus continues to exist and be operative. When the time comes to travel, I may recall what I said I would do, and regard myself as bound to do it. Believing that I have committed myself to traveling on the six o'clock bus, and wanting to execute my commitments, I might now form the intention of traveling on that bus, even if my original intention had somehow lapsed in the interim, or even if other considerations would normally have caused me to give up my intention.

Something similar can occur outside social contexts. Recalling that I had made up my mind to travel on the six o'clock bus, and wanting to do what I have made up my mind to do, I might take that bus independently of the operations of any simple (purely first-order, non-normative) intention. For I might think that people *ought* to follow through on their intentions, in general. And then given that this ought-belief generates a corresponding motivation, in the manner outlined in Section 2, I have a *new* reason for undertaking the action that I believe I formed the intention of performing, even if I am misremembering the event, or even if I have lost that intention meanwhile.

---

[5] As we saw in Chapter 4.6, some philosophers think that beliefs and intentions are normative in a much richer sense than this—they think that the very capacity to *have* beliefs, or to *have* intentions, depends upon one's general adherence to norms of rationality (McDowell, 1994). I am committed to rejecting such a view, of course.

For many of us, it is an important part of our self-conception that we should be steadfast, or strong-willed. We think that we shouldn't change our minds too easily; nor should we be easily deflected from our plans. Hence if I think to myself, 'I shall finish that piece of writing tonight', I might thereafter have sufficient motivation to finish my writing even if my initial thought didn't truly reflect the formation of a (simple) intention. It is enough that I should *believe* that I have formed that intention. For then, wanting to do what I (take myself to) intend to do, I may settle down to complete my writing nevertheless.

There are therefore two distinct causal routes to the formation of an intention, paralleling the two distinct routes to the formation of belief that we discussed in Chapter 6.7. And these different routes result in two different kinds of intention. One route is first-order, and needn't involve any beliefs *about* my intentions or commitments. But the other route is higher-order, depending on my beliefs about what I intend, or my beliefs about what I have committed myself to doing; and in the normal operations of this second route, normative beliefs will generally play an important part.

5 Desires *Versus* Reasons

All of my discussion so far in this chapter has been premised on the assumption that human practical reasoning has a belief / desire / planning / intention structure. I have assumed that human practical reasoning involves the integration of beliefs with desires to generate intentions and actions. But some have argued that human theoretical judgment can itself be directly practical. Some think that beliefs about what it would be *good* to do are directly motivating, without requiring the intervention of any desire (Dancy, 1993, 2000). Others have argued that it is our perception of *reasons* for action, rather than our desires, that provides the motivational element in practical reasoning—with desires themselves only being motivating to the extent that they involve the perception that we have a reason for acting (Scanlon, 1998). These claims mount a radical challenge to the account of the architecture of the human mind that I have been defending throughout this book.

5.1 Weaker Claims

It is important to keep these claims about motivation separate from claims about the nature of reasons for action themselves, however (which are often made by the same authors). Thus Dancy (2000) argues that desires are never reasons, and that reasons for action don't depend upon, nor need to be grounded in, desires. He argues that the mere fact that someone desires something is never a reason for them to pursue it, independent of any claim about the value of that thing, or about some value that can be promoted by achieving it. Indeed, Dancy (2000) also argues, not only that reason-explanation isn't really a species of causal explanation, but also that reasons themselves aren't psychological states of the agent, but are rather features of the world. Since these claims about the nature of reasons entail nothing about cognitive architecture, nor about belief / desire psychology, they aren't relevant to the topic of this book. I therefore shan't discuss them here. For one could agree that reasons for action are provided by facts about value, or facts about obligation, while maintaining that our best psychological account of how actions are produced, and causally explained, always involves the integration of beliefs with desires.

Dancy (2000) also argues, however, that desires are often caused to exist via the agent first coming to believe something. He argues, in short, that desires are often caused by beliefs. And likewise Parfit (1997) argues against what he calls 'the Humean theory' that beliefs can only motivate us when combined with some desire whose existence is causally independent of beliefs. These claims might appear to have architectural implications. They suggest that the causal route can go from belief to desire to intention and action, rather than beliefs and desires *interacting* with one another (in 'side-by-side' fashion) to produce intentions and actions. And this does look like a challenge to the sort of belief / desire architecture that I have been assuming throughout.

These appearances are deceptive, however. On the contrary, precisely what my sort of modularity-thesis predicts is that beliefs can and do cause desires. For notice that beliefs will generally be included amongst the inputs to our desire-generating modules. (See Chapters 2.5, 3.6, and 3.7.) For example, coming to believe for the first time that a particular woman is my mother might cause in me feelings of sexual revulsion towards her. (And one might say, in consequence, that it is the fact that she is my mother that provides my *reason* for avoiding sex with her.) Indeed, *all* desire-generating modules are *information-based*, in the sense that they depend for their operations on receiving information about the world, or about the subject's own body, as input, where that input is provided either by our perceptual systems or by our belief-generating modules. So *all* activated desires will be at least partly caused by informational states, even if those states aren't always beliefs, but are sometimes perceptions.

Recall from Chapter 3.7, too, that those of our modules that have been designed to deal with normative issues are likely to have a complex structure, enabling them to straddle the belief / desire divide. One set of components will be cognitive, devoted to discerning the norms that are operative in one's culture, as well as to figuring out whether the current circumstances are such that a given norm does or doesn't apply. But another set of components is connotative, attaching intrinsic motivation of various sorts to the non-normative components of our activated normative beliefs.[6] So on this model, too, one might expect a belief (such as the belief that a particular action would be wrong) to give rise to a desire (such as the desire not to perform the action in question). Yet the two states are still distinct existences, each with its own intentional content and causal properties.

We can therefore concede that reasons for action can often be beliefs; as well as conceding that our beliefs can often cause us to have certain desires. (And notice that in conceding this we are conceding that reason is *not* 'a slave to the passions'. For if reasoning can give rise to a novel belief, which in turn causes us to have a novel desire, then 'passion' has here been 'controlled' by reason.) But it is quite another matter to say that either reasons or beliefs can motivate action *independently of desires*. (I propose to call this 'the doxastic theory of motivation'.) This really would mount a challenge to the belief / desire architecture presented in this book. And it is on this claim, accordingly, that I shall focus.

More needs to be said in elucidation of the doxastic theory of motivation, however, before we can turn to evaluate the arguments for it. For those who defend such a theory will often concede that there are desires *involved in* all motivated action, but not as independently motivating causal factors. Nagel (1970), for example, allows that whenever there is motivated action, there is desire. But he claims that these desires are often mere logical consequences of the motivation to perform the action. On this account, a judgment that I ought to do Q can itself be sufficient to motivate me to do Q. And as a result of me being so motivated, it can truly be said of me that I want to do Q. But here the 'desire' is a mere logical consequence of my state of motivation, it isn't an independent source of motivation. On this account, the doxastic state—the judgment that I ought to do Q—can itself provide all the motivation that is needed.

On the contrasting picture to which I have committed myself in this book, on the other hand, the difference between belief and desire is an architectural one, built into the basic causal 'flowchart' of the mind (see Figure 2.1). Beliefs and desires are here conceived, not as mere aspects of the *interpretation* of action, but as discrete, structured, causally effective content-bearing states. And the claim is that all action is a causal consequence of at least one desire interacting with at least one belief, or of at least one desire interacting with perception. So

---

[6] Thus a normative belief with the content, *that I should help this person now* will tend to give rise to a desire with the non-normative content, *that I help this person now*.

the difference between the two accounts turns, not on whether desire is always present when there is action, but on whether desires (realistically construed) are always causal factors in the production of action. I claim that they are; the opposing doxastic theory of motivation claims that they are not.

5.2 The Case for Motivation Without Desire

The most explicit set of arguments in support of the doxastic theory of motivation is provided by Scanlon (1998). A good number of these focus in one way or another on the phenomenology of (conscious) desire. Examining what it is like to feel thirsty, for example, Scanlon argues that it cannot be the sensations of dry throat and so forth alone that motivate drinking. He argues that the real source of the motivation consists in the judgment that the future pleasure of drinking (assuaging the dry throat) *counts in favor of* drinking. But what justifies this exclusive focus on *conscious* events? It is perfectly consistent with the phenomenology involved here that the conscious judgment, *that a drink would be good*, is itself the expression of an underlying desire-state. And the latter gets expressed in doxastic form by virtue of our general disposition to express desire-states in such a way as to enable them to be processed by the resources of theoretical reason (as I suggested in Section 3).

Likewise, the *absence* of any phenomenology characteristic of desire in many cases where we are nevertheless motivated to comply with a moral judgment is no argument in support of the doxastic theory of motivation, either. People will often say things like, 'I *must* do it, but I really don't *want* to.' It doesn't follow that there isn't a non-conscious desire accompanying (and perhaps caused by) the normative judgment involved. Moreover, recall that on Damasio's (1994) account, the mental rehearsal and self-monitoring system can often operate in swifter 'as if' mode, in which no actual bodily response gets caused. Nevertheless a simulated or predicted response can be used to ratchet up the desirability of the rehearsed option. So exactly what we might have predicted is that desires without any associated phenomenology are often caused in us by conscious reflection.

Scanlon (1998) also distinguishes and defends a common-sense notion of desire that he calls 'desire in the directed-attention sense'. When I am thirsty, my attention might keep returning to the thought of drinking, where drinking is cast in a favorable light. Thoughts of potable liquid will keep intruding into consciousness, even when I am resolved to concentrate upon other things. Likewise when I have a strong desire to do my duty, or to achieve posthumous fame—my thoughts will keep returning to considerations of duty, or of fame, with these considerations casting their objects in a favorable light, as good, or as valuable, or as 'to be done'. And in all such cases, Scanlon thinks, it isn't the desire itself (the continual focusing of my attention) that motivates the action, but rather the *reasons* for action that occur to me when I do so attend. It is the perception of some consideration as *a reason* that motivates me when I act, not a desire in the directed-attention sense of desire.

I very much doubt whether there is any such thing as the directed-attention sense of desire, however. That is, I doubt whether ordinary folk believe that in such cases their desire for something is *identical with* the fact that their attention keeps returning to thoughts of that thing. Rather, they surely believe that their strong desire is the *reason* (in the sense of 'cause') why the object of their desire keeps grabbing their attention. It is *because* I am very thirsty (that is, have a strong desire to drink) that I keep finding myself thinking of glasses of cool water or beer; my desire isn't to be *identified with* the fact that my attention keeps returning to thoughts of drink. And likewise it is *because* I want posthumous fame that my thoughts keep returning to that topic. And whatever the folk might believe, this is certainly a consistent and possible position, and one that Scanlon has done nothing to undermine. On this account, so far from the motivation for action being provided by the 'favorable light' in which the object of desire is cast when I attend to it, the motivation is provided by the desire, which merely gets expressed consciously in the form of thoughts of goodness, or valuableness, or to-be-done-ness (or which is caused by such thoughts, perhaps—recall that according to the ideas sketched in Sections 2 and 3, judgments of what it would be best to do, or of what I ought to do, might cause in me a desire to do that thing).

Scanlon (1998) does provide one direct argument *against* the view that motivations are always provided by desires. He considers the example given by Quinn (1993), of the man who continually feels the urge to turn on every radio that he comes across, but without seeing anything *good* about radios being turned on. Scanlon claims that such a desire doesn't rationalize the man's actions—we aren't satisfied when we are told that what the man wants is, *that radios be turned on*—and he concludes that it is the missing perception of some *reason* for the action to be undertaken that is the crucial component of desire, whenever desires *do* succeed in rationalizing actions.

There is an alternative construal of this example that seems equally valid, however. This is that the explanation for why we aren't satisfied when told of the man's intrinsic desire to turn on radios isn't because desires, as such, don't explain actions, but rather because the desire in question is so unfamiliar to us. We *are* familiar with *extrinsic* desires to turn on radios (e.g. to hear the news, or the results of a ball game, or to listen to music); but we are told that none of these are applicable in this case. So of course we are puzzled. For there isn't a familiar generalization under which we can subsume such an intrinsic desire, of the sort that we have available to us in the case of thirst and other such desires. ('When people haven't drunk anything for a long time, then they have an intrinsic desire to drink.') It doesn't follow that the real motivations for action lie in the perceptions of value that so often accompany our intrinsic desires.

Perhaps the most challenging of the arguments in support of the doxastic theory of motivation goes as follows, however (Scanlon, 1998, pp. 33–4). In the case of belief, a process of reasoning that leads to the judgment that there is compelling reason to believe that P can issue directly in the belief that P—when we form the judgment, we form the belief (*ceteris paribus*). Likewise, then, in the case of intention: why shouldn't a process of reasoning that leads to the judgment that there is compelling reason to do Q similarly issue directly in the intention to do Q, independently of any other motivational state (and in particular, independently of any desire)? What Scanlon has in mind here, of course, is conscious 'System 2' reasoning, rather than the sort of reasoning that occurs within conceptual modules.[7] And the question is thoroughly apposite: we have already allowed (in Chapter 6.7) that System 2 reasoning can issue in belief; so why shouldn't such reasoning issue likewise in an intention to act? And then given that intentions can cause actions without the activation of any desire, as we argued in Section 4 that they can, it will follow that reasoning can lead to action without the causal contribution of any desire, and the doxastic theory of motivation will be established as true.

Recall from Section 4 that there are two kinds of intention, however: simple and normative. That processes of reasoning should give rise to intentions of the normative sort is neither surprising nor challenging. For these intentions have unconscious desires embedded within their realizing-conditions. (And so do the corresponding System 2 beliefs, of course. Recall that when I make up my mind to believe P, this can become a 'virtual belief' provided that I thereafter recall that I have committed myself to thinking and acting as if P were true, and *want* to honor my commitment.) Suppose that after reflection I conclude, 'There exists overwhelming reason to do Q.' Thereafter if I remember this judgment, and want to be the sort of person who does what there is overwhelming reason to do, then I shall be sufficiently motivated to do Q, and it will be *just as if* I had formed the intention to do Q. So

---

[7] This is partly because he barely even nods in the direction of *un*conscious processes of reasoning. But even if we set this to one side, there is no reason to think that there are any doxastic modules that can issue in intentions independently of desire. Recall the normative reasoning modules discussed in Chapter 3.7, for example. There is every reason to think that these regularly issue in states of emotion and desire of various sorts (guilt, anger, and so forth), and that their contribution to action-determination should depend upon the causation of such states.

here the intention will be *realized in* a suitable set of unconscious beliefs and desires (Frankish, 2004).

It is thus easy to see how someone might be tempted to think that beliefs can be directly motivating. For all that need be manifest to me through introspection is that I reach a theoretically framed conclusion—'Doing Q would be best, all things considered', 'I ought to do Q', or, 'So I shall do Q'—and then I act. We aren't normally aware of any separate desire to do what is best, or to do what we ought, or to do what we believe we have committed ourselves to doing. But some such desire may be operative nonetheless.[8]

The real question is why processes of deliberation can't lead directly to the formation of a *simple* intention (i.e., one that does *not* involve any sort of normative belief or higher-order desire). In the case of belief we allowed that the parallel phenomenon is possible: we allowed that processes of System 2 reasoning can issue in a first-order belief, in something like the way that the testimony of others can issue in belief. (See Chapter 6.7.) So why not in the case of intention as well? If reasons alone can be compelling in the case of theoretical reasoning (issuing in belief), why should they not also be compelling in the case of practical reasoning, issuing in an intention without the intervention of any desire?

The two cases are by no means symmetrical, however. It is entirely to be expected that a process of reasoning that implicates only beliefs, perceptions, and other informational states should lead to belief. There is nothing at all puzzling in the idea that reasoning from beliefs as premises should lead to the formation of a novel belief as conclusion. (This only *became* somewhat puzzling once we drew the System 1 / System 2 distinction, and asked how System 2 reasoning could issue in belief *simpliciter*.) But it surely *is* puzzling how any purely doxastic process of reasoning could issue in an intention. For an intention is a state whose causal role is to initiate and organize action. How can reasoning from beliefs as premises lead to the formation of a state that doesn't have the mind-to-world direction-of-fit characteristic of belief, but rather a state whose function is, not to represent the world, but to change it? This is, intuitively, an entirely different matter.

Recall from Chapter 6.6 our account of the way in which System 2 reasoning can issue in a simple belief. We said that in the case of theoretical reason there was, very likely, already in existence a set of processes for evaluating and testing a putative item of testimony, and then storing that item as a belief if

---

[8] And something of this sort *must* be the case if we are to share the same basic belief / desire cognitive architecture that is common to the rest of the animal kingdom. This point will be elaborated in Section 5.3.

it should pass muster. And the theoretical use of reason can then piggyback on these processes, using cycles of self-generated imagery and inner speech until a content is found that meets the various testimony-based criteria of acceptability, at which point that content is stored as a novel 'simple' belief. But there is, in contrast, no such thing as testimony that issues in intention.

Of course, people do issue orders and imperatives (and probably they always have), thereby instructing others to do things. But it is very doubtful whether there is any mechanism that takes another person's imperative utterance as input and delivers an intention to act as output, without the intervention of any desire. On the contrary, what happens when people decide whether or not to obey an order is that they consider whether or not they *want* to do what this person tells them; whether if they *don't* do what this person tells them, they stand to lose anything that they want; whether they are *obliged* to obey this order, given the authority of the person who issued it; and so on. And even if there were such a mechanism, it would in any case only take one from an *imperative* sentence to an action, not from an indicative ('doxastic') sentence to an action. So there simply isn't the makings, here, of a mechanism that might take one from a verbally expressed doxastic judgment that concludes a piece of deliberation straight to an intention to act, by-passing all need for desire.

This isn't to say that such a mechanism is impossible, of course. But we do lack any account of how that mechanism might have evolved. In the case of abductive reasoning leading to belief, there are good reasons to think that there would already have been some abduction-like processes involved in the use of language for purposes of testimony. There is no similar story to be told about how purely doxastic deliberation might lead to intention. And there are, in contrast, independent reasons to believe in a variety of systems that would take one from theoretical reasoning involving evaluative language to a *desire* to do the thing concluded upon, as I have tried to show in earlier sections of this chapter. At the very least, we have sufficient materials here to answer Scanlon's 'Why shouldn't there be?' challenge to the opponents of the doxastic theory of motivation.

5.3 The Case Against the Doxastic Theory of Motivation

I have argued that the considerations that are supposed to support the *reasons* alternative to belief/desire architectures do not, in reality, do so. (See also Smith, 1987; Brink, 1994; Copp and Sobel, 2002.) But there are also direct arguments against that proposal. For the proponents of the doxastic theory display an unfortunate disregard for the constraints on theorizing that should be provided by comparative and evolutionary psychology. Since we have good reason to think that the minds of animals have a belief/desire architecture, it ought to require some showing how a reasons architecture could be grafted onto the back of, or in place of, that. And there should be discussion of the evolutionary pressures that would have necessitated such wholesale changes in our mental organization. Not only is none of this to be found in the writings of the authors in question, but it is very hard to see how any such story might go.

According to the account that I have been developing over previous chapters, a belief / desire modular architecture, which we inherited from previous animal species, became enriched in the hominid line through the addition of further modules—for language, for mind-reading, for normative reasoning and motivation, and so on. Utilizing these additions, together with a pre-existing (but now enhanced) capacity for creative mental rehearsal of action, humans have evolved a disposition to engage in extended cycles of rehearsal and intra-modular reasoning, giving rise to the distinctive creativity and flexibility of the human mind. And in the present chapter I have tried to show how minor alterations to this same arrangement would give rise to everything that is distinctive of human *practical* reasoning, as well.

What, in contrast, is a defender of the doxastic theory of motivation to say, at this point? Some, like McDowell (1994, 1995), will attempt to finesse the issue altogether by denying that animals possess genuine beliefs and desires—claiming that such states are inherently normative in character. My rebuttal of such claims is to be found in Chapter 2. And if the existence of belief / desire architectures in animals is granted, then it looks as though the defender of the doxastic theory will have to claim something like the following. In addition to the mechanisms that existed in animals for reasoning and for integrating beliefs with desires to determine intentions and actions, somehow in the course of human evolution a whole new route to the determination of intention and action was added. This involved a new sort of mechanism for theoretical reasoning about values and obligations which is capable of leading straight to intentions, by-passing the pre-existing belief / desire architecture altogether.

Already this seems to violate one of the robust principles of evolutionary biology, which is that evolution characteristically proceeds by conserving and making incremental additions to existing structures. At the very least we need to be told about the selection pressures behind the evolution of a doxastic intention-determining mechanism, and to be told why those pressures couldn't have been met (more conservatively) by adding components to the existing belief / desire intention-creating system. I have been unable to think of any plausible story here that would fit the bill. And certainly the defenders of the doxastic theory of motivation make no attempt to provide one.

On any account, of course, there are significant cognitive differences between ourselves and other animals, and I have emphasized a number of them in the course of previous chapters. But any acceptable explanation of those differences should also preserve the extensive commonalities between us. And other things being equal, an account that preserves a basic common cognitive architecture while adding differences of detail (such as additional belief-forming or desire-forming modules) is surely preferable to one suggesting that the evolutionary transition from other animals to ourselves involved the creation of a whole new—reasons employing—cognitive architecture.

6 The Illusion of Conscious Will

There is one final question that I now propose to discuss before leaving the topic of practical reason and intention. This is the question whether conscious will is an *illusion*, as Wegner (2002) argues at length that it is. I shall separate a number of distinct strands in Wegner's discussion, before showing how one of them receives at least partial vindication from the positions that I have defended in this book.

6.1 Wegner on the Illusion of Conscious Will

Wegner (2002) argues for the illusoriness of conscious will across a broad front, and presents a wide array of evidence. But he has a number of different illusions in mind at different points in his discussion, not all of which, arguably, really constitute an attack on conscious willing. One is the traditional idea of a *metaphysically free* will, as an uncaused cause of action. But on this he has nothing to add to traditional philosophical critiques, I think (e.g. Dennett, 1984). Another is the idea that we have direct awareness of the *causality* of conscious will. The claim under attack here is that we have non-inferential and immediate awareness of the causal relationship between our conscious acts of deciding or intending and the actions that result. So even if our conscious decisions do cause our actions, on this account conscious will would still be an illusion if we weren't immediately aware of the *causing*-relation.

Wegner (2002) makes out a plausible case that there is no such immediate awareness. In part he tries to do this by drawing on Hume's (1739) claim that we never perceive causal relations themselves, not even when one billiard ball bounces into another, causing it to move. But this claim is eminently deniable for anyone who thinks that perception can be to some degree theory-laden. Given suitable background theories of the causal processes involved (some of which are, very likely, innate—see Baillargeon et al., 1995; Spelke et al.,

1995), we surely *can* perceive the causal efficacy of some physical events. And if physical, why not mental too? Wegner is on stronger ground when he points out that the causal connections between our conscious thoughts and our actions are too complex, and too variable from case to case, to count as perceivable.

Even if Wegner's claims on this were made out, however, it is doubtful that the idea of conscious will would thereby be undermined. Granted, there would be no such thing as conscious will if our conscious thoughts were never, or only rarely, the causes of our actions. For causal efficacy seems built into the very idea of what a *will* is. But provided that these conscious thoughts are often enough amongst the causes of our actions, then I think that the reality of conscious will needn't be undermined by our lack of awareness of the causing-relation. For these events would, by virtue of their frequently causal status, constitute the operations of a *will*. And, by hypothesis, they are conscious. So there *would* be such a thing as conscious willing, even if we aren't conscious of the *causal efficacy* of our acts of willing.

Yet another idea that Wegner (2002) defends is that, very often, the conscious events that we take to be the operations of our conscious will, causing our actions, aren't really doing so. Often, both those conscious events and the actions that we subsequently perform have a *common* cause in some set of *unconscious* mental events. These events cause both our conscious 'willings' *and* our actions. In which case what we are aware of isn't what causes our actions. For example, an intention activated by our practical-reasoning system might cause *both* the action intended *and* an appropriate verbalization of the intention ('I'll go *that* way'). The latter is mentally rehearsed and globally broadcast, thereby becoming conscious. Although it is easy for us to mistake this conscious event for the act of willing itself, in reality it doesn't play any causal role in the production of the action (or not always; I shall return to this point in a moment). Rather, there is a common underlying cause—the activated intention—which causes both the action and the conscious verbalization of the intention to act.

However, unless the present argument collapses into the previous one, it would have to be claimed that our conscious 'willings' and our actions are *always* the effects of a common underlying cause, and not just that they sometimes are. For otherwise, in those cases where our conscious thoughts *do* cause our actions, there *would* be such a thing as conscious willing. But Wegner doesn't really do anything to defend this stronger claim, I think, unless via the idea that I discuss next. And that strong claim is surely inconsistent with the reality of System 2 reasoning and decision-making, in which conscious verbalizations of intention do play a causal role.

The final claim that Wegner (2002) makes—which I propose to spend some time in Sections 6.2 and 6.3 elaborating and defending—is that our access to our own will (that is, our own acts of deciding or intending, which cause our actions) is always *interpretative* in character. Our awareness of our own will results from turning our mind-reading capacities upon ourselves, and coming up with the best interpretation of the information that is available to it—and this information doesn't include our acts of deciding themselves, but only the effects of those events. On this account, then, the events in question don't count as *conscious*, or at least not by the intuitive criterion that requires us to have non-inferential, non-interpretative, access to a mental event if the latter is to qualify as a conscious one. I shall say just a little about this latter claim here, before turning to discuss the main point.

There is, of course, a great deal of dispute about the nature of consciousness. By far the major part of this concerns the nature and best explanation of *phenomenal*, or experiential, consciousness. This is a topic on which I have well-developed views of my own (Carruthers, 2000, 2005). But it isn't the one that concerns us here. For our topic isn't conscious experience, but rather conscious thought: and in particular, conscious acts of *deciding* or *intending*. And here it is arguable that our common-sense understanding of what it is for a thought to be a conscious one is that it is a mental event *of which we are immediately and non-interpretationally aware* (Carruthers, 2005, chs. 7 and 8). It is this that gives us the contrast between our conscious thoughts and our unconscious ones. For the latter, if they are known to us, are only known via a process of self-interpretation. And it is also what gives us the asymmetry between our own conscious thoughts and those of other people. The latter, too, are only known to us through a process of interpretation, whereas our own thoughts, when conscious, aren't, we think.

At any rate this is what I propose to assume in what follows. I shall take for granted that if it can be shown that the only form of access that we have to our own intentions and decisions is interpretative—in this respect like the access that we have to the intentions and decisions of other people—then there is no such thing as conscious willing or conscious deciding. Conscious will would, indeed, have been shown to be an illusion.

6.2 Is All Awareness of Willing Interpretative?

Recall the account that I defended in Chapter 3.3 of the way in which our mind-reading faculty is embedded into the overall architecture of the human mind. (This was represented diagrammatically in Figure 3.2.) On that account, the mind-reading faculty is focused 'outwards', via the perceptual faculties, on the world (and the agent's own body). Its primary function is the attribution of mental states to other people, together with the prediction and explanation of their behavior. Accordingly, the main inputs to the mind-reading faculty are perceptual ones. It can, no doubt, access stored information of various sorts, and it can query other systems for information. But it has no access to the inferential processes that take place within those other systems, including the practical-reasoning system. And even when other inferential systems are co-opted for purposes of prediction by *supposing* that one is in the position of, or has the beliefs or goals of, another person and reasoning accordingly, the products are only made available to the mind-reading module when they are globally broadcast in the form of visual or other imagery, or in the form of inner speech.

If this account is on the right lines, then the mind-reading module won't have any direct access to the agent's own decisions and acts of intention-formation, either. It will have to rely on interpreting indirect cues of various sorts. These include perception of bodily movements and actions; monitoring of bodily changes of various kinds preparatory to action; the use of action schemata to globally broadcast images of the movement to be undertaken (hence making those images accessible to awareness); and verbalizations of intentions in inner speech. In all such cases, what is made available to the mind-reading system isn't the decision itself, but events that occur prior to, or subsequent to, that decision; and the occurrence of the decision can only be known by *interpretation* of those events. And it will follow, therefore, that there is no such thing as conscious deciding. For there will be no events occupying the causal role of decision that are immediately available to awareness, in a manner that doesn't involve self-interpretation.

If this were the last word on the matter, then Wegner (2002) would be correct: there would be no such thing as conscious will. There would exist conscious events of various sorts, and there would exist *willing* events, such as acts of deciding, but the two classes would be disjoint. For the lat-ter—*willing*—events would only be knowable by the subject via interpretation of the former—conscious—ones. But in fact this isn't the *last* word, because the distinction between System 1 processes and System 2 processes is here being overlooked. Acknowledging this distinction will complicate the argument, but will leave Wegner's conclusion essentially untouched. Let me elaborate.

6.3 Complicating the Argument

Suppose that at the conclusion of an episode of System 2, conscious, reasoning I say to myself, 'So I'll do Q.' The motor schema for an utterance of this sentence is used to generate an auditory image of the words, 'So I'll do Q.' This image is then globally broadcast. It is, *inter alia*, received as input by the language comprehension system, which attaches a content to it that is made available to the mind-reading system. The latter interprets the image as constituting a *decision* to do Q. Either immediately or at some point thereafter I recall that I have decided to do Q, and because I want to do what I have decided, or because I think of myself as a resolute individual who always does what he decides and I want to conform to this self-image (or whatever), I set about doing Q.

Here there is a conscious event, namely the event of hearing myself say the words, 'So I'll do Q.' And that event does play a causal role in producing the subsequent activity of doing Q, by virtue of being interpreted as a decision, recalled, and fed into a further decision process (which remains unconscious) involving other beliefs and desires of mine. Hence if by a conscious decision or act of will we just mean a conscious event that causes the action that is picked out in the intentional content of that event, then it will turn out that the act of saying to myself the words, 'So I'll do Q', *is* a decision to do Q, after all. And then conscious will would be a reality, albeit only in connection with System 2 forms of practical reason.

However, surely our idea of a decision to act, and our idea of what it is to form an intention to act, is the idea of an event that causes action either immediately, or through the operations of further reasoning processes that are purely first-order in character (such as figuring out a necessary means to the execution of that act). But the event of saying to myself, 'So I'll do Q', doesn't have this character. On the contrary, it only leads to action via processes of reasoning that are higher-order in character, including such events as *believing that I have decided to do Q*, and *wanting to do what I have decided*. In which case, while the act of saying to myself, 'So I'll do Q', is conscious, and does play a causal role in the production of the behavior of doing Q, it doesn't have the causal role characteristic of a genuine decision to do Q. And so it turns out, after all, that there is still no such thing as conscious deciding.

Let me develop this argument in a little more detail. Consider, first, an intention to perform an action that is to be completed here-and-now, as when I decide to open a window for the breeze. We surely think that, in such a case, a genuine decision must be the last *deliberative* mental event in the causal chain that leads to the action. A genuine decision is something that might cause a motor schema to be activated, which is then guided and updated in the light of ongoing perceptual input. Hence a genuine decision to do something here-and-now needn't be the last *mental* event in the causation of the action. But once the decision is made, we think, then there is no further role for the interaction of beliefs with desires in any sort of process of practical reasoning. Rather, a genuine decision, in these sorts of circumstances, should *settle* the matter (subject, of course, to problems arising in the execution of the action—e.g. I find that my legs have 'gone to sleep', and that I can't walk—and subject to unforeseen circumstances leading me to revise the original decision—e.g. I find that the window is swarming with biting ants). But saying to myself, 'So I'll do Q', *doesn't* settle the matter. It only results in an act of doing Q via further deliberation, given that I have further beliefs and desires of the right kind.

Now consider a decision that is taken for the more distant future. Often such intentions are 'incomplete', in the sense that they don't yet contain a full specification of the means to be taken in executing the decision. So some further reasoning needs to take place. For example, I decide to purchase a particular book after reading its description in the press's catalog. But this doesn't yet fix *how* I should make the purchase—should I place an order on-line through Amazon, phone my local bookstore, or complete and send off the order-slip from the catalog itself? So in such a case a decision *isn't* the last deliberative step in the causal chain that leads to action.

All the same, we still think that a decision in this sort of case should settle *what* I do (subject, of course, to the usual qualifications about unforeseen difficulties and changes of mind). It just doesn't settle *how* I do it. Put differently, we think that while a decision, if it is genuinely to count as such, can be followed by further deliberation, this should only be deliberation about the *means* to execute the action, not about the action itself. So if the act of buying a book is Q, the deliberation that follows a decision to do Q shouldn't be about whether or not to do Q (that should already have been settled), but merely about *how* to do Q in the circumstances.

In a case of System 2 decision-making, in contrast, the conscious event of saying to myself in inner speech, 'So I'll do Q', *doesn't* settle that I do Q, and the further (unconscious) practical reasoning that takes place prior to action *is* about whether or not to do Q. For on the account of System 2 practical reasoning sketched above, the sentence, 'So I'll do Q', first needs to be interpreted *as* a decision to do Q by the mind-reading faculty, and it only leads to the act of doing Q via my desire to do what I have decided, in combination with my belief that I have decided to do Q. So this is surely sufficient to disqualify the conscious event, here, from counting as a genuine decision, even though it does play a causal role in the production of the action. For the role in question isn't the right *sort* of role appropriate for a decision.

I can imagine two replies. One is that the event of saying to myself, 'So I'll do Q', might be the last mental event that occurs *at the System 2 level* (albeit with further practical reasoning taking place thereafter in System 1). So it *does* directly cause my action at that level of description, unmediated by any System 2 practical reasoning. But this isn't enough to qualify it as counting as a genuine decision, in my view. Our common-sense notion of a decision doesn't make any allowance for the System 1 / System 2 distinction. It is the idea of an event that causes action without the mediation of any further reasoning about whether or not to act. And given this idea, saying, 'So I'll do Q', plainly doesn't qualify.

It might also (and relatedly) be replied that my development of Wegner's argument overlooks the fact that System 2 processes are supposed to be *realized in* the operations of System 1. My decision to do Q is a System 2 event that is realized in a set of System 1 events, included in which is the belief that I have made a decision and the desire to do what I have decided. So again, the System 2 event directly causes my action *at that level of description*. But this reply, too, is off the mark. It is true enough to say that System 2 processes in general are realized in those of System 1. But surely the realizing conditions for an event cannot occur subsequent to that event itself. And it is only once the conscious event of saying to myself, 'So I'll do Q', is completed that the System 1 reasoning leading to the action kicks in. Moreover, if we opt to say that the decision to do Q isn't *that* event, but rather the more extended event that also includes the subsequent System 1 practical reasoning, then *that* event isn't a conscious one. So either way, there is no one event, here, that is both conscious and a decision.

I conclude, then, that Wegner (2002) is correct: conscious will is an illusion. Given that the mind-reading system has no direct access to events that take place in the practical-reasoning system (as we argued in Chapter 3.3), but only to their globally broadcast effects, then our access to those events is always interpretative. Hence those events within practical reason don't qualify as conscious ones. And even where a conscious event (such as saying to myself in inner speech, 'I'll do Q') does play a causal role in the production of the action, through System 2 processes, that role isn't of the sort that is characteristic of a 'willing' event of deciding or intending. For it doesn't settle anything by itself. Only if I want to do what I have decided and *believe* that by saying to myself, 'I'll do Q', I *have* decided, does the action get settled upon.

6.4 Whence the Illusion?

How does the illusion of conscious will arise in us, however? And why is it so persistent? This isn't so difficult to explain. For the mind-reading module only contains a limited, highly simplified, model of its own operations. Recall that the mind-reading system's model of the architecture of the mind as a whole is highly simplified, but nevertheless accurate enough for most everyday purposes of prediction and explanation. (Compare Figures 4.1 and 4.2.)[9] Likewise, it

---

[9] This simplified model explains the perennial pull of general-learning / faculty-psychology models of the mind, I think. At least part of the reason why such accounts seem so *intuitive* is that they mesh with our innate or innately channeled common-sense psychology. See the discussion in Chapter 4.1.

is plausible that the mind-reading system's model of the sort of access that the mind has to itself and its own operations is highly simplified. That model appears to be quasi-Cartesian in character: it pictures the operations of the mind as *transparent* to itself, in such a way that the events within a mind are immediately known by the mind. This model can be modified as a result of experience and subsequent System 2 reasoning, no doubt, and many people nowadays end up allowing for the existence of unconscious mental processes, to some degree. But the default is transparency, and that default might actually be adaptive in various ways (Gazzaniga, 1998; Wilson, 2002).

So when the mind-reading system sets to work interpreting the inner verbalization of the sentence, 'So I'll do Q', as the formation of an intention to do Q, it doesn't represent the fact that it engages in such a process of interpretation. Rather, its results are couched in terms of the simple transparency model. So its output—if required to report on its own operations—would be something along the lines of, 'I (the person) am immediately aware that I have just formed the intention to do Q.' But in fact there is no such immediate awareness, if the arguments outlined above are correct.

7 Conclusion

Much had already been done in previous chapters to explain how the flexibility and creativity of human practical reasoning is both consistent with, and explicable in terms of, a massively modular account of the architecture of the mind. The present chapter has mostly been focused on the distinctive *forms* that human practical reasoning appears to take, with much of that reasoning being cast in terms of judgments of value or obligation. I have argued that we can make sense of the fact that we rarely express our desires in the optative mood ('Would that P!'), and instead use the indicative ('It would be good if P', 'I want P to be the case'), if we suppose that this is an evolved disposition designed to make those contents accessible to our *theoretical-reasoning systems*. I have argued, moreover, that there are no good reasons for believing in a *reasons* architecture that would conflict with the sort of belief / desire architecture that we have been assuming throughout. Along the way there has been discussion of different forms of intention, of the way in which the System 1 / System 2 distinction applies within the domain of practical reason, and of the likely illusoriness of conscious will. The take-home message, however, is that there is nothing here that can't be accommodated within a massively modular model of mind.

8

Conclusion to the Volume

I take myself to have achieved three things, over the course of this book. First, I have shown that there are powerful reasons for believing that the human mind is massively modular in its organization, given a quite specific (and relatively weak) understanding of 'module'. Secondly, I have shown that there are no reasons of principle why the human mind *shouldn't* be massively modular, hence answering the main 'How possibly?' challenge to massive modularity. And thirdly, I have proposed and defended a fairly detailed architecture—or 'flowchart'—for the human mind, specifying many of its modular components and their modes of connection and interaction. Let me say just a little about each of these in turn, by way of summary and reminder.

The *argument from design* suggests that the mind should be composed of a great many distinct, or partially distinct, functional components, whose properties can vary independently of one another, and whose operations can be differentially effected and differentially damaged. For this is true of biological systems quite generally, and we have every reason to think that the mind is such a system, subject to just the same constraints on piecemeal evolvability. Moreover, complex systems in AI and computer science, too, display a similar organization—and for a similar reason, since designers need to be able to tinker with the parts without affecting the functionality of the remainder. So we should expect the mind to contain almost as many distinct components as there are evolutionarily ancient functions to perform. (And these are myriad, plainly.) In addition, a similar argument suggests that a constraint of piecemeal *learnability* will result in a great many additional acquired modules (e.g. for distinct skills and abilities), built by modular learning mechanisms.

The *argument from animals* delivers a similar conclusion. We saw that animal minds contain a great many different learning mechanisms, specialized for particular tasks. Not only this, but there appears to be no such thing as *general* learning, since even the results of so-called 'associative conditioning' are best seen as a reflection of the operations of a specialized rate-estimation system. Likewise, animal minds contain a great many different desire-generating

mechanisms, which are designed to take perceptual representations, representations of bodily states, and/or beliefs as input, and to deliver an intrinsic
desire as output. Even the practical-reasoning mechanisms that select an action
in the light of the organism's beliefs and desires appear to be multiple, and
to be functionally specialized for particular types of task. And we should
surely expect that most of this complexity would have been conserved in the
evolutionary transition to the human mind. In addition, although there is good
reason to think that a multitude of new modules would have been added to the
pre-existing primate repertoire in the course of human evolution, there isn't
any reason to believe that what got added was some sort of holistic (a-modular)
general-purpose reasoning system or central executive system.

The *argument from computational frugality* supports these conclusions further,
but places some additional constraints on the nature of the various modular
systems that make up the human mind. There is good reason to think that
mental processes are realized in computational ones. And computations that
are effected using neural hardware, and that are completed (for the most part)
in seconds or fractions of a second, would need to be divided up amongst
processing systems that are *frugal* in the complexity of their algorithms and
the amount of information that they need to access for their operations. We
should therefore expect modules to be wide-scope encapsulated, meaning that
they can only access a small subset of the total information that is available
in the mind when executing their tasks. (They won't necessarily access the
same subset on different occasions, note, but might rather use a variety of
frugal search heuristics—so this isn't encapsulation as it has traditionally been
understood.) Moreover, we should expect that the internal operations of these
modules will be inaccessible to other systems. Modules will query one another,
and deliver information to one another, and hence be capable of reading the
outputs of some others, but for the most part they will know nothing about
the internal processing that serves to generate those outputs.

None of these arguments (neither singly nor combined) provides any sort of
proof of the massive modularity hypothesis, of course. For the arguments are
all broadly abductive in form (they are 'inferences to the best explanation'),
and are hence defeasible. It was therefore crucial for us to confront the various
arguments *against* massive modularity. The main one of these takes the form
of a 'How possibly?' challenge. For many people find it difficult to see how
any mind that was organized along massively modular lines could *possibly*
display the sorts of creativity and flexibility that are distinctive of the human
mind. A successful answer to this challenge required us to make a number of
commitments concerning the likely components of the human mind, together
with their modes of operation and interaction with one another.

I have argued that the basic architecture of the human mind, inherited from our primate ancestors, is organized into systems of perception, belief-generation, desire-generation, practical reasoning, and motor control. Perceptual systems in each modality (vision, hearing, and so on) bifurcate into those that globally broadcast their outputs to all the various central / conceptual modules for belief, desire, and practical reason, on the one hand; and those that make their outputs available to the motor systems for the fine-grained control of action, on the other. Feedback loops and cross-talking enable motor schemata to be used to drive imagery of the intended action, which can then be globally broadcast to the central / conceptual modules for evaluation, hence making possible both the *mental rehearsal* of action, and open-ended cycles of such rehearsal. (See Figures 2.5 and 2.8.)

While it is likely that a number of novel modules were added to the human mind in the course of hominid evolution, the most important one for our purposes is a language faculty. This probably has a tripartite internal organization, including a comprehension sub-system, a production sub-system, and a database of acquired information about language that can be accessed by each. The comprehension sub-system receives its input from perception and makes its output available to the central / conceptual modules. The production sub-system can receive its input from any belief-module, any desire-module, or from practical reason. And in common with other action-controlling systems, the production sub-system can use its speech-act schemata to generate imagery of the intended speech act. These mentally rehearsed utterances will then be fed as input to the comprehension sub-system, which will globally broadcast its output (a representation of the content of the intended speech act) to all of the various central / conceptual modules. (See Figures 3.4 and 4.3.)

The language faculty is uniquely well positioned, then, to link up and unify some of the mind's computational resources. I have argued that the production sub-system is likely to have acquired the power to combine two or more sentences that encode the outputs of two or more central modules, hence unifying thought-contents that might otherwise remain separate. And I have suggested that the limited primate capacity for *creative* mental rehearsal is greatly boosted in human beings, through the childhood disposition to engage in pretend play. The result is that novel sentences (and other action schemata) can be generated and rehearsed creatively, without having to encode or combine any previously existing thought, perhaps utilizing a variety of learned heuristics and creative strategies. And I have suggested that principles originally employed for speech comprehension and the evaluation of testimony might be co-opted to give rise to a sort of virtual faculty of inference to the best explanation, conferring on us a disposition to believe self-generated sentences whose contents are suitably accurate, simple, consistent, coherent, fruitful, and unifying.

In such a manner the flexibility and creativity of the human mind is explained in outline, at least; as is a significant part of our capacity for science. Other distinctively human modules take up the slack. One is a mind-reading faculty, which not only makes possible much of our sophisticated social interactions, but is also at least partly responsible for our distinctive capacities for learning through imitation. Another is a module for normative reasoning and motivation that underlies and explains the norm-saturated character of all human societies. And then both mind-reading and normative reasoning are implicated in creating System 2 reasoning processes out of patterns of mental rehearsal and the global broadcast of such rehearsals.

In conclusion: since there are powerful arguments supporting the massive modularity hypothesis, and since there are no convincing arguments against it (in particular, since the 'How possibly?' challenge can be answered, in outline), a massive modularity theorist is what every good cognitive scientist should be. Or rather, since in science generally it is fruitful for more than one research program to be pursued, even when one of them is in the ascendant and the remainder are degenerating (Lakatos, 1970), what we can conclude is that a great many *more* cognitive scientists should begin exploring the massive modularity hypothesis, and conducting their research within its framework. For that is where the future action, and future success, is likely to be.

References

Able, K. and Bingham, V. (1987). The development of orientation and navigation behavior in birds. *Quarterly Review of Biology*, 62, 1–29.

Adams, C. and Dickinson, A. (1981). Instrumental responding following reinforcer devaluation. *Quarterly Journal of Experimental Psychology*, 33B, 109–122.

Aggleton, J. and Pearce, J. (2002). Neural systems underlying episodic memory: insights from animal research. In Baddeley et al., 2002.

Aglioti, S., DeSouza, J., and Goodale, M. (1995). Size-contrast illusions deceive the eye but not the hand. *Current Biology*, 5, 679–85.

Aiello, L. and Wheeler, P. (1995). The expensive tissue hypothesis. *Current Anthropology*, 36, 199–221.

Amabile, T. (1996). *Creativity in Context*. Westview Press.

Ambrose, S. (1998). Late Pleistocene human population bottlenecks, volcanic winter, and differentiation of modern humans. *Journal of Human Evolution*, 34, 623–51.

Anderson, M. (forthcoming). The massive redeployment hypothesis and the functional topography of the brain. *Philosophical Psychology*.

Ans, B., Rousset, S., French, R., and Musca, S. (2002). Preventing catastrophic interference in multiple-sequence learning using coupled reverberating Elman networks. In *Proceedings of the 24th Annual Conference of the Cognitive Science Society*, Lawrence Erlbaum.

Anzai, T., Shiina, T., Kimura, N., Yanagiya, K., Kohara, S., Shigenari, A., Yamagata, T., Kulski, J., Naruse, T., Fujimori, Y., Fukuzumi, Y., Yamazaki, M., Tashiro, H., Iwamoto, C., Umchara, Y., Imanishi, T., Meyer, A., Ikeo, K., Gojobori, T., Bahram, S., and Inoko, H. (2003). Comparative sequencing of human and chimpanzee MHC class I regions unveils insertions/deletions as the major path of genomic divergence. *Proceedings of the National Academy of Sciences*, 100, 7708–13.

Atkinson, R. and Shiffrin, R. (1968). Human memory: a proposed system and its control processes. In K. Spence (ed.), *The Psychology of Learning and Motivations*, Volume 2, Academic Press.

Atran, S. (1990). *Cognitive Foundations of Natural History: towards an anthropology of science*. Cambridge University Press.

——— (1998). Folk biology and the anthropology of science: cognitive universals and cultural particulars. *Behavioral and Brain Sciences*, 21, 547–609.

——— (1999). Itzaj Maya folk-biological taxonomy. In D. Medin and S. Atran (eds.), *Folk Biology*, MIT Press.

_____ (2002a). Modular and cultural factors in biological understanding: an experimental approach to the cognitive basis of science. In Carruthers et al., 2002.

_____ (2002b). A meta-module for conceptual integration: language or theory of mind? *Behavioral and Brain Sciences*, 25, 674–75.

Baars, B. (1988). *A Cognitive Theory of Consciousness*. Cambridge University Press.

_____ (1997). *In the Theatre of Consciousness*. Oxford University Press.

_____ (2002). The conscious access hypothesis: origins and recent evidence. *Trends in Cognitive Science*, 6, 47–52.

_____ (2003). How brain reveals mind: neuroimaging supports the central role of conscious experience. *Journal of Consciousness Studies*, 10, 100–14.

_____ Ramsoy, T., and Laureys, S. (2003). Brain, consciousness, and the observing self. *Trends in Neurosciences*, 26, 671–5.

Baddeley, A. (1986). *Working Memory*. Oxford University Press.

_____ (1990). *Human Memory*. Lawrence Erlbaum.

_____ (1993). Working memory and conscious awareness. In A. Collins, S. Gathercole, and M. Conway (eds.), *Theories of Memory*, Lawrence Erlbaum.

_____ and Hitch, G. (1974). Working memory. In G. Brown (ed.), *The Psychology of Learning and Motivation*, Volume 8, Academic Press.

_____ Conway, M., and Aggleton, J., eds. (2002). *Episodic Memory*. Oxford University Press.

Baillargeon, R., Kotovsky, L., and Needham, A. (1995). The acquisition of physical knowledge in infancy. In D. Sperber, D. Premack, and A. Premack (eds.), *Causal Cognition*, Oxford University Press.

Baker, M. (forthcoming). The creative aspect of language use and non-biological nativism. In Carruthers et al., planned for 2007.

Baker, R. and Bellis, M. (1995). *Human Sperm Competition: copulation, masturbation, and infidelity*. Chapman and Hall.

Barkow, J., Cosmides, L., and Tooby, J., eds. (1992). *The Adapted Mind: evolutionary psychology and the generation of culture*. Oxford University Press.

Baron-Cohen, S. (1995). *Mindblindness*. MIT Press.

_____ and Swettenham, J. (1996). The relationship between SAM and ToMM: two hypotheses. In Carruthers and Smith, 1996.

_____ Leslie, A., and Frith, U. (1985). Does the autistic child have a 'theory of mind'? *Cognition*, 21, 37–46.

Barrett, C. (2005). Enzymatic computation and cognitive modularity. *Mind and Language*, 20, 259–87.

_____ (2006). Modularity and design reincarnation. In Carruthers et al., 2006.

Barrett, L., Dunbar, R., and Lycett, J. (2002). *Human Evolutionary Psychology*. Princeton University Press.

Barton, R. (2001). The coordinated structure of mosaic brain evolution. *Behavioral and Brain Sciences*, 24, 281–2.

Barton, R. and Harvey, P. (2000). Mosaic evolution of brain structures in mammals. *Nature*, 405, 1055–8.

Bechara, A., Tranel, D., Damasio, H., Adolphs, R., Rockland, C., and Damasio, A. (1995). Double dissociation of conditioning and declarative knowledge relative to the amygdala and hippocampus in humans. *Science*, 269, 1115–8.

———Damasio, H., Tranel, D., and Damasio, A. (1997). Deciding advantageously before knowing the advantageous strategy. *Science*, 275, 1293–5.

Bednar, J. (2003). The role of internally generated neural activity in newborn and infant face preferences. In O. Pascalis and A. Slater (eds.), *Face Perception in Infancy and Early Childhood*, NOVA Science Publishers.

Bekoff, M. and Byers, J., eds. (1998). *Animal Play*. Cambridge University Press.

Bellugi, U., Lichtenberger, L., Jones, W., Lai, Z., and George, M. (2000). The neurocognitive profile of Williams syndrome: a complex pattern of strengths and weaknesses. *Journal of Cognitive Neuroscience*, 12, 7–29.

Bem, D. (1967). Self-perception: an alternative interpretation of cognitive dissonance phenomena. *Psychological Review*, 74, 183–200.

——— (1972). Self-perception theory. In L. Berkowitz (ed.), *Advances in Experimental Social Psychology*, Volume 6, Academic Press.

Beneczki, T. and Dunbar, R. (1997). Female-biased reproduction strategies in a Hungarian gypsy population. *Proceedings of the Royal Society of London*, B, 264, 17–22.

Bennett, J. (1964). *Rationality: an essay towards an analysis*. Routledge.

Berliner, P. (1994). *Thinking in Jazz: the infinite art of improvisation*. University of Chicago Press.

Bermúdez, J. (2003). *Thinking without Words*. Oxford University Press.

Bickerton, D. (1990). *Language and Species*. Chicago University Press.

——— (1995). *Language and Human Behavior*. University of Washington Press.

Birch, S. and Bloom, P. (2004). Understanding children's and adult's limitations in mental state reasoning. *Trends in Cognitive Sciences*, 8, 255–60.

Blackburn, S. (1993). *Essays in Quasi-Realism*. Oxford University Press.

Blackmon, J., Byrd, D., Cummins, R., Poirier, P., and Roth, M. (2005). Atomistic learning in non-modular systems. *Philosophical Psychology*, 18, 313–25.

Blake, R., Turner, L., Smoski, M., Pozdol, S., and Stone, W. (2003). Visual recognition of biological motion is impaired in children with autism. *Psychological Science*, 14, 151–8.

Bliege-Bird, R. and Bird, D. (1997). Delayed reciprocity and tolerated theft: the behavioral ecology of food-sharing strategies. *Current Anthropology*, 38, 49–78.

Bloom, P. (2002). *How Children Learn the Meanings of Words*. MIT Press.

——— (2004). *Descartes' Baby: how the science of child development explains what makes us human*. Basic Books.

Bloor, D. (1976). *Knowledge and Social Imagery*. Routledge.

Boden, M. (1992). *The Creative Mind: myths and mechanisms*. Basic Books.

——— ed. (1994). *Dimensions of Creativity*. MIT Press.

Boehm, C. (1999). *Hierarchy in the Forest*. Harvard University Press.

Boesch, C. (2002). Cooperative hunting roles amongst Taï chimpanzees. *Human Nature*, 13, 27–46.

Bogdan, R. (2005). Pretending as imaginative rehearsal for cultural conformity. *Journal of Cognition and Culture*, 5, 192–214.

Boyd, R. and Richerson, P. (1985). *Culture and the Evolutionary Process*. University of Chicago Press.

——(1992). Punishment allows the evolution of cooperation (or anything else) in sizable groups. *Ethology and Sociobiology*, 13, 171–95.

——and Silk, J. (1997). *How Humans Evolved*. Norton.

Boyer, P. (2001). *Religion Explained: the evolutionary origins of religious thought*. Basic Books.

Bratman, M. (1987). *Intentions, Plans, and Practical Reason*. Harvard University Press.

——(1999). *Faces of Intention: selected essays on intention and agency*. Cambridge University Press.

Bridgeman, B., Kirch, M., and Sperling, A. (1981). Segregation of cognitive and motor aspects of visual function using induced motion. *Perception and Psychophysics*, 29, 336–42.

Brink, D. (1994). A reasonable morality. *Ethics*, 104, 593–619.

Brooks, R. (1986). A robust layered control system for a mobile robot. *IEEE Journal of Robotics and Automation*, RA-2, 14–23.

Brosnan, S. and de Waal, F. (2003). Monkeys reject unequal pay. *Nature*, 425, 297–9.

Brown, D. (1991). *Human Universals*. McGraw-Hill.

Bryson, J. (2000). Cross-paradigm analysis of autonomous agent architecture. *Journal of Experimental and Theoretical Artificial Intelligence*, 12, 165–90.

Buller, D. (2005). *Adapting Minds: evolutionary psychology and the persistent quest for human nature*. Harvard University Press.

Burge, T. (1993). Content preservation. *Philosophical Review*, 102, 457–88.

Buss, D. (1989). Sex differences in human mate preferences: evolutionary hypotheses tested in 37 cultures, *Behavioral and Brain Sciences*, 12, 1–49.

——(1994). *The Evolution of Desire: strategies of human mating*. Basic Books.

——(1999). *Evolutionary Psychology: the new science of the mind*. Allyn and Bacon.

Butterworth, B. (1999). *The Mathematical Brain*. Macmillan.

Byrne, R. (1995). *The Thinking Ape: evolutionary origins of intelligence*. Oxford University Press.

——and Byrne, J. (1988). Leopard killers of Mahale. *Natural History*, 97, 22–6.

——and Whiten, A., eds. (1988). *Machiavellian Intelligence: social expertise and the evolution of intellect in monkeys, apes, and humans*. Oxford University Press.

——eds. (1997). *Machiavellian Intelligence II: extensions and evaluations*. Cambridge University Press.

——Henzi, S., and McCulloch, F. (1993). Nutritional constraints on mountain baboons: implications for baboon socio-ecology. *Behavioral Ecology and Socio-ecology*, 33, 233–46.

Cahill, L., Babinsky, R., Markowitsch, H., and McGaugh, J. (1995). The amygdala and emotional memory. *Nature*, 377, 295−6.

Callebaut, W. and Rasskin-Gutman, D., eds. (2005). *Modularity: understanding the development and evolution of natural complex systems*. MIT Press.

Camp, E. (forthcoming). Who can think conceptual thoughts?

Campbell, A. (2002). *A Mind of Her Own: the evolutionary psychology of women*. Oxford University Press.

Campbell, J. (1999). Schizophrenia, the space of reasons, and thinking as a motor process. *The Monist*, 82, 609−24.

Capitani, E., Laiacona, M., Mahon, B., and Caramazza, A. (2003). What are the facts of semantic category-specific deficits? A critical review of the clinical evidence. *Cognitive Neuropsychology*, 20, 213−61.

Caramazza, A. and Mahon, B. (2005). The organization of conceptual knowledge in the brain: the future's past and some future directions. *Cognitive Neuropsychology*, 22, 1−25.

Carey, D., Harvey, M., and Milner, D. (1996). Visuomotor sensitivity for shape and orientation in a patient with visual form agnosia. *Neuropsychologia*, 34, 329−37.

Carey, S. (1985). *Conceptual Change in Childhood*. MIT Press.

Carpenter, M., Nagell, K., and Tomasello, M. (1998). Social cognition, joint attention, and communicative from 9 to 15 months of age. *Monographs of the Society for Research in Child Development*, 63, 1−176.

Carroll, S. (2005). *Endless Forms Most Beautiful: the new science of evo devo and the making of the animal kingdom*. Norton.

Carruthers, P. (1992). *Human Knowledge and Human Nature*. Oxford University Press.

――― (1996). *Language, Thought, and Consciousness*. Cambridge University Press.

――― (2000). *Phenomenal Consciousness: a naturalistic theory*. Cambridge University Press.

――― (2002a). The cognitive functions of language. *Behavioral and Brain Sciences*, 25, 657−719.

――― (2002b). Human creativity: its evolution, its cognitive basis, and its connections with childhood pretence. *British Journal for the Philosophy of Science*, 53, 1−25.

――― (2003). On Fodor's Problem. *Mind and Language*, 18, 502−23.

――― (2004a). Practical reasoning in a modular mind. *Mind and Language*, 19, 259−78.

――― (2004b). On being simple minded. *American Philosophical Quarterly*, 41, 205−20.

――― (2005). *Consciousness: essays from a higher-order perspective*. Oxford University Press.

――― (2006a). Simple heuristics meet massive modularity. In Carruthers et al., 2006.

――― (2006b). Why pretend? In S. Nichols (ed.), *The Architecture of the Imagination*, Oxford University Press.

――― and Boucher, J., eds. (1998). *Language and Thought: interdisciplinary themes*. Cambridge University Press.

――― and Chamberlain, A., eds. (2000). *Evolution and the Human Mind: modularity, language, and metacognition*. Cambridge University Press.

――― and Smith, P., eds. (1996). *Theories of Theories of Mind*. Cambridge University Press.

—— Stich, S., and Siegal, M., eds. (2002). *The Cognitive Basis of Science*. Cambridge University Press.

—— Laurence, S., and Stich, S., eds. (2005). *The Innate Mind: structure and contents*. Oxford University Press.

—— eds. (2006). *The Innate Mind: culture and cognition*. Oxford University Press.

—— eds. (planned for 2007). *The Innate Mind: foundations and the future*. Oxford University Press.

Cartwright, N. (1983). *How the Laws of Physics Lie*. Oxford University Press.

Carvalli-Sforza, L. and Feldman, M. (1981). *Cultural Transmission and Evolution: a quantitative approach*. Princeton University Press.

Casati, R. and Varzi, A. (1999). *Parts and Places: the structures of spatial representation*. MIT Press.

Castiello, U., Paulignan, Y., and Jeannerod, M. (1991). Temporal dissociation of motor responses and subjective awareness. *Brain*, 114, 2639–55.

Ceponiene, R., Lepisto, T., Shestakova, A., Vanhala, R., Alku, P., Naatanen, R., and Yaguchi, K. (2003). Speech-sound-selective auditory impairment in children with autism: they can perceive but do not attend. *Proceedings of the National Academy of Sciences*, 100, 5567–72.

Chalmers, D. (1996). *The Conscious Mind*. Oxford University Press.

Chandler, N., Fritz, A., and Hala, S. (1989). Small-scale deceit: deception as a marker of two-, three-, and four-year-olds' early theories of mind. *Child Development*, 60, 1263–77.

Chao, L., Haxby, J., and Martin, A. (1999). Attribute-based neural substrates in temporal cortex for perceiving and knowing about objects. *Nature Neuroscience*, 2, 913–19.

Chater, N. (1999). The search for simplicity: a fundamental cognitive principle? *Quarterly Journal of Experimental Psychology*, 52A, 273–302.

Cheney, D. and Seyfarth, R. (1999). Recognition of other individuals' social relationships by female baboons. *Animal Behavior*, 58, 67–75.

Cheng, K. (1986). A purely geometric module in the rat's spatial representation. *Cognition*, 23, 149–78.

Cheng, P. and Holyoak, K. (1985). Pragmatic reasoning schemas. *Cognitive Psychology*, 17, 391–416.

Cherniak, C. (1986). *Minimal Rationality*. MIT Press.

—— Mokhtarzada, Z., Rodriquez-Esteban, R., and Changizi, B. (2004). Global optimization of cerebral cortex layout. *Proceedings of the National Academy of Sciences*, 101, 1081–6.

Chomsky, N. (1957). *Syntactic Structures*. Mouton.

—— (1959). Review of *Verbal Behavior* by B.F. Skinner. *Language*, 35, 26–58.

—— (1965). *Aspects of the Theory of Syntax*. MIT Press.

—— (1975). *Reflections on Language*. Pantheon.

—— (1986). *Knowledge of Language*. Praeger.

—— (1995). *The Minimalist Program*. MIT Press.

Church, R. and Meck, W. (1984). The numerical attribute of stimuli. In H. Roitblatt, T. Bever, and H. Torrance (eds.), *Animal Cognition*, Lawrence Erlbaum.

Churchland, P. and Sejnowski, T. (1992). *The Computational Brain*. MIT Press.

Clark, A. (1987). The kludge in the machine. *Mind and Language*, 2, 277–300.

_____ (1998). Magic words: how language augments human computation. In Carruthers and Boucher, 1998.

Clark, D., Mitra, P., and Wang, S. (2001). Scalable architecture in mammalian brains. *Nature*, 411, 189–93.

Clayton, N., Griffiths, D., Emery, N., and Dickinson, A. (2002). Elements of episodic-like memory in animals. In Baddeley et al., 2002.

_____ Emery, N., and Dickinson, A. (2004). The rationality of animal memory: the cognition of caching. In S. Hurley (ed.), *Animal Rationality*, Oxford University Press.

Clements, W. and Perner, J. (1994). Implicit understanding of belief. *Cognitive Development*, 9, 377–95.

Coady, C. (1992). *Testimony*. Oxford University Press.

Collett, T. and Collett, M. (2002). Memory use in insect visual navigation. *Nature Reviews: Neuroscience*, 3, 542–52.

Connor, R., Smolker, R., and Richards, A. (1992). Dolphin alliances and coalitions. In A. Harcourt and F. de Wall (eds.), *Coalitions and Alliances in Human and Non-human Animals*, Oxford University Press.

Conway, M. and Pleydell-Pierce, C. (2000). The construction of autobiographical memories in the self-memory system. *Psychological Review*, 107, 271–88.

_____ Turk, D., Miller, S., Logan, J., Nebes, R., Metzler, C., and Becker, J. (1999). A positron emission tomography (PET) study of autobiographical memory retrieval. *Memory*, 7, 679–702.

Copp, D. and Sobel, D. (2002). Desires, motives and reasons. *Social Theory and Practice*, 28, 243–78.

Cosmides, L. (1989). The logic of social exchange: has natural selection shaped how humans reason? Studies with the Wason selection task. *Cognition*, 31, 187–276.

_____ and Tooby, J. (1992). Cognitive adaptations for social exchange. In Barkow et al., 1992.

_____ (2002). Unraveling the enigma of human intelligence: evolutionary psychology and the multi-modular mind. In R. Sternberg and J. Kaufman (eds.), *The Evolution of Intelligence*, Lawrence Erlbaum.

Coward, L. (2001). The recommendation architecture: lessons from the design of large scale electronic systems for cognitive science. *Journal of Cognitive Systems Research*, 2, 111–56.

_____ (2005). *A System Architecture Approach to the Brain*. Nova Publishers.

Cowie, A. and Stoerig, P. (1995). Blind-sight in monkeys. *Nature*, 373, 247–9.

Crutchfield, J. (1984). Space-time dynamics in video feedback. *Physica*, 10D, 229–45.

Csibra, G. (2005). Mirror neurons and action observation: is simulation involved? <http://www.interdisciplines.org/mirror>.

Cummins, D. (1996). Evidence of deontic reasoning in 3- and 4-year-old children. *Memory and Cognition*, 24, 823–9.

Currie, G. and Ravenscroft, I. (2002). *Recreative Minds: imagination in philosophy and in psychology*. Oxford University Press.

——and Sterelny, K. (2000). How to think about the modularity of mind-reading. *Philosophical Quarterly*, 50, 145–60.

Curtiss, S. (1977). *Genie: a psycholinguistic study of a modern-day 'wild child'*. Academic Press.

Daly, J., Emery, N., and Clayton, N. (2006). Food-caching western scrub-jays keep track of who was watching when. *Sciencexpress*. Published on-line May 5, 2006, Science DOI: 10.1/26/science 1126539.

Daly, M. and Wilson, M. (1988). *Homicide*. Aldine Press.

——(1995). Discriminative parental solicitude and the relevance of evolutionary models to the analysis of motivational systems. In M. Gazzaniga (ed.), *The Cognitive Neurosciences*, MIT Press.

——(1998). *The Truth about Cinderella: a Darwinian view of parental love*. Weidenfeld and Nicolson.

——(2005). A reply to David Buller. Published on the web at:<http://psych.mcmaster. ca/dalywilson/>.

Damasio, A. (1994). *Descartes' Error: emotion, reason and the human brain*. Papermac.

——(2003). *Looking for Spinoza: joy, sorrow, and the feeling brain*. Harcourt.

Dancy, J. (1993). *Moral Reasons*. Blackwell.

——(2000). *Practical Reality*. Oxford University Press.

Davidson, D. (1970). Mental events. In L. Foster and J. Swanson (eds.), *Experience and Theory*, Duckworth.

——(1973). Radical interpretation. *Dialectica*, 27, 313–28.

——(1975). Thought and talk. In S. Guttenplan (ed.), *Mind and Language*, Oxford University Press.

Davies, M. (1991). Concepts, connectionism, and the language of thought. In W. Ramsey, S. Stich, and D. Rumelhart (eds.), *Philosophy and Connectionist Theory*, Lawrence Erlbaum.

——(1998). Language, thought, and the language of thought (Aunty's own argument revisited). In Carruthers and Boucher, 1998.

——and Stone, T., eds. (1995). *Folk Psychology: the theory of mind debate*. Blackwell.

Dawkins, R. (1976). *The Selfish Gene*. Oxford University Press.

——(1986). *The Blind Watchmaker*. Norton.

Deaner, R. (2006). More males run fast: a stable sex difference in competitiveness in US distance runners. *Evolution and Human Behavior*, 27, 63–84.

Dehaene, S. (1997). *The Number Sense: how the mind creates mathematics*. Penguin.

——and Naccache, L. (2001). Towards a cognitive neuroscience of consciousness: basic evidence and a workspace framework. *Cognition*, 79, 1–37.

Dehaene, S., Cohen, L., Bihan, D., Mangin, J., Poline, J., and Riviere, D. (2001). Cerebral mechanisms of word priming and unconscious repetition masking. *Nature Neuroscience*, 4, 752–8.

____ Sergent, C., and Changeux, J. (2003). A neuronal network model linking subjective reports and objective physiological data during conscious perception. *Proceedings of the National Academy of Science*, 100, 8520–5.

Dennett, D. (1978). *Brainstorms*. Harvester Press.

____ (1984). *Elbow Room: the varieties of free will worth wanting*. MIT Press.

____ (1987). *The Intentional Stance*. MIT Press.

Dennett, D. (1991). *Consciousness Explained*. Penguin Press.

Diamond, J. (1997). *Guns, Germs, and Steel*. Norton.

Diaz, R. and Berk, L., eds. (1992). *Private Speech: from social interaction to self-regulation*. Lawrence Erlbaum.

Dickinson, A. and Balleine, B. (2000). Causal cognition and goal-directed action. In C. Heyes and L. Huber (eds.), *The Evolution of Cognition*, MIT Press.

____ and Charnock, D. (1985). Contingency effects with maintained instrumental reinforcement. *Quarterly Journal of Experimental Psychology*, 37B, 397–416.

____ and Shanks, D. (1995). Instrumental action and causal representation. In D. Sperber, D. Premack, and A. Premack (eds.), *Causal Cognition*, Oxford University Press.

Dienes, Z. and Perner, J. (1999). A theory of implicit and explicit knowledge. *Behavioral and Brain Sciences*, 22, 735–808.

Dreyfus, L. (1991). Local shifts in relative reinforcement rate and time allocation on concurrent schedules. *Journal of Experimental Psychology*, 17, 486–502.

Driver, P. and Humphries, N. (1988). *Protean Behavior: the biology of unpredictability*. Oxford University Press.

Dummett, M. (1973). *Frege: philosophy of language*. Duckworth.

Dunbar, K. (2002). Understanding the role of cognition in science: the *Science as Category* framework. In Carruthers et al., 2002.

Dunbar, R. (1996). *Grooming, Gossip, and the Evolution of Language*. Harvard University Press.

____ (2000). On the origin of the human mind. In Carruthers and Chamberlain, 2000.

Dupré, J. (2001). *Human Nature and the Limits of Science*. Oxford University Press.

Durham, W. (1991). *Coevolution: genes, culture, and human diversity*. Stanford University Press.

Dyer, F. and Dickinson, J. (1994). Development of sun compensation by honeybees. *Proceedings of the National Academy of Science*, 91, 4471–4.

Eagly, A. and Claiken, S. (1993). *The Psychology of Attitudes*. Harcourt Brace Jovanovich.

Eaton, M. (1982). A strange kind of sadness. *Journal of Aesthetics and Art Criticism*, 41, 51–63.

Ebersberger, I., Metzler, D., Schwarz, C., and Paabo, S. (2002). Genome-wide comparison of DNA sequences between humans and chimpanzees. *American Journal of Human Genetics*, 70, 1490–7.

Edel, M. and Edel, A. (2000). *Anthropology and Ethics*. Transaction Publishers.

Ekman, P. (1992a). An argument for basic emotions. *Cognition and Emotion*, 6, 169–200.

—— (1992b). Facial expressions of emotion: new findings, new questions. *Psychological Science*, 3, 34–8.

Ellis, B. (1992). The evolution of sexual attraction: evaluative mechanisms in women. In Barkow et al., 1992.

Elman, J., Bates, E., Johnson, M., Karmiloff-Smith, A., Parisi, D., and Plunkett, K. (1996). *Rethinking Innateness: a connectionist perspective on development*. MIT Press.

Emlen, S. (1969). The development of migratory orientation in young indigo buntings. *Living Bird*, 8, 113–26.

Ericsson, A. and Simon, H. (1993). *Protocol Analysis: verbal reports as data*. (Revised edition.) MIT Press.

Euler, H. and Weitzel, B. (1996). Discriminative grandparental solicitude as a reproductive strategy. *Human Nature*, 7, 93–107.

Evans, G. (1982). *The Varieties of Reference*. Oxford University Press.

Evans, J. and Over, D. (1996). *Rationality and Reasoning*. Psychology Press.

Farah, M., Mayer, M., and McMullen, P. (1996). The living/nonliving dissociation is not an artifact: giving an a priori implausible hypothesis a strong test. *Cognitive Neuropsychology*, 13, 137–54.

Farrant, A., Boucher, J., and Blades, M. (1999). Metamemory in children with autism. *Child Development*, 70, 107–31.

Feagin, S. (1983). The pleasures of tragedy. *American Philosophical Quarterly*, 20, 95–104.

Fehr, E. and Gachter, S. (2002). Altruistic punishment in humans. *Nature*, 415, 137–40.

Felleman, D. and Van Essen, D. (1991). Distributed hierarchical processing in primate cerebral cortex. *Cerebral Cortex*, 1, 1–47.

Fessler, D. and Navarrete, D. (2003). Domain-specific variation in disgust sensitivity across the menstrual cycle. *Evolution and Human Behavior*, 24, 406–17.

—— (2004). Third-party attitudes towards sibling incest: evidence for the Westermarck hypothesis. *Evolution and Human Behavior*, 25, 277–94.

Festinger, L. (1957). *A Theory of Cognitive Dissonance*. Stanford University Press.

Fiddick, L., Cosmides, L., and Tooby, J. (2000). No interpretation without representation: the role of domain-specific representations and inferences in the Wason selection task. *Cognition*, 77, 1–79.

Finke, R. (1995). Creative realism. In S. Smith, T. Ward, and R. Finke (eds.), *The Creative Cognition Approach*, Cambridge University Press.

—— Ward, T., and Smith, S. (1992). *Creative Cognition*. MIT Press.

Finlay, B., Darlington, R., and Nicastro, N. (2001). Developmental structure in brain evolution. *Behavioral and Brain Sciences*, 24, 263–308.

Flavell, J., Green, F., and Flavell, E. (1995). Young children's knowledge about thinking. *Monographs of the Society for Research in Child Development*, 60, 1–95.

Flombaum, J., Junge, J., and Hauser, M. (2005). Rhesus monkeys (*Macaca mulatta*) spontaneously compute addition operations over large numbers. *Cognition*, 97, 315–25.

Fodor, J. (1975). *The Language of Thought*. Harvester Press.

_____ (1983). *The Modularity of Mind*. MIT Press.

_____ (1992). A theory of the child's theory of mind. *Cognition*, 44, 283–96.

_____ (1998). Connectionism and the problem of systematicity (continued): why Smolensky's solution *still* doesn't work. In J. Fodor, *In Critical Condition*, MIT Press.

_____ (2000). *The Mind doesn't Work that Way*. MIT Press.

_____ (2003). *Hume Variations*. Oxford University Press.

_____ and McLaughlin, B. (1990). Connectionism and the problem of systematicity. *Cognition*, 35, 183–204.

Fodor, J. and Pylyshyn, Z. 1988. Connectionism and cognitive architecture. *Cognition*, 28, 3–71.

Foucher, L., Mallon, R., Nazer, D., Nichols, S., Ruby, A., Stich, S., and Weinberg, J. (2002). The baby in the lab-coat: why child development is not an adequate model for understanding the development of science. In Carruthers et al., 2002.

Frankish, K. (2004). *Mind and Supermind*. Cambridge University Press.

Frisch, M. (2005). *Inconsistency, Asymmetry, and Non-Locality: a philosophical investigation of classical electrodynamics*. Oxford University Press.

Frith, C. (1992). *The Cognitive Neuropsychology of Schizophrenia*. Lawrence Erlbaum.

_____ Blakemore, S., and Wolpert, D. (2000). Explaining the symptoms of schizophrenia: abnormalities in the awareness of action. *Brain Research Reviews*, 31, 357–63.

Gallese, V. and Goldman, A. (1998). Mirror neurons and the simulation theory of mind-reading. *Trends in Cognitive Sciences*, 12, 493–501.

_____ Fadiga, L., Fogassi, L., and Rizzolatti, G. (1996). Action recognition in the pre-motor cortex. *Brain*, 119, 593–609.

_____ (2002). Action representation and the inferior parietal lobule. In W. Prinz and B. Hommel (eds.), *Common Mechanisms in Perception and Action*, Oxford University Press.

Gallistel, R. (1980). *The Organization of Action*. Lawrence Erlbaum.

_____ (1990). *The Organization of Learning*. MIT Press.

_____ (2000). The replacement of general-purpose learning models with adaptively specialized learning modules. In M. Gazzaniga (ed.), *The New Cognitive Neurosciences*, Second Edition, MIT Press.

_____ (2003). Conditioning from an information processing perspective. *Behavioral Processes*, 61, 1–13.

_____ (forthcoming). *The Blackwell Lectures*. (University of Maryland). Blackwell.

_____ and Gibbon, J. (2001). Time, rate and conditioning. *Psychological Review*, 108, 289–344.

_____ (2002). *The Symbolic Foundations of Conditioned Behavior*. Lawrence Erlbaum.

_____ Mark, T., King, A., and Latham, P. (2001). The rat approximates an ideal detector of rates of reward: implications for the law of effect. *Journal of Experimental Psychology: Animal Behavior Processes*, 27, 354–72.

Gangestad, S. and Thornhill, R. (1997). The evolutionary psychology of extra-pair sex: the role of fluctuating asymmetry. *Evolution and Human Behavior*, 18, 69–88.

Ganis, G., Keenan, J., Kosslyn, S., and Pascual-Leone, A. (2000). Transcranian magnetic stimulation of primary motor cortex affects mental rotation. *Cerebral Cortex*, 10, 175–80.

Gardner, H. (1983). *Frames of Mind: the theory of multiple intelligences*. Heinemann.

Gathercole, S. and Baddeley, A. (1993). *Working Memory and Language*. Lawrence Erlbaum.

Gaulin, S. and Robbins, C. (1991). Taivens-Willand effect in contemporary North American society. *American Journal of Physical Anthropology*, 85, 61–9.

Gazzaniga, M. (1998). *The Mind's Past*. California University Press.

Geary, D. (2005). *The Origin of Mind: evolution of brain, cognition, and general intelligence*. American Psychological Association.

Gergely, G. and Csibra, G. (2003). Teleological reasoning in infancy: the naive theory of rational action. *Trends in Cognitive Sciences*, 7, 287–92.

——Nadasdy, Z., Csibra, G., and Biro, S. (1995). Taking the intentional stance at 12 months of age. *Cognition*, 56, 165–93.

Ghahramani, Z. and Wolpert, D. (1997). Modular decomposition in visuomotor learning. *Nature*, 386, 392–5.

Gibbard, A. (1990). *Wise Choices, Apt Feelings*. Oxford University Press.

Giere, R. (1992). Cognitive Models of Science. *Minnesota Studies in the Philosophy of Science*, 15. University of Minnesota Press.

——(2002). Scientific cognition as distributed cognition. In Carruthers et al., 2002.

Gigerenzer, G. and Hug, K. (1992). Domain-specific reasoning: social contracts, cheating and perspective change. *Cognition*, 43, 127–71.

——Todd, P., and the ABC Research Group. (1999). *Simple Heuristics that Make Us Smart*. Oxford University Press.

Gill, F. (1988). Trapline foraging by hermit hummingbirds: competition for an undefended renewable resource. *Ecology*, 69, 1933–42.

Giurfa, M., Zhang, S., Jenett, A., Menzel, R., and Srinivasan, M. (2001). The concepts of 'sameness' and 'difference' in an insect. *Nature*, 410, 930–3.

Gladwell, M. (2005). *Blink: the power of thinking without thinking*. Little and Brown.

Glover, S. (2004). Separate visual representations in the planning and control of action. *Behavioral and Brain Sciences*, 27, 3–24.

Glymour, C. and Cooper, G. (1999). *Computation, Causation, and Discovery*. MIT Press.

Golding-Meadow, S. and Zheng, M. (1998). Thought before language: the expression of motion events prior to the impact of a conventional language model. In Carruthers and Boucher, 1998.

Gomez, J. (1998). Some thoughts about the evolution of LADS, with special reference to TOM and SAM. In Carruthers and Boucher, 1998.

Goodale, M., Pélisson, D., and Prablanc, C. (1986). Large adjustments in visually guided reaching do not depend on vision of the hand or perception of target displacement. *Nature*, 320, 748–50.

Goodale, M., Milner, D., Jakobson, L., and Carey, D. (1991). A neurological dissociation between perceiving objects and grasping them. *Nature*, 349, 154−6.

____Jakobson, L., and Keillor, J. (1994a). Differences in the visual control of pantomimed and natural grasping movements. *Neuropsychologia*, 32, 1159−78.

____Milner, D., Perrett, D., Benson, P., and Hietanen, J. (1994b). The nature and limits of orientation and pattern processing supporting visuomotor control in a visual form agnosic. *Journal of Cognitive Neuroscience*, 6, 46−56.

Gopnik, A. (1993). The illusion of first-person knowledge of intentionality. *Behavioral and Brain Sciences*, 16, 1−14.

____(1998). Explanation as orgasm. *Minds and Machines*, 8, 101−18.

____(2001). Theories, language and culture. In M. Bowerman and S. Levinson (eds.), *Language Acquisition and Conceptual Development*, Cambridge University Press.

____and Glymour, C. (2002). Causal maps and Bayes nets: a cognitive and computational account of theory-formation. In Carruthers et al., 2002.

____and Meltzoff, A. (1997). *Words, Thoughts, and Theories*. MIT Press.

____and Schulz, L. (2004). Mechanisms of theory formation in young children. *Trends in Cognitive Sciences*, 8, 371−7.

____Choi, S., and Baumberger, T. (1996). Cross-linguistic differences in early semantic and cognitive development. *Cognitive Development*, 11, 197−227.

Gordon, R. (1997). Everyday life as an intelligence test. *Intelligence*, 24, 203−20.

Gottfredson, L. (1997). Why *g* matters: the complexity of everyday life. *Intelligence*, 24, 79−132.

Gould, J. (1986). The locale map of bees: do insects have cognitive maps? *Science*, 232, 861−3.

____and Gould, C. (1988). *The Honey Bee*. Scientific American Library.

____(1994). *The Animal Mind*. Scientific American Library.

Gould, S. (1991). Exaptation: a crucial tool for an evolutionary psychology. *Journal of Social Issues*, 47, 43−65.

____and Lewontin, R. (1979). The spandrels of San Marco and the panglossian paradigm: a critique of the adaptationist program. *Proceedings of the Royal Society of London*, B 205, 581−98.

Gouteux, S., Thinus-Blanc, C., and Vauclair, S. (2001). Rhesus monkeys use geometric and non-geometric information in a re-orientation task. *Journal of Experimental Psychology, General Proceedings*, 130, 505−19.

Gowlett, J. (1984). Mental abilities of early man: a look at some hard evidence. In R. Foley (ed.), *Hominid Evolution and Community Ecology*, Academic Press.

Griffiths, P. and Gray, R. (2001). Darwinism and developmental systems. In S. Oyama, P. Griffiths, and R. Gray (eds.), *Cycles of Contingency: developmental systems and evolution*, MIT Press.

Grush, R. (2004). The emulation theory of representation: motor control, imagery, and perception. *Behavioral and Brain Sciences*, 27, 377−442.

Gunther, Y., ed. (2003). *Essays on Nonconceptual Content*. MIT Press.

Haidt, J. (2001). The emotional dog and its rational tail: a social intuitionist approach to moral judgment. *Psychological Review*, 108, 814–34.

——and Joseph, C. (forthcoming). How a thousand virtues might bloom from five moral modules: uniting cultural and evolutionary approaches to moral intuition. In Carruthers et al., planned for 2007.

——McCauley, C., and Rozin, P. (1994). Individual differences in sensitivity to disgust: a scale sampling seven domains of disgust elicitors. *Personality and Individual Differences*, 16, 701–13.

Hala, S., Chandler, M., and Fritz, A. (1991). Fledgling theories of mind: deception as a marker of three-year-olds' understanding of false belief. *Child Development*, 62, 83–97.

Hamilton, W. (1964). The genetical evolution of social behavior. *Journal of Theoretical Biology*, 7, 1–52.

Hamman, S. (1990). Level-of-processing effects in conceptually driven implicit tasks. *Journal of Experimental Psychology: Learning, Memory, and Cognition*, 16, 970–7.

Hansen, R. and Skavenski, A. (1985). Accuracy of spatial localization near the time of a saccadic eye movement. *Vision Research*, 25, 1077–82.

Happé, F. and Loth, E. (2002). 'Theory of mind' and tracking speakers' intentions. *Mind and Language*, 17, 24–36.

Hare, B., Call, J., Agnetta, B., and Tomasello, M. (2000). Chimpanzees know what conspecifics do and do not see. *Animal Behavior*, 59, 771–85.

Harper, D. (1982). Competitive foraging in mallards: ideal free ducks. *Animal Behavior*, 30, 575–84.

Harris, P. (2000). *The Work of the Imagination*. Blackwell.

——(2002a). What do children learn from testimony? In Carruthers et al., 2002.

——(2002b). Checking our sources: the origins of trust in testimony. *Studies in History and Philosophy of Science*, 33, 315–33.

——and Núñez, M. (1996). Understanding of permission rules by pre-school children. *Child Development*, 67, 1572–91.

——and Brett, C. (2001). Let's swap: early understanding of social exchange by British and Nepali children. *Memory and Cognition*, 29, 757–64.

Hart, J. and Gordon, B. (1992). Neural subsystems for object knowledge. *Nature*, 359, 60–4.

Hartmann, G. and Wehner, R. (1995). The ant's path integration system: a neural architecture. *Biological Cybernetics*, 73, 483–97.

Haruno, M., Wolpert, D., and Kawato, M. (2001). Mosaic model for sensorimotor learning and control. *Neural Computation*, 13, 2201–20.

Hauser, M. (1996). *The Evolution of Communication*. MIT Press.

——(2000). *Wild Minds: what animals really think*. Penguin Press.

——(2001). Review of *Folk Physics for Apes* by Daniel Povinelli. *Science*, 291: 5503, 440–1.

Hauser, M. and Spelke, E. (2005). Evolutionary and developmental foundations of human knowledge: a case study of mathematics. In M. Gazzaniga (ed.), *The New Cognitive Neurosciences*, Third Edition, MIT Press.

―― Chomsky, N., and Hitch, W. (2002). The faculty of language: what is it, who has it, and how did it evolve? *Science*, 298, 1569–79.

Hawkes, K. (1991). Showing off: tests of another hypothesis about men's foraging goals. *Ethology and Sociobiology*, 11, 29–54.

―― (1993). Why hunter-gatherers work: an ancient version of the problem of public goods. *Current Anthropology*, 34, 341–61.

―― O'Connell, J., and Blurton Jones, N. (1997). Hazda women's time allocation, offspring provisioning, and the evolution of long postmenopausal life spans. *Current Anthropology*, 38, 551–77.

Hempel, C. (1966). *The Philosophy of Natural Science*. Prentice Hall.

Henrich, J. (2004). Demography and cultural evolution: why adaptive cultural processes produced maladaptive losses in Tasmania. *American Antiquity*, 69, 197–214.

Henrich, J. and Boyd, R. (1998). The evolution of conformist transmission and the emergence of between-group differences. *Evolution and Human Behavior*, 19, 215–41.

―― and Gil-White, F. (2001). The evolution of prestige. *Evolution and Human Behavior*, 22, 165–96.

―― Boyd, R., Bowles, S., Camerer, C., Fehr, E., and Gintis, H., eds. (2004). *Foundations of Human Sociality: economic experiments and ethnographic evidence from fifteen small-scale societies*. Oxford University Press.

Hermer, L. and Spelke, E. (1994). A geometric process for spatial reorientation in young children. *Nature*, 370, 57–9.

―― (1996). Modularity and development: the case of spatial reorientation. *Cognition*, 61, 195–232.

Hermer-Vazquez, L., Spelke, E., and Katsnelson, A. (1999). Sources of flexibility in human cognition: dual-task studies of space and language. *Cognitive Psychology*, 39, 3–36.

Hernstein, R. and Murray, C. (1994). *The Bell Curve: intelligence and class structure in American life*. Free Press.

Higginbotham, J. (1985). On semantics. *Linguistic Inquiry*, 16, 547–93.

Hikosaka, O., Sakai, K., Nakahara, H., Lu, X., Miyachi, S., Nakamura, K., and Rand, M. (2000). Neural mechanisms for learning of sequential procedures. In M. Gazzaniga (ed.), *The New Cognitive Neurosciences*, Second Edition, MIT Press.

Hill, K. and Kaplan, H. (1988). Trade-offs in male and female reproductive strategies among the Ache. In L. Betzig, M. Borgerhof-Mulder, and P. Turke (eds.), *Human Reproductive Behavior*, Cambridge University Press.

Hitch, G. (1980). Developing the concept of working memory. In G. Glaxton (ed.), *Cognitive Psychology*, Routledge.

Hobson, P. (2002). *The Cradle of Thought: challenging the origins of thinking*. Macmillan.

Hodges, J. and Graham, K. (2002). Episodic memory: insights from semantic dementia. In Baddeley et al., 2002.

Holloway, R. (2002). How much larger is the relative volume of area 10 of the prefrontal cortex in humans? *American Journal of Physical Anthropology*, 11, 399–401.

Hrdy, S. (1999). *Mother Nature: a history of mothers, infants, and natural selection.* Pantheon.

Hubel, D. and Wiesel, T. (1970). The period of susceptibility to the physiological effects of unilateral eye closure in kittens. *Journal of Physiology*, 206, 419–36.

Huffman, K., Nelson, J., Clarey, J., and Krubitzer, L. (1999). Organization of somatosensory cortex in three species of marsupials: neural correlates of morphological specializations. *Journal of Comparative Neurology*, 403, 5–32.

Hume, D. (1739). *A Treatise of Human Nature.* Many editions now available.

——(1748). *Enquiry into Human Understanding.* Many editions now available.

Hummel, J. and Holyoak, K. (1997). Distributed representations of structure: a theory of analogical access and mapping. *Psychological Review*, 104, 427–66.

——(2003). A symbolic-connectionist theory of relational inference and generalization. *Psychological Review*, 110, 220–64.

Humphrey, N. (1986). *The Inner Eye.* Faber and Faber.

Hurlburt, R. (1990). *Sampling Normal and Schizophrenic Inner Experience.* Plenum Press.

——(1993). *Sampling Inner Experience with Disturbed Affect.* Plenum Press.

——Happé, F., and Frith, U. (1994). Sampling the form of inner experience in three adults with Asperger syndrome. *Psychological Medicine*, 24, 385–95.

Hurley, S. and Chater, N. eds. (2005). *Perspectives on Imitation: from neuroscience to social science*, Volume 1. MIT Press.

Jackendoff, R. (1996). How language helps us think. *Pragmatics and Cognition*, 4, 1–34.

——(1997). *The Architecture of the Language Faculty.* MIT Press.

Jacob, P. and Jeannerod, M. (2003). *Ways of Seeing.* Oxford University Press.

Jacobs, R., Jordan, M., Nowlan, S., and Hinton, G. (1991). Adaptive mixture of local experts. *Neural Computation*, 3, 79–87.

Janzen, D. (1971). Euglossine bees as long-distance pollinators of tropical plants. *Science*, 171, 203–5.

Jarrold, C., Boucher, J., and Smith, P. (1993). Symbolic play in autism: a review. *Journal of Autism and Developmental Disorders*, 23, 281–387.

——Carruthers, P., Smith, P., and Boucher, J. (1994). Pretend play: is it metarepresentational? *Mind and Language*, 9, 445–68.

Jensen, A. (1998). *The g Factor: the science of mental ability.* Praeger.

Johnson, S. (2005). Reasoning about intentionality in preverbal infants. In Carruthers et al., 2005.

Johnson-Laird, P. (1983). *Mental Models.* Cambridge University Press.

Jolly, A. (1999). *Lucy's Legacy.* Harvard University Press.

Joyce, R. (2001). *The Myth of Morality.* Cambridge University Press.

Kahneman, D. (2002). Maps of bounded rationality: a perspective on intuitive judgment and choice. Nobel laureate acceptance speech. Available at:<http://nobelprize.org/economics/laureates/2002/kahneman-lecture.html>.

——Slovic, P., and Tversky, A. (1982). *Judgment Under Uncertainty: heuristics and biases.* Cambridge University Press.

Kamel, R. (1987). Effect of modularity on system evolution. *IEEE Software*, January 1987, 48–54.

Kanazawa, S. (2004). General intelligence as a domain-specific adaptation. *Psychological Review*, 111, 512–23.

Kaplan, H., Hill, K., Lancaster, J., and Hrutado, A. (2000). A theory of human life-history evolution: diet, intelligence, and longevity. *Evolutionary Anthropology*, 9, 156–85.

Kaplan, M. (1981). A Bayesian theory of rational acceptance. *Journal of Philosophy*, 78, 305–30.

Karmiloff-Smith, A. (1992). *Beyond Modularity*. MIT Press.

Karni, A., Meyer, G., Jezzard, P., Adams, M., Turner, R., and Ungerleider, L. (1995). Functional MRI evidence for adult motor cortex plasticity during motor skill learning. *Nature*, 377, 155–8.

Katz, L. and Shatz, C. (1996). Synaptic activity and the construction of cortical circuits. *Science*, 274, 1133.

Katz, L., Shatz, C., Weliky, M., and Crowley, J. (2000). Activity and the development of the visual cortex: new perspectives. In M. Gazzaniga (ed.), *The New Cognitive Neurosciences*, Second Edition, MIT Press.

Kawai, M. (1965). Newly-acquired pre-cultural behavior of the natural troop of Japanese monkeys on Koshima islet. *Primates*, 6, 1–30.

Kelly, S. (2001). Demonstrative concepts and experience. *Philosophical Review*, 110, 397–420.

Kertesz, A. (1988). Cognitive function in severe aphasia. In L. Weiskrantz (ed.), *Thought without Language*, Oxford University Press.

Keysar, B., Shuhong, L., and Barr, D. (2003). Limits on theory of mind use in adults. *Cognition*, 89, 25–41.

Kharraz-Tavakol, O., Eggert, T., Mai, N., and Straube, A. (2000). Learning to write letters: transfer in automated movements indicates modularity of motor programs in normal subjects. *Neuroscience Letters*, 282, 33–6.

Kirschner, M. and Gerhart, J. (1998). Evolvability. *Proceedings of the National Academy of Sciences*, 95, 8420–77.

Kitcher, P. (1985). *Vaulting Ambition: sociobiology and the quest for human nature*. MIT Press.

——— (2002). Social psychology and the theory of science. In Carruthers et al., 2002.

Koechlin, E., Ody, C., and Kouneiher, F. (2003). The architecture of cognitive control in the human prefrontal cortex. *Science*, 302, 1181–5.

Köhler, W. (1927). *The Mentality of Apes*. Harcourt Brace.

Koltermann, R. (1974). Periodicity in the activity and learning performance of the honey bee. In L. Browne (ed.), *The Experimental Analysis of Insect Behavior*, Springer.

Korsching, S. (1993). The neurotrophic factor concept: a re-examination. *Journal of Neuroscience*, 13, 2739–48.

Koslowski, B. (1996). *Theory and Evidence: the development of scientific reasoning*. MIT Press.

_____ and Thomson, S. (2002). Theorizing is important, and collateral information constrains how well it is done. In Carruthers et al., 2002.

Kosslyn, S. (1994). *Image and Brain*. MIT Press.

_____ Thompson, W., Wraga, M., and Alpert, N. (2001). Imagining rotation by endogenous versus exogenous forces: distinct neural mechanisms. *NeuroReport*, 12, 2519–25.

Krackle, W. (1978). *Force and Persuasion: leadership in an Amazonian society*. University of Chicago Press.

Kreiman, G., Fried, I., and Koch, C. (2003). Single neuron correlates of subjective vision in the human medial temporal lobe. *Proceedings of the National Academy of Science*, 99, 8378–83.

Kuhlmeier, V., Bloom, P., and Wynn, K. (2004). Do 5-month old infants see humans as material objects? *Cognition*, 94, 95–103.

Kyburg, H. (1961). *Probability and the Logic of Rational Belief*. Wesleyan University Press.

Lahr, M. and Foley, R. (1998). Towards a theory of modern human origins: geography, demography, and diversity in recent human evolution. *Yearbook of Physical Anthropology*, 41, 137–76.

Lakatos, I. (1970). The methodology of scientific research programs. In I. Lakatos and A. Musgrave (eds.), *Criticism and the Growth of Knowledge*, Cambridge University Press.

Lakoff, G. and Johnson, M. (1980). *Metaphors we Live by*. Chicago University Press.

_____ (1999). *Philosophy in the Flesh*. Basic Books.

Lamm, C., Windschberger, C., Leodolter, U., Moser, E., and Bauer, H. (2001). Evidence for premotor cortex activity during dynamic visuospatial imagery from single trial functional magnetic resonance imaging and event-related slow cortical potentials. *Neuroimage*, 14, 268–83.

Landau, B., Spelke, E., and Gleitman, H. (1984). Spatial knowledge in a young blind child. *Cognition*, 16, 225–60.

Langley, P., Simon, H., Bradshaw, G., and Zytkow, J. (1987). *Scientific Discovery: computational explorations of the creative process*. MIT Press.

Larson, A. and Losos, J. (1996). Phylogenetic systematics of adaptation. In M. Rose and G. Lauder (eds.), *Adaptation*, Academic Press.

Latour, B. and Woolgar, S. (1986). *Laboratory Life: the construction of scientific facts*. Princeton University Press.

Laurence, S. and Margolis, E. (1999). Concepts and cognitive science. In E. Margolis and S. Laurence (eds.), *Concepts: core readings*, MIT Press.

Lazarus, R. (1994). Universal antecedents of the emotions. In P. Ekman and R. Davidson (eds.), *The Nature of Emotion*, Oxford University Press.

Learmonth, A., Newcombe, N., and Huttenlocher, J. (2001). Toddlers' use of metric information and landmarks to reorient. *Journal of Experimental Child Psychology*, 80, 225–44.

Ledoux, J. (1996). *The Emotional Brain*. Simon and Schuster.

Lemmon, E. (1965). *Beginning Logic*. Van Nostrand Reinhold.

Leslie, A. (1987). Pretence and representation. *Psychological Review*, 94, 412–26.

_____ and Polizzi, P. (1998). Inhibitory processing in the false belief task: two conjectures. *Developmental Science*, 1, 247–53.

Levelt, W. (1989). *Speaking: from intention to articulation*. MIT Press.

Levenson, R. (1994). Human emotion: a functional view. In P. Ekman and R. Davidson (eds.), *The Nature of Emotion*, Oxford University Press.

Levinson, J. (1982). Music and negative emotion. *Pacific Philosophical Quarterly*, 63, 327–46.

_____ (1997). Emotion in response to art: a survey of the terrain. In M. Hjort and S. Laver (eds.), *Emotion and the Arts*, Oxford University Press.

Levinson, S. (1996). Language and space. *Annual Review of Anthropology*, 25, 353–82.

_____ (2003). *Space in Language and Cognition: explorations in cognitive diversity*. Cambridge University Press.

Levinson, S., Kita, S., Haun, D., and Rasch, B. (2002). Returning the tables: language effects and spatial reasoning. *Cognition*, 84, 155–88.

Lewis, V. and Boucher, J. (1988). Spontaneous, instructed, and elicited play in relatively able autistic children. *British Journal of Developmental Psychology*, 6, 315–24.

Li, P. and Gleitman, L. (2002). Turning the tables: language and spatial reasoning. *Cognition*, 83, 265–94.

_____ Abarbanell, L., and Papafragou, A. (2005). Spatial reasoning skills in Tenejapan Mayans. In *Proceedings of the Cognitive Science Society*, Lawrence Erlbaum.

Liebenberg, L. (1990). *The Art of Tracking: the origin of science*. Cape Town: David Philip.

_____ (forthcoming a). The evolutionary roots of science.

_____ (forthcoming b). Persistence hunting by modern hunter-gatherers.

Locke, J. (1690). *An Essay Concerning Human Understanding*. Many published editions now available.

Lorenz, K. (1950). The comparative method of studying innate behavior patterns. *Symposia of the Society for Experimental Biology*, 4, 221–68.

_____ (1970). *Studies in Animal and Human Behavior*. Harvard University Press.

Lucy, J. and Gaskins, S. (2001). Grammatical categories and classification preferences. In M. Bowerman and S. Levinson (eds.), *Language Acquisition and Conceptual Development*, Cambridge University Press.

McBrearty, S. and Brooks, A. (2000). The revolution that wasn't. *Journal of Human Evolution*, 39, 453–563.

McCloskey, M. (1983). Naive theories of motion. In D. Gentner and A. Stevens (eds.), *Mental Models*, Lawrence Erlbaum.

_____ and Cohen, N. (1989). Catastrophic interference in connectionist networks: the sequential learning problem. *The Psychology of Learning and Motivation*, 24, 106–64.

McDermott, D. (2001). *Mind and Mechanism*. MIT Press.

McDowell, J. (1994). *Mind and World*. MIT Press.

_____ (1995). Might there be external reasons? In J. Altham and R. Harrison (eds.), *World, Mind, and Ethics*, Cambridge University Press.

McGrew, W. (1992). *Chimpanzee Material Culture*. Cambridge University Press.

Mahon, B. and Caramazza, A. (2003). Constraining questions about the organization and representation of conceptual knowledge. *Cognitive Neuropsychology*, 20, 433–50.

Mann, J. (1992). Nurturance or negligence: maternal psychology and behavioral preferences among pre-term twins. In Barkow et al., 1992.

Manoel E., Basso L., Correa U., and Tani G. (2002). Modularity and hierarchical organization of action programs in human acquisition of graphic skills. *Neuroscience Letters*, 335, 83–6.

Marcel, A. (1998). Blindsight and shape perception: deficit of visual consciousness or of visual function? *Brain*, 121, 1565–88.

Marcus, G. (2001). *The Algebraic Mind*. MIT Press.

—— (2004). *The Birth of the Mind: how a tiny number of genes creates the complexities of human thought*. Basic Books.

Mark, T. and Gallistel, R. (1994). The kinetics of matching. *Journal of Experimental Psychology*, 20, 1–17.

Marr, D. (1983). *Vision*. Walter Freeman.

Martin, A. and Chao, L. (2001). Semantic memory and the brain: structure and processes. *Current Opinion in Neurobiology*, 11, 194–201.

—— and Weisberg, J. (2003). Neural foundations for understanding social and mechanical concepts. *Cognitive Neuropsychology*, 20, 575–87.

Mates, B. (1965). *Elementary Logic*. Oxford University Press.

May, M. (1991). Aerial defense tactics of flying insects. *American Scientist*, 79, 316–28.

Mayes, A. and Roberts, N. (2002). Theories of episodic memory. In Baddeley et al., 2002.

Maynard-Smith, J. and Szathmáry, E. (1995). *The Major Transitions in Evolution*. Walter Freeman.

Mayntz, D., Raubenheimer, D., Salomon, M., Toft, S., and Simpson, S. (2005). Nutrient-specific foraging in invertebrate predators. *Science*, 307, 111–13.

Meltzoff, A. (1995). Understanding the intentions of others: reenactment of intended acts by 18-month-old children. *Developmental Psychology*, 31, 838–50.

Menzel, C. (1991). Cognitive aspects of foraging in Japanese monkeys. *Animal Behavior*, 41, 397–402.

Menzel, E. (1974). A group of young chimpanzees in a one-acre field: leadership and communication. In A. Schrier and F. Stollnitz (eds.), *Behavior of Non-Human Primates*, Academic Press.

Menzel, R., Brandt, R., Gumbert, A., Komischke, B., and Kunze, J. (2000). Two spatial memories for honeybee navigation. *Proceedings of the Royal Society: London B*, 267, 961–6.

—— Greggers, U., Smith, A., Berger, S., Brandt, R., Brunke, S., Bundrock, G., Hülse, S., Plümpe, T., Schaupp, S., Schüttler, E., Stach, S., Stindt, J., Stollhoff, N., and Watzl, S. (2005). Honey bees navigate according to a map-like spatial memory. *Proceedings of the National Academy of Sciences*, 102, 3040–5.

Michel, F. and Peronnet, F. (1980). A case of cortical deafness: clinical and electrophysiological data. *Brain and Language*, 10, 367–77.

Miller, G. (1997). Protean primates: the evolution of adaptive unpredictability in competition and courtship. In Byrne and Whiten, 1997.

_____ (2000). *The Mating Mind: how sexual choice shaped the evolution of human nature.* Heinemann.

Milner, B. (1966). Amnesia following operation on the temporal lobes. In C. Whitty and O. Zangwill (eds.), *Amnesia*, Butterworths Press.

Milner, D. and Goodale, M. (1995). *The Visual Brain in Action.* Oxford University Press.

_____ Perrett, D., Johnston, R., Benson, P., Jordan, T., and Heeley, D. (1991). Perception and action in visual form agnosia. *Brain*, 114, 405–28.

Mithen, S. (1990). *Thoughtful Foragers: a study of prehistoric decision making.* Cambridge University Press.

_____ (1996). *The Pre-History of the Mind.* Thames and Hudson.

_____ (2002). Human evolution and the cognitive basis of science. In Carruthers et al., 2002.

Miyashita-Lin, E., Hevner, R., Wassarman, K., Martinez, S., and Rubenstein, J. (1999). Early neocortical regionalization in the absence of thalamic innervation. *Science*, 285, 906–9.

Molnar, Z., Lopez-Bendito, G., Small, J., Partridge, L., Blakemore, C., and Wilson, M. (2002). Normal development of embryonic thalamocortical connectivity in the absence of evoked synaptic activity. *Journal of Neuroscience*, 22, 10313–23.

Montague, R. (1974). *Formal Philosophy.* Yale University Press.

Morreall, J. (1985). Enjoying negative emotions in fiction. *Philosophy and Literature*, 9, 95–103.

Morris, R. (2002). Episodic-like memory in animals: psychological criteria, neural mechanisms, and the value of episodic-like tasks to investigate animal models of neurodegenerative disease. In Baddeley et al., 2002.

Moshman, D. (2004). From inference to reasoning: The construction of rationality. *Thinking and Reasoning*, 10, 221–39.

Moss, C. (1988). *Elephant Memories.* Houghton Mifflin.

Mulcahy, N. and Call, J. (2006). Apes save tools for future use. *Science*, 312, 1038–40.

Murphy, D. and Stich, S. (2000). Darwin in the madhouse: evolutionary psychology and the classification of mental disorders. In Carruthers and Chamberlain, 2000.

Myers, D. (1993). *Social Psychology.* Fourth Edition. McGraw-Hill.

Nagel, E. (1961). *The Structure of Science.* Harcourt and Brace.

Nagel, T. (1970). *The Possibility of Altruism.* Oxford University Press.

Nersessian, N. (1992). How do scientists think? Capturing the dynamics of conceptual change in science. In R. Giere (ed.), *Minnesota Studies in the Philosophy of Science*, University of Minnesota Press.

_____ (2002). The cognitive basis of model-based reasoning in science. In Carruthers et al., 2002.

Nettlebeck, T. (2001). Correlation between inspection time and psychometric abilities: a personal interpretation. *Intelligence*, 29, 459–74.

Newton-Smith, W. (1981). *The Rationality of Science*. Routledge.

Nichols, S. (2002). Norms with feeling: towards a psychological account of moral judgment. *Cognition*, 84, 221–36.

——(2004). Imagining and believing: the promise of a single code. *Journal of Aesthetics and Art Criticism*, 62, 129–39.

——(forthcoming). Just the imagination: why imagining doesn't behave like believing. *Mind and Language*.

——and Stich, S. (2003). *Mindreading: an integrated account of pretence, self-awareness, and understanding other minds*. Oxford University Press.

Nijhout, H. (1991). *The Development and Evolution of Butterfly Wing Patterns*. Smithsonian Institution Press.

Nisbett, R. (2003). *The Geography of Thought: how Asians and Westerners think differently... and why*. Free Press.

——and Wilson, T. (1977). Telling more than we can know. *Psychological Review*, 84, 231–95.

Núñez, M. and Harris, P. (1998). Psychological and deontic concepts: separate domains or intimate connection? *Mind and Language*, 13, 153–70.

O'Hear, A. (1997). *Beyond Evolution*. Oxford University Press.

O'Neill, D. (1996). Two-year-old children's sensitivity to parent's knowledge state when making requests. *Child Development*, 67, 659–77.

Onishi, K. and Baillargeon, R. (2005). Do 15-month-old infants understand false beliefs? *Science*, 308, 255–8.

Origgi, G. and Sperber, D. (2000). Evolution, communication, and the proper function of language. In Carruthers and Chamberlain, 2000.

Owens, D. (2000). *Freedom within Reason*. Routledge.

Owens, T. (1995). *Bebop: the music and its players*. Oxford University Press.

Packer, C. (1994). *Into Africa*. University of Chicago Press.

Paillard, J., Michel, F., and Stelmach, G. (1983). Localization without content: a tactile analogue of 'blind-sight'. *Archives of Neurology*, 40, 548–51.

Pan, Q., Bakowski, M., Morris, Q., Zhang, W., Frey, B., Hughes, T., and Blencowe, B. (2005). Alternative splicing of conserved exons is frequently species-specific in human and mouse. *Trends in Genetics*, 21, 73–7.

Papafragou, A., Massey, C., and Gleitman, L. (2002). Shake, rattle, 'n' roll: the representation of motion in language and cognition. *Cognition*, 84, 189–219.

Papineau, D. (2000). The evolution of knowledge. In Carruthers and Chamberlain, 2000.

Parfit, D. (1997). Reasons and motivation. *Aristotelian Society Proceedings*, Supplementary Volume 71, 99–130.

——(2001). Rationality and reasons. In D. Egonsson, J. Josefsson, B. Petersson, and T. Ronnow-Rasmussen (eds.), *Exploring Practical Philosophy*, Ashgate Press.

Parsons, T. (1990). *Events in the Semantics of English*. MIT Press.

Passingham, R. (1993). *The Frontal Lobes and Voluntary Action*. Oxford University Press.

Paterson, S., Brown, J., Gsödl, M., Johnson, M., and Karmiloff-Smith, A. (1999). Cognitive modularity and genetic disorders. *Science*, 286, 2355–8.

Paulescu, E., Frith, D., and Frackowiak, R. (1993). The neural correlates of the verbal component of working memory. *Nature*, 362, 342–5

Pearl, J. (2000). *Causality*. Oxford University Press.

Pelegrin, J. (1993). A framework for analyzing prehistoric stone tool manufacture and a tentative application of some early stone industries. In A. Berthelet and J. Chavaillon (eds.), *The Use of Tools by Human and Non-Human Primates*, Oxford University Press.

Perenin, M. and Vighetto, A. (1988). Optic ataxia: a specific disruption in visuomotor mechanisms. *Brain*, 111, 643–74.

Perner, J. (1991). *Understanding the Representational Mind*. MIT Press.

＿＿＿ Ruffman, T., and Leekam, S. (1994). Theory of mind is contagious; you catch it from your sibs. *Child Development*, 65, 1224–34.

Peterson, C. and Siegal, M. (1999). Representing inner worlds: theory of mind in autistic, deaf, and normal hearing children. *Psychological Science*, 10, 126–9.

Piaget, J. (1927). *The Child's Conception of Physical Causality*. Routledge.

＿＿＿ (1936). *The Origin of Intelligence in the Child*. Routledge.

＿＿＿ and Inhelder, B. (1948). *The Child's Conception of Space*. Routledge.

＿＿＿ (1966). *The Psychology of the Child*. Routledge.

Piattelli-Palmarini, M. (1994). *Inevitable Illusions: how mistakes of reason rule our minds*. John Wiley.

Pietroski, P. (2005). *Events and Semantic Architecture*. Oxford University Press.

Pillow, B. (2002). Children's and adult's evaluation of certainty of deductive inference, inductive inference, and guesses. *Child Development*, 73, 779–92.

Pinker, S. (1994). *The Language Instinct*. Harper Collins.

＿＿＿ (1997). *How the Mind Works*. Penguin Press.

＿＿＿ (2002). *The Blank Slate: the modern denial of human nature*. Penguin Press.

Posthuma, D., Neale, M., Boomsma, D., and de Geus, E. (2001). Are smarter brains running faster? Heritability of peak alpha frequency, IQ, and their interrelation. *Behavior Genetics*, 31, 567–79.

Povinelli, D. (2000). *Folk Physics for Apes: the chimpanzee's theory of how the world works*. Oxford University Press.

Prinz, J. (2004). *Gut Reactions: a perceptual theory of emotions*. Oxford University Press.

Pylyshyn, Z. (2003). *Seeing and Visualizing: it's not what you think*. MIT Press.

Quine, W.V. (1953). *From a Logical Point of View*. Harvard University Press.

Quinn, W. (1993). *Morality and Action*. Cambridge University Press.

Raff, E. and Raff, R. (2000). Dissociability, modularity, evolvability. *Evolution and Development*, 2, 235–7.

Ramachandran, V. and Blakeslee, S. (1998). *Phantoms in the Brain*. Fourth Estate.

Ramos, J. (2000). Long-term spatial memory in rats with hippocampal lesions. *European Journal of Neuroscience*, 12, 3375–84.

Ramsey, W., Stich, S., and Garon, J. (1990). Connectionism, eliminativism, and the future of folk psychology. In J. Tomberlin (ed.), *Philosophical Perspectives 4: action theory and philosophy of mind*, Ridgeview Publishing.

Rasskin-Gutman, D. (2005). *Modularity: jumping forms within morphospace*. In Callebaut and Rasskin-Gutman, 2005.

Ratcliff, G. and Davies-Jones, G. (1972). Defective visual localization in focal brain wounds. *Brain*, 95, 49–60.

Rawls, J. (1972). *A Theory of Justice*. Oxford University Press.

——(1980). Kantian constructivism in moral theory. *Journal of Philosophy*, 77, 515–72.

Repacholi, B. and Gopnik, A. (1997). Early understanding of desires: evidence from 14 and 18 month olds. *Developmental Psychology*, 33, 12–21.

Rey, G. (1997). *Contemporary Philosophy of Mind*. Blackwell.

Richerson, P. and Boyd, R. (2005). *Not by Genes Alone: how culture transformed human evolution*. University of Chicago Press.

Richter, W., Somorjat, R., Summers, R., Jarnasz, N., Menon, R., Gati, J., Georgopoulos, A., Tegeler, C., Ugerbil, K., and Kim, S. (2000). Motor area activity during mental rotation studied by time-resolved single-trial fMRI. *Journal of Cognitive Neuroscience*, 12, 310–20.

Ridley, M. (2003). *Nature via Nurture*. Harper Collins. (Re-published in paperback in 2004 with the title, *The Agile Gene: how nature turns on nurture*.)

——(2004). The DNA behind human nature: gene expression and the role of experience. *Daedalus*, Fall 2004, 89–98.

Riedel, G., Micheau, J., Lam, A., Roloff, E., Martin, L., Bridge, H., de Hoz, L., Poeschel, B., McCulloch, J., and Morris, R. (1999). Reversible neural inactivation reveals hippocampal participation in several memory processes. *Nature Neuroscience*, 2, 898–905.

Rizzolatti, G. (2005). The mirror neuron system and imitation. In S. Hurley and N. Chater (eds.), *Perspectives on Imitation: from neuroscience to social science*, Volume 1, MIT Press.

——and Gallese, V. (2003). To what extent does perception depend upon action? Three visual systems for action and perception. In L. van Hemmen and T. Sjnowski (eds.), *Problems in Systems Neuroscience*, Oxford University Press.

——Fogassi, L., and Gallese, V. (2000). Cortical mechanisms subserving object grasping and action recognition: a new view on the cortical motor functions. In M. Gazzaniga (ed.). *The New Cognitive Neurosciences*, Second Edition, MIT Press.

Roeder, K. (1962). The behavior of free-flying moths in the presence of artificial ultrasonic pulses. *Animal Behavior*, 10, 300–4.

——and Treat, A. (1961). The detection and evasion of bats by moths. *American Scientist*, 49, 135–48.

Rogers, E. (1995). *Diffusion of Innovations*. Fourth edition, Free Press.

Rolls, E. (1999). *The Brain and Emotion*. Oxford University Press.

Rorty, R. (1979). *Philosophy and the Mirror of Nature*. Princeton University Press.

Rossetti, Y., Rode, G., and Boissson, D. (1995). Implicit processing of somaesthetic information. *Neurological Reports*, 6, 506–10.

Rozin, P., Haidt, J., and McCauley, C. (2000). Disgust. In M. Lewis and J. Haviland (eds.), *Handbook of Emotions*, Guildford Press.

Rumelhart, D. and McClelland, J. (1986). *Parallel Distributed Processing*. MIT Press.

Russell, J., ed. (1998). *Autism as an Executive Disorder*. Oxford University Press.

Sacchett, C. and Humphreys, G. (1992). Calling a squirrel a squirrel but a canoe a wigwam: a category-specific deficit for artefactual objects and body parts. *Cognitive Neuropsychology*, 9, 73–86.

Sachs, O. (1985). *The Man who Mistook his Wife for a Hat*. Picador.

Sak, U. (2004). A synthesis of research on psychological types of gifted adolescents. *Journal of Secondary Gifted Education*, 15, 70–9.

Salmon, D. and Butters, N. (1995). Neurobiology of skill and habit learning. *Current Opinion in Neurobiology*, 5, 184–90.

Samsonovich, A. and McNaughton, B. (1997). Path integration and cognitive mapping in a continuous attractor neural network model. *Journal of Neuroscience* 17, 5900–20.

Samuels, R. (1998a). Evolutionary psychology and the massive modularity hypothesis. *British Journal for the Philosophy of Science*, 49, 575–602.

_____ (1998b). What brains won't tell us about the mind: a critique of the neurobiological argument against representational nativism. *Mind and Language*, 13, 548–70.

_____ (2002). Nativism in cognitive science. *Mind and Language*, 17, 233–65.

_____ (2005). The complexity of cognition: tractability arguments for massive modularity. In Carruthers et al., 2005.

_____ (2006). Is the human mind massively modular? In R. Stainton (ed.), *Contemporary Debates in Cognitive Science*, Blackwell.

Sanders, M., Warrington, E., Marshall, J., and Weiskrantz, L. (1974). 'Blindsight': vision in a field defect. *Lancet*, April 1974, 707–8.

Sanz, C., Morgan, D., and Gulick, S. (2004). New insights into chimpanzees, tools, and termites from the Congo basin. *American Naturalist*, 164, 567–81.

Scanlon, T. (1982). Utilitarianism and contractualism. In A. Sen and B. Williams (eds.), *Utilitarianism and Beyond*, Cambridge University Press.

_____ (1998). *What We Owe to Each Other*. Harvard University Press.

Schacter, D. (1995). Implicit memory: a new frontier for cognitive science. In M. Gazzaniga (ed.), *The Cognitive Neurosciences*, MIT Press.

_____ and Buckner, R. (1998). Priming and the brain. *Neuron*, 20, 185–95.

Schaller, S. (1991). *A Man Without Words*. Summit Books.

Scheuffgen, K., Happé, F., Anderson, M., and Frith, U. (2000). High 'intelligence', low 'IQ'? Speed of processing and measured IQ in children with autism. *Development and Psychopathology*, 12, 83–90.

Schiller, P. (1957). Innate motor action as a basis of learning. In C. Schiller (ed.), *Instinctive Behavior*, International Universities Press.

Schlanger, N. (1996). Understanding Levallois: lithic technology and cognitive archaeology. *Cambridge Archaeological Journal*, 6, 75–92.

Schlosser, G. and Wagner, G., eds. (2004). *Modularity in Development and Evolution.* Chicago University Press.

Schooler, J. and Melcher, J. (1995). The ineffability of insight. In S. Smith, T. Ward, and R. Finke (eds.), *The Creative Cognition Approach*, MIT Press.

Schroeder, T. (2004). *Three Faces of Desire.* Oxford University Press.

Searle, J. (1992). *The Rediscovery of the Mind.* MIT Press.

Seeley, T. (1995). *The Wisdom of the Hive: the social physiology of honey bee colonies.* Harvard University Press.

Segal, G. (1998). Representing representations. In Carruthers and Boucher, 1998.

Sellars, W. (1963). *Science, Perception, and Reality.* Routledge.

Semendeferi, K., Armstrong, E., Schleicher, A., Zilles, K., and van Hoesen, G. (2001). Prefrontal cortex in apes and humans: a comparative study of area 10. *American Journal of Physical Anthropology*, 114, 224–41.

Shallice, T. (1988). *From Neuropsychology to Mental Structure.* Cambridge University Press.

_____ and Warrington, E. (1970). Independent functioning of verbal memory stores: a neuropsychological study. *Quarterly Journal of Experimental Psychology*, 22, 261–73.

Shanahan, M. and Baars, B. (2005). Applying global workspace theory to the frame problem. *Cognition*, 98, 157–76.

Shapin, S. (1994). *The Social History of Truth.* University of Chicago Press.

Shatz, M. and Wilcox, S. (1991). Constraints on the acquisition of English modals. In S. Gelman and J. Byrnes (eds.), *Perspectives on Thought and Language*, Cambridge University Press.

Shennan, S. (2000). Population, culture history, and the dynamics of culture change. *Current Anthropology*, 41, 811–35.

_____ (2001). Demography and cultural innovation: a model and its implications for the emergence of modern human culture. *Cambridge Archaeological Journal*, 11, 5–16.

Shepher, J. (1983). *Incest: a biosocial view.* Academic Press.

Shergill, S., Brammer, M., Fukuda, R., Bullmore, E., Amaro, E., Murray, R., and McGuire, P. (2002). Modulation of activity in temporal cortex during generation of inner speech. *Human Brain Mapping*, 16, 219–27.

Shusterman, A. and Spelke, E. (2005). Investigations in the development of spatial reasoning: core knowledge and adult competence. In Carruthers et al., 2005.

Siegal, M. and Surian, L. (2006). Modularity in language and theory of mind: what is the evidence? In Carruthers et al., 2006.

Simon, H. (1962). The architecture of complexity. *Proceedings of the American Philosophical Society*, 106, 467–82.

Simpson, R. (1988). *Essentials of Symbolic Logic.* Routledge.

Singer, P. (1989). *Practical Ethics.* Cambridge University Press.

Skinner, B. (1957). *Verbal Behavior.* Appleton-Century-Crofts.

Slobin, D. (1987). Thinking for speaking. *Proceedings of the Berkeley Linguistics Society*, 13, 435–44.

Slobin, D. (1996). From 'thought and language' to 'thinking for speaking'. In J. Gumperz and S. Levinson (eds.), *Rethinking Linguistic Relativity*, Cambridge University Press.

—— (2003). Language and thought online: cognitive consequences of linguistic relativity. In D. Gentner and S. Goldin-Meadow (eds.), *Language in Mind*, MIT Press.

Smith, J., Shields, W., and Washburn, D. (2003). The comparative psychology of uncertainty monitoring and meta-cognition. *Behavioral and Brain Sciences*, 26, 317–73.

Smith, M. (1987). The Humean theory of motivation. *Mind*, 96, 36–61.

Smith, P. (1982). Does play matter? Functional and evolutionary aspects of animal and human play. *Behavioral and Brain Sciences*, 5, 139–84.

—— (1986). Language and the evolution of mind-reading. In Carruthers and Smith (1986).

Smith, S., Ward, T., and Finke, R., eds. (1995). *The Creative Cognition Approach*. MIT Press.

Smolensky, P. (1991). Connectionism, constituency, and the language of thought. In B. Loewer and G. Rey (eds.), *Meaning in Mind*, Blackwell.

—— (1995). Constituent structure and the explanation of an integrated connectionist/symbolic cognitive architecture. In C. MacDonald and G. MacDonald (eds.), *Connectionism*, Blackwell.

Sober, E. and Wilson, D. (1998). *Unto Others: the evolution and psychology of unselfish behavior*. Harvard University Press.

Spelke, E. (2005). Sex differences in intrinsic aptitude for mathematics and science? A critical review. *American Psychologist*, 60, 950–8.

—— and Tsivkin, S. (2001). Language and number: a bilingual training study. *Cognition*, 57, 45–88.

—— Phillips, A., and Woodward, A. (1995). Infants' knowledge of object motion and human action. In D. Sperber, D. Premack, and A. Premack (eds.), *Causal Cognition*, Oxford University Press.

Sperber, D. (1996). *Explaining Culture: a naturalistic approach*. Blackwell.

—— (2000). An objection to the memetic approach to culture. In R. Aunger (ed.), *Darwinizing Culture: the status of memetics as a science*, Oxford University Press.

—— (2002). In defense of massive modularity. In I. Dupoux (ed.), *Language, Brain and Cognitive Development*, MIT Press.

—— (2005). Massive modularity and the first principle of relevance. In Carruthers et al., 2005.

—— and Girotto, V. (2002). Use or misuse of the selection task? Rejoinder to Fiddick, Cosmides, and Tooby. *Cognition*, 85, 277–90.

—— and Wilson, D. (1995). *Relevance: communication and cognition*. Second Edition. Blackwell.

—— (1996). Fodor's frame problem and relevance theory. *Behavioral and Brain Sciences*, 19, 530–2.

—— (2002). Pragmatics, modularity, and mind-reading. *Mind and Language*, 17, 3–23.

—— Cara, F., and Girotto, V. (1995). Relevance theory explains the selection task. *Cognition*, 57, 31–95.

Squire, L. (1992). Declarative and non-declarative memory: multiple brain systems supporting learning and memory. *Journal of Cognitive Neuroscience*, 99, 195–231.

—— and Knowlton, B. (1995). Memory, hippocampus, and brain systems. In M. Gazzaniga (ed.), *The Cognitive Neurosciences*, MIT Press.

Srinivasan, M., Zhang, S., Altwein, M., and Tautz, J. (2000). Honeybee navigation: nature and calibration of the 'odometer'. *Science*, 287, 281–3.

Sripada, C. (2005). Punishment and the strategic structure of moral systems. *Biology and Philosophy*, 20, 767–89.

—— and Stich, S. (2006). A framework for the psychology of norms. In Carruthers et al., 2006.

Stanovich, K. (1999). *Who is Rational? Studies of individual differences in reasoning.* Lawrence Erlbaum.

Stein, E. (1996). *Without Good Reason.* Oxford University Press.

Sternberg, R., ed. (1988). *The Nature of Creativity: contemporary psychological perspectives.* Cambridge University Press.

—— ed. (1999). *Handbook of Creativity.* Cambridge University Press.

Sternberg, S. (2001). Separate modifiability, mental modules, and the use of pure and composite measures to reveal them. *Acta Psychologica*, 106, 147–246.

Stich, S. and Nichols, S. (1998). Theory-Theory to the Max: a critical notice of Gopnik and Meltzoff's *Words, Thoughts, and Theories. Mind and Language*, 13, 421–49.

Stoerig, P. and Cowie, A. (1997). Blind-sight in man and monkey. *Brain*, 120, 535–59.

Stone, V., Cosmides, L., Tooby, J., Kroll, N., and Wright, R. (2002). Selective impairment of reasoning about social exchange in a patient with bilateral limbic system damage. *Proceedings of the National Academy of Sciences*, 99, 11531–6.

Striedter, G. (2004). *Principles of Brain Evolution.* Sinauer Associates.

Sugiyama, L., Tooby, J., and Cosmides, L. (2002). Cross-cultural evidence of cognitive adaptations for social exchange amongst the Shiwiar of Ecuadorian Amazonia. *Proceedings of the National Academy of Sciences*, 99, 11537–42.

Tager-Flusberg, H., ed. (1999). *Neurodevelopmental Disorders.* MIT Press.

Tarsitano, M. and Andrew, R. (1999). Scanning and route selection in the jumping spider Portia labiata. *Animal Behavior*, 58, 255–65.

—— and Jackson, R. (1994). Jumping spiders make predatory detours requiring movement away from prey. *Behavior*, 131, 65–73.

—— (1997). Araneophagic jumping spiders discriminate between routes that do and do not lead to prey. *Animal Behavior*, 53, 257–66.

Tautz, J., Zhang, S., Spaethe, J., Brockmann, A., Si, A., and Srinivasan, M. (2004). Honeybee odometry: performance in varying natural terrain. *Public Library of Science: Biology*, 2, 915–23.

Thaler, R. (1992). *The Winners' Curse: paradoxes and anomalies in economic life.* Free Press.

Thoenen, H. (1995). Neurotrophins and neuronal plasticity. *Science*, 279, 593–8.

Thornhill, R. and Gangestad, S. (1999). The scent of symmetry: a human pheromone that signals fitness? *Evolution and Human Behavior*, 20, 175–201.

Tomasello, M. (1999). *The Cultural Origins of Human Cognition*. Harvard University Press.

———— and Call, J. (1997). *Primate Cognition*. Oxford University Press.

Tooby, J. and Cosmides, L. (1992). The psychological foundations of culture. In Barkow et al., 1992.

———— (1996). Friendship and the banker's paradox: other pathways to the evolution of adaptations for altruism. *Proceedings of the British Academy*, 88, 119–43.

———— and Barrett, C. (2005). Resolving the debate on innate ideas: learnability constraints and the evolved interpenetration of motivational and conceptual functions. In Carruthers et al., 2005.

Trivers, R. (1971). The evolution of reciprocal altruism. *Quarterly Review of Biology*, 46, 35–57.

Tulving, E. (1983). *Elements of Episodic Memory*. Oxford University Press.

Turnbull, O., Carey, D., and McCarthy, R. (1997). The neuropsychology of object constancy. *Journal of the International Neuropsychology Society*, 3, 288–98.

Tye, M. (1995). *Ten Problems of Consciousness*. MIT Press.

———— (2000). *Consciousness, Color, and Content*. MIT Press.

Vallortigara, G., Zanforlin, M., and Pasti, G. (1990). Geometric modules in animals' spatial representations: a test with chicks. *Journal of Comparative Psychology*, 104, 248–54.

van der Lely, H. (2005). Domain-specific cognitive systems: insights from SLI. *Trends in Cognitive Sciences*, 9, 53–9.

Vargha-Khadem, F., Gadian, D., and Mishkin, M. (2002). Dissociations in cognitive memory: the syndrome of developmental amnesia. In Baddeley et al., 2002.

Varley, R. (1998). Aphasic language, aphasic thought. In Carruthers and Boucher, 1998.

———— (2002). Science without grammar: scientific reasoning in severe agrammatic aphasia. In Carruthers et al., 2002.

Vaughan, W. (1985). Choice: a local analysis. *Journal of Experimental Analysis of Behavior*, 43, 383–405.

Verhage, M., Maia, A., Plomp, J., Brussaard, A., Heeroma, J., and Vermeer, H. (2000). Synaptic assembly of the brain in the absence of neurotransmitter secretion. *Science*, 287, 864–9.

Vernon, P., Wickett, J., Bazana, P., and Stelmack, R. (2000). The neuropsychology and psychophysiology of human intelligence. In R. Sternberg (ed.), *Handbook of Intelligence*, Cambridge University Press.

Vygotsky, L. (1961). *Thought and Language*. MIT Press. (First published in Russian in 1934; republished and translated, with portions that were omitted from the first English translation restored, in 1986 by MIT Press.)

———— (1971). *The Psychology of Art*. MIT Press.

—— (1978). *Mind in Society: the development of higher psychological processes*. Harvard University Press.

Waal, F. de, (1982). *Chimpanzee Politics*. Jonathan Cape.

—— (1996). *Good Natured: the origins of right and wrong in humans and other animals*. Harvard University Press.

Wagner, G. (1996). Homologues, natural kinds, and the evolution of modularity. *American Zoologist*, 36, 36–43.

—— and Altenberg, L. (1996). Complex adaptations and the evolution of evolvability. *Evolution*, 50, 967–76.

Ward, T., Smith, S., and Finke, R. (1999). Creative cognition. In Sternberg, 1999.

Watson, J. (1924). *Behaviorism*. Norton and Company.

Webb, S., Monk, C., and Nelson, C. (2001). Mechanisms of postnatal neurobiological development: implications for human development. *Developmental Neuropsychology*, 19, 147–71.

Wegner, D. (2002). *The Illusion of Conscious Will*. MIT Press.

Wehner, R. and Srinivasan, M. (1981). Searching behavior of desert ants. *Journal of Comparative Physiology*, 142, 315–38.

Weiskrantz, L. (1980). Varieties of residual experience. *Quarterly Journal of Experimental Psychology*, 32, 365–86.

—— (1986). *Blindsight*. Oxford University Press.

—— (1997). *Consciousness Lost and Found*. Oxford University Press.

Welker, C., Schwibbe, M., Shafer-Witt, C., and Visalberghi, E. (1987). Failure of kin recognition in Macaca fascicularis. *Folia Primatologica*, 49, 216–21.

Wellman, H. (1990). *The Child's Theory of Mind*. MIT Press.

—— Baron-Cohen, S., Caswell, R., Gomez, J., Swettenham J., and Toye, E. (2002). Using thought-bubbles helps children with autism acquire an alternative theory of mind. *Autism*, 17, 343–63.

Wertsch, J., ed. (1981). *The Concept of Activity in Soviet Psychology*. Sharpe.

—— ed. (1985). *Culture, Communication, and Cognition*. Cambridge University Press.

West-Eberhard, M. (1996). Wasp societies as microcosms for the study of development and evolution. In S. Turillazzi and M. West-Eberhard (eds.), *Natural History and Evolution of Paper-Wasps*, Oxford University Press.

—— (2003). *Developmental Plasticity and Evolution*. Oxford University Press.

Whiten, A. (2001). Review of *Folk Physics for Apes*, by Daniel Povinelli. *Nature*, 409: 6817, 133.

Whorf, B. (1956). *Language, Thought, and Reality*. Wiley.

Wicklund, R. and Brehm, J. (1976). *Perspectives on Cognitive Dissonance*. Lawrence Erlbaum.

Wilcox, R. and Jackson, R. (1998). Cognitive abilities of araneophagic jumping spiders. In I. Pepperberg, A. Kamil, and R. Balda (eds.), *Animal Cognition in Nature*, Academic Press.

Wilson, D. (2006). Human groups as adaptive units: towards a permanent consensus. In Carruthers et al., 2006.

_____ Wilczynski, C., Wells, A., and Weiser, L. (2000). Gossip and other aspects of language as group-level adaptations. In C. Heyes and L. Huber (eds.), *The Evolution of Cognition*, MIT Press.

Wilson, M. and Daly, M. (1992). The man who mistook his wife for a chattel. In Barkow et al., 1992.

Wilson, T. (2002). *Strangers to Ourselves*. Harvard University Press.

Wimsatt, W. and Schank, J. (2004). Generative entrenchment, modularity, and evolvability: when genic selection meets the whole organism. In Schlosser and Wagner, 2004.

Winter, W. de, and Oxnard, C. (2001). Evolutionary radiations and convergences in the structural organization of mammalian brains. *Nature*, 409, 710–14.

Wittgenstein, L. (1953). *The Philosophical Investigations*. Blackwell.

Wolpert, D. and Flanagan, R. (2001). Motor prediction. *Current Biology*, 11, 729–32.

_____ and Ghahramani, Z. (2000). Computational principles of movement neuroscience. *Nature Neuroscience*, 3, 1212–17.

_____ and Kawato, M. (1998). Multiple paired forward and inverse models for motor control. *Neural Networks*, 11, 1317–29.

_____ Doya, K., and Kawato, M. (2003). A unifying computational framework for motor control and social interaction. *Philosophical Transactions of the Royal Society of London*, B 358, 593–602.

Woodward, J. and Cowie, F. (2004). The mind is not (just) a system of modules shaped (just) by natural selection. In C. Hitchcock (ed.), *Contemporary Debates in the Philosophy of Science*, Blackwell.

Wrangham, R., McGrew, W., de Waal, F., and Heltne, P. (1994). *Chimpanzee Cultures*. Harvard University Press.

Wulff, S. (1985). The symbolic and object play of children with autism: a review. *Journal of Autism and Developmental Disabilities*, 15, 139–48.

Wynn, T. (2000). Symmetry and the evolution of the modular linguistic mind. In Carruthers and Chamberlain, 2000.

Xu, F. (2002). The role of language in acquiring object kind concepts in infancy. *Cognition*, 85, 223–50.

Yonelinas, A. (2002). Components of episodic memory: the contribution of recollection and familiarity. In Baddeley et al. (2002).

Zhang, S. and Srinivasan, M. (1994). Prior experience enhances pattern discrimination in insect vision. *Nature*, 368, 330–3.

Zola, S. (2003). Memory, animal studies. In R. Wilson and F. Keil (eds.), *The MIT Encyclopedia of the Cognitive Sciences*, MIT Press.

Index of Names

Index of Subjects

CPSIA information can be obtained
at www.ICGtesting.com
Printed in the USA
BVHW01s0143080318
R8544300001B/R85443PG509771BVX1B/1/P